GURDJIEFF'S EMISSARY IN NEW YORK

GURDJIEFF'S EMISSARY IN NEW YORK
Talks and Lectures with A. R. Orage 1924–1931

ISBN: 978-0-9954756-1-8

Acknowledgement is gratefully made to A. R. Orage and Leeds University Library; Charles Sumner Greene and University of California, Berkeley; Jean Toomer, Muriel Draper, Blanche B. Grant, Lawrence Morris, Carol Brown, Margaret Anderson, Kathryn Hulme and Yale University. Special thanks to Frank Brück for assistance with the text, to Matthias Buck-Gramcko for redrawing the illustrations, to David Kherdian for encouragement, support and the foreword, to Gert-Jan Blom for generously sharing photographs from his archives, and to Neil Rhodes for photo restoration.

Front cover photograph of the bookshop in the Yale Club building, East 44th Street, reproduced with the permission of Special Collections, Leeds University Library. Classmark: BC MS 20c Orage/54

British Library Cataloguing-in-Publication Data.
A catalogue record for this book is available from the British Library.

bookstudio.co.uk

CONTENTS

CONTENTS

CONTENTS

FOREWORD

The disciples of Gurdjieff each brought their own essential and indispensable gift to the Work: de Hartmann—The Note, de Salzmann—The Foot, Ouspensky—The Pointed Finger, Bennett—The Voice, Nicoll—The Cross, and Orage—The Pencil. Orage was not only a writer and thinker, but an editor, a developer of talent, and more important than any of these, he was Gurdjieff's brilliant translator. He sculpted Gurdjieff's opus into its final shape and form as no one else could have done: P. L. Travers saying of it upon publication that it resembled "a great, lumbering flying cathedral."

This was Orage's greatest contribution to the Work, and also, very importantly, his exegesis of the *Tales*, as recollected from talks to his pupils, published in great part by C. S. Nott in his book, *Teachings of Gurdjieff: The Journal of a Pupil*, later published as a single volume by Two Rivers Press, and more recently, and definitively, by Book Studio, under the title, *Orage's Commentary on Gurdjieff's "Beelzebub's Tales to His Grandson": New York Talks 1926–1930*.

Although America would become one of the growing points of the Work, following its start in Fontainebleau, France, there were none inside Gurdjieff's magic circle who were American born. One has to wonder if there would have been an American presence if it weren't for the man who was in essence himself an American—Orage, who was able to make a blossoming of the Work in America because of his spirit, which found its correspondence there, where he formed his first group, that became for him a family in ways he had never experienced before. Orage claimed he had left the life he knew behind, in order to find God. With his American family he found love, which must have come to him as a resounding answer to his striving for God. Not surprisingly, he married an American woman, with whom he fell in love at their first meeting upon his arrival in New York.

It was a case of mutual recognition: these were his people and he would be their leader. This occurrence, this birthing, this episode in time, was captured brilliantly by Louise Welch in her book, *Orage with Gurdjieff in America*.

Gurdjieff had said of Orage that he was his brother. America might have said the same.

David Kherdian

INTRODUCTION

Alfred Richard Orage (1873–1934), whom G. B. Shaw declared the most brilliant editor of the past century, suddenly laid down his pencil in 1922 and sold his famous journal *The New Age* to work with the mystic G. I. Gurdjieff. The lifelines of these two exceptional men crossed at a time when Gurdjieff was at the height of his powers and Orage was desperately looking for a more fundamental understanding of the human species. Even before the First World War and the following events, he was disillusioned by Western civilization. He saw that it lacked, in spite of all its achievements, both knowledge and methods, and, what was even more frustrating, the intellectual integrity and will necessary to come to a comprehensive understanding of human nature. And without this understanding, no further development was possible. But without something really new and promising, and attractive, he was convinced that the very will to live would decline. So it was no surprise when he wrote in 1915: "Anything that inspires to the practice of Mysticism is all to the good, since it is certain in my opinion that with the faculties we already possess Man has come to the end of his tether. Progress must continue, if at all, horizontally instead of perpendicularly, until a new faculty is developed to apprehend the world in a new way."[1]

Gurdjieff was moving along the same line, but claimed to have found a way to develop new and even higher faculties trained in the necessary methods, with knowledge that has its sources in the hidden wisdom of the East. His claim was supported by his behavior, which was so deeply rooted in reality that some people called him no longer a man but a natural phenomenon.

When Orage encountered Gurdjieff, he was accustomed to dealing with famous men and gurus. He was never distracted by them, since he was able to penetrate quite simply and unpretentiously—according to T. S. Elliot—to the heart of the moral rottenness or intellectual dishonesty of the most acclaimed man. Hence, there is reason enough to proceed on the assumption that Orage was not simply charmed by Gurdjieff's powerful personality. He must have recognized something eminently authentic in Gurdjieff and his teaching, including a practical method with a hitherto unknown degree of vitalizing sanity and coherence. Certainly he was aware that working with a man like Gurdjieff was an unique opportunity, a chance that was offered only to a few, but once in a century, that would never come again in his lifetime. Hence he gave up everything for it—his career, fame, social and material security. For more than a year he worked intensively with Gurdjieff in his *Institute for the Harmonious Development of Man*, and it seems that Orage had finally found what he had sought.

Gurdjieff, on the other hand, found in Orage someone that he considered

---

1   The New Age, 15 July 1915

a brother in spirit. A spirit that was defined by Orage some years before as: ". . . displaying itself in disinterested interest in things; in things, that is to say, of no personal advantage, but only of general, public or universal importance." [2] To find a man of such spirit in the West must have been a joyful surprise to Gurdjieff. And after the disappointing performance of Ouspensky, who, impelled by self-importance, separated from Gurdjieff to establish a sort of rival school with himself as its headmaster, he needed someone who would formulate the teaching for western ears. So when Gurdjieff expanded his activities into the New World, it was only consequent that Orage became his emissary there.

When Orage arrived in New York in December 1923, he was fifty years of age. According to Gorham Munson,[3] he gave no sign of middle age. No hint of grey in the dark hair, and only a slight recession of the hairline near the part on the left. His first impression of Orage was that this man's *note* was intelligence. The hazel eyes, alive and challenging, were intelligent. The strong nose was intelligent. The mouth, ready to smile at paradox, was intelligent. He had never met a man before who struck it with as much clarity. A thought came to his mind: that Orage was a Pico della Mirandola of the twentieth century.

Munson was not the first one who was so eminently affected by Orage's presence. Some years before Holbrook Jackson, an early friend of Orage, has given a similar and more detailed description of the personal impressions that Orage made upon his contemporaries:

In appearance Orage was tall, and, at that time, slim and dark-haired, and he dressed conventionally.... His hair was straight and worn short except for a long tuft which sometimes strayed over his forehead. His eyes were hazel, lively, and challenging, and in moments of excitement they seemed to emit a red glint. It was a feline face and there was something cat-like in his movements. He walked as though he were going to pounce on something, much as his mind pounced upon an idea or an opponent. His expression was earnest, without being solemn. There was wit in his poise and manner and he was good to look at without being good-looking. But he did not impress by his features so much as by that which was outside and beyond his features. You were conscious of his aura; you felt his presence so much that you forgot details, even the vague birthmark which broke into his complexion like an irregular sunburn, and seemed to become deeper when he was bored or out of humour. This appearance, so lively and so earnest, was a perfect background for his conversation. You expected a man who looked like that to talk well, and I am not alone in thinking that his better genius expressed itself in talk.

---

2   The New Age, 31 October 1918
3   Gorham Munson, The Roaring Twenties

Even his small talk was fascinating. The odd remarks and unpremeditated sallies, often trivial, were always amusing and sometimes something more.[4]

Without doubt, Orage's charismatic aspect was one of the reasons why the Gurdjieff-Teaching found a way to take root in America's intelligentsia. But another aspect was his ability to elucidate Gurdjieff's ideas in such a manner that his listeners found the teaching more and more essential to their lives. Orage was interested in every member of his group as an individual and so his answers to their questions were individual. He never lost himself in esoteric generalizations. At the same time, he could show them the bigger picture of which they were a part, and out of this new perspective, they could find a solution to their problems by themselves. Orage never expected blind faith or obedience, on the contrary, he always encouraged scepticism—neither believe nor disbelieve.

In 1925, Orage was talking to a growing group of interested people from different professions. They met once a week in the barnlike quarters of Muriel Draper at 24 East 40th Street. Members were, among others, the short-story writer Israel Solon; the literary critic Van Wyck Brooks; businessmen Stanley Speidelberg and Sherman Manchester; the rich heiress Blanche Rosette Grant; detective-novel writer and psychologist C. Daly King; music reviewer Muriel Draper; actor Edwin Wolfe and actress Rita Romilly; architects Claude Bragdon and Hugh Ferris; poets Melville Cane and Edna Kenton; and the author of *Cane,* Jean Toomer; painters Boardman Robinson and Claire Mann; publishers Amos Pinchot and C. S. Nott; writers Waldo Frank, Carl Bechhofer Roberts, Gorham Munson, Lawrence Morris, Scuyler Jackson, Lawrence S. Hare, T. S. Matthews and his sister Peggy (son and daughter of the Bishop of New Jersey); editors Carl Zigrosser, Herbert Croly, John O'Hara Cosgrave, Margaret Anderson and Jane Heap; concert pianists Carol Robinson and Rosemary Lillard; physician Dr. Louis Berman; Helen Westley of the Theater Guild; historical novelist, Mary Johnston; mathematician John Riordan, and chemist Willem (Wim) Nyland. Of the legal profession were Reese Alsop and Allan Brown; impresario Lincoln Kirstein; the Swiss consul in New York, Robert Schwartzenbach and his wife Marguerite, and Katie Powys, sister of John Cowper Powys.

Unlike Gurdjieff, Orage encouraged his students to make notes of his lectures, and many did. The present volume is based on the papers of Jean Toomer, Muriel Draper, Charles Sumner Greene, Blanche Grant, Lawrence Morris, Carol Brown, Kathryn Hulme and Margaret Anderson. We are grateful to the notetakers and their prudence to leave their papers to the universities of Yale, Berkeley and Leeds, who guaranteed the survival of these papers in their archives. Without all this combined effort they would otherwise be scattered all over the world and largely unknown and "upon the verge of being irre-

---

4   Phillip Mairet, A. R. Orage A Memoir

coverably lost" as C. Daly King once wrote. Along with the commentaries on Beelzebub, this edition completes the record for Orage's meetings, talks and lectures on Gurdjieff's teaching.

The notes have been edited with an emphasis on readability. Illegible words, missing or wrong punctuation and grammatical errors have been corrected. Missing letters and words have been reconstructed using the context where possible. In cases where no meaning could be deduced, no changes have been made.

Frank Brück
Weyhe near Bremen, June 2016

Clockwise from top left: Muriel Draper, Boardman Robinson, Amos Pinchot, C. Daly King, Carl Zigrosser, T. S. Matthews, Hugh Ferris, Margaret Anderson, Carol Robinson, Willem Nyland, Waldo Frank, Gorham Munson, Philippa Powys, Lincoln Kirstein, Rita Romilly, John O'Hara Cosgrave, Mary Johnston, Jane Heap, Charles Sumner Greene, Jean Toomer, Claude Bragdon, Melvin Cane, Helen Westley, Herbert Croly, and A. R. Orage.

G. GURDJIEFF'S INSTITUTE FOR THE HARMONIOUS DEVELOPMENT OF MAN.

CERTIFICATE OF MEMBERSHIP No. 625.

Mrs. Muriel Draper *with sons* 21 E 89 st.New-York

The bearer of this, a member of the GURDJIEFF INSTITUTE, has the following privileges:

Free residence, with all the rights of permanent members, at the chief centre of the Institute at Fontainebleau, as well as at the Institute's boarding-houses in other places;

Free attendance at all classes, lectures and conferences, wherever held under the auspices of the Institute, except those lectures etc. specially held for permanent members;

Free subscription to the Institute's journal and all the literature issued by the Institute;

The right of enquiry and reply concerning the ideas of the Institute.

Any member may, if he or she wish, use any of the sanatoria or hotels of the Institute for him or herself, and family, at one half the regular rates.

This certificate is valid for One Year from June 1st, 1924 to June 1st, 1925.

(Signed)   Founder: *G. Gurdjieff*

Person issuing: *A.R. Orage.*

This document is authorised for American citizens only over the personal signature of the Founder, Mr. Gurdjieff, and that of one of the following persons:
Mrs. Rublee, 242 East 49 st., New-York.
Professor Comstock, Harvard University, Boston.
Mr. Edgar Hamilton, 245 North Kenilworth Ave, OakPark, Chicago.
Mr. A. R. Orage, c/o. Mr. F. R. Whoteside, 1510 Waverley st.,
                                                    Philadelphia.

71 West 23 St.
June 24, 1930.

You may know of some one who, if approached by you, would avail him- or herself of the opportunity to assist Mr.Gurdjieff during his revision of the book. We are still short the sum of $792 in pledges of the required $4200, for the six months period.

It may help you to learn whom you might approach by going over the below list of names. We believe this list to be complete of all those who have in any way pledged themselves to support this fund.

You will be interested to know that we have thus far collected $2396, and that we have sent off to Mr. Gurdjieff $2100, and that we have a balance of $296 for the August 1st, or fourth, installment of the required $700. It will assist the committee materially if you will send on your August installment as soon as possible after the receipt of this circular, if you have not already done so.

Very truly yours,

The Committee:

Allen R. Brown	Louise Michel
Ehler Dahl	Marguerite Schwarzenbach
John J. Hefti	Israel Solon, Secretary.

Mr.& Mrs. Reese D.Alsop	Mary Johnston
James Amster	Mariska Karasz
Paul Anderson	Marjae Marston
Lewis Benson	Mavis McIntosh
Gwendolyn Bjornkranz	A.R.Orage
Allen R. Brown	Donald Peterson
Florence Cane	Margaret Price
Ehler Dahl	John Riordan
Muriel Draper	Mr.& Mrs.Boardman Robinson
Mr. & Mrs.Hugh Ferriss	Marguerite Schwarzenbach
Naomi Gottlieb	Dorothy Seamans
Blanche B. Grant	Israel Solon
Dorothy Harris	E. Thompson
John J. Hefti	Edwin R. Wolfe
Annette Herter	Carl Zegrosser
Schuyler Jackson	Caesar Zwaska
Lillian Jacobs	Book Readings

TUESDAY, 1 JANUARY 1924

First you must understand that the story I have to tell you can never be *told* in the ordinary sense of the word.

"Mysticism," I said—"Then you have been in the East?"

"Science," he replied. "Yes, I have been in the East."

There was a long silence. We apparently gave our whole attention to our cigars and our drinks.

"Science," I mused, "facts, then. Why cannot it be told if it deals with facts?"

"Perhaps you have eyes yet ye see not, ye have ears yet ye hear not."

"Ah, religion then," I said.

"Well, if you could properly call Jesus religious—perhaps."

"You might employ the words Christian science as an accurate designation possibly," I speculated.

"Christian science," he said, "is our ignorant brother."

"Oh," I finally murmured. Another silence.

"You see it, but probably I had best tell you how I got started on this quest?" He looked at me quizzically, smiling that rare and lovely smile, which lights up his saturnine features, yet indicates no abandon, being thereby rare and lovely.

I melted instantly. "Please," I said, making appropriate gestures, with glasses and fresh cigars.

It began with a dream. I was spending the summer eight years ago, wasn't it? At Woodstock. It is a beautiful little village near the Hudson River in the foothills of the Catskill Mountains. One night returning from a party in the Maverick, the musicians' colony there, I felt a queer restlessness. It was nearly dawn so I walked on past my studio, turning up a country road which leads to a favorite spot of mine. It is a hill top from which there is a view in all directions. Off one side the distant Hudson was dimly visible through the mist, and beyond, the high hills, blue against a pale gold sky. On the other hand there were the Catskills, dimly outlined, massive, huge. Between these ranges are valleys, streams, grain fields, houses, roads, stone walls, and always great trees in groups around the houses, in lines along the roads, and streams and lanes, occasionally a giant standing alone. Reaching the summit of the hill I sat down. There on clear days one can see all manner of men moving about in any means of locomotion—steamers on the Hudson, automobiles, wagons, horses, even ox teams and carts on the roads; men riding horses and men walking idly and or briskly.

A girl had been playing strange music on the piano that night. She had said the pieces were accurate transcriptions of temple music, ritualistic dances, dervish dances brought out of the Far East from Afghanistan, Tibet, the Gobi desert, China, Hindustan.

They had affected me strangely. What was it that held me, the music or only another girl, I wondered. I closed my eyes. A queer, vivid person this girl. Mysterious, yes, and that is always alluring. A friend and guest of Schlayter (Schweitzer?), famous organist and teacher. She wore a turban, I remembered, of strange color—orange.

Here I must have fallen asleep. I saw a strange man come striding up the hill—wearing an identical turban. He came straight to me and sat down crossing his legs in Hindu fashion.

"What the devil!" I thought and stopped abruptly. For he looked more like the devil than the devil himself. A great head, yet not out of proportion to his great figure. A high wide forehead over heavy black brows, deep set black lustrous eyes, prominent cheek bones and strong cleft chin. A thin nose with strong nostrils; a wide mouth, guarded by vertical lines and a black mustachio, sweeping left to right above it.

He spoke:

"First there is the sun" he said. "Then the earth, the planets, the moon, the infra-moon, mankind, animal, vertebrates, invertebrate, vegetable, mineral, metal."

"Quite comprehensive," I said politely.

"Words are really fun, aren't they?" he said and smiled so brightly it was like looking into the sun itself.

"Apprehension versus comprehension. Asleep versus awake. Dullness and ecstasy. Apathy and sustained elation. Sickness and health. You and a complete human being. Futility and fulcrum. Three and six. That was my music," he added.

"It was extraordinary," I said, again quite politely.

"It might be equally well said that all other varieties of music are extraordinary. Music is held to be the best of the arts, for it expresses in its scales the cosmic law."

"So does the fish," I said very politely.

"Quite right," he replied, beaming a smile down at me, as though I were a child who had unwittingly said something quite profound. I felt abashed, even a bit fearful.

"Sorry, please go on with the tale," I said.

"The fishes of yours," he inquired, "they are really much the same, you know."

"The musical scales, please," I spoke very, very politely.

"In the scale we have eight so-called whole notes and two half notes: do, re, mi—then a missing half note—fa, sol, la, si—then a missing half note again.

The millennium, so to speak, is just over that half note. All history shows that civilization after civilization has progressed to a certain level, where a millennium seemed to be the very next step. Then without exception each lapses into a period of retrogression. Do, re, mi, re, mi, re, mi, re, do, etc. This is not to say that mankind may not sometime cross this line and become as far above the men of today as the men of today are above the animals."

"Certainly not," I exclaimed with polite emphasis.

He regarded me with a sort of glowing amusement which made me quite uncomfortable.

"Man is the product of two forces—biological and sociological, and reacts automatically exactly as any other automaton. The Behaviorists have amply demonstrated *that* from conclusive studies made of animals and infants. But man differs from animal; he possesses potential power for real thought. The animal is a two-centered being—instinctive center and emotional center. Man is composed of instinctive, emotional, and intellectual centers. To be sure, the intellectual center in most men is hardly discernible, but every man possesses the possibility of developing a third or lower intellectual center, whereas this is invariably lacking in the animal. These centers may be said to be contained within the instinctive center, though this is not strictly accurate. The body is the physical structure of the instinctive center. It is only through the instinctive center that the emotional and intellectual centers can be manifested. Of course, each man or animal has a different emotional content, deposited at the time of his conception by the planets and determined by their configuration."

"Of course," I interjected politely.

"Though men of the same race may be structurally much the same there never is any essential identity. Brothers, even twin brothers, possessing practically identical physical structures at birth immediately begin to display essential differences which in maturity have often brought about marked differences both external and internal. For the essence of man is not determined by his ancestry either immediate or remote. Nevertheless, since we are so nearly or always automatons, and since each one inherits his physical structure, it may be said that the sins of the father or mother may affect the sons or daughters even through the third or fourth generation. By that time it will have been washed out."

"So that's a wash out, too," I commented courteously.

"Everything in these three centers is a washout eventually."

"Eventually? Why not now?" I inquired mildly.

"Because mankind serves a cosmic purpose, of course. Take food. It goes up the scale, solid, liquid, gas, i.e. do, re mi. Then it is carried by the blood from the stomach to the lungs where it is transmuted into life energy by the shock of its contact with air and is distributed through one's body and runs itself up the scale fa, sol, la, si. So we grow and live. In the same way mankind

3

provides the shock which transmutes the sun's energy into food for the earth, the moon, and the infra moon."

"Exactly," I concurred with exceeding politeness.

"How politely you speak," he remarked, eying me obliquely. "Except for misunderstandings, politeness would never be necessary. For if I understand my friend, politeness between us is never necessary, i.e. of course if he understands me. But if we do not agree through a lack of understanding we must be polite to each other or fight. And since few people like to fight and few of these are evenly matched, everyone must be polite to his neighbors. Thus the degree of politeness proper and necessary to employ depends always on the extent of the lack of understanding involved. We are particularly polite to the ladies."

"Perhaps you are right," I remarked without emphasis.

"Perhaps," he said, and was silent for a while.

Presently he motioned toward the next hilltop where a flock of sheep were grazing and from which the sheep bells occasionally sounded. But still he said nothing.

At last "Sheep?" I queried idiotically.

"Yes, sheep" he said.

"Suppose those sheep were to discuss their purpose and their relation to the cosmos. Such a speculation would no doubt arouse most of them to fear and wrath by its impious tendency.

"'How can you ask such a question', they would bleat angrily. 'Isn't the evidence sufficient for you? Don't the men-gods give us a warm shelter in the winter, good food from their stock, when the earth is covered with snow, sheer our heavy coats in the spring when otherwise we should be too unbearably hot, and constantly take the righteous away into the Promised Land?'

"And no doubt they would ostracize and even butt and kick such questioners. Yet if these agnostics persisted, and by determined investigation, would find that man kept them solely for mutton and wool—that would be considered as a cruel and impossible conclusion.

"Yet it is the law of life that every living thing must live by the death of other living beings. You yourself as a man cannot live without going through the same process. Why then should you suppose that you do not yourself further the life purpose?"

"It is so," I admitted.

"Perhaps," he said.

"Yet there is this purpose," I remarked. "The life of a sheep is without purpose and utterly futile. Whereas, men are constantly improving themselves and their environment."

"Oh, are they really?" he asked with great politeness.

"Hm, you do not understand it that way, I perceive by your manner."

4

He smiled, and despite my valiant effort I was pleased, thrilled and stimulated by that smile.

"You happen to be living, shall we say, in a state of society that is just approaching its zenith. The war represented the first signs of the wave breaking, just as the white crest of the wave appears when it is near the shore. Presently it will touch the beach, its limit, and come tumbling crashing down—as it always has done in the past. Even in your conception of history you can see this. Various so-called civilizations have achieved a high point of development, only to lapse into a retrogression which took them down to the lowest point from which they had risen. From that point there would be an upward turn and so on over and over. Even this has only the appearance of upward or downward trend since all things are in constant balance."

"From this maelstrom of futility then," I said, "my only escape would be self annihilation?"

"Suicide is sometimes possible," he replied, "but self annihilation not."

"Then I live forever?" I queried? "And must live forever?"

"Can a fire extinguish itself? Yet it does not burn forever. The life of a piece of radium is estimated to be fifteen thousand years. Your span of individual life may be fifteen thousand years or centuries but unless it is replenished and sustained by your own successful efforts and by the addition of outside accidents, such as my talk with you this morning—your being at the Maverick last night, your accidental equipment resulting in your reaction to my music etc.—even with these factors given you will probably eventually reach the vanishing point and vanish. Though you cannot by choice either vanish or not vanish."

"But how?" I interjected.

"By hearing me," he continued.

"Choice is not possible to three-centered or four-centered man. For every one of your thoughts, feelings, and acts are predictable in any circumstances. The fact that you are unable to predict them and that you have never met anyone able to predict them does not mean that they are not definitely and actually predictable."

"But look here," I interrupted angrily, thrusting out my arm.

Undisturbed he continued.

"Obviously you either will or will not," he remarked. "What will be the cause of your extending your arm if you do? Obviously the act will have been motivated by your reaction to the idea of automatism. It will be apparent to you that you could not act except as that act is the result of your own limitations. Unless, of course, you become perchance a complete human being."

"A complete human being?" I exclaimed.

He was silencing me with a glare.

"The cosmic man," he continued, "differs from the world man in that he has developed his three higher centers. For as you know, food is transformed into life-energy through processes that are gratuitously provided for the world man. However, every man has three higher centers—higher instinctive, higher emotional and higher intellectual—e.g. potentially. Also there is food for the growth of the higher centers available but it is rarely or never absorbed."

"But how *know*?" I stammered angrily.

He continued serenely.

"The harmonious development of men—that is the nectar and ambrosia of life. First one must realize that he knows only one or two things actually. For example that there are two thousand million people on this earth and that all of them will die. Second that man is the only interesting object of study, and that you can only truly know one man—yourself. To learn about yourself, first you must establish your identity in the higher intellectual center and from this point of view observe your behavior. Not with disapproval nor with approval. Simply observe. You must be simultaneously aware of your complete state of mind, emotions, and body. You must be aware of them but not identified with them. This is not impossible.

"You can, by an effort of real imagination, conceive yourself coming up the hill now toward our two figures seated here. You can from that point of view perceive certain aspects of Orage, whom you have always mistakenly considered to be yourself. He is only one possible phase of you.

"You will most easily observe at first, five things about him: the posture of his body, the expression of his face, the tone of his voice the gestures of his hands, arms, or other members of his body, and his carriage as he moves through life. Those are the external things about a man which others can see. But one must be simultaneously aware of them and of a score more of internal aspects are only to be known by you.

"Then your emotions must be observed—not directly, for this is not possible. But one can and must observe the physical evidences of one's emotional states. Then one must add to this an awareness of one's intellectual processes.

"All of these observations will narrow down eventually to the study of your habits. Gradually it will become possible to vary one's behavior by changing one's physical states or by placing one's self in new circumstances or by supplying a new stimulus by means of mood. Now the key, if there be one, particularly at the beginning, will be the realization of simultaneous awareness of as many as are possible.

"The memory film must be rolled back—first for an hour, then a day, a week, a year, until it may be possible to go back to one's virgin state and discover one's real essence. For it will be increasingly evident that we are more conditioned in actions, feelings, and thoughts, than we have supposed.

"An immoral act, thought, feeling or life is one that fails to produce simultaneously profit, pleasure, and understanding. The difference between right and wrong is determined by whether or not, whatever it may be, is agreeable to you. This means if it really agrees with you, in the sense that some foods happen to agree with one person and perhaps not with another.

"When you were an infant you could not use your hand for any of the useful things you now do so deftly and easily. Suppose you could use your whole equipment, mind, emotions, and body as deftly and easily as you now use your hands? This you can do if you can establish your identity in your higher intellectual center and develop the potential powers in your higher emotional and instinctive centers. There is food incessantly available for anyone under all conditions.

"You will find that it is easier to observe yourself when you are doing something you do not automatically wish to do or when you are engaged in gratuitous effort."

"Still," I objected, "such a course would seem to make one obnoxiously self-conscious?"

"No. Not if one says: 'I am not that man. I will observe this mechanism, but not with approval nor with disapproval, but with an impartial unprejudiced external attitude.'"

Silence.

"Since this man is entirely automatic and merely a product of say two forces—biology and sociology—and nevertheless is one phase of the real 'I' then I will observe him and all his actions and reactions. I shall study him because man is the only mystery in the world and since I have a specimen, myself, I am content. Absorbing experience in the process which will provide food for the higher centers. I must go."

The sun peeping over the rim of the horizon seemed to kindle a hundred fires in his lusterful black eyes.

"It will here become apparent to the real 'I' that the behavior of your organism is absolutely automatic, and that it is most undesirable to be at the mercy of the chaos produced by the almost constant quarrel of the three centers among themselves. They constantly fight, agitate, and trick each other, to their equal discomfiture."

"But damnation," I shouted, "will you listen?"

"Yes?" he said, pleasantly.

But I had forgotten what it was I wanted to say.

After a short silence, he proceeded.

"Take your own case for example, and let us discuss your organism between us. The real 'I' in your organism and myself. At the moment your instinctive center is weary and it is tired of reclining against that rock and it is hungry and thirsty.

"Those states are known to the emotional center which is agitated by them. The intellectual center is however able and willing a participant in this conversation and resolutely ignores the other centers endeavoring to give its whole attention to our ideas. It is not strong enough as you can see and is caught by

7

the emotions and made to turn to angry shouts. Meaningless, dangerous, and actually injurious.

"It will be evident to you, i.e. to the real 'I' in you, that this is an inevitable and undesirable state, which nevertheless cannot be changed by an effort of will. Thus we say a world man has no free will or power to choose, and that he never will and never can have."

"Unless?" I said.

"Unless you observe and study your organism without identifying yourself with its three centers. It is possible and necessary however to make real effort, to realize every thought, feeling, and action. To accomplish this, a kind of fire is necessary. This fire will be present whenever you are, so to speak, awake. That is whenever the real 'I' is conscious and aware of, though entirely void of identity with your thoughts, feelings, and actions simultaneously. The effort necessary may now be made by you, for you have heard the truth. It will be difficult if not impossible, for all your organism is so much dead weight. And every current and phase of life as you have hitherto known will be counter to these ideas and will present itself so to you in future."

"But are there no absolute moral values?" I asked. Thoughts and emotions were seething within so that I was powerless to formulate even one question. I finally stammered: "For the love of God don't go!"

"For the love of God I go!" he answered.

His expression seemed to me to be a divine blending of truth, beauty, love and laughter.

He rose, faced the rising sun for an instant then strode away down the hill. His figure moved swiftly and gracefully but instead of diminishing with distance it seemed to take on greater dimensions, though its outlines were less and less visible. I did not exactly lose sight of him, but I could no longer discern any details. He seemed to have merged with the hills and streams, the mist and sunlight, the gold and blue of the sky and the green and brown of the earth.

I rose; my body was cramped and cold but I was nevertheless glowing with the warmth of celestial ecstasy.

Orage ceased speaking and sat regarding the embers of the fires with a curious absence of concentration that was the exact opposite of dreaming. He seemed extraordinarily at ease yet completely alert and alive in a way hardly comprehensible to me.

"Have you met that man since?" I asked.

"Oh, yes," he replied.

"In a dream?" I demanded.

"In a recurrent dream," he replied, "Life."

There are twelve physical types—but essence is not the same in the same types.

Behavior is the result, usually if not always, of biology and sociology. Do not commit yourself to any wish or ambition of today. It almost surely will not last. A pianist went to the Institute—became and is now a farmer in New Zealand.

Do, re, mi of the emotional center is related to emotions, impressions, sex of the instinctive—so, la, si of the astral or emotional center is related to do, re, mi of the intellectual. See if in your actual experience you have had an emotional experience of greater intensity than sex—i.e. so, la, si, of the emotional scale.

Fa—is earth in E (emotional?) scale.
Do, re, mi—is moon.
So, la, si—is sun.

So every time my "fa," i.e. "I" falls into do, re, mi it is contributing something to moon—and when by an effort "I" goes into so, la, si, it is contributing something to the sun. If "I" comes to have a separate existence, responses will be so, la, si, (of the emotions) but the organism always has the reaction do, re, mi (of the emotions).

Suppose you find yourself in a negative emotional state (hitherto we have said "observe etc.") now you can turn your mind to one of these ideas:

Order of the Cosmos.
Relation of sun and moon.
Cosmic scale.
Enneagram.
Any cosmic ideas, i.e. to think in terms of cosmos.
Objective morality.

The fact is, we can have no higher emotions in the presence of negative emotions.

We do not hold these ideas in suspense—that is a passive attitude. We are experimenting with these ideas—a positive attitude.

Words are difficult to employ. We must take words and find out what they really mean, out of our present experience.

9

Higher emotion—what does this mean? The organism can never experience a higher emotion.

Appetites are not wishes. Appetites are in the emotional sub-center of the instinctive center.

Wishes only come from the emotional center. I am not hungry yet I wish to eat. This is from the emotional center. Will is the power to change attitudes.

We have a choice at the present moment of choosing another image than the one now held in the cerebral system which now determines attitude (i.e. emotional rest). Same result achieved by contemplating something purely reasonable—taking a walk is retreating into the instinctive center.

First shock is self-observation. Second, contemplating the rational of the universe or of existence.

If you can non-identify with all organisms—you do not have an emotional approach to mankind (i.e. how terrible everyone's life is etc.) you will take an intellectual attitude. You will study your own organism and that of others. But you must not expose this attitude to others. You have to behave "as if" you were a reasonable being. But if you become a reasonable being you have to play a role again—this time "as if" you were not a reasonable being.

Emotions are always responsive to ideas, but these ideas are not compatible with the emotion common to man.

To do more and more, and better and better, and to think less and less of it (i.e. in the sense of estimate) will be the result. (I.e. to be less and less satisfied by the results.)

Unless your righteousness shall exceed the righteousness of the scribes and Pharisees you shall by no means enter into the kingdom of heaven.

We must know:

1. Ourselves
2. The world
3. Our station in the world.

We wish to know, in order to be, in order to do. In groups we can learn to know—in life we can learn to be—then we can learn to do.

Three tests—thinkable, feelable, sensible.

If I can co-ordinate my three centers—thinking, feeling, and doing, perhaps I can do something.

Self-observation, participation and experiment will develop this ability.

Try to imagine a circle of chairs, one for each year of your life. Try to imagine yourself in the first chair for one year than in the second for the second year. The same person, but in a different form, then in each chair the same person, but in different forms. The same person is at any given time all those things he has been and all those things that he will become. Call these chairs birthdays.

Those figures that we see in passing around this succession of chairs must be regarded as the inevitable result of potentialities. What is it that passes around through those successive molds or figures? I. But I am identified with each figure at that given moment. When I am at any given point it is, so to speak, illuminated. Last year is only memory. To me there seems to exist only the present instant. A present doomed to recur, i.e. actualize the same things over and over again, from birth to death. There is also an "I" potential attached, so to speak, to animals (re), vegetables (do), men (mi). No suggestion from anyone in the circle is of any value to "I."

The trick of getting out of this circle or maze is self-observation, participation, and experiment. Unfolding the pentagon, realizing the enneagram, "I" is the actualizing principle relative to itself. Essence is the source of all possible bodies—the physical body, the astral body, and the mental bodies are essence.

Simultaneity is the second dimension of time. The first is succession; the third, recurrence; then eternity.

The first center of "I" is individuality; the second, consciousness; the third, will.

The order of development of centers is number one, then a piece of number two, then the completion—do, re, mi, of number two.

To non-identify would be to be indifferent to any forms actualized. Buddha (it is supposed) passed from the state of human being as we know it to all degrees of actuality in the universe.

The etheric body, composed of what we call magnetism, principally can after death be sometimes materialized by some varieties of incense. But this body is no part of "I" but of the organism. The difference between being stimulated or drained is due to the types of etheric bodies of two individuals in contact. If a positive etheric body contacts in conversation or other association with a negative etheric body—naturally the positive body will be drained, unless he knows how to protect himself.

The actual home to "I" is in the sixth dimension. It lives (or should live) in do, re, mi and fa, so, la, si, but "I" is not now able to be conscious in do, re, mi. In one second after death, before recurrence, "I" sees his past and future lives.

Except for prejudice or habit we could see our whole past lives at a glance.

Plato said our aim is to learn how to die every day, i.e. to see back and foresee at a glance the whole of our lives.

Potentialities are imperceptible, but determine the form of the result of positive and negative elements. We see the positive and negative elements but see only the result—not the significance.

As far as we are concerned, neutralizing force is always psychological—i.e. not susceptible to sense perception.

There is no phenomenon without significance but we can seldom know or realize it.

We exercise all three forces, positive, negative and neutralizing. When we exercise consciously only positive and negative forces we are in the world of phenomena only, it is our work to realize the significance of the world of phenomena.

The neutralizing force is always the silent partner to positive and negative forces.

(CARL) ZIGROSSER: How is it that the neutralizing force in going up and down the scale is always different?

ORAGE: The neutralizing force going down, is to the negative absolute—in going up, to the positive absolute.

Be aware plus questioning attitude as to significance, be expectant of a meaning to appear.

Try to make every little episode in your daily life meaningful. Always have a reason if you are walking on one side of a street and if someone should tap you on your shoulder and ask why you are walking on this side of the street, you should be able to give a reason for it.

• Self-observation—trying to be aware of all your phenomena with non-identification.

• Participation is observing and acting purposively still with non-identification, i.e. as if one were choosing to go.

• Experiment = awareness to phenomena plus participation plus having a reason, still with non-identification.

We wish to identify significance in its cosmic relation. We wish to regard our organism as being a cosmic machine for the transmutation of energies to which "I" is attached.

Children are more in essence than grown-ups. But children are unfortunately very corruptible.

We wish to become incorruptible children, having known sin and rejected it. Chief feature is a pretence that you have now the development that you wish to have.

Chief feature is the relation between essence and personality. The idea is ultimately to detach "I" from personality. An ulterior motive in this work is one identified with the organism held for its welfare against that of "I."

All lower emotions are those we share with animals—all those peculiar to man are higher emotions. Lower emotions come from response of the organism to the external world. Higher emotions come from response of "I" to the organism. There are negative higher emotions, for example remorse.

This method is directed toward regularizing what has occasionally already occurred. Higher emotions for example have occurred. We wish to regularize them—to evolve a science of living.

Orage said Jesus Christ used this method; perhaps "Saint" specialized. The conversion of water into wine means—we now run on water—but by this method we run on wine.

The miracle of the loaves etc. means the scientific use of all the energies of food and of all foods.

Do = God. Si = the sum of all milky way's—i.e. all possibilities.

Three forms of reason dealing with objects.

Dealing with concepts of objects.

Dealing with potentialities.

Objective reason sees what must be if it ever actualizes.

Orage working on the Study House at The Prieuré.

THEORY

Man is a product of *heredity* and *environment* and hence is a mechanical organism determined by these two factors. All that comes through heredity is called *essence*. While that which is the result of the interplay between essence and environment is termed *personality*. Essence and personality constitute what man takes to be "*I.*" In man there is not as assumed one but three "*I's.*" These different "*I's*" are the product of three different centers in man, any one of which may be temporarily in control of the organism. The real "*I*" is potential and it may be imagined as existing some distance behind the biological and social product. The effort must be made at present to conceive the "I" as outside the organism. This effort is the effort made to achieve *non-identification*. The effort to non-identify and the effort to self-observe are to be made together. These two constitute the alpha and omega of the system.

SELF-OBSERVATION

A new psychological function existing in none of the now recognized faculties of man. It is the function of a potential "I" which may become actual by virtue of its operation. Its object is the so called shell. Since the I exists only potentially it is hardly to be expected that this faculty should immediately begin. Hence it would seem necessary to make an effort with some existent faculty to this end. In this method, and particularly in this point, the *effort to observe* must be emphasized, not result of observation. This shell is threefold, consisting of the following centers:
1. The Instinctive.
2. The Emotional.
3. The Intellectual.

These differ in their degrees of sizeableness. The instinctive being the most sizeable. In fact, the only one that can at first be sized at all, hence one begins with an observation of the instinctive center. That the observation of this center may proceed, it is necessary to divide the instinctive center into two classifications:
1. The body as a three-dimensional body.
2. The body in terms of inner sensation.

There are about ten classifications in each group. These are to be observed at first singly and then combinations of two, three, four, etc., are to be made, *the being made to achieve simultaneity of observation.* The practice of self-observation should lead from isolated to simultaneous observation. After simultaneity has been achieved in the instinctive center, it is then necessary to achieve simultaneity in the observation of the emotional and intellectual centers. The final purpose of observation is to obtain simultaneous observation of all three centers.

The real "I" is attached or stuck on to the organism (that is three centers or sub-centers of these centers). The degree of attachment usually varies in the individual, that is, I may be more stuck on to the intellectual than on to the emotional or instinctive centers, and vice versa, and it varies with individuals, hence the variety of attachments. According to the degree of attachments you will find it difficult to non-identify. In the process of achieving non-identification, the total difficulty is equal for all. For, by way of example, if one finds it relatively easy to non-identify with the instinctive center, for the reason that the "I" is stuck on to it rather loosely, it usually follows that the "I" is stuck more tightly to either the emotional or intellectual centers and hence, one will find it relatively difficult to non-identify in these cases. (Phase difficulties vary—difficulties are equal.)

THE ORGANIZATION OF MAN

Man has three centers, each sub-divided in three:

Instinctive	a. Instinctive b. Emotional c. Intellectual	Semi-amorphous—Vegetable
Emotional	a. Emotional b. Instinctive c. Intellectual	Amorphous Animal
Intellectual	a. Intellectual b. Instinctive c. Emotional	Human

Relationship between three centers:
1. They are imitative.
2. They are successive in action, giving the illusion of simultaneity.
3. No single center in man can function without the successive functioning of the other two centers. (Example of beads on a string.)
4. The instinctive is the only center that has reached the human level, the other centers are relatively undeveloped.

Man is a microcosm within the macrocosm. Therefore man has his own scale—the first three notes are the three centers.

Difference between first three and second three centers: first three are filled in life without man's effort.

a.   Man is born with the instinctive partly filled.

b.   Two other centers empty at birth.

Second three centers only filled by man's conscious effort. It is only possible to develop these higher centers by a special method (Gurdjieff system or such as this). This effort to develop the "I" by formulation, self-observation, and non-identification leads to the awakening of these three higher centers. These three centers become the emotional, intellectual and instinctive centers of the "I." This development of higher centers raises the focus of consciousness.

ATTITUDES

1.   Attitudes—mental images—induce corresponding emotions, and the emotions in turn cause actions.

2.   Each one of us has some dominant attitude toward life. The attitude placed in us by education, reading, conversation, etc., must be found. The act of finding it, trying to find it, may be called the peeling of the onion. For we have many attitudes that are superficial to the basic one. When found, this attitude will be seen to be childish and not corresponding to the facts of the real world. It is usually the product of fancy, and it is fancy. For even the scientific and philosophic attitudes are fanciful. Because it is childish, our emotions must necessarily be immature, and our behavior in line with our emotions. The method then is to change the attitude. But not merely change it; change it strictly in accordance with the real world. The cosmogony given by the Gurdjieff system is an inscription of this world.

3.   Hold in the mind, among other things, these facts, the fact of death, the fact that there are two thousand million people on the earth today.

ENERGY

All energy is one. The various manifestations of energy are merely modifications of this one. Sex is the central energy of man. The instinctive, the emotional and intellectual centers of man are the transforming stations of this energy. Man is the sex cell of nature. All living forms are screens through which energy passes.

MAN'S FUNCTION IN THE UNIVERSE

Man is a transmitting agency of energy from the planets to the moon. The moon needs an aid which is human pain.

THE FORMULATORY CENTER

The intellectual or formulatory center is the driver, the emotional center the horse, and the instinctive center the cart pulled by the horse and directed by the driver's reins.

MISCELLANEOUS

1.   The sense of time for us is produced by our breathing.

2.   One plane is all planes. Such things as inclined planes, etc., are subjective determinations. In particular, we derive the conception of an inclined plane (in fact all inclines) from what we call inclination, from a psychological (subjective) state.

3.   Potentialities are actualities. Whatever is to be, exists now. A thing is potential solely in reference to our (limited) consciousness.

4.   Most emotion and thought, instead of coming from the emotional and intellectual centers respectively, are but projections from the instinctive center.

5.   Man may be seen in terms of the triangle, each center being a side. But no one side or combination of sides can see and comprehend the entire figure. For this, it is necessary that a fourth center existing outside of the triangle act. This center is the "I."

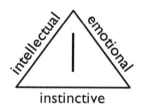

ESSENCE

Essence is that part of us with which we are born. It contains all particles of planetary matter corresponding to all planets by which we are affected at the time of conception or at the time of birth. Since the planetary influences are never the same, it follows, that each person in essence is constituted differently.

THE LIMITS OF THE SOLAR SYSTEM

Is defined by the extent of the suns influence. Sunlight is energy, therefore matter. Twenty tons are deposited by the sun on this globe each day. Sunrays deposit matter in us. In like manner the substance of other planets whose influence reaches us deposit matter in us.

There are two assumptions—

1.   That experience is good in itself.
2.   That it teaches.

In fact, however, experience may prove harmful to the extent that something is damaged beyond repair. And though *we* may *learn* from experience, it, being passive, teaches nothing.

THE OCTAVE

The scale is a symbolical expression of the relationship that exists throughout the universe—do, re, mi, *fa*, sol, la, *si*, do.

Fa and si are half tones—the rest are whole tones. A half tone indicates a difficulty or that the original impulse is diminished, exhausted or slowed down at that point. The scale is composed of two tetra cords, composed of tone, tone and semitone.

Each note in the scale may be considered as the note of a new octave. Between any two notes there is another and innumerable inner octaves. Do is at once the end of one octave and the beginning of another. Can do therefore be isolated to any one octave? No. An impulse has no sooner struck do than it passes on to re. Energy can run either up or down the scale. Does the impulse descending the scale travel through the identical notes as the one ascending?

I. THE GREAT OCTAVE — AUM — OM

The earth is mi.
The moon is re.
The planet forming behind the moon is do.
The planets are fa.
The sun is sol.
The milky way is la.
All the milky ways are si.
The entire universe is do.
(Our sun is a planet to the sun of the milky way.)

The moon is younger than the earth. As the earth moves up the scale to the position of planets, the moon becomes earth, and the planet behind the moon becomes moon to the present moon. (Their earth.)

2. THE NATURAL OCTAVE

Metals	do		1
Minerals	re	Metals	2
Vegetable	mi	Minerals	3
Invertebrates	fa	Vegetable	4
Vertebrates	sol	Invertebrates	5
	la	Vertebrates	6
Man	si	Man	7
	do		8

(Something lower than metals still unknown, really do.) Or fa not existing would complete the scale with metals at 1.

Man is the mind of nature.

THE HUMAN OCTAVE

Man's three centers are the first three notes of the octave.

1st Center	Instinctive	do	Planet forming
2nd Center	Emotional	re	The moon
3rd Center	Intellectual	mi	The earth
4th Center	(Self-observation,		
	its function)	fa	The planets
5th Center		sol	The sun
6th Center		la	The milky way
7th Center		si	All other milky ways
		do	The great universe

Only the first three centers of man are awake. Man has a sun, moon, etc., analogous to the great scale within himself.

Where is man in his own scale?

MONDAY, 5 JANUARY 1925

ORAGE: Questions?

ZIGROSSER: As to the octave?

ORAGE: Will someone repeat the great octave?

G: Planet behind the moon—do, moon—re, earth—mi, planets—fa, sun—sol, milky way—la, all milky ways—si, the totality—do.

Question as to the first do being in a formative phase.

ORAGE: Impulse started from the top do.

Florence K. questions this statement, (the great octave). Orage answers by reminding of what he has said about attitudes. This given as corresponding to facts certain of which are already generally accepted, namely that the moon, which is earth's satellite, revolves about it. The earth revolves about the sun. The sun as a planet in this (our) milky way. The many milky ways. What is new, is the relation between these things as given by the Gurdjieff-system: the octave. And, by implication, the elaboration of this octave, which followed:

1. What is an epitome of a thing can know it.
2. A seed is an epitome of a tree, and hence can know it.
3. Man is an epitome of nature, and hence can know it.
a. Nature is an epitome of our globe.
b. Our globe of the planets.
c. The planets of sun.
d. The sun of the sun of the milky way (situated in the constellation of Hercules).
e. The sun of the milky way of all milky way suns.
f. These suns of the absolute.
g. Hence, man is an epitome of the absolute.
4. Man is an epitome of nature.
a. Cells within man, categories of cells in his body correspond to each category of nature. Hence man contains cells corresponding to the metals, minerals, plants, invertebrates and vertebrate animals, and the human species.
b. Man's brain contains numerous animal cells—monkey cells—and a small number—twenty perhaps—of human cells. It is by virtue of these hu man cells that he is human.
c. Mankind as a whole is the human cell or cells in the brain of nature.
5. For nature is a being whose body we perceive.
6. While the organic kingdom is or are, the sense organs of our globe, by means of which our globe communicates with other globes.
7. And the globes are analogously related and perform corresponding functions for the sun. The sun for the sun of the milky way. And so on.
8. Just as we are beings of definite forms, so too are nature, our globe, all globes, the sun, all suns, the absolute, beings (or one being) with indefinite forms (a definite form). We, however, because of our limited perception, do not see these other forms as they actually are. *(Illustration)*: I sit in my chair. I revolve at rates 500 revolutions per second. I will see myself as I actually am but to onlookers I will appear as a globe—a sphere.
a. The absolute is a definite being and must not be confused with the conception of infinity.
9. Just as the potential "I" in man stands in relation to his body—not being conscious in relation to it, not knowing it, not being able to control it, so the "I" of nature exists in relation to its body, the "I" of our globe in relation

to its body, and so on, up to the absolute. And at the end we may find that the whole thing was simply this great being, *dreaming*.

a. In so far as our "I" becomes conscious, the "I" of nature becomes conscious. And so on. In so far as our "I" gains control of the organism, the "I" of nature gains control over its body. And so on.

10. All this, a statement of fact. Let the attitude be accordingly. Then emotion may really mature. Etc.

Zigrosser questions as to the relationship, our globe—mi, planets—fa. For are we not of the planets?

ANSWER: Analogy—I, Jean Toomer, am one thing, and, while I am of humanity, yet humanity is certainly not Jean Toomer, hence, from this point of view, the two things are different.

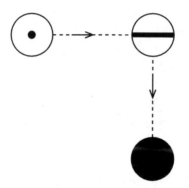

GRACE POTTER: Limitation of attitude due to partial facts.
ORAGE: Need of view of *wholes*. Spengler.
EDNA KENTON [as to observation]: Long intervals between "flashes."

Orage relates the discussion on brain cells to the problem of observation.

The potential "I" has an ally in the organism; the human brain cells. These, once stimulated, carry on its work as best they can, during its long periods of sleep or absence—recall one to observe, impel one to make the effort etc. and, though they do not actually observe—in the sense that only "I" can observe—yet they do much work, and the "I" whenever it partially or more fully awakes, will find that much "business" will have been done by these allies. In addition to their acts specifically connected with observation, they set about the controlling of the organism. They are the cells capable of responding to and retraining the truth as regards the real world. Hence, they are the vehicles of mature attitude. Hence too their *indirect* power to control. And as a very important task, they can set about the task of subduing the monkey cells—the formulatory center—to the service of the higher intellectual and emotional centers, to the control of the "I." As it is, these cells, this center is really nothing more than the slave of the lower (emotional instinctive centers). They generate phantasies (fancies) and every childish attitude which man is capable of. In themselves, it is their nature to be this way, and they are this way in response to the lower centers. The method of subduing them, of *humanizing* them, is to force them to formulate in words the various observations, etc.

(Depression is the pain of growth, growing pains. One must work through it, constantly applying the method.)

GRACE POTTERS: Recalling the events of the day in pictures.

ORAGE: Repeat numbers, or a poem.

In the monasteries: monks, fingering beads and mumbling prayers, to occupy the instinctive and intellectual centers, thus freeing the emotional center for sainthood.

("I" is absolute: a cat, or an apple is absolute.)

MONDAY, 12 JANUARY 1925

COLLECTIVE ACCIDENT

Adam Kadmon—Totality of Man

M: How to make a working fact of two thousand million people?

ORAGE: Corresponding to the number of brain cells there are two thousand million people on this earth. Conceive of these as divided in races, then nations, etc.

Take an ordinary globe in your mind, locate all countries mentally, the inhabitants history, life, distribution, characteristics, etc. Then twist rapidly and try to get a simultaneous sense of all these.

This discussion is associated with recalling one's childhood. First to be recalled sequentially and then an effort made to get a simultaneous picture. (Refers to writing biography up to present time and then extend to a novel which would portray the future.) Each of us is all that we have been and what we shall be, it now actually exists, but in time we are unable to perceive it. Four-dimensional perception would give you a complete picture of the past and also the future. But the future is not so certain as the past, for the reason that any situation has a number of possibilities, from among which, theoretically, any choice can be made. Example of get out of chair, theoretically all is possible, actually only one is possible because of heredity and past experience.

Time is the actualization of one possibility.

The number of probables however are not infinite, and hence free choice is not an infinite choice but a choice limited to possibles. Such a choice may be called the *lesser freedom. The greater freedom* is choice among *sets of possibles.* The lesser of freedom though limited to the organism may decide as to what that organism within its limitations may do. This means the control by the "I" of the three lower centers, i.e. the power to make them act, rather than mechanically react. (Intellectual is the weakest and highest center.) The greater freedom is not limited to this organism but has choice of organism, i.e. choice with respect to reincarnation. (Choice among sets of possibles.)

GREAT OCTAVE REPEATED

Addition—any whole is an octave, any whole is an epitome

Man is such an octave, a whole.

But other kingdoms of nature below man are not (mineral, vegetable, etc.)

The natural octave is placed in the great octave between mi and fa, the half tone between earth and planet, i.e. man is between earth and planets. He is subject to the influence of both sun and moon.

Any do has two aspects, positive and negative. A positive struck means an ascending impulse. A negative struck leads down the scale.

The top do on a great octave was struck in its negative aspect. In consequence of this fact the impulse is down the scale to the planet forming behind the moon. Therefore man is being drawn toward the moon. If man subserves this cosmic impulse he will run down the scale become successively unconscious of his intellectual and emotional centers, just as he is now unconscious of his higher centers. Communication between the centers will be cut off. The sun stands for joy, the moon sorrow and pain. The result will be increasing pain and suffering for man. Man because of this function is given the possibility of moving toward the sun against the downward impulse.

The sun is a plateau—once you reach it you are safe.

Example: *Seven Indian boxes within each other.*

The outermost box corresponding to all milky ways being one. And successively down the great octave, each being subject to a group of laws, the innermost box equals do or seven, is subject to all the laws. Re is six. Break into the next box, and it is subject to one less law, mi is five etc.

When an impulse dies out one becomes subject to inclination, i.e. he follows the line of least resistance, the movement being circular.

Within man certain of the cells are human, whole cells, and are therefore a complete octave. Within these cells are other cells, atoms, or electrons, likewise whole or octaves. Because these cells are octaves within man there is the possibility that man may do this work and rise in the scale towards the sun.

Man's Scale

Do	Re	Mi	Fa	Sol	La	Si
		Instinctive	Emotional	Intellectual	"I" Center	"I"
					Super-conscious	Super-super-conscious
		Earth	Planets	Sun	Milky Way	Sun of All Milky Ways

Human cells are like Machiavelli's prince, they must use much strategy and control of an unwieldy kingdom.

TUESDAY, 27 JANUARY 1925

Business redistributing people in two groups.

Gorham reads report on last meeting.

Orage asked for questions stimulated by reading.

SIG: *Please develop idea about time.* Mr. Munson seemed clear in his statement as to the mechanism of film unrolling, but is that the correct explanation?

ORAGE: *The work of unrolling the film is the work of the emotional center as a whole.* The emotional center and its instinctive and intellectual sub-centers, a complete non-identification in unrolling the film would eliminate emotion. The practicing of the film is a good exercise in non-identification. Facing one's self occurs when the fourth center, the "I," faces the other three centers objectively. The organism or any part of it cannot face itself. No one of the three centers can truly judge each other. Real judgment can only take place in the fourth center. Only rarely do we *experience purely* in one center. Usually we are between two or three centers. Under extreme or unusual circumstances a single center can be brought into play. The need of placing the organism in such circumstances for experimental purposes. (Gurdjieff experience in robber band and Russian convict camp.)

The constructive imagination can also be used to induce such experience. States of fear, nightmare etc., can be consciously induced for the sake of observation. *If you did observe these things in a state of non-identification these things would not occur.* An examination of one's life would reveal a constant recurrence of similar circumstances. The only way to change this pattern is by withdrawal of the "I," thus changing the chemical combination. The pattern can be changed in no other way, for we can neither add a new chemical nor control a given combination. Man can do only what he cannot help doing. Example of a severed arm. For therapeutic purposes past emotion connected with an experience may consciously be re-induced, to observe it for the purpose of eliminating it.

Past time does not exist nor does future time exist. If you worry about what happened yesterday you will be certain to repeat it today. It is useless to waste energy over the past which no longer exists and the future which may not exist.

The idea of mechanicality if continually and consciously maintained will filter through to the emotion, the higher emotion situated in the heart as contrasted the lower emotion in solar plexus. Until this happens no real work can be done. *This creates a sense of tragic urgency* that drives one on in itself. If the group stopped if everyone died, one would go on alone. *Will, judgment, desire,* etc., are simply mechanical compensations for the purpose of re-establishing balance.

TIME AND DIMENSIONS

(Mental gymnastic problems.)

The dot, the line, the plane. References to Hinton.

Framing stick twirled in circle, continuous line, cannot tell where real stick is.

Silver globe and apple rotating round, creating impression of band. Movement of both upward would result in a cylinder covered with green (from apple.) Moving in a third direction, it creates a sphere cased in green. This relationship of casing within casing applies to all the bodies of the universe like skins of an onion.

The law of effects is based on chemical affinity rather than continuity or gravitation.

PSYCHOLOGICAL TIME

Time is the actualization of one possible. The three aspects of time are: *time, eternity, duration*. Time and dimension are properties of matter as related to our perceptions.

Israel Solon digresses: truth cannot be perceived by one center alone. Orage agrees. Places this conception of time not as an achieved reality but as a mental gymnastics until it was tested.

Continuity is reality. Truth is the last illusion. When you finally arrived at the seventh dimension you would find a point moving simultaneously in six directions which do not exist. Moving in three opposite directions of time, eternity and duration as dimension.

MISS KING: Wasn't there *more about time?*

ORAGE: *The physical scale represents the working of the law of man in time.* From do to mi man moves mechanically and returns to do in a circular movement unless some outside agency draws him up to fa. Man is bound in this circle of time unless he breaks it to reach fa. If you are born in 1886 and you die in 1930, you wake an instant but fall asleep again. You will still then be in 1886. You can do nothing but live over the identical life in time. But if you step from mi to fa you are out of time. You wake up, escape the dream. To step over into the second tetra-chord places you in eternity. *The difference between time and eternity* being whereas in time you are determined in your choice, in eternity choice is free. But even in eternity or being a God you are only free to choose within a definite and limited range of possibilities.

Second birth—immaculate conception.

Akashic records—man is in his emotional center. Nature's is located similarly.

TUESDAY, 3 FEBRUARY 1925

1. Question regarding inhibitions—the necessity of breaking through them—first questions an inhibition once broken through cannot against present itself as formerly.

2. Difficulty in finding third movement.

3. Not necessary to achieve the result; but necessary to make the effort.

a. *General question of effort.*

Life as a gymnasium—the effort, not the result.

Reversal of world process—heaven, earth.

Mabel Collins—work as one whose desire is success.

Development of muscle.

Distinction between effort impelled or helped by the prospect of the end-product, and the effort made gratuitously.

Religious practices for consciousness:

1. Laying one's self down to measure the way.

2. Jesuits in missionary activities.

Walking all night.

Making money when no need for it.

Impossible tasks.

b. *The three types of effort.*

1. Ascetics—instinctive, but with no regard for other centers.

2. Saints—emotional, but with no regard for other centers.

3. Yogi—intellectual, but with no regard for other centers.

This system demands all three types of effort.

4. *Essence—heredity.*

Three types of chemicals: active, passive, neutral. (Chemicals due to experience; active.)

Essence, at present passive.

Self-observation transforms these passive chemicals to active, releases them. Thus introducing and producing new combinations in the organism.

Essence located in the emotional center.

5. *Essential Wish.*

a.   We cannot really wish in the present state, for an essential wish involves the harmonious, (but not necessarily equal), desire of all three centers. As to this work none of us really wish it with all of our three centers, for if we did, then this wish could be stopped (destroyed) by nothing, but must achieve its end. For *this is the nature of an essential wish.* (Gravitations: the wish matter. Example: a drop of water wishing the center of the earth.) The intellect wishes it, but the intellect which is the highest is also the weakest center. The infantile emotion does not wish it. (This will come when the intellectual wish filters through.) The monstrous instinctive does not wish it.

b.   Image: driver—intellectual, cart—instinctive, horse—emotional. Driver, not only cannot control, but he is usually in the public house chattering with the other drivers while the horses and cart may rear about as it pleases them. The use of words, in the face of the inability to act.

6. *Reality is the object of this method.*

Beginning of actual content to what are at present empty words. Examples: The "I," an empty word, for if this organism (by means of which we now realize ourselves) were abstracted, then the "I" would have no means of realizing itself, practically it would not exist. *The "I," virtually a literary image.*

Grace questions this, claiming that it has a real meaning, a real content for many people in terms of their orientation to life—true, but somnambulist, man under anesthetic, the idiot, are likewise orientated to life.

The idiot is on three wheels, the normal man on four, but both are mechanically orientated.

7. *Devolution—Evolution.*

(Idiot loss of human cells.)

Man in devolution; nature in evolution. Man drawn to moon, then in waking state a condition that we now call sleep. Now man's waking state is sleep to the state above. He must break this sleep, to really awaken.

Nature in evolution: physical body now evolved by nature to the human phase. The instinctive complete—emotional infantile, intellectual practically not born. Nature has done all she can. If man is not to continue devoluting he himself, of his own effort, must mature the emotional and intellectual centers. From another point of view he must recover them, that is, regain a consciousness of them.

8. *Was man once conscious?*

Yes, but not during the period covered by the historic races.

Adam—the garden—the organism.

Once its gardener. Put out. The "I" put out. It must return. The second Adam.

The Indian tale, the infant before birth sings: "Let me remember who I am." Its first cry after birth, I have forgotten who I am.

Christ method. Saint Paul—trying at first to compromise.

The Pythagoreans, Plato, Catullus.

9.   *Formulating* as to objects.

a.   All you know about an object—sequential.

b.   The effort to hold this data simultaneously.

c.   Thinking, sequential.

d.   Conscious: all one knows, simultaneously known.

e.   The development of "I," a necessary forerunner of consciousness. This life as a means to the "I."

10.   *Distinction between logic and psychologic.*

a.   Logic—line.

b.   Psychologic—plane—consciousness.

c.   Heart—knowledge.

11.   *Language.*

a.   Sounds—pattern.

12.   *Gorham as to happiness*—craftsmanship—selection—humanism.

Orage:

a.   Subjective.

b.   Happiness an accident due to a certain relationship subsisting between the centers and the environment.

c.   Not a result of choice but in all ways determined.

d.   The ten wishes.

e.   Happiness: lower. Bliss: higher emotional.

f.   Happiness as by-product.

13.   *Weight of opinion*—Memory of truth.

a.   Common language expressing all thought, opinion, being matter, has weight.

b.   According to weight, opinion received through conversation, reading, etc., goes to some center or sub-center.

c.   Observe opinions as to their weight, the tone of voice which expresses them.

d.   Illustrations of different degrees of weightiness—ending in facing a trip to London.

e.   Observe emotions as to their weight.

Comparison on Gurdjieff to standards of ordinary life: What are by-products of this system are regarded as objectives of ordinary life.

Non-essential wish: That which can be displaced or altered by superficial circumstances: meal, (food), conversation, reading, etc.

Essential wish: That which cannot be displaced or altered by these things, which sustains itself even in the face of powerful externality.

SUNDAY, 8 FEBRUARY 1925

GERTRUDE: Does essence enter into the formation of the "I"?

ORAGE: Yes, *Essence is heredity, and through heredity we get everything we are or can be as potentials,* at birth includes elements responsive to sun, planets, etc. But circumstances permit the actualization of certain of these potentials. The actualized potential correspond to our existing three centers. In the process of actualizing these three centers by means of experience the personality is formed. By an extension of this personality the higher centers cannot be actualized. It is therefore *necessary to dissolve this personality or in other words to make it transparent.* And begin again with essence—"As little children."

ESSENCE

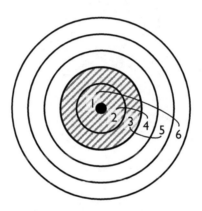

Plan of centers—1, 2, 3, lower instinctive, emotional and intellectual. Instinctive center only one filled. At first observation within first three centers. As these are filled a center in circle 4, the "I," begins to form. It can observe all three centers together as if outside the organism. As the fourth center fills, a center in circle 5 begins to grow. Then 5 fills etc., through circle 6.

Law of triads—1, 2, 3. No. 2 is neutral and forms the beginning of the next triad.

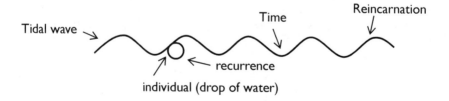

The two pre-requisites for this work: magnetic center built up accidentally by favorable circumstances and encounters, and by reading of folk tales, mystic and occult literature—a sense of time, a sense of urgency (contact with the real method).

ANALYSIS OF CIRCULAR MOTION

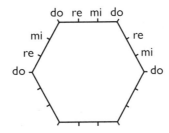

Zigrosser asked how this circular motion occurred when movement appeared linear.

Movement of each drop of water in tide carried from do to mi, then momentum died and it dropped at mi. Each time beginning of another new do. Circular because of habit and lack of effort to cross fa. If one can maintain straight line one breaks the circle and gets into the stream of time. If a straight line can only be maintained for a certain distance this only widens the circle.

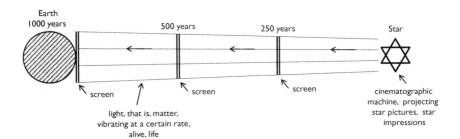

Conceive the star as being a cinematographic machine projecting picture, impressions, composed not of a single substance, but of complex matter. The earth as screen. These pictures then reach us 1,000 years after they have taken place on the star. If one were in position to be at the same time on the star and on the earth, we would perceive what was then taking place on the star and, from the earth, what had taken place on the star 1.000 years previously. These pictures are our life, ourselves. We are then nothing more than what transpired on some star or group of stars thousands of years ago. Hence, the illusion involved in our thinking that we exist, as we perceive ourselves.

THREE KINDS OF FOOD

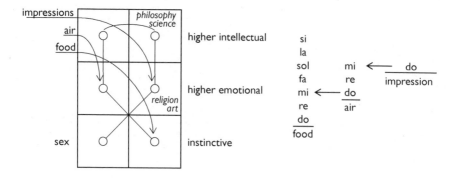

Three types of food needed to feed the organism.

1.   *Regular food*—which we are able to select, avoiding rotten and choosing most suitable food. This feeds the instinctive center.

2.   *Air as a food*—can also be selected and controlled by those who have been taught through special breathing exercises. Possible to breathe so as to draw sun, air, planetary, etc., separately. Air feeds the emotional center.

3.   *Impressions*—come to us through hearing, sight, smell, touch and taste, from this and other worlds. Impressions feed our intellectual center.

SCALE OF EACH FOOD

Food goes from do to mi in instinctive center. At mi it is pushed over the half step by air, where do starts, at the mi of food, and sends food on to si, but as impressions are only a thin film-like surface of soap bubble quality, it does not even fill do, and has no momentum, therefore problem is to develop impressions of lower intellectual center in order to eventually feed the "I," the upper centers.

The impressions we usually receive are empty, or, of them we receive only the name, at most, the husk. Hence they are not real food for us, nor can they function as a shock to lift air from its mi to fa. They do not strike a full do. They must be made conscious, that is, filled with content. The method is to make the effort to have present in the mind all we know of an object when we perceive it. (The mind gives content to impressions.) Conscious impressions feed the higher centers.

We are ordinarily subjected in the functioning of our three lower centers. In the two higher centers—art and religion, science and philosophy are divided. Mathematics is the only pure and objective-subject within our experience. Science, art, and religion are subject to as definite a measurement.

Sex is a center in touch with the cosmic store or reservoir.

Instinctive center is the machine.

Emotional is heat.

Intellectual is light.

Each draws off energy from sex and transforms it according to its nature. This they store in a reservoir. If center is in good working condition it utilizes its store. Defective working conditions will leave a surplus which then tends to overflow into another center. Example: emotional coloring of ideas. Cause of neurosis, lack of functioning of machine and overflow. *Sex cannot be touched directly*, nor can the centers touch themselves. The functioning and balance between the three lower centers can only be achieved by the action of the two higher centers. These can only become active through the development of the "I," i.e. feeding them through formulation of impression and observation.

Fall

Deluge

Tower of Babel
$$\uparrow$$
Satan, Christ—equal exertion necessary to each.
$$\downarrow$$
We are in growing branch.

At present, our tip, the moon.

The final tip, the planet behind the moon.

TUESDAY, 17 FEBRUARY 1925

Re-reading of stenographic report—two meetings before. One half read.

Orage wishes that in future the major part of meetings be taken up with experience through self-observation. Only one half hour to be given to theory.

MRS. ARMSTRONG: Does self-observation tend to increase emotional disturbance? If sense of pleasure was experienced, was this activity not gratuitous? Is it usual to experience sense of deadness at times?

ORAGE: Yes. If act truly gratuitous, if pleasure accompanies it, all the better. (Example: Day in the country, Orage talking to man on train.) Yes, see diagram.

DIAGRAM OF MAN IN PROFILE

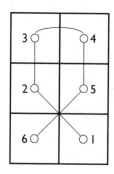

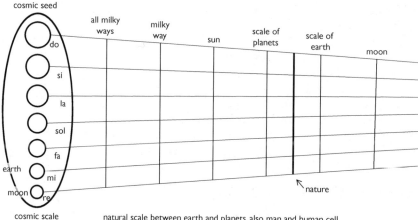

cosmic seed

all milky ways · milky way · sun · scale of planets · scale of earth · moon

do · si · la · sol · fa · mi · re

earth · moon

nature

cosmic scale   natural scale between earth and planets, also man and human cell

In waking consciousness three lower centers connect in such a way that when one acts the others tend to act correspondingly. One drags the other after. Only in sleep are the centers disconnected and their action then is separate. There is noticeable intensification in the action of three centers in sleep. The somnambulist, instinctive center works alone—walks, chasm, no fear. Terror from nightmare, emotional center alone. Mind in sleep, its isolated power greater than Shakespeare. Tendency of observation in waking life to disassociate centers and produce intensity of condition comparable to that occurring in sleep. This fact, applied to the emotional center, answers Mrs. Armstrong's first question. In order to gain state of consciousness of other higher centers we would have to wake up twice. These two higher centers cut off by some malign force with shears. From the point of view of re-establishing the connection, this work is simple. All you have to do is to re-establish the connection with the lower centers by observation. For these two centers are active. In other ways this is difficult—meaning the way we are going.

ORAGE: All these things come to us through heredity.

EDNA: Which type of heredity, greater or less?

ORAGE: You mean cosmic heredity. Parents are the only means of transmission, without the cooperation of cosmic energies they could not conceive, (see diagram). The feeling of deadness referred to by Mrs. Armstrong is explained on the diagram.

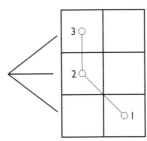

Instinctive center—partly filled, others not at all at birth.

Emotional center—filled, by impressions from parents, world of people and objects, includes like and dislikes, positive and negative, optimist and pessimist.

Intellectual center—basis of thinking is the recognition of like and dislike, i.e. discrimination. Training in discrimination—method of teaching children to select grades of colors, difference of form, etc. (Placing of words in a pattern as act of thought.)

Each of us records impressions at the rate of 30,000 per second. At the most over our life we may record a million. In contrast to the sum total this amount is negligible. When we try to explain reason for action we only know minor elements therefore, mechanicality of our nature is obvious.

Three centers are simultaneously affected by three impressions from one object. For example chair—color, quality, etc.

If one consciously holds and thinks about a true idea, it registers first in intellectual center, then in the emotional, and finally in the instinctive. This filtering through from the intellectual center, creates groups of allied cells in emotional and instinctive centers, and these allied cells form a triple alliance, (this being possible because the connection between the centers is already given). This triple alliance, which because of its consciousness is capable of affecting its desires upon the organism.

Hereditary differences registered in the different size of centers.

Example: Musicians. Large emotional, small intellectual and instinctive.

Neutralizing element equals potentiality.

This relates to the law of the triad. Any of three centers can be neutralizing element.

Third force blind.

Not to know potentials. Example: Man has gold in his pockets, does not know where it is, and then does not know where to find it.

MAN FROM BIRTH

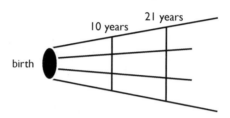

We can only see man at a given age at one moment, but they all exist. All a matter of realization.

MRS. ARMSTRONG: How could the two upper centers be active and not connected with the lower center?

ORAGE: You are mixing your terms—*confusing actual and potential, both being real,* but existing according to their natures.

The necessity of being able to distinguish between actuality and potentiality, both being real, both exist, for nothing can be except what already is.

Example: acorn—actual, oak tree—potential, but existing and capable of being seen by a higher rate of perception.

But our task is not to deal with potentials but with actualization of the one possible. Our life in time being the actualization of one possible.

MISS COUTS: Were human cells in higher intellectual center?

ORAGE: No, higher intellectual center contains no cells, was a controller of other centers and had allies in the organism, i.e. human cells.

Example: Man training dog, humanizes him, but does not himself become a dog. As stated previously, these human cells transform a certain number of monkey cells and chase a certain number up trees. This is a way of accounting for missing link between monkey and man.

Higher intellectual and emotional centers do sometimes break through.

Example: Falling in love.

Separation of centers, emotion intensified, both negative and positive, "as a little child," not having all lovely emotions.

Birth can only follow after death.

Essence of all include chemicals from all planets, but proportions of chemicals is determined by the position of stars at time of conception. Planets are

36

related to the emotional center, sun to the intellectual, milky way to higher intellect center. The planets change their positions and this factor accounts for emotional instability. By knowing one's emotional states it is possible to determine the position of the planets.

TUESDAY, 24 FEBRUARY 1925

Consciousness in three higher centers as compared to other three involves a difference of light. The lower ones are like a shadow. There are always three centers in all four phases of consciousness—sleep, our present waking, two later waking's into real consciousness, and cosmic consciousness. Three centers remain—their function change.

Example: A man pressing against different states of matter; air, fog, water and treacle. The pressure is always the same. The matter resistant, different in degree—the effect therefore different. So it is with three centers on various planes of consciousness.

Living in one of the three higher centers meant vibration increase. (30,000 times greater than usual.) With this vibration it is possible to see minute substances and distant objects such as planets with the physical eye. We are in treacle—what's the condition of getting out? We must realize that we are asleep and not merely intellectually. There were only a few; I will not mention number who have yet gotten their real sense of their mechanicality. Again recalls quantity of impressions per second.

Example: Difficulty getting out of chair. Telling have to stand up.

Free will argument. Mrs. A. and Miss C. try to squirm out—Mrs. A. says it is not true of little things.

METHOD AS A BRIDGE

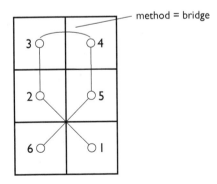

Actual application of method is necessary to form this bridge. No matter how developed a person's lower centers were, it did not help them to carry on the method. Often a deterrent, Pythagoras probably had difficulty because of his Greek egoism. Probably spent fifteen of seventeen years breaking down his pride, in Egypt. *If you can continually observe organism for a week, self-consciousness would be reached.* Emphasis on continued awareness rather than on detailed observation. Self-observation is simple, and in order to be able to do it, all this necessary irksome and preparatory exercise needed.

LUCY C: You spoke of wheat in empty jar—would result of effort in this life, resulting in the growth of the "I," be carried over to the next life?

ORAGE: It most certainly would, and would mean practically that you would meet the method sooner and carry it on more effectively. Store up treasure in the kingdom of heaven.

FORMATION OF MAGNETIC CENTER

Formation of magnetic center is formed by one's accidentally coming in contact with ideas, whose source is in the higher center. These ideas have same specific gravity without effort from the individual. They group themselves, and then they tend to crystallize about the parent idea when introduced by the method. The method comes from a self-conscious source from above. We are not going to need teaching forever. It will not be necessary to continue always observing this way, once a certain state is reached. (See back, Miss C.'s question as to how we can get on without a teacher, when Pythagoras was taught in Egypt for seventeen years.)

GRACE: Will you please explain how the idea of being born again in time with same parents occurs?

ORAGE: I will give a gross example. Though this has been answered before.

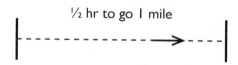

If a man move one mile in one half hour it would be possible for a dog to trace his scent, this is so, not because the dog is intelligent, but man leaves behind him fragments of his "aura." Wherever man moves he leaves the stamp of himself, a ghost of himself exists all along the route, which he successively realizes. He really exists over a complete path, and is perceptible to those having adequate perception. This straight line diagram is really a circle. The figure of the lighted point of stick swung in ring produces a circle. We do not know where the point is. To us, to our perception, the point passes through an already existent circle. We are both point and circle, this equals our life in time. (Note: read the epistles.)

GRACE: Didn't poet prophecy—the high rate of vibration could see past and future.

ORAGE: No, accidental touch of higher centers—what may be registered as a result may be inaccurate, because he is not trained to receive this thing. Something Blake says may hit the truth from higher center. He may feel it to be true, but he can neither tell the reason why it is so, nor how he arrived at it. Neither can he construct a method to attain it. Blake: "To taste bread is to taste the stars and all the eternity." Also Plato and Plotinus were touched accidentally from higher center and formulated these things. Genius also touched by it. But with this method, what with genius was an accidental flash, must be developed and sustained.

OBSERVATION

Edna questioned whether her type of observation same as Orage's. She questioned whether her type was non-identified, as point brought out by Jessie V.

Orage discusses distinction between effort to observe and moment of result. Test of conscious action—ability to arrest it. Shorten time of observation from day to one half day, get in as much as in a day. In an hour as much as half a day. Same in half hour. Thus by reducing length of day and increasing number of observations you lengthen your psychological time.

Observation of somnambulistic waking state—intellectual center still asleep.

Consciousness on a self-conscious plane does not involve complete knowledge and ability to do on it, no more than an ordinary waking from sleep implies mastery of this plane.

How can one wake up. One can wake by having a bad dream. There are illegitimate ways of waking to self-consciousness. Such an awakening is terrifying for the organism which has not been properly prepared for it. Just as we wake from sleep to waking, so we wake to self- and cosmic-consciousness.

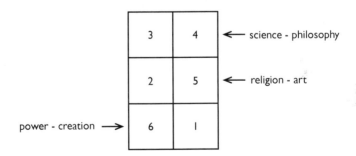

Identification all occurs at emotional center. One can drink all night with right attitude in proper psychological state without ill effects.

ZIGROSSER: If one should perceive the many existences in a single place, would he then not become confused.

ORAGE: He would have the ability to concentrate on a single figure to make selection.

Example: Smoking of cigarette—doing one thing in the presence of multiplicity.

TUESDAY, 3 MARCH 1925

Man's Pattern

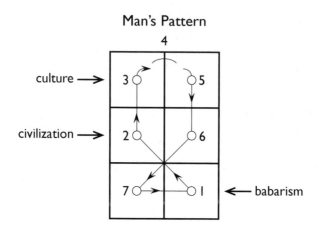

Starting point = sex = conception.
1. Instinctive—earth.
2. Lower emotional—planets.
3. Lower intellectual—negative sun.
4. State of transition.
5. Higher intellectual—positive sun.
6. Higher emotional—galaxy.
7. Cosmic sex—all stars (all milky way's).

See oneself as actually consisting of this complete pattern.

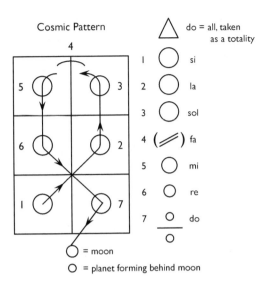

Cosmic Pattern

do = all, taken as a totality

1 — si
2 — la
3 — sol
4 — (fa)
5 — mi
6 — re
7 — do

◖ = moon
○ = planet forming behind moon

Starting point = all star = cosmic sex.
2. Galaxy—higher emotional.
3. Positive sun—higher intellectual.
4. Transition.
5. Negative sun—lower intellectual.
6. Planets—lower emotional.
7. Earth—instinctive.

See the world, our particular universe, as actually existing according this pattern.

The diagrams are maps.
A knowledge of them is a boat, (steamboat).
Taken together they provide the means for one's conscious movement in the world. They are a charted course therein.

MAN'S PATTERN

This pattern is given, complete in the moment of conception. The projection of this pattern in the world is actually what conception is. The term is to be understood literally.

Likewise the six centers are empty cups, varying in size. Capacities are given at the moment of conception.

The pattern, containing cups of various sizes, quite without content, is

41

man's heredity element. It is given by biology. The moment immediately after conception, biology ceases and sociology begins. The mother is an environment for the growing seed, the embryo. The centers receive their first content from the mother. (Now science also is beginning to recognize the mother in terms of environment.)

The content of the centers is man's environmental element. All content comes from this source.

The seed-man is conceived. Content is given to his instinctive center while he is an embryo. (A precise knowledge of this content, together with a knowledge of what—if any—content is given to the other centers (in embryo) can only be derived from man's ability to consciously project back into the embryonic phase.)

After birth, the instinctive center is the first to grow. It is given growth. It is taught movements. Secondly, the lower emotional center is given growth. It receives content from parents on all objects, in the form of likes and dislikes. Third is the lower intellectual center. Its content comes in the form of words. It holds opinions and thoughts and makes comparisons between the other two centers.

In general it may be said, that impressions constitute the content of the above mentioned centers. These enter the organism (the pattern, the empty cups) at the rate of ten thousand per second, from the moment of conception. It is these impressions, accumulated, which react to any new stimulant. These reactions are what we usually call our life. Our life then, is simply a compound reaction, it is mechanical. But each of these three centers is really three-fold, possessing a dominant center and two sub-centers. In a given case, these sub-centers correspond to the other two main centers.

For example: in the case of the intellectual there is a dominant intellectual center and an emotional sub-center (corresponding to emotional center) and an instinctive sub-center (corresponding to the instinctive center). Because of this fact, this series of correspondences, the three main centers exist in a magnetic relationship to each other. That is, if the intellectual center holds a certain idea, the emotional center will tend to feel accordingly and the instinctive will tend to act in the same fashion. To any given stimuli the three main centers tend to react together, sequentially. Hence the impossibility, save by accident, for us in our present state to experience the pure function of a single center. For example: the intellectual center, by itself, could have an emotion about an idea that is held. It is in fact necessary to try to obtain awareness of such emotion. And if thought moves rapidly, it does so because of the notion of the instinctive sub-center and so on.

TUESDAY, 3 MARCH 1925

CENTERS OF COSMIC PATTERN

The growth of these centers is provided for by natural evolution. And we are more or less aware of them. We have some knowledge of their content. But though we are not conscious of our three higher centers as existing, they do so in reality. But their development will not be carried on by nature. This must come by the conscious effort of man himself. As was said, the higher centers are in active existence and are receiving influence from the corresponding centers of the cosmic pattern. Once man was aware of these. But twice he fell asleep. That is, first the connecting link between 7 and 6 was broken and second between 6 and 5.

And then he fell asleep a third time. The gap from Sol (5) to Mi (3) was bridged downwards. Great effort necessary for this fall. Now he, who is three times asleep, is awake only in 1, 2 and 3. A similarly great effort will be needed to bridge the gap and again place him in 5, the higher intellectual. Meanwhile all that he can do is to begin at 1, run up to 3 and run down again. Likewise with nations, civilizations and races. But the number of times, that man can thus traverse the notes is limited. If he does not pass the gap within the number, then as a species he becomes extinct. The odds are against him, for the cosmic urge is downward. He may fall asleep again. That is, have the connection link broken between the lower intellectual and emotional center. Then he would dwell on the moon, in a bad condition. And then still another step—to inhabit the planet forming behind the moon.

It is doubtful that the mass of any race will bridge the difficulties. It is only necessary, however, that a certain minority affect this. For then these could accomplish the desired end.

THE SCALE

It is held that a projectile dropped from a height (gravity equal in all directions) would uniformly increase its velocity. It is held that a projectile shot from a gun would uniformly decrease in velocity.

In fact, however, the motion of an impulse is never uniform. Rather all motion whatsoever, including the one which attended the creation of the universe and those impulses which are daily occurring in the life of man, proceed according to the law of the octave, to the intervals as formulated in the scale: tone—tone—semitone—tone—tone—semitone. This is no arbitrary scheme devised for measurement. It is an acute expression of the laws which relate to impulse. An impulse actually does proceed for two steps, as it were, and encounters a difficulty. If no (additional) shock is introduced, the line is broken, then after two more steps in the new direction, this line too is deflected and so on, until the impulse, describing (more or less) a circle, returns to the point it originally started from. For instance, the figure that human life describes is a

43

twelve sided polygon. It is necessary to know this law and be able to apply it, to the end that a straight line is maintained. For even if an impulse does not die, at Mi, even if it be strong enough to maintain itself (comparatively) the danger is that, not being aware when a critical phase is (Mi) has been reached, it will end by going in the opposite direction to that which it started with. Example: the Christian religion. First break in the straight line, when it compromised with those who were in other ways desirable, but could not bring themselves to wholly accept and practice: love thy God and love neighbor as thyself. Second break: when for secular power it compromised with the Emperor Constantine and so on. Now its direction is opposite to Christ's teachings. The Grand-Inquisitor, doubtless sincere in the belief that he was doing right and strictly in line with the original doctrine.

Be conscious of the octave as it operates in one's own impulsive life.

The descending impulse is quite right and good from cosmic view point. But for the individual consciousness it is evil. Illustration of the Indian boxes: from the outmost, a progressive constriction of consciousness until the inmost one is reached. References to the earth have been thrown out by the sun and thus becoming an inferior planet. The moon having been thrown off from the earth and becoming inferior thereby.

The bull-dog grip. Emotional center. This strength and tenacity is not always good, for it often happens that a strong impulse will lead to just the opposite direction from that it started with.

The necessity for maintaining a straight line. This implies the ability to know when Mi has been reached and then (the intervention of a lucky Fa, or) the application of a conscious one.

The diagram as an interpreter of all genuine occult or religious teachings.

Active perceptions fill the higher intellectual: observation, the assembling, simultaneously, of all one knows about an object. Suppose one is dominated by an object. This lamp, for instance, just dictate what I shall see of it. But I must make it yield an active perception.

When one is not actively doing some aspect of the work, going against some inclination, etc. he is either suspended, or more likely, is regressing.

The three steps: knowledge (of the diagrams etc.), realization, constant effort and application.

To get at the source of the impulse and control it.

Pain is located in the emotional center; it is placed in man by the planets.

Due to two planets being in hostile opposition at the time of conception. The planets demand pain on earth. It may be variously distributed, but among the two thousand million people, a constant amount is obtained, always. Planetary deposits: quantity, quality and variety.

MAN'S PATTERN

1, 2, 3—Dog	5—Individuality—Holy Ghost
4—Child	6—Consciousness—The Son
5, 6, 7—Heavenly Man	7—Will—God, the Father
4 is a State	

The course in man's pattern and in the cosmic pattern is in the reverse order. Consequently, if man is to develop, he must go against the cosmic impulse. The difficulty is apparent. In fact, just in his present state, man is in the worst hot-bed of this universe.

When man dies, his instinctive pod (cup) flies open and all the seeds (impressions) fall out. Likewise with the lower emotional and intellectual center. The content of the higher centers is retained.

The occultist is one who can conceal his operations. Among men he is an ordinary man, giving no indication of what he is doing.

You walk backward, as it were. There are so many going downstream; your own progress is so slow, that the descending cosmic impulse takes no notice of you. Pushing backward to the higher centers.

Sincerity is a correct formulation of one's reactions. It may be true, it may be untrue. It has no necessary relations to objective truth.

All who really apply this method are in the fourth position, that is, in a state of transition. They are, or becoming as little children.

The higher centers are likewise in a magnetic relationship. Consequently the higher emotional center (for example) will tend to feel in accordance with an idea held by the higher intellectual.

There are cosmoses. Of the names of these only two have come to us—through Pythagoras: these are macrocosm—the milky way and microcosm—man.

These are wholes: atoms, cells, men. The whole of nature, the earth, all planets, the sun, the milky way, all milky ways, the absolute, take as the totality.

The content of the centers can be altered by some very great experience.

Taste involves both lower intellectual and emotional centers.

Scale of Food

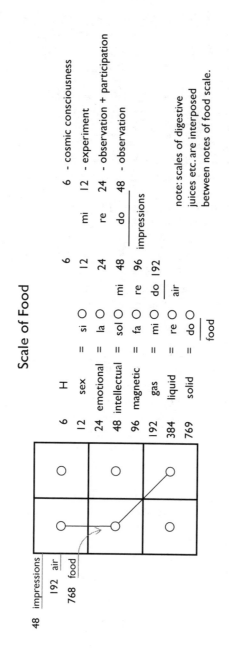

					6 - cosmic consciousness
6	H		6		6 - cosmic consciousness
12	sex = si O	12	mi	12 - experiment
24	emotional = la O	24	re	24 - observation + participation
48	intellectual = sol O	48	do	48 - observation
96	magnetic = fa O	96	impressions	
192	gas = mi O	192		
384	liquid = re O	air		
769	solid = do O			
	food			

48 impressions
192 air
768 food

note: scales of digestive
juices etc. are interposed
between notes of food scale.

46

Orage suggests that everyone take this opportunity to use this system in their own minds and ask questions on any blanks that occur.

MR. BARNES: By-products themselves would be an encouragement to effort; hence can you give me a rationale of how they occur?

ORAGE: This can be answered by explaining food, which is of three kinds (see diagram).The organism runs on energy, it does not pick it up from nowhere, but it draws energy from three forms of food. These have numbers which indicate the number of atoms in the molecule or the rate of vibration. The principle from which these numbers are derived will be given later. By applying it one can arrive at these numbers by one's self, and similarly with all the principles. Not all to be remembered but they can be reconstructed. The three forms of food enter through the head. Once they have entered and struck their do, they are then subject to the law of the octave. Food runs its octave because of the intervention of air at mi. It runs to si which is sex, where it encounters a difficulty. It is possible to bridge this difficulty. This is the transmutation of sex. But it may not be done by any of the methods ordinarily given to this purpose. The sex referred to is the lower form of sex.

Air strikes do and runs to mi. It cannot pass from mi to fa because impressions are dead. They must be changed from passive to active in order to strike their own do, likewise complete the octave of air. By-products are the result of the development of the air scale. Active perception is the observation of the organism by the "I." The "I" fed by such perceptions can actively perceive objects.

If air did not enter food scale at mi, animals and many plants could not live, the world would consist of lower forms of plant life. Air is necessary for emotion and thought. Since there is no air on the moon, the form of life possible there is unknown.

Foods affect various centers. Dietary plans of occult schools and monasteries are based on this knowledge.

The effects of foods on psychologies is not absolute in a physical sense as dieticians imply. Environment and the state of the individual condition affect food. (E.g. Man living on meat for six month in the Arctic against the advice of dietician.)

Without a certain type of digestion, certain modes of feeling and thought are impossible. (The Turks say coffee becomes poison taken in relation to certain foods, not otherwise.)

FASTING

GERTRUDE: What about the effects of fasting?

ORAGE: Effects of fast to reduce fatting tissues which surround the organs. For while fasting man feeds at first on his own fat. It is only safe to fast until the fatty tissue of the least covered organ is consumed. After the fat is removed

TUESDAY, 10 MARCH 1925

the tissue of the organ itself is used. The damage may be irreparable. The only way to fast is under competent observation, if you cannot tell. I challenge anyone to tell from the tone of his voice, sound or taste, what the states of organs under fast were in. The good effect of fasting is not to stimulate the mind, but simply remove impediment to its action. The fatty cells are parasites. They demand things for their good but not for the good of the organism. Clean organs would allow one to rely upon his taste. As it is, parasite and functional appetites mingle in our taste.

Barnes asks for an explanation of *non-identification* and *awareness*.

ORAGE: We are nothing but elements formed by nature as a product of biology and sociology. For we had no part in creating the pattern, its content or it reactions. We are a process. In point of reality, one individual not differing from another. We are ghosts. The three higher centers are however real though asleep, but they are real only in virtue that they non-identify with the lower centers. For in identity they are the lower. Hence the necessity of non-identification to establish what is real in us.

Figure: Three boys playing in a room $\left\{\begin{array}{l}\text{Instinctive banging around}\\\text{Poet reading}\\\text{Studying philosophy}\end{array}\right.$

Their main energy spent in interference with each other. The father—fourth center—he looks through the window and all attend their own business. But he must not enter the room nor try to correct them with missionary zeal.

Sleep is not positive gaining of strength, but cessation of interference of centers—connections cut. The effort to do pure work is largely in fending off interference rather than the work itself.

The body continually giving a marvelous complete record of all that is happening to it. (See Bible—Daniel, the handwriting on the wall, same as writing on body.)

GRACE: Can you teach this method to children?

ORAGE: No, it is difficult to teach it to adults, if they do it by suggestion, then its certain that they are not doing it. The most that can be done for children is the conditions where the development of centers is harmonious. This is difficult to judge in our present state of lack of knowledge. For with a harmonious development there would be no prejudice against the ideas of the system, such as most of us have to combat in one of our three centers.

Instinctive—lazy.
Emotional—dislike.
Intellectual—scientific training.

Also a wider range of experience, tastes, etc., are possible for children. Gypsy child's education ideal. Variety no falsity. Standards of conventional upbringing false. Values set up untrue, reward for truth work and virtue.

MR. BARNES: When you are angry, drink a glass of brandy.

ORAGE: Just the wrong thing. Never drink when you are down, only when you feel gay. If you running down the scale it drives you lower.

Image of stalk, sheaf, an ear—we are this, instinctive, emotional and intellectual. The stalk begun, sheaf slight, ear hardly exist. Just as the instinctive is the starting point or stalk for the lower emotional and intellectual, or stalk of its triad, so the higher intellectual is the starting point of the upper triad.

The two types of fatigue—real and imaginary.

Christian science part of truth turned the wrong way.

TUESDAY, 17 MARCH 1925

We are in a similar state as the savage, but on a higher plane. We need to be given language, fire and tools. For us, language is the understanding of the precise meaning of terms according to the Gurdjieff-system. Our tools are the use of our centers. Fire is energy. Then it is necessary to plough, plant and cultivate. As to language, it is now necessary to examine it and see what fresh meaning it holds for us in light of the system.

Orage then asked for our understanding of certain words prominent in the system. This process resulted in accurate definition. He suggested the following words to think about before being questioned. Man, world, life, consciousness, time, occult, dimension, thought, emotion, sensation.

MAN

LUCY CALHOUN: Man had possibility of immortality.

ORAGE: Yes. You mean within man's patterns. All right to begin with.

(Jean thought, but didn't say, man is a whole in the natural kingdom, being used as a transmuter of rays to the moon.)

DEGREES OF MAN — MAN DEFINED

No. "1"	No. "4"	
No. "2"	No. "5"	1, 2, 3, lower centers
No. "3"	No. "6"	4, transition, students
	No. "7"	5, 6, 7, higher centers

This tells where man's center of gravity is located.

Varieties of man determined by combination of center and sub-center.

WORLD DEFINED

ZIGROSSER: World not cosmos.

LISA: World is seven bodies related in a scale ascending from moon to the absolute forming one particular cosmos. World's pattern related to man's pattern.

LIFE DEFINED

Life exists within the organic kingdom. Man does not think of life as existing in other terms than his own (moon seems dead, etc.). There is an organic kingdom on moon, earth, sun, located on the surface of our earth between sun, earth and moon. These organic kingdoms form the food (scale) of the cosmic being. The difference in degree of development of nature on moon, earth and sun correspond to the three scales of food, air and impressions of man. The moon feeds on food, the earth on air, the sun on impressions. Follow up this analogy in our own feeding and digestion (see diagram last time). The sun is both active and passive in relation to the planets. The active sun sends out a growing ray. We are in such a ray. The earth of sun, moon of earth, planet behind moon. Passive sun's ray does not grow. Example ray to Venus.

CONSCIOUSNESS

Man only conscious three dimensionally—one and two dimensions effect of imagination.

Time—three dimensions—time, eternity, duration.

Time realization of one possible.

Eternity is the continued realization of that possible. A plane is an infinite of lines. A line cut across a sensitive plate would send out a wave which would reproduce this line all along a plane. Actually not a plane but a circumferences of a cylinder. The lines produced are similar so it makes no difference at what point you start. Doctrine of recurrence applies. We live in eternity. Nothing lives in time. Theoretically possible to choose among possibles, actually possible is chosen for us. Could we select a possible not predetermined, then in so doing, we would create another plane.

A sufficient freedom of choice would allow us to create in such a way as to create a solid. This would be free will. We would exist in duration.

Example: Orange, proceed with needle. Freedom to push needle in at any point.

(Create planes) = duration.

Thing always active in all six planes, but in point of consciousness it might exist in special planes.

Four forms of consciousness. Consciousness is a relationship between centers.

1. Waking (only one we know)—magnetic relationship.
2. Sleeping (by report)—centers are disassociated.
3. Simultaneous activity of all three centers, fourth center active—all three centers are one—not three in one.
4. Three higher centers—are one as opposed to three lower centers as one = Christ- Jesus.

SENSATION, EMOTION, THOUGHT

1. Sensation—first element.
2. Emotion—interpretation of sensation in terms of like and dislikes.
3. Thought—interpretation of other two centers in terms of comparison.
4. Simultaneous interpretation of all three above.

ORAGE: After the "I" has been given sufficient content to start its growth, what are its activities, what does the "I" like to play with? (Any action not contained within the existing centers.)

1. True ideas, life, death, humanity.
2. Wholes.
3. Microcosm, macrocosm.
4. Thinking about the doctrine.
5. Making passive impressions active.
6. Giving real content to words (making two centers work together will give content to words).
7. Constructive imagination.

51

8.   Formulatory work.

9.   Breaking up associative thinking and effort consciously, to bring things together.

10.   (Horse described by Job. All gospels formulated.)

11.   Going against inclination.

12.   All attempts at simultaneity.

13.   See things in relationship.

Gorham answers as to what activity of higher centers is, by naming by-products of his personal experience.

Instinctive—overcoming self-consciousness.

Emotional—becoming aware of childishness.

Intellectual—gaining more muscle.

Eight types of observations—four types with sub-group

I	a.	Instinctive
	b.	Experimenting
II	a.	Emotional
	b.	Experimenting
III	a.	Intellectual
	b.	Experimenting
IV	a.	Simultaneous observation
	b.	Experimenting

While observing instinctive, increasing amount of emotional and intellectual enter in.

No single object exists. Effort to see everything in terms of relationships. As for instance a cigarette related to the universe—tobacco being vegetable in organic kingdom.

Heat is matter in increased vibration. To beings of higher consciousness, what appeared to us as heat, would not affect them.

One of the important by-products of the application of the method is a reduction of waste energy.

RECURRENCE

Possibility of expansion or contraction of circle. Relate this to circular movement of earth round the sun.

WEDNESDAY, 23 MARCH 1925

A peasant has as much mental activity (thought) as cultured man. Cultured man perhaps has more images.

Energy uselessly spent in ordinary thinking. Three types of thinking:

1.   Ordinary.
2.   Feel no and say yes.
3.   For profit, pleasure and consciousness.

Morality—one center activity is immoral, create conditions for morality if none are provided (profit is anything that feeds the instinctive center).

FIRE

Fire created by friction—for instance, feeling no and saying yes.

Lawful fire—fire created for individuality, consciousness and will.

Unlawful fire—created for personality.

We become fiery men in proportion as we create this fire.

The futility of mere information.

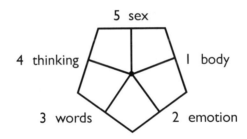

Necessity to utilize the energy drawn off (put aside) for each and all of these, else the energy turns upon itself, becomes poison, and poisons the organism.

1.   Physical activity: walking if done consciously.
2.   The range of feelings: hate, fear, love, pain, joy, etc. (pleasant if possible, if not, then unpleasant).
3.   Talk: ordinary conversation. (Women gossiping necessary to their general health and other activities.)
4.   Thinking about facts: formulating facts.
5.   Sex.

All that we have is life, and an organism, an instrument by means of which we can contact life.

Real thinking is the application of imagination, (real imagination not fancy) to fact or facts. The attempt to think of the two thousand million people. Each one of these may be taken as the missing member of any given unit. The complete human being would be Adam Kadmon. Any given human being needs all the rest to complete his humanity. In so far as one does not understand any person, who may present himself, one is incomplete.

We need to change our state of being in order to increase our range of understanding. The state of being is dependent upon the relation of the centers, alter it by observation.

MONDAY, 30 MARCH 1925

How does the previous definition of morality fit in with the social morality.

ORAGE: Society is concerned with itself not with individual needs. Group reactions are mechanical, not real.

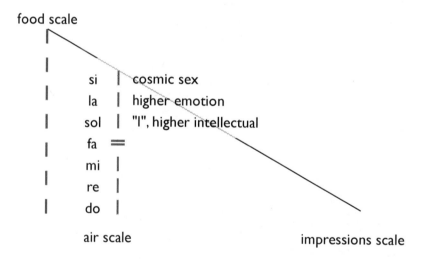

We are only what we are in virtue of food. Hence the development of higher centers or completion of our humanity is dependent on food. Specifically completing of an octave. Complete development of the food scale places us as animals. If not for the coating of education this would show clearly. For our enemy is animal. This becomes evident in proportion as work is carried on.

When these things are uncovered, there are always two centers to balance it. (Remain in instinctive and intellectual—essence = emotional.

ZIGROSSER: If the possibilities one person could actualize were limited by the fact that they were being actualized by the rest of humanity, two thousand millions necessary to realize all possible. Humanity taken a whole—called Adam Kadmon in Kabbalah. Humanity is actualization of all the possibles contained in one man. These possibles limited by mans pattern, for obviously he's not a tree, cat or tiger. Necessity of seeing whole humanity not simply as anthropologist would see them, but as all they had been, were and attempt to see what they would be, must be seen in terms of three centers, instinctive, psychic and psychological. Seeing with one center was not seeing at all. Comparable to seeing one side of triangle = line. Seeing with two sides = angle. Attempt to see threefold, man utilizes threefold nature of one who makes the attempt.

DEATH

None of us know whether we would get home tonight without dying. Image of man living on thread over precipice—is conscious with his whole body of situation. We are in relation to death hanging on thread over precipice. But that is not even real. We are mere sociological bubbles.

All that is real are our sensations. Refers back to ten internal, ten external movements and sensations. Suggest isolating and observing each for day, voice, expression, gesture. Observe our expression while talking to others (transparent).

The world is what we imagine it to be, judging from sensations. That unreal, get back to observing sensation. Only way to increase knowledge and experience of external world and things to observe oneself. The subject and not the object. This may appear round about method but really short cut. Houdini memory training, shop window all wrong. Don't pursue imagination, formulation, etc., as such.

MR. ANDERSON: How were impressions made active?

ORAGE: By observing them. 10,000 impressions—our opinion is naturally wrong based on so few conscious ones. As we observe, area of the conscious impressions increase, thus reducing the unconscious area. In proportion as one becomes conscious of present area of impressions, he likewise becomes conscious of unconscious impressions in his past life, for the two areas are identical.

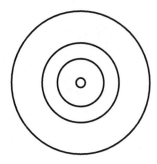

Occult—Words occur in groups associatively. To be pulled out like a bunch of grapes.

A. E. using this image. Heavenwards = heaven occult.

Suggests this diagram relates to milky way. Real thought would involve breaking of old roads (associative) and making free choice from the totality.

We think only about words. But real thought would involve thinking about words, pictures (emotional center), senses (instinctive center).

OBSERVATION

EDNA: Wouldn't it be better to observe all gestures and movements for a few minutes than our present type of observation?

ORAGE: But can you?

GRACE: Was it all right to stop and enjoy fruits of observation?

ORAGE: Better plow it under. You can spend it. Analyst who improved by it, used it to profit and let method go. Orage himself after one year might not have enough material to write for five. Test again to try out suggestions, and the test of it is if it worked. Theory might be true. But if it didn't work in practice, it was useless.

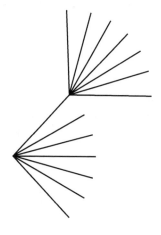

THE BEGINNING OF NUMBER

Say man has seven possibilities. In order to achieve all seven you would have to multiply yourself seven times. You would appear as seven people to an on-looker. Then at the end of each one of those seven there would again be seven possibilities. Man is a multiple figure. In this way number originated. The aim of man is to be the multiplier (No longer passive multiplying).

But are we nothing but what food produces. Man digesting air.

In proportion as one becomes aware of the impressions (all of them) which he receives, he will have added facts (factors) to base his reason on.

Life is a series of obsessions.

Under pain—act as insanity.

Millions of social restrictions.

TUESDAY, 7 APRIL 1925

Questions asked for:

EDNA: Wider meaning of being is related to three centers.

GRACE: What is conscience?

GERTRUDE: As to number in relation to food scales.

As to genesis of number in relation to the diagram of seven possibles for man.

The fivefold star as diagram of man with labels, construct—it leads to sixfold star—two triangles—see diagram higher and lower centers.

GORHAM: As to the position and control of sex in relation to the system.

Types.

Orage presses for questions from group. Explains need for making effort to formulate questions. We are each of us surrounded by a vague fringe of ignorance. Formulation of questions is the beginning of biting through that ignorance, but true formulation brings an answer which is knowledge. It is like hands stretched forth to grasp. The answer may come in unexpected ways.

Growth is a form of bursting. We should be pressing out on all five sides. If we are really doing so, this pressure will beget questions. The questions are therefore the outposts of growth. Gurdjieff describes this condition as puffing out. It is the condition of seed expanding to burst.

Lisa—question as to the correspondence between milky way and diagram of intellectual center in word associations.

ORAGE: We are only three centers. Each center is two in one. Each center is a milky way. It passes through this phase of chaos moving toward the coming of Cosmos. Centers also have a state in which they exist as nebula. (Reference—Ephesians verse to relation to higher and lower centers.)

ESSENCE

What is a real formulation? Formulation is the expression in words of the essence. That is of one's reality. Formulatory center is usually in the service of the personality, the emotions, likes and dislikes and of the sensations. It is necessary to peel off these superimposed crusts until we uncover what it is that we essentially like and think about a subject.

A practical method of discovering one's real attitude is to find out what you really think and feel about a certain person and write it down. To reach this attitude is more difficult than might appear on the surface. This means striping oneself of emotional prejudices and stating what one is ready to stand by for all time as one's own estimate of the individual concerned. In order to do this, one must be willing to be honest with oneself in proportion as one becomes aware and admits to oneself one's own real tastes and wishes. One touches essence. It is necessary to uncover and know one's own essence. Through accepting this, growth becomes possible. This does not mean necessarily admitting such knowledge to the outside world, however. One may do as one chooses. One may do as one chooses provided he knows what his real attitude is in a given case. Machiavelli is an example of a man who was honest with himself. Matthew Arnold was also an essential man.

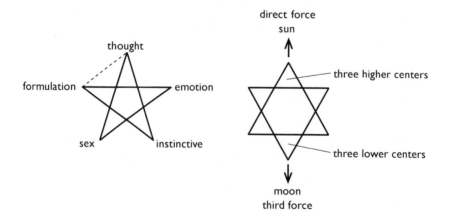

GORHAM: What about the position of sex in relation to the system? The problem of continence control, full use of energy.

ORAGE: The fact is that in the fivefold needs of man, (see diagram above) only three of the five functions are really being used directly—sex, instinct, emotion. Formulatory is only in the service of emotion and instinct, it is not real thought at all.

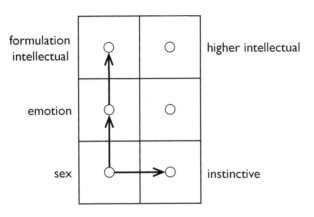

Diagram shows this, whereas actually the formulatory should be in the service of the higher intellectual, i.e. real thought drawing directly from the sex center. When this occurs we no longer throw back unused sex energy onto emotion and instinct, but use it for formulation and thought. The result of this is to create a balance which may eventually lead naturally to continence. Continence is not a cause and effect. It may be an effect eventually of the work; that is very different. As one of the Masters said, the translation of many of the Eastern classics has led to a subtle misinterpretation of cause and effect in relation to esoteric teaching. Example: in the pseudo yogi training method of left and right nostril alternation of breathing has touching results that are utterly pathological. This type of breathing is eventually obtained in the method, if previous work is pursued.

When thought is actually functioning, i.e. using its quota of differentiated sex-energy and with the formulatory center in the service of thought, and thus using its quota of sex-energy, unused energy from these centers ceases to spill back in the lower centers and sex itself ceases to be a problem. It becomes no more of a special problem than instinct, emotion or ordinary thought.

Inhibition is inertia.

THE GENERATION OF FIRE

The general method opposes the wish of the "I" to what the organism wishes.

Opposition = friction = fire = will.

Two methods:

To the organisms 'yes' opposes the nay of the "I"

To the organisms 'nay' opposes the yes of the "I."

Third method

To the organisms yes add the yes of the "I," that is drive the organism in what it wants to do considerably past the point it naturally wishes.

(The origins of Epicureanism. The attempt to generate fire by consciously going beyond what is ordinarily pleasing.)

(Orage—what an amateur collection of celebrities you have!)

Asceticism—The nay of the "I" to the yes of the organism.

Essence

Live essentially, according to one's essential wish. This leads to growth, or at least know what the essence wishes, though conscious considerations demand a different type of action. For a dog, the condition for passing upward from this state is first to be a dog.

Types—a question as to number.

ORAGE: You can calculate the possible number of types from this diagram:

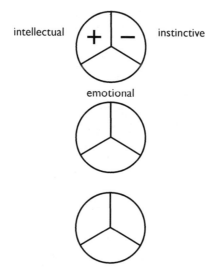

intellectual   instinctive

emotional

Each center has three sub-centers each of which contains positive, negative and neutral. All possible combinations are theoretically possible (78?) but actually they are not. For example a creature with all three centers negative would be a monstrosity. Nature attempts to create a form for such creatures but they die. Similarly all three centers balanced would be an impossibility for the very conditions of the stars at birth preclude it. They are never in such positions to make it possible.

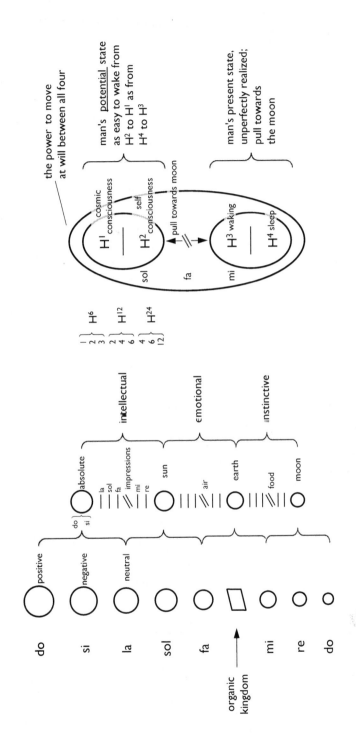

MISS C: Don't all people have all planetary matter in them?
ORAGE: Only certain ones have certain matter.

HUMANITY — ADAM KADMON

Humanity is the sum of possibles contained in one man. This is Adam Kadmon. He contains all of humanity in its seven degrees.

Seven Types of cells: human, monkey, invertebrate, vertebrate, vegetable, mineral, metal.

Just as the seven types are to be found in the being Adam Kadmon so they are to be found in us in the varying types of our cells. Our "I" is the Adam Kadmon to our Cosmos within ourselves. Our attention is mainly devoted to the monkey and the human cells. So it is with Adam Kadmon in relation to monkey and human types of humanity. And he is just as conscious of these types and no more so than we are of the monkey and human cells in our body. As it is only necessary to convert a limited number of monkey cells to human in us so it is with humanity to Adam Kadmon. The rest of the cells are needed to form other functions.

One must be able to enter experience of all humanity, men, woman, and child, past, present and future.

As to this diagram (page 61):

The organic kingdom interposed between the earth and the planets is not of this cosmic ray. It is introduced into it from the outside so to speak just as our food is introduced from without the organism and only becomes a part of the organism in virtue of digestion and assimilation. It is not a planetary body, it is not a celestial being, it is of a different order of being.

The neutral element or third force is a potential subsisting in the relationship of a positive and negative element. The positive and negative can subsist in this relationship only because the neutral is potential.

Starting with the absolute, the great octave is grouped according to the three forces as shown on the diagram. The last or neutral force of one triad becomes the first or positive force of the succeeding triad. In all, the great octave is grouped into four triads. Each one of these triads gives rise to a single note. Thus from this grouping, four notes or centers are produced, named, the absolute, the sun, the earth, the moon. Interposed between them, are, in all, three octaves, the octave of the absolute or the intellectual, the octave of the sun or the emotional, the octave of the earth or the instinctive. These correspond to the three centers in man. Each one of the four main notes is both do, and si. Therefore, on the octaves there are only three semitones, one each. These are called (starting from the bottom), food, air and impressions. Of the three octaves, the instinctive is fully developed. The emotional only as far as mi, i.e. instinctive, emotional, intellectual. The intellectual not at all. Placement in one or the other of these octaves defines the given nature. A being living in the instinctive octave is instinctive, in the emotional, is emotional,

(Angles), in the intellectual is intellectual, (three centers, all of which are intellectual).

There can be no act, no function, without the necessary matter. One's psychology is determined by matter. The above diagrams give the complete psychological possibilities in man, and any given man may be defined in accordance with his placement in them. And each type of matter has a number. Therefore, a man containing given types of matters, (given psychic and psychological functions) has corresponding numbers. In fact he is these numbers. An accurate description of him would be a mathematical formula containing these numbers.

Since man is matter, since all functions are material, the importance of food is evident.

Ouspensky leaving out the step of self-consciousness between ordinary consciousness and cosmic-consciousness. This is characteristic of many writers on the subject of consciousness.

Distinction between sympathy and compassion:

Sympathy—feeling with, hence identification with object.

Compassion—feeling for, hence non-identification with object.

TUESDAY, 14 APRIL 1925

Premium placed on the acquisition of new ideas was putting them into practice.

Make energy trough observation, and spend it through experiment.

MISS R: *How do the three centers waste energy?*

ORAGE: Energy wasted in two ways by the centers.

1.   By reacting sequentially to an external stimulus, one center dragging the other two after. Example: Three lights shining when only one is necessary. The explanation of this goes back to the manner in which an external object has a meaning for all three centers. So that now when an external stimulus touches one center, the other two tend to act.

Diagram of Three Centers

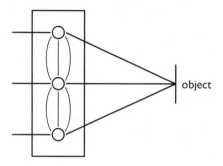

object

2.   The centers leaking when there is no external stimulus.

a.   Intellectual—day dream.

b.   Emotional—worried.

c.   Instinctive—fidgeted—contracted muscular tension. They bleed or drip blood. When two centers interfere with the third the balance of centers is interfered with in this way:

Instinctive—self-consciousness.

Emotional—shame or embarrassment.

Intellectual—stammering.

The method of eliminating this leaking is observation. In this case the waste energy is transferred to the "I," which has a use for it, it must however, be pumped up, for it is going against gravity. Gravity pulling toward the moon, this method toward the sun.

ZIGROSSER: How to keep awake?

GRACE: On contraction?

Orage asked why contraction would keep one awake—then answered that at least two centers must be in conjunction for that purpose.

GERTRUDE: As to waking up at time desired?

ORAGE: Instinctive center had a timepiece but in order to wake oneself at a given time it is necessary for the wish to penetrate the emotional as well as the other centers.

MISS R: What is *intuition?*

ORAGE: Intuition is an accidental conjunction of two centers, there being as many types of intuition as there are combinations possible among the three centers. *When all three centers come into conjunction you get intuition with certainty or certainty.* Three are necessary because reality is threefold. In the case of intuition two sides are known, the third unknown. Toward this unknown side the intuition may be right or wrong, but it does not *know.*

Realization. Try to realize *"I" have a body* not *"I" am a body.* This is the direct way, a short cut. It is not a method it cannot be taught. The method teaches the slow sure way around the mountain by which we will all surely reach the summit, but realization is the straight ascent more difficult but briefer, the other way may take many lives. Realization is what the Christians meant by faith. But this is impossible—realization that we have a body cannot be obtained. Anyone may find this for himself. In ancient times men rolled over on themselves for twenty or thirty miles in order to attain this realization. In the middle ages the monks abused this means to realization and made it an end, losing eventually its purpose altogether.

Example: Figure of a field rented and a field owned. Difference in man's attitude to plot of land, same as if you own this body or rent it. This body is a sociological and biological product given to us. Try to realize that the "I" owns it and that society does not. In this way you become an individual and not a social personality.

Creation (see diagram on page 61). Creation was a progressive densification of matter descending from the absolute to the moon. The planet behind the moon a denser composition than metal.

Creation is the progress of an original single atom through molecular combination. Each successive plane consists of hydrogen atom, doubling in size from the absolute down to the moon. Each atom indivisible on its own plane. If divided, the matter passes up to the next higher state.

MISCELLANEOUS

The sun—complete recollection.
The moon—memory.
The past exists only in memory.
The future only in the imagination.

The configurations of the planets at the time of conception deposit a certain rhythmic pattern in man. This pattern subject to periodicity. So that, when the planets subsequently arrive at the same configuration, an event similar in importance to conception will take place.

Non-receptivity in most people to the ideas. Less receptivity as time goes on. Within a thousand years, impossible.

TUESDAY, 21 APRIL 1925

MORALITY

Morality is a means not an end. It is determined by its end. Good and bad seem in relation to that end. If the ends conflict, then the moralities conflict. At present there are two moralities—the prevalent, with the moon as its object, the other with the sun. Every action not consciously directed toward the sun is within the moon's morality, is "moon meat."

Psycho-analysis has in mind only one life, and in that life simply an adjustment of an individual to the external world. And though the analysts say they are working for consciousness, they have not the means to arrive there. And though they wish to develop the ego, they have not the means of developing it. They come within the moon's morality and are opposed to the Gurdjieff system.

G: What is the Ego in relation to the "I"?

ORAGE: "I" is the germ of the ego. The difference between actual and potential. Image of egg. The partially formed chicken in the egg is the actuality. The completed chicken is the potentiality. The method is the attempt of the "I" to observe the actual and thus to actualize the potential.

Need for puffing out—exert as much energy in all ways as possible in order to speed up. In this way the body becomes prepared to withstand the shock of the "I"'s awakening. When the "I" awakes it does not have full control of its powers. Compare the "I" to an infant. A child on our plane in awaking state is as conscious as we, the difference is that adult has three centers more filled. He, "I," may wake up for a moment, and again fall asleep for a long period. This is a power and not a fully realized state. It is not lost in sleep but can be recaptured. A state like that of swimmer who has power to swim though he does not swim all the time. Also man who is super-conscious exerts power at will, not constantly. Need of speeding up all one's activities. Because if one stops one did not stop. One did something else. You keep on spending on anyway, only when there is no conscious effort it leaks out. You lose the value of what you spend.

REST

It is necessary, however, to rest. There is need for a conscious relaxation. This does not add energy but prevents dispending it. We know what bodily relaxation is. *There must be a positive relaxation for the emotions.* (G. P. gives effects but not means for attaining this, by freeing from inhibitions and repression.)

Emotional relaxation brought about by conscious imagination. Picture a lovely landscape and place yourself in it. This is the "garden of rest." Example: In the Mahabharata—oases which warriors travelled to in intervals between battles, were not real places, but imaginary ones.

Imagination consciously projected.

Fancy the accidental injection of images.

Individual at mercy of fancy—two trains of fancy colliding interfere or destroy each other. Never know here you will end on fancy.

(Relaxation for intellectual center not given.)

Orage criticizes academic questioning for information, when we cannot apply practical suggestions already made.

Question of consciousness during embryonic period—G. P.—"Let me remember who I am. I have forgotten who I am, at birth, quotes

Orage says this legend is symbolic. The difference of centers is a matter of content. After moment of conception three lower centers make earth contact and begin to be filled, whereas higher centers receive no contact. Possible higher centers underwent this to see if they could maintain consciousness while asleep.

Three Forces—Positive, Negative and Neutral.

Neutral is third force blind.

Positive element—initiation to act, but it must act against some relatively inert substance. There must be resistance. The conception of force involves a resistance to be overcome, cannot work in a vacuum. *This inert object is the negative element.*

The neutral is the motive, object or purpose of the act.

There are two ideas regarding the neutralizing element.

1.   That the neutral element is a potential, subsisting in a relation of positive and negative. Without this potential the positive and could not exist in a given relationship. To any act, there are an infinite number of possibles. One of which will be actualized. Example: Get up from the chair.

The desire to rise—positive

Inertia in body to be overcome—negative

Rising in one of possible ways—neutral

The neutral is different from the other two.

2.   We do not know what potential it is we are going to actualize, hence we are called third force blind. Even after actualization we are not aware of it, we don't see it. The motive is this third force, neutral force, yet we explain in all sorts of erroneous ways. We do not know why we act though we may explain an act in various ways. Our motive is already apparent in the act. "By your works shall ye be known." Example of man who unconsciously is determined to slay a man. He does not know that he is going to or even that he wants to.

THREE CENTERS — TWO DIAGRAMS

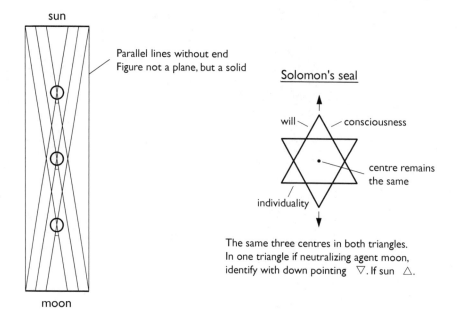

sun

Parallel lines without end
Figure not a plane, but a solid

moon

Solomon's seal

will — consciousness

centre remains
the same

individuality

The same three centres in both triangles.
In one triangle if neutralizing agent moon,
identify with down pointing ▽. If sun △.

Anyone of three centers may be the neutralizer. The neutralizing agent is not necessarily the same. In this work the motive are of four kinds, to satisfy:

Instinctive—desire for help etc.

Emotional—desire for art, pleasure, etc.

Intellectual—desire to apprehend the ideas.

For consciousness—which has no end.

Everyone starts from a base, (see triangle diagram, Solomon's seal). The one whose motive is in the instinctive will drop off soonest, emotional next, and intellectual third. Only those working with this system can move toward the sun, in all others the process is reversed towards the moon.

Definition of individuality is consciousness of will.

Milton—"Wages of labor or effort?"

Sunward—"Motive is to be able to continue making the effort."

Neutral Idea is one of the Hardest to Formulate. Comparable with conception of time. So difficult to grasp because we are third force blind. But it is necessary to try to know what the purpose is.

The Positive Element is one's strongest center. But it does not mean that this strongest center is the object of acts.

Springs running down.

Neutralizing agent applied to the great octave.

Food octave—our cells on moon or moon in us.
Air octave—earth in us—or ourselves on earth.
Impressions octave—sun in us, or ourselves on the sun.

TUESDAY, 28 APRIL 1925

ATTITUDE

ORAGE: Necessary to have an attitude toward the organism, as expressed by the phrase "I have a body." In order to control all three centers, you must have this attitude, and in order to control someone else you must have this attitude. By means of this attitude we can know what centers are controlling them and employ a different center in yourself for their control. For you can never control another person if you use or meet them with a similar dominant center. By knowing this you can produce an effect in them, joy, pain, anger, sorrow, etc.

WILL — ANALYSIS

Will used by the analyst on a patient comes from external source. Whereas in this method the method is defined, the application of it or the will must be exercised by the person himself. A person has will just in proportion as he can apply it

PSYCHO-ANALYSIS

Psycho-analysis is primarily therapeutic, it aims to better conditions in this waking state whereas in the Gurdjieff-method it is a matter of indifference as to what this state is. The object is to wake up from this state, i.e. second birth. Though you never lose the idea, this fact does not mean that you never cease applying it. If you don't try to push ten to eleven, you will drop back from ten to nine. (Shortening the day, increasing a closed period of hour or half hour for required work.)

Death and suicide equally mechanical as we know it.

ZIGROSSER: *What is the base in connection with the Three Forces, Positive, Negative, and Neutral?*

ORAGE: The base of the triangle is the "I" and the body. Neutral element is consciousness, i.e. sun pull.

Down pull equals moon. If you realize "I have a body" without consciousness as a neutral element the forces generated or released will sink into the unconscious, and produce madness. (Swift, an example of accidental realization without consciousness as to third force.) Gurdjieff said he could give drug which could produce the realization. You could survive the drug, but not the premature awareness.

Bakti Yoga is given after a person practices Raja, when realization comes of incompleteness of the emotional, after self-consciousness in intellectual is attained. This method is sequential. Gurdjieff-method simultaneous. Note: when the words Hatha, Bakti, Raja, are used without the word Yoga following it means the separate training in that branch of Yoga.

When a given center is dominant, why is it dominant?

The motive or third force is in the emotional sub-center of the dominant center.

Type is a matter of essence, of the centers prior to content, hereditary. Each type has a number. As we become more conscious we ought to be able to tell what twelve main types are through ourselves. Hundred and Four types are mathematically possible. Only seventy-eight viable.

FOODS

food   air   impressions = knowledge

The term *knowledge* only to be used as ladder to reach understanding of impressions, then thrown away. Digested knowledge is understanding. Understanding is to knowledge as digestion is to food. We have more knowledge than we can use. This explains why Gurdjieff gives out so little information, saying that we already have more than we can use. One may have much understanding and little knowledge. *Knowledge is digested into understanding by observation* not by any intellectual process.

METHOD

There is no association or suggestion in our lives to make the path seem desirable. Money has its associative appeal hence we desire it, mechanical. A savage could not respond to this symbol without association for him. Since this way has no associations, it is necessary to apply *real will* to it. The amount of will needed becomes greater, hence the amount of effort must increase.

WEDNESDAY, 6 MAY 1925

Edna as to perception and knowledge.
  ORAGE: I see the lamp, I know I see it, I know it.
  (My hand may learn to do a thing, then my hand knows it.)
  Actualization equals identity and vice versa.
  All possibles being actualized at given moments.
  The present Jean Toomer, this particular possible has been actualized. Theoretically it was possible to actualize anyone of the large number. This particular one was actualized *but the others likewise are being actualized, for any given moment all possible are being actualized.*
  Should I step out of this, one must of necessity continue to be actualized. Example I step off a train, the train continues. To be able to step out of this one does not mean necessarily our stepping into a better one. It does mean that I will have the power to step out of the second one if I find it to be worse. I cannot guaranty your adventure.

CHIEF FEATURE

What animal. Review of past life. This only possible by use of the unlawful energy generated by self-observation. Since this energy is not generated by the organism it is not prejudiced, and can therefore undertake a candid examination. (Unlawful—contrary to nature.)
  Stream of behavior. Habits determining subsequent acts. Learn what the creature is, that we may predict future actions, and not demand impossible of it.
  The animal not to be taken literally, that is, no attempt should be made to describe behavior in animal terms, but in terms of human psychology.
  In virtue of air—animal emotions, fear, rage, anger. These are real. Chivalry, altruism, etc. are sociological virtues, the verbal (ideal) continuation of the air octave.
  Do not identify with the animal or chief feature. The tendency will be to do so, more even than in the case of the personality, for essence is more intimate.
  Essence, same substances, but different patterns, hence individual differences.—Horoscope.

71

Chief feature introduced by Orage asking everyone to form him opinion as to everyone else present. But this of no first value. *One's own chief feature is* only minor of importance.

GRACE: Interference of instinctive with observation. (Breadth held)

TUESDAY, 12 MAY 1925

THE WHOLE IS THE "I" EQUALS THE ABSOLUTE.

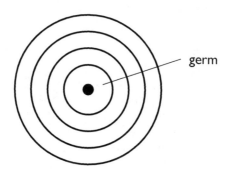

The attempt of the "I," the given Absolute to observe that part of itself (the germ) already actualized. The germ is the organism, equals M. or J. *Because it is actualized it is mechanical.* Introversion would be an attempt of the mechanism to see itself from within. True observation could be more accurately state as being extraversion, for the "I" which carries on the real observation, must be thought of as existing outside the organism.

(In reply to Zigrosser's paper formulating observation in terms of introversion.) The "I" is carrying the organism within it, as if the organism were an embryo. What the "I" is we can't define. Nor can we specify what part of itself is doing the observing. The fact that we have a word for "I" means that it is potential.

Orage continues to talk from Zigrosser's paper.

Observation cannot be characterized as being "aesthetic", for aesthetics is merely like and dislike. It is morality transferred to the plane of beauty. The method is scientific, for it is interested not in whether a thing is pleasing or displeasing; it is concerned with the *observation of behavior as such.* All things become of equal value. (See Watson "Behaviorism" for method.)

MORALITY

This morality and social morality. We must subscribe to social morality, since social morality is the condition under which we are forced to work for our purpose. Example: A man who has to live in Japan, and must earn his living.

We should follow the eleventh commandment which is: "Do what you wish, but do not get caught," for that is what the whole world believe in doing. The ability to practice the eleventh commandment depends on subscribing outwardly to the ten others.

Purpose of man—*Example of Sheep*. Sheep exist not knowing what their purpose is. Then some few wise ones really find out that they are being used by human beings for their wool and mutton. So some wise ones among them found out that the human race is being used to transmit energy from the sun and planets to the earth and moon. The reason for this being that the sun is growing. It is sensing forth a branch whose tip is the moon. Like a tree, one branch grows at the expense of another (some branches are dead having subserved their purpose.) In the example of the tree a relatively large amount of its material goes into pulp and bark than into the amount of seed. Humanity as a whole make up this larger proportion. Some few are seed. This is so, because the sun desires seed.

G: *Isn't this due to the law of accident?*

ORAGE: Yes.

G: What is law of accident?

ORAGE: Can't explain. Then added, it is a law for one person and an accident for another. Example: Person for whom it is a law decides mathematically upon a plan for distribution, He says every third person will get a package. He follows his plan without respect of persons. So far as the persons themselves are concerned it is accidental. Who are the third persons?

Example two of Law of Accident: A magnet which attracts only a certain type of metal—magnesium. The magnesium is strewn about. It is accidental where it falls. There is only a certain amount of it. All people cannot contain it, hence there is this difference. This magnesium is the magnetic center, when the time comes the magnet can draw it all back to itself.

Phosphorus was necessary for mentality. Let us suppose that Radium is necessary for higher mathematics. If you haven't got radium, then you haven't got it, it's no use worrying about it.

(Put under purpose of man) It is said that the first 100 feet down from the earth's surface has all passed through man, been part of man's organic life at one time or another. Petroleum is the mineralized fat of myriads of pre-historic fish or animals. Coal is the mineralized product of an ancient vegetable kingdom.

Man furnishes the shock to the moon's mi. Man helped create metal on the moon. Man is analogous for moon to the shock we received through air.

Our behavior is a current record of all our experience. We cannot possibly come to know all the details of experience as such, but we can observe behavior, which is a record of this experience. By such observation we can come to digest and assimilate all that has hitherto remained undigested.

THE ORGANISM AS A WHOLE IS THE HUMAN OCTAVE

Everything in us, all cells, all systems, all centers, are at some point in the octave. And the organism taken as a whole is at some point in its octave either running up or down the scale. The organism as a whole is the human octave. The cells, systems, centers, etc., are the inner octaves in the human octave. If this octave is at mi, then it is susceptible to the method. If people are at re it is useless to tell it to them, but they wouldn't want it. It is neither necessary nor inevitable that all organisms reach mi or that they pass beyond it.

TESTS FOR MOVEMENT UP OR DOWN SCALE.

You are either running up the scale or momentarily static or you are running down the scale. The following are the tests. If you are running up the scale there is effort and it is difficult. If you are running down the scale it is easy. If you are static you cannot stay there long, you must either drop or make the effort to mount. Increased ability to observe means you are going up the scale. (*Power of observation is a measure of one's will.*)

ESSENCE

G: [*Asks relation of heredity to essence*]

ORAGE: *Structure is given by Heredity.* When you speak of essence you speak of it in relation to the personality. Personality depends upon temperament, and temperament may be defined as the configuration or constellation of wishes deposited in us by the planets at the time of our conception. Planets deposit matter which functions psychologically as wishes. We are wishes and our life is a fulfillment of our wishes. (In this psychoanalysis is right.)

A structure might be given but without wishes it would not live. The wish to live is planetary. Heredity did give a structure—the physical body (the instinctive) composed of muscular, nervous and cerebral systems, but not until emotional and intellectual centers are formed do we have emotions, do we feel and think. *The formation of centers is planetary.* The capacity of centers is given at birth, (due to heredity.) The actual functioning is due to planetary influence. The wishes may be consonant with the structure, but may be directly contrary to it.

Example: Man in structure is created to go on all fours. Wishes have placed

74

him on his hind legs, but the structure has not as yet completely adapted itself to this upright position. (Reference to Secret Doctrine, of the descent of God's into animals. And our present state due to the fact that we have forgotten what we came into them for.)

Man is really his own wish. That is why we call that essence. It is the whole life of man.

Actual and potential are similarly real.

The actual, real in terms of our limited perception. Our potentialities are being realized somewhere to some perception. Both are equally real, and we must get used to conceiving of potential and actual as both real.

Example: Three ways of getting out of chair. To his senses he actualizes only one.

But all three were actualized through other perceptions.

It is said that the first hundred feet . . .

SUNDAY, 17 MAY 1925

ORAGE: *Our present state of being is determined by two, three-centered states.*

In one of these, the three centers exist in magnetic connection in such a way, that if one acts the other two follow suit. In the other, the magnetic connection between the three centers is broken. The former is the waking, the latter the sleeping state.

Growth pertains to change within the limits of the threes-centers. *Development* aims at a four center, outside of these three, which is not magnetically connected with them.

Our aim in development is the transformation of our state of being. Change occurs; a tree grows within the limits of natural growth. In transformation a wholly new form occurs. Examples of transformation are to be found in nature. Such an example is the phases of a caterpillar, (egg, caterpillar, chrysalis, butterfly). In man the corresponding states, sleep, waking, self-consciousness, cosmic consciousness. We are now at the caterpillar stage.

BARNES: If the beginning of interest in this work depends upon questions, may not the intellect stop it.

ORAGE: Yes.

Miss C. did not think the approach was intellectual, because she was moved by the truth spoken by Gurdjieff.

ORAGE: Approach could be through any of the centers. But if one followed up the work, whatever the approach, sooner or later the other centers would be affected, because the centers are magnetically connected. The ideas would filter through to the emotions, etc.

THE THREE CENTERS

We cannot observe them separately, but we can observe their totality as manifested in instinctive behavior, for this totality being in magnetic connection is manifest in instinctive behavior.

WILL AND WISHES

All wishes relate to the organism whose neutralizing element is the moon. In wishes there is no will. Will relates to development whose neutralizer is the sun (consciousness). Will has one wish: to become aware of, to develop and control the organism, and in the process of doing so to increase itself or attain self-consciousness. When the neutralizing element is the sun it includes them not as ends but as means or by-products, therefore those who pursue art, success, fame, affection, happiness, etc., are feeding the moon. Furthermore since the moon is only a reflection of the sun, those who pursue it, pursue appearance, and hence are certain to miss the very realities they aim at. While those who forsaking the pursuit of appearance, seemingly miss reality actually achieve it.

SUBJECTIVE AND OBJECTIVE ART

Almost impossible to speak of objective art to subjective people. An outstanding example of outstanding art is the crucifixion. Those who took part in the Crucifixion were conscious and deliberate creators. Note the lasting effect of their performance.

ORAGE: [to Jean] Examples of objective art are rare in so called fields of the arts, but are more frequent in life. Example: In the conducting of a group. The manipulation of the scale, perhaps for ten minutes, a genuine atmosphere will be created.

MAN ON THE NATURAL SCALE

So far as his instinctive center goes man is at si. But his two interior systems or bodies, astral and mental are at mi and do respectively. Man has astral matter, but the astral body is undeveloped. Man's obligation is to develop this astral matter to human form. At present he is merely vegetable and must still pass through—invertebrate, vertebrate, and monkey, up through human. In doing this he will complete that natural scale. Counting on his ability to remain non-identified and retain an understanding of his purpose, man entered our bodily prison. Instead of expanding his prison and bursting out of it, he became identified with it. He fell asleep within its limitations. At one time we all possessed self and cosmic consciousness. We possess it now, only we cannot realize this possession. The higher centers already have content.

G: Did higher centers lose their content when man fell asleep?

ORAGE: No. The difficulty is to awake. If we could we would find our higher centers complete. At present time we are spending all our energy in behavior of the organism under external pressure. Observation transfers the energy and the pressure to the fourth center, the "I."

The weakness in our essence—determines that we repeat our pattern. It is not lack of strength but fear of hurt that drives us in this way.

1. Example—person who says he would rather walk a mile, than see someone.
2. Example—of man with wounded leg who has to circle up the mountain, instead of going straight up the steep way.

Neutralizer: top of the mountain is happiness, which should be a by-product. The way of weakness is not the line of least resistance. Our motive is our weakness. Types of motive, negative and positive, positive only rarely. Our *chief feature* is our sore spot. It can be tested by the resistance we oppose to uncovering it. In searching for *chief feature* in past conduct, necessity for being objective.

The method is more objective than science. Subjective elements, however, tend to be subtly incorporated in it. (Think of the time and effort it took to eliminate the personal equation from science.) One must constantly be on guard against these elements. Some of them are: analysis, viz.-attempt to find causes; thought—the tendency to utilize visualization or some other mode of awareness rather than awareness itself; judgments, that is, like or dislike, corrective attitudes, etc.

Observe the twenty forms, interior and exterior, progressively combing them until a simultaneous observation of all twenty is achieved. Such progressive efforts will progressively diminish waste energy.

Questions of Mr. Mann:

1. Why only six centers?

ORAGE: No definite limit set. Perhaps more after six are realized, not infinite in number, but finite to the absolute. The limits of one form must be fully realized before there can be a progression to the next. But when on form is thus realized, another one is then found to be present.

Example: full realization of the egg—caterpillar
Full realization of the caterpillar—chrysalis
Full realization of the chrysalis—butterfly.

2. Why the theoretical ideas?

ORAGE: Many ideas not necessary. Given, in order that each one may take up those that interest him. The method the main thing.

3. When did we posses self and cosmic consciousness?

ORAGE: Not in time.

4.   Why do you say that nature or natural processes will not produce development? Is not this very method itself a part of the processes of development, that is, natural? And may we justly conclude this present civilization will not achieve development? For surely, since its time has been so short, we may not conclude the contrary.

ORAGE: Races and civilizations have come and gone. No evidence of development. Generally, this statement made on the basis of facts available to everyone. Perhaps the human race will achieve the development within the course of the next twenty million years. But while this, if a fact, might be interesting to a sociologist, what immediate concern is it of the individual? In truth whatever future development takes place will be dependent upon individuals becoming self-conscious now.

Two things necessary: a seed capable of sprouting, that is, a germinal seed, and, circumstances from without—sun, moisture, suitable soil.

MISCELLANEOUS

Everything is in a process of growth. But there are two forms of growths: growing larger, up, and growing smaller, down. Example of latter: ants, once very large, who still imagine their ant hill to be one of the five continents; man, who once had the whole range of the universe, and who now imagines his globe, this earth, to be the universe.

Ordinary dreams enter the Gate of Horn. These ideas enter the Gate of Gold. Both are equally fleeting and difficult to retain. At the moment of hearing the ideas, one seems to understand them perfectly. In a few minutes, they are gone.

Will is the germ to develop.

MONDAY, 25 MAY 1925

Orage asks for questions from everyone.

BARNES: Are "observation" and "awareness" interchangeable terms?

ORAGE: Yes, only with this distinctions: that observation implies an active awareness.

A recapitulation of the method, adding, as emotion is different from sensation, so thought is different from emotion. As thought or cognition is different from emotion so awareness is different from thought. How long it took human beings to differentiate between thought and emotion. Even now, in fact, if you ask a person what he thinks about a certain thing, he is likely to reply by telling you what he feels about it, that he likes or dislikes it.

As the emergence of thought produced a scientific age, so an emergence of awareness would produce a conscious age.

Structure defines function. Structure presupposes function. Nature has provided us with structure. We function instinctively. We function emotionally to mi. We must initiate and carry on from this point by our own efforts. Example of the egg. White of egg and yolk given. The question is, will the germ fully utilize the given white and yolk (food).

The distinction between humanity and mankind, The former a fancy, the latter a fact.

5 awareness

4 thought   3 words

1 instinct   2 emotion

Five Pointed Star—Man is sick because the energy differentiated for 4 and 5 is not utilized by 4 and 5, and hence seeks expression through 1, 2, or 3, and thus throws them out of gear.

Man is structurally designed for real thought. (Sir Arthur Keith, the size of man's brain—how relatively a small portion of it is being used in the ordinary demands placed upon it.) It is his duty, so to speak, to think.

Mankind may reach civilization and culture about 200 times. If at one of these times it does not pass up the scale, it will degenerate or become extinct. It is possible that the monkeys are former human beings who failed to pass up.

Example of a snow-flake. All of a given shape, but exhibiting various types or crystallization. It is a matter of accident how it crystallizes. The types of crystallization equal the types of personality. Simpler crystallization not inferior to more complicated.

SECOND YEAR — MONDAY, 9 NOVEMBER 1925

If we have really observed for at least a moment, we have experienced "I" as a point existing outside the organism. We should have convinced ourselves by experience of *the separability of "I" from the organism.* Not that "I" is yet separate or can control. The periods of the separability of "I" from "It" should be intensified and lengthened. Method of strengthening the "I" is non-identification, intensifying it, and increasing the time of its waking periods to be given later.

A new phase begins in the group work, wherein Orage's "I" speaks not to our organisms but to our "I"'s. All esoteric teaching is based on this condition in which our organisms are deaf whereas our "I"'s can hear. "He who hath ears let him hear." As long as the teaching was to the organism, the organism would interpret it in its own subjective terms. If, for example, the five points of objective morality were given, they would be subjectively understood. Although the "I" can only be awake for moments, the organism, like a dictaphone, will hold the impressions for the "I" until it wakes again. These ideas are self-evident and need no demonstration for the "I." They have the familiarity of recollected truths, as you will discover when I tell you what objective morality is.

Our "I's", observing our organisms, should make effort to be like consulting physicians over a patient. Our "I's" should have the same impersonal disinterested attitude, seeking to understand in order that they may control the organism. Personality should be absent as though we had hung it on a hook with our overcoats before entering the room.

Visualization of 2 dots—one is the organism, one is "I." At time of conception the "I" dot not even a spectator, it is only a potential existence. And it remains as such, while the dot of the organism, by means of terrestrial digestion grows into its threefold structure. The organism, which is nature, grows from do to mi, and then runs down again to death. Running the scale from do to mi and back again satisfies nature's purpose. At this point "I" receives a sun-ray in the form of an idea, it may become active and begin the work of completing the octave. The "I" is capable of running from sol to si. If the "I" completes its octave, then it is the whole octave having redeemed and transformed the organism.

Steps of "I"'s acquisition of control:

It attempts to understand.

It attempts to control.

Example of Asquith picking men with cabinet minds capable of impersonally judging the interest of the group rather than of self.

Distinction between theoretical understanding and realization. Example: a friend's death.

In thinking how difficult this is to control the organism, we must remember that it has evolved over a course of a million years. The circulation of the blood in the veins, nerve force in the nervous system, and electricity in the cerebral system, having been established over countless centuries. Organic habits fixed and established over same vast period.

The figure of the prince as the infant "I." The heir apparent. Note Machiavelli's Prince. Then multiply the subtleties needed by 30.000.

We rationalize what the organism does from subjective feeling. We not really reason. The aim is to make reason produce conduct, rather than conduct produce rationalization.

In a sense, the organism wishes to be controlled by the "I" because at the present time it is subject to circumstance, which circumstance may prove painful, injurious, or even kill the organism. This leads again to the realization of urgency for the control of "I" over organism.

Will can be defined as the absence of all wishes: it is activity without wish. Will is necessity. A necessity arising from the profoundest nature of "I." Will, if successful, induces gratification. If it fails, there is no disappointment, for there is no wish. Organically there is pleasure and pain. But for will, only pleasure is possible. For in certain worlds there can be pleasure or pain without its opposite. For example, in Hell there is all pain. On earth they are mingled, with slightly more pleasure than pain. In heaven, all pleasure.

The essential wish leads to chief-feature. The organism seems complicated but in fact the chief-feature is the mainspring and key to everything since all wishes arise from it. Hence it is the point of focus for control of the organism. The preliminary steps of observation are essential to the creating of energy for the unearthing of the chief-feature. It is only from *continued observation* of the organism that chief-feature can be found. Chief-feature, when discovered, has no connection with the "I" relation to the twelve types of "I"'s.

With all "I"'s there is one objective. And they are indifferent to which function they perform. This will depend upon their type.

The whole universe is determined. But this very determinism includes opportunity, so that, opportunity recurs as well as determined patterns. Unactualized opportunities are equally real with actualized possibles. Circular recurrence in times exists. But there is a distinction between the metaphysics and the facts of this recurrence. In the facts there is a slight change. (?) A metaphysical treatment of recurrence involves time. Time is the incomprehensible mystery to beings. God Himself is subject to time. The discovery by Beelzebub that God must end, but was unaware of the time, was the cause of Beelzebub's expulsion from heaven.

Detachment.

Example: Goldsmiths Traveler—Persian B.

Gurdjieff on all human beings.

The qualities necessary to "I."

The Sphinx, a copy imported into Egypt, is a symbol of the powers necessary to "I."

1. Woman's head and breast—mother-love.
2. Body of bull—indefatigable effort.
3. Legs of lion—fearlessness and certainty.
4. Wings of eagle—aspiration.

Religions are based on one quality only—love, or faith, or hope. Any one quality is insufficient, because, in order to control the organism, the "I" should have at its disposal all these qualities simultaneously, together with their opposites.

Example: The "I" must have the power to hate the organism, or anything else necessary to discipline it.

MONDAY, 16 NOVEMBER 1925

CONSCIOUS OR OBJECTIVE MORALITY

We will talk to "I" about "It." "It" is left outside. Use conscious imagination to leave it outside. It is for the moment dead. But it is to be re-entered shortly. What should I do in relation to it?

Ordinary morality is a matter of social convention. In relation to ordinary morality the organism is subject. But the organism becomes the object of conscious morality. In ordinary perception and observation, the organism is the subject, external objects are the objects. But with us, the organism becomes the object of observation, since we observe it observing. So the organism becomes the object of conscious morality.

The five elements of conscious morality, which define the duty the "I" is obligated (under the necessity of reason) to perform with respect to the organism, are:

1.   The preservation and maintenance of its life and well-being. (Self-preservation the first law of life.)

a.   No destructive acts or pursuits are to be engaged in.

b.   No suicide.

For it has been given to us by nature on trust and it is necessary to the life of "I." Moreover, should we quit it, we should pass on a good and even better organism to the next "I."

Figure: The duty of a responsible tenant towards the house rented from a landlord.

2.   The improvement of the organism

a.   Acquiring new technics.

b.   Discovering possibilities and realizing them.

For we must turn over to the next "I" or to our own "I" at the next recurrence, a better equipped vehicle. (The necessity of acquiring new and many technics, not for the sake of the technics but for the purpose of preparing the body to be used by the "I," that is, pliant to demands of the technics of technics.)

These, 1 and 2, can be and are subscribed to by ordinary subjective morality. Everyone admits them, and displays this acceptance by evincing the corresponding wishes, namely, to preserve and improve themselves. The organism itself has these wishes. But 1 and 2 of conscious morality may go against or disregard the ordinary canons, not simply for the sake of disregarding them or being unconventional, but for the purpose of experiment. Ordinary convention and conventional morality are equally mechanical. Not even as contrasts can they serve as guides to conscious morality.

3.   To understand the nature of man, the nature of the universe and their

mutual relations, is the *duty* of the "I." (To understand the nature of the organism and its relation to nature.)

Philosophy and science are not mere interests or inclinations (as they are generally considered to be), but obligations, from an objective point of view. Energies are differentiated for curiosity, that is, philosophy and science. If these are not used they turn back on some other avenue of functioning and derange it. Nervousness and sex perversion, cannot be dealt with directly, but can be cured by stimulating and pursuing the curiosity to understand the nature of man and the universe. The five types of energy. The five pointed star. Each person and situation should be made to yield an understanding of principles (psychological, social etc.) not only mere likes and dislikes.

The capacity for reason is the saving faculty of mankind.

The spectacle of life is the great drama which "I" should approach to understand. Every contact should yield something more than a subjective response. It should yield an understanding of habits, traits, motives, etc.

4.   The fourth duty of the "I" is to discover and discharge its function. (To pay for its existence.) The discovery of function can only follow from having discharged duties (1), (2), and (3).

Figure: wheel, nut, wagon. A wheel is such, not a nut. The wagon is such. Taken together, their relationship defines an inevitable function for the wheel.

5.   The fifth duty of "I" is to aid others in their efforts to apply (1), (2), (3), and (4).

Each one of these follows from the other, and, taken relatedly, they are axiomatic, self-evident to objective reason. Although the organism may reject these five obligations, the "I" knows as true.

The effort should be to apply (1) (2) (3) (4) (5) simultaneously, that is all in any one given action. It is the duty of the "I" to select, from among a number of possibles, the *one* which will allow an inclusion of all five. The organism will be determined to select one by past experience. The "I" must make the effort to non-identify, select, and actualize the *one* in which its purpose will be served.

This fivefold effort superseded the threefold one (designed for personality) of profit, pleasure, and religion.

These five elements pass quickly from the memory since society is hostile to them, does not aid them. The difficulty is to remember. This is the main difficulty.

The difficulties in separating and developing "I" are equal for all. But organic capacities may differ by accident, one being better equipped for certain purposes than another, and hence more suitable for the conscious object of such a one as Gurdjieff. (These capacities may be: strength of personality in influencing people, many languages, diverse crafts, talents, etc.)

Can the "I" ever be completely separated from the organism? No. There are two forces at work, simultaneously, between the "I" and the organism, one, separating and one joining the two more closely in union (Separation and union). This antinomy always exists, so that an application of the method will yield in actual experience, at once, a sense of a greater separation and a closer union.

Remember do, re, mi (organism), fa (transition) sol, la, si ("I"). Interposed at every semitone are triangles: positive, negative and neutral forces, purpose being the third or neutral force.

ENNEAGRAM

Jesus: do, re, mi. Christ: sol, la, si. Jesus Christ, the two in one—do, re, mi, becomes one in—sol, la, si.

We are now one. We must become two, in order to become one. Duality is the pre-condition of Oneness.

The upper room of the early Christians. The place where psychological conditions are favorable to the "I's" learning their duty.

Governments: Due to accident. All within the organism.

Democracy: The domination of the organism by first one center and then another, due to some chance and uncalculable external stimuli. So we now exist.

Socialism: The continued control of the organism by the instinctive center. Physical appetites leading to chaos and anarchy.

Monarchy or Aristocracy: The continued control by the emotional center. The best feelings.

As Plato wished: Continued domination by the intellectual center. Philosophers.

Government: Conscious. By a fourth center not contained in the organism.

Theocracy: Our "I's" becomes gods to the organisms.

Some beings are responsible for the whole of nature.

Some beings are responsible for man. Remember the place of man in the scale of nature that is, si. Man a sex cell. Si of the food octave is sex.

So we are responsible as gods to our organisms.

God, for his purpose, in order to maintain perpetual motion, designed that each order of being feed on some other and be fed on.

Unfits among men are symptomatic of disease in nature. They are the pimples through which poison is drawn off. A number of "I's" becoming conscious might so utilize the energies designed for conscious usage as to being health, as, for analogy, energy used for thought cures nervousness and perversion.

MONDAY, 23 NOVEMBER 1925

1. TYPES

Learn them from experience. The materials thus gained will tend to classify according to the twelve main types. Some few types are not possible here, owing to unfavorable conditions in the west.

First, group according to similarity: this person similar to that one.

The types themselves are determined by the centers, the positive and negative aspects of each of the three centers.

Positive intellectual—positive attitude towards ideas

Negative emotional—negative attitude towards feeling.

Positive instinctive—positive attitude towards doing.

Etc.

2. ESSENCE

a.   Negative essence—all of us are murderers, liars, treacherous ones, etc.

b.   Positive essence—all of us have real feelings of impartiality, love, etc.

Our essence now manifests in these extremes because it is not grown up, not developed. We are bitter, poisonous plants which may grow up to be sweet and marvelous.

3. CHIEF FEATURE

a.   What did you do as a boy?

b.   "He had himself on his mind."

c.   Tests of non-identification.

d.   Did you have a sense of strangeness?

e.   "He had himself on his mind."

Test of non-identification

Did you have a sense of strangeness?

Did you have a sense of fear?

Did you feel that he could move without you and that you did not know what he would do next?

Did you have a sense that you did not know him?

4. SIGNATURES

a.   Plants

b.   Man si, *seed,* of natural octave. All natural kingdoms epitomized in him. Correspondences. Bean corresponds to some group of cells, or organ or function in man. They have negative effects.

What type of situations could you be trusted to handle and carry off well?
What type of situation could you not be trusted to handle and carry off well?

MONDAY, 14 DECEMBER 1925

1. *How to relax*
a. Muscular strains and tensions.
Generally, more than necessary. Or if necessary for a given work, then they tend to be retained for sometime after the period of their need. But they relax much sooner than either nervous (emotional) or cerebral (mental) tensions. And they can be relaxed easier. The need for the taste, the actual experience, not of comparative relaxation, but complete relaxation. To this end, someone who knows must aid the experience. We cannot at first give it to ourselves.
b. Nervous tensions.
Which come often in the form of worry. Long after an event has passed, we worry about it. Example: rook with frozen eyes—looking long after the owl had passed. To relax: find out from your own individual experience what image is so associated with pleasurable feelings as to induce a state of emotional relaxation. Then, creatively imagine.
c. Cerebral tensions.
No real mind to relax, nevertheless, we experience cerebral fretting: the annoying recurrence of same day dream or phrase, etc. The monkey cells at incessant chatter. To relax: give the human cells the occupation of observing symptoms, of trying to recall the past and present nature of the organism, unrolling the film, etc.
2. The aim is to contain the energy which now passes through us as through as sieve. For only in the presence of a quantity of contained energy can the cells of which we are composed pursue their evolutions. It is necessary that they evolve (they are the kingdom of nature within us). For upon their evolution, the evolution and transformation of our state of being depends.
3. An emotion of displeasure, a negative emotion is an emotional comment upon, or interpretation of, a physiological (or muscular) waste of energy. Of physiological destruction. An emotion of pleasure, a positive emotion, is an emotional interpretation of a physiological containing of energy. Of physiological construction.
4. We are pursuing observation (and simultaneity of observation) to a definite realization, which is: that we will at sometime experience the organism as being a diminutive manikin (Tom Thumb, homunculus). And ever after we will carry, not a full sized organism (as now, *to us*) but a diminutive manikin along with us.
5. *Participation*
The experience of participation induces an experience of increased or decreased weight, smoothness, etc. Not because the objects have changed char-

acter, but because our registration of them has changed, that is, become more conscious and intense.

Participation presupposes observation and non-identification. It is not a substitute for these. Participation is not a substitution; it includes them as running includes walking. When we participate, we must, and do, observe and non-identify—only, observation is in the background, so to speak,- our main attention is upon participating.

The attempt of the "I" to participate in the work of the instinctive center will, in time, produce pure instinctive work. That is, it tends to effect a conscious separation of the instinctive from the other two centers. (The instinctive center, of itself, is very much aware.) Likewise, eventually, with participation in the work of the emotional and intellectual centers.

6. At present, the skin is on wires which are attached to, and commanded by the three centers. These centers are wired with each other, so that, when one moves, the others follow suit. While the centers themselves are on wires which are attached to, and commanded by the external world.

We aim to detach these wires, one by one, place them within the organism, under the control of "I."

To this end, gradually begin to experiment. (The three steps: (1) observation and non-identification, (2) participation, (3) experiment.) Seek to prevent mechanical reactions to external stimuli. Change the tone of voice, to see what happens to one's own and to other organisms. Try to change attitudes, emotions, conduct, for experimental purposes.

We cannot be *intelligent* in experiment. But the aim and act to be so are themselves intelligent. They are indeed, the first proofs of intelligence.

At first, we may spoil material, but this is allowable, *provided,* that the spoiling of material comes as a consequence of conscious experiment. Just as it is allowable to spoil wood in learning the craft of carpentry. But unconscious spoiling is held to our account.

7. To observe others with the aim of understanding them contributes to knowledge. To interfere with the conduct of others for the purpose of experiment contributes to being. Thus, the two essential aspects, which are the reciprocally pursued: to know, to be.

All knowledge which is in excess of being is theory.

Know, in order to be. Be, in order to know.

Increase knowledge in order that being (through experiment) may be increased. Increase being in order that knowledge may be increased.

Of the two forces, which seek to increase knowledge and being, the third force is the neutralizer: and this neutralizer is understanding.

Orage started by asking Donald what use he had made of his day. Donald started by telling how he allowed himself two cigarettes after breakfast and tortured himself the rest of the day with none. Orage pressed him back to beginning of day. His state on waking, attitude as to ideas, what centers disaffected at rising. How he used dressing process to break habits. How did he use quarreling of family at table to gain positive energy? Donald explained that he succeeded, at least by observing, in not getting up his usual negative irritation. Donald asks whether the energy gained is not really stealing one's own, and not gaining from negative energy of others.

Orage explains if we achieve a positive state ourselves, we can actually attract by that condition the loose negative energy of others and turn it into our own positive. His idea is the neutralizer. Nobody has asked me to explain as yet. Orage continues to question Donald as to his day. Shows him how his intensification of pleasure over playing records while smoking is hedonistic and subjective. An intensification of pleasant accidental state. His trip downtown on bus, the study of other people neglected. Did Donald have a conscious plan as to how he would deal with people he met at office, etc.

The neutralizer is the conscious object, plan, or idea. Each situation with people should contain the three elements: positive, negative, and neutral. One must learn to deal with every situation consciously, so as to inject the one that is lacking. For instance, tonight, Orage said, I started with a question positive as to how Donald spent his day. I might have asked how you are getting on with the work, negative. Or I might have asked for questions concerning the system, neutral (ideas form).

The neutralizer is the invisible plan, idea, form, or organization, within which positive and negative function. For example, hydrogen is the form of two elements, a nucleus, and a part that moves about it. The pattern of this relation is the neutralizer. We are third force blind because we can never see the neutralizer. The form contains positive and negative, but is not visible in itself.

Socrates always in his discussions used the negative approach, reducing pupils to what they did not know. Because he was only a junior member of the Pythagorean school. (Also analogy to Gurdjieff.)

Our "I" consists of an invisible triangle—will, consciousness, and individuality.

Self-consciousness is the only possible neutralizer to our positive and negative states. It is the only apex to our own triangle, distant enough to act as neutralizer for more than a life. Triangles with by-products placed as objects or neutralizers, fail of their purpose, as too easily attainable. It is necessary to find a neutralizer to gradually pull together the positive and negative base of our triangle to a long distant objective. And this apex, self-consciousness, tends of itself to pull the positive and negative towards it.

Mistake to assume that negative and positive states equally inevitable. In our present state, we regard negative and positive emotional states as opposite of same thing. This work strives to attain a condition where ultimately there will be no negative states of emotion. All emotion to be positive. And when otherwise negative states would have existed, there should be ultimately a condition of emotional neutrality, that is, death. But this has nothing to do with swinging from negative into positive. For by observation, non-identification, etc., a neutral state conditioned instead of negative. Then when a later positive reaction occurs, this stored up energy can be released to intensify the positive reaction. (M. N. surprised how this explains her recent state of no emotion whatever, as to J's trip after first 24 hours.)

THE ENNEAGRAM

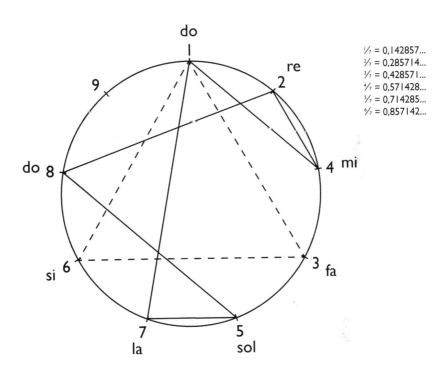

Plotinus wrote Enneads on the subject of this same enneagram. The nine-fold aspects of man. The invisible triangle, dotted, equals: consciousness, will, individuality. Food, air, impressions. The dotted triangle equals the invisible

"I," equals: aspects of $3-3$, 6, 9. This is injected at semitones on the scale to help complete it. The "I" acts as shock. Thus one of "I's" possibles may be realized in completing the scale without taking away from it its potentialities. The scale can only be realized after the triangulation occurs, with self-consciousness accepted wholly as neutralizer.

The invisible triangle equals: Krishna in the Gita—although creating the universe (scale), ""I" remain separate."

In the scale of nature the:

First shock   at 1 equals—food
Second shock at 3 equals—air
Third shock   at 6 equals—impressions

Food carries the scale of nature up to mi. Then air enters and carries it up to la. But impressions cannot become active in the scale of nature. It takes conscious efforts of man after he has been taught the method. After he passes this semitone he can pass others without being taught.

Note that beyond man's scale there is an opening at 9, which includes other potentialities in man beyond the human. This is the foundation of the next scale above man. It is the beginning of another circle.

Orage enlarges on meaning of seriously placing self-consciousness as objective. Subordinating all life to conscious effort and experiment.

The need of distinguishing between the subtleties of motive for in by-products, or willingness to risk all in life for the uncertain chance of self-consciousness. Orage describes king in Mahabharata convinced that he can only know justice by risking, gambling all. Orage explains how we are not real true gamblers, but dealers, who always held a little back in reserve. This king gambled his children, sold into slavery, his wife whom he loved, his kingdom, his own freedom, and lost all. Convinced of the inevitability that what would be, would be. And accepted willingly each step as he lost. After a period of 99 years slavery, all restored to him, not only intact, but with his own added consciousness of realization. *This was conscious faith.*

Orage refers to his own similar experience of the octave being carried through with the triangulation of the invisible "I." Surprising interrelations, coincidences, thought transference, etc., seem to occur. Actually, where we had existed as discordant notes before, the "I," the triangle at the semitones, now draws notes into relation on our own scale, so that other notes do not touch us.

Arrangement of our 3 centers, such that instinctive is positive, emotional negative, and intellectual scarcely existent.

The rate of vibration of the:

Intellectual center is 30,000
Emotional center is.$30,000^2$
Instinctive center is $30,000^3$

These figures explain why the relative weakness of intellectual vibration has little effect at the emotional. And also why the instinctive vibrations, which are the cube of the number of the intellectual, control and dominate the emotional. The problem therefore is to create a fourth center whose vibrations on will be the square of the square of the intellectual, that is, 30.000 to the fourth power. This center will therefore be strong enough to gain control of all 3 centers. The emotional is now negative, under positive instinctive control. Emotional should eventually come under a positive intellectual. Then the emotional will be the neutralizer, since within it lies essence, equals pattern, etc. And instinctive become negative.

At present, the emotions of even the most passionately intellectual types are under the control of the positive instinctive. Positive emotions about ideas fade into insignificance against control of the instinctive center. Imagine yourself struck suddenly blind, and try to find any emotion about ideas that is comparable. In man's present stats this holds, but it does not mean that from another center outside it is not possible to have other overwhelming emotions.

Orage cites experience of discovering chief-feature as such. Places one in an entirely new plane. State arising from such an experience, slips. Can only be regained with great effort. One goes about after discovery with a sense of amazement, that every one doesn't see it. And a readiness to admit it, whenever it is spotted. Agrees that one has a sense of being a beggar. Chief feature as being the opposite of what one likes to pretend is ones chief characteristic. One who seems to act independently, really most dependent. When you come nearer to chief feature, will give you more examples of those confessed by others.

Metaphysical distinction between real and actual. As to the triangle, the "I," we may actualize one possible as in the case of getting out of a chair, the number of possibles is fixed. But all the un-actualized possibles remain real. These are potentials.

Magnetic center—repeats, to question, that without magnetic center no one can be seriously interested in this work. Describe the way materialist scientist Clifford and "Lewis Carroll" mathematician, (Alice in Wonderland) wrote fantastic stories, etc. Specify gravity of ideas group them in exact groups in intellectual center. If person is without magnetic center, it is possible in recurrence for him to attain it in childhood from association with fairy tales, etc., that contain germs of this. It is always associated closely with emotional connection—affection for mother, nurse, etc. For remember, centers closely related—though in intellectual center, these ideas are charged with feeling.

MONDAY, 28 DECEMBER 1925

Orage opens with announcement of reading of book with him, beginning 1st Jan. Goes over importance of aiding publication by raising money, etc.

Eventually may be enough copies to be read in small groups. All may have to help conducting groups or reading book. (Explains how it is necessary to risk everything. Some may not increase in being until they are absolutely forced in desperation to make effort, and risk failure.) Emphasizes great importance of book. As aid to constructive imagination. Speaks of marvelous chapter not yet read aloud on purgatory, etc. Orage says he has read thousands of books and nothing in philosophy, not Plato or Plotinus, compare in lucidity, concentration, subtlety, etc., to this chapter. It leaves all philosophy behind. Try to imagine the kind of intensity and concentration necessary to produce such writing. The wonder is that Gurdjieff could do more than a line a day.

Orage suggests that maybe the most important work of the Institute is the completion of this book, which it is possible for us to contribute towards, for others in the future if not for ourselves.

Remember that the Bible which has had such an enormous influence was not any of it the direct writing of Christ. But merely the notes of his disciples.

For two years, many have been asking why there was not a book on the ideas. Now here it is. But your own experience of the difficulty to try to write what you know about true ideas, individuality, consciousness, etc., can give you some conception of what it meant to try to concentrate the ideas of this system, the method, and the sifting of Gurdjieff's experience with various occult teachers, etc.

Orage suggests the importance that everyone in the group considers the making of a vow for the coming year. The word vow is the same as the word devotion or de*vow*tion. It is now almost completely associated with religion. Something holy. He is at his devotions. Though we do say he is devoted to his business. In ancient times in India etc., people undertook to carry out vows, a pilgrimage etc., in order to cure themselves of disease, nervousness etc. Not psychoanalysis but a vow was prescribed for all sorts of disturbed conditions. But the making and carrying out of a vow is a serious matter. We are not considering it in a religious, but in a psychological sense. It must not be undertaken lightly. Not unless one has sufficient strength to risk it. For the effects of a vow is a pledge to oneself. It is of no consequence to the rest of the world if it is kept or broken. But to oneself it is of great consequence. For the failure to keep a vow is weakening, affecting seriously one's own self-confidence. But the making and fulfilling of a vow is enormously strengthening in the growth and development of being. Example of man who recently told Orage with pride of having fulfilled a vow to write 100 articles in the last year. He had done so—the articles had been in demand. But the purpose had not been one to increase being. The necessity of making a vow to carry over a period like a year, long enough to test oneself under varied conditions. As the phrase goes: "One does not know a man until one has summered and wintered with him."

Orage then reviews two types of effort at constructive imagination, which follow, and suggests that it would be a wise vow to spend a half hour, or at another time he said ten minutes, each day, or as much time and energy as possible each day, in these acts of constructive imagination. The result in the course of a year for all of us would be a remarkable change in our state of being. So that those ideas which we can now only speak of in words would be realized.

CONSTRUCTIVE IMAGINATION

In summarizing the two main points to work on for the New Year, beyond making a vow, Orage spoke of:

1.   Once again trying to envisage all of mankind, in all conditions of race, culture, emotions, etc., simultaneously. Remembering that the particular condition of this organism was a mere cell in man takes as a whole, which consisted of the two thousand million taken as one—Adam Kadmon.

2.   To attempt to envisage the universe as stated by Gurdjieff to consist of a series of related planets, satellites, etc., the moon, subordinate to the earth, the earth to the sun, the sun to the milky way, etc., and each of these places inhabited by various types of three centered beings. Orage recalls tale of ants reduced in size to present stature. Because dangerous in former proportions to equilibrium of world. Orage suggested that the relative size of beings depends on condition of thyroid and could be affected by those having the proper knowledge. He suggests that certain Atlanteans were changed in size, when moved to another continent. The "little people" of Ireland Leprechauns, also come under this category. Orage says it is an interesting idea to speculate upon that creatures could be reduced to manikins if a species of so called poison gas were introduced into the air, before birth, to affect their stature. (This makes M. wonder, though she did not ask in group, whether this reduction of the figure of this organism under simultaneous observation and non-identification, to manikin size, is not similar, and therefore connected with change in thyroid secretion?)

TYPES

The senselessness of any exact diagram. It would be purely academic. It is only through one's own effort that one can approach it. Use any type of classification to group people—generous, mean, calculating, domineering, etc. Finally there will be a few that will not fall into any of the classifications you can make. Then the diagram of classification becomes useful to place these.

Our three higher centers exist although they are not in our service. The organism, do, re, mi, is played on by nature, moon and planets.

But sol, la, si, the "I" is played on by a higher super-nature, the sun and the milky way. This will help us to relate ourselves to the cosmic struggle. To realize that every step we take towards constructive imagination, etc., real

93

thought, draws up towards the sun, every identification with subjective emotion etc., is a pull towards the moon. We are constantly in the midst of this combat.

Definition of man—as the type of being that could reason.

Man—manas—intellectual center still undeveloped.

Battle of Mahabharata.

Field of battle—emotional center.

Kurus—Intellectual center.

Pandavas—Instinctive center.

The struggle between the two families for the control of the essence. Stationed in the emotional center, but containing elements of other centers also.

Essence cannot be controlled or developed directly. Remember image of driver, cart and horse. Essence is at mi. Instinctive at si. But the intellectual must still strike do, and go up the scale to mi, in order to control essence and develop it up to si. Therefore the necessity of all these efforts of constructive imagination, observation with non-identification, participation and experiment. All the exercises given to practice are meant to help start the intellectual center moving up the scale—begin real thought.

Essence is the basis of all that subjectivity in us that interferes with pure thought. There is no devil in the world except essence.

Atonement in time. Occurs when as above described, the intellectual center by various conscious efforts starts to move up the scale and in consequence pulls the other centers up. The result is the real digestion of our past. The rechewing of it, as the cow chews its cud. We are able by this act to bite off and eat away our past. Things rearrange themselves and fall into proper groupings. Nothing in our past is then lost or wasted.

Distinction between, actual, potential, and real.

Actual can be seen.

Potential can be imagined.

The real cannot be seen or imagined. It is in other terms and is the source of the actual and the potential. (Plato's world of ideas.)

Jean Toomer

Need to exercise all five centers.

Attitude, positive.

1. Sex: positive attitude, though one were continent.

2. Instinctive: care for it, in food, and so on. Responds to good care, even should its needs be only partially met, and will bide its time until more suitable activities can be provided for it.

3. Formulatory: mathematics, formulating, other philosophies in one's own terms – exercises as already given.

4. Higher Emotional: indirectly exercised, by virtue of one's [...] Directly exercised by religion and art. The truly tragi-comic Higher Intellectual: in trying to comprehend the system by all types of simultaneous effort.

One have no fear as regards the lower emotional being exercised.

Guard against an inclusion of the fanciful.

1. The actualization of one possible: living in time

2. The actualization of all possible: living in eternity

3. The actualization of all unpossibles

The "infinite" is a concept, a mere fiction. The absolute is finite, let us say, as to number. And in point of time, finite, calculable. Man: 80 years. The natural kingdom: 80 x 30.000. The earth: 2400.000 x 30.000. And so on.

 swinging into the ascending current
by means of this system

Swinging into the ascending current by means of this system.

All do's have three aspects: positive, negative, and neutral. Dead do?

The "I" on the same plane with the higher intellectual and emotional centers, and hence, can control them. It must control them, equally with the lower centers. They function according to planetary influences. They may impress themselves upon a passive mind.

The "I" not located in the same place in all people. With some, definitely within the body. With others, some inches outside the body, in the aura.

The case of Nietzsche, etc.

Self remembering. Direct method. Gurdjieff to Orage.

1. Sounding

2. Try to locate the "I". Say "I", and endeavor to find where it locates. If

intensity is produced in forehead above the eyes, try to relax this, and then search for the "I".

3.   The organism, comprising the centers, is the cosmos of "I". Pull the cosmos into the "I". Whenever saying "I" do this.

4.   More radiant than the Sun,
       Purer than the Snow,   corresponding to centers
       Subtler than the Ether,
       Is the Self,
       The Spirit within my heart,
       I am that Self,
       That Self am I.
       Repeat 500 times a day

QUESTIONS TO ORAGE, MONDAY, 23 FEBRUARY 1925

A. Formula

1.   Repeat by voice? Repeat by mind?

a.   Simultaneous: effort to hold these descriptive lines in consciousness at same time.

2.   Eyes open?

3.   Eyes closed?

a.   The closed eye consciousness.

1.   Description: disassociation from the physical, then from the psychic.

2.   What is it? Does a ray from higher center come through and inform it, or is it nothing more than the over-must produced by the three centers in temporary association?

3.   Should the "I" of the formula be related to it, and its expansion attempted? Or should it be disregarded altogether, being negligible, and the "I" related to the strictly potential centers?

Answer: Realization through contemplation of itself. Expansion: Trying to move it towards the higher centers.

4.   Loss of identity. Distinction between non-identity and loss of identity.

5.   Difficulty of isolating "I" in conversation.

6.   Is it good to sit and work from closed-eye consciousness?

7.   Effort to wake up. Pure psychological effort?

B. Psychic

1.   Formula does stimulate activity.

2.   Withdrawal from physical.

3.   Withdrawal from psychic.

a.   The psychic goes on, providing amazing phenomena for observation.

4.   Phenomena in forehead. Description.

5.   General phenomena. Description.

6.   Sense of tautomer. Formation of psychic body?

C. Doctrine

1.   Recurrence.

a.   Does fourth-dimension contain all necessary explanations and recon-
ciliations?

D. Talk of group, people.

1.   Answers, and diverse elements

A.   Generally, for the purpose of realizing that we are in fact as radiant
as the sun, etc. The need to hold a balance between consciousness of the fact
that the organism is mechanical, and the fact that the self is radiant. Neither
the denial of the first fact, as in the case of certain mystics and yogis, nor denial
of the second, as in the case of the modern exponents of mechanical behaviorism. But both affirmed. The formula as a means of suggestion, of suggesting to
oneself, ones true state. A counter to the conscious suggestions which induced
our present state, for the purposes of nature.

(A master can give this suggestion, thereby producing consciousness in the
disciple, even in a disciple with personality! Christ to his disciples. Upon this
is founded the emphasis of faith in the Christian religion.)

1.   Perhaps it has a sound value, and therefore it may be well to repeat it
subvocally.

3.   (a) (2) Orage does not think that the higher centers enter into it.

6.   To be carefully watched. (My own deduction, from general remarks ,
particularly with reference to the chief feature.)

B.   6. Yes, formation of psychic body. Orage's experience. This body
usually exists, its constituents in a loose and diffused state. Wasted and disor-
ganized by worry, fear, etc.

Integrated by means of conscious effort, the elimination of waste energy. A
by product. Astral (emotional) body next to form.

C.   1. (a) Yes

Somewhere we are solid. To locate the true solid.

Essence: irrational passion, an inward desire, springing from no external
suggestion.

When it has been uncovered, the need for a matured intellect to protect the
organism from destructive passions, to mediate for truly conscious purposes.

The race between the uncovering of the essence and the maturity of the
mind.

Temporary insanity produced by freed essence with no intellectual maturity to temper it.

Chief feature: Watch for it, and watch out for its operations.

Exercises: instinctive (the movements), intellectual (simultaneity) for the purpose of rendering the organism muscular and plastic for the manifested "I".

FRIDAY, 20 MARCH 1925

QUESTIONS FOR ORAGE

1. What is the congested or relatively sluggish state in the morning, upon awakening, due to?
2. The question of denying sleep. What effects more than the obvious ones? How should we gauge the effort?
3. What is "chief feature"?
4. Is there any active thing to be done in connection with the growth of the vital body? The vital body? What is to be guarded against? What feeds it? As an impulse, it is subject to the law of the octave. The semitone will mature. Bridge the difficulty or must I? If I must, then how?
5. Is the formation of a body the same thing as the maturity of a center, or is formation prerequisite to maturity?
6. Does the mental body form after the astral body? Is the mind dependent on it for maturity?
7. Do the bodies form in this sequence? Or may there be another order? Or does growth occur in all three at the same time, simply differing in degrees, or degree of obviousness?
8. Do the three lower centers revolve about the 5th? The instinctive? Does sex revolve about the lower centers? The instinctive? Is sex then the moon?
9. The problem of sex as it is experienced in my present phase of work. Stimulated. The organism diminished subsequently.
10. The question of energy. Diminished saving during sleep, because of shorter hours. I do wish to resort to sleep for it. What then?

ANSWERS AND ADDITIONAL CONSIDERATIONS

1. Perhaps a faulty (an imperfect) connection of the centers. The connection between them imperfectly established upon awakening. Some damage may have been caused by my forced athletics and physical exercises. By my general tendency to overdo.
2. It developed that I was too much of an ascetic. Too much given to forcing things. Too much cerebral domination. In general, special disciplines should be naturally possible as a result of the psychological work. In time, the centers will harmoniously wish to do things. The cerebral center should not bully the other two. The distinction between doing a thing for discipline and for experimentation. At this stage, do not force experiment, but let these also

come naturally, that is, make use of favorable conditions for the purpose of experiment.

3.   The chief feature and the essential wish are identical. It is the mainspring of action. Why do you do things? For what do you do them? For example, Gurdjieff, when challenged to tell a distinguished Russian general what his chief feature was, said: Fear. The general finally admitted that he did fear to face his wife, unless he had been heroic. This fear in connection with his wife was the motor behind all he did. I decided that my chief feature was the desire for power. Orage thought that this came pretty close to the nest. And added; we say that the chief feature must die. Meanwhile, observe it in all acts.

4.   The etheric body is practically formed. It is the magnetic center. The natural processes take care of it. In another talk, however, Orage told me that it was generally in a somewhat loose state. I conclude then, that some sort of conscious effort is needed to tighten it. My own experience points to this as true. The astral body, however, can only be formed by conscious effort. Not effort direct upon it, but the practices which the system gives. The completion of the air octave.

5.   The formation of a body and the maturing of a center are identical. When it is formed, the center is mature. From this point of view, there may said to be only three centers. The lower center being the root, that from which the body springs and grows.

6.   Yes, yes.

7.   Yes. Work goes on in all at the same time, but growth is completed in the given order.

8.   The distinction between generation (for the moon) and creation (for the self).

10.   Though this work is run on sex energy, there is enough sex generated for all purposes, including its expression in the sex act. My attitude wrong.

————

Avoiding Karma. Gurdjieff.

Individuality – the effort to find out what I really want, in a given situation, even though I do not finally act upon this desire.

Consciousness – doing what you have to do, consciously; accompanying each act with awareness.

Will – going a little faster than you have to go.

As an actor – acting a situation that pleases you, acting a situation that displeases you, as perfectly as if it pleased you.

Trembling – etheric body – good. Much magnetism.

The need to treat the body well.

The need for as long and continuous a sleep as the organism will stand.

My writing: emotional figures. Illustration in a book. Illustrations and comparisons serve to convey a meaning. Once the meaning is grasped, these things should be eliminated.

Insanity touched off by the work.

Planetary deposits at conception, perhaps.

Work uncovers them. But, if work is undertaken as directed, these germs will be uncovered under a glass jar, as if it were. Otherwise . . .

Gurdjieff: What is the use of pouring energy into you when you leak like a sieve? Stop up your holes, first. Stop the leakage, the wastage. In a word, become continent.

A master idea among the usual assemblage, is like a wolf among lambs: it devours them.

There are a groups of ideas. Many groups. To each group there is associated a group of emotions. It may happen that the ideas of a given person have joined to them all the available emotions. In this case, a new idea could stimulate no emotional response. But if it were powerful enough, it would displace some old idea, and take over to itself the emotions freed by this act.

The octave of a group, and its control, can only be learned by experience. Recognize *me*, and invent a suitable shock. Some special person for this purpose. Others initiated by her talk. (Coater). Ouspensky taking someone out for a talk, etc.

Have the plan for an evening, and make the group carry it out. Progress according to suspense

SUNDAY, 19 APRIL 1925

Dear Orage,

I enclose a tentative program for the Wednesday group, subject to your modification and directives.

And too, ten pages of an attempt to triangulate.

Jean (looks like "I saw" but could very well be Jean)

It is necessary to bluff (within limits) in order that you be forced by this act to live up to it, ie, actualize the bluff.

The higher intellectual : positive

The formulatory   : negative

The external world   : neutral, or neutralizing agent.

If the activity is only between the positive and negative elements, they wear on each other and may produce pathological symptoms. It is essential, therefore, that one set oneself a task in the external world, that is, employ the neutral element.

Did Napoleon set himself the *conscious* task of unifying Europe?

The ordinary will is not the strongest desire; it is a compound of desires, tending to go in the direction of the strongest, but being somewhat deflected because of the hangers-on.

Figure:

Man as a planted root. This root composed of the three higher centers. From it grow the stalk, leaves and flowers. These, are our ordinary life. When they are cut off – we call that death – another plant will start to grow, from the *same* root, and this is another life, and so the process continues. The types of plant may differ, due to the circumstances it springs to. This time good; perhaps another time bad. We must change the root if we wish real change. The growth is a plant, we are vegetables. It is necessary that the growth form; invertebrate and vertebrate animals, monkeys and then the human form: man. We must develop the growth that it may correspond to the root. I am in an Emersonian phase. Apply the ideas, but do this more concretely.

The question of Karma.

Karma is generated in group work. But it is necessary *to do*. Only, do not make mistakes. Mistake is Karma. If one learns from a mistake, the Karma is cancelled.

Material spoiled for consciousness is not spoiled. A conscious gain justifies the wastage. Otherwise, it is not justified. (Paper wasted in effort to write essay.) An increase of consciousness is to our credit.

Our obligation to biology is conscious; it is not biological.

ORAGE TO J. TUESDAY, 19 MAY 1925

Do not start (in detail) a larger subject if, before you get it, the meeting is ¾ over. There will soon be so much negative energy released that, if a person be intense enough, and non-identified, that is, if he be in a condition to utilize it, he could become self-conscious.

Food enters the body negative. Within the organism there must be a corresponding positive element. But even given the positive and negative elements, nothing will happen unless there is a neutralizer. Say Do is struck by positive and negative; there must be Re. In fact, without Re, Do cannot be struck. As regards people and these ideas – I am positive, they are negative. These are given. But nothing will happen unless there is a neutral element. In this case, the neutralizer will be the *wish* of the other person. (Wishes are always the neutralizers.) This wish may sometimes be induced by a questioning of the individual.

THE OCTAVE

Each given unit is an octave, that is, it has its own octave, and at the same time is a note of some other octave. In the octave of nature, the vertebrate animals are at Sol. Sol is an octave. But animals are not wholes, hence should they completely realize Sol, they would progress to La, but they would not pass out of the natural scale. Man, however, is a whole.

Should he realize (completely) his octave, he would pass out of the natural scale. Only wholes, upon the complete realization of their octave, pass on to another scale. Man is a note in the scale of nature, and nature is a note in the scale of man. (For man is a cosmos. His is the great octave.) Man is at Si. All impulses have their inception at Si. In the case of the impulse to practice the method, it starts at Si. The effort is to strike Do. But between Si and Do, there is an octave. The impulse must pass the difficulties at Fa and Si of this inner octave before it can strike Do. It often runs up to Mi immediately, and one experiences, say, ten observations the first day after the method has been given. But it quickly runs down the scale, 7 per day, 5, etc. until it is at Do (of the inner octave), that is at Si. If it manages to pass Mi to Sol, this fact is evident in the person. If it really strikes Do, this fact is evident. The person feels that he is committed to this work forever. Neither Gurdjieff or anyone else is needed to persuade him to continue. But he may stay at Do.

A person with essential energy. He may not be over intelligent, but he makes his presence felt. He is certain that is he is doing the work.

There is no use to stop a projectile in flight, that is, a person somewhere between Do and Mi. The thing to do is to is to speed up his flight. If he now writes one book a year, let him undertake to finish three. When he comes to rest at Fa, then he is ready to be approached by, an approach this system.

We are elementals. We who have survived death are elementals. In the process of developing the "I", of becoming self-conscious, it is necessary that we humanize the elemental. I must make a human being of Jean Toomer. For all rungs of the ladder must be filled.

Every time that I conduct a group there is a master cell within my brain carrying on similar work with a group of brain cells.

ORAGE TO J. MONDAY, 25 MAY 1925

From Do to Re is a whole tone
From Re to Mi is a whole tone 1st tetra chord
From Mi to Fa is a semitone
From Sol to La is a whole tone
From La to Si is a whole tone   2nd tetra chord
From Si to Do is a semitone

Between Mi and Fa, (and Si and Do) there are broken octaves. Into these, the ray (is it solar or cosmic?) enters. It is by this means that the single unit partakes of everything. For instance , into the semitones of the natural octave the ray enters, and, among other matters, nature here receives influences from the other planets. The bee is said to be of Venus, that is, to display Venus characteristics. Nature upon earth receives its *dominant* influence from the earth. Hence it is peculiar to the earth. But it also receives influences from the other planets. Hence it is also planetary – universal. Nature upon Venus receives its dominant influence from Venus. Hence it is special to Venus. But it also receives subordinate elements from the other planets, among these, the Earth. Hence, though primarily characteristic of Venus, it nevertheless is also composed of earth-matter, etc. In this way, any given octave is at once distinct and universal.

The caterpillar is a specimen of objective art introduced into nature to serve as an example.

What will happen when air passes up its octave, what emotions we will have, what type of invertebrate and vertebrate animals we will be, we cannot tell. It is certain, however, that we will have no real control over them. For what is to control them, in the absence of an "I". At best, the lower intellectual and instinctive centers will effect a partial balance.

Whereas we react to the strongest attraction, *Will* will enable us to act towards the greatest advantage.

The procession of magnets. It is determined, (by our past experience), which one or one's we will be attracted to.

If a thing does not attract us, we cannot *create* an emotional response to it. In general, we cannot create emotions.

ORAGE TO J. MONDAY, 8 JUNE 1925

J: The human brain cells are the allies of the "I" in the organism. But even these allies go to sleep quite often. When awake, they are the vehicle of self-awareness, the ideas of the system. They likewise set about the control of the organism. Their attempted control is not only legitimate, it is their real function to control, as emissaries of the "I". Because of their motive (which is two-fold: self-consciousness – an experiment, in order that they may learn their business) and the true ideas that they possess, are they distinct from other brain cells. And by means of these same factors their operation can be distinguished from the ordinary types of intellectual center dominance and "self-control".

O: Think of the "I" as being a catalyzer. Through observation, for the most part, proceeds from the intellectual center (the human brain cells), observation takes place (in our sense) only in virtue of the presence of the "I".

O: Bring in the figure: driver, horse, and cart – passenger sleeping. The idea is to have a complete equipage. Whereas now the passenger (the "I") is asleep, the driver likewise sleeping or in a pub house talking (having fancies with) other drivers, and the horse and cart either running wild or cutting figures to illustrate the drivers fancies, the driver must get on the job, learn and practice his business. And the passenger must awake to find a driver who can take his orders. Passenger ("I") to driver (intellectual center) to horse (emotional center) to cart (instinctive center).

At the present time, the centers, though magnetically related and mutually affecting each other, neither are aware of what one does to the other nor what is done. For example, the emotional center does not know what it does to the instinctive , nor does it know what the instinctive does to it. The horse might kick the cart to pieces, unaware, etc.

The instinctive center has only enough energy for its own special purposes. Likewise with the intellectual. The emotional center supplies the motive for all (so to speak) extra functions. Common sense arises when the three intellectual sub-centers work together.

Satisfaction from the solution of a mathematical problem is an illustration of the functioning of the emotional sub-center of the intellectual center.

The performance of a piece of mental work, mechanically or by habit, illustrates the working of the intellectual sub-center of the instinctive center.

Mental gymnastics, the attempt at simultaneity (assembling) – moving sub-center of the intellectual center.

The next but one. To arrive at the next, implies and necessitate the next but one. For without this third, nothing can happen. Thus, air must be present in order that food pass from solid to liquid. Magnetism must be present in order that it pass from liquid to gas, etc.

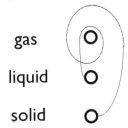

gas

liquid

solid

The positive reaches up, so to speak, and gets its spark or germ from the neutralizer. It then doubles back to the negative. The substance must bring the germ forth. The potential is only actualized in this way. Father +, mother -, child

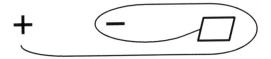

The solar ray enters broken octaves.

Cosmic sex (energy) pertains to the pattern. Food, air, impressions pertain to the systems, the structure (organism). We will be released when we have developed all structures to the human form, that is, when we have completed the air and impression octaves.

Make an emotion say of depression or grief, do something. This emotion will evoke corresponding reactions in the instinctive and intellectual centers. But these two centers will be merely imitative, that is passive. Make them active. Make the instinctive express grief by some positive action. Make the intellectual express grief by some positive action. Make it accurately, formulate observations, or formulate ideas relative to the state.

ORAGE TO J. TUESDAY, 16 JUNE 1925

Our one possible human act at the present time is: the formulatory center can report the behavior of the organism to the "I". The "I" exists. It has a state of being. But it has no life, for we refer life to the organic kingdom. Hence for life, that is to live, the "I" must function through some unit of the organic kingdom. This unit is the organism. Only the relation, however, between the "I" and the organism is now established. Function implies the active use of the organism by the "I". But at present the "I" is inactive as regards the organism. Consequently, it does not function in the given sense, and has no life.

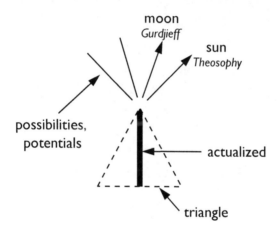

Humanity has reached a certain point, having actualized what we call the history of man. At this point, there are a number of possibilities any one of which may or may not be actualized. Among these possibilities is that man will reach the sun. The theosophists have stated this possible as though it is certain to be actualized. But it is by no means certain. Another possibility is that man will reach the moon. This is the Gurdjieffian assertion. But neither is this *certain*, though there are more indications of it than there are of the theosophist possible. The uncertainty lies in this: that behind the manifested line there is always the unmanifested triangle. This triangle is in touch with the entire universe. It is subject therefore to cosmic influences. And there is no telling for certain what may happen in the cosmos beyond our solar system, beyond the certainty of the our solar god. Such an unforeseen and unknowable occurrence would necessarily have an unpredictable effect upon the triangle, which in turn would similarly effect [...] upon humanity.

Likewise with the individual. Behind the organism there is the [...] pattern. And, though from the evidence of the organism, the chances are a million to one against the persons really doing this work. There is always this one chance. Something may happen in the triangle that would cause the one possible to be actualized.

[...] something can be done. Learn to know just what [...] states

[...] Experiment with it. Find out what is [...] and experimental circumstances.

Man's number is 24. The number of the planetary god is 12.

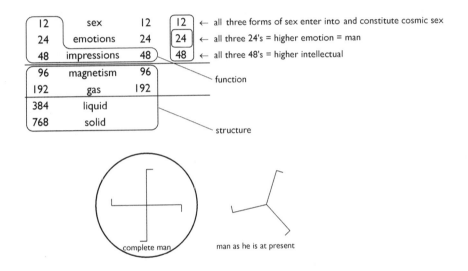

complete man

man as he is at present

Ordinary earth belongs to the globe and is not part of the organic or natural kingdom. (A homogenous form determines inclusion in the organic kingdom).The organic kingdom = metals, minerals, vegetables, etc.

Man is the sex cell of the organic kingdom. Every individual is an appendage in the body of nature. That is her mind, men are the brain cells of the kingdom of nature. The formulatory center is simply the higher sex organ. Procreation and words are both sex. Sex, Si, differentiates into these two. The sex differentiated for the formulatory center is transmitted when the formulatory center is in the service of the "I", that is, when it ceases to be a merely mechanical instrument of external information for the organism and becomes a reporter to the "I" of the behavior of the organism.

The lower emotional center is simply that portion of the higher center which at the present time can manifest itself [...] with the lower intellectual.

107

There is enough metal in a man to make a small sized nail.

In the course of this work physiological changes are actually taking place. It is necessary to meet them with conscious adjustments and adaptations.

There are three hundred billion sperm cells to each ejaculation. The number of ova are quite limited. The number of ripe ova are [...] than three. There is a relation between the three hundred billion sperm cells and the two thousand million people.

The attempt on the part of 24 to make 48, 24
24= the back of the head
48 = the front of the head, the formulatory center
24= man's number
48= the number of the higher animals

ORAGE TO J. WEDNESDAY, 24 JUNE 1925

Consciously organize and pursue a (so to speak) irrational and impossible task or object in the world. In this way you will create your moon and utilize it for solar purposes. An institute, a renaissance, etc.

The whole natural octave is a transmitting station. Beings supply the material of or for manifestation. Other beings supply the materials for the (terrestrial?), the astral, mental and causal bodies.

But the triangle is "I" – the "I" is "I".

To a woman: "It was your chief feature which said that." That is, it was her chief feature which determined what she thought to be her chief feature.

Close group with the idea of chief feature, which can be found by self-observation.

ORAGE TO J. THURSDAY, 29 OCTOBER 1925

1. The non-associational state (referring to and interpreting my own experience at Lake George): wherein words are neither related to themselves in verbal patterns, nor to objects. A given word is no longer associated to another word or group of words. A given word is no longer associated to a given object, as, for example, the word sensation a mode of consciousness.

This non-associated state precedes and is a necessary prerequisite to free associations. It is, therefore, a forerunner and foreshadower of real thinking.

2. (Referring to the same experience) The state wherein names forms, and modes are dissolved into the one, homogeneous, conscious pulp of the non-existent "I". Observation is impossible because there are no objects to observe. All is one, subject and object are identical. And this one something can hardly be called conscious. It seems not to exist. In such cases, be aware of the dim changes of states. Try to be continually aware of these changes. In

this way, experience itself is observed, not objects of experience. Whatever is, is, to the extent that is, aware. it was a good sign that, in this state, the sun was tried to be identified with.

3.   The need for the *function* of serving the moon no longer exists. But, this need having passed, the *habit* persists. And education, that is sociology, through its *suggestion*, enforces the habit.

4.   External suggestion: moon-ward, towards unconsciousness
Auto-suggestion: beginning towards the sun
The "I" on the sun plane.

The function of these ideas is to counteract mass- or social-suggestion. They are a means to auto-suggestion.

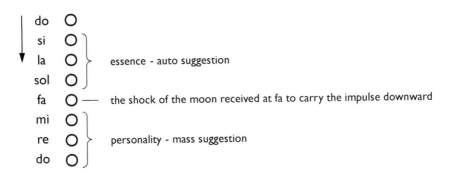

The "I" exists in lesser freedom. The organism determined. These ideas, however, initiate an upward movement, through Sol, La, Si, to "I". By means of them therefore a conduit is established with the plane of freedom. Consequently, this plane is able to extend its influences to the determined plane.

ORAGE TO J. WEDNESDAY, 25 NOVEMBER 1925

Each thing done or participated in should be purposive according to one or more of the elements of objective morality. Therefore, we should have a reason (and be conscious of this reason) for everything we do. If asked we should be able to tell just why we are engaged in this and that. Or, if we have walked into a situation unconsciously, then, upon awakening to it, we should ask and discover which of the five elements can be lived here. Having discovered it, we should act accordingly.

Not only cast a role for Toomer, but also cast a role for "I", a proper not through, Toomer. (Gurdjieff identifying with Beelzebub.)

There are two, and only two aspects of the universe, one, an existence, the other a function, namely, "I", and eating.

Essence is the germ plasm. There can be a redistribution and development of its elements, but the essence itself cannot be changed until after the note Sol of its own scale has been reached. At present, it is subject to the planets. When Sol has been reached, it will subject to other cosmic bodies (the sun?).

The scale of essence:

Do= physical body

Re=astral body

Mi= mental body

Sol= causal body

All of the bodies are potential in the germ plasm. Further, the germ plasm contains actual astral and mental (causal?) matters or material.

Reason relates to the lower intellectual center.

Understanding relates to the lower intellectual center and emotional center.

The ego can withstand the transformations of essence. Only with causal body there comes a permanent identity. Then, all and everything that has ever happened to one is recalled and held continuously.

Toomer is lazy. He has not had an emotional realization of the necessity to pay, in terms of money, to made money.

The $\triangle$ is a psychological state.

The attempt of the $\triangle$ or "I" to assemble in one act of consciousness all that is known about that which is actualized, namely, the organism. To assemble only *a part* of what is known, to select a certain aspect of the organism and assemble what is known of this *aspect* — such an act is psychic. To assemble *all* that is known with reference to the whole organism, such an act is psychological. Psychic activity is smoke. Psychological activity is fire.

ORAGE MEETING, THURSDAY, 25 JUNE 1925

ORAGE: Describe your experiences after the stimulus of the groups was withdrawn. Ask any personal questions that may have arisen in the interval. Ask any questions in relations to the ideas.

The need to create fire by friction in order to help a given impulse over Mi. No use to try to take the impulse over directly. Another type of energy, that is, fire is necessary. Generally, it can be generated by opposing the "I" to the wish of the organism. The Gurdjieff work may be taken as a fourth type of yoga, one that aims to employ the other three types more or less at the same time. Generate fire (will) by punishing the body, making it take the Buddha posture, etc. These simple exercises would not do in the case of the failure of an impulse directed, say, at simultaneous observation. For this, much more drastic exercises.

As to our behavior, a test of real observation is that we cannot remember what we have observed. Nevertheless, data concerning our behavior collects, forms itself, and in time yields its own deductions.

Two exercises: experiment with the organism, deliberately place it in different circumstances for conscious purposes. Try to formulate what some other and other people think of you. The back of the head, the higher intellectual center knows what they think. But the lower intellectual does not. This is an attempt to make the formatory center know and transcribe what the higher center knows. It knows most things, the lower does not, and since we only aware of the latter, we are not in possession the higher's knowledge.

THE CHIEF FEATURE

Sometimes when found, one is not certain of it until he has been told so, confirmed in his finding by another (capable of giving this confirmation).

Much time is wasted, and hence much time and effort can be saved by knowing the chief feature. The chief feature is the configuration, *conformation* or patterns of our wishes, both the wishes themselves and the pattern having been determined by the position of the planets at the moment of conception.

Vanity – vain in regard to just what? Precisely how does this vanity express itself?

Are you self-confident? Are you the reverse? Towards what are you self-confident? In what way?

Are you treacherous? In regard to what? How?

Do you fear? What do you fear? How do you fear it?

Vanity, fear, etc. – these are some of the backgrounds of chief features. They will manifest according to the seventy-odd types. But even within these types, the features will not be exactly similar. For each point on the globe and each minute marks a different configuration of the planets.

The feature, when found, will usually be "criminal". But there are higher crimes, and low crimes. (The distinction between a bold highwayman and a sneak-thief. Between a dangerous man, and one who is merely troublesome.) It will usually be meanly criminal. One can escape really touching it by identifying with high crime.

One is never the same person after having discovered it. It may be uncovered prematurely. Normally, a number of months of observation must precede its discovery. A quality, like cruelty is not a chief feature.

Carl Zigrosser

OUR COSMIC RAY

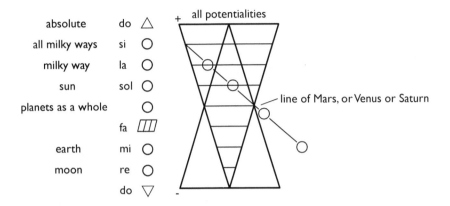

The earth is one of seven planets. Pattern of seven planets a more complex structure. Any one planet is do. Planets taken as a whole are complete octave of any one planet. When planets speak of world they refer to the sun. The sun is their creator. Each of seven planets derived from material of the sun.

Our sun is merely one of the stars in the milky way. The milky way contains innumerable suns millions of times larger than our sun. The sun is one in myriads in belt or tract or as we should call it, *organ* of the milky way.

There are seven milky ways.

Allowing planets, nebulae, etc. [...] nothing higher than suns, totaled in sum of milky ways.

The Absolute is the universe taken as one—concrete not metaphysical. Possible to follow line in different suns, line Mars, Saturn, etc. Diagram equals triangle.

Diagram all this—neutralizing forces of a positive and negative absolute—occurs on any given octave or dimension.

We can say object of creation to run down scale.

Why does one thing grow out of another?

Why is the following less than the one before?

There is a contraction of consciousness—involution.

Each is a fall down—movement is towards a negative state of being, by sacrifice of positive elements.

"I" starts from top absolute, and is successively contracted by each step in definition.

Evolution - positive.   Movement up scale.   △

Solomon's seal.   ✡

Triangles identical.

God contracts   ▽   goes down scale.

Man expands   △   goes up scale.

All rungs on ladder always occupied.

If we became gods tomorrow, we should not enter an empty world, but would find that there were gods before us. Just as if a horse should become a man, he would find two thousand million men before him.

Ladder always occupied by 2 sets of beings, one going up the scale, the other going down. So it is impossible to tell whether the beings you meet at some point are going up or down with you.

All moons occupy a particular note, so earths, so suns.

This is how God found himself: /\

Since he came to exist subject to some power. Discovered it was time. He set to work to create a universe to cheat time. Perpetual motion involved no matter wasted. Food of one person depends on another.

All beings live by taking in each other's washing.

Bottom do—negative absolute—absence of potentiality.

Sin against Holy Ghost—absence of potentiality. (To destroy potentialities. But one can only destroy one's own.)

Positive do contains all potentialities.

Negative do contains no potentiality—actuality without any potentiality—place where inability to move or change, but to be moved or to be changed—zero of inertia. Frozen air nearest approach to this state, zero of inertia.

This diagram ought to show world no chaos. Example—articles thrown on floor—there is a scheme of colors of rainbow.

We may die helpless, but we will not die hopeless if we begin to realize the pattern behind the spectacle.

Self like woman in revelation. Sin on head. Moon below feet.

Real cosmic emotion—emotion from feeling of relation with cosmos.

The law of the 3—positive, negative and neutralizing forces.

Modern physics aware of 2 forces, positive and negative, that implicitly assumes third force. Mechanics—neutral—point of application where stress can be asserted. Example: tug of war—on rope tie handkerchief in middle and watch stress of both forces. Everything is tug of war between positive and negative forces. All we see is handkerchief.

We human beings, same 3 centers. 2 centers are related to positive and negative. Emotional center, where we feel alternate pulls between other two centers, equals, handkerchief. Don't see strength or agents that pull. But by watching handkerchief can measure stress.

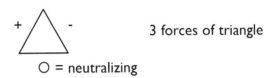

3 forces of triangle

We humans—third force blind.

All phenomena—neutralizing forces—we don't see what gives them a shape.

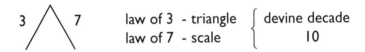

In every phenomenon there are positive, negative and neutralizing forces—positive, negative and form. Example: hydrogen-atom—nucleus, electron. The neutralizing force is the force which maintains them in that relation with each other. Why is its order a circle?

What is it that makes cells in our body keep their shape? Why do we cohere? How did a germ cell know where to stop? It is as though it were growing into a pattern. It couldn't grow into two mere arms or legs. Plato spoke of ideas-pattern previous to things—neutralizing force.

1 is only 1. 2 is 2 because its position of being presupposes another 1. The relation between these 2 is the sum of 1 plus 2 equals 3. 1 and 2 are juxtaposed—to make a three—hydrogen atom.

Before matter—there was 1 and 2. But there was no actualized relation. Actualized relation—the selection of 1 potentiality which makes a form.

St John. In the beginning was the word (1). The word was with God (2). The word was God (3).

The octave divides into three—always 3 neutralizer—acts as beginning of next triad. All subsequent matter presupposes hydrogen atom as H. presupposes trinity—3—neutralizer—child of 1 plus 2. Then neutralizer of previous triad becomes positive of succeeding one. This makes our planets neutralizer.

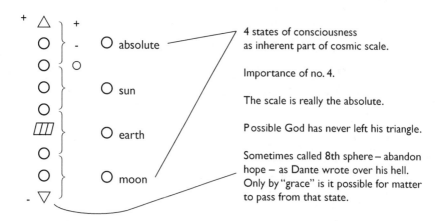

4 states of consciousness as inherent part of cosmic scale.

Importance of no. 4.

The scale is really the absolute.

Possible God has never left his triangle.

Sometimes called 8th sphere – abandon hope – as Dante wrote over his hell. Only by "grace" is it possible for matter to pass from that state.

Each group taken as 1.

At fa—had to be introduced an artificial transmitting station.

It will serve equally upwards or down.

Organic kingdom on this planet—life.

Life began as single cell—two directions (1) vegetable {2} animal

Acting as transmitting agent from the sun through the planets to the earth and onwards to the moon. We exist to attract and held influences from all the planets. To deposit in earth when we die. Earth absorbs planetary matter through agency of what we call protoplasm. As earth gets more magnetized etc., it may shift up in scale to become sun, etc.

Scale equals 9—with one semitone—enneagram.

Each step down is a converting station, is a machine for changing energy from one rate of vibration to another.

A difference of form does not necessarily mean a difference of nature. Bird form can be a 3 centered being.

Semitone between mi and fa.

 Machine derived from substances of all other planets.

Our organic kingdom contains representatives of all other planets.

Fa indicates absence of natural transition.

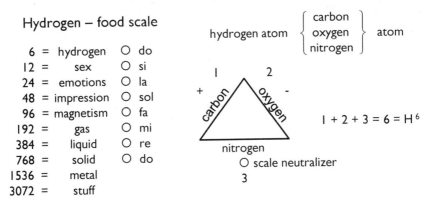

Hydrogen – food scale

6	=	hydrogen	○ do
12	=	sex	○ si
24	=	emotions	○ la
48	=	impression	○ sol
96	=	magnetism	○ fa
192	=	gas	○ mi
384	=	liquid	○ re
768	=	solid	○ do
1536	=	metal	
3072	=	stuff	

hydrogen atom $\left\{ \begin{array}{l} \text{carbon} \\ \text{oxygen} \\ \text{nitrogen} \end{array} \right\}$ atom

$1 + 2 + 3 = 6 = H^6$

○ scale neutralizer

○ 1 absolute – all cosmoses superior to sun

○ 2 sun – sun as center of gravity of its △

○ 3 earth – earth as center of gravity of its △

○ 4 moon – moon as center of gravity of its △

The 4 states of consciousness inherent in the cosmic scale. Explains importance of no. 4.

This diagram applies to man and his centers and sub-centers. We must find earth, sun, moon, planets, etc., in ourselves.

The octave divides into three triads, 3 is always neutralizer and acts as beginning of the next triad.

The scale is really the absolute expanded. It is possible God has never left his triangle.

Octave starts as law of 3. Exhibits itself as law of 7. Divide octave into threes and it represents 4 states of consciousness possible to earth, sun, etc.

Higher center—use of whole center, and not mere confinement to sub-center.

(do)	1		H^6	6
(si)	2			
la	3	2		
sol		4	H^{12}	12 = 3
fa	4	6		
48) ///	8		H^{24}	24 = 6
mi	12	8		
re		12	H^{48}	48 = 3
(do)	16	24		
(si)	32		H^{96}	96 = 6
la	48	32		
sol		64	H^{192}	192 = 3
fa	64	96		
192) ///	128		H^{384}	384 = 6
mi	192	128		
re		256	H^{768}	768 = 3
(do)	256	384		
(si)	512		H^{1536}	1536 = 6
la	768	512		
sol		1024	H^{3072}	3072 = 3
fa	1024	1536		
768) ///	2048		H^{6144}	6144 = 6
mi	3072	2048		
re		4096	H^{12288}	12288 = 3
(do)		6144		

12 = 3

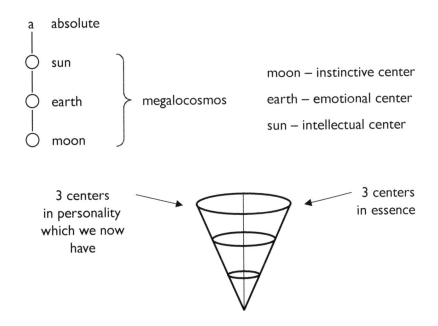

Eventually our three centers in personality and our three centers in essence should become one.

Origin of matter in time—matter will certainly end in time.

Within God's life there are subsidiary cycles. Each of 19 followed by 31 cycles—to be life period of cosmos—each no of each cosmos multiplied by 30.000. Ours equals 80 times 30000, gives life period of organic kingdom. 80 times 30.000 times 30.000 give life of earth.

Each higher cosmos is multiplication of lower one by 30.000.

Identical repetition of a thing is same as same thing continuing.

Time is 1.

God began as 2—positive and negative: will and consciousness of will. God became 3 by inclusion of base line △ neutralizer.

The absolute equals 1.

Whitehead—God, the principle of concretion, makes visible what had been an idea.

1 equals un-manifested Brahman. Nobody describes. Thing ability—that which contains possibility of becoming something. It first became 2.

2 equals 1st manifestation—will and consciousness—positive and negative.

In a state of dream—forces materialized in dream but not in substance.

Mirror called consciousness. By actualizing possibility in dream—2—it would be too soon over.

3 By concretizing—arrangement of universe—for prolonging His own life.

Octave is only △ rearranged all center as neutralizing force.

△ + and △ - at end of scale only seen.

Base of God's triangle equals God's dream projected.

Hydrogen atom—infinite multiplication of God Himself.

Every particle of dream itself a triangle and therefore a dream.

This is the ingenuity of the creation.

God finds himself—originally it was a trinity—principle of 3 to start. Principle of 7, the most economical method of handling 3.

$$\begin{Bmatrix} 1 \\ 2 \\ 3 \end{Bmatrix} \begin{array}{l} 6 \text{ parts} \\ 1 \text{ total} \end{array} \quad \bigstar \quad 6 + 1 = 7$$

All combinations of 1, 2, 3 equals 6 as parts
equals 1 as whole
7 all together

Negative absolute—base of matter of universe. No potentiality of further degradation.

Contracting parts of will and consciousness

Before cell, in world—great evolution in world if only crystallization. Food for cells raises minerals to organic kingdom.

Object—consciousness—project our dream into reality.

Definition of man—a being who can do. One of possible neutralizing forces.

Scale of being:
God
Angels
Seraphim
Cherubim
Solar gods
Planetary gods
Man

Angel always negative force.

Earth positive to moon negative.

Scale—notes are celestial body, semitone character—the whole of the universe enters there.

Only purpose of our organic kingdom—serves as condenser of radiations not collectable by earth in vegetable and mineral forms.

Organic kingdom — specialized film for transmission—is senses of the brute body of the earth—by means of it the earth comes in contact with planets, sun, etc. Earth's object is same as ours: by use of its senses to learn. Earth sees its other people—planets, suns, etc.—as we see other people, though its sense organs, that is, us. We have no more responsibility towards earth than our cells towards us.

Other planets, etc., conscious also by means of their organic kingdom.

Fa—need of transmitting station—passage from matter to matter

Si—nothing to transmit—taking whole of octave as one—this interval is passage from will to matter—passage of a *force* into *radiation*, not matter to matter—matter of will—psychology

Planets for us represented as organic kingdom

Fa—organic kingdom plus planets

Scale

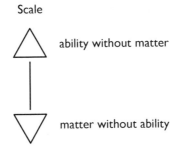

ability without matter

matter without ability

absolute (do / si)
       la
       sol
       fa
      ▦ – impressions = organic kingdom – supports our intellectual body at do
       mi   – no digestion at all
       re   – received mechanically – react mechanically
    sun (do / si)
       la
       sol
       fa
      ▦ – air = organic kingdom – supports emotional body at do, re, mi
       mi
       re
  earth (do / si)
       la
       sol
       fa
      ▦ – food = organic kingdom – feeds physical body – scale complete
       mi
       re
  moon (do) – no si left – no possibility left to actualize
              – desperation
              – far from hope
              – despair of matter

Our Ray in the same state as we—physically complete—food scale—emotionally—do, re mi—intellectually—no digestion

God of ours may only like a man in relation to his possibilities.

3 centers of gravity for universe   1 /\ 2   1 /\ 2
                                                     3

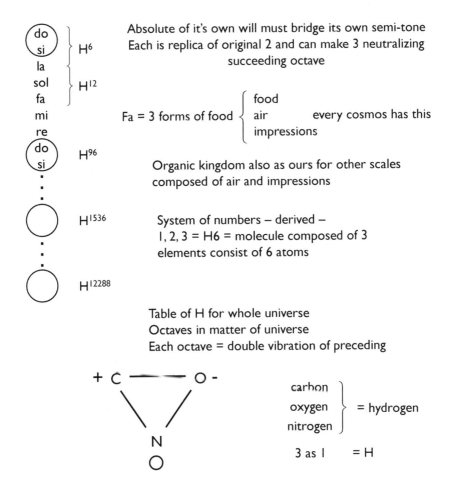

do
si H^6
la
sol H^{12}
fa
mi
re
do H^{96}
si
.
.
.
○ H^{1536}
.
.
○ H^{12288}

Absolute of it's own will must bridge its own semi-tone
Each is replica of original 2 and can make 3 neutralizing
succeeding octave

Fa = 3 forms of food { food, air, impressions } every cosmos has this

Organic kingdom also as ours for other scales
composed of air and impressions

System of numbers – derived –
1, 2, 3 = H6 = molecule composed of 3
elements consist of 6 atoms

Table of H for whole universe
Octaves in matter of universe
Each octave = double vibration of preceding

+ C ———— O -
\   /
N
O

carbon
oxygen   } = hydrogen
nitrogen

3 as 1   = H

Difficult to work with figures as big as this.

Our business: to make as much emotion, sex in order that it be possible that there be "I," that begins with H^6.

Economy = utilization of everything with no waste whatever. Reason is that judgment, that anybody in given circumstance would repeat it if he could.

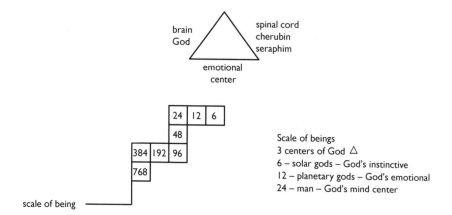

Scale of self-observation
do cosmic consciousness

.

.

.

.

mi—experiment
re—participation
do—self-observation and non-identification
Impressions scale
Scale of self-observation

At mi of the self-observation scale an outside shock must come. This shock: the attempt to imaginatively conceive oneself to be a being of the populated cosmos, to conceive oneself to be more or less formless, but crystallized into a form suitable to life on this particular planet. On another planet a different form. When mi has been reached, this effort necessary to carry self-observation up its octave. One then attends to cosmic consciousness; one no longer *attends* to self-observation. But the effect of thus attending to cosmic consciousness will be, that self-observation runs up, that is, we will actually observe more and more. Just as, when we transfer attention from the organism to self-observation, the octave of the organism run up their scales, without our attending to them.

God's emotional center or solar plexus is the solar plexus of all beings.

Our astral body is just past mi, almost, or at sol, that is, invertebrate, worm, snake. For it to show signs of becoming vertebrate, a dog, a cow, a horse, a cat,

Octave 1 — Food / physical body / positive

12	genitals	si	sex
24	solar plexus	la	emotions
48	brain	sol	impressions
96	?	fa	magnetism
192	liver	mi	gas
384	intestine	re	liquid
768	stomach	do	solid

Food
physical body
positive

Octave 2 — Air / astral body / negative

si		man
la		monkey
sol	vertebrate	intellectual
fa	invertebrate	emotional
mi	vegetables	instinctive
	minerals	
	metals	

Air
astral body
negative

Octave 3 — Impressions / mental body / neutralizer

mi	experiment	study diagrams
re	participation	being visiting earth etc.
do	observation	
fa		

Impressions
mental body
neutralizer

cosmic consciousness

do

a tiger, these are good signs. Sometimes it is subject to swift metamorphoses, becoming, for instants, any one of a number of vertebrate forms, or even becoming human—and then dropping back again.

The food-octave gives us our physical body. The air octave gives us our three centers.

Magnetism in the food octave is that which decays us.

Brain—positive.

Spinal cord—negative.

Solar plexus—neutralizing.

And the solar plexus or emotional center is controlled by the chief feature.

Sometimes one has to spank a baby in order to make him take his first breath. So a spank may be needed to make take his first impressions.

The self-observation scale, once started, the other two notes would naturally occur to one.

The two brains (passage over, that is, between them, equals, fa) equal milky way, the spinal cord planets, the solar-plexus sun.

God's master devices:

Our cosmic ray, at the organic kingdom, receives influences from all the other rays of the entire universe. (The many in one.) And likewise, every other ray receives influences from all other rays. Thus the rays are dependently and reciprocally related.

The double base of God's triangle. The base of the positive absolute is also the base of the negative absolute, thus:

We can only see of other beings what we can see of ourselves. We can see our core, that is, physical body. We can only see the core, (perhaps the heart or nucleus) of the planets, sun, stars, etc.

No shock is needed at si because do is simply the summation of the octave. Si being the end of the scale, no external shock, but an interior act of will is necessary. This will attempt to realize the scale as a whole, that is, simultaneously. When this realization has seen achieved then this realization is do. Movement from one scale to another must be effected, not by an external shook, but by an act of will (from within).

In the scale of beings, man is God's intellectual center, the planetary gods his emotional, and the solar gods, his instinctive center.

Man's cells correspond to the whole scale of beings, from arch-angels, angels, gods, supermen, men, down to and including metals. Not all men have, say, the higher types of cells. If a man has, then God realizes himself in man in this scale of development. If a man has not, then God realizes himself in man in this scale of development.

Of all the three foods, that is, chemicals, introduced into the blood, impressions are the most important. When the blood receives impressions it is then able to condition the body to receive and stand the shock of higher conscious states.

I, as an organism, am literally the product of my past digestion and indigestion.

At the present time we have, at best, only positive and negative food energies. Impression is the neutralizer. Only with all three forces moving or present can sex be transformed. Celibacy or any direct form of attempting sex transformation is impossible, since it, or they, simply involve the use of positive and negative, only two forces.

When we are only taking in two kinds of food our triangle is open—as God's was before creation.

By starting the impressions octave, a conscious base is supplied and our triangles are closed.

Man is made up of innumerable triangles.

A speck of protoplasm was introduced into our ray, at mi of octave of nature. It contains elements from all cosmic rays. Its pattern, magnified, and cast on a screen is seen to be identical with the pattern of the milky way (and all other cosmoses). (Temple in Egypt.)

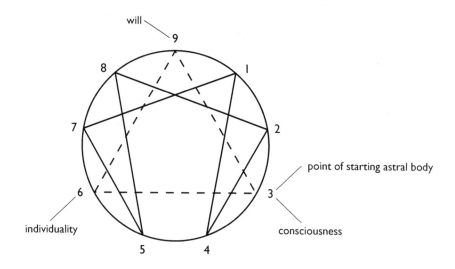

Enneagram—9—*It is man*—not merely represent man—a dynamic diagram. Enneads—Plotinus—commentary on cosmology of Plato. Ouspensky says that this diagram is never found in any literature or in any other method.

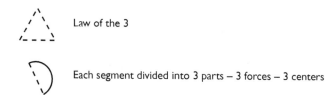

Law of the 3

Each segment divided into 3 parts – 3 forces – 3 centers

Man's development: to realization of triangle plus realization of all three points—to complete our development we must go round circle.

At any given moment we ought to be able to place ourselves, to tell at what point we are on this clock-like arrangement.

Double binary.

Binary: a pair—2 halves exactly alike—fold over to sides, right and left aide—gives them a difference, though similar we are symmetrical as human beings because we are on this model—biped beings.

Ternary: trinity: each side of triangle: 3

Quaternary

Triangle is dotted because we do not realize it.

Symbol of octave—7 tones.

Spiral ascent of octave: 8 repetitions of 1; 2 shocks—si, do; 9 closes cycle and completes symbol at a whole; 8, taken as 1 makes 9.

Closed circle of change of life of things considered. Circle infinitely recurrent.

is the nought of our decimal system.

is 10—a thing taken as a whole, equals, cipher.

(Life must contain consciousness and potentialities.)

1 is the active principle.

0 is the circle, is the neutralizing force.

These together give 10. What is there between 1 (active) and 0 (neutralizing)? This: 1—2,3,4,5,6,7, 8,9,—0, that is, 9 steps.

(From 2 to 9 is the negative principle.)

The decimal system—of same occult origin as musical scale.

Top of ternary closes the binary.

The apex of the triangle multiplies eternally.

9th step closes and starts cycle.

Law of structure of diagram 1/7 equals 14285; 2/7 equal 285714 etc.

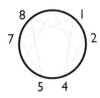

Circle is equal to 7 parts if triangle is omitted.

Infinite approximation to an integer but not it.

7/7 approximate but never reaches or equals 1.

Read Bertrand Russell on Mathematics.

7/7 equals 99999—point 9 recurrent.

If 7/7 were same as 1, then it would be possible, that, when completed, there would be no future.

Infinity of spiral due to fractional difference between integer and sum of its parts.

Infinite is infinite in an infinite number of (words) ways.

Our recurrence in this life—around same circle, but differing in the way we jump series of numbers, skipping, alternating, etc. Plato said we have 10 fingers because the decimal system is predetermined.

1/7, 2/7,—142857—etc. The order of these numbers is the order in which our .....functions. If you know impetus of act, you know order it is bound to pass. If it goes forward—progressive series. If it goes back—retrogressive series. Progressive is order in sun wise turn, that is, to right. Retrogressive is to left. The movement must go to right or left.

Example—solar plexus. If to right, progressive. If to left, retrogressive. The idea is to discover the direction of the movements in ourselves. All purposive acts to move wheel to right. It is difficult to move to right because the momentum is the other way, due to pull of moon.

Plato: the atmosphere of the earth is such that all ideas rust. Everything that has ever been in the world (earth) runs down—decomposes. We are on the most difficult planet in our solar system, perhaps in the universe.

Will is related to state of being.

Wish is related to some object.

Emotional center: power house. Now under control of instinctive center, should be under control of reason. Emotional center both solar plexus and heart. Depends on type.

State of inertia in emotional center—death.

3rd center—Reason. 3 sub-centers when complete. Reason contains the wish to gratify itself.

Distinction between reasoning process and reason. Example—Bhagavad-Gita. Arjuna—instinctive center dead—student. Krishna says: now act *as if* you wish to battle—according to reason. (The Lords Song.) Arjuna: I am enlightened—fight as if.

Example: Light on Path—action without wish is will.

Phil. of As If —Weniger.

Try to think in terms of these ideas without the preconceptions of current science.

Let us try to distinguish in ourselves, in our personal experience, between: wish and will, bodily wish and other wishes. From this, a body of personal knowledge will arise, separate from theory.

All 3 centers should have all 3 kinds of food. At present, only the instinctive enter has all three sub-centers developed. Emotional center—only emotional sub-center developed. Intellectual—only intellectual sub-center developed.

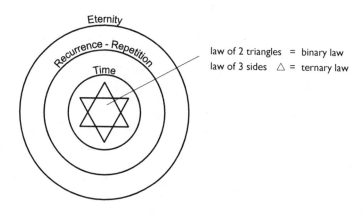

law of 2 triangles = binary law
law of 3 sides △ = ternary law

Time
Time—line—1st dimension
Recurrence—plane—2nd dimension
Eternity—solid—3rd dimension
The three kinds of time, space and energy.
Time: time, recurrence, and eternity
Space: linear, superficial, and solid
Energy: positive, negative, and neutralizing

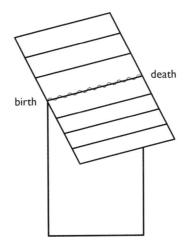

Depends on plane of actualization—which is recurrence.
    Take sphere of time—cut in any direction, a plane is made.
    Cut plane, it makes a line.
    Eternity: the sum total of all potentialities that can be actualities.

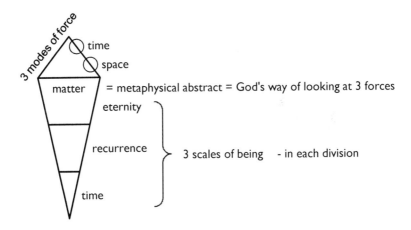

Such a symbol is a shock to understanding—effect on emotional center to give shock to reason.

"I" wishes - yes ⎫
                      ⎬
"It" wishes - no ⎭

1. yes ⎫
2. no ⎬ (struggle) ⎫
3. dispute ⎭   ⎬ 4. resultant

Binary through ternary converted into quaternary.

Since this organism is the diagram, this struggle is taking place any time, at all times—in emotional center. And from this struggle, deposits are made in the emotional center. The character of these deposits will depend on which triangle triumphs. And the character of the deposits will determine whether the struggle has taken place for consciousness and individuality, or for the opposite of these.

Material for further development depends on struggle between "It wishes" and "I wish." The strongest struggle takes place over "I's" wishing to become self-conscious. Material for the development of astral body beyond mi—and for mental body.

Two triangles: ▽ moon △ sun

Earth the place of struggle.

This mill (of the two triangles) grinds fine or coarse. If fine, the material enters the astral body. If course, the physical body.

Mental body: not mechanical—purely act of will.

Astral body: mechanical—develops sequentially (and along with) after do, re, mi of mental scale.

5 main centers in man

sex

thinking   formulation

feeling   moving

All 5 centers developed in one man, locks up the pentagram. 5 in 1. He can live like 1 of 5 or all together.

Man is 6 pointed star. 5, and 5 taken as 1—6. He becomes personal realization of Solomon's Seal.

SYMBOLISM

(Word, number, form) combined, more perfect system.

Tarot cards, Magic, astrology, alchemy—each a symbolical system.

It is necessary to *experience* symbols.

Symbolism of words—our speech—dream utterance, not essential.

Truth is taken by force and it is possible to him who uses force to get it (effort not reason). Use force of understanding.

Tone of voice. Organs participate in tone of voice, Whole organism speaks. Locate where the voices is placed in ourselves and others.

Digestion. State of health located in throat. Feeling. Sincerity.

TWO MINDS

Formulatory: we have but haven't cultivated—reasoning according to concepts—generalization.

Formless mind: we know nothing about—reasoning based on principles—reasoning according to mathematics.

In absence of examples, generalizations mean nothing. Going from general to particulars—deduction—contrary to modern science. Reasoning by generalization—summation of examples. Reason: the discovery of relations between generalizations.

Every negative emotion disintegrates organism. Nature's business: to keep as integrating and disintegrating periodically. Now disintegration always wins.

Mechanism—is struggle between I and It.

Lion and unicorn fight for crown.

Emotional center—field of battle—Mahabharata.

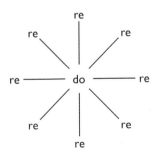

Only 7 potentialities in any act—scale

do—initiation of act the number of possible re's are limited. One will be actualized.

Four known ways to truth:

1. Hebrew 2. Egyptian 3. Persian 4. Hindu

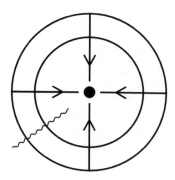

Any of 4 ways will take one to the center. Truth—point in the middle. Intermediate ways: Theosophy, Occultism, etc., may or may not take to center.

The 5th way—all 4 simultaneously—Gurdjieff's way.

Eclectic mind—a little mixed with all 4 ways - chancing to wander to the middle.

The enneagram is numbered as follows:

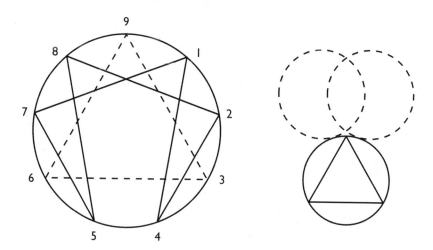

By using the numbers of 1/7—142857 - and drawing the line in this sequence, back to 1, the interior figure of the enneagram, the figure within the circle, is formed—by means of this single, continuous line. Between 3, 6, and 9 is formed the triangle.

This diagram is the key to many things.

3, 6, and 9 can be seen to be the neutralizers to 1, 2, 4, 5 and 7, 8 respectively.

The opposing angles in the double triangle (excluding 3, 6, 9 of the triangle) always add to 9:

8 plus 1

7 plus 2

5 plus 4.

Addition of any two sequential angles on double triangle will give a multiple of 3:

1 plus 2 = 3

4 plus 5 = 9

5 plus 7 = 12

8 plus 1 = 9

The addition of 142857 equals 27 equals 9 equals 3 times 3—including the law of the 3 within the law of the 7.

These remain unchanged in form—while the others go through their circle of 142857 etc.

1/3—333333 etc.

2/3—666666 etc.

3/3—999999 etc.

Since everything is constructed and moves according to the law of 7, and the law of 7 is 1/7 equals 142857, 2/7 equals 285714 etc., therefore all movement, all life, is in this circle. And this explains the law of recurrence mathematically.

The movement can be circular both ways, running round from 1 through 7, as above, and also at right angles to each number, thus:

```
7 1 4 2 8 5
5 7 1 4 2 8
8 5 7 1 4 2
2 8 5 7 1 4
4 2 8 5 7 1
1 4 2 8 5 7
```

These 6 numbers placed in their order of increase:

1 2	4 5	7 8
4 8	2 7	1 5
2 5	8 1	4 7
8 7	5 4	2 1
5 1	7 2	8 4
7 4	1 8	5 2

Insert 3, 6 and 9 as neutralizers. 1 is positive, 2 is negative, 3 is neutralizer. 4 is positive, 5 is negative, 6 is neutralizer. 7 is positive, 8 is negative, 9 is neutralizer.

This form used in gymnastics—each person given a number on top row and follows the sequence. 1 4 2 8 5 7. Note positive and negative position. This sacred dance evidently express the law of 7 and the added vibrating rhythm in each position—the law of 3.

See enneagram.

1 2 3—tone, tone, semitone.

4 5 6—tone, tone, semitone.

7 8 9—tone, tone, semitone.

3, 6, 9 become the shock in the scale of 1 4 2 8 5 7 placed in their correct sequence.

The difference (on the enneagram) between the angles opposite each other and joined by a line, on the double triangle, is 3 or a multiple of 3.

8 minus 5 = 3

4 minus 1 = 3

8 minus 2 = 6

7 minus 1 = 6

MONDAY, 22 FEBRUARY 1926

Just as we cannot understand the cells of our body (we can understand centers, system, organs, down to tissues), so God cannot understand us, who, relative to him, are cells. But our "I," which is, as it were, a delegated cell of His reason attached to this cell, namely, our organism, can understand this cell, this organism. In proportion as my "I," the various "I"'s understand their organism, so God understands them. In seeking to understand them we are in this way helping God. Each time that we make the effort to understand our organisms, to see its behavior, to penetrate and illumine it psychology, we are at our devotions. Psychological exercises are therefore devotional exercises. We should have continually the passionate desire; we should always be making the effort to understand more and more of this organism.

By comparing the meaning we attached to certain words two years ago with the meaning we now attach to them, we can measure, not necessarily our progress, but certainly our change.

Try to give a definite content to at least fifty of the more important words. With fifty main words so defined, one begins to live in an intelligible, definitely thinkable, cosmos.

Knowledge consists of (1) right opinion (2) personal experience, that is, personal realization. Until we have achieved personal realization we are not entitled to say we know.

We have no special technical terms; we have technical meaning for ordinary terms.

Observation is our one possible conscious act. All else is mechanism.

One may intellectually discover chief-feature without realizing it. Realization comes from a repeated seeing of it in action. The intellectual discovery gradually filters through to the emotional center. The realization of it is comparable to the devastating effect of shell-shock, only in our case, our preparation for its realization deadens the shock. If, on its realization, we could then switch our attention on to physical behavior, we would insure that it would never operate without our anticipating it and being conscious of its actions.

One crystallization has been reached, then we can carry on.

Astral body—swift moves from mi to sol, la, si, and down again.

Gurdjieff's music. Once the astral body has permanently reached sol, then it can consciously exist apart from the physical body. To be able to observe continuously for one week would mean that either prior to or in the course of the observation, the astral body reached sol. A completely developed astral body would be in complete control of the physical body. Gargoyles are undeveloped astral bodies. The astral body's mode of perception is simultaneous.

You are either feeling the urge to do more, to observe more, or else you are beginning to do less.

Split Essence.

Essence is split, as it were, in two parts. The organ of Kundabuffer so split the essence that a part of it, susceptible to the influences of this organ together with social influences, is now in opposition to the part of essence which remained in its true state. In any given individual this split may be found. It manifests thus: the pure part of essence wishes to do a certain thing, or to like a certain thing. The impure part does not want to do, does not want to like this thing. Thus essence is in conflict, and the two parts may thus effect a dead-

137

lock, forcing the individual to some compromise. In time, the negative aspect may, as it were, wear down. Whereon, the individual is released to act according to positive essence. Example: W. de Morgan, who only found it possible to do what he really wished to do, namely, write, towards the end of his life.

In some individuals, almost the whole of essence may be in conflict in this way. In some individuals, perhaps only a few essential wishes are thus blocked.

In some few individuals the negative aspect may offer practically no resistance to the positive. It is then as if there were no split.

MONDAY, 1 MARCH 1926

Compare - past and present mental (frame of mind) and emotional (attitude) postures.

Emotional postures (attitudes)—defensive, positive, weak, etc.

Intellectual posture—point of view not yet colored.

Realization—emotional attitude towards something known.

Is response emotional or intellectual or both to words read?

Consciousness—4 states—exact method.

Cosmic consciousness awareness of our occupancy of a universe along with other beings.

Scheme of cosmoses—octaves. The universe is a cosmos, not a chaos. We have a personal realization of this. But we have diagrams which represent this order. And we hope to realize these diagrams.

We are a small key fitting into an ascending series of locks.

Garden of Eden—Snake "fell" into being a worm. Snake combines worm plus wisdom. Reason does this. The snake is a transformed worm.

Scale of matters.

Everything except (1) is phenomena. 1 is the triangle, noumenal. The triangle will never be aware of itself. All things we are aware of are matter.

H^6. Series of octaves of matter. No experience possible without matter. Our experience depends on the existence of definite matters within us. The matters now exist in the external world. When we attain these matters, then we will experience the world which corresponds to them, and not till then.

H^{48} to H^{964}—is range of man's present experience.

The external universe is like a ladder which I may climb up by acquiring the corresponding matters.

Law of the 3—Positive, negative, and neutralizing forces. Third force—foreordained mould into which the struggle between positive and negative forces are bound to fall. 3rd force blind, because of our mechanical nature. Definition is always the result of neutralizing fore.

Trinity in action.

Need of purpose—improvising a mould. Neutralizing force the most important. Change from pull of moon to pull of sun. Change negative to positive.

Reason is superior necessity.

If ten men possessed reason, they would all act similarly in any given situation. It might appear that they were imitating each other. In fact, they would be acting independently. And their similar actions would be due to conditions imposed by an identical mathematical necessity.

LAW OF SEVEN

Experience is circular. All experience returns to its own opposite, under same name. If negative to start, then it completes its own circle and ends positive. If positive to start, then it ends negative. In heaven there are no opposites.

"Continent." Energy contained—original meaning. Under observation energy is contained. Negative transformed to positive. And when lower container is full, it overflows into higher center.

The 4 means of development of foods. (These correspond to the 4 states of consciousness.)

Respiration—ordinary breathing

Perspiration—2 forms (a) physical body, (b) astral body—panting, puffing, breathless, keyed up.

Aspiration—thinking—practical activity towards end—effects instinctive center.

Inspiration—all 3 enters work together. Participate in cosmic creation.

We can only change through food. We are always exemplifying the state and degree of our digestion.

To change state of being, change digestion.

Conscious and unconscious energy feed each other reciprocally.

The 3 centers are related to 3 systems: the sensory-motor, the nervous, and the cerebral. We are not aware of the independent control of each system or center.

Personality: a procession of changing "I"'s.

Individuality: the continuity of a single "I."

Man—7 degrees—each degree—12 types.

The 7 degrees of men:

Ascetic

Saint

Yogi

Ordinary person

Self-consciousness and individuality

Higher emotional center developed

Will—Man capable of consciousness and individuality

No. 5 man—still determined by type, but if he contained positive, negative and neutralizing elements of all sub-centers positive, then he could contain 12 types within himself.

No. 6 man—still determined by type.

No. 7 man—the only one free from type, he can reincarnate as he chooses, independent of planetary circumstances.

Types belong to essence.

Culture is a by-product of occult training.

Do more and more and better and better and think less and less of it.

Art

Two types of subjective

(a) minor—presentation of objects.

(b) major—representation of concepts of objects - abstract.

Objective art deals with the ideas of objects before they become objects.

Words to define: life, time, space, 3 types of reason, purpose, method, automaton, occultism, soul, yogi, saint, ascetic, sleep, waking, octave, essence, personality, inertia, magic, religion, love, conscience, fire.

Attitude

The ability to realize our present attitude is an agent in its change. The secret of this work in change of attitude. Attitude most important.

An emotional attitude is the configuration of the emotional center at any moment.

An intellectual posture is a point of view not yet colored by emotion.

The attempt is to arrive at, not merely a full content for the terms used, but an absolute content for these terms.

Through definition of these terms, an exact language is formed.

An agent of the Institute brings to the barbarians (ourselves):

Language (an exact and technical terminology)

Number (by means of the octave and the table of matters)

Fire (by conscious effort)

Through the use of these three, we who are at present barbarians, may begin to civilize ourselves.

Attitude is the most important of all. The ability to realize our present attitude is an agent of its change. The secret of this work lies in change of attitude. If the attitude or posture is recumbent, laying down, inert, despairing, and one is not aware of it, as is subject to unconscious defeat, and is incapable of meeting circumstances which demand other postures. Example: the body lying down.

If we could identify with the triangle of the enneagram, then we might achieve a telescopic view of the movement of the circumference, see the law of the octave in operation, and supply the necessary shocks at the critical phases. This would mean the correct application of observation, participation, or experiment according to the nature of this phase. In this way we could break the circle of experience which turns everything into its opposite. We could maintain a straight line (higher emotions). This circular movement of the octave is what is meant by the Buddhist Wheel of Life. When you get off it, you are on, or make a straight line. Man makes five breaks, as a pentagram which, according to law, breaks or deflects at every three steps—(do, re, mi). A straight line, started, does not naturally maintain itself so; it can be kept straight only by the continued application of will or consciousness at the critical phases. All experience is circular, this means that all that happens in the organism proceeds according to the circle. All higher emotion is sustained as a straight line. It is not subject to its opposite. Heaven is a straight line. In heaven there are no opposites.

ESSENCE

Purgatory is that place where a being frees himself from planetary essence, from the deposits of planets in his essence, from the influence of planets, that is, from constriction to any special type.

EXPERIENCE MATTER

All possible experience is determined by the coincidence of matter in myself and matter in the external world. All matters, that is, all possible (potential) experiences already exist in the external world. It is simply a question of my forming within myself the corresponding matters. For example, H^6 exists in the world. When I develop H^6 in myself, then I shall have such experiences as are determined by or are inherent in, H^6. At present, man's experience is confined within these matters which range from H^{48} to H^{964}. This range is like a ladder, which one may either climb up or down. To climb up, means that we at once leave old or lower experiences behind and attain to new higher ones.

CONSCIOUSNESS

The capacity to assemble, in one act, all that one knows about a thing. Thus, a conscious man would not necessarily know all about any given thing, but he could give you a complete and instantaneous report of what he does know.

MONDAY, 8 MARCH 1926

These ideas, having their source in the fourth center, are arch-types. They are, as it were, empty when we receive them. That is, they are empty—without meaning—to our third center, and it is only with our third center (for we have, actualized, no fourth center) that we can receive them. It is our work to fill them, to give them content. The content is always the same, namely, personal experience.

Only impressions above 48 can contribute to the development of essence. For the astral body is already at mi, that is, at 48. And the only way we can get impressions above 48 is by means of self-observation. The organism cannot vibrate above 48. The most intense third center thought only reaches 48. Most often our thoughts are much below this.

Divine contemplation is seeing impartially, without judgment, without rationalizing, without corrective or tutorial attitudes. It is, simply, awareness. But awareness of what? Awareness of the organism. For we cannot be aware impartially of another person or object. True, we have an instant of impartial awareness of, say, another organism, but immediately thereafter we are sidetracked into thinking or feeling about it. In short, divine contemplation is self-observation or awareness of the organism; there is nothing else (for the present) that we can divinely contemplate.

Who has realized that he can no more control this organism than the behavior of an elephant in India? Yet this is the fact. The organism either will or won't look after itself in any given situation. And until an "I" is formed and developed, all that even self-observation can do is to polarize the organism positively, thus making it better capable of caring for itself.

If the body were in perfect well-being, we should be pulled the more to identify with it, and we would perhaps have no motive for self-observation.

Purpose is positive—intellectual center. Inertia is negative—instinctive center. The resultant of these two forces will be determined by the quality, quantity, and intensity of these two forces, respectively. The mould or form of the resultant is the third force or neutralizer—emotional center.

The resultant can be changed by changing the quantity and intensity of either the positive or negative forces.

At the present time, the negative force (instinctive center) is much the more powerful determinant. There is just enough positive force in opposition to the negative to produce visceral stress, i.e. emotions. The purpose of this psychological work: thinking about the ideas, etc., is to increase the positive force to the degree where it can be and is the determinant. Then reason will prevail over the instinctive center.

Attitudes are emotional postures. They are the actual material postures of the astral body. And we should think of, or try to see them as such. There are three postures:

Attracted, like, positive

Indifferent, neutral,

Repulsed, dislike, negative

See the astral body actually being attracted or repelled.

Posture is fixed. It is only action that changes, or changes place.

A difference in point of time does not makes a difference in the character of the three forces called forth. In point of time, the positive may become operative first. But implicit in this positive force are the negative and neutralizing forces, which correspond to it in character.

Within the configuration of the chief-feature there may be any number of attitudes or postures, and these may change or shift. At the present time our emotional center is made up of fixed attitudes. It is crusted or solidified to its present form. It must be broken up, and fire applied to it, in order that its substance may evolve from solid, to liquid, to gas, and so on up the octave. The aim is to fit the body so that it can give reasonable service, that is, be an instrument for reason.

MONDAY, 15 MARCH 1926

Physical type—determined by heredity and sociology.

    Essential type—determined by essence.

    These two may be in conflict.

    Chief feature relates do, re, si, (emotional center) to instinctive.

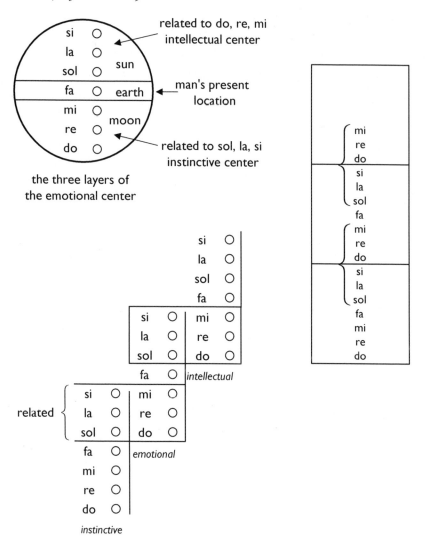

the three layers of
the emotional center

Emotional center is in 3 layers. We are in do, re, mi of the air scale, and it is related to sol, la, si of the instinctive scale. We are now at fa—earth—we can move down to moon or up to sun. Sol, la, si—air scale—higher emotions. Any emotion up through mi of air scale does not go beyond sex, si of instinctive. All higher emotions are above sex. Similarly, do, re, mi, of intellectual parallel sol, la, si, of air scale. There remains alone at the bottom, do, re, mi, of instinctive, and at top, sol, la, si, of intellectual.

THE SECOND SHOCK

The development of higher emotions utilizes the same energies that are now lower emotions. As long as we have lower emotions we cannot have higher emotions. They are the same centers. The transmutation of lower emotions to higher emotions can occur in to two ways:

By self-observation.

By using the energy generated by observation in the attempt to think about the order of the universe, the enneagram, the octave, etc.

This, (2), is the second shock. This is especially to be practiced in the case of negative lower emotions. Try to think of and about the enneagram while in a state of negative emotion. (Use the negative emotions released by the war and you will become self-conscious.)

The organism cannot experience higher emotions. The "I" experiences them, not *through* the organism but *from* it.

Energy generated by self-observation if not used in an attempt to understand and be reasonable, will do either one of two things: it will either prevent further observation or be switched into the organism for utilization in the pursuit of by-products, thus intensifying this pursuit and the more committing one to it.

Appetite and need are of the instinctive center and are related to physiology and organs. (Aim to develop *appetites* and *needs* in the intellectual center. Aim to have these needs stronger than instinctive needs.)

Wishes, wants and likes are purely of the emotional center. Appetites and wishes may be, and most often are, in opposition in man. Example: Man may want food, but not need it, have no real appetite for it. This is not true of animals which have only appetites and needs. (Save in the case of domesticated animals which have received a sort of psyche by their association with men.)

Habits pertain to the emotional center.

There are also muscular habits, muscular reflexes.

While we are unreasonable we must act (try to) as if we were reasonable. When we become reasonable, we must act as if we were unreasonable.

To say what you think you should say. This, is in accordance with objective morality. At the present time, we mechanically say what we think.

Recurrence illustrated by means of a circle of chairs. Try to get a simultaneous picture of yourself as all the forms in all the chairs. If I get out of this circle, I do not have to take a circle, a potential form, adjacent to it, but can jump, say, to some distant one. But the released positive and negative energies must actualize one of the *possible* forms.

The positive, negative and neutralizing move in the way indicated below: from 1 to 2 to 3 and back again to complete 2.

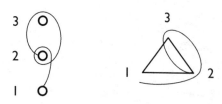

Essence gives rise to the physical, astral, and mental bodies, but it is no one of them.

To do more and more and better and better and think and fell less and less of it—Orage.

"Unless your righteousness shall exceed the righteousness of the Scribes and Pharisees." To do rationally by will infinitely more of righteous things, than they did by mechanical wish.

We wish to know, in order to be, in order to do.—Gurdjieff

We all wish to act perfectly in every situation according to reason, which wish would be sol, la, si—air scale. Essential wish.

MONDAY, 22 MARCH 1926

The etheric double is composed of physical matter, that which corresponds to the note of magnetism in the food scale. It can be positive, and attract. It can be negative, and suck. Whether a person after contact with another person feels stimulated or used up largely depends on the respective bodies. (One can protect oneself by observation.) Crying is negative emotion manifesting through the etheric body.

The neutralizer is meaning or significance. At the present time, we usually only see objects; being third force blind we do not "see" their significance. But since all the forces are necessarily present in all objects, all objects have significance. As we advance in this work, significance will be more and more manifest to us in all things.

Improvising is giving a reason, a meaning, a significance to each single act and all we do. We should have a reason for even our smallest actions. In this way, we provide conscious neutralizers. In proportion as we do so, our own behavior becomes significant. And as our behavior, so we become individuals and significant. (3rd note of observation-scale.)

There is a relational difference between the three forces. This difference is symbolized by the three sides or points of the triangle. (At any one of the sides or points the whole triangle is concentrated.) One may pass into another, as for instance, the third note of one triad becomes the first of the next: the neutralizing becomes positive. But always the *relational* difference is maintained. Whatever is manifest, materialized, concretized, actualized, is the positive and negative force. The neutralizer is always the form of the positive and negative forces. Positive and negative forces are phenomenal. The neutralizer is noumenal. It is always so. The instant a force is phenomenal, then by definition it must be either positive or negative. In this sense, the neutralizer may *be actualized*, (by positive and negative forces), but it is never actual. It is the actual which is subject to change, to birth and death as it were. The potential or neutralizer is eternal. No actualization or "passing away" of an actual can ever destroy the potential. (Actualize a possible and the possible still remains to be actualized at another time or by some other.) Actualization is a process in time. The potential exists outside of time, that is, is eternal.

Do, re, mi—the actualized—the personality or organism.

Sol, la, si—the potential—"I."

In order to determine relations, we must have a scheme or system of relationship. For instance, we must first have the decimal system, and then we can see what relation the various numbers bear to each other.

Sense perceptions pertain to the positive and negative forces. Feeling and thought pertain to the neutralizer, to significance.

To be elastic, to be formless, in the sense, that, like water, we can take the form or shape demanded by any set of necessities.

Objective reason is related to the neutralizer. It is deductive. It says that if such and such a potential is actualized, then so and so must be so, and not otherwise.

There are two types of subjective reason, both inductive. The first type is related to and deals with single instances. (Is this intelligence? The intellectual sub-center of the emotional center? J.T.)

The second type is related to and deals with concepts, with generalizations. (Is this intellectual? The third center? J.T.)

Memory and all other psychological functions have their ultimate seat in "I."

Memory has its own scale and will pass up to finer matters, to finer forms, as we move up to sol, la, si.

The three intellectual sub-centers, taken as one, give the higher intellectual. The three emotional sub-centers, taken as one, give the higher emotional. The three instinctive sub-centers takes as one give higher instinctive.

The significance of the machine.

Just as we had to eliminate criticism, correction, etc., from observation, so will we have to eliminate (organism-) motives from observation. An ulterior motive seeks something for the organism.

Mental awareness, awareness without non-identification is dangerous, tending to produce, among other things, self-consciousness in the wrong sense.

The organism will never serve "I," but I" can use it, just as a gymnasium will never become the servant of the organism, but the organism can more and more use it and develop thereby.

(To Margy: Increase the objective: do as you think it should be done, trying to be perfect in the execution of (even) all details. Decrease the subjective: feeling less about it in subjective terms. This is objective art, which has the effect of creating adoration in the object (person) for which it was intended.)

MONDAY, 29 MARCH 1926

At present, "I" is embryonic. When it is actually born, then an altogether different type of instruction is not only possible but certain. This type will be strictly personal, that is, esoteric in the real sense.

Images, accidentally received from experience, grouped together according to their similarities, form concepts. The lowest type of reason deals with concepts and is dependent upon personal (subjective) experience. The second type of reason, astral reasoning, deals with abstractions, with empty forms, as it were, the contents of which are not dependent upon experience in the ordinary sense and hence are not limited by it. Objective reason deals with the nature of things in terms of the law of 3 and the law of 7.

These laws are symbolized in the enneagram. We are enneagrams. Let us try to realize ourselves as such, "I" being the triangle, "It" being the circle.

How a Russian realized, by a shortcut, that "I" is separate from "It". How he became 'desperate' in this work. He hung to a rope insecurely suspended over a precipice. During a very short time "It" died many times, and was quite dead by the time be pulled himself up the rope and set feet on firm ground. The direct method to realize: I have a body.

What we see is merely an actualization relative to our perceptions, that is, we have sense imagination. We see what is really a stream, a becoming, only at the present point of actualization. We should be able to see, at will, anyone or all of the actualizations of any given thing, say a chair or a person, past or future.

Each one of the three centers is continually dreaming. When the magnetic current is negative they dream separately. When it is positive their dreams interfere with each other.

Between each center there is an octave. Many of our experiences are not definitely related to anyone center, but correspond to some note of the octaves between the centers. As, for example, reverie, meditation and so on. Some fall between the intellectual and emotional centers. Some between the instinctive and emotional centers. According to their character, they will be nearer one center than the other. Take a list of psychological terms and determine their positions.

A talent may be due to something wrong with the organism. Its loss, through observation, will be felt as a relief.

Objective art: the use of words, forms, sounds, colors, etc, to produce an intended effect. Mantras—their magic lay in nothing mysterious, but in the fact that by science and conscious design, it was necessary that they produce the given effect. It will be possible for us to hear, understand and use mantras upon ourselves and others when "I" is born. The syllable OM, how to pronounce it? Open the mouth wide and vocalize an Ah which perfectly grades down as the mouth closes to and on M. The gradation downwards must be perfect as regards the balance and proportion of the intervals, notes, and curve of diminution. No consonants must be thought of, nor must they be formed by tongue or mouth. "Ah" is the sound of the Positive Absolute. "M" is the sound of the Negative Absolute. Between them is the great octave. The fixed points or machine-cosmoses of this octave are the consonants. Each cosmos has a corresponding consonant. Conscious art, deliberately used for this purpose, disrupted a civilization which, unaware of what was happening to it, took pleasure in the process.

Before men were on this planet, ant forms held the highest place. These, having failed, were gradually diminished in their size by the use of conscious art. Of course the ants knew nothing of what was happening to them. Nor do they know what has happened.

It is said that one of the possibilities of men is that they too will be similarly reduced, so that, at the end of the process, a whole family could dwell within a thimble.

Conscious art would be one of the technics used by "I" in order to effect its purpose. It would contain in itself all means for reaching its objects: through sight, the arrangement of syllables and words, through hearing, rhythm, through speech, sound, through understanding, the arrangement of ideas, the weights of ideas, etc. No one, whatever his condition, could escape it, and the intended effect would necessarily come about.

The most that we can do is to experiment; we cannot guarantee results. The fact that we experiment defines us as pupils. Only masters, having passed beyond experiment, can work for results. If we, as pupils, assume that we can achieve results, then we presume to be masters and become bad pupils. We are pupils just to the degree that we can experiment. Hence experiment break habits, etc. But without criticism, without the aim of improvement, etc. Observe the organism, but keep your thoughts about it to yourself. This is the Pythagorean vow of silence, imposed for the purpose of pure observation and pure experiment. It is to this organism that we must be silent.

If I shove this chair, it will move, because a certain energy has been brought to bear on its inertia. In exactly the same way and with equal certainty, if I speak or live from essence, I will move the other person essentially: his essence will be moved.

MONDAY, 26 APRIL 1926

If this is a real method, then it means that it is bound to affect the physiology and magnetic currents as well as the psychology of the organism. Physiological and magnetic changes are certain to occur. We may interpret them as being distressing. But it should be remembered that we have consciously induced these changes. And more than this, no attention should be given them. They will last, off and on, during this convalescent phase. If we continue to observe, then we will get well.

The center of essence is "I," is do, and it is the place of calm, the "hut upon the mountain." Round about this central place or spot, essence is arranged in concentric circles. Si, la, sol, higher emotions belong to "I." Fa is the bridge. Mi, re, do, lower emotions belong to personality, to "It." The circles increase in turbulence as they move outward. At the present time "I" is identified with do, re, mi, occasionally it may retreat to the nest. But the aim is that it should be able to move at will anywhere in the full octave of essence.

Emotions are evoked by, and respond to, mental images or pictures. These, the emotions, perceive and then react accordingly. But they perceive *all* the images present in the mind at any given time, not merely those that I, so to speak, am mentally aware of. I am aware of only a few. And hence my difficulty in knowing just what provoked a given emotional state.

"I" cannot control or affect the organism directly. But if "I" observes "It", then will change.

Some chickens are egg or shell-bound. They are full formed within the shell, but for some cause they do not break through and come out the shell. They die. Similarly some human beings are shell-bound. They do not break through and come out. They do not really wish to non-identify with the organism. They do not wish to come out of it. Strictly speaking, their "I" does not will. And nothing can be done for them.

Gurdjieff says that not God Himself can force or help them.

A point will be reached, where, looking backwards, it will be seen that "I" controlled and directed even the accidental and mechanical sequence of phases.

When we break the circle, we will be androgyny. Perhaps some of us were commissioned prior to this birth, as it were. (Certainly all "I"'s knew why and what they were doing in the beginning.) But we will have to go through this training before we can regain consciousness of what our commission is.

We must first grow personality, because it is by the effort required to disentangle ourselves from it, that "I" develops will.

Sociology supplies our gymnasium.

The earth is called the planet of sin and the ridiculous planet.

Whatever emotion is related to the body is a lower emotion. The ordinary fear of death is a lower emotion because it is concerned with what will happen to the body. But the fear of what will happen to "I" after death is a higher emotion. All higher emotions are related to "I."

Let us die now by conscious separation, and not by death which will cause a mechanically enforced separation. This is non-identification. Non-identification, in a sense, is more difficult than observation. Because something in us does not want to let go. But from now on we should make increased efforts to non-identify. Prior to observation there was nothing to non-identify. (Now we will assume there is.) If we continue to observe, only, we will be sure to become more stuck on.

There are some people who make all the movements, all the gestures, but never do it. Of these some are deluded into believing that they are, while others, somewhere in themselves, know they are not.

We can let go without fear that the organism will be unable to take care of itself, since it, apart from us, must do as it must and will continue to do.

MONDAY, 12 APRIL 1926

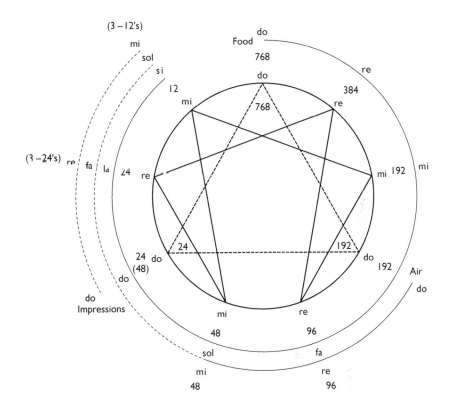

Any point of the triangle is do. At each point the whole triangle is concentrated. The points differ because of their placement or pull, one pulling up, one to the right, one to the left.

Each segment cut off by a side of the triangle represents a center:

151

Right—instinctive.

Base—emotional.

Left—intellectual.

Each of these centers is composed of three sub-centers: do, re, mi. Anyone of these centers or sub-centers is an epitome of the whole.

In nature there are only three notes: do, re, mi. Sol, la, si are simply repetitions of the former three at a higher position in the octave. Sol sounds like do, is the do of the second tetra chord. La is the re. Si is the mi. Hence, sol, la, si, equals do, re, mi (in a higher position). Mi is the summing up of do, re, as si is the summing up of sol, la.

Man's difference from animals.

We digest air (to mi) animals do not. Because of this, we have two forms of magnetism (96), one from food (animal) and on from air (human). We have two forms of perceptions or impressions. Animals, with only one form, simply register impressions. (Their impressions are (96)). We, with two forms,—one serves as a mirror to reflect the other, that is, we can reflect. The second form mirrors the first. Man's impressions are 48.

If impressions begin to be active, then air scale is enabled to continue up its octave, and when this octave is fully developed, it will give us two forms of emotions and two forms of sex. And as impressions go up, there are three forms of emotions (24) and three forms of sex (12)—three elements: positive, negative and neutral. And these equal higher emotions and higher sex. Higher sex equals creation. Creation is then possible because all three forces of sex will then be present. When the three foods are as fully digested as possible, then we get: single products—instinctive center; double products—emotional and triple products—higher centers. Three times around the enneagram complete the three food scales.

At the moment of conception there are deposited in us (essence), substances derived from the three cosmic octaves of matters. The essence of man is composed of matters of the three octaves of matter in the universe. In the cosmic octave there is a continuous involution and evolution, a circular movement from the positive absolute to the negative absolute and from the negative to the positive. Similarly, there is a circular movement in essence, taking place between its two poles. It moves either up or down, the direction of the movement depending on wish. Essence is indifferent as to whether the movement is towards consciousness or unconsciousness. Essence can aspire upwards if we attempt to play roles which are higher than any of our present actualizations.

Essence contains all actualizations plus all potentialities. Ordinary circumstance is sufficient to actualize only a few of the potentials originally deposited in us at the moment of conception.

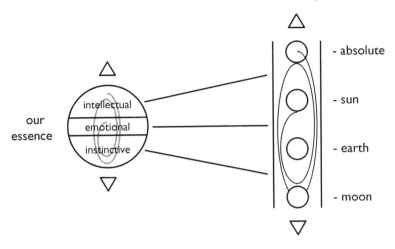

The moment after conception the environment (in the form of the mother) begins to deposit layers of social impressions around essence. At birth and for a year or so afterwards the layers are still thin enough for impressions to strike essence. It is during these years that we are really "impressed." But before long sociology so covered essence that impressive experiences occur less and less. Personality is grown, and thereafter most impressions merely strike it. Fee strike deep. Active impressions are impressions which strike essence. We must get back to essence—little children—wonder—capacity to be impressed. But in our case the wonder must be accompanied by an active, intense and continuous questioning. This is the attempt to add (mature) psychology to the essence of a child.

All identified impressions, impressions received while identified with the organism, are passive. All non-identified impressions are active.

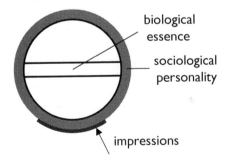

Forms of Impressions – Specific Weights

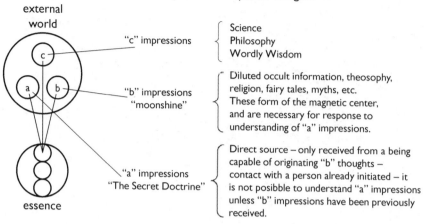

An "a" person comes into the ordinary world for an individual reason, personal to him (a means of his moving up his own scale), and which at the same time has in view an objective effect—upon the ordinary world, upon "b" persons. He fishes amongst "b" persons. "b" persons of a special type will be attracted to him. He will want "b" persons to help him in his work. But in order that they may help him, he must train them. He will initiate those who can be of special help to him.

An "a" person can recognize all three types. A "b" person can recognize his own type, mistake "b" for "a" persons. Believe himself to be an "a" person, and recognize "a" as "c" type, but a "b" person cannot recognize an "a" person. He will be fortunate if he comes in contact with a real "a" person. A "c" person can recognize his own type, but neither of the other two, nor will he be able to understand "a" impressions and he will be intolerant of moonshine.

A "b" person can understand the doctrine of an "a" person.

An "a" person is one who has arrived at a development of essence wherein he can formulate his own doctrine wherein he can originate "b" impressions. He is the direct source, and is capable of acting as such. He is the Secret Doctrine. This doctrine may be given by him in a matter of fact form. It is in class "a" impressions.

"C" "B"   "A"   Motives

"C"—one enters and continues the work for personal, individual motives, for his own improvement understanding, etc.

"B"—the personal motive widens to include the interests of the group. What will be of real advantage to the group?

"A"—the individual and group moves from "b" to "a" and here the interests of the work at large are motives. For us, this would be to aid in the actualization of the Institute, which now exists only in prospectus. (Read the prospectus and see what you can do in terms of it.) What function will you fulfill in the Institute?

Cast a role for the organism, and among other things you will realize how difficult it is to make the organism actualize it. The organism will most often in fact break out. (A realization of mechanicality.)

Cast lower roles (roles below its present actualizations) for the organism in order to increase its mobility and render it mere pliant to the control of "I."

Cast role higher than any present actualization for the purpose of making the organism actualize a possible higher than any new actualized.

Whether it is a lower or higher role, whichever we identify with we tend to become. Hence, if we identify with a reasonable, a higher role, a Beelzebub, a Karatasian, we will tend to become it.

The same essence recurs. But it will be modified by the active impressions received during the previous recurrence.

A dead essence drop to the bottom (goes to the button hole maker) and has no possibility of evolving during this cycle.

An ordinary person is "attractive," "influential," because of magnetism, not because of essence.

The East educates types, and places value on type difference. The West educates for a standardized type.

MONDAY, 19 APRIL 1926

1. Time.
Three dimensions: time, eternity, and duration.
Eternity: simultaneous perception of one line.
Duration: simultaneous perception of many lines (a plane) of potentialities as well as actualities.

2. Time is relative to modes of perception—all modes of perception are within space.

3. Time is superior to space—space (the three dimensions) do, re, mi—time (the three dimensions) sol, la, si.
Time conditions existence; space conditions ....

4. All three centered beings of similar development have similar time perceptions. All have the same background of time and space, though materials differ.

5. The reason our sense of time is sequential, not simultaneous. The 3 centers vibrate at different rates and they do not act together: first see—a slight pause—then we feel—a slight pause—then we think.

6. Only because a re is present, can a do pass up to re. Only because a mi exists (potentially) can re pass up to mi and so on. The potential must be present—it is the neutralizer. Higher beings supply the potentiality, that is, make

possible the movement up the scale beyond our present actualizations. The Holy Ghost is all potentials. Nature is always do, re, mi.

THE MEANING OF SAYING GRACE

Eating food for three centers—eating in which all three centers participate. Approach food with attitude of effort and aspiration. The three centers participate physical—savoring, emotional—the wonder of being kept alive by food, thankfulness for its provision. Intellectual—scientific attitude—in terms of chemicals and the law of the octave. (Sacrament—bread and wine.)

CROSSING ONESELF

The swift crossing oneself a remnant of what was once a psychological exercise, practiced by the few attending the esoteric schools. Meaning: the cross—the four states of consciousness—the triangle, the "I" crucified in these four states. The "I" crucified, dead and buried. Purpose of exercises: to remind oneself that "I" is crucified and that there must be a resurrection.

We are punished for either voluntary or involuntary sin. Punishment is Purgatory; where one's reason is fully realized, but finds himself unable to do. All humanity is actualizing the potentials of any one of us. So if we hurt or destroy a potential in someone else, we necessarily destroy it in ourselves.

MANTRAM

I want to remember myself. Repeat not more than 4 minute's once a day.
I—totality of past, present, and future life. It is the string and the beads.
Myself—organism at this moment, this present bead.
Want—recall a state of vivid and intense wanting.
To remember—recall a state of vivid recollection.
Between I and myself, want to remember is to be placed, connecting these two. Each word to be associated with its own intense meaning, distinct from the remainder of the sentence. These to be repeated:
1. I wish to remember myself
2. wish to remember myself I
3. to remember myself I wish
4. myself I wish to remember
This circular motion forms do, re, mi, fa, repeated in a series of 4.
This is alchemy associating two emotions with two ideas, stealing the emotions from the context given them by nature, and, by a trick, making them and our own psychology serve a conscious purpose. This is stealing unlawful fire. Stealing fire: Mercury stole but was too swift to be caught.

This mantram has to be dropped when constant wishing for self-observation has been achieved.

Actualization means activation—activity. To actualize, we must make active. That is, use, what was heretofore a potential center, faculty or function. The fourth center, like all centers, has 3 sub-centers, and these are to be developed by self-observation, non-identification and experiment, respectively. Located at back of head.

All centers have two aspects.

The throne: one master cell, the center of focus, the "I" of any given moment. Who occupies it? One or another of the 3 centers, but usually all centers contribute a quota to its occupancy. The more human cells we have the wider and more intense our focus. This is not to be developed by ordinary means, by concentration of the given quantity on something external, but by a new order of focus, namely, attending to it.

All cells are self-conscious. They hold and continue to repeat whether we are or are not aware of it, all the experience or images that they have ever had. All the images contained in one cell, are simultaneously perceived by it.

WORK

1. Triangulating

Work to be done for three purposes:

Profit.

Pleasure.

Consciousness.

Profit, an economic return, not for money, per se, but simply in order to place oneself as a productive economic units to earn one's bread by the sweat of one's brow. Pleasure, the satisfaction or higher pleasure derived from an activity prescribed for the organism by a method the object of which is consciousness. Consciousness. . . as described by the method.

2. The fourfold work.

(1) Formulating. The act by means of which the formulatory center is divorced from its slavery to the lower three centers of and placed in the service of the higher emotional and intellectual centers. That it may become the scribe, the amanuensis of these centers. (These centers are described in abstract terms, and are called, respectively, art and science. At present they are active, and contain fact or reality as felt and know. Their manifestation however is prevented, owing to the fact that they have no organ for expression on this plane.) What then to formulate? All accurate, scientific description is formulation. Therefore describe, as accurately as possible, experience in generals: events, conversations and so on. Describe what is observed. Let the description or formulation of observations be concurrent with them. Try to formu-

late the doctrine. And take fragments of the doctrine as staging points for reflection. Describe experience, reflect on doctrine.

(2)   Conscious effect. Make such selections of material as will affect the reader or readers in the given way; prepare them for some forthcoming activity.

(3)   Spread Institute ideas.

(4)   Profit, as explained.

(5)   The sum of these for consciousness.

Imagine that a certain person, dead, that is, uninterested, but whom you wish to interest, to be sitting in the room with you. Write in such a way as to catch his interest, stimulate and sustain it.

LETTER FROM ORAGE TO TOOMER

There is a very important task for you to accomplish in getting the right relation between your wife and your work. It is another example of G.'s favorite conundrum—of getting a sheep and a wolf and a cabbage across a river.

You have obligations in each direction and you cannot meet them without extra trouble to yourself. The trouble you were prepared to give to make your wife happy without the work for yourself, is not sufficient now. You have to make a special demand on yourself. You have not only not to be lazy but you have to be very intelligent.

To succeed in the task you have to convince *all three parts* of your wife that the work will not come between you. She must think and feel and sense that she receives more and not less from you.

Now you cannot accomplish this by *quantity*. Some time has to be sacrificed for your visits to NY. Therefore only *quality* will help. Quality means attention. It means self-remembering. It means a far greater effort to enter into *her* emotional situation.

I know what such a task means. It puts a different kind of pressure on you. It belongs to what G. used to call: "Externally play role inwardly not identify." But the role must be so perfectly played that no one can possibly see the conscious work. This means that, you must *at all times* genuinely *feel* what you are doing.

That is the extraordinary part of such a task that if you forget and are careless for one minute you undo the result of many days or even weeks of work.

Once G. put me in front of such a task and it taught me more than almost anything.

In your case, it is not I that put you in front of the task, but the work itself. All that I am doing is to make sure that you recognize it.

It will not do to win from your wife a reluctant acceptance of your interest in the work. She must not notice that the work takes up your time, because of the additional interest and warmth that you bring into her relationship with her. The interest and warmth must be real; that is, you must really *feel* a stronger and richer bond with her.

I write all this without having met your wife and without knowing the circumstances. I write *on principle* because I understand the *principle* and have seen how it works.

Photo from the archives of GJ Blom, Amsterdam

Orage at The Prieuré.

It sometimes happens that there is an essential wish, as it were behind chief feature. This wish, originally belonged to and concerned with essence, has been turned outward, not only to personality, but further, namely, to the external world. It then seeks its fulfillment by trying to do for another person what it was originally intended to do for one's own essence. My wish to instruct, teach, and develop other people may be of this kind.

The way to transcend identification, both with oneself or another, is to die each morning. There are a number of ways to do this, among them, this: Imagine that you are leaving the Earth for Karatas perhaps forever, knowing no one who is going to take the trip, no one there.

The only types of sexual relation possible are either with someone who is not vitally in the work, or else with someone who is advanced and capable as oneself. In either case, there will be no feeling of responsibility in regard to progress in the work to interfere. Such a feeling of responsibility should not cut across a sexual relationship. Real sex is impossible if it does.

We are not entitled to entertain ideas of development or reform for another person. We should not have them. Eliminate them from the man-woman relationship.

"I" dreaming that is waking up. It must really wake up, and to this, in such a state, make the effort for more and more active observation and non-identification. An active series of efforts produced it, but *keep active*. In this way, eventually, the organism (the mother) will drop out of "I" (the infant) just as the child at birth drops out of its mother. The "I" will then be a substantial existence.

Distinction between a state of observation, a state of non-identification, and an act of observation, an act of non-identification. The one is passive; the other, active.

We should be sources of "A" impressions. Most often we merely give the shadow of "B's." We lack the force to give "A's" on all occasions.

The masculine attitude, the masculine purpose. "Impress", procreate always. Demand this of oneself. This, the higher role. The condition of observation and non-identification wherein he, as objective as a very good friend, is the constant friendly companion.

What do you mean by her? Define your purpose, your wish, your intentions.

What we say aloud is personality. What we say aside or to ourselves is essence. The aim is to speak what we now withhold, and withhold what we now speak.

Each center has a wish, but these three wishes, due to the differences of the educations of the centers, never coincide, and the resultant — a sort of fourth wish, is always a compromise. To make all three coincide. I wish. I dare not. I ought. I wish. I can. It is reasonable.

Complete development: a coincidence of higher thinking, feeling, and action. He thinks, and does what he thinks, thought and act coincide.

There are as many chief features as there are attitudes in human relations. Names of a few chief features: self-importance (to feel so); self-on-mind; fairy prince or princess; lady bountiful; Jesus Christ. The questions: to reduce to a realization of not- knowing.

What should he do? Be practical in the worldly sense? Undertake experiments, which, without committing him, would exercise his weakness? What type of experiments?

1.   What role did his early sickness play?

2.   How is his picture of himself related to his weakness?

3.   Is the type of his essence revealed in all this?

4.   Precisely how is color related to his weakness?

5.   Do all people have defects in either one or another of the sub-centers? And are all "sore" emotions related to this main defect? So that, a means to knowing their chief feature or dominant motive would be to determine in what sub-center this defect lay? He wishes to know for power.

6.   Is this his dominant motive? Or is there something under this?

7.   Marriage?

8.   What should be the attitude towards the weakness? Should it be seen in terms of the organism, as a defect in the organism? Or is it more intimately concerned with "I," "I" having been attached to this type of organism precisely because its weakness is similar?

9.   Is the attitude a resultant of the weakness? Or does the attitude, the chief feature suggest this weakness?

10.   Sex weakness, in act, in attitude? How related?

11.   How related? Formulatory, emotional, sub-instinctive?

Our attitudes towards our weaknesses or defects are not based on facts derived from an objective observation of the organism. We are not only subjective towards the world, we are entirely subjective towards ourselves. There is a given mould, a preconceived idea towards organism in the emotional center. This mould is actualized or filled by sociology, by social suggestion. This attitude has no relation to facts. There is no "weakness" in the instinctive center, though its sub-centers may be or are undeveloped. The "weakness" is in emotional center, in attitude. We "feel" that we have no ability. To be aware that this is mere feeling, to be aware that we have ability, is to dissolve the attitude. What parts of us are really undeveloped will only be found as a result of continued objective observation. When found, then we will understand the organism and know what to do in order to develop it. We have never seen the organism as it is in fact; we have only seen it through an attitude, subjectively, under suggestion. Hence, what we consider to be our weak points may be not so, while what we consider to be our strong points may be our weak (undeveloped) points.

"Weakness" is subjective and comparative.

The organism is a dream of "I."

(I now see this method as a means for the successive peeling of *fictions*, until "I" is reached. Put differently, the dream is progressively thinned out, until only "I" is left. Again differently: *this method troubles the dream, and finally induces such as nightmare that "I" wakes up.* Or, it is method for making it possible for "I" to get along with a shorter period of sleep.) J.T.

Only thought or understanding which vibrates at the rate of 24 or 12 really counts. 48 mere "philosophy" does not. Orage can only *think* of the book for half an hour a day. After this period, he merely thinks about or reads it. Ordinary thinking and reading are wastes of time. After half an hour, he gets at something else.

Most wishes are for *ability*. There are many things we do not want to actually do, or to actually have; we merely want the *ability to do, the ability to have them*. (It is our *attitude* towards *ability*: we may have an attitude that we have no ability whereas in fact we have: we may have an attitude that we have ability, whereas in fact we have not). If this or these attitudes were based on fact, then we might say that the emotional center wishes its own development. J.T.

It is when essence, released from its dream, actually enters in that we both have ability and feel that we have it.

The first and fundamental ability is the ability to make real effort. But real effort is *essential* effort, the effort of essence. Essence, however, is for the most part dreaming, and it is particularly cut off from special sub-centers which differ with individuals. Or at least we feel that it is cut off. And here it is that we particularly feel that we have no ability.

Because essence is dreaming (passive) and attitude, chief feature, personality are active, we all doubt that we have ability. But, being lunatics, we try to overcome the doubt by intensifying personality (that which causes it), instead of releasing and developing essence.

Attitude causes doubt and then drives us to intensify it.

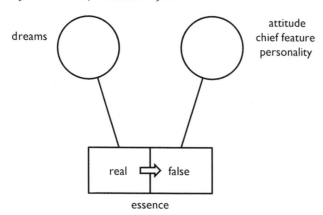

Ability resides in real essence. The first of real essence is to make real, not sham, or personal, effort. But all that personality can do is to make sham or personal efforts. And since almost all of us is personality, it is no wonder that we doubt real ability and the ability to make real effort.

In time, the wish to live supersedes the wish to dominate, or to coerce, compete, rival. The wish and need to work supersedes the wish to be ahead in, or get ahead in the work.

The attitude that we can't do or get is based on a disinclination to make effort, not an actual lack of ability, save perhaps lack of ability to make real effort.

More and more I am amazed at the exactitude with which *this*, a *shadow*, has been and can be understood and defined. This *shadow*, with all of its complexities is a subject of mathematical exactitude. And this more and more amazes me. I am amazed that the mathematics have already been worked out and are understood, so that, for all my real discoveries, there are the perfect formulae waiting to confirm them. I am amazed that I can make any real discoveries – discoveries which can be objectively verified, concerning this shadow. I am amazed that other shadows have or have had similar if not identical experiences and understanding.

A nostalgia for vegetation, which is increased by the sight of the 'I' and the consequent desire to imitate those who are still vegetables.

The secret wish, as long as it is secret, is a goad, but not an effort. It goads us to fulfill it, but since we never admit it, we can never make effort to fulfill it.

1.   The desire to forget the unfavorable aspect of the body.

2.   The desire to escape into some field or way of life where this aspect would not be called to the front.

3.   The desire to be in such a way that even this aspect, though present and evident, must be accepted.

The types of approach: (1) circling (2) looking one way but going another (3) snaring (4) zigzagging (5) over-shooting or stepping the mark (6) two steps forward, one step backward.

We will not use the highest level of our intelligence to look at ourselves. Just as it is possible for a person to wake up as it were, and, with his eyes open, for the dream or nightmare to continue on, so "I" wakes up, and this dream, the organism, continues on before its open eyes. Through observation of physical behavior one grows able to see emotional behavior and postures as if they were physical.

The wish for ability is the wish for character, for will. Necessarily, it is the will for individuality.

This is the lesser freedom: to be free of all inner inhibitions.

This is the greater freedom: to be free of, that is, to be able to control external circumstance.

The chief feature or the solar plexus is "the heart," that is, what we take to be the heart, the false heart. It is this that identifies.

Do, re, mi, of essence belongs to personality. *Sol, la, si,* of essence belongs to "I." I am at *fa*. But fa is an octave. I am somewhere on this octave. Where?

The chief feature or *fa* is the Dweller on the Threshold.

Education is that which extracts from a biological specimen sociological values.

Distinguish between *must* and *ought*.

Must = conscience; ought = social conscience

Weight of ideas, of emotions – possibility of exact discrimination.

What is the source of this light?

Conversations between the centers continually going on; dispute, one finally falls asleep and there is a conclusion.

It is this conversation that makes us subjective. Three centers differentially educated, hence cannot agree.

The body can only get an image of a thing by trying to actually take the form or shape of the thing. That is, it tries to imitate whatever it sees. And the tendencies or habits which are implied in these mechanical imitative efforts constitute a part of its inertia, positivity or inertness being only one form of inertia. In short, there is the inertia of momentum as well as the inertia of inertness.

Our emotional conditions, our psychic states, are related to the planets, and undergo changes corresponding to planetary changes. These planetary changes constitute what are called the planetary or psychic weather. Since the configurations and influences differ for each person, two people may be sitting in the same room, one experiencing stormy weather, the other, clear skies and sunshine.

Each phenomenon, each person, event, situation, is a set of answers awaiting questions. It is our work to supply the questions, whereon, the answers will come forth. The book impossible, but for Hassein. The master is not an answerer, but a questioner.

God awoke to realize that Time would defeat the actualization of all His potentials. These, He wished to actualize, and to this end, it was necessary that He, first of all, defeat Time. One of his possible was that of endlessness. This, he has now actualized.

The glands are the second reservoir of energy, which may only be tapped when, that is, after the first reservoir has been exhausted. The pineal gland will supply energy to the back of the head. But only the activity of the back of the head can use this energy.

We are patterns, and at any given moment we are located in some center of this pattern. We should be able to tell where we are located: sex, locomotive, emotion, words, back of the head, heart.

There are three types of dreams: (1) Instinctive – we act, are actors in the dream. (2) Emotional – we are spectators, usually we cannot move, nightmare. (3) Intellectual – we carry on discussions, read, think, talk, etc.

It is only when we can induce these three types at will, during our waking state, that an accurate interpretation of dreams becomes possible.

Generally, it is impossible for us to use yesterday's supply of energy. Only the energy generated by observation will "keep" for a month. Half an hour of observation at night will draw off all the unused energies from the three centers.

Any physical manifestation is a complex phenomenon, containing intellectual and emotional as well as instinctive elements. For the present, we can only observe the physical elements. Later on, the emotional and intellectual elements will become objects of observation.

Emotions are evoked by and respond to mental ideas or images. Change the image – change the emotion. But only "I" can change images.

(The chief feature, then, is associated with one constant image. Herein, the function of experiment, casting roles. One dominant role, one dominant image has been cast for us. We, ourselves, must cast all others. To cast a role, means precisely to cast an image. J.T.)

1.   More and more he "wriggles" in life. Is this an indication that his essence is beginning to, actually receive impressions? The worm is nerved, and the nerves are exposed, but not negatively exposed.

Are the gaps in the octave explained by: triangle = ½ note between *si* and *do*: triangle = ½ note, and external shock from outside = 1 note, in all, 1½ notes between *mi* and *sol*?

Is sex included in the instinctive center as negative force? What type of mind have I?

5.   More and more, the postures of my physical body seem to be determined by, and correspond to and be expressive of, what appear to me to be astral postures. Is this only fancy? Or is it a fact that with the simultaneous

breaking up social moulds, social restrictions and corrections, and the development of essence, my physical body will actually tend to an increased parallel with, and expression of astral postures?

1.   Yes. The first impressions are astringent.

5.   Try to obtain a complete disassociation between the two bodies, so that the coming astral movements will not produce cramps and strictures in the physical, so that the physical body will not reveal what is taking place in the astral.

"After all that she has done for me."

The feeling of sex jealousy.

This is sex identification.

Never identify, but act *as if* identified.

Any sex relationship should be broken immediately upon "something wrong" with either party.

Unless the sex relationship is right and positive, all other things will go wrong.

According to Gurdjieff, there are two types of women, namely, the wife, and the promiscuous type. By nature, by essence, the wife will only desire one man, the possibility of other relationships is not entertained. By nature, the promiscuous type will desire accordingly. The wife type may be promiscuous; the promiscuous type may be a wife. Try to be able to recognize and distinguish them, and handle them accordingly. The wife type is often found in the East, but rarely met with in the West.

Act or bluff the adult, and in the course of doing so, you will develop the power to be one in fact.

Miscellaneous

1.   Two ways of affecting self-consciousness: indirect, objectifying the organism: direct, repeating a verse . . . which tends to intensify the sense of "I" and lead to it directly.

2.   Observation of functions: how a thing works. Relationship. The cause, the mechanical effect. The organism seen as evil, that is, mechanical. Illustration of cause, effect. Someone smiles: my face smiles. This observed in non-identification.

3.   Associative thinking: one brain cell sets in motion a (linear) chain of brain cells. A mechanical-chemical process. Real thinking: Simultaneous awareness of all brain cells (and thought processes and functions?), simultaneous consciousness, that is, real consciousness of the entire mass of brain cells, together with the power to make selections from amongst them.

4.   The planet behind the moon; absolute evil: no potentials.

5.   Through heredity:

(a.)   An instinctive center, partially full of content. Even so, the greater number of movements which will later characterize it, must be taught it: walking, and more complicated gestures etc.

(b.)   An emotional center, endowed with capacity, but no content. Hence, our emotions are the product of environments.

(c.)   An intellectual center, likewise with no content.

6.   Since the formulating center is the weakest, the "I," through the agency of the human brain cells, can get control of it. And through it, control the emotional and instinctive centers for emotions are determined by attitude, and acts take their orders from emotions.

7.   The method makes the personality passive in order that the "I" may become active. The present organism is the seed. When planted (when it becomes passive), suitable circumstances will cause the plant "I" to sprout. Blade, ear, corn within the ear.

8.   Emotions will be chaotic as long as there is a chaos of attitudes. But no stable attitude is possible unless it be founded on fact.

9.   Emotion may "luxuriate" while still upon the ground, i.e. childish. For maturing, they must have a pole to climb upon, i.e. an attitude based on fact.

10.   "Fields of influence" are composed of matter. The influences of planet converge, overlap. According to these overlappings, will various forms of matter be produced. Man is possible only in virtue of certain conventions. And the "I" may be developed only with reference to suitable planter influences.

11.   Humanity as a whole, with the exception of […] and those annihilated will reach a fully developed phase outside of time. While those who are successful in this method will attain consciousness in time, thereby possessing choice as to claim matters, the range of choices and the types of activities that […] incarnation have not yet been touched upon.

12.   All centers have a digestive system. These systems vary with individuals and in the individual. Some good, some bad. Rarely in an individual are all these found in good condition. Perhaps that instinctive will be good, emotional defective, the intellectual moderate, and various combinations.

(a.)   The content of a center depends, first, upon the food received, second, upon what use can be made of this food, i.e. how well it can be digested.

(b.)   As to food received, the instinctive receives food sufficiently good for its purposes. Emotional – bad food. Intellectual – no food at all – mere words, no facts, paper.

Mary Johnston

DISCUSSION ON "GOOD AND EVIL"

WITH A.R. ORAGE

SATURDAY, 5 NOVEMBER 1927

PART I OF 3

[Eleven numbers were taken.]

REESE: As I remember, there was originally no such conception of good and evil as we have now; it grew out of the idea of positive and negative. It's a degeneration of these ideas, in which such a state as hunger, for instance, can be thought evil.

ORAGE: You remember that these concepts of good and evil never came into man's experience until objective reason had degenerated. There was discrimination of values before then but it was disinterested—qualitative differences arising from differences of nature. After the decline of objective reason, this discrimination became associated with emotional center and its interests and there came good and evil in place of positive and negative.

LUCILLE: There was no neutralizing element present, was there?

ORAGE: You remember that a certain being was supposed to have introduced good and evil into the world. His mistake was pointed out, that he had insufficiently stressed the neutralizing element. The question arises whether in his mind he thought of good and evil as one neutralizing force—a force beyond good and evil, as it were. But the fact is that his hearers had no concept of neutralizing force in good and evil. We shall perhaps see what the neutralizing force is in these ideas—something which is neither good nor evil but partaking of both.

MARY JOHNSTON: If good is fulfilling potentiality of essence, then evil is falling short of this. I wasn't here when that chapter was read, though.

ORAGE: That's all right—this is a definition of the purposes of values. The objective merit of a being is his realization of the values which he was created to fulfill. Added to that is the criterion of direction—a being's state is good if it stays statically good, but a being with potentialities must be constantly in a state of becoming to be good. Progressive values arise out of this process of actualizing possibilities. So we have both static and dynamic concepts of good. A perfectly good being would be one whose cross section—the cross section of his time tube—would always be in the direction of fulfilling its objective. But we may find that we need another word to describe a being's responsibility to the nature of its being—the design of its creator. In this discussion try to exercise simultaneity of understanding, holding all statements in mind and contemplating them in one pattern.

EDNA: Evil is definitely the problem God faced when he worked out the laws of 3 and 7, life and death. Good is maintaining the 3—7—9 functions, reciprocal feeding.

ORAGE: But where does good and evil come in? I invite comment on this as a contribution.

EDNA: You ask where good and evil come in, but I spoke of making effort at a time of crisis, through pondering, which is certainly good.

ORAGE: We are close to the ascetic school when we equate good with effort.

EDNA: But pondering is an equalizing force.

ORAGE: Pondering is a process. If there is a misdirected effort then effort alone is not necessarily good, there can be good and evil effort relative to the result. There was an idea in the original statement you made—about the government of the universe by the laws of 3, 7 and 9. Nine introduces effort against time. This presupposes that the creator thought the universe worth the effort of maintaining. What we have to consider concerning objective good and evil is whether life in this universe is worth maintaining at the cost of the effort of the semitones 3, 7 and 9.

SHERMAN: Are you speaking just of this planet, or all the universe?

ORAGE: All the universe. Life doesn't go absolutely smoothly elsewhere—the only difference is that elsewhere provision is made for securing the effort necessary to the universe at these semitones—through schools, teachers and so on. We reach majority without becoming aware of the nature of our life as adults, and if we have the desire for self-improvement (the first semitone) or to help God (second semitone) we find no one and no school deputed to help us. On other planets youths find such schools. In other respects, we are the same as other beings.

MR. BROWN: The book says no grandmother ever told us.

ORAGE: We haven't even tradition, you see. It is hopeful to know that we are really normal, but depressing to know that our environment provides no help for development.

HUGH: Why is our environment so unattractive to teachers?

ORAGE: It isn't. But imagine going to this planet to preach peace, for instance. The people don't even think that they don't want it—they say they want it and then they immediately go to war. Imagine how much more impossible it would be to teach objective duty to the Creator.

[At this point Edna brought up her question about something Beelzebub had said to Hassein. Orage said it was irrelevant—said her type of "mind" was the obstacle to teaching—then modified this a little to keep from hurting her feelings.]

ORAGE: I pass up Edna's somewhat irrelevant question to answer Hugh and Edna doesn't listen. You understand now, Mr. Ferriss, some of the difficulties of teachers. I thought we were on the high road to a discussion of good and evil—and here we are.

EDNA: But it is an absolutely good question—absolutely. [Everyone laughed]

ORAGE: I had thought that in my 1000th incarnation to be a religious teacher, but I am already getting cold feet. Everyone hears questions and answers from the center of gravity in which he is at the moment. His interpretation depends on this only. Essence has the form of being of the center of gravity—it is animal, child or barbarian—and every second the psyche is changing form. To such beings, doctrines are addressed! You can imagine how such a being transforms a doctrine having heard it in three centers. The difficulties of a world teacher are so tremendous that no wonder it took the Son of God—and he failed—to explain to men a few simple ethical doctrines.

HUGH: It has been said that we should become as little children—is this childlike?

ORAGE: I explain that something as meaning that if any motive exists for pursuing self-knowledge, then the objective is distorted. It must be pursued as children pursue an interest—without comment or motive. We are not to become like children, but as children. To be like them wouldn't be the kingdom of heaven, but the kingdom of the nursery.

SHERMAN: You mean we should become, as children should be, not as they are?

ORAGE: No—as they are. You remember—art is like nature, but it is not nature. Well—you can puzzle it out for yourself.

LEWIS: Do many potential teachers abandon the idea?

ORAGE: Hundreds.

SHERMAN: May I ask if good and evil concepts came into being after the removal of Kundabuffer?

ORAGE: The concept was a consequence of the organ. We haven't as yet reached a definition of good. Were you thinking of what I said about a being's responsibility to his nature?

SHERMAN: I was thinking of that being who was banished to an evil island for his mistake.

ORAGE: I would suggest that the denial of the possibility of being of value is the only objective evil. When a machine is scrapped and is totally useless it is bad. Its suffering is like that of the beings on the planet where nothing they do has any value to the universe—literally nothing.

HUGH: Could you say that the absence of neutralizing force between good and evil, in the sense of the lack of possibility of making a choice, would be evil?

ORAGE: That's good formulation.

JOHN: Heropass is the source of all evil in that it is the great depriver of possibility.

ORAGE: In that sense it is.

[Mary Johnston suggested that in the universe as a whole the good might outweigh evil, since good is native to the sun absolute.]

ORAGE: Yes, but there are planets for beings that have absolutely no use in the universe, and yet preserve their being. The idea put forth is too optimistic from our point of view. Some beings refusing to be of value, maintain their being but cease to exist in the mind of God—cease to have any value.

NAT: In a way they are better off than we are; we don't know why we exist.

ORAGE: We don't know yet. But we have a wish to be needed—to contribute values and to wish this but be incapable of it is the state of beings on those planets we have mentioned. We are of unconscious value, at least, as manure for the moon.

HUGH: Even the people then who just go out to raise hell contribute at least negative values—they aren't evil, but merely bad.

ORAGE: Exactly.

CARL: By the corollary to the scrapped machine being absolutely evil, absolute good must be fulfilling function.

ORAGE: Yes, but we must decide what function to fulfill. If I could draw a diagram of this concept it would be:

.   .

.   .

.   .

Positive neutralizing force is absolute good. Negative neutralizing force is absolute evil. Unconscious neutralization has value to the moon.

MELVILLE:: Is minus another word for negative here?

ORAGE: Yes, a good word. Plus and minus.

JOHN: There is no connection—no triad—between plus and minus neutralizing forces.

ORAGE: Yes, there is present in each being a neutralizing of positive and negative forces constantly manifesting in being. But the state of being depends on serviceability to God, and lacking this serviceability beings do not cease to exist but cease to be.

CARL: A description of this state would be life in death.

ORAGE: Yes, a living death.

CARL: How do minus beings escape Heropass?

ORAGE: They are bound to last as long as God, if God has suspended Heropass in all his sphere.

[Mary Johnston suggested that the threat of evil, threatening God's existence provides the drama of life.]

HUGH: How does all this effect us practically?

ORAGE: Only as we realize this drama of the possibility of non-being, and the struggle to develop our being. Plus neutralizing force has the function

173

of coordinating positive and negative forces in any being so that that being fulfills its objective. Animals, having no conscience, run no risk as man does, whose consciousness makes it possible for him to actualize the development of conscious plus neutralizing, or to fall into minus neutralizing. In the book's objective critique of man, he is literally inferior to animals in that he can make a positive contribution to absolute evil by not consciously contributing plus neutralizations. Ashiata started with the assumption of subconscious dormant values—objective conscience. The discipline for waking this conscience starts with self-observation.

LEWIS: Then objective conscience isn't a pulling power toward consciousness?

ORAGE: Objective conscience is a sense of being-duty and the discharge of this duty, which requires a higher state of consciousness than one has. So consciousness demanding plus neutralizations is required by objective conscience and is its motive in discharging its obligation.

LEWIS: Then conscience isn't a neutralizing force.

ORAGE: No, it can be said to be an urge toward the development of neutralizing force.

LEWIS: But if we finally lose all our negative motives for self-observation, such as wish for power, etc., we are left in a sort of barren state.

ORAGE: But if you finally uncover an urge toward self-observation—the uncovering of objective conscience—it doesn't matter with what motive you started. Self-observation, as a matter of fact, could be taught and practiced merely as a technique in ordinary psychology. Watson might very likely take it up. But when we strike objective conscience we shall realize the falsity of all motives.

NAT: The labor of self-observation would be the same after uncovering objective conscience, wouldn't it?

ORAGE: Yes, but it then becomes a sacred duty—the highest value in your experience. Values are transvalued.

HUGH: Isn't there a connection between the urge and magnetic center so that after uncovering magnetic center and objective conscience, trick motives are no longer necessary?

ORAGE: Yes, that can be added.

HUGH: But don't some people uncover this and then lose their interest?

ORAGE: In Gurdjieff's terminology, faith equals magnetic center. Persons with developed magnetic center "smell" the hidden treasure to be found through further self-observation.

SHERMAN: You have spoken of this faith stage as a "desert," but it doesn't seem so to me, thank God.

ORAGE: Roses, roses all the way! So much the luckier.

NAT: Knowing what good is, we still don't know our function.

ORAGE: Yes. We can ask—what is the nature of our organism? Function is defined by structure and this takes us to the question of norms. It presupposes self-study and this presupposes a state of disinterestedness. Only in this state is self-study possible and only when this exists can the objective value of the structure of the organism be discovered. If we self-observe long enough a state of disinterestedness—of non-identification—does occur. And by reason of the presence of our consciousness it is implicit that we are intended to development of the understanding of our function.

MILLIKEN: We aren't intended to be driven, like motor cars?

ORAGE: Unconscious, we are driven.

HUGH: Do you assert that self-observation will lead to non-identification?

ORAGE: Yes.

MARY JOHNSTON: Is non-identification synonymous with impersonal self-observation?

ORAGE: Yes. Your word is better. Without this non-identification self-observation takes a long time to produce the state; the conscious effort to introduce the state of impersonal self-observation shortens the process.

HUGH: I don't question this, but who introduces non-identification?

ORAGE: Suggestion. I suggest it—by saying how long plain self-observation takes to produce the state, and so on. Disinterestedness is not lack of interest, but absence of bias. Bias presumes a moving object. It is the neutralizing force.

SALLY R: Can you say self-observation is blowing air in the pig to make it bigger, but it is still a pig?

ORAGE: Yes, the features of the psyche become clearer.

EDNA: Real disinterestedness is passionate interest in any observed facts, whatever they prove.

ORAGE: Exactly.

LEWIS: There is no evil, but only the deprivation of good.

ORAGE: In view of what we have said, we must change that to "deprivation of the possibility of good."

BLANCHE: Until we live by essence, we cannot be concerned with good and evil. Now we are concerned with right and wrong.

ORAGE: Yes, in the discovery of essence, the right thing is that which leads to uncovering essence, and the wrong thing is the opposite—that which further conceals essence. We can be statically good, but we must also be dynamically good in developing potentialities. God must maintain the universe this way—not just statically. Sun Absolute is not the abode of absolute good except as it contains the state of dynamic good.

MILLIKEN: Then the inhabitants of that planet you mentioned are a standing condemnation of the creator.

ORAGE: And so God has no use for them.

REESE: Isn't static good negative and dynamic good positive?

ORAGE: When static good is wholly static it ceases to be that and becomes minus neutralizing. The sin against the Holy Ghost is the suppression of dynamic good.

REESE: Or of static good?

ORAGE: Thereby hangs a tale I won't tell you now.

SOMEONE: I can't conceive of a being without potentiality, as a representative of evil.

ORAGE: Well, let us say that we are not apt to meet such a being for a long time. The state of such a being is not being nor non-being, but minus being.

GERTRUDE: How can a minus-being be actualized, or continue to be actualized?

ORAGE: It remains statically actualized. It is no longer in the stream of becoming; it is fossilized in its actualized form.

GERT: It can become separated from the law of seven?

ORAGE: Yes, on that particular planet. It is the scrap-heap of the universe. Whether willfully or ignorantly, these beings have failed to actualize their potentialities; their fate is the same. And they may be a standing condemnation of their creator. Eddington says some atoms exist so—without time's arrow. They are something like hearts that go on beating outside the organism to which they belong.

MILLIKEN: What keeps them beating?

ORAGE: Ask Eddington.

SATURDAY, 12 NOVEMBER 1927

PART 2 OF 3

ORAGE: We will continue with Good and Evil in order to try to reach firmer conclusions than we arrived at last week. Our present views are wholly subjective; tell me your family income for two generations, the schools you have gone to and so on and I will tell you your real ideas on good and evil. Does there exist in the objective world any element corresponding to our subjective good or evil? It's too bad that the stimulation of these evenings so often fades leaving nothing. First let's have questions.

ALAN BROWN: I remember once we were given three stages of morals, and eventually right and wrong. These weren't mentioned last week except when it was said that until we have objective conscience we have no sense of good and evil, but only of right and wrong, as though these latter were lower states. It seemed to me that much of our discussion was of right and wrong.

ORAGE: Right and wrong are subject to pragmatic proof.

BROWN: But in seeking for an absolute, can't we say that pragmatic judgment may come from objective understanding?

ORAGE: Oh no. Any result in a world that is perpetually becoming may depend on where you draw your line and say that at that point something is right or wrong; but later on this judgment may be reversed. The only center in which absolute judgments are possible is the one where we feel our absolute identity—in the emotional center. Instinctive judgments are based on like and dislike; the intellect says right or wrong. They are both based on the absolute center—the emotional. This says if the thing is good or evil.

HUGH: Are our emotional centers capable of such absolute judgments?

ORAGE: Capable of them potentially.

MAN: This gives the emotional center some element of timelessness.

MILLIKEN: What about the activity of discrimination—isn't this intellectual?

ORAGE: Discrimination of likeness and unlikeness is intellectual, and without moral value. The development of what we call reason has no connection with what the book calls reason. Any elongation of a single line of the triangle does not increase its triangularity.

HUGH: Is essence in that absolute center?

ORAGE: Essence is a particle of the center of conscience of the universal being. It is the voice of God in the individual—that is, objective conscience.

SHERMAN: How can we know that the values of this being are absolute?

ORAGE: You use absolute too metaphysically. Absolute means taking all things as one. All suns collectively are said to be Sun Absolute; all planets are taken as one absolute planet.

SOLON: If we assume then that the emotional opinion is non-educable—a native response—it makes an absolute judgment?

ORAGE: Yes.

MAN: Isn't emotional education possible?

ORAGE: Oh yes, but its judgment wouldn't come from discussion; it would not be derivative, though it would naturally be similar to other judgments.

MAN: Do we ever have such experiences?

ORAGE: If emotional center were not distorted by the education of the other two centers, we would have such experiences. All essential impulses arise in the emotional center. Our natural likes and dislikes are not related to essence; but at the moment of experiencing them we can be aware of them as good or evil.

DALY: Why isn't this just a conflict of emotions?

ORAGE: There is no element of discrimination in pure emotion. We simply find an internal monitor that condemns what we like.

DALY: It seems to me like external training.

ORAGE: That is so. In the absence of objective conscience in essence, judgments of emotional center are influenced by sociological training.

SHERMAN: My judgments seem to be based on a feeling of safety or peril.

ORAGE: Purely instinctive, Sherman.

SHERMAN: Isn't a sense of death—such as Gurdjieff advises us to cultivate—a sense of peril?

ORAGE: It was never meant as a bogey; it was meant to evoke objective conscience by a sense of duty undone.

SHERMAN: How does this differ from a mechanical urge?

ORAGE: It doesn't except in so far as it is conscious. Animals are said to be without sin because they have no choice in the matter; men who are conscious of the possibility of choice are under the same obligation to fulfill their objective duty. They have both mechanical and conscious obligation—parallel. The question of evil arises only when this possibility of split occurs. And it is perfectly easy to discriminate between sociological guilt and being shame.

HUGH: I don't see why acting according to essence wouldn't be according to unrealized essence.

ORAGE: Essence is part of the absolute as a drop of water is of the sea. Insofar as it is capable, it goes through the process of self-understanding and development.

SHERMAN: Then there is a difference between essence and 'I'?

ORAGE: Yes. Essence is a particle of the active principle of life; 'I' is forever non-participant in the life of essence—untouchable.

MILLIKEN: We ought to say that a judgment is absolute relative to its part in a group—of one universe. We know there may be more than one universe.

MARY J: You can't speak of the 'relative absolute'!

ORAGE: Maybe in one sense you can. Imagine you are nothing externally—just a point of consciousness. Recollections remain but have no use to you. You are not now existing, you could not be perceived, are not phenomenal. You can't be said to occupy space, but you do occupy time. This point is 'I,' persisting in time, not in space. It has a field limited by recollections and possible states of consciousness. The world it then inhabits is its absolute world, having lost all possibility of contact with other processes. There is no growth, no shrinkage.

LOUISE: Can't it create out of its memories?

ORAGE: We come to that. Assuming it has imagination, its world is spun from its own subjectivity.

NAT: It makes new combinations of recollections?

ORAGE: Yes. What happens in its isolation—

SOLON: Why isolation. I think that means it is bounded—not absolute. It has to be actualized to be isolated.

ORAGE: It is isolated by its limits of recollecting, its self limitations are absolute. This comes to Mr. Milliken's question of whether an absolute can be relative.

DALY: I think we use the terms absolute and relative in unusual ways. Relativity in Einstein isn't used in this sense.

MILLIKEN: Relativity existed before Einstein.

ORAGE: The question of relativity inheres even in the concept of the whole and its parts. In this sense we use relative. Absolute is the whole taken as one;

relation of the parts is relativity. There may be a relation of two absolute suns. An absolute may still develop.

SOLON: You said it could shrink but not grow.

ORAGE: I'm not speaking now of the 'I' point of consciousness. Since it does not exist, it has no possibility of relation with anything else.

LARRY: There is nothing, then, but imagination?

ORAGE: That is all.

SOLON: In this case imagination is the only reality?

ORAGE: Yes—periods of pure imagination between manifestations.

LARRY: What are we to suppose happened to this 'I' that evidently once had experiences?

ORAGE: Death.

LARRY: Then we are all brain cells of a ghost?

ORAGE: Exactly!

LARRY: Very amusing!

ORAGE: Being in a state of pure imagination which was beginning to decline, the being had to make an effort to arrange his world. To arrange images in a cosmos instead of having them a chance series of recollections. I hope you see where this leads us in the question of good and evil. The existence of pattern presupposes a value on its actualization. To the extent to which the pattern is recognizable to its parts, the cosmos becomes awake—conscious. It is implicit in the plan that this world shall be His body with three brains, in one of which we shall live, and that He shall become concretely conscious.

DALY: If a body is to be created, what will its environment be?

ORAGE: Read the last chapters of Eddington, or Whitehead's *Process and Reality*. We have to use "body" as Whitehead does—as any organization of knowledge, an ordered relation of parts.

SOLON: As twelve units make a dozen?

ORAGE: Yes.

LARRY: Did He discover this pattern or devise it?

ORAGE: He devised it—it might have been another.

MAN: Where did God get his recollections? Was He part of another cosmic system?

ORAGE: Yes—it might have been that there were many other universes, and they may be existing now.

MAN: We might eventually have cosmic systems of our own?

ORAGE: Well, eventually! Every wish we experience can be regarded as a psychological entity—every impression a unit, playing the same role in our psychical being as we as individuals play in the life of the planet. Gurdjieff said that if one could be anatomized psychologically, he would see myriads of beings—wishes, thinking organisms. He would see his entire population.

MARY J: Isn't that personalizing the passions, as the Elizabethans did?

ORAGE: This is a bit more subtle. This is projecting on a screen the concretized contents of mind. In this way we are one of the ideas in God's mind. Conflicts in our minds represent internecine conflicts in His mind. We defined good as whatever design God had in composing his pattern as he did. In one sense this is arbitrary, in another it is absolute since no other pattern is possible for the constituents. Evil is the failure on His part to realize progressively, or dynamically, this pattern.

SOLON: Then God alone is capable of evil?

ORAGE: We'll come to that. The question arises of the degree of participation in that plan and the possibility of participating in good and evil.

MAN: Then he does good catalytically and evil when he interferes.

ORAGE: No—when he fails to interfere—fails to produce catalysis. Evil arises from the weaknesses of God; when these weaknesses manifest they are in the forms of beings. This is where religion comes in—divine service—to save God from "nodding."

MARY J: Then Beelzebub was the manifestation of such an aspect?

ORAGE: Yes—a fallen angel.

LARRY: Evil seems an odd word to use, since God's arrangement of the cosmic pattern was voluntary on His part; and if he sometimes nods he pays the penalty. Good and evil imply a sense of obligation imposed by the very nature of the case.

ORAGE: No—unless you use "nature of the case" as the totality of the world for us. He does evil in his own judgment. Evil is related to less-being, or non-being; good to more-being.

DALY: You said God preferred more-being; isn't this, then, just a like, not a good?

ORAGE: This judgment of God's is from emotional center; it is an absolute preference for absolute good. If the growing end of his pattern is toward more-being, then the being participating in it is on the side of absolute good.

SOLON: This is much like St. Augustine's words on human responsibility, man as a channel for God's will.

ORAGE: Channel is a bad word from our point of view. Man should be an agent in God's will. This point led to Quietism and the heresy based on men as the servants rather than the sons of God.

WOMAN: Is God's failure our failure?

ORAGE: We are so constituted as to save him from His failure—this is our potentiality. Our failure is in not realizing this potentiality. Any three-center being can be co-conscious with God.

DALY: I understand that absolute good or evil for the creature is participation in or failure to participate in consciously this pattern of God's. But isn't this simply like or dislike for God?

ORAGE: Well, maybe so.

DALY: Do you think so?

ORAGE: No, I don't. That is the same kind of good and evil—he has defined by his will absolute good as more-being, and absolute evil as less-being. For the original being this choice is arbitrary.

DALY: For us there is no such choice?

ORAGE: No. As an absolute being you could defy absolute good and call it evil for you. For subordinate being there is no choice.

LARRY: It seems more likely that instead of preferring being over non-being, God was compelled to choose being as good.

ORAGE: Oh no, there was no compulsion.

LARRY: But he was terrified—he must have been terrified at the possibility of non-being.

ORAGE: I once brought up this point with Gurdjieff. He said that God's mind was not compelled to follow His emotions; it was not a choice under necessity, though the stimulus to the choice was a necessity. So we cannot say anything compelled God to make this decision. Will is not in emotional center—he could have willed to choose evil. Will excludes wish.

MAN: What would be the picture if God never nodded?

ORAGE: We wouldn't exist. We are one of his nods, and have a special lot of work to do to become normal.

DALY: Then God would be better off without us, since we are a mistake. He may get some value from us, I suppose, but I doubt it.

ORAGE: When no value is possible the being goes to that planet we spoke of. This is the ash heap of the universe. The third point I wanted to make tonight is that three centered beings have the possibility of understanding the universal plan, as God understands it. A private in an army can participate in any sphere of function provided he has a conscious appreciation of the fact that the particular status he occupies is unimportant.

DALY: And the being's absolute good or evil is determined by his part in the great absolute?

ORAGE: Yes—in modern terminology this is "relativity."

SATURDAY, 19 NOVEMBER 1927

PART 3 OF 3

ORAGE: So far we've agitated the bushes in this discussion of good and evil, but I doubt if we've startled the hare. Instead of recollections to start off with, I wish one or two of you would attempt formulations of the ideas so far thrown out. This last discussion is staged really for Larry Morris, who was so dissatisfied with the first two. Larry, would you summarize what you think we've arrived at?

LARRY: Last time we started with a resummary and ended by discussing new things. It's much better I think to start where we left off last week. I recollect that we stopped with a discussion of God's situation at the inception of the universe and considered the conditions under which he was forced to invent some design for it.

ORAGE: Forced?

LARRY: He was driven by his state of fear to form this purpose.

ORAGE: Not driven. Is a motive called a force?

LARRY: He desired to escape a disagreeable situation.

ORAGE: It was a free desire. He had the alternatives of passing to extinction and of willing to overcome it.

LARRY: But he was terrified of extinction.

ORAGE: Not terrified. There was no compulsion in the matter. The reason Gurdjieff insists on this point is that the universe is non-mechanical, and maintained by a will.

DALY: But He had to find extinction disagreeable according to His nature.

ORAGE: That *was* compulsion, but His doing something about it was not.

LARRY: Am I wrong in imagining that the story goes that having been satisfied with things as they were, He realized that this would cease, felt fear and took measures to ward the end off?

ORAGE: Yes.

LARRY: That is all I meant to imply by compulsion.

ORAGE: You can say that this situation provoked Him, but did not compel Him. It is like not being forced to get up by an alarm clock. It isn't having to do one thing or another, but doing something or something else.

SOLON: It seems to me that that is the way we use "compulsion."

ORAGE: That is because we are perfectly mechanical.

MARY JOHNSTON: He would know that His 'I' remained, though, even if the universe dwindled out or not.

ORAGE: Yes. He couldn't decide to do nothing because to do nothing was part of time's inevitable flow. He had to do one of several things that were possible. You can't decide to *let* time take its course; time *is* taking its course.

MARY J: His was a decision to Be.

ORAGE: Yes. He was under the compulsion (laughter)—well, the logical necessity to Be one thing or another.

LOUISE: I thought God was in a state of pure being non-manifested. How did he run down in that state?

ORAGE: The state is purely psychological. His power of imagination was running down. The images in His mind depended on subjective activity, and, losing this activity, He had to create a source for these images by concreting them.

Imagine a state of pleasant dream interrupted by nightmare from which 'I' concludes that the powers of imagination are waning due to the influence of time. Further waning and more nightmare is foreseen. 'I' makes a selection of dreams and gives them substantiality—makes a durable pattern of them. Then there is no fear of waning dream power.

REESE: If God had sufficient power to maintain His images concretely, why couldn't He go on imagining them?

ORAGE: Because will was necessary; the dream state was one of only consciousness and individuality. Will is necessary to stabilize. Will was present potentially.

SOLON: God and the angels had to objectify their imaginings in order to get the reflexes from the concretions?

ORAGE: Where does this "objectifying" come in?

SOLON: When the imaginings were simply projected from God they were purely subjective; concreted they were objective.

(Daly [raised an] objection; mentioned Santayana and asked for a "summary" of his ideas. The argument trailed off in confusion.)

ORAGE: All this links up with our personal problem: of selecting an ideal or dream to realize. God's dream actualized is our world. The individual makes a dream come true by concretizing it.

SOLON: When God was young He took no thought on the morrow—then He began to save up for the rainy day!

ORAGE: The first part is all right—not the last.

SOLON: But our universe is the result of His saving up—of His taking thought.

ORAGE: Yes—our universe is an actualized dream, like a cathedral—only it is made up of beings.

MILLIKEN: Was the idea of this universe new to the archangels?

ORAGE: Yes.

MILLIKEN: To God?

ORAGE: Until the crisis, no thought of will was in His consciousness. This system implies the same in us; there is no actualization of will in us, but there is the potentiality.

REESE: Was the act of will caused by fear?

ORAGE: No more than I am caused by it to get up by an alarm clock. Ashiata Shiemash spoke of the "terror of the situation" in order to rouse activity, but not to cause the results.

MILLIKEN: Isn't the universe running down according to Eddington?

ORAGE: Eddington is in the position of God's angels asked to report on the running down—they reported the second law of Thermodynamics. There is now beginning to be a doubt that that law is the decisive law of physics.

JOHN: These dreams were taking place in subjective space—

ORAGE: Yes, and the objective dream is in curved space. Imagine a sphere in which every atom is a being. Atoms at any point have the possibility of occupying the whole sphere—a totality enriched by this conscious activity. To go back to Gurdjieff's image—imagine a sphere of every type of being—the mass making up the world of being. This has a Queen Bee—we assume—which is God. His will is that sphere, until every being in it shall *be* all sphere, and iden-

183

tified with Him. Since it is a being, the sphere has the possibility of Being All being. Until it actualizes this it remains just sphere.

DALY: Then the end of being is non-being after all potentialities are realized?

ORAGE: There is a difference between positive and negative states of non-being—the positive is the conscious end of actualization. These are the two ideas of Nirvana, with stress on different syllables when the word is spoken.

JOHN: God conquers the passing of time, rather than time, because in the conquest each moment of time occupies the whole of space.

ORAGE: Good, John. Have we reached the point now where we know when the ball has stopped rolling?

LARRY: We were discussing the perpetuation of pattern and the terms good and evil, and identifying good with what carries out the pattern.

ORAGE: What maintained the pattern and developed the static and dynamic aspects?

LARRY: We discussed how the pattern became the objective necessity to all its component parts.

ORAGE: Would this be absolute good for all beings in the design, with or without their consent?

LARRY: Yes—consent is implied in their being parts.

SOLON: Insofar as they tend to destroy the pattern are they evil or wrong?

ORAGE: Wrong. They are right when they happen to be in harmony with absolute good, and wrong vice versa.

SOLON: To what does evil apply?

ORAGE: To beings who escape from the pattern.

DALY: I thought last week we said only God could do evil?

ORAGE: Did we say so? Oh—on the supposition that God's choice is to Be, He alone can unmake it.

BLANCHE: I thought you also said God does wrong when He nods?

ORAGE: To nod is not to change the decision. I prefer to call it a mistake, or wrong—it is not an impingement. The will is constant, but the consciousness occasionally nods.

DALY: Then can anyone do evil?

ORAGE: No, they have to drop from the pattern to do evil.

SOLON: A part can fall into a state of evil, rather than do evil.

ORAGE: That's better. The Hasnamuss type drops into this state and loses the potentiality of will, ceasing to be actuated by will and dropping out of the dynamic pattern.

LARRY: I think the next step is clearing up right and wrong.

ORAGE: Well, suppose that in an army a plan of campaign is made which constitutes a guide for all; subordinates have no part in the decision, though it takes them into account. Good is now defined as accomplishment of the plan, and evil as the opposite. The subordinates have nothing more to do with it, but their decisions to cooperate or not are right or wrong, good and evil having been determined by the decision on the plan. Good and evil is impersonal for all beings.

HUGH: But the beings don't know the plan, and can't consciously cooperate or decide if good and evil are predetermined, or even right and wrong.

ORAGE: The history of religion and ethics show that what purports to be called the plans of campaign are handed down, through priests. Privates think they are cooperating by obeying conventional standards of right and wrong—the subjective standards of morality. But we can't be satisfied with the plan of campaign of a leader who is in dispute.

SOLON: Does the individual's being right unconsciously bring about good?

ORAGE: No—it brings about right.

HUGH: Can we discuss this humble soldier who gets conflicting orders?

CRAMPTON: A knowledge of good and evil is necessary before right and wrong can be known.

ORAGE: Yes, in subjective morality the interpretations are therefore idiotic.

HUGH: Then we must try to discover the plan of campaign through observation, voluntary suffering and conscious labor?

ORAGE: Exactly so.

JOHN: The plan of campaign for the universe is the same for each part rather than a separate function for each?

ORAGE: Yes.

SOLON: Isn't any obedience required?

ORAGE: Voluntary suffering only; a means to an end.

LARRY: How can the private find an objective criterion of right and wrong?

HUGH: I think that in his desire to know the campaign he might observe himself and discover the purpose of the macrocosm in his microcosm.

NAT: The important thing is to learn this technique before you get shot!

DALY: I understand that before he can choose, even incorrectly, the individual must know the plan of campaign.

ORAGE: Yes, consciousness may be developed in advance of will.

DALY: I thought will was the last thing developed.

ORAGE: There is a difference in the capacity of will according to development; it doesn't mean that there is no will to begin with.

DALY: Then full development of will is dependent on consciousness?

ORAGE: That is true, but they develop simultaneously. The seed is last developed, but it is already in the bud. The development of will, consciousness and individuality is both simultaneous and successive.

DALY: I thought Purgatory was the state of consciousness without will.

ORAGE: Not enough will for what is understood.

DALY: The beings there can't participate in the conscious plan of God?

ORAGE: They participate but suffer because they know more than they can do. To avoid Purgatory, will, consciousness and individuality should develop

185

harmoniously and simultaneously. This development of three at once is anti-Yoga. As Beelzebub told Hassein, cease activity in one center when the rate is too high and bring up the other centers, under order of the fourth center—this is Iransamkeep—I keep myself in charge of three centers.

Let me give you this brief summary:

The absolute by definition is the whole considered as one. The absolute to which we refer is the whole of our world. This self-contained unitary absolute presents two features, its status quo and a movement—the static and dynamic features. These two presuppose a plan or design necessitating the maintenance and development of the universe. This development can be called the plan of campaign, and the status quo is the army for carrying it out.

The plan has as its objective the development of the potentialities of all the constituent beings of the total plan. The realization of the plan is objective reason—the fulfillment of the being of each being. This plan of campaign is being carried out by all beings, conscious or unconscious, to the extent to which they remain beings at all; they might cease to be contained within this absolute. One potentiality of beings is to be conscious of the plan of campaign and to develop the will to cooperate with it. Regardless of their consciousness, they are all included in the plan, however. The attainment of a state of conscious cooperation with the plan is defined as right. Failure to attain this state is wrong. The plan of campaign by nature and by the nature of the beings operating it is discoverable. In the absence of this discovery, all reports of its nature must be regarded in the category of conventional or religious morality. Obedience to conventional morality constitutes wrong-doing.

The Gurdjieff text claims that the principles of right and wrong as laid down are derived from a prime source by a being having access to it. It doesn't follow that they are right. From that point of view, Gurdjieff's view of objective morality is only one of many of similar claims. However, a technique is given not involving obedience to these commandments, but designed to bring into consciousness the criterion of conscience so that the individual can appreciate the plan for himself. This technique starts with self-observation and proceeds in maintaining the objectification of body and the development of three centers simultaneously. The technique is designed to help the individual understand the plan of campaign and to cooperate in will with it. This excludes all possibility of team responsibility. Nothing, however, exempts the individual from his responsibility of development.

The only objectively right thing we can do is to practise the method and bring conscience into consciousness. This is claimed to develop all three centers. Other methods aim at a lop-sided development.

Do you feel that these three evenings have been wasted? Is the hare we started a March Hare? It may be we shall be dissatisfied with our conclusions and have to admit that we cannot produce the Truth, like Hamilinadir, who turned to growing the first being food, which is impressions; the second being food is intentional suffering, and the third food, conscious labor, for the being which informs the planetary body.

LARRY: Would you say that objecting to a lack of criterion is the beginning of objective conscience?

ORAGE: Yes.

Orage and Gurdjieff, 1922.

ORAGE MEETING NOTES OF CAROL BROWN

THIRD SERIES, TALK I

FRIDAY, 27 JANUARY 1928

Three groups:

Exoteric: or outer group (beginners)
Mesoteric: or middle group (theoretical Information not accessible to ordinary man. Search for objective truth, subjectively good.)
Esoteric: or Inner group (Initiation, self-perfecting)

THIRD SERIES CALLED "LIFE IS REAL ONLY IF 'I AM'"

First "Initiative factor" to endure manifestations.
"It weeps in me" — Skridlov.
Brother Sez = says (speaks from mind)
Brother Ahl = all (speaks from essence)
Senses limbs of the mind"
Free one's self of an experiencing of the outer senses,
then free one's self of an experiencing of the inner senses,
(contemplation and meditation).
The desire of my mind becomes the desire of my heart.
Kindness, pity, compassion, love, justice.
I will die, he will die.
(All lead to real faith and objective hope.)
Gurdjieff gave this:
Sit in straight chair, easy posture, erect, small of back (base) against and always in contact with chair. For *one hour* think of just *one* special thing, allowing no wandering dream state to take possession.

LECTURE TALK IV (THIRD SERIES)

... "As the correctness of the functioning of any relatively independent organ proceeding in us depends on the correctness of the tempo of the general functioning of the whole organism, so also the correctness of our life depends on the correctness of the automatic life of all the other external forms of life arising and existing together with us on our planet.

As the general tempo of life on the earth, engendered by the cosmic laws, consists of the totality of all the tempos both of our human life and also of all the other external forms of life, therefore the abnormalities of the tempo of any one form of life, or even only the disharmony, must inevitably evolve abnormality and disharmony in another form of life" . . .

LECTURE III (OR SEVEN IMPULSES CHARACTERIZE GENUINE MAN)

"Seven psychic factors proper exclusively only to man."

"I shall speak about three: CAN, WISH, and THE-ENTIRE-SENSING-OF-THE-WHOLE-OF-MYSELF."

It is necessary first to learn to divide one's attention into three approximately equal parts and to concentrate each separate part, simultaneously for a definite time, on three diverse inner or outer "objects."

"Soil-preparing" exercise.

Americans begin with Exercise 4, thus:

First of all one's attention must be divided approximately into three equal parts, each of these parts must be concentrated on three fingers of the right or left hand, for instance: the forefinger, third and fourth; constating in one finger the result proceeding in it of the organic process called "sensing," in another the result of the process called "feeling," and with the third making any rhythmical movement and at the same time automatically conducting with the flowing of mental associations a sequential or varied manner of counting.

Feeling-center = Nervous sympathetic nodes. The solar plexus is the chief agglomeration.

Sensing-center = Moving center = Nervous moving nodes, partly spinal column and partly head brain.

(Most difficult of all the exercises of this series but necessary for the Americans. At the beginning one must all the time try only to understand the sense and significance of this exercise without expecting to obtain any concrete results.)

Essence changes in form as often as the center of gravity changes.

Faith = Christian term for Magnetic center = Gurdjieff's use of the word "smell."

First semitone = impetus to self-development

Second semitone = how to serve God.

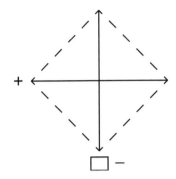

The horizontal line is the popular idea of Good and Evil.
Absolute Evil = absence of serviceability and functioning.

TUESDAY, 19 NOVEMBER 1929

GOOD AND EVIL

Orage's formulations at the end of the evening:
  The absolute by definition is the whole considered as one.
  The absolute to which we refer is the whole of our world.
  The self-contained unitary absolute presents two features: a *status quo,* (i.e.,
its condition at any given moment) and a *movement* (1. Static / 2. Dynamic).
  Note: Two kinds of will: Static = to stabilize
  Dynamic = to develop
  These two features presuppose a plan or design which necessitates a main-
tenance and a development and = a plan of campaign and an army to carry out
the campaign.
  Objective of plan of campaign is development of the ability to use body's
forces. Total plan = objectiveness = fulfillment of potential of each being.
  The plan of campaign is being carried out by all beings consciously or unconsciously to the extent to which they remain beings. Only possibility of
escape from plan is that they should cease to be.
  The potentiality of beings is to be conscious of the plan, and to develop at
the same time will to co-operate with it.
  Attainment of this state of conscious willing to co-operation is defined as
right. Failure to develop is defined as wrong.
  This plan of campaign by its nature and by the nature of beings, is discoverable by all beings. In absence of personal discovery of the plan of campaign all
reports are under suspicion of being subjectively determined. Consequently,

obedience to any standard of morality (religion, society, etc.) risks the wrong-doing of the individual.

In Gurdjieff's text the claim is made those principles of right and wrong as laid down are from the prime source—formulated by being Divine (by divine Being).

[...] He said can be found only in conscience.

Five Commandments to follow:

The objective is the attainment of objective reason.

1. To be just to the body. (state of fitness for the plan of campaign)
2. To improve one's "being." ("being efforts")
3. To understand the meaning and aim of existence.
4. To pay our debt to nature.
5. To serve. (service)

Or

1. To preserve one's life
2. To find one's place in the scheme
3. To develop one's self
4. To help others to develop
5. To pay back

There are three foods for planetary body:

- Food
- Air
- Impressions

They have their psychological equivalents in three being foods:

- Self-observation
- Voluntary labor (stroked out)
- Conscious suffering (stroked out)
- Conscious labor
- Voluntary suffering
- Unobtainable for us as yet

THE FIVE FACETS OF THE MIND (ORAGE)

(Five ways of reading G.'s book.)

I. Sex power.—We read to extract a method, support for our arguments, not to get at the truth.

II. Mental.—Critical. Newspaper. We compare with everything we have heard before and reject everything that does not conform. This facet is scribbled over so that the truth can't go through.

III. Mental.—The position of the esoteric scholar G.R.S. Mead. Accepts but merely to compare with other systems.

IV. Emotional, Aesthetic.—Looking for purple passages,

V. Emotional, Wonder.—Become as little children. Here the truth enters so that it appears as though nothing happened.

(To attain V. the Book must be read aloud. In reading aloud we can avoid II. That is why the Catholic Church permitted the Bible to be read only in church.)

WEDNESDAY, 4 DECEMBER 1929

SPIRITUALISM

Octave of first plane of matter:

Do, Re, Mi—our material body

Fa—the bridge

Sol, La, Si—our etheric body (also physical). (Not the astral or second body, but part of first body.)

The etheric body surrounds (3 or 4 inches) and interpenetrates the material Do-Re-Mi body we know. It is of rarer substances and coherent. It has its own five senses, and senses differently. It can separate from other body in life.

Mediums and mediumistic persons are in a state of misplaced center of gravity—dangerous.

Extreme fatigue, illness, excitement puts one on this state of seeing the etheric body.

The body dies—the etheric body remains a day, a year or thousands of years—speaks the words that are old records, turned on by accident. So entirely automatic, decomposing etheric force is the conversation reported from the spirits. (The real reason for its banalities.)

Cremation destroys the etheric body.

By blood fumes (so-called black magic) one sees etheric bodies or amas.

The function of the etheric body is to refine grosser substances, Acts as forces—super-dynamo for tuning our special forms of consciousness—(emotional and mental centers).

Mediumship is induced by change of blood currents (stream)—also drugs, hysteria, certain nerve pressure - makes a different state of consciousness.

Consciousness is *not* dependent upon constituents of blood but on channel or blood streams. (Determines races, nations, even family.)

Channel of even smallest blood vessel may change—makes different state—of consciousness.

There is a second blood stream for etheric body—color is steel blue—quite separate from other blood. Absence is said to cause anemia. Doctors prescribe sunlight.

The etheric body has its own senses—sight, hearing, etc.—but these senses are of entirely different range. What is called second sight, for instance, is due to etheric body. The etheric body is responsible for what we call nervous tone.

Blake in his "Marriage of Heaven and Hell" described the angel with whom he talked as changing color repeatedly—Aura.

In Tibet the Lama was about to divulge an important legomonism, when sudden death came. For him consciousness could continue in the etheric body, but on condition that there should have been left before death some of his physical blood with which his etheric body could make contact. Prevented by his sudden death, Jesus accomplished this in the upper room. Judas purposely led the soldiers to Gethsemane to cause a delay, in order to make possible the necessary preparations, now preserved in the legend of the Holy Grail and the Sacrament of the Eucharist.

TUESDAY, 15 OCTOBER 1929

MAN CONSIDERED CHEMICALLY, PHYSIOLOGICALLY, PSYCHOLOGICALLY, SOCIOLOGICALLY

These are four stages, the quaternary of man. He must complete the octave in each department. At present he is complete in the first two departments, but psychologically he is at the note Mi and sociologically he is at note Do. This unequal development accounts for his oddity.

MAN CONSIDERED CHEMICALLY:

From one point of view every action, every thought, is simply a change in chemicals. A cosmic chemist, in an impartial way, might consider all human activity as simply a series of chemical phenomena. To so view man is an exercise in imagination.

Man already has in him all the chemicals necessary for his complete development. The trouble is that he is not conscious of a large part of them. But the chemicals latent in him (if evolved) would make possible for him a large extension of experience. For instance, he has never become aware of or experienced the chemicals going into the makeup of his second and third body. Man's potentiality of experience is limited by the range of chemicals in him. He has all the chemicals in him for all the experience appropriate to the species man, but he can actualize these experiences only if he becomes aware of the chemicals.

Man considered chemically is a transforming station for the chemicals within his range. This range for man is H24. This is one of seven octaves in the scale of being. It is man's objective duty—that is, his function—to transmute the chemicals in his octave. In this octave the process is failing, to the damage not only of man but of beings in every octave. The proper performance of his function is what is properly known as divine service—"Helping God." A man may have every virtue from a planetary point of view and still be failing in his real principal cosmic function. The damage to beings in other octaves is what St. Paul refers to when he says that the whole creation groaneth awaiting the manifestation of the sons of God.

In music each octave has vibrations just twice those of the octave below. So it is with the scale of being. We begin with H3—God. This is not manifest in matter. It consists of one atom each of consciousness, will and individuality.

Consciousness is passive and has the No. 1

Will is active and has the No. 2

Individuality is neutralizing and has the No. 3

This gives us the next octave—H6 with twice the density and half the rate of vibration of the octave above.

H6   Solar gods (These were once given as archangels and angels and are synonymous - Orage.)

H12   Planetary gods

H24   Man

H 48 Apes

H96   Vertebrate

H192 Invertebrate

H384 Vegetable, etc

Do   Stuff (Ethernokril)

Re   Metals

Mi   Minerals

Fa   Vegetable

Sol   Invertebrate

La   Vertebrate

Si   Man

Orage says a being of a certain octave cannot recognize a being of a higher octave as such, and that we view a planetary god as a planet. A cat views a man wrongly in the same way. (Denied by Daly King.) Suggested that a cat has higher development, is on his way to 24, whereas we are not on our way to 48. It seems that within 24, for instance, there may be a whole octave of development. (Also special gap between Si and Do, man and god.)

Orage further stated that a being of a higher scale could affect the lives of beings of a lower scale without their knowing it. Thus man might shoot a cat and for the cat it would be an accident. So our "accidental" deaths are not accident but due to act of planetary god. Orage said no death was accidental (from chemical point of view).

MAN CONSIDERED PHYSIOLOGICALLY:

Man's position is not Si in the evolutionary scale given. Man is nature's sex cells (free to wander).

Orage-discussed the Norse mythological tree, Yggdrasil—all parts of which are beings.

Man is seed:
1. Nature's objective and culmination
2. free, falls from tree
3. the epitome of all the life that has gone before

Chemically the unit is the atom
Physiologically the unit is the cell

We are terminal nerve cells of the planetary god and so responsible for his development.

TUESDAY, 22 OCTOBER 1929

MAN CONSIDERED PSYCHOLOGICALLY

In all our four phases man's duty is to upgrade. The contrary is objective sin. We may consider the function of the race as bacterial—a collective transforming. Conscious cooperation with this cosmic process has the further result of aiding the individual.

In considering man psychologically we depart from the visible. But still we must discover a unit or our work will be unscientific, like alchemy before chemistry, or physiology before Harvey discovered the circulation of the blood.

A chemical unit is the atom.

Physiological unit is the cell.

Psychological unit is an impression.

What defines man is the field of his impressionability. The external world is the totality of vibrations. Some of these, man cannot receive. Others, he alone can receive.

It is man's duty to receive the impressions within his range in his three brains and to transform them to higher vibrations. The use of one brain by one, a second brain by another, a third brain by another, will not do, for then the reconciling is not there.

Three-brained beings are designed to use their three brains in conjunction. This transforming process is really the evolution of the psychology of God.

We receive vibrations that He cannot receive unless we transform the rate of vibration. The failure of the process is like the failure of the cells in our brain resulting in a lapse of memory. This is not fatal with God. He may have other ways of getting around it, just as we may have a notebook.

Nature is a being whose function it is to create machines to do the necessary work. The three-brained machines are perfect. They receive ALL the impressions within their range. But the being in the machine must transform them. This is where the failure lies. The reception is mechanical and perfect. But we do not transform to higher rates.

There are three forms of impressions. Our psychic life is this:

We experience thought responses, emotional responses and conative responses. These are all passive. (This gives thought as to the meaning of voluntary suffering. We "suffer" impressions passively). These experiences build up our psychology. It is not growth, not evolution, but a coral structure, an aggregation independent of the individual. (Compare the different methods of receiving intellectual impressions, the difference between knowledge and understanding.)

Man collects impressions and excretes behavior like an earthworm. Like the worm, he does not himself change in the process. He is unaware of his function. But if he co-operated he could change. For God is not a monster like sociology. Man has two purposes—one for God, one for man. For the glory of God and man's estate.

Man—H24—operates within range 48–24. Planetary god is also three-brained but in another field. He operates 24–12. We receive impressions at the rate of 48 and should transform them to 24, ready for the planetary god. But we leave them at 48. The result is a mere mechanical aggregation, part nature's and part sociology's. (Buddha called the soul an aggregate of conditions.)

In transforming the process goes not by 24 steps from 48–24, but by 7 notes of the scale, as 48-44-40-36-32-28-24. The terror is that as in quantum theory a full note of the scale must be actualized or nothing is done. Thus a transformation (transforming?). Many are called but few are chosen.

There are four stages in the going from 48-24

1. Egypt—Do, Re, Mi   Mechanical man
2. Desert—Fa   Self-conscious man
3. Promised Land—Sol, La, Si   Cosmic consciousness

Fa is arid. Nothing drier and emptier than to be aware of the physical behaviors of the body. Third stage—transfer of center of gravity. Impressions actively taken.

Man, as he is, receives the impression of the two higher stages, but unconsciously.

Do—is primitive man
Re—the great herd
Mi—the better, divided into two classes:

197

1.   With a tendency, back to Re

2.   With aspirations to Fa. These have magnetic center. It is said that many wish to escape from Do, Re, Mi, but have no aspirations to Sol, La, Si.

SOCIOLOGICAL MAN

What is the unit? The family. It is the smallest unit representing the interaction of man and society. There is no individual, therefore the family is necessary to provide the trinity which the one-sided man cannot represent. The duty of society is to develop individuals. The family ought to make the one-sided man three-sided. (Note St. Paul's reference to the Father "from whom all families on earth are named.") Eventually the ideal form of state organization is anarchy, the temporary voluntary association of individuals for the accomplishment of specific purposes. Meanwhile considering that it is the instinctive center which is to be ruled, there are three possible forms of state organization:

1.   Theocracy—as established by Ashiata Shiemash, is governed by 4th center, by priests, real initiates, consciously recognized as superior in being.

2.   Monarchy—government by a hereditary class, by the intellectual center, has the advantage over democracy of continuity. The king may have some sense of objective duty and compel his subjects to live according to it.

3.   Democracy—is government by the emotional center, a preponderance of wishes. Lentrohamsanin's proposal was anarchy—an absence of all control and pursuit of happiness.

ON TIME:

Though the Eternal is changeless, all change and time, growth and evolution are contained in it as an abiding reality, whereas in our world-image we see them unrolled on the endless scroll we call time. What we experience in our time-consciousness is but the ever-shifting section of reality which we term the present.

Thus our individual cycle of time, our evolution, is our experience of eternal Reality within the greater cycle of time which is the experience of reality by the in-dwelling life of our universe, but none of these cycles of time are objectively real, they are experiences of reality.

Eddington ("Nature of the Physical World"): "When I close my eyes and retreat into my inner mind, I feel myself *enduring*, I do not feel myself extensive. It is this feeling of time as affecting ourselves and not merely existing in the relations of external events which is so peculiarly characteristic of it; space on the other hand is always appreciated as something external."

INCARNATION AND REINCARNATION

"Reincarnation presupposes incarnation." Stress falls first on Incarnation. It is a completed fact or a fact in process. Not yet subject to a repetition until completed process. (G's method is a technique for speeding up a process in activity—not to be identified with the process itself.)

Not a process of "materialization"

Not a process of "taking on a body"

Not a process of "embodiment

Whitehead: It is a process of "concretizing."

"Coating" is Gurdjieff's word, provisionally satisfactory for the word "incarnation." A more subtle word than any above synonym.

"As long as we have remained a sleeping passenger, the process is still taking place." Orage continued the driver, horse, cart analogy, the owner (master), "I," asleep.

Forms of consciousness . . . being . . . "being" is incarnation.

Analogy:

Tree, seed   = Reincarnation

Leaves   = Incarnation

Orage says he used this—leaves—for recurrence as against reincarnation. Each succeeding leaf differs by totality of tree. Gurdjieff speaks of "blocks of essence" = the tree. Blocks of essence = human life, and leaves = each life. Leaves recur—not to be confused with reincarnation. But seed falls from tree and entire cycle is repeated = principle of reincarnation.

Gurdjieff: Every one of us recurs. Not a reincarnation of previous leaf or a continuation—we do not inherit any of the virtue or experience. Issues from a common essence—but no continuation of individuality. So we only recur like leaves -no continuity of progress except as the (tree) human essence has undergone development.

Individual can pass from wheel of recurrence by identifying himself with another part of tree—seed, relative freedom. But oak to oak—type.

God is subject to three laws—the nature of His will, consciousness, individuality (primordial, or existing from the beginning).

Next order of creation is under 6 laws: 3 laws of his own and

3 laws proceeding

Next order of creation is under 12 laws: 3 of its own

9 of two series before (6+3)

(Hydrogen) 24 laws for us; 3 being the primordial laws for our being

+3+6+9. (3+9+9?)

If we were to pass from 24 to 12 laws, that is gaining relative freedom. 12-6 + 6-3 as far as we go.

"Time-tube"—Eddington. Concretize any cross-section of one's past or future, and every cross-section in time-tube remains constant. (1) with static

199

pulsation, but there is also (2) dynamic movement. And any cross-section if understood, reveals the whole time, simultaneity, all that has been and that will be is implicit.

1st dimension of time = repetition without change—or constancy of any process.

2nd dimension of time = movement in which change even small, or repetition in a spiral, takes place.

3rd dimension of time = cross-section in which any changes are seen, or totality of tube, or whole sum of cross-section, or "timelessness."

(At another lecture Orage said the first two dimensions of time were: 1—Succession; 2—Simultaneity, with a third to be added later).

Reincarnation = transfer from one cycle with potentiality of spiral, to another circle with spiral potentiality. Don't confuse Re-incarnation with single spiral which can either expand or contract.

Viewing a single slice or cross-section or identifying with a single slice of time-tube is to recur without progress. To identify with a slightly different slice is what many do—slight progress. To identify with totality. Our time-tube = a totality of our essence.

(Cornucopia—old idea of expanding time-tube).

Time was first—the mother of space.

Space, smaller, is our field for (of?) consciousness. There exists for man potentiality of three-fold embodiment, and to have fully actualized that potentiality is to be fully incarnated. The means is the "method."

Incarnate = take on flesh.

A stone is *incarnated*, a tree is _____(?) (Word ruled out by G.) What word for this? When a psyche actualizes one of its potentialities as *ability to manifest. Not* manifestation. "Coating"—Gurdjieff's word finally used = superimposition (electrolysis) upon a real object (psyche), not perceptible, which renders (makes) it sensible or sensible perceptible. Converts it from the noumenal to the phenomenal (sensible or perceptible), but not from the subjective to the objective. The process of deposit is not the same as result of deposit, i.e., mineral (petrified) forests = a coating on vegetable. Coating—co-extensive with being—not peripheral (bounded].

Psyches go back into group psyche. Diffused, dispersed into its constituent elements. Does not reincarnate—enriches individualized psyches which arise later. We should say *psychic matter*. Until it begins to be coated we have no psyche which can be incarnated.

LAW OF ASSOCIATIONS

Observe only the end phenomena—overt behavior contains ingredients of three centers.

Gurdjieff's "Movements" (dance) designed as readiest means of access to emotional and mental centers by way of motor (physical) center and = *gospel* for motor center.

This *initiation* of instinctive-center type brings about accompanying activities in other two centers. To a type capable of being initiated in emotional center brings about sympathetic vibrations in other two centers. Third type—Impetus to intellectual type—echoing stimulation of corresponding groups in other two centers.

In waking state there is a magnetic tie between the three centers. This is broken in sleep. Sometimes this tie wears very thin, e.g. Hamlet—third center only. N*ear*, dream state with delayed responses in other two centers. Usual order is physical experience with two following.

Think of 3 spheres in each of which are the letters A-Z. If, for example, A be struck in one center it calls out A in other two (overtones). This is normal (usual?).

The Legomonists *made* art (artificial) in which three rhythms, e.g.

A in one center
B in another
C in another

Were played, each a strong experience affecting incongruous groups.

Removing conditioning = the independent working of each of the three centers while each is still magnetically associated with the other two.

Memory—three different keyboards of vibrations. All impressions are images. Images in each center (not visual). Image = power of recall or re-experience of anything that the three centers have already experienced, becomes a perpetual activity and continues as long as the organism lasts.

Gurdjieff's example of the boxes, one within the other. Any impression received in first box passes through and into the second and third box. = Blossom, fruit and seed, operating in simultaneity and succession.

So—ultimate seat of memory is (in?) center of psyche—middle box—mental matter.

Fields of memory = spheres in which impression continues to act as it originally began to act.

An atom of ether is simultaneously in all parts of ether at once. Psyche = an epitomized cosmic field = ideal form in which each atom of ether is both localized and eternal.

The Akashic records (or cosmic memory) consist of field of cosmic ether.

The psyche is indestructible (with one exception—see Chapter "Purgatory").

The psyche = the material instrumentation of "I."

The psyche = both the form of the field and *contents* of the field. (Field of Ethernokrilno and has 3 Emanations—God the Father, God the Son, and God the Holy Ghost).

In any given psyche the contents of Ethernokrilno have 3 potentialities, but only in developed psyche are these 3 forms differentiated into centers and only when each center has become the root of a body is the psyche said to be a soul.

Three bodies:

Etheric = Blossom

Astral = Fruit

Mental = Seed

Completed soul = completed seed.

The above 3 bodies, plus physical or planetary body, make man what was called quaternary in Pythagorean teaching—on this planet, men 4-sided instead of only a trinity.

The planetary body (modeled atom for atom on the etheric body) thus being 4 sides, for calling us tetartocosmos beings, tetar meaning four. It is necessary to have this kind of body on our planet.

The etheric body is the definitive body. The planetary body is put on it (patterned on it) and is the double of it. The etheric is the original. ("Coating"—Gurdjieff's electrolysis.)

AIUEIOINA (Remorse) (from chapter "Arch-Absurd")

(Psyche—crystallized essence)

"Djartklom" is the first peculiarity of the holy Okidanokh. Djartklom—the process of scattering electricity into its 3 prime sources.

Ethernokrilno (prime source substance) = primary matter from emanations from the Sun Absolute from which all things are made. Basis for everything that exists.

MONDAY, 20 JANUARY 1930

LAW OF ASSOCIATIONS (CONTINUED)

Impression newly arriving in center hitherto unoccupied has nothing to associate with. Simile—violin:

1. Bow is stimulus for impression
2. String is nerve tract
3. Violin is receptacle (or our body)

Tone is the impression deposited.

Nerve tract may be cut—illness, intoxication, etc.

Laws of association in each center are according to octave, but three centers taken as unity are law of Triamazikamno—as the three notes Do, Sol, Do form octave of 7.

Negative impressions we call "deprivation" quality; not just minus quantity, but absence of quality. Related to + being and—non-being.

First Law: Law of contrast or polarity (+ and -). Electricity polarized—center is now mopped out.

An incoming charge is modified by character of charges already in globe or center, which can be described as "swirls," but not chaos. Divided into hemispheres—swirls and anti-swirls.

(Word dicotying (?) used several times. Can't find in Oxford) Carol

Second Law: Law of propinquity in point of time.

Third Law: Law of propinquity in point of space.

Fourth Law: Law of Similarity of rates of vibrations—all positives, all negatives. Grouping of impressions per se in each center—same law as governs human units in society—basis

(two and a half line of text is blacked out)

of Gurdjieff's book. All this (above) antecedent to the introduction of a new element or catalyst—not conscious, no superior agency or force.

Similarity includes concordance (e.g., recognition of any major chord as *major,* also examples of words, etc).

(Law 1 is major law—refers to the *whole*—two hemispheres. Laws 2.3,4,3—Minor—refer to single hemispheres.)

Fifth Law: Density, weight, gravity, gravitation (consider this as regards tones, planets, notes in the scale, etc.).

Sixth Law: Law of rising and falling. One impression or group of impressions is running up the scale, another impression or group of impressions is running down the scale. Will determine whether association of similarity is momentary or lasting—or whether it falls into dis-similarity. Development of center depends upon ascending order. Reciprocal feeding. Descending impressions food for ascending impressions and vice versa. Complexity is also a unity, i.e., resultant from any orchestra can be taken by totality as one impression, a unity.

Is b-flat absorbing a-sharp, or a-sharp absorbing b-flat? Which is a higher rate of vibration?

NOTE: Foote and Spalding's "Modern Harmony." Page 2: F-sharp is higher in pitch than g-flat by a very small interval called "Comma of Pythagoras," which is about one quarter of a semitone.

Question of vivifyingness. Vitamins to food. (?) Vivify organism.

All objects including our own physical body are materialized vibrations and set in vibration by external objects according to the relations between them (piano accessible to stimuli of vibratory order from external world).

Where a number of different rates of vibration (Ethernokrone) happen to cross each other, the point at which they cross is called matter.

TUESDAY, 10 SEPTEMBER 1929

"I" AND "IT"

"I" is forever unobservable and therefore "subjective." Subject can never be object. (Subjective can never be objective)? Think of "I" as an emanation—it can never direct. Whatever "I" can become will be by being aware of "It." "I" is non-sensible, non-passive, non-receptive.

"I" is under the Law of Three—individuality, consciousness and will. The reality which produces impression on "I" is expressed in the octave. We see only so much of the world as "I" (eye) is capable of seeing. We can also relate "I" to being. Being is the range of susceptibility of objective reality.

An adult is one who wished to separate himself from himself. This does not mean that an adult is fully conscious but he has simply entered into the state of the spiritual adult. A boy entering manhood is not a fully grown man.

Never while in the body does one reach objection or objective reason. (Carol puts a ? here). This is after the psyche is developed. While in the body the present only is possible. When "I" looks at the organism, God looks at "I." (We must be an equilateral triangle, the same as God.)

In the story of the Equipage, the reins are the driving pattern of images, the control of images. In which direction does the driver drive? The purpose of his driving is to carry the passenger. "I" is not in control. This is not the function of "I." The responsibility is with the driver. The driver is at the disposal of the passenger, is for the sake of the passenger. The driver is asleep—his motion is always at the disposal of the horse and the horse is at the disposal of the cart. The horse is not reined, but is bound to respond, to the casual images of the Mind—of the sleeping driver. Only when the cart is smashed does the driver awake (if then); until then he dreams that he is accomplishing his object, quite unaware that he is constantly frustrated and arrives at just where he does not wish to arrive.

Gurdjieff's method applies to the passenger. The passenger wake up when he realizes he is in an equipage. He next wakens the driver. Why an equipage? That the passenger may realize the meaning and aim of existence.

There must always be a means, a ship, a vehicle on every plane. The fore-ordained vehicle in this plane is the three-centered planetary body. The passenger, having taken the ship, goes below in calm and falls asleep through the voyage.

"I's " work is not to harmonize. Harmony is a by-product of "I" agreeing.

"I" on one side, electricity on the other.

The communication of electricity (the whole of the external world) and "I" is the understanding vibrations.

"I heard a beggar yell and it was me."

"I" is sometimes awakened by accidental shock but "I" does not remain awake except by use of the method.

"I" is attached to "It" through essence.

"I" is a potentiality of essence. The function, of "I" is objective—is objective knowledge.

Individuality is the consciousness of will. Personality is the awareness of a wish. To be conscious of will is to have individuality; to be aware of wish is to have personality.

"I" am equilateral when aware; any other triangle is out of harmony. God is equilateral and therefore can only see us when we are aware.

"I" cannot sense, feel, or receive impressions. Body does.

In the FIRST BODY, we have instinctive reason.

In the SECOND BODY we have subjective reason.

In the THIRD BODY we have objective reason.

PONDERING

Pondering is the neutralizing force. In the absence of pondering all impressions go into either intellectual (positive) or instinctive (negative) deposits and leave the emotional (or neutralizing) center vacant. Pondering is the food of the emotional center. The difference between thought and pondering is that pondering includes clarity (thinking center) with emotional element (emotional center) which is the seat of essence.

Pondering has weight and value.

Without emotion there is no value, only logic—weighing clarity against clarity.

Thinking octave or three notes in thinking scale:

Sol = concentration

La = meditation

Si = contemplation

QUESTION: What relation do meditation and contemplation have to pondering?

ANSWER: None.

Our emotions are at root—based upon our being or non-being. Positive, expanded; negative, contracted.

Emotions: The thermometer of state of being at the moment.

What is weighed in *pondering* as against what is weighed in *thinking* are our experiences of preference and disinclination in the emotional center; likes against dislikes, pleasure against displeasure, relative to the criteria of being.

Happiness can be described as the conscious experience of Becoming.

Pondering is nearer being than anything that goes on in either of the other two centers (one and three).

No 9 in scale of centers is the intellectual sub-center of the emotional center.

Am I creating those objective values that I was created to create?

There are three approaches to knowledge of the aim of existence:

1.   Values according to likes and dislikes. (Infantism.)
2.   Welfare of planetary body—state of being called existence. (Physical)
3.   *Being*—continuity of being—expansion—state of becoming—experiences of happiness (real), experiences of pondering. (Related to permanence of being.)

Planetary existence related to *trogoautoegocrat* value.

Being related to God.

Essential element in pondering is the very center of being.

Gabriel's (?) measuring rod: Where do I stand?

Blessed are they who have intense experiences.

PURPOSIVE THOUGHT

Higher mental center is so-called because it has the power to command and control the lower mind—our thinking center.

Purposive thought takes places in higher mental center. Result = more being.

Purposive behavior = purposive manipulation of body = playing roles. Called center of will (higher center). This controls the emotions which are results of external stimuli or reflex emotions.

NOTES ON PARABLE

Parable is the language of mythical figures. (Beelzebub, Hassein, etc., are mythical figures.)—conscious representations of a fully-developed three centered being. Their speech is natural speech, as opposed to literary speech.

Jesus spoke in parable.

Objects are then in three planes interchangeably. (Note our tendency to attribute added meaning (other than verbal) to those who seem to speak with some degree of understanding.)

Allegory is the simplest form of parable—crude parable.

Parable can be read seven ways (e.g., take "Secret Doctrine"):

1.   Psychologically
2.   Physically
3.   Chemically
4.   Astrologically
5.   Religiously
6.   Transcendentally
7.   ?

This then, complete, is parabolic form raised to its octave. Then it passes to oracle.

Scripture told in parabolic form because simple language does not change—lasts over long periods. Whereas doctrinal language—referring to things of higher plane is constantly changing value and cannot be explicitly or safely (because liable to change) stated.

Parable cannot be thought.

Swift's "Tale of a Tub" is a crude parable because every reference can be checked. Usually information does not help in reading true parable. Example chapter on "Bolshevism" (G.'s book)—rebellion of three centers is referred to but where is the evidence?—requires understanding.

Significance of allegory is topical, whereas the interest of parable is universal.

Question: What about the key?

What is the Bible? Thrown into the hands of group (the Church) supposed to have the key.

Meaning of word "testament"?

The gap (Fa) between the Old Testament (Do, Re, Mi) and the New Testament (Sol, La, Si) was the miraculous appearance of the universe incarnated (shock from outside). So narrative can proceed from history of Jesus (or genealogy) to the . . . .

Parabolic account of the nature of man's development of first three centers is Old Testament, and nature of man's development in three higher centers is New Testament; and the correspondences

1, 2, 3 (Old)

5,6,7, (New)

St Paul takes myths from the Old Testament and translates them into meaning of New Testament, e.g., Hagar cast out daughter—symbol of pseudo-center, refers to it as allegory.

Jesus does the same—refers to Old Adam and New Adam.

The word "promise" seldom used in Old Testament. Had very special and important use = exhibiting symptoms of potentiality.

Only historic plausibility in Old Testament, but don't take it as history—only allegory. But we can say: Old Testament = historical parable. New Testament = psychological parable (miracles as text)

New Testament: It was characteristic of disciples to astound former companions by resourcefulness, illustration, apt example, etc. "He that shall practice this method shall find himself bringing out of his treasury things both new and old." (A symptom—embarrassed with riches of latent memory (memories?).

What is the advantage of stating a method by parable, instead of by fact?

Answer: Gurdjieff: "I bury the bone so that the dog, if he smells it, must scratch for it—and deep, so that with much scratching understanding comes."

Method — "new sense of smell" (Gurdjieff)

Method — divining rod, or measuring rod. Gurdjieff also says: "Plenty of keys in the book, but I never put a key near the lock."

Israel Solon attempted to argue that Einstein was really parabolic No, said Orage, purely symbolic language; not even language—a code.

Three-centers parable: horse (3), cow (2), goat (1)

Allegory: the three bears—only a picture.

Example of trans-solar ships (first Gurdjieff book)—astral and spiritual to make communication possible outside this sphere.

Example: Cart, horse, driver, passenger. Best of all parables. Orage discussed use of reins, taming horses, etc. Plato speaks of charioteer, chariot, drawn by two horses, one white (positive emotions), one black (negative emotions).

Fairy tales begin to fill magnetic center of child. New fairy tales ("Alice in Wonderland" only exception) cannot compare with old. It is to be supposed that the writers had knowledge, cast it into popular language.

Allegory is parallel.

Fable is not parallel (because the original is distorted).

We are incapable of writing parable.

Old meaning of parable—"An earthly story with an heavenly meaning."

Content = cosmic truth. Instead of "heavenly" meaning call it "cosmic" meaning or universal truth, facts of objective kind; if less than that, it becomes moral or scientific, etc.

Story told on instinctive plane must have its emotional and intellectual counterparts.

Referred several times to Wagner, who has written eight or ten volumes of prose, including his own dramas to all the operas. "The Ring," elaborate allegory. In all he shows himself to be a sentimental moralist of the worst sort. (Read Nietzsche's "The Case of Wagner") The allegory is so bad that his music must be equally bad (aroused a fury). Bombastic, sentimental platitudes, almost infantile.

Music weighed like literature. Two things:

Content, as stated in terms of prose

Form—pleasure of its poetic expression

Shelley's own comment on "Queen Hap" is as intelligent prose as the poem is a poem.

Swinburne—infantile

Joyce—disease

Stravinsky—very bad

Bach (2), Palestrina (1), Beethoven (3)

Blake's "prophetic books" are not parable. Spoke of Saurat (who wrote "the

Three Conventions")—new book on Blake's mythology, in which he traces it to its sources in Swedenborgian religion, which was Blake's religion.

Being refers to the movement up and down the scale.

Existence refers to the movement up and down the scale.

Evolution = actualizing of potentialities

Involution = potentializing of actualities

Major scale = scale in which totality of objects or beings is represented.

Evolution-involution	Other Octave	
Do = megalocosmos	Man	
Si = Sun Absolute	Monkey	(Is matter for science
La = all suns	Vertebrate	and of less interest to
Sol = sun	Invertebrate	the system.)
Fa = all planets	Vegetable	
Mi = planet	Minerals	
Re = organic kingdom	Metals	
Do = man		

Can be various octave diagrams—each differs according to subject of interest (Do). If it is MAN, he is Do, and not Mi, as in a different frame of reference. But we are always talking about the same phenomena.

Gurdjieff method: Man's interest in himself is the first premise. Man = do.

Two things about the Trogoaftoegocrat:

1.   Its maintenance.

2.   That maintenance, or progress, subserves its development.

When expert in the method, one can enter into one's instinctive center and discover a replica of the organic kingdom.

Question: Where do we now stand? Eddington: "Science and the Unseen World"—page 20 (or 70):

"The moat flawless proof of the existing of God is no substitute for it; and if we have the relationship the most convincing disproof is turned harmlessly aside."

SECOND SERIES

"Remarkable persons who I happened to meet during my preparatory age and who, somehow or other, voluntarily and involuntarily, were "vivifying factors for the complete formation of one aspect or another of my present individuality."

Chapter III. "My Father" (inscription for his grave):

"I am Thou

Thou are I

He is ours
We both are His
And all will be
for our neighbor."

Chapter IV. My First Tutor. Father, Dean Borsch of Kars Cathedral, said: In order that at responsible age a man may be a real man and not a parasite, his education during childhood must be without fail based on the following 10 principles. From childhood there should be installed in the child:

1. Belief in receiving punishment for disobedience.
2. Hope of receiving reward only for merit.
3. Love of God, but indifference to the saints.
4. Remorse of conscience from ill-treatment of animals.
5. Fear of grieving parents and teachers.
6. Fearlessness toward devils, snakes and mice.
7. Joy in being content merely with what one has.
8. Sorrow at the loss of the good-will of others.
9. Patient endurance of pain and hunger.
10. The striving early to earn one's bread.

Chapter V. Bogachevsky—later Father Evlissi of the Essene Brotherhood—said: "Objective and Subjective Morality." (*Copied elsewhere.*)

Chapter VI. Mr. X or Captain Pogassian (first comrade and friend of my youth) said: "I do this because I like work, but I like it not with my nature, which is just as lazy as people in general and which never wishes to do anything useful. I like work with my common sense." "Please always bear in mind," he added, "that when I use the word "I" you must understand it not as the whole of me, but only my mind. I like work and have set myself the task of being able through persistence to accustom my whole nature to love it, and not my reason alone. Further, I am really convinced that in the world no conscious work is ever wasted. Sooner or later someone must pay for it. Consequently if I now work in this way I achieve two of my aims. First, I shall perhaps teach my nature not to be lazy, and secondly, by this, I wish to secure my old age. I also work so, because one's only consolation in life is to work not by compulsion but consciously; that is what differentiates man from a Karabakh ass, who also works day and night."

Chapter VII. Abram Yelov. "It is not a question to whom a man prays, but a question of his faith. Faith is conscience, the foundation of which is laid in childhood. If a man change his religion he loses his conscience, and conscience is the most valuable thing in man. I respect his conscience, and since conscience is sustained by his faith and his faith by his religion, therefore I respect his religion and for me it would be a great sin if I should begin to judge his religion or to disillusion him on it; and thus destroy his conscience which can only be acquired in childhood.

Chapter I—Ekkim Bey

Chapter II—Peter Karpenko
Chapter III—Professor Skridlov
Chapter VIII—Prince Lubovedsky (includes account of Vitviskaia and So-
loviev and beginning of Prof. Skridlov—archeologist—on trip to Gobi desert
where Soloviev was killed by wild camel.
Steiner:
"An Outline of Occult Science"
"A Knowledge of Higher Worlds"
"The Story of My Life" (ends 1912; died 1925)
"The New Art of Education"
"Lectures to Teachers"
"Essentials of Education"
"The Education of the Child"
Occultists believe in three kinds of clairvoyance!
1. Hereditary
2. Karmic (transmitted from our own previous incarnations)
3. Conscious
Rudolf Steiner claimed karmic clairvoyance.
Delphic priestesses or pythonesses had clairvoyant gifts.

CHAPTER ON ART

Music now creates mechanical associations in one single center only, the center which changes to dominate at that moment (where your center of gravity temporarily is), but may vary at another moment. Same music call forth
another response in same being. Perhaps only an emotional sub-center of instinctive or intellectual affected.
The artist pulls one stop at a time.
Babylonian sacred melodies—as if sounds entering in combinations were
afterward sorted out—all equal intensities, producing 3 quite separate prompt-
ings (or manifestations?), e.g:
Third center—Joy (intellectual sub-center)
Second center—sadness (emotional sub-center)
First center—religious posture (instinctive sub-center)
Three influences simultaneously combined by a melody.

THE COMMUNICATION OF FORM-THOUGHTS

There is a certain grammar of associations—thinking in words and thinking
in forms.
A verbal thought by definition is one which can be formulated, that is, it
can be accurately expressed in words. In fact, the verbal thought really is noth-

ing more than the formulated word-pattern and so of course is directly communicable.

The formulation of a verbal thought may be illustrated by the analogy of painting. On his canvas the painter can make a direct reproduction of any surface pattern, it is only a matter of care and technique, Also a verbal thought can be reproduced in words, it is a plane surface. It represents the pattern by which the thought process moves from point to point by suggestion.

A form thought, on the other hand, cannot be directly reproduced in words, because it is something more than a plane. It is not a mere location but has actual substance and dimensions. It cannot be adequately reproduced by a verbal pattern—just as a solid body cannot be *reproduced* by the lines upon a canvas. Where in painting it is attempted to *represent* a solid body, a conscious convention is used, whether distortion (as in the case of the Egyptians), or perspective, or the use of planes to represent solids (as in the case of the so-called moderns). So also words can be used merely to suggest a form-thought; never to reproduce or *embody* it. Our error as hearers lies in conceiving that the words used to represent a form thought are intended to be a direct embodiment of the thought and not merely an indication of its presence.

The added dimension of the form-thought is due to the fact that a form-thought represents something more than an intellectual process. The emotional center must be engaged. There must be an entrance of being into the process or the thought remains merely intellectual or verbal. In thinking in forms, the thinker does not merely ruminate about something, but he actually places himself emotionally in the thick of the situation. He dramatizes. The thought does not remain a mere hypothesis or intellectual conception. It becomes real—the difference between thinking about something and thinking something.

The fact that a form thought, a thought of real substance, cannot directly expressed or communicated in words is very well illustrated by the reaction of the group to the attempted formulation of the ideas implicit in the book. For instance, in the lectures an example was given of pondering on the subject of Creative Imagination. Although the words used in exposition were extremely precise and explicit, when the group later came to discuss the incident, a substantial proportion was of the opinion that the exercise in question was not pondering. The most careful use of words had failed to express the reality of the thought. It was noted that the group's difficulty was found primarily in the query whether pondering must be related to experience or not—a purely verbal distinction. Some members were of the opinion that pondering must not only be directed to the meaning and aim of existence, but that it must be related to experience. The failure to realize that pondering is not related to experience but is itself experience, shows that the careful words used had been totally inadequate to engage the emotional center and effect a real understanding of the thought.

So in general the group discussions have disclosed wide differences of opinion as to the verbal expression of the most fundamental propositions even after the precise explanations repeatedly given. If it were at all possible to give verbal expression to substantial thoughts, certainly enough skill was used in the exposition and enough attention was paid in the hearing to have affected a far greater degree of uniformity than actually resulted. It is significant to note that when differences arose they were rarely resolved by a formulation quoted directly from the lectures. When, on the other hand, a incident in the book could be adduced with a direct bearing on the point at issue, that almost always cured the difficulty. This may be taken as a sign not that there was a complete failure to grasp the ideas, but that words are inadequate a means of expressing the ideas. In other words, a real thought must be grasped directly or rather it must be entered into. It cannot be embodied in words. It can only be talked *about*.

If then it is impossible to formulate a form thought in words, how can it be communicated? Of course this may be accomplished through art forms, such as painting etc. But discarding these, let us consider some possible methods of communicating form thoughts by words, even though words are incapable of reproducing the thought directly.

Gurdjieff's book is an illustration of the first method. (*Something must be missing here.*) There is no attempt at a direct formulation of the ideas behind the book. The words are used consciously as an intellectual shock whereby the emotion is aroused, so that the being is sufficiently expanded to assimilate the thought or idea This result is accomplished even though the immediate ideas actually formulated in the book may be rejected intellectually by the hearer. This is the method of parable. It is the method employed by great teachers again and again. It is the method of Jesus. He never attempted to formulate his idea of the kingdom of heaven. He merely indicated the idea by parable and it is stated that "without a parable He spoke not unto them." In other words, he understood perfectly the inadequacy of direct formulation.

Another suggested method of communicating a form-thought, or of indicating its presence, is the method of the literature of simultaneity. This technique recognizes that a thought has substance, is a solid, is an organism. It attempts therefore to represent in simultaneity the various aspects of a thought and thus to attain more verisimilitude than is attainable by merely painting one side of the thought, as is done in ordinary literary forms. Basically the method of orchestral literature is the method of paradox. What paradox does in an epigram, orchestral accomplishes by the actual simultaneous production of the necessary number of voices appropriately placed. Preliminary attempts at the use of words in simultaneity by the experimental group has appeared to be fruitful, and it is believed that further experiments along this line on a more developed scale would bring large results. As a matter of fact the recent group discussions were nothing more nor less than unconscious exercises in simultaneity. From the various formulations, antagonistic and erroneous, and expressed almost in simultaneity, the hearer might make out the form of the underlying thought. But he would never reach the thought if he relied on any of the formulations as its embodiment.

A third method of communication, a form thought or the presence of a form thought is the Sutra-method, employed particularly in Indian literature. This method avoids imprisoning the thought in the words employed. The words indicate the presence of the thought but do not confine it.

John O'Hara Cosgrave

The normal being wishes to live forever.

Normal man is one who not only has actualized his inherited potentialities but has freed himself from his subjectivity.

The happy person is one who is striving to actualize his potentialities.

The psyche never passes out of existence which has been neutralized.

Literally we are living in the Body of God. God is not a perfected thing. He has given Himself eternal time to accomplish His perfection.

We are made in the image of God. God's fancy is immortality.

Implicit is it in the pattern that man should find himself in the same situation that God found himself in. He has shared with us His suffering that we might also share in His creation.

God can maintain the universe by Himself without help, but God is also good and He wished a fulfillment for beings in the universe that they also may enjoy bliss and become Sons -that they may enter into the psychology of the being who created the world.

Suffering is the price of endlessness. Our fulfillment is imposed upon us. This may be called Justice.

This wish to live constitutes a Being. If God wished to live He has shared that wish with all of us. He has also provided the means by which that wish to live may exist forever.

Once being alive there is no choice; we must live forever. The representative of God in any individual is that which tells him how or what God would do in any situation. Your powers are to actualize your presence. This is your money in the bank, your cash, and your earning ability.

To advance in this sphere you must act as God's emissary. This is life eternal, to know the living God.

The being in essence is in the moving sub-center of the emotional center. This is where one's pure acme is found, and is said to be of the material of God. His movements are straight from the Heart. God, as being, is there in The Heart.

Essence is a chemical deposit from the sun and planets of the solar system entering earth beings at the time of conception. In man this affects the region of the solar plexus. It is unlike any of the chemicals found on this planet and links man to the Cosmos. As the chemicals of man return to their natural state at death, so do these chemicals return to their sources.

The leaves of a tree recur annually, but not the same leaves. There is leaf ability. The leaves are recurrent but not the identical leaves. The change between each leaf and its predecessor differs only by the change in the tree from season to season. The tree is the block of essence, the leaves are the human

216

beings; the tree remains not by its leaves but by its seeds. When the seed falls it has the potentiality of repeating the whole tree. The leaf is recurrent, the seed reincarnates. A leaf cannot be said to inherit anything from the life of the previous leaf; there is no use made of the previous leaf, no continuity, but it springs from the same block of essence. We, like the leaves, recur without any continuity.

Time is the most important thing next to awareness. The flow of time through us gives us our chance to extract what we can. Time is a threefold stream passing through our three centers. We fish in the stream, what we catch is ours, what we don't is gone. Time does not wait for us to catch all in the stream. If we catch enough we have enough to create the three bodies and become enduring.

Time is the sum of our potential experiences, the totality of our possible experiences. We live our experiences successively; this is the first dimension of time. To be able to live experiences simultaneously is adding another or second dimension to time. To be aware of this simultaneity is called solid time, or the third dimension of time. When we have identified ourselves with time it will be as Revelation says: "And time shall be no more."

Just at that moment when we can say: "The thing that is happening to me," will we be safe.

I beg you before starting on this journey to question you are plunging into the dark; here is a little lamp; I show you how to rub it; make sure you know how to rub it.

Conscious labor consists of having an objective in life as a life aim, an aim which can be pursued the whole of your life. It does not depend on the vicissitudes of life. It is the aim for which you took the trouble to be born. You assume first of all that you are an immortal being, you give yourself unlimited time. If you keep this aim through this life you will I have an aim strong enough to persist after this life - an aim big enough to persist through an immortal existence.

Compiled from my four note books on Orage's "Group" talks, for you, Jessie.

Are they not wider and deeper in significance than anything we are likely to find?

Blanche
9 November 1934

MONDAY, 7 OCTOBER 1929

I

We take it for granted that one of the major interests of man is the study of mankind.

Our relations with others and their relations with us are our prime interest. Some may claim to be or seem to be more interested in art but we will find even with them 90% of their interest is in human relations.

As important a part of life as human relationships play in life, still they are governed according to whims. Our likes and dislikes of people are arbitrary.

When we are shown that this is so we are at a loss for a criterion. That we have no better criterion is childish. This in children is childlike but this stare in adults is childish and unsuitable.

For the moment there seems no other standard than "I like" and "I don't like." What standard is there for judging otherwise? This is a difficult question to answer because we have not considered it.

This method, which we call "The Method of Objective Judgment," applied to ourselves, is very much simpler than we might imagine.

Conjure up a picture, see in your mind's eye someone you know; a friend, a relative you know well, and then estimate them without curiosity about them. Repeat this with other friends, a hundred, the more the better. You will find you have more content in your own mind.

There is little difference in the experiences of different people but the difference consists mainly in what they do with their experiences.

One form of food is what we eat. The Importance is not so much in the quality and quantity as in the digestion of it. Experience is another form of food.

"The understanding of a human being according to my understanding is the beginning of wisdom."

When you have given your best and impartial judgment of people the chances are you are wrong. We may hope to arrive at a judgment a little less biased but the chances are our judgment about our most familiar friend is completely wrong. This is to say our present judgment is doomed to be not just fragmentary, but completely wrong. The quality to judge impartially is something to work toward. Now we are judging on the same basis as the animals.

It may be said with the equipment of science, with laboratory methods, one might be expected to be nearer correct - with the history and inheritance before us, etc. We say, the greater the variety of material you collect, the less liable are you to be right. It is not in the quality and quantity of your equipment brought to bear that you arrive at correct judgment of the material.

We do not propose in these classes to collect facts about other people. We

218

are satisfied with the smallest amount of material. We are not interested in psychoanalysis; that is barking up another tree. We are interested in the quality of the judgment brought to bear on our material, much or little. We are primarily interested with ourselves as judging agents. The proper study of every individual is himself or herself.

This is an absolute statement.

Only he who has attempted to judge himself can have an idea of judging anyone else. Otherwise his judgments are made by his subjective self. The first subject of study for anyone, who aims to be adult, is himself or herself.

How do we know anyone at all? By what means did you arrive at such conclusions as you have made about the person you have in mind? Not under what circumstances did you meet them but how did you come to know them?

Have you a claim to a private approach intuition, clairvoyance?

We none of us have any knowledge of the state of emotion in which our dearest friend may be standing only a few feet away. (If interested in the scientific side read McDougal, "Psychology of the Crowd.")

Illustration: The man blinded in a raging crowd was serene until his blindfold was removed.

The only evidence you have that I am here is my manner of behavior, tone of voice, posture, gesture, movements and facial expressions. Suppose it was dark, would you know I was here? Suppose I was bursting with emotion would you like to sit in the dark and read my mind?

The work of reason is not completed when you discover something is untrue. When you think you have intuition, disclaim it; disclaim your prejudice; clip away all such preconceived ideas and feelings - this is the beginning of your education—to remove obstacles to your discovery of truth.

The only material for judgment we can collect regarding others reduces itself to the five manners of behavior. Change your tone of voice and you deceive the other person. Many friendships have been made and broken by tones of voice. When we hear a tone of voice, like that of a nurse in childhood or our mother's voice, we say: "I like that person" or "I don't like that person" without the slightest idea of why.

You don't go to Columbia to study tones of voice of others, but among your friends you give your attention to tones of voice. You will learn tones that issue will be as exact as tones issuing from a motor car.

We might say as you interest yourself in theoretical psychology you lessen your interest in practical psychology and vice versa.

A Columbia professor has written a book on gestures. There are gradations of tones of voice of which we know nothing and do not use.

We have all been taken by the smile of Mona Lisa; perhaps it was not her smile, that Leonardo just put it there.

Facial expressions are constantly changing. A poker face can be read by a poker reader. Faces change slowly sometimes; we say "her face lit up" or "her face fell" but generally the change is slow and the one least conscious of the change is oneself.

A facial expression is a dial or a total barometer of the person at the moment. It is a threefold compound of the state of the works of the total mechanism of the organism. A clock dial changes progressively; a face changes successively according to the organism.

Over a period of time, being with a person, we arrive at conclusions. By any one of these manners of behavior understood we can arrive at judgment; by any three, we certainly can.

Movement is the passage between postures. Carriage, department. Our postures are characteristic of our training. (Illustration: Ironworkers in England sitting on their heels.)

Each of these is a language with grammar, syntax, style. These are the only occult languages in the world. There is nothing occult, nothing concealed. Everything is open to those who can read the text, no one can trick them.

It is not what they say but what they do which is the language people speak sincerely.

Whether you think it now or not, when you have to think about it you will realize all your judgments of others are based on these five languages, badly, incorrectly read.

If I have taken from you your belief in your intuition, clairvoyance, emotional understanding, I have given you something in its place.

We are not here, if you continue to attend, primarily to get to know others by these languages. We are not interested in anyone else; we are interested in ourselves that we may come to form objective judgments.

By the only means by which we can come to know others can we come to know ourselves.

I do not expect you to agree with me at once.

Nothing which you know of yourselves, emotions, trains of thought, is probably true. When you think you have an understanding of yourself, your facts are wrong, your conclusions are wrong. These conclusions lead to feelings of superiority and inferiority. People are suffering under the illusion that they have an understanding of themselves. It is one chance in a hundred that one reports something correctly about himself. No one is more misinformed about A and B than A and B.

Only when one has passed beyond the stage of passing subjective opinions does one see he has been living in a fool's hell (or a fool's paradise) because he has a subjective state as evidence about himself.

If this has had any meaning for you, you will see the next step.

Introspection is a form of lunacy. If this is written in letters of fire some will still say what I am going to say is introspection even though I say to think about yourself, your actions, etc., is already beginning a form of lunacy. We must disclaim to read the minds of others; we must disclaim to read the minds of ourselves. What is there left? There is left the same field to trade in that we trade in in thinking of others: tones of voice, postures, gestures, facial expressions and movements. This method intended eventually to arrive at self-knowledge and then knowledge of others, begins with observing these five forms of behavior, to be aware while they are taking place. You ask, "What is to be arrived at?" I answer, "What is it you want?" We prescribe nothing you shall want, we only ask, "What do you want?" You wish to excel, to be successful in this, that or the other, to have power. It does not matter; every wish from our point of view is holy. To attain whatever you wish, you will need self-knowledge and self control. You will need what this method will infallibly bring about. This method is of practical value to bring about a wish. Some wishes may change under the method. A criminal wish cannot survive the observation of your five manners of behavior.

MONDAY, 14 OCTOBER 1929

II

These evenings are more classes than lectures.

QUESTION: What does anyone remember from the last meeting?

ANSWER: Observe concurrently the five manners of behavior, tone of voice, posture, gesture, movements and facial expressions. Why are these five isolated and exclusively dealt with? We are aware of the reception of impressions in others by deductions from these five manners of behavior. We imagine we can report about ourselves what we are feeling and thinking, that we have some intuition or clairvoyance which enables us to know and report our own thoughts and feelings correctly. The vast majority of people cannot report their own thoughts and feelings correctly. Not even with special training. A trained person uses a telescope; the result is he sees some things more plainly but the telescope limits his range.

QUESTION: How about reading hand writing for evidence?

ANSWER: Why take anything so minute to read when there are these five languages shouting at us which, if we can read, tell us everything?

We cannot depend on what people say, for what they say now they may not say tomorrow.

We do not take as evidence about ourselves what we take as evidence about another.

This method suggests studying ourselves through the same medium which we use in studying others.

We propose an objective method not introspection. We propose observing our objective forms of overt behavior.

We are not concerned with reading others; this would be impertinence un-

221

til we can do it competently; when we can read ourselves then can we do something about reading of others.

We propose first of all to introduce you to yourselves. You may have a craze for this person walking under your hat; you take a goose for a lion - this is a superiority complex. Or you take a lion for a goose - this is inferiority complex. Or you may have both. If your portrait sat side by side with the sitter you would not recognize the portrait. We say, "I will fell the unvarnished truth about myself," and what we tell is mere flattery. Again we say, "I will be frank and tell the good about myself," and this is humility.

When we begin to report on our own posture, gestures, etc. we and others can check up on them. We are not reporting on introspection; we are reporting on something objective. Our movements are few in number.

Our habitual postures are only three or four.

The range of our tones of voice instead of being what it should be - seven octaves forty-nine notes - is limited to four or five notes.

Our facial expressions "Oh, for a new face"—Charles Lamb. We have one face for the breakfast table, another for the office etc.

Gestures: We have all suffered from gestures in others we do not like. Marriages have been broken up because of some little gesture.

Our self-ignorance results in great catastrophes to others and to ourselves. We come to conclusions subjectively about ourselves. Our proposed remedy will make things worse because we have misjudged.

There can be no self-improvement without self-knowledge. The aim of this group is self-improvement without self-knowledge. The beginning step is to keep your eye on the 'ball': the ball is tone of voice, gesture, posture, movements and facial expressions. When you can report on these you can report on the kind of person under your hat.

By introspection you get a caricature; by this method you get a correct picture. This is a safeguard against self ignorance and ignorance of others.

We may not always understand ourselves and others and may then say: "I do not understand" but we must not misunderstand.

It is hopeless to try to trace the origin of our postures, gestures etc. We did not get them from our college, our parents or our friends.

QUESTION: With what do we observe?

ANSWER: Who are you? Who you are is who observes.

QUESTION: What advantage is there to this?

ANSWER: At present we are under the disadvantage of making many errors in our judgments of ourselves and of others. This is the one exercise which combines in itself all the advantages of all exercises for mental growth.

QUESTION: What evidence did you have for these advantages?

ANSWER: We have to collect evidence as to these advantages before we can pass judgment on this method. All judgment must be reserved until evidence is collected. Illustration: a court.

222

What is your own account of your five manners of behavior? If you cannot report we rule you out in a court of essence beings.

A properly trained boy should be able to understand the Einstein theory of curvature and space.

There is no thought in telling about our small personal experiences of all kinds - how much money we have made, what we have been busy about, etc.

The technique of self-knowledge is the technique of techniques. To begin with its use, select one of your manners of behavior tone of voice, and say: "I will hear every word I speak as if I were listening to another person." In listening to your own voice, you do not change it, but it changes - becomes more nearly the truth and will give a more truthful report of your thoughts.

QUESTION: *Text missing*

ANSWER: Don't play with algebra when you have not studied arithmetic. "Seek ye first the kingdom of heaven." Be as a little child is - concerned with himself. Philosophy goes, psychology goes - nothing is left but animals exhibiting. We never propose to make any use of material we collect; it is the collecting that counts.

When we say, "I have a complete list of my manner of behavior," then we are getting on.

Don't classify. Don't change your manner of behavior when aware, but try to continue it. You will find your manners of behavior change; they undergo change - not that you will change them. It isn't your emotional reaction that is to bring about the change. Change comes if it isn't your motive. If you change because of motive you are not observing correctly - objectively.

Illustration: Case of stammering at Johns Hopkins's cured by professor telling patient to wait for the stammering and observe it. This released his self-consciousness in his emotional center, the attention being in the mind.

When you find a manner of behavior in yourself which you do not like, try to repeat it. You make the mistake of saying, "I don't like it." Instead, repeat the manner you do not like, until you cease to dislike it.

QUESTION: Should one repeat a bad action, say murder.

ANSWER: This does not mean an action - an action is a compound of manners of behavior. We prescribe no change of yourself and to give no time to observation.

It takes no time, it takes no thought. It suggests no change in your present life. Continue doing exactly what you are doing. Do not trace the stream entering into the exhibition of behavior - the visceral, the spinal, the cerebral. A gesture has three prime colors in it: cerebral, visceral, spinal. These we do not consider; we are interested in the white light the gesture. Every movement is the epitome of your entire state at the moment.

QUESTION: Do all start alike?

ANSWER: "I heard a beggar cry and it was me." —Kipling. He didn't hear; it was an overtone he heard. This is different than intending to hear. When you begin to observe objectively with intent no one is any better off than anyone else. Observation occurring accidentally is no advantage. In intention to observe, we are all, literally every one, at the same point. No one makes more headway than another except by effort. No one can foretell the amount of effort anyone will make not God Himself. No one knows why one, seemingly least probable, makes more effort than others. Dr. Watson, with his training, after listening to a lecture, thought he could continue listening to his voice, after hearing himself say: "how do you do" he soon returned, saying he had failed.

If you will be aware, hearing the words flowing from you, you will find yourself saying things more clearly, more logically. It is like taking off a clutch. It relieves the bugbear of what is called: "Self-consciousness," which is consciousness of others, and you are at ease.

MONDAY, 21 OCTOBER 1929

III

We have two states of consciousness: sleeping and waking. When dreaming, one is not aware of being asleep. The material for dreams arises from something that has been in the mind during the previous twenty-four hours.

Try to realize man is a being with three centers: thinking, feeling and instinctive. Seldom does it happen that the three centers are ready to fall asleep at the same time. Two centers go on working after one has fallen asleep. Perhaps one of the other two falls asleep about two o'clock in the morning and the other stays awake until four, in the same order the centers fall asleep as they awake. For this reason, when one comes down for breakfast, one is third awake; along in the middle of the forenoon one is two thirds awake and by luncheon time one is fully awake. After twenty-four years of age people are seldom fully awake in the three centers at once for more than a few minutes during the day. Only in times of stress, war times or times of death are people awake in three centers at a time, for more of the day.

Insomnia is caused by one center's not having had enough exercise during the day and keeping the other centers awake.

Whatever involves intellectual, emotional or physical waste we call immoral.

There are three forms of sleep: sleep in one center, sleep in two centers, sleep in three centers. Sleep in three centers we call complete sleep, or sound, dreamless sleep.

Anyone who dreams is a little pathological.

One of the terrors of psychoanalysis is that it tries to induce sleep by other means, instead of prescribing exercises for the underused center or centers.

Sleep powders affect the blood stream.

When you are asleep nothing should happen in your consciousness. When you report your dream to us we should be able to tell in what center you were not asleep. If it is your emotional center which is not sleeping, you are shirking disagreeable emotional situations in life.

What is spoken of as sex sublimation is not correct. Sex energy in the physical center may become normal and not dominating if the sex energy is also used in the two other centers.

So far human beings are only one form of transforming machines, but there are two other centers capable of transforming sex energy.

QUESTION: What about the catalytic center?

Answer? This is the fourth center.

There is an "I," a fourth center, a potential soul. If we can say with the same simplicity: "I have a body," as we say, "I have a car," we can begin to realize that this body is a possession. "This body is a transforming machine which I have; just as I have a car or a refrigerator, I have a machine to use." It does not mean, "I am a machine."

The emotional center is our impressionability ability; our responsiveness to environment.

The intellectual center is our ability to think clearly.

We start life with three relatively blank centers. These centers differ through heredity. We all start with much the same potentiality of experiences in these three centers, but difference in circumstances make it impossible for all to actualize the same experiences. Being born in China our possibilities of having certain experiences are limited; experiences easily possible in the West are not so in the East, and vice versa. It is said English women are cold; it means they are limited in affection, in passion. At birth these experiences are possible but circumstances make them impossible.

No one ever actualizes all his possibilities of experiences, only a fractional part.

The fourth center does not work miracles; it does not give us any possibility which was not placed within us at birth. Fourth center is consciousness—consciousness is something quite exact.

We start life hereditarily limited and with three blank centers. In life we fill up these three centers. We should derive from them all we can.

The Gurdjieff School was called: "The School for Harmonizing the Three Centers of Man." It was not for developing one center. There are other schools for actualizing one center at a time. The Three Schools of Yoga.

This method actualizes all three centers simultaneously. Developing one center at a time you become a monster. While all have three centers at birth we might say they vary in size. We all started at a single note at the beginning, at birth. We say a full sized center at birth is 3. A proper distribution at birth of center potentialities would be 3,3,3. But we are never born 3,3,3. We are born with centers limited to a development of 3,2,1; 2,3,1; 2,1,2, 2,2,1; etc. These arrangements at birth make 28 types. These possibilities at birth cannot be changed during life. We cannot change heredity. Man has been on this planet thousands of years and never has one been born 333 in possibilities.

How do the three centers become relatively filled? All centers can be developed according to their potentiality for experiences - according to the inherited pattern.

A child is not in a position to realize its movements, its feelings, its thoughts, or to decide what they should be. The fact of speaking depends on environment; the ability of speaking depends on heredity.

The musical scale was originally taken from the laws of nature.

Energy in any given space is almost identical with the quantum theory.

The first interval is comparatively easy: do re mi. Most people go: do re mi mi fa do.

A baby born with the possibility to experience 3,2,1 or 2,2,1 does not mean he ever fills these centers to these points, that he ever actualizes his potential possibility for experiencing.

The idea of this method is to develop beyond do, re, mi.

QUESTION: When we have reached the second do, does it mean we have the whole octave?

ANSWER: "Curb Ideas in questions to the sequence in which the argument is going. I am not evading the argument. I am only attempting to keep the sequence of the octave."

What will be the next step is I say everyone is born with one of these arrangements in centers: 3,2,1; 2,1,3; etc.

QUESTION: How can we improve if born 1,1,1?

ANSWER: That comes later at note la, and is not now in the sequence.

We are the three centers; what experiences should we have? What do babies begin to receive in their centers? This is the sequence.

Remember the story of Goldenlocks and the Three Bears? We are given empty bowls of different sizes to be filled. Environment will evoke in the child only the experiences of which he is capable.

There are three forms of stimuli which exist in the environment. We are limited in responsiveness to these.

There is the whole external world, we can only know as much as we can respond to. We can only know reality through thought, feeling and sensing.

This external world is threefold for us and begins to evoke in us three kinds of experiences.

We should be lucky if the environment in which we were born provided us with stimuli in proportion to our inherited possibilities. Because this seldom happens we are "at cross purposes with ourselves" as we say. We receive from our environment stimuli out of proportion to the inherited arrangement. Born 1 in the thinking center, society tries to develop a scholar, scientist, philosopher, but born 1 in the thinking center, one will never become more than

1. One may fill this center ¼, ½ or ¾ or completely, but never will one become 2 in this center.

A 1,2,3 man should be placed in circumstances where he can develop or fill his centers according to their inherited possibilities.

QUESTION: Are centers inherited from one parent or another?

Answers: No.

A 3,3,3 environment is good for everybody. At 3,3,3 one would be a man, a normal man; everything else falls short. "Potential" means a certain possibility. Say 2,3,1 is potential at birth; the possibilities are that no one thus born will actualize this 2,3,1 of which he was capable.

QUESTION: Would one seek naturally the environment which he needs?

ANSWER: Unfortunately being already over weighted in one center he is dominated by this center and seeks naturally for the environment for this center and neglects the other two. He will then become more unbalanced all the time, more lopsided.

QUESTION: Would it not be good for society for the dominating center to go on developing, excelling, perhaps becoming a genius?

ANSWER: What we propose to do is to help the integration of what one has at birth. We may hope this may do something for society but to suffer and become distorted that society may benefit is doubtful as to good results.

3,3,3 never exist according to nature; such are not born. The chances statistically are infinitely against it. To be 3 in more than one center is rare.

All human beings are born three centered animals and differ in the potentiality of the three centers. This is the note Do.

There are many 1,2,3 people at birth, but the 3 it more rarely found than the 2 and the 1. There are no fractions at birth but in the actualizing there are fractions.

3,3,3 is not a potentiality of nature. Nature can occasionally make a 3 in one center, rarely in 2 and never in 3. "I" can make 3,3,3. This is the work of art, the work of "I."

In the Orient we say in general the environment plays for essence; in the West environment plays for personality, and plays to make all personalities alike. With us if any person shows any sign of being a genius he is hit on the head; if he shows a sign of being a saint he is not allowed in politics. In the East they are inclined to exhibit lopsidedness, in the West to conceal the truth. There are no psychoanalysts in the East.

You are hearing "3,3,3." How can one become 3,3,3? It can be answered.

What we are now is a hereditary and sociological fact. That we are hurt, angry, jealous etc., is due to the fact that we are struggling to be something which, we are not born to be, thanks to society, instead of striving to be that to which we were born. We are quarreling with our potentialities.

The happy person is one who is striving to actualize his potentialities. This happiness is rare because one never sees his potentialities. If you choose you choose from a distorted idea. It is impossible for us to arrive at a judgment of ourselves through introspection, this judgment is sociologically formed. You must depend on the same kind of evidence in judging yourselves which you depend on in judging others. We do not ask a person his opinion of himself. We must ignore the subjective opinion we have of ourselves.

There are impressions which evoke thought, impressions which evoke emotions, impressions which evoke sensations. We learn to talk thanks to environment. We learn to hate, love, suffer thanks to environment. We walk, run, rest in a chair thanks to environment.

All our impressions have been collected passively; this is why we are machines. We are not agents; we are reagents of what has been stimulated by environment. The machines are run by environment. The same dynamo runs every little machine.

There is a fourth center called "I," but never will we receive passively an impression in that center. All impressions in this center are taken actively and even God and all his angels cannot put an impression there. Only "I" can put impressions there. Someone has to direct our attention to the fourth center but only "I" can fill it.

<h2 style="text-align:center">MONDAY, 28 OCTOBER 1929</h2>

IV

Threefold Brains

Consider yourself as a psyche. We cannot break the walls of death to find what is beyond, but we can try to strip the psyche of a body.

I invite you to consider the types of body that are ordinarily associated with that octave of beings we call human. You are contemplating with an idea of incarnating the nature of the body with which for ordinary purposes you are to be associated. You will inquire—What is the character of the body I am supposed to incarnate to? What experiences will it be possible for me to have if I succeed in having mastery over it? I am assuming you would ask what experiences would you be bound to suffer and what experiences you would choose to have if you could choose.

Let us disabuse ourselves of the idea that there is or ever will be anyone who can choose for us with authority. You must not believe this; you must know. You must check, by experiment. To live by personal experience, by personal knowledge, means almost to be a normal human being.

If you are keeping in mind these two questions, the first thing I would say is that this human being is structural on a plane, not just cells and atoms but an organism. An organism is a whole which acts through its parts. One suggestion: this structure presents itself as an octave. Analyzing the human structure we find the first form is atom, the next form is molecule, the next cell. It began with one single cell composed of atom and molecule. The next form is tissue, the next bone. We go on in sequence to total aggregation. Each note supposes a previous note not like it. Next come organs; next systems, the coordination of organs, and the next is not so familiar. It is here we introduce an element about which you must think. We call it "system of brains," three in number. The cerebral located in the head, the spinal brain located in the spine and there is a third brain the center of which is in what is called the solar plexus.

We are aware of our solar plexus. We have a certain sudden experience and we say "I was hit in the stomach," or "my stomach turned over." Observe and you will find that no matter how intensity you have been feeling, the trouble is invariably there in the solar plexus. When next you find yourself wrought up, observe where it originates.

The waiting soul, which is watching to incarnate, has this bind of an organism, in which to manifest in building up this organism we have come to the note SI in the ascending scale. The seven controls the six, the six the five, the five the four, etc. By the time we arrive on this planet, we find these bodies prepared for us; machines to inhabit or to experience what is potential.

We ask "who am I"? For the moment all we will say is "I am that which coordinates all that is in the body before if arises, the principle of coordination of the seven." This principle is not of the same element as any part of the body, it is not a component part of the body, but it is not a stranger to it. This element it is which makes the unit.

We now pass on to the second QUESTION: "what experiences must I suffer with such a body and what experiences would I quote?"

First, I am limited in experiences to the pattern of the organism. Such as that body is, will be the definition of my passive experiences.

God alone knows what environment really is. In the absence of a medium between us and God, we are limited to the possible experiences of the body.

There are three brains; each can be said to yield a form of experience. We find we have thought; we claim to be able to think, we pride ourselves on this particular fact. We have the experience of connation (a modern psychology term). It is that experience we have when making exertion, making an effort against resistance, the experience of muscular exertion. All these experiences take place in the third brain, called "spinal brain." From this brain also come our movements; we also call this the instinctive brain. The second brain we call the solar plexus. Do not just listen to these words, but try to distinguish your states in this brain: hatred, anger, fear, shrinking, etc.

Recall the different qualities of your states in these three brains.

It is because we have these three brains that we can have these three kinds of experiences. Given another brain we might have another class of experiences, but we cannot conceive of what these experiences might be; we cannot imagine. We are cut out of knowing reality because we are limited to these three

229

brains. It is only to use words to admit that there may be other experiences of which we have no knowledge. All this begins to answer the first question. We are doomed to suffer experiences in these three categories: to think, to feel, to move.

QUESTION: What about the duality of man?

ANSWER: This organism is threefold. We have been in the habit of calling ourselves a duality because we have taken feeling and mind as one, and the body as the other; that mind consisted of two elements, thought and feeling. Thought is a comparison of images to discover their likenesses and differences.

QUESTION: What is memory?

ANSWER: We have 10.000 impressions of three different kinds making 30.000, entering our minds every second. These make chemical impressions; the body registers, remembers them all. This is the tact of memory. The ability to recall, to collect, is entering another field, the field of psychology.

We can say this body is the epitome of its physical history. Our bodies bear the marks of being battered about. Illustration: we make a dent in a tray. It carries the mark of that experience. The power of recollection is quite another matter.

The novelty of three-foldness is that each one of these brains is interdependent with the other two and independent of the other two. Each brain can act independently, but generally each brain acts interdependent. An activity begun in one brain is very likely to pass on to the other two brains. Nothing ever starts in the visceral brain; everything starts in either the cerebral or the spinal. Muscular exercises, massage, produce emotional states. This method is used by psychoanalysts. They manipulate muscles and release tensions which cause certain emotional states. In an emotional state we say "change your posture - you may be pressing on your solar plexus." An emotional state may be brought about quite physiologically. The cerebral brain can also control emotions. This is done by change of images. Our emotional brain is blind; it responds only to images, on the one side, and pressure on the other. We say the second brain is not a part of the other two but is the neutralizing force between the other two. When the other two are in perfect balance, there is no feeling.

Should there be the same quantity on both sides, there would be no emotion whatsoever. Emotion is merely the relation between the more and the less of brain and spine.

Everyone has experienced the emotion of anger. You are angry with a friend, with an officer, with an equal, with a superior, with an inferior, with an animal. Every one of these states of anger is different; the difference being determined by your image of the so called cause of your state of emotion.

QUESTION: How do you provoke a desired emotion in another?

ANSWER: By these two methods:

Change the visceral by, say, a good meal. The cerebral takes no part; but also no wish is evoked.

Evoke different images by changing the physical state; then other wishes may also be provoked.

We have a picture of this organism as being in a very bad way. Nature has not done us proud at all. The most valuable element, feeling, is at the mercy of two brains over, which we, as "I," have no control. This second brain is the register of the other two. Unless we can obtain control over the spinal or the cerebral or both, never will we have control over the second. Every honest hypothesis has its justification. There are certain justifications for the duality ideas.

There is one over two; this is the duality.

These statements are not speculations in the minds of those who make them, but statements of facts. They are not asking belief, but acceptance.

QUESTION: What experience is it possible for the psyche to have if the human organism is in control?

ANSWER: It is almost impossible to realize what consciousness is, it is to near. We are aware of two states, the state of sleeping and the state we call waking. Dreams may take place in a phenomenon of our waking consciousness. (I am speaking of consciousness in the ordinary sense).

Intuition (nosegays), subconsciousness, intuition of higher life, sixth sense, the time dimension, - all these precious and semiprecious ideas are only phenomena occurring in consciousness.

Distinguish between an event and an experience. The unconscious has no experiences; just a procession of events. Events are converted into experience by consciousness.

It is affirmed that the plane of waking consciousness, in which we experience three kinds of experiences, has as its possibilities the two other planes:

Regular consciousness

Self-consciousness

Super, or cosmic consciousness

These last two are not on the same plane as waking consciousness. In each of these fields you also can be aware of three forms of experience, but these differ not in degree but in kind. Also, on the cosmic plane, a being thinks, feels, moves; but how he thinks, feels, moves - that is different.

The potentiality of the organism is that it should experience thought, feeling and movement on three planes instead of on one only. The difference is in kind, not in degree.

V

When you come to the realization that the totality of yourself, what you have treasured, what your friends have admired, is totally useless, you will suffer, but we say, that it is only from this point that there is any hope for your becoming. We are so incredibly small, mere specks in our whole solar system.

Illustration; three flies in the Grand Central station; we are as a speck on one leg of one fly. This is an interesting theory, but the theory means nothing. Yet, speck of a speck of a speck that we are, we worship this speck of a speck of a speck that we are.

The speck comes of value only when you ask "what am I"? There is a turnover in the solar-plexus; one is as if stabbed in the heart, when it is truly felt that one is useless, worthless.

Never again, even by accident, can you expect anything pleasant to happen to you. Nor can you ever feel that your life is significant or that your life can have anything others do not have. Thereafter you can be content with what you get, regarding yourself as insignificant and worthless.

The difference between religion and the word. Religion is from the bed-rock of nothingness, an aspiration. A prayer is the wish of a being who knows himself. A wish is the appetite of a self-unknowing person. St Paul says:"They alone can......

If you are not in this state, perhaps one of the fears you had when coming to the place was that you would lose something, be robbed of something worthwhile. "I will do my best to rob you of it."

This is a matter of pure reason, just as you do not pretend to have acquired yourself, your stature, your color, etc., these being hereditary, so I go a step further and say you have acquired nothing, anymore than you have chosen the color of your eyes, hair, etc.

You pride yourself on your knowledge, your discrimination in art, etc, when all these things have been thrust upon you. You have had given to you a free gift, lust the data that you have sitting here, in a chair. Your cells, body, etc. is your data given you.

There is a science of changing your being and there is an art of changing it. An engineer deals with theory, mathematics, etc.; likewise, there is the technique of this method and the application. There are two steps: the theory and the application. The object of the method is the art of self-exploitation; the theory is the creature to be exploited. There is:

1.   The structure of the creature - how it is put together how it has come to be what it is - what has been put into it - the strength of the working structure

2.   Some recipe for working the creature

It is ridiculous to think that after a few moments work in a workshop that we can manipulate machines, as a motor car can be taken apart and put together. Maybe we will have to work a long time in the workshop, with patient study of the organism's structure, before we try to do anything about it, lest we find something worse than we had to start with.

Test: can you look at an image in the glass and forget that it is you? I will say that you will be surprised and say "is that me?" Illustration: trick mirrors. The only person we could allow to proceed with safety with an objective report of himself, is one who can thus look in a mirror. We are not yet speaking of the art of self-exploitation; we are only speaking of getting acquainted with the creature to be exploited.

We prescribe a certain method. I regard myself as recurring decimals, point 3, etc. This method consists in the attempt of being simultaneously and continually aware of movements, tone of voice, posture, facial expressions, and gestures. This technique will bring about in the " shortest length of time that state which will make it possible to go on with exploitation. We look in the mirror. We do not say "I wonder what it is going to do, etc." We take ourselves as an image. When we begin to be aware of ourselves as an image, we have completed the first step.

Our first step is to empty the body of psychology and confine it to the phenomenon of the physical behavior it exhibits. The first step is the knowledge of the physiology, and the overtones are the manner of behavior, - so simple, that five forms of exhibition complete the list.

There is to be no analysis of hopes and fears, no recollection of the past, no picturing of the future. Our manners of behavior are not to be described; they are to be noted. One is not to describe the angle of an arm in a posture, but to note the angle, i.e. be aware. You do not make a list of your habitual behavior, you collect facts of behavior. It is the fact that is to be noted. This gives you ability to attend, and this ability to attend will make it possible to attend to other things.

Illustration: Gymnasium work for a weak back weak from disuse. Do you remember the record of the exercises you have done? No! You say "feel my muscles." You acquired strength though the exercises have been forgotten. In continuing these exercises, you will have gathered strength to use in exploiting yourself.

We are not to observe others, but, because our eyes are open, we are bound to see others; only, we say, "I see because I look". I must look, here, acutely, not passively.

Observing does not grow easier. Memory plays the role of calling, but few get up. The alarm clock goes off, but few get up. There is satisfaction in the ability to attend, regardless of what is going on. One interesting thing to discover is how little there is that you observe that you are not interested in. You see a gesture; immediately you say "I don't like that gesture," it is like some other person's gesture. When you can make a pure observation, without comment, you then have a pure, an immaculate perception. In this work you refrain from making all the mechanical observations. The self-observation must be pure. All scientists talk about disinterestedness, but it is almost heartbreaking to see that all have their own subjective idea. There are none I would trust to make a disinterested report of a human being.

There is a certain amount of objective truth in all beings, there truly is.

The degree of disinterestedness in the approach to any problem is in taking a mental attitude. This is the method of achieving disinterestedness toward this precious self.

The outline of this talk this evening.

Each sentence has been unnecessarily elaborated. Illustration: one tree giving the impression of a whole forest. One tree in a dooryard—a man walking around lost as if in a whole forest.

I do not wish you to be lost in a forest.

First: you are the most important person in the two thousand million people on the earth.

Second: you are the object of all that there is in life.

Third: you are the person about whose abilities and desires you know least.

Fourth: you are the person

This is the theory and application.

Illustration: Calf love converted into bull hate, both without identification. With this method you love yourself less and hate yourself less. This is not toleration, but recognizing a fact. It is not proper to love, it is not proper to hate, it is not proper to be indifferent toward oneself. So long as you are in any of these states, you cannot be happy; you cannot discharge your function as a human being. Self-respect, complacency, is an artificial grafting. When we can say "I alone did it," we can have respect for self. About all my accomplishments I can have no pride. That, from day to day, I can more simultaneously and continually observe, this is my pride, - this is laying up treasure, where moss and rust do not corrupt. The ultimate objective is to manipulate imagination - - conscious self-exploitation.

You are concerned with the maximum satisfaction. We don't care two pence about cosmic consciousness, or divinity, or God; but in our own maximum satisfaction; perhaps this is your objective duty. Make it a continuation worthy of its biological and sociological beginning. Think of the time and labor involved before biological man appeared. Then consider the further time required for this sociological development.

We have a physical body which is not mean.

We have a soul which is not barbaric.

Can you perfect this; carry it on its way?

You say "I have a passion for an automobile, for money, etc. - I say "what for?"

We cannot get far until we have classified ourselves as to type. I see before me many types, like a dog fancier at a show. The dog fancier sees Newfoundland's, Terriers, etc. I see those before me who personally wish to be, to do, to know. Which one are you essentially? Do you wish to be something more than you are? Do you wish to do something more than you do? Do you wish to know something more than you know?

We begin self-study by trying to classify ourselves according to these three large classes of types.

If death should overtake a million people, only two or three would have any reason for continuing life. We live from day to day, for nothing other than to meet the happenings of the day. None ever asks what he is living for; what keeps him alive; what he is hoping for.

Questions that cannot be answered:

When you come to die, what is it that would be an alternative to life? What do you hope to accomplish from continuing to be alive?

If your ultimate object is to *be*, you also must know and *do* if your prime object is to *know*, you must know as much as possible, do as much as possible and be as much as possible. All types have their field for work.

For each end the other two are sublimated. Your type determines the base of your triangle. If I ask: What is your work to be? I will not ask for reply.

There are possible states of being and impossible states of being. I cannot be an apple tree or a giraffe, no matter how much I may wish to be. There is a limit to the possibilities for each person.

What do you wish to know? What do you wish to do? This field is over-populated. Examine yourself quite honestly before God.

The major part of our life is taken up in filling up time. Like spoiled children, to live is to be spending our time to gratify wishes. The importance is not to fulfill our wish, but to pursue its fulfillment. Perhaps the best therapy is to find out our wish and to begin on its fulfillment.

Supposing you were doomed to immortality, - nothing could destroy you, - you are you,- and nothing can make you another. You are struck suddenly with the realization that you have to continue - what would you do? You have infinite time. You say: "I would like to learn languages." You could learn all languages, but the time would come when you would pray to cease to be. I ask again: "What work would you wish to do"? We now say that we wish to live, But what reason have you? What are you living for? This method is intended primarily for those who have an inkling of what they are living for. Someone may say he is interested in painting, but in fact, he is interested in wheelbarrows. This method is for those who are looking first of all to know "what kind of a being am I?

These bodies you have brought with you tonight are no more yours than mine. Everything is a gift. Your status as a doer, a knower and a being is what use you are making of this body, this organic mechanism, which is a present to you. What can you do to have full use and control of this body, which is a gift to you?

I consider time but a few moments. Thirty, forty, fifty years ago, there would be sitting on your chair a single, tiny cell. At the crisis of birth, there is a fully formed infant. But a long history goes before. There is a state in which it is invertebrate, vertebrate, monkey, human. This is its biological history. The child comes with no memories, no experiences of the senses, no intuition. It now enters the sociological environment of his parents, and on the conditions of its environment depend its sociological development.

We learn to speak, to walk, etc. up to the age of majority. Here we reach the end of a certain phase and the being is then considered to be responsible. This is the time when life is supposed to begin. The first stage is biological; the second is biological and sociological, and the third stage is sociological. At this age, the age of majority, in 99 out of 100 cases, contraction sets in. We know what to expect - a return to the womb. This is what psychoanalysts also say. How for a word used by Eddington, Whitehead and Jeans, not a word used in the Sunday papers— "time-tube."

We were all only red, wrinkled infants. We begin to resent nurse; we begin to go to school, to college, to think we know it all. We grew up from a cell, say, dressed for a party, limbs, arms and all the rest, and we arrive and for twenty, forty, sixty, ninety years, we go through a series of forms, with which form do you identify yourself? You find it difficult to answer. So we suggest the use of the time-tube. We say "when I was a little girl," etc. Each individual makes his own tube.

(Fourth dimension states are called time, read Hinton.)

We should see the forms through which an object has passed; it's history. This requires imagination, facts and measurements. We do not say at the moment when this is involution and when evolution. We simply advise people to look at objects in this way. From the footprints of our civilization, a million years from now, our civilization could be built up. We should look at cross-sections and build up the rest. We call this looking at the fourth dimension. God alone knows what anyone of us may be.

We are a procession of fate in time.

Next step: why is it that our original seed turns out to be a human being?

236

We say a human being is an organism with three brains. Had we been born monkeys, we would have two brains, or, had we been born fish, we would have one brain. We have a brain for being, a brain for doing, and a brain for knowing. Up to the age of majority, our physiology is set in a general form which will last the rest of our lives. Nature does all this; we do not attend to this. But nature says "I provide you with a body and three brains." What you do inside your body, do with your three brains, nature does not care.

We are ceased on first by parents, second by teachers, etc. By all this you must see what kind of brain one will have at twenty-one. If his brain has not been used by himself, at twenty-one it will be undeveloped. If his emotions have been curbed or indulged, etc., he will be infantile. The first center will be very large in comparison. He can walk to his office, smoke, drink, drive a car, be a regular Robinson Crusoe, build a hut, fish, and all this with only two brains developed and one brain artificially developed. No wonder we may be regarded as inferior.

It is so ridiculous that other people take their eye off the ball. It is serious that we take our own eye off the ball. We are infantile. It would raise my hair to say about myself what I say about Orage. I look in the mirror; I know no one more hateful, or more despicable than Orage. A creature so lopsided, so infantile in its sociological development, there is nothing to retrieve him. The only comfort is that I have infinite time to develop a mechanism which society has almost completely spoiled.

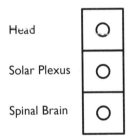

This is a correct portrait of every individual.

One who is moved only by the descriptions of the emotions of others is dying in the emotional center. Illustration: Shelley's "Ode to the Skylark." Contrast Shelley's "Ode to the Skylark" and Charlotte P. Gilman's poem on Shelley's Skylark. His was real emotion; hers was not evoked by the skylark but by his emotions about the skylark.

One who is not interested in boats, being in a boat, about a garden, being in a garden, is dying in the instinctive center. One who is not interested in the new discoveries of science is dying intellectually. We develop three centers; interest should be shown in all three types of interest.

Edison is 50,000 years old. What do you suppose a man may be in another 50,000 years? His physiology may be much the same; perhaps a third eye might be added.

Reformers are dreaming without making a picture of what the results of their reforms may be, when 50.000 years have passed. Would it be a world of pugilists, Platos or Jesus Christs?

We come back to what the individual can do in his lifetime. We say "only the potentialities which we realize today can be realized by the future race."

Actualize all wishes only at your own choice, voluntarily and on your own terms. To have complete understanding, complete feeling, complete ability to do, is to fill up the three brains. Merely because an emotion is provoked by an image in the mind, or by a feeling in the body, does not matter. An emotion is always evoked by one or the other, but they are genuine while they last. Illustration: reading a book and blubbering. Show me someone who is moved by a work of art and I say his emotion is still alive.

You are looking at the world through three mediums simultaneously. You get a sense of images in one medium, in another, feeling, in another connation. Seeing ourselves this way we will, every one of us, change, not metaphorically but psychologically. We shall begin to think more, we shall begin to feel more, we shall begin to do more.

There is a possibility of 343 emotions (7 times 49) Generally speaking, an individual experiences about 27. The hope is to experience every species of emotion.

The race cannot do more than what is potentially in the race. Only what the individual can do, the race can do.

There are vestigial organs - for which we have no more use, like the appendix, - and anticipatory organs for which we do not know the use yet.

in the back of the head: consciousness
in the heart: individuality
in the spine: will
Consciousness is determined by our actively taken impressions.
A will is a purpose pursued irrespective of any wish.
Time.
Consciousness is the simultaneity of thought processes.

MONDAY, 18 NOVEMBER 1929

VII

You have only to change in one of your centers and you see this room differently.

This external world may be called a very large X or unknown. The external world for us is unknown because we are conditioned as we are.

We differ from the animals only because we have three screens; the higher animals have two screens, the lower one screen and the vegetables have no screen.

Environment is the seed of possible stimuli. Environment gives you your ideas of the external world. We collect what we wish through our senses and create our sensations and stimuli.

"I" only contacts the external world through these three screens. Without all the senses it does not mean that the world has changed, it only means that the organism is changed. The world does not change because one is blind or deaf.

The first screen is our body. We come in contact with the world through our senses, two, five or ten, whatever we have. This is our only experience with the outside world. We depend on these senses - taste, sight, smell, etc. in this way we do not differ from the reptiles. The reptiles have one screen only, one center for external conceptions.

Another screen is the feeling or emotional center. Our first classification of the external world is in this center and is " I like" and "I don't like" an elemental classification. There is no such thing in the world as an unpleasant taste, touch, etc. there is only taste, touch, etc., and we make the classification "I like" and "I don't like." One rate of vibration makes an unpleasant face, another a pleasant face; there is nothing of mathematics in this which makes the difference; it is the emotional center, positive and negative emotions, (I like and I don't like) and they have nothing to do with electricity or....

There is an octave in emotions ranging from low to high like the keyboard of a piano, and the notes struck in this octave of emotions are lasting in the same way. Our emotions are unpleasant or pleasant according to vibrations. When these—"I like and I don't like" are assembled, we have the contents of our emotional center. There are two elements in the motional center states of pleasant and unpleasant emotions.

Negative emotions spend your energy without profit to yourself. Negative emotions are devitalizing. Indulgence in them breaks down cells and destroys the body.

The two-screened animals also like and dislike. With the endowment of the third screen human beings is given a responsibility not given to animals and reptiles. The wretched thought screen in us is no longer "I like" and "I don't like" but raises the question of "is it right or is it wrong that I like or don't like?" It begins comparison. Thought is a classification of sensations.

QUESTION: What is judgment?

ANSWER: How can I judge without comparison? The word "judgment" implies the final conclusion on comparisons with respect to likenesses and differences. My judgment is a final verdict of a series of comparisons. You cannot help your judgments any more than you can your likes and dislikes. But in the third center is the possibility of making conscious judgments.

We each have three center or brains. The total number of sensations coming into these brains since birth is given as ten millions per second by way of each sense. Endowed with ten senses, each of us has received 100 million per second since birth. By this you will see how complex our bodies are from the point of view of sensations. These sensations are classified in infancy into "I like" and "I don't like"; already we have this second screen; it begins to operate in the cradle. It is the origin of spoiled children and of all our prejudices. Long before we have judgment we begin the emotional classification automatically. How many emotional experiences have we? As many as we have sensations. Divide sensations into two halves positive and negative then judgment enters.

Sensation, feeling, thought are three possible responses to reality. They are forever different in kind but not unrelated in interest; there is an interblending. The three screens are not of the same strength in ordinary individuals; all depends on their relative inherited strength. One screen may become defective but the scheme has not gone wrong.

An instinctive center may have the strength to live 500 years; an emotional center to live 100 years; a thinking center to live 20 years, we are at any moment at a different age in the different centers. We may be approaching old age in one center and comparatively young in another center. A common phenomenon is the cessation of life in the thinking center while emotional and instinctive centers are still strong. A man has been to college, attains business success and the mind dies; he cares only to live in the other two centers. He likes to be entertained, to go to the theater, etc or to play golf like a boy. You know at one time he had exercised his mind. The answer is he is dead in his thinking center. Our fate is that the three centers differ in each individual; this difference depends on heredity and the winding up of the three centers by environment.

We are not deceived beyond a few years as to the age of a person, as to body; but to estimate the age emotionally and intellectually is more difficult. You can't treat an adult as an infant or vice versa, nor can you treat old age as an adult. We treat everyone according to their physical age, regardless of their emotional or intellectual age. When you are capable of seeing their emotional or intellectual age, you can treat people fairly, according to their three ages. Ask yourself, whatever his physical age may be, what is his emotional and intellectual age.

We say that we cannot change these three centers except by new consciousness. By chance they may be renewed temporarily - we sometimes speak of one as raised from the dead.

QUESTION: Is there not such a thing as affinity?

ANSWER: Affinity is following inclination. There certainly is - this is like vibrations attracting each other. Illustration: the magnet drawing the metal. It is the fate of the metal to be drawn by the magnet. Fate is an accident. Read any of the latest books on psychology. It is by accident that the future for anyone of us will be glorious or inglorious. We can acquire no new faculty, no new sense, no new center; we can only develop what faculties, what centers we have. The only way we can change is voluntarily not by being spoonfed by others and not by our forbears who in turn were also conditioned.

Up to nineteen years of age, the three centers march together; then one may begin to drop out, say the intellectual center. A real educational system would guard against spending emotional and intellectual energy and would also strengthen both. In such an education, the centers would march together, say to the age of ninety - this would be a ripe old age. We do not die in a center from using it but from waste and fatigue.

There is what is called a second wind and a third wind, a new lease on life. This may be brought about by chance or design. There are glands which can be opened up and give new energy for a time. You get your second wind between openings of "cans" (I can).

There is a second physical wind, a second emotional wind and a second intellectual wind. Illustration: someone from the physical point of view can lift 500 pounds; he says he can lift no more. It is possible to put him into such a state that he can lift twice that weight but this would not mean that he would have the use of it. In a certain emotional state, one can lift beyond one's natural strength. There are emotional states when you feel you have superhuman strength - we say "in tune with the infinite."

Intellectually there are times when you feel you can understand anything - things extraordinarily clear to you. Everyone has experiences of power greater than they ordinarily use.

Our aim in this method is to develop these three centers. We do not say as Freud does that these centers have been sublimated when we find our second wind. We do not find our second wind necessarily by exhausting our first wind. So we do not speak of supermen. We do not say "higher thinking center," "higher emotional center" and "higher instinctive center" because this suggests these three centers have been sublimated. Instead we say will, consciousness and individuality. Use second wind instead of sublimation.

The three Yoga develop each center separately. Saint Francis of Assisi had extraordinary emotional experiences, but physically he was weak and intellectually ordinary.

QUESTION: What about Samson?

ANSWER: Samson had a momentary physical experience.

Plotinus, Gnani Yoga, is an example of a developed third center but was ordinary in the other two. Jesus was supported almost entirely by his disciples, who were chiefly Bhakti Yogi and we have no report on him physically or intellectually; somethings, however, do creep through. It was said to the Jews he was a stumbling block and to the Greeks foolishness.

While our schools are all of the same pattern, the ancient schools aimed at developing one or the other of the three superstates.

Hatha Yoga developed the instinctive center.

Bhakti Yoga developed the emotional center

Gnani Yoga developed the intellectual center.

Each produces a monster. Plotinus was weak, probably could not shake himself. The Bhakti Yogi we call "silly saint." The Hatha (or Raja) Yogi produces the ascetic.

There is a fourth Yoga, the aim of which is to produce simultaneously and harmoniously the effect of the other three Yogas, the technique of which is this method. There cannot be a school in this method.

There are plenty of monks who wish to achieve contact with Jesus. Each Yoga cannot promise results.

A Hatha Yogi can show pupils who after one or three years can perform certain things. These schools are always full.

(The psychological exercises are elemental Yoga exercises).

The first exercise in the Bhakti Yoga schools is to manifest the opposite of what you feel. If you feel a pleasant emotion, you exhibit an unpleasant one, and vice versa. You contradict your own inclinations. Try this as a simple exercise. As a practice exercise, stop with the first, there is less waste of energy.

There are dual schools for developing two centers at once, but no triple schools. There is no salvation in any Yoga; each should be taken with a grain of salt. To take them with a grain of salt was whispered information given to Princes.

The schools of Egypt were different, for they took Egypt to be a physical body and divided it geographically accordingly. In Thebes were only admitted those who had been through all schools (here they approached the teaching of the fourth Yoga).

There is another way of reaching super-consciousness but its aim is for one center to rule over the other two; generally this occurs in the emotional center, this being the most fragile shell-shocked. Only people in this state wish to be back in their normal state of emotions.

The Whirling Dervishes whirl until they get into a super-state of body the body identifies with the psyche. In this state they can cut the body, see blood and stop its flow. Their physiology has become a part of their psychology.

The fourth Yoga is to do the work simultaneously of the other three. It is more ambitious and at the same time more modest.

No genius, no matter on which plane, can deceive us into wishing to be like him. How can three be developed simultaneously? The difficulty lies in simultaneity.

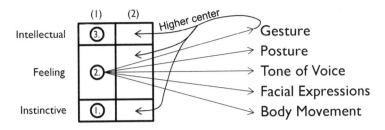

Remember the diagram

Through self-observation each of the three centers will send impressions to their equivalent higher center.

Faculty is the evidence of experience.

Transient emotions are lower emotions. Lasting emotions are higher emotions.

The first step is observation of your own behavior. The three centers no one sees. We will never see our own centers. When you look at someone else you do not see three brains; you see five manners of behavior; out of their organs come five manners of behavior the totality of their behavior.

You say: "I must be aware of my five forms of behavior." In doing this you will become aware of all three centers. Through all five manners of behavior come primarily from one center, they all have elements of the three centers. All three centers blend to produce every form of behavior. Every gesture blends the three centers. If it arises in the first center, it is 3 in the first center and, say, 2 in the second center and 1 in the third. Its elements have these proportions. If aware of such a gesture we build in the three centers individuality, consciousness and will, in the same proportion.

(The clairvoyant reads shades of voice, etc.)

The Mona Lisa's smile is a compound. The portrait is a diagnosis of her by the painter; whether the smile was in the subject or was intentionally put there by the painter we do not know. Therefore we go to the person and not to the portrait for the truth." From this point of view a diagnostician cannot find anyone uninteresting.

Any person contains a key to read not only themselves but all others. We check one language of behavior against another. Any person may be affected in one manner and not in another.

QUESTION: Does imagination have its source only in emotion or also in thought?

ANSWER: Imagination is the source of the material upon which the thought acts.

MONDAY, 25 NOVEMBER 1929

VIII

QUESTION: What do we mean when we say "our potentialities"?

ANSWER: We mean something quite concrete, something which everyone can see. It is your body - harmless, apparently despised body - that is the subject of our study.

What body or bodies? There are those that claim to diagnose - astrologers, for instance, or handwriting readers, etc. 999 answers out of a thousand are wrong. Diagnosing others, as diagnosing ourselves, is equally wrong.

Our life depends on the understanding of ourselves. Who is there that never commits errors so that his friends suffer? Who has never behaved in such a way that he has afterward felt regret?

The skill we use in handling ourselves is as amateurish as that used by a person given an automobile to drive who has never driven.

As far as direct self examinators go there are none in civilization. There is no one here who knows himself or herself as well as anyone who has known them for five minutes. Still we act on the supposition that we know ourselves. We make every variety of mistakes and then wonder who has made the mistake. We always put the blame on others or on circumstances. We have neither the courage nor technique to observe ourselves and this is the price we pay for not looking at ourselves in the same way we look at others. Give yourself your name and imagine you see that person and ask: Can she be trusted? Is she a liar? Is she capable of loyalty? Is she serious about anything? Has she intelligence? Is she where she wishes to be? Is she lazy? Is she self-indulgent? Is she selfish? Is there any one she loves? Is there anyone for whom she would put herself to real trouble? Could she take a vow to do any work? Is she a snob? Has she any idea of why she is alive? Could she tell, if at the point of death, what she would do if she were given another ten years to live? Has she ever wished to excel in anything to be of service? Or has she been in pursuit of pleasures? Do the words "conscience," "responsibility," "religion," "womanliness," mean anything to her? Is she complaining? Does she think the world owes her anything? What does she do for society? How does she spend her day? Before going to sleep does she review the day or pass into oblivion? In waking does she have a purpose for the day? Does she ever make effort against inclination? What character did she have as school girl? How does she appear today? Could she write on a piece of paper what others say of her? Has she a pleasant temper, or morose? Has she ever had the strength to apologize? Has she used words as a snake uses its sting, to throw at someone whom she hates? Has it occurred to her at night to recall her remarks during the day and ask what kind of a person was this who said these things?

One who asks these questions is truly a new species, not one which springs up in evolution.

This self candor is different from candor about others. Is Orage a person who has the tendency to say things to please others? Is he inclined to lie? I could not answer these questions if attached to myself.

You cannot answer these questions accurately at first - this is not important; it is necessary that you give answers. You can say: "Yes, I am deceitful; I shall lie to my best friend" and then pass on to another QUESTION: "Am I a person who can be relied upon?" You say: "Yes, she can be relied upon." You will be pleased and begin to purr in answering these questions that someone (your-self) has taken interest in you.

I see scars on your faces; you have suffered in your pride. If I could tell you of a beauty parlor where you could be freed from scars you would go. I am offering you something which will take the sting out of every possible thing which could be said to you or about you: it is that you have discovered all these things first for yourself and can say, "Yes, it is true."

Socrates asked his friend what he saw in his face and received the reply: I see greed, hatred, malice, etc." Socrates said, "Good. Shake hands. I have seen them all there too."

If you discover yourself first you will not suffer.

When you have so diagnosed yourself you will ask, "What is to be done?" You may think you will be hopeless and in despair but it will not be so. You know how to say such things as will depress an enthusiastic friend. You see their spirit depart; you know the effect that is produced on one's self when hostile remarks are made from the outside; but the effect on yourself will be the reverse when you have stated about yourself: "I am weak, lazy, etc. Then when others say these things to you, you feel relief - you can be yourself and like a little child - innocent. You can never fall below your diagnosis but can have new courage, new spirit by the hope that you can become better. You cannot become worse.

I stress this because without some effort at self candor there is no hope of arriving anywhere. All the rest may be philosophy. You can go to the theater, to lectures, etc., and think you are being educated by churning over and over what you already have. The vast number of people after twenty years of age never progress but they go back; and back not to childhood but to childish-ness.

Evolution is an accepted fact.

This is highly prejudiced and leaves out the millions of creatures who have lived on this planet and are extinct. Nature does not care. What takes place in nature is a number of changes.

We have been in a state of optimism - one of the superstitions of the nine-teenth century and which the twentieth century will refute.

If you do not do something for yourself, nothing will be done. You will grow worse as time goes on. By luck this may not be, but most people will grow worse until time to die. The subject to study is one's self; the technique such as you use on anyone else for whom you feel responsible; brother, sister, children; anyone emotionally in your charge.

Think of someone whose welfare is some concern of yours. What effort do you make to better their condition, to know their character, their weaknesses, their strength, their needs? What have you done for them, I ask you in God's name, compared with what you have done for yourself?

Now see someone for whom you care and you wish to help, but it is beyond your being able to help them. I say you cannot help them until you have come to be the person who knows himself. It is absurd to try to help others when you cannot help yourself.

The educators are all so prejudiced they cannot help imparting their prejudices to pupils whether they are good for the pupils or not. The subjective element is so great that no one can be trusted to help others.

A psychoanalyst will begin to attribute to patients the very complex he himself has. If this is the case with trained minds imagine how wrong it would be for the untrained to attempt help. They would give the worst advice that could possibly be given.

This subjectivity - self ignorance - is the beam with which we try to cast out the mote which is in our neighbor's eye. The beam is self ignorance; we cast it out by self-observation. You look at the creature bearing your name and say about it what you would say with long acquaintance. It will be relative truth if not actual truth. Then only will you venture to prescribe for others.

In judging yourself all depends on the mood you are in; according to your mood you will be extreme in condemning or praising yourself. It will not be pure judgment; it will be relative to your emotional state.

"When a man begins to study others he will color his conclusions by his own subjectivity." James discussions. There is a simple person, a concrete figure, for me to study. I don't need a book or introspection.

Always the difficulty occurs of expecting a logical proof instead of a fractional result. "Once I was blind; now I can see" — pragmatism, result following cause; not logic, preceding cause.

Psychoanalysis, in my opinion, is a form of Voodoo with obscene rites...

A psychoanalyst at seventy years, head of one of the largest institutions in the world his wife became insane, his son a criminal, his daughter married three times unhappily. He did not know that he was the cause. I say the world is literally crazy; knowledge of others is of more importance than self-knowledge is the state. "The eyes of the world are on the ends of the earth."

Illustration: You have cancer. You do not say, "How interesting. Now, how did I acquire that?" I find an inclination to lying. I do not inquire how I came to have it.

QUESTION: Is this self-knowledge done alone?

ANSWER: Yes, it needs no jargon, no text books, and no group meetings.

All that we are, we are because of heredity and sociology. We wish to know what kind of joint heredity and sociology is here in us. What the being is at the moment we call pragmatic psychology.

To the one interested we prescribe that you be continuously and simultaneously observing the five manners of behavior of the body you take with you. You will be performing the greatest usefulness you can be to yourself and human society because you are doing this.

QUESTION: Shall we take all this you have been saying on faith?

ANSWER: No. Either you leave it or you experiment; either you are interested in the experiment or not interested. The skeptical - inquiring - will personally experiment or find out if it is so or not. It is not a question of logical truth. It is a question of practical truth.

Watson said about this method: "This is not—come see, it is—go do."

If you are skeptical, do not believe what was said, I ask you in the next state of temper to continue your state but listen to your tone of voice, etc. One experience of this kind will do more than a thousand years in the group. Just listen to what the other person has to listen to from you you suddenly have a feeling of stark amazement - your tone of voice immediately changes; your vocabulary will fall into a different kind.

Some blame others for disagreeable states or if they have grown beyond this stage they blame sociology, heredity; this is also stupid.

Being aware of states here and now the states begin to change.

QUESTION: Does the method applied to such states wear out?

ANSWER: Every state of negative emotion is like a blown up rubber animal. There are different kinds of negative emotions but all are inflated. Prick any kind of a rubber animal and it collapses. Self-observation is like the prick; the principle always works. However, this habit of using pins may make it impossible to blow up the same animal (negative emotion) again and again.

A negative state is one personally unpleasant to you. Also whatever things we do which would be disagreeable to us if we saw them, we will stop when self observing.

Illustration: A public official, on seeing himself on the screen, soon after some public occasion in which he figured, resigned from office.

Second illustration: The cure of a case of stammering at John's Hopkins, (watch for the stammering and observe, and it ceases.)

We defy you to continue to talk disagreeably if you hear yourself.

"Self-consciousness" so called, is acute awareness of somebody else not acute awareness of self. The more truly self-conscious you become the less conscious you are of others.

The more you attend to what you are doing the more you will understand what others are doing.

Everybody's portrait, standing erect, is a tower of three stories:

247

Thinking story

Feeling story where is all wishing etc.

Doing story – where chores are done
kitchen – food, drink – new clothes for parlor use.

In this bottom story the most of us live habitually.

In the feeling story, or parlor, we live a large part of the time.

In the thinking story, the study, we live infrequently.

Ordinary beings live: 9/10 in kitchen, 9/100 in parlor, 1/100 in study.

The way to control our thoughts, feelings and actions is to establish here (see above) "I." This is not theoretical psychology but practical psychology. So try to see if you can continue an ill temper when aware of its manifestations. This is a receipt for continuous happiness.

When you are in a state of worry will you go to the mirror (not go over the circumstances) and say, "Ah, now I see how you look when you are worrying." You see the droop of the mouth, the color of complexion, the eyes. You walk and feel constriction. It is as interesting as being pregnant - there is pressure of blood at the back of the head, etc.

Then suddenly you discover you have lost your worry; before you have exhausted your symptoms, you wait for more, they do not come.

Illustration: A professor at Columbia lay in wait for another toothache; he had discovered sixteen symptoms, he wanted to get them all.

Any negative emotion should be taken as the professor took the toothache; instead of apprehending the next attack you will be looking forward to it but it won't appear.

One reason for the value (necessity) of these groups is because the world is rotten with negative emotions, so it is almost impossible to live in it, and here we learn of a simple way of curing negative emotions.

QUESTION: What happen to positive emotions when observed?

ANSWER: Observe yourself in a positive state and you enhance that state. A positive state is one which is pleasurable to you. You would like it repeated.

Negative emotions you do not like, they are at the expense of your well being a debt you have to overcome them. In one bank account there is a balance; in the other account a debt.

$1000	
$500	$500
minus	plus

In a positive state I add to the balance.
In a negative state I diminish the minus.

(A new idea, not ever given before in other groups, now given for the first time.)

When I observe my tone of voice, movement of arm, etc. since there are three centers involved, the impression is threefold.

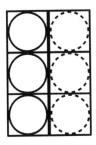

The element of the third center in the impressions goes here.

The element of the second center goes here.

The element of the first center goes here.

By the simple act of observing you are taking three orders of impressions and so all the centers begin to develop.

We have no "I" in these three centers and never will we take an impression here.

Faculty is the evidence of experience. Transient emotions are lower emotions. Lasting emotions are higher emotions.

MONDAY, 2 DECEMBER 1929

IX

We have a sense perfectly real that we share the soil of the planet with two thousand million people who are born at the rate of one every three seconds and die at the rate of one every three seconds.

It is literally inconceivable that we should realize this and have an idea that we are of any great Importance. Astronomy will tell us that our earth is only a remote planet revolving about a remote sun which is only a speck in a universe where there are millions and millions of suns.

Physicists will tell us atoms....(text missing)

Illustration: A fly on the ceiling of the Grand Central Concourse; we are as a speck on one wing.

I am trying to approach this from another way. We can travel around the world and meet a specimen of every race. Make this an effort in concrete imagination - while we sit here there are two thousand million people on the planet, being born and dying at the rate of one every three seconds. Every moment of our day is a present moment for everyone else. Every disease possible to man is occurring, being suffered, somewhere at this time. No one can have an experience that has not been experienced by someone a moment before us or a moment after.

There is no unique accident.

There is no unique deformity.

There is no unique experience.

There is no unique being.

You will begin to realize there is a community of total experiences which we share to a certain extent. This realization gives a person a perspective on himself.

No experiences are of any value. The organism remains what it was before though the effect may be integrating or disintegrating. Only purposive, intended experience brings about change:

-transformation

-development

-understanding

We do not compare human beings with atoms or with the universe but human beings with individualities. Each individual is a cell in total humanity. I wish you to turn your attention to the one cell in the human organism which happens to bear your name and say: "there is one being in the universe that I can turn my attention to" and say:" I am responsible for that cell."

I say "you have brought your bodies with you." By virtue of the use of the word "I" it is possible to look at the body. I can look at my hand; I can look at my arm, I can be aware of my body walking—back, legs, arms in walking. But how much of myself can I get into focus as I can my arm? Can I see my organism as clearly as you see it? No, I cannot see the totality of Orage as clearly as you can, not in the same way you can see him, but I can have the same image in every other sense except sight.

Close your eyes—how clearly can you see my image? It blurred. There is the possibility that your mind can project the image as clearly, as an image in a dream and hold it for a time and turn your attention to something else and then back and see the image still there. Now will you try seeing yourself and saying: "There walks the (image) being which is myself, there walks the creature which is my chief responsibility among two thousand million creatures that are now existing." Saying this you would not say: "There walks the most colossally important person in the universe and for this person I am responsible" instead you will see yourself as an ordinary creature.

It is a fact, that you know yourself better than anyone else knows you, you history, your ambitions, etc., though it's also true that you know yourself less you do not know how you look to others - you cannot for the moment make any comparative judgment - you have on the other hand the advantage of knowing its history, its plans and many of its secrets. On one side you have this knowledge; on the other you have none. Out of the materials you have, you can create the portrait of the one creature for which you are destined to be responsible.

Still having this image before you, what is this being from point of view of ability of mind? ability of feeling? ability of doing? What has this image to make it capable to handle this creature?

Within fifty years, one hundred years, everyone here will be dead (do not accuse me of metaphysics) but change will take place between now and the grave which will not be a change pleasing to our friends, to ourselves. This is one reason of our infantile state - we dare not project our imagination into this picture of what is going to happen to us. Instead of doing this, we have a child's imagination that all will go well for us, our friends will help us out, etc., when we should be planning what we should like to become in mind, body and emotions, five, ten, fifteen years hence, in respect to quality.

What is the force of your wish about the future of this creature? What is the amount of effort you are making to become the kind of person you would like to be? Or are you leaving it to hope?

An ideal is an instrument for measuring ideals and it should register the kind of emotional experiences etc., which you would wish to have - the kind of person you would wish to become.

Here is the moment when the human psyche is as slippery as an eel. There is a reason for facing these facts about ourselves but we prefer to consider others when we try to pin ourselves down to facts about ourselves and this is the primary downfall in trying to see the clear picture of oneself in point of view mentality.... in human relations.

If you are pleased with the picture of yourself, find self-satisfaction, I would not crack the ego of this superiority complex. If you are not pleased, what step are you taking to become that which you would be?

The urge of self perfection is the shame of self dissatisfaction the urge is not the allurement of perfection.

There is what we are, what we wish to become, what the means are to become what we wish.

QUESTION: What is the means?

ANSWER: This is the picture of what we are now.

So that the now can be transformed into the hence

NOW   MEANS   HENCE

What we are now transformed into the hence, five, ten, fifteen years, when we will still be human beings.

We think, we feel, we act, how do we think, feel and act?

I am not inviting you to look into a mirror which shows you as you think you are but into a mirror showing what you really are. When this portrait

251

which is real is reflected in our glass instead of the one we ordinarily see there, the feeling of self satisfaction will not be great and we will wish to change the portrait.

We say our state is this:

Mental ability

Emotional ability

Ability to do

I invite you to say in which respect you do wish to improve.

The "I" means the lowest marks a generous allowance. What is your ambition to be more of in the future than you are now? This will settle your type.

Do you wish more understanding of books, art, Einstein? This is the type "1," whose ambition it is to improve in mind.

Type "2" is one who wishes to feel more, more delight, more happiness, etc.

The "3" type wishes to do more, to be more practical.

You must belong to one type but all types are mixed, for to belong to one pure type would be a misfortune. It would mean one of the Yogas monsters.

Types are generally a mixture of two centers preeminent. If three centers were equally developed it would mean a well-rounded person.

The desire to improve in one center is largely hereditary. We might say every one of us is an incarnated wish or set of wishes.

There is in man an urge for growth because he is not developed. What makes the tree go on? The fact it is alive. The animal is satisfied to live. "Man has the wish to live, the wish to live well, the wish to live better." (The function of reason in man)

Orage

WILL AND WISH

(CONTINUED FROM 11 APRIL 1938)

We have experienced, at least in our psychological registration of processes, the difference between doing and not-doing. There is here no real distinction, because both are in the field of reaction. We distinguish by the quantity of inertia overcome by constant effort that is analogous to our experience of overcoming inertia.

Next: Character of inertia overcome. Again, we must fall back on our mechanical experience. How do we distinguish not only between quantity but also quality of effort? Do we not often say: I had to put a quantity of effort into that; or: you have no idea the kind of effort, I had to make. That is we *do* commonly distinguish both in quantity and quality.

Someone in the group questions: Isn't it always really quantity?

Orage asked him to compare the kind of effort needed by Milton in beginning Paradise Lost and that of an equally voluminous writer of a modern novel.

The difference between quantity and quality is as absolute as the difference between the components of a picture and the making of the picture.

Quality is the arrangement of quantity. It is impossible that the multiplication of quantity could give quality. There is a difference between the effort to assemble quantity and to arrange quality. This differentiates two types of activity. When both are involved the two taken together are superior to either alone. There must be a greater amount of effort as well as kind in trying to introduce design into quantity than in merely assembling.

Obviously there is a greater range of freedom in the range of potentialities of arrangement. Taken in its broadest sense, we have here the whole physical world. So far as we know, quantities are fixed but the potentialities of arrangement are almost infinite. The effort involved in exploiting possibilities of arrangement are greater in quality and in kind than mere assembling. Now will in one of its aspects must be concerned with an arrangement of quantities since this is the only field in which a wide range of possibilities occurs.

If we say that all assemblages of quantities are the way of nature and are mechanical, we can begin to define will as an assemblage of matter (inertia). Unfortunately it can be shown in our experience of overcoming inclinations that this overcoming is itself an inclination. We register the inclination of our organism in relation to a given environment as *wishes*. If we oppose an inclination it can generally be shown on analysis that it is an stronger or previously unconscious *wish* which is doing the opposing. Can we conceive of opposing without inclination? A wishlessness, which yet can overcome *wish* is called *will*. It is a force not conditioned by the organism or the environment nor any relation between them, which yet can rearrange quantities producing a different relation. *This conception is inconceivable, from the point of view of reason it is unintelligible.*

This is the great difficulty of every great religious Teacher. He cannot explain this kind of will which he is talking about yet maintains that it is and has been experienced. All esoteric books turn on it. It is the mystery of mysteries. We say the world was created by an act of will and is so maintained. This is rationally inconceivable. Here the intellect plays with words. It must be approached practically. It can be realized.

All discussions of will end in paradox, for it defies analysis. It is like the statement "I am." "I will" is not susceptible of proof except by experience. The field of will in respect to its practical experience like every field must begin with small things and proceed through small things to greater things. But the character of the effort is always the same: *an arrangement of quantities in a non-natural way.*

Objective art is an act of will and ordinary art is the result of inclination. Non-natural does not mean it is arbitrary. It is under laws and contains order, but such order as nature alone would not produce, exemplifying the laws of the will that caused it. Nature is under the law of seven, art under the law of three. It is only against nature in the sense that what are inexactitudes under the law of seven are exactitudes under the law of three.

For proper object of will Orage proposes the attainment of consciousness; since this is the nearest man can come to having an object devoid of attraction as his goal—effort without wish. This involves a subtle point since every living being is the incarnation of a will toward consciousness. But this will is different from any wish the creature may have. Its wishes are natural to it. This will is the cause of its existence. This will cannot be one of its wishes. Here an illustration was given used by Hegel and Schopenhauer: Light (white) refracted through a prism. None of the refracted lights are the original white. Schopenhauer said that man's will is refracted into wishes. A will to consciousness cannot be a wish yet every wish presupposes that will. Consciousness must be the object of will since it cannot be the object of wish. In self-observation as an act, is the first step of will.

CONSCIOUSNESS, INDIVIDUALITY AND WILL

(NOTES ANNETTE HERTER)

One cannot make conscious products from unconscious material. No impression can be received in the fourth center unless we put it there ourselves. This center is inviolable—it is individuality. No power external or internal can affect it, except you. It is the essence of our complete freedom and the essence of our responsibility. A faculty of self-consciousness is developed consciously by impressions of the physical organism's behavior. Positive impressions do not consist in focusing attention—but conscious and waking impressions can only be taken by a positive act, difficult to maintain, and become the material for active thought.

The highest definition of 'man' is "a being who can do." This implies possession of the three higher active centers:

Conscious thought = individuality

Higher emotions = consciousness

Will = the power to do—not to 'react'

Unconsciousness and waste of energy through the leaks in our centers make us grow old—never purposively spent energy.

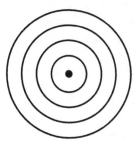

By practicing all we *can* do (self-observation and awareness) we will develop around the "I" center : awareness, consciousness, will, until it will dominate the organism.

Conscious moral conduct is the means to contribute in accordance with the cosmic scheme.

The moment you die, you immediately are re-born again at the same day, year, from the same parents, in the same environment—unless you consciously break the circle. Then you begin to exist in real time and go on in a spiral.

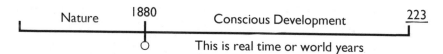

Consciousness of other people is really the definition of what we call generally self-consciousness.

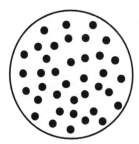

Mind: Myriad of impressions. I write: one word strikes another through association and thus from one to another a set of ideas is formed. Six months later the same word might strike other associations which are mechanical. The thought glides over the surface of the unconscious where are kept all the words known—all we know. Real consciousness will give me at will the immediate use of all I know. The real man is he who can at will in any circumstance play the reasonable part.

As there are three skins around the embryo child, so are there three skins around "I"—individuality, consciousness, will. The final state of instinct is will—will is the last thing to be conquered—the end of all.

In the back of your head is already the complete pattern of all your thoughts—so even that is mechanical—everything is mechanical until you

256

reach the state of will in which you realize that this pattern you laid down is the discharge of your will.

The idea of the method is not the development of cosmic consciousness but to wake us up from the drugs that have made us pathologic, degenerate—self-imaginative.

We are three-centered beings with four possible states of consciousness. The second of the five rules of objective morality is conscious effort.

As there are two modes of thought, and two modes of style, so are there two modes of consciousness. There is however a third mode of thought and consequently of consciousness. It is impossible to acquire it mechanically—we cannot define it in usual words. It necessitates an act of such character as never made before. Our first octave is waking and sleeping. Our second is self-consciousness, which makes possible cosmic consciousness. Octaves are never mechanically completable. The two intervals are efforts—shocks. In some cases they can be given from outside—in other cases they must come from will. The second interval is always an act of will.

The advantage of the terrible disadvantage of being human is to be able to be glad—whether happy or unhappy—and—by achieving consciousness to become greater than the angels. We, conscious, are the mind of God—angels are his emotions.

The law of three: individuality, consciousness, will. This is the only planet where these do not work together normally. Therefore, man must labor and suffer (to feed the moon). Here beings *must* labor and suffer, but by doing so consciously can win a higher plane than the angels and archangels.

Daly King asked what catastrophe might come about if everyone became conscious and refused to feed the moon. Orage said this was impossible since we can only furnish conscious effort by the use of certain chemicals in our atmosphere which are limited in quantity just as radium, phosphorus, etc. are limited. That, if it were conceivably possible to interest all beings in this effort, the atmosphere must change. At present there exists enough material for those working on these lines.

Why have we not a normal development of self-consciousness and cosmic consciousness fitting our human form? Some catastrophe has occurred in us (just as to former civilizations—Atlantis), for that is the nature of this planet and of all organic life on it since the first collision of the comet with the earth, and the premature birth of the moon and Anulios. Everything here repeats this same history. The moon—self-consciousness, awareness in my body—Anulios, cosmic consciousness, awareness of world in which we live -- and these normal adjuncts have been struck off from us. To attain them we must make a special effort. Why? It is a unique tragedy and a unique opportunity.

(Regarding 'reforms'): Establishment of self-consciousness as an individual aim would bring about a strictly just valuation of all subsidiary reforms, down the octave. To bridge the interval between the unconscious and the conscious has been the aim of all religious teachers.

Voluntary undertaking brings conscious reaction.

From the moment that one begins self-observation, it is as if a certain psychological function begins to germinate from the seed in a characteristic pattern—goes through certain phases, which have time limits (ample for the normal person)—and 'effort-food' must be given, or the original seed is destroyed. There are many seeds, i.e. potentialities for developing self-consciousness, so one can often respond anew and start again—but only as long as all seeds are still available. No one knows his responsibility in propounding this method to someone who cannot be kept in touch with 'the food'—since we cannot know how many potentialities each may have. The sin against the Holy Ghost—involuntarily or consciously—is the destruction of a last potentiality for self-consciousness.

The attainment of individuality, consciousness and will are the essential aims of man.

The birthright of a human being is the desire for self-consciousness, coming around the age of majority. Then, at about thirty, comes a sense of the world in which we live, the dawning of cosmic consciousness. After this, according to one's gifts, conditions, circumstances, etc., one should become a conscious agent in the functions of the cosmos, which is a total scheme of which we have a relative comprehension.

At birth we come in a state of super-consciousness. Our first cry is: "I have forgotten." After education it is completely gone except in moments of remorse, extreme anguish, in which moment's *only* man has the sense of the aim and meaning of his being.

A thinking process is a chemical process—formulations are chemical—philosophies, doctrines, are a substance of a very high vibration that may be poisonous or fatal to the body. A few years of yoga exercises can destroy forever the possibilities of development of objective conscious being.

The third form of 'art,' or major art, which is the only 'art' is conscious art: the art of producing consciousness (for more see under 'art'). Minor art is subjective; its only object is the gratification of the artist himself. The Babylonian school's objective was to produce conflict of the three centers, because only then is there a possibility of reconciliation or a real thought. In all forms of art an element of disturbance was purposively introduced in order to arouse questions, leading to answer in regard to consciousness. To us a work of art is a stimulus to harmonious associations. Disharmonious association is to us an experience, a novel impression. The first criterion of a real work of art is that it is forever memorable.

Purpose: consciousness.

Means: experience of a memorable kind.

Result: they who had undergone these (spectators) would in turn become a work of art. The spectator so is expected to introduce voluntary, intentional variation in his natural behavior, making him so a conscious being. If he can make the sequential objective he becomes himself a work of art.

The thesis of Gurdjieff's book is: we as humans suffer and make efforts—this is obligatory. We are doomed from our position in the cosmos to suffer and labor; this is our fate and it is absolutely inescapable. Though the quantity may be distributed so as to appear that from time to time some of us escape, as a whole it is always the same. Whether it is for the moon or for other purposes, the fact remains that the human race must produce a certain amount of suffering distributed among them as they like or as they *can*. Lifting of suffering or reducing effort is impossible: it *has* to be borne. If suffering is voluntary and effort conscious, in addition to our inescapable debt, it is possible to obtain personal advantage in the form of consciousness and will—through observation, participation and experience, it is possible to acquire individuality. The perfect soul has: consciousness, individuality and will. Moments of feeling the emptiness of one's life—of failure—a feeling of having missed the road—a moment of objective consciousness buried in the unconscious: Ashiata Shiemash worked to evoke this state and build upon this. The Platonic method: anamnesis, or recollection. Socrates never stated anything; he always interrogated; the idea is that we really *know* but need to be reminded.

The objective universe (all that there is knowable) is a work of conscious creation, consciously maintained, for a conscious purpose. In that respect it differs from a machine only in degree. As in our own plane we construct machines 'consciously,' in the other plane God created a machine (universe) with the conscious object of deriving from that machine something that he wished.

Orage's comments on Gurdjieff's chapter 'The Mountain Pass of Impartial Judgment': the passion for understanding and for perfection—with a conscious desire to cooperate with the Creator's cosmic job is the highest function of a human' being and therefore those who attain a certain objectivity—or impartial judgment—can sacrifice the most precious thing in themselves, to take part in the evolution of the fittest.

The 'horns' symbolize *real will* and the whole 'giving' must be done without any hope of any kind of reward or arrière-pensée. In the old prospectus of the Institute there was a treatment mentioned which, translated means 'cure by slavery.' It is inconceivable that anyone consciously willing to be servile can destroy his will—but he can give up all 'appearance' of will, which is what usually seems the most important, and, if by doing so he makes any kind of bargaining, unconsciously hoping to become better, wiser; hoping to gain in any way—his sacrifice is *not* impartial and has no worth.

The unconscious has no experiences. It has only a procession of events. We are a procession of fate in time.

All the race potentialities are contained in the individual. Unless the individual *today* can develop all his potentialities, the race cannot realize its. There are vestigial organs (for which we have no more use like the appendix) and anticipatory organs (for which we do not know the use yet).

In the back of the head: consciousness

In the heart: individuality

In the spine: will

Real consciousness is determined by our *actively* taken impressions.

A *will* is a purpose pursued irrespective of any *wish*.

Consciousness is the simultaneity of thought processes.

What the English language calls 'self-consciousness' is an acute awareness of others. What Gurdjieff calls 'self-consciousness' attains just the contrary from what we are used to calling it.

"Gold" is the *use* of personality by individuality.

It is not necessary to strive for consciousness too obviously (story of London lady who had been told she was over careful and who threw some very valuable china on the floor in the presence of guests and husband and made herself so notorious in the newspapers thereby that the London group was forced to be dissolved!) Psychological 'obscenity' is to be caught trying to *exhibit* devices for attaining consciousness.

Consciousness is a simultaneous awareness of all the thoughts that we can think.

The attainment of self-consciousness is the condition of truth. Dulo-therapy is a regime under which one becomes a slave of one's own resolution.

Will is the ability to produce in yourself states of consciousness, and have control over them.

To sweep a floor consciously is performing better service than to have written half a dozen masterpieces (unconsciously).

Our life is just waiting for death without a 'raison d'être. Conscious labor is setting yourself an object of being alive. The formulation of an object for which your life is worth living and its pursuit: that is conscious-labor.

There are two movements: time and space. Where they meet there is an object. If they meet low it is a vegetable, higher an animal, etc., in each case a being. We are the embodiment of the conflict between these two forces. A small part of us is resisting, pushing against unconsciousness (conscious effort) a larger part is pulling us into complete inertia.

When you write, make for your readers a much more *real* experience than they have had. Conscious writing should be in such a form that makes it impossible for a reader to remain the same. He must get out purified. This is the creative power of the logos, or speech.

Gurdjieff says the universe is non-mechanical—not rationally dictated. It is a free creation maintained by a will.

There are three primordial laws : will—consciousness—individuality. God himself is under these three laws.

In our present state we only 'recur'—like leaves from year to year. Only through conscious effort at self-development do we cease to recur—and begin to incarnate our essence-body.

Our state of consciousness is determined by a state of body. It depends upon a state of the blood—its currents, within the blood vessels themselves. The 'I'—the 'ego' is in the blood—the blood is the 'life,' the 'vehicle' of the ego. What we call self-consciousness is never induced by a state of the blood. Our blood contains the same substances we find in all other sources of our planet. Mental—astral—etheric. Consciousness is not dependent upon the constituents of the blood but upon the *channel*.

The seed of essence is the root of individuality.

Real will is not acquired by nature. Will is developed by initiatives. Always, continually, use initiative. The overcoming of the illusion of the possession of will is the method by which to attain will or salvation of sin (realization of our mechanicality).

What is true of the megalocosmos is true of every particle. Every being must of necessity have a particle of God's purpose—consciousness—individuality—will. The scale of having it depends on the scale of 'being.' (Being is a perpetual self-initiated momentum.)

(Regarding differentiation between quantity and quality): It is practically impossible to change the quantity, but the quality or arrangement of quantities is free. Not meaning absolute freedom but range of possibilities. We never speak of freedom in the absolute sense—only in the relative sense, as we say that a locomotive animal is freer than a stationary vegetable. Will in one of its aspects must be concerned with the arrangement of quantities. Gurdjieff's book states that 'will' is the arrangement of matter.

The first state of will is the absence of wish. Will is paradoxical—inconceivable—the mystery of mysteries. It invents, sustains and destroys the world. It seems rationally impossible and yet it is said to be necessary and again not acquirable......Will alone is beyond analysis—it is therefore to be approached practically and not intellectually. The "solveter insulendo." Will is an arrangement of quantities in non-natural order. 'Art' must be according to formal laws imposed by will—not by nature. Against nature does not necessarily mean arbitrarily only. Any act of will is a work of art. Will operates within the law of three. Nature operates within the law of seven.

If you take consciousness for the motive of your willing it cannot be of the nature of a wish or inclination as all other motives are. A creature's wishes are natural to it. Its will is the foundation of its being, the cause of its existence. The will of man is refracted through his organism into wishes (as a white light ray is refracted through a prism in colors that never have any of the original white in them).

Robinson: How comes the wish for self-observation?

ORAGE: The being as such is already a concretization towards the will for consciousness. This goes to say that an act of self-observation is always an act

261

of will. The wish to have no wishes is will (like self-observation in a difficult emotional situation)—it kills wishes—but it is done out of the *wish* to have no wishes.

Go from the verbal logic about will to the formal logic of experience.

What has been 'conditioned' can be consciously 'unconditioned.' In this method when we speak of suffering we mean effort, conscious intentional effort. Overcoming inhibitions—or the doing of what you wish (will?) to do—this is voluntary suffering. To be able to will to do what you damn well please is our definition of freedom.

Conscious labor is a life objective—a raison d'être.

Voluntarily or involuntarily everybody repays everything. If involuntarily, he extracts unconscious or involuntary suffering—if consciously, there is the compensation of consciousness.

(Megalomania) Whim is the beginning of will. Whim is a mouse—will an elephant. Gurdjieff's elephant is nothing less than a complete change in the course of human history; to make humans attain consciousness as the supreme aim of their life.

When you can at will non-identify with your body—this is 'Iransamkeep' beginning of self-consciousness.

MONDAY, 12 MAY 1930

The meeting was held at the Greenes.

Absent: Mr. Greene, Mrs. Bathen, Mrs. Kirk.

The Confession hour found Miss White less given to self-observation.

Mrs. Skene found that what ability she had acquired previously toward self-observation had been of great help in recent lessons in acquiring correct posture as the teacher's method involved self-observation as to this detail.

Miss Braley was steadily at work.

Mrs. Greene intermittently so.

Mrs. Stanton told of difficulties.

Mr. Skene amused us by saying he had tried "sitting on a planet," and from this lofty vantage had observed Ralph Skene going about his daily business. He said that he was gratified to notice that now he saw not only his own body but his immediate environment in this picture.

As to "Vows"

Miss White continued to clean up irritating small jobs.

Miss Braley was working on many small things with a view to getting the ground cleared for a large one.

Mrs. Greene was getting many family chores out of the way.

Mrs. Stanton had attacked her desk.

Mr. Skene spoke of his difficulties in finding where to be elastic and where to be determined in carrying out his plans.

The main discussion of the evening was on the words "objective" and "subjective." M. E. B. owned to confusion as to the correct meaning of "objective." Subjective seemed plain enough, but there was the possibility of a double interpretation to "objective." An object in its general sense is a thing, a concrete unit. In work according to the philosophy we are studying, we are trying to build such a unit in the emotional body. This now is but a potentiality to be realized. When realized it would become an experience and hence subjective. Objective, as generally used in philosophy, means something viewed impersonally. In this philosophy it is consistently used not only to mean this but to have the added meaning of something potential, not yet realized.

In this philosophy subjective is our personal point of view; this is also thus used here as it always means that *which we ourselves experience.*

The phrases with the word objective were carefully gleaned from the Morris notes and were carefully considered:

Objective time—This phrase is a paradox for time never comes objectively and never can be an object. It becomes subjective the moment it is experienced. It can therefore be objective only in potentiality.

Objective reason—Something to be developed. At present our reason is purely instinctive and a function of our planetary body.

Objective conscience—An awareness of our possibilities and the possession of an urge to fulfill them. It is spoken of as a "personal anguish." Most of the occupations of life are substitutions to divert us from this which should be our real purpose.

SUNDAY, 25 MAY 1930

The meeting was held at the Greenes and advanced one day in order that Mr. Skene who was leaving for four months abroad, on Monday, might be with us.

Absent: Mrs. Skene, Mrs. Stanton, Mrs. Kirk, Miss White.

Our ranks were reinforced by the accession through unanimous consent of Dora Hagemeyer.

The Confession hour brought reports:

Mrs. Greene—Some success.

Mr. Greene—Much discouraged and a very difficult week.

Miss Braley—Nothing new.

Mr. Skene—Could be detached when alone but not when others were present.

Mrs. Bathen—Could work in moments of stress.

Mrs. Hagemeyer—when fatigued or irritated.

Various reports of different vows made with varying success.

The group spent the evening in considering the meanings of two words "sincere" and "spontaneous." Defined:

"Sincere"—Being in reality as in appearance. Intending precisely what one says.

"Spontaneous"—Arising from inherent qualities, without external efficient cause, i.e. without special premeditation.

The question was first considered "Is spontaneity necessarily sincere?" This was illustrated by the story of a friend who might come to me full of some happening of interest to us both; but coming at a time when I am preoccupied or perhaps ill. His news arouses no apparent interest, and he goes away rebuffed. The fact may be that I am really greatly aroused by it but expression is crowded out by my preoccupations. Sincerity seemed to be a word having to do with the mind while spontaneous was affiliated with the emotions.

This cleared the way for the question which had arisen before relative to the sincerity of practice in "As If" for "As If" manifests external behavior in the absence of a corresponding emotion.

"As If" has a three-fold purpose:

To train the body as a tool to be used for a conscious purpose; instead of allowing ourselves to be used by the body.

An exercise to increase one's realization of the present mechanicalness of behavior. The effort to behave non-mechanically is itself a "conscious labor." By mechanicalness we mean our customary conditioned reflexes. The effects of these reflexes may ordinarily be good or bad, e.g. they are good when they lead us to jam on the brake to prevent collision; bad, when we wink our lids during eye surgery. It is wise to seize such opportunities for conscious labor.

A training to enable us to act with *real* sincerity.

At present, we, being at the mercy of current stimuli are literally incapable of any genuine sincerity. Also we are quite ignorant of our own motives; and not even capable of manifesting our true feelings. We continually perform acts untrue to our deeper selves. Yet others have to depend on our manifestations for an understanding of our real state.

If these manifestations are not in accord with our real feeling our friend will take us in a way which differs from our wish and our conception of how this wish has been manifested. In "As If" we suppress one form of behavior to be able to manifest another which is more in accord with our true selves. It is naive to suppose that sincerity means being spontaneous. Spontaneity may be merely giving way to moods. It is a real art to be truly sincere.

The acting of commedia as done at the Drama Guild is very like the tasks set his students by Pythagoras. He had them familiarize themselves with the differing types of planetary bodies; they could then step into the part and manifest a given behavior.

"As If" will open a line of conduct for you with those to whom you feel unsympathetic. You act "As If" not with intent to deceive but to put oneself in a proper attitude to bring about a change. If you produce no response it is

264

a proof of your inadequacy in your part. Do this persistently and establish smooth relations with effort to see the other's good points.

In opening relations with people, the appearance is more than the reality, for the reality must be created. In this method we use the lie "I have a body." If we can hold this long enough we can go far toward the creation of the "I." It is impossible to love one's enemies but it is not impossible to act as if we did.

MONDAY, 23 JUNE 1930

Absent Mrs. Bathen.

The meeting was with M. E. B.

In the Confession hour:

Mrs. Hagemeyer found she could use self-observation more frequently.

Mr. Greene felt he was acquiring something more of detachment.

Mrs. Stanton reported too many vicissitudes in experience and environment to have achieved much success.

Miss Braley reported less success in effort.

Miss White found some improvement.

Mrs. Greene felt herself able to be more impersonal and spoke of the spiritual experience she had had in seeing "Journey's End."

As to "Vows" various degrees of success were reported:

Mr. Greene had pondered much on the behavior of metals and materials.

Mrs. Stanton had just returned from the Camp in the Ojai Valley where the theosophist leader, Krishnamurti gives daily lectures. She gave us some of his sayings:

Pure action is action without reaction.

The ego is a mass of unconquered reaction.

We came from unconscious perfection through conscious imperfection, to conscious perfection.

Truth is the one goal which cannot be organized.

Churches and organizations crystallize belief and kill.

After much interest was expressed in Krishnamurti, Mrs. Stanton promised to give us more of him later.

The group then proceeded to try to discover the possible causes for man's unequal development in his three centers. His functions in these are:

Doing—physical or instinctive

Knowing—mental

Being—emotional.

The fact that one of these predominates does not at all mean that it is over-developed; but merely that the others are underdeveloped. Each of our three centers seems to have had its own history unrelated to the others and not keeping step with them. Almost all great thinkers at present reach their prominence at the expense of motor and emotional centers. We are accustomed to the artist with the mentality of a child and to the athlete with neither mind nor heart.

The whole aim of this method is the harmonious development of our nature in the increase of being. Being is of the emotional center; being cannot be developed by any direct means. That this is a fact is proven by the inability of the Christian religion, whose aim the cultivation of this center, to show any mass success after two thousand years. According to this method, the emotional center, which is the neutralizing force, can only grow through friction between the mental and the instinctive centers. In all the work in this method there runs the work of the positive, the negative and the neutralizing. Here it is claimed that the emotional center is helped by the carrying on of motor activities while exercising mental activities on their proper material, being an effort to understand.

It is claimed that when impressions are received passively as we usually do receive them, these three electric forces, positive, negative, and neutralizing are not distributed to their proper centers. Hence the uneven growth.

We frequently have an adult instinctive or motor center, are adolescent in our emotions and infantile in our intelligence. We are thus torn apart and find ourselves thinking one thing, feeling another, and often doing a third. St. Paul: "That I would not, that I do."

But it is claimed that when impressions are received consciously, that is we are aware of them, the three forces are distributed properly and the three centers equally fed. Our first job is to restore the balance; for each of us is a sort of monster. In the world at present all the high rewards are for doing and knowing. There are none for being and yet being is the result of doing and knowing properly applied. No development of any one center will serve. Before becoming highly developed we must become *ordinary* men and women, that is people who are harmoniously developed. No one who is extraordinary can be harmoniously developed. The world at present calls only those successful who are freaks. To be ordinary is a step toward becoming *normal*; for a normal being is one who is ready to meet every situation as a united being, think, feeling, and acting in unison and toward one purpose. Such an one does not use his energy up in internal conflicts; he is not a battle-field but is a dynamic force.

The failure of reforms is usually explicable by the one sidedness of the reformers. This leads to such ridiculous situations as priests blessing battle-flags and senators voting dry and drinking wet.

The expounders of this method believe that if at any time, in any age, a few hundred, even a few score people could be developed through this method to be harmonious and normal beings, that they could move mountains of social difficulty and the world might know what the gospel of Christ really means.

Talk of plans for summer and fall

"Doing." Try to got clear of idea of principle involved. Effort to under-stand "formally." Never to rest unless deliberately after exertion; but never to rest if you can help it, trying to find in variety of effort what we would ordinarily seek in rest.

QUESTION: Why?

ORAGE: To learn to distinguish the real need for rest and a pseudo need. If one stops effort as soon as one has an impression of fatigue one will never learn the extent of one's own capacity, e. g.: the man who thought he could wheel a barrow only a certain distance was shown that by shifting weight to another set of muscles he could continue much longer. If he had rested he would not have learned this shifting. This is especially important when one learns to shift from center to center; when one center is tired devise an activ-ity for another, a voluntary invention of activity. But one must learn to know oneself, experimenting, to be able to do this and to recognize true fatigue and rest when it is really necessary.

QUESTION: What about the poisons in the blood caused by fatigue.

ORAGE: Consciousness is of itself a prophylactic. If one is acting purposive-ly, consciously these fatigue poisons are much less. They occur more in the absence of a catalytic agent (for analogy consider how much less fatigue we feel after voluntary effort of some kind than after same task undertaken under compulsion).

QUESTION: What is the relation between this and our "debt to nature"?

ORAGE: Payment of the debt does not come until we are mature in relation to nature. Not mature until we are in a state of "I keep myself," that is a state capable of non-identification at will.

There is objectivity of this debt, e. g. the foods you eat determine your later chemical constitution. The effect is the price paid for a cause. In growing up, you are the cause of a variety of efforts. True, you are not consciously the cause of these efforts. The payment is that in coming into the possession of a planetary body, which the effect of long series of causes, biological, cosmic, etc., payment is to make the maximum use of it. Do not quarrel with the planetary body received but make use of it. When you are dealt a hand of cards, you do not quarrel because there are no trumps but you learn to play cards. This is what we call a debt. This cannot be conceived intellectually but can be felt. Experience of indebtedness must be felt, through the awakening of consciousness before it can be recognized intellectually. For mind can work only on material supplied by sensation and emotion.

QUESTION: Does the Gurdjieff-System preclude racial recollections?

ORAGE: There are no impressions carried over from the past to the pres-ent but there is impressionability, i. e. previous impressions subsumed in the structure of the immaterial container; by Jung's theory of ancestral memories. There is confusion between impressions and impressionability. Examples: Mozart and a Japanese boy with a brush.

The body is made up of materialized vibrations, i. e. possible response to impressions. Inherit a piano whose possible range is determined by heredity. What tune will be played on it is determined by circumstance. The condition of this inherited piano will make one person more responsive to certain impressions than another, i. e. range of impressionability. The body is an electrical phenomenon, matter is wave lengths. The kind of body determines impressionability and effects. In absence of experience of debt the mind cannot conceive, but only register. We cannot conceive a color. I repay a debt because of fear of consequences, should I fail to pay. Here there is no sense of debt but only calculation.

Voluntarily or involuntarily everyone repays everything. If voluntary we may extract conscious advantage; if involuntary there is involuntary suffering. Karma—compensation—justice. Human "justice" is often objective injustice.

QUESTION: When people lead unhappy lives what is their compensation?

ORAGE: Gurdjieff has said that all suffering is either repayment of old debts incurred or preparation for future conscious or unconscious satisfactions.

QUESTION: Does all that happen within one life?

ORAGE: The psyche never dies; once a being always a being. It is never the planetary body that suffers but the being that inhabits it. Continuity of being; may be paying debts acquired before. But still this is all aside from voluntary suffering which is consciously undertaken to carry out a purpose.

QUESTION: Does the being remember the previous experience?

ORAGE: When it is non-identified with the planetary body, the memory is that of being and not of planetary body. In that state it does not suffer from vicissitudes.

QUESTION: But if it cannot suffer how can it experience anything else, joy, etc.?

ORAGE: But it can. State of non-identification is defined as bliss. It is positive not dependent or negative. Remember that the word suffering is not used in the ordinary sense; but in the sense of effort to overcome conditions of inertia. On arriving at a certain stage we naturally assume certain responsibilities. Herbert Spencer gives example of wild bulls that put cows in the center. Spencer says: who told them they were bulls? They have a realized state of being.

We have practically never had experience of ethical obligation, consequently when the idea is proposed it is analyzed by our ideas of ethical obligation already sociologically determined.

All possible experiences are at every given moment are experience-able; you do not have to go somewhere; but what a being experiences depends on what he is; i. e. radio waves are filling the air but what you get depends upon what you tune in on. Experiences are beating their wings in the ether.

QUESTION: If we had been conscious in a previous state of existence, would we not remember it now?

ORAGE: Yes. It is the being, not the psyche that remembers. A being is defined as a particle of His Endlessness and is coated with three bodies, thus we have:

Being—mental

Astral body—the psyche

Planetary body—a continuity of being with intermittence of existence

When all three coatings are dropped off being is non-existent but not annihilated. Differentiated by will, consciousness and individuality according to its development.

See chapter in Eddington when he tries to conceive what ether must be if it exists. Any given particle of it not only may be but must be omnipresent. This is inconceivable and must be so because our intellectual analyses are based on experience. This is an analogy for a being. Each particle of it is also the Whole. Not that the drop absorbs the Sea nor the Sea the drop but that the drop always was the sea. The whole purpose of this method is to transfer identification of being in planetary body to identification of being with being. Until being makes a conscious effort it has materials for psyche, but no psyche. We are invertebrate psyches.

Have I fully developed this planetary body?

My astral body is in the state of development of a slug.

The mental body that is only a stone, not even an amoeba

Conditions are often bad but not irremediable, so far as development of being is concerned. God supplies time and conditions of perfectibility.

QUESTION: But there are irremediable conditions for the planetary body?

ORAGE: The planetary body does not experience but it is always the being that is the experiencer. Consider the stops in the process of receiving impressions: electrical charge can be traced along neurons, over synapses etc. to brain, then a gap and image. The image is our experience.

QUESTION: In what does "doing" consist?

ORAGE: Always pressing against the yoke, e.g. Orage arrived at home at 5.45 after an exhausting day with an engagement at six. Filled in the time by overcoming his inclinations with a resolve to with inclination to remove obstructions, willing to make effort. There is a certain self-satisfaction in carrying out a whim. Whim is the beginning of will. Whim is a mouse and will is an elephant. Begin with mice. Psychological effort, not merely physical effort, which may be only a sort of fidgeting. Voluntary suffering is a voluntary effort. Giving oneself the trouble. "Always trouble trouble before trouble troubles you." Not merely resisting inclination but substituting a positive. When swimming against the current it is true one meets resistance but the purpose of swimming is not the overcoming of resistance but arriving at a goal. Our goal is consciousness ability at will to regard the planetary body with non-identification, as an instrument.

"Doing" always to be on tip-toe, eager, experimental, positive.

The Greeks used the word "spirit" in the sense in which we use the word "spirited." A spiritual man meant a spirited man. The Body Kesdjan is spiritedness; psyche in a state of puff. Gurdjieff once said "Roll your triangle"!

There are three forms of activity: During the day, roll your triangle. You must have thought actively; you must have been or have put yourself in situations, where you *felt;* must have exercised your planetary body and you must have done something useful. Bur without self-observation there is no doing. If every particle of being is the whole being and the being has a purpose, every being shares this purpose.

How can a fore-appointed experience appear to be totally original? To the person experiencing it? The obligation is imposed, yet seems original. Consider your first experience of adolescent love. How difficult for any one experiencing this to realize it is not original, absolutely; to realize, it has lain potentially in one all the time. We talk about obligation as those do who talk about love but have never had its experience.

TUESDAY, 13 MAY 1930

Group vs. Circle

Group has one leader, circle has no leader. Each one on own center of gravity. For three motives:

Personal advantage

To be of help to others

To help a common cause of promoting consciousness

Few of us have this triple state of obligation. Not intellectual, this thing can be done "as if" but fact or not.

Feeling that if a day has passed without an effort toward consciousness, we have slipped. This is the first side of the triangle of consciousness.

Feeling a duty towards one's neighbors, that is to others who are sincerely striving toward objective development. There are some members of the group who lose interest in the method, when suffering; that is just when they could make an experimental effort, fair weather sailors. But when the waves are never too high, when one can stand alone in the world - this is the first crystallization of individuality, the establishment of a center of gravity.

A passion for the Work, such as Jesus showed when he moaned "Jerusalem, Jerusalem." This is divinely pattered. Or the Elder brothers spoken of by some theosophists; not elder but indicating a state of being.

When one has established a center of gravity in each of the three one comes into the membership of a circle, of which one may be at any moment either at the center or circumference. Here is organization without machinery; communication without speech. Six years is a short time, this group is not a circle. The London group, ten years old, is not yet a circle.

Orage is coming back the next January, but group meetings will be of a different kind. There will be no money fee. Never again will one be taken.

The second condition: Continued Attendance

This will be a sign of the work done. Orage will know what sign to look for. A definite experience as vivid as drowning and being revived. This comes when one feels all that holds one to the body cut off: the experience Beelzebub had in Gornahoor Harharkh's Laboratory, when he felt that he was in danger of losing his being; when, perhaps for only a few seconds one feels that one is dying in the body.

No vow of secrecy will have to be imposed because no one could possible repeat what is said in such a group. Our "personal" problems not our own but a joint responsibility.

Orage's discussion of personal problems is not a matter of patience but a conviction that every personal problem impedes the formation of a circle. The matter must be considered objectively. The person involved is responsible for the action taken and also has a duty to get what light possible. In absence of "other-trust" this cannot be done. No member of a circle is sworn to secrecy but has attained to secrecy that is to an inability to betray or misuse facts about fellow members. Yet this stage must be reached if this work in New York is to continue, not by repetition but by progress or development.

The third condition: The Group must make greater impression on the places where they live. After six years our impression (effects) are chiefly bad, associated with ideas of personal behavior and of a cult instead of the dignified standing of the Akhaldans. We are insignificant caricatures etc. In every established organization Orage finds at least one enemy, primed with false reports. Because things have been said in wrong circumstances, in ignorance of the laws of association, for no idea ever stands alone but in association with ideas at that moment in the hearer's mind. There must be in New York something corresponding to the Pythagorean Institute but not under one building. P. made the mistake of founding an organization, with the certainty that it would run down the scale and become the opposite of itself.

Orage has tried to exemplify what members might do; take one subject in which you are relatively skilled and gather others. If actually striving a magnetic influence will trickle through to the members to the extent to which they are susceptible of being magnetized and will become interested in the background of mind. Each one starting a school in the subject in which he is skilled and in which his own language is spoken. This will not be an organization. But each like a planet with relation to the sun (that is the source of life and ideas). There may be no explicit discussion of these ideas but magnetic communication. One of the conditions for next year.

271

Only those who are candidates for these three kinds of work will be eligible. Those who are not, will either have to attend beginner's classes or no groups, since Orage will have no financial obligation to the Institute nor will he be dependent on the members. There will be no need for members. He will also be free to be candid and will expect candid replies not only in private but in public. The first step is to be serious, to be determined. If we are not serious Orage cannot be serious with us and if not serious an end is put to expansion of understanding.

This is now to remind you of certain principles which we understand at our peril, peril because of the same reason that St. Paul gave to those who are hearers and not doers of the word. Having heard we are responsible. This reminding is in the hope that understanding may force us to do something.

1:—End of the method is to attain a state of being in which the planetary body and all its potentialities becomes yours to exploit objectively. You as psyche have this body in charge to feed on it i.e. to transform it up the scale as we transform up the scale the molecules that we take in as planetary food up to emotions and sex. Transformation into higher substances. We do not harm our food. Similarly when "I" feeds on "It" by self-observation, participation, etc., we do not injure it or destroy it but step it up. The self-creation by reciprocal feeding between the "I" and the "It" of a God who can exploit the potentialities of every given planetary body.

It follows from this that this is not merely a personal achievement but a common obligation, laid on all three centered beings. His Endlessness is engaged in discharging the same function for the total body of the universe. Perhaps cosmic development awaits one individual's passing through the same function.

The five rules of objective morality which Orage thinks may be set against any rules of morality ever formulated. There is no one who cannot assent to them. They permit many codes of behavior which conventional codes condemn. On the other hand they make obligatory things the omission of which would not be condemned by usual codes. Try to grasp the principles involved; not imitate somebody else's behavior. Understanding the principles, try to act out of oneself.

"Follow yourselves and ye will find me; follow me end you will lose both me and yourselves." This is given as of Christ in an un-canonical gospel. It means that no being's external behavior is to be taken as a model.

Story of a distinguished disciple of Buddha who asked Buddha a question. Buddha said: I cannot tell you the answer. The man urged:Buddha told him, But I know a man who can answer you. He turned out to be the butcher (low caste). The question was satisfactorily answered. Afterward Buddha said: Now you have your answer and also you know that an objective being may do what he pleases.

Proposing to become a butcher in order to have that man's wisdom would be no more foolish than trying to imitate any man's external behavior; e.g. Gurdjieff's.

Having grasped principles we must act according to oneself; to be free of Kundabuffer which is merely susceptibility to hypnotic influence. Ponder each of the five rules. They will become a five-fingered hand with which to grasp the situations of life.

QUESTION: Will you repeat the Five Rules?

ORAGE: Keeping all three brains of the body fit, i.e. preserving ability to think by practice; preserving ability to feel, by engaging in enterprises and relationships where we will be exposed to feeling; keeping the body fit.

Constantly to be pondering the meaning and aim of existence—not with any hope of solving it but keeping the mind oriented, Why this rule which seems to have no practical use? Because preoccupation with this problem makes other problems relatively easy.

For the artist, art is the pursuit of an unattainable goal; and in this pursuit what we know as works of art are thrown off like shaving. In one of the Upanishads Brahma himself did not know. But in aiming towards this unattainable truth, which perhaps His Endlessness himself does not know, ordinary truths appear in the mind like shavings.

Obligation to make being-effort, doing. Doing not necessarily any visible effort, anything concrete—Partdolgduty; exercising; effort-making.

Perhaps between November and the first of January Orage will work out a set of exercises not psychological but in will. Beginning with those of mice towards those of elephant Not mental will—the ability to carry out whims, what it takes your fancy to do.

Cooperation with those engaged with yourself in the same task of attaining objective reason (the Circle). "That I may not cause the feet of a little one to stumble."

The next is unfortunately mystical unless associated with the definition of "suffering" given before. We asked Orage - why must I make all this effort to reach a stage of being. Because if you do not make it for yourself it will be made for you by somebody else. At present the burden is mostly on His Endlessness.

Summary: given above

1.   Aim

2.   Rules that shall guide one when he is in the way of becoming responsible, becomes an individual, developing in responsibility through practice of the Five Rules.

The other items in the system chemistry, tables of food, physics, vibrations, cosmology, etc. are of professional interest to those interested in specialist study but the Five Rules are of practical technique for all.

But having once "understood" we are capable of sin. This is failure to make effort in proportion to understanding; a refusal to convert a verbal understanding to formal. This meeting is merely the end of one phase. Next January we begin a new phase of work. Whether we continue against the Yoke.

OUR PRESENT STATE OF CONSCIOUSNESS

All our physical and psychological phenomena are interactions between the organism and environment. If we consider them in this state we would not say there was any element of inner "control" beyond structure and nature, i.e. nobody has "will" meaning ability to do, which is a self-initiated activity. Taking Gurdjieff's definition of man as *a being who can do* and since all men are in a state of will-less-ness, there are no men in Gurdjieff's sense of the term.

Let us discriminate first between reaction and will; then let us consider if there is any way to pass from reaction to will. It is difficult to realize that not only physical processes (heart-action etc.) but also all our psychological processes (thoughts and their trains, emotions and their consequences, overt behavior) are of the same order as physiological conditioned reactions. This would apply to the present discussion, statement and reception of ideas. When we have the sense of touch on the coming into contact of two bodies, we do not the sensation due to will, it is dependent on touch. Similarly, Orage saying what he is saying and we thinking what we are thinking. We have been so conditioned and wound up with no more real will than characters in dreams. Who wills the deeds of figures in our dreams? On waking, the dream may be vivid, but we do not attribute to the dream figures the initiation of their acts; and since the dream occurs to us in our sleep we did not will them. They are figures of the sub- or un-conscious. They are not puppets because there is no puppeteer. They are figures apparently acting on their own initiative, not the victims of a master will yet with no will of their own. Applying the dream-image to our own lives we find the same situation. How does this come about? In Gurdjieff's book an effort is made to explain it in the myth of the breaking off of the moon and Kundabuffer, but this myth may be no better than the myth of the Garden of Eden.

It is not a surprising thing that man is will-less, but that he has the illusion that he has will. This illusion is supposedly the effect of Kundabuffer. One of the first results of the practice of self-observation is the removal of this illusion. This conviction of mechanicality is a conviction of sin which is an overcoming of the illusion of having will. This is precedent to formulating a technic for attaining will or arriving at salvation.

Assuming that this conviction exists, is it possible to pass from this state of reaction to real living? If so, by what means? At the threshold of this inquiry stands the question of will. What definition can we now give? We have no data from our present experiences which are exclusively composed of reactions, for the definition of this novel process. Our first intellectual difficulty is to conceive the nature of will. If the word is intended to convey some meaning we can begin to look at its associations.

Will is associated with doing, not primarily with thinking or feeling. We must therefore begin to look for some new kind of doing in which the reactive element gives place to active. Have we any analogous aspect of doing that is active? We have experience in our psychological registration of processes of the difference between doing and not-doing, being active or passive, although mechanical in all. We can perhaps define will in advance of its realization as *inertia being constantly overcome*; that is, analogous to our experience of overcoming inertia. Next; we can distinguish the character of the inertia overcome. Again we must fall back upon our mechanical experiences to get a purchase on a conception not yet experienced.

How do we distinguish not only between quantity of effort but quality of effort? Do we often say, "I had to put a lot of effort into this" and "You have no idea of the kind of effort that I had to make." This shows that we do distinguish between quantity and quality.

Someone in the group questions: "Isn't it always really quantity?"

ORAGE: "Compare the difference in the quality of effort made by Milton writing Paradise Lost and an equally voluminous writer of a modern novel."

The difference between the quantity and the quality is as absolute as the difference between the components of a picture and its design— *Quality is the arrangement of quantity*. It is impossible that the multiplication of quantity should give quality. There is a difference between an effort to assemble quantity and an effort to arrange quantity. This differentiates two types of activity. When both are involved the two taken together are superior to either alone. It takes a much greater effort to introduce design into quantity than merely to assemble. In which of these two activities is there, relatively speaking, more freedom, that is, a greater range of possibilities? (Let us never speak here of absolute freedom.) Obviously there is a greater range of possibilities in arrangement. Taking it in its broader sense in the whole physical world, so far as we know, quantities are fixed. But arrangements are possible and may be as numerous as the combinations and permutations involved. These are not infinite.

The effort involved in exploiting the possibilities of arrangement are greater in quantity and different in kind from those exploiting possibilities of assemblage. Now *will* in one of its aspects must be concerned with the arrangements of quantities since this is the only field in which a wider range of possibilities occurs. If we say that all assemblages of quantities are the work of nature and are mechanical we can begin to define will as an arrangement of matter (matter equals inertia).

Someone in the group asks if matter excludes thought.

Answer: Everything is material. All the arrangements of matter that we experience take place quite automatically. Can we conceive of experience in

275

which matter ceases to be arranged automatically and is arranged against nature?

Unfortunately in our experience of overcoming inclinations it can be shown that the overcoming itself is always an inclination. We register the inclinations of our organism in relation to a given environment as wishes. If we oppose an inclination it can be shown on analysis that it is a stronger or unconscious wish that is doing the opposing.

Can we conceive of opposing without inclination? The first characteristic to be marked of "will" is the absence of "wish." When we oppose what we usually call will to wish, it is usually only another wish. This wish-less-ness which can yet overcome wish is called will. It is a force not conditioned by the organism nor the environment nor the relation between them yet it can re-arrange quantities producing a different relation. This conception is inconceivable, for from the point of view of reason it is unintelligible.

This is the difficulty of every great religious teacher, that he cannot explain the sort of will he is talking about, and yet he maintains that it not only can be but has been experienced. All esoteric books and gospels turn on this. It is the mystery of mysteries. While it is said that the world is created by an act of will yet this is rationally inconceivable. All intellectual speculation on it is merely playing with words.

Someone speaks of Nirvana, which is defined as both non-existence and all-existence. This was the dispute between Northern and Southern Buddhists. All popular conceptions mistakenly link it with extinction.

All discussion of will ends in a paradox for the intellect; because it defies analysis. Only the subsequent processes initiated by an act of will are subject to analysis. They must therefore be approached not intellectually but practically; they cannot be analyzed intellectual but can be realized. Like the statement "I exist," "I will" is insusceptible of proof except by experience. The field of will in respect of its practical realization, like every field, must begin with small things and proceed through small things to greater. But the character of the effort is always the same: it is an arrangement of quantities in a non-natural way. The reason why ordinary art is attacked in the book is because of a conception of real or objective art which is an act of will. Ordinary art is the work of inclination. But non-natural art or against nature does not mean arbitrary. It is under laws and contains order; but such order as nature alone would not produce. It exemplifies the laws of the will that caused it. Arbitrariness is ruled out because the willing agent is subject to the laws of the order of will. Nature is under the law of seven; art is under the law of three. It is only against nature in the sense that inexactitude is according to the law of seven and exactitudes are according to the law of three.

It seems as if we had been talking about trying to fly elephants; let us begin with flying flies. As a substitute for an object of will Gurdjieff proposes the attainment of consciousness. Since that is the nearest we can come to having as our goal an object devoid of attraction. Effort without wish.

I give you an image employed by Hegel and Schopenhauer; white light refracted through a prism. None of the refracted lights are the original white. Schopenhauer said that man's will is refracted into wishes. A will for consciousness cannot be a wish! Yet every wish presupposes that will. Gurdjieff takes as an object of will consciousness, since it cannot be the object of a wish and implicit in the act of self-observation is the first step towards will.

A discussion here of self-observation. It is not pure until it is non-identified. When non-identified it is outside the field of wish. That is, it is non-identified with the refracted wish but is identified with "I." It could identify directly with "I" but would then be unnecessary to non-identify with the personality. There is a possibility of doing this in a flash, so to speak, as shown in the story of the Thief on the Cross which is followed by non-identification with the personality.

In that case the slow method of non-identification is unnecessary.

Going back to the point that it is not a question of theory but of practice. Self-observation with non-identification is the first step but it is not yet "Doing"! When Gurdjieff said: "Method? I know nothing about it," he meant, it is about time for our next step. But doing is impossible until the first step of complete self-observation with non-identification has been gone through. Consider now not the nature (theory) of will, but the practical steps to be taken to attain this power. Next week we will set out the practical steps to be followed for personal realization.

MONDAY, 14 NOVEMBER 1927

NOTES TAKEN BY M. E. B. FROM ORAGE'S LECTURE IN NEW YORK

The so called "mind" has form and members, and the movements of the physical body are analogous to the movements of the mental body, for example: *attention* may be considered the right arm and *observation* the left.

Pondering may be considered an attempt to bring the body of the mind into actuality, the attempted use of the mental body, whose existence is postulated, to form potentialities into actualities.

We now arrive in the reading of Beelzebub at the chapter on time but will rehearse first steps.

The result of "ponderings" was asked for and the group was told that in reality "self-consciousness" was merely a consciousness of other people. If there were true self-consciousness, the individual would be too absorbed to notice even the presence, apart from their re-actions, of those present. Those group meetings to be used to their best advantage should be a psychological laboratory; but so far this has not been done. To get real self-consciousness, take yourself as a machine, and observe these phenomena. As we said the mind is a complete organism and a duplicate of the physical organism.

At first the endeavor to be "aware" will preclude anything else; but the amount of awareness possible is unlimited. Orage said that his first attempts at reading while becoming aware of his behavior resulted in inability to comprehend the page. But, later after persisting, he was able to become concurrently aware, gaining greatly in clearness and in quantity of attention available.

He illustrated with an experiment in which people were asked to close their eyes, then open them for a counted period; then close again and list what they had seen on a wall before them. Most would go from one object to the next single object, focusing and memorizing singly. The better way was to try to get one inclusive impression at once. Attention may definitely be stretched. The effort should be to increase the size of the lens and not the intensity of the focus. We should all be continuously occupied with same train of thought to which we should snap back, after interruptions.

One of the group offered a pondering on the "ordinary woman," classifying her by her (middle-class) occupations. Orage's comment was that a woman cannot be defined by her occupations. An animal is always an animal, and a woman is always a woman, just as men are men, apart from what they are doing. Man he defined as an interrogation directed to intelligence; and a woman as an interrogation directed to the emotions.

An organism is an instrument for wish fulfillment. Freud is wrong as to causes of nocturnal dreams; but would be right if we applied his theory to the objective dream of living.

In man a single wish breaks into a chaos of desires. It is believed that in the embryo, sex is not developed until after three months.

Going back to the idea of thorough women and man, our concrete experience is to form the image of a matriarch and patriarch, someone who does not take a position of responsibility but has it given to them involuntarily. There is a specific gravity of essence. Man is in essence, a passion for the reasonable understanding of the meaning and aim of existence.

Since the order in which our experiences occur depends on chance and not on logic or reason, e. g. a motorcar run properly is subject to wear and tear and its life is determined by this wear and tear but if it is misused, occupied as a hut for boys, or as a source for spare parts, the rate of wear and tear under such circumstances is not determined by its original structure. The incidents of our life are not graded in the order from which we could derive real understanding. But with the development of essence, experience begins to flow in the right order. "Coincidences" occur more frequently. So that the old Christians used to feel that their lives were directed by Providence. As a matter of fact what looks like Providence is a coincidence of octaves.

The planetary body exists for two purposes:

As a transformer of energies between the sun, earth and moon, just as trees are.

To provide a soil in which soul can develop. At present only in a physical sense does the cosmos make use of the planetary body; and it is in this sense that we are "agents" for a supply of food to the moon.

"The kingdom of heaven is within you; and if ye know yourselves ye shall find it." This saying was discovered on a parchment forty years ago and is attributed to Jesus, also: "Know yourselves and ye shall be aware that ye are the sons of the Father." These parchments were written about 350 *AD*.

Pondering seek to know why.

Ratiocination to know what.

Why am I alive? Start by eliminating all the familiar answers, finding all useless. We are left with no answer except our craving for an answer.

The body can only dream, who can deliver me from the body of this death? We can only escape the dream by dis-identifying. Then "I" can wake up though the body continues to sleep.

All undirected thought is waste of time, organism and energy, the daily ration. In the intervals when not thinking of anything, think of something. If not pondering on these matters, then on practical problems. "The material of pondering is the forms of experience, and requires thinking in forms."

All verbal communication is really impossible or at least relative, We communicate by recognition of similarity of experience. All experience is ineffable. Certain forms of thought "at which we throw words," but the formulation is not the form; there are many possible formulations for each form.

The wish of wishes in man is the wish to understand; but this wish is broken up into a variety of wishes; it is a bush instead of a tree, accomplishing nothing. The myth of Osiris cut in pieces and scattered over the planet; and the work of Isis (wisdom) to integrate and make whole. Then man is man.

The turning to the "section on time" in "Beelzebub":

Time is a process which cannot be sensed, felt or understood. Only its phenomena can be known. Time is the unique subjective, never a subject to be known.

"I am," is an ability to experience. This ability to experience is determined by the organization. The potentialities of my personal experience are conditioned by the winding of my three centers or three brains. At the present time our three brains act according to chance and the result is that experience teaches us nothing because the order in which experiences occur is dependent on chance and not on reason or logic.

Thought varies in weight and rapidity.

Emotion varies in intensity.

Movements, in muscular stress.

Try to catch some of the thoughts you have had and distinguish their relative weight. Compare the intensity of some emotions. Compare muscular movements as to tensions. Each idea has its specific gravity and finds its place in the brain accordingly. A weighty idea is balanced.

Sentence: "Man is in essence a passion for the reasonable understanding of the meaning and aim of existence. Life is an objective dream, acting out wishes. An essential wish is for understanding. The objects of desire may be deduced from objective dreams.

Man is the fighting edge of an expanding universe.

Introspection is trying to think about our emotions.

A desire in psychology has the same function as a force in physics.

Reason is a faculty of our planetary body.

Emotion, of our astral (spirited) body.

Consciousness, of our mental body.

We have reason and emotion but no consciousness. Reason may be used to increase our being.

Gurdjieff uses "Reasonable understanding." A being's reason is the sum of his normal functions, these are:

The necessities of the body.

The necessities of the feelings.

The necessities of the intellectual, to understand; but we are doped by slogans and nine-tenths of us are in trance, subject to words.

When truth is experienced emotionally there is heat.

When truth is experienced intelligently there is light.

Gurdjieff claims that no *unconditioned* being who is part of the flux can possibly make any effort against it. If a man understood himself as the victim of blind chance, which he is, he would not consent to live.

If two beings meet, the superior must dominate. A "normal" man might enter a jungle and never come to harm—if he met only "normal" beasts.

The Gurdjieff method relates to potentialities and is not logically demonstrable. If you really *do* anything, you *know* and can communicate with any other *doer* or *knower*.

The wish of wishes in man is a desire to understand; our understanding is based on the number of our ideas and we can only speak or think in terms of our vocabulary.

Peace of mind without understanding should be impossible. Complete understanding uses three centers. This never happens, but may be brought about.

MONDAY, 21 NOVEMBER 1927

Orage began by saying that while theory was good, practice was necessary. He urged discussion, for an inability to discuss with others was a lack in oneself.

This evening was spent in discussing with the group individual experiences and results of work with self-observation. One man who had not attended for a year began by telling the cause of his absence. This was that he flattered himself that he got on well with people and was a good mixer, he noticed that he was becoming different; and as this grew he withdraw from the meetings. Orage said that Pythagoras is said to have enjoined a seven year vow of silence on his disciples. He said that it was clearly evident that the speaker feeling himself different had probably become a nuisance. That always with people, negative emotions must be turned into positive and that there was a natural dislike in most for anyone who felt himself "different" in ways they could not observe. They would turn on him and hence his own annoyance. This was a real confession of failure on the part of the disciple; and a good example of the folly of revealing what one was only learning to do.

Orage elaborated at some length a line of conduct to be followed, with those to whom one felt unsympathetic. One could always act "as if," not with intent to deceive but to put oneself in the proper posture to bring about a change. If you produce no response, it is usually a proof of your own insufficient technique. Do this persistently: establish smooth relations with effort to see good points.

Story of Gurdjieff who went to a monastery where he believed there was value and was rejected. Went to the vicinity and after much labor established himself, conquered their prejudice and got himself taught by the monks.

In the beginning of relations with people, the appearance is more than the reality, for the reality must be created. In general it is true that we have no "I." The aim of this method is to create this "I." Start with the lie "I have a body," when there is no "I" but if you persist in this, an "I" will become a reality. To love one's enemies is impossible but it is not impossible to act as if one did. Eventually, one may. The Coue method is like this although confined to the one matter of health. Autosuggestion is an active agent.

Of a thousand who hear "I have a body," but a few try to carry it out. "I" cannot be developed by any external aid, but by self-observation as a result of independent regular effort. "Live the life and know the doctrine." It is a terrible thing to assume. While the body is functioning, its values contribute to "me"; but when in dissolution, "I" am as little responsible as a rider whose horse has been shot from under him.

Food in general is a need. Any especial food is a want. Drink may be either.

FRIDAY, 25 NOVEMBER – MONDAY, 28 NOVEMBER 1927

Each of the following texts is to be like a fish line in a pool. They are to be pondered at various times and with varying results. Real pondering if properly directed will then be carried on in the unconscious and the results brought to mind.

There is a certain grammar of association. Such words as home, duty, love, romance use this fact. Home is a Nordic word and has deep connotations with northern peoples. These are Words of Power to such but they are just words to others. Other races in turn have their words which mean little to us.

Man is a being designed to create, encounter and overcome difficulties.

Man is in essence a passion for the reasonable understanding of the meaning and purpose of life.

Creation began but will never end.

The whole objective universe is a work of conscious creation, consciously maintained and for a conscious end.

There are three orders of location in the cosmic universe:

The Sun Absolute—corresponding to intelligence.

The suns—corresponding to emotions.

Planets—corresponding to the planetary body of man.

There are souls on most planets of the megalocosmos; but forms vary according to the form of the planet. Other planets, other forms. Each living thing has its own form. Story of Algernon Blackwood standing with outstretched arms, trying to feel how it was to be a tree.

There are between all planets inter-relations, just as between people. Planets have likes and dislikes, affinities and dis-affinities. Their forms we never may know. If a man in a chair were made to revolve, he would give an impression of a hazy roundness.

Planets have means of communication. Radiation is giving off matter (influence with matter).

Emanation, giving off immaterial substance (influence without matter).

There is an especial relation between the earth and the moon and this relation is abnormal. The earth met with a catastrophe and like a too young mother was prematurely delivered of a premature child. There is a mother complex.

All through the Gurdjieff text, the same words always mean the same thing.

Two planets may mingle radiations yet seem one at a distance.

"Reasonable understanding"

A being's reason is the sum of his normal functions. His normal functions on a physical plane are eating, sleeping, and all necessities of the body; on the emotional plane, to feel; on the intellectual plane to understand.

To try to change oneself by affecting one function will upset the totality.

Man's genuine duty is to fulfill the function for which he was created. Purpose is always inherent in structure; and the duty of the structure is to fulfill this purpose. You can tell the purpose of a motor car from its structure.

MONDAY, 28 NOVEMBER 1927

It is the same with humanity. Man's threefold function may be predicated from his three brains. This is strictly mechanical.

Very special conditions have made the earth what it is. A large part was struck off by a catastrophe and the moon and the earth were both impoverished. The earth was called upon for more emanations. This was brought about by conscious agencies, invisible beings with malign intentions which brought about Kundabuffer. As a patient in hospital needs a strong friend, full of hope and courage, so the moon, poor and sick, needed uplifting radiations which could only be supplied from the earth. Hence the earth must produce beings capable of this effort.

There are two kinds of unconsciousness. We surely furnish much of one kind.

There was enormous (unconscious) suffering in the late war. It is possible the moon needed it. In the absence of compulsion, people will not make effort. It is possible, the Flagellants saved the world much suffering and may have saved the world.

There is voluntary Suffering and through this you also gain power for yourself.

Escape you cannot; but one may make conscious effort. It is unbelievable that adults that lead a quiet life can be persuaded to go into war where they suffer themselves and kill as many as possible. No sane nation can fight; they must first be driven mad. Sakaki and Kundabuffer and hence the distortion. The moon must be surfeited with such buffering. Now comes the idea of universal brotherhood to counteract this.

Life evolved according to a sevenfold scale; but human life was slightly distorted. In consequence humanity ceased to learn from experience.

Words of power are just suggestibility. We are always under their influence. We are doped, and are thus suggestible to slogans, etc., 99% of our consciousness is in a trance, subject to words.

There is now no active pondering in the human race. There are probably not over twenty human beings who can. Why? Because the result of pondering might be disagreeable. One work of Kundabuffer is an obstacle to any attempt at pondering.

Egoism is measuring others by our likes and dislikes. We would despise a doctor who gave medicine because he liked its taste.

Self-love is preferring ourselves to our betters. How dare you carry on if you have never made an attempt to pay your debts or done a day's work? Self-love is such a preference for the body that it must be wrapped in luxury.

Pondering should never "take time." It should be done consciously. Self-observation is to use a part of the brain never before used and so to train it that pondering may be done consciously. It might be analogous to say that breathing takes too much time.

Pride is an ignorant presumption that qualities of the organism are due to merit. All organs are handed over to the behaviorist. They are the results of Ancestry plus Society. Literally, I am not responsible for my conduct. It is an impertinence to be either proud or apologetic.

Efforts at self-improvement are often disastrous because of the identification of "I" with the organism.

An offer of a million dollars to anyone who can observe himself for one hour. A trained observer once tried to listen to the sound of his own voice and was shocked at this inability to do so after a few moments. The reason is that self-observation presupposes the development of certain parts of the brain. Understanding can only be acquired by voluntary effort and conscious suffering. Everything else is the result of environment and heredity.

Modern beings do nothing, but evolution is done through them. There can be no peace without understanding. There is no one to blame. Kundabuffer has been reproved but its offices remain the same.

TIME

Time is a process which can be neither understood, felt nor sensed. Time is the ability to experience, time is the sum of potentialities in that plane, time is the unique subjective.

The Creator found himself running down. He had to do something, to observe himself. The phenomena of his body came to consciousness and He created the world and had to support and feed it.

Before consciousness we eat to transform substances into matter with radiations and emanations. This we do in common with trees and plants. If it is done voluntarily we gain.

Time is one's own possibility of experience.

Life ordinarily lived is merely passing time until death. Make time, do not pass it. The planetary body exists much as an electric transformer to "step up" a low form of matter to a higher. We transform food, air, impressions involuntarily. This may be made voluntary and a means for self creation.

To make a soul by self-observation, voluntary suffering and conscious labor; but in our form of understanding, truth itself becomes absurd. Beelzebub says man has been hardly treated and he shows heart over this cosmic circumstance.

The sun is a cold body which contains neither light nor heat, these are due to emanations from the sun to our atmosphere. What are these substances? Electricity or Okidanokh. When emanations reach the substance they feel "remorse" or an aspiration to raise the vibration (emanation from the sun is effort to understand). If you succeed, you have light; if you fail you have heat. When truth is experienced emotionally there is heat, when intellectually, light. Heat is failed light. To one who has attained, the day should never be long enough for this cold intensity. "Quiet puff" or great effect in quietness. One should have a heart of fire but head and feet of ice. Cold brain is light; a cool demeanor lets no energy waste. Okidanokh is in the very substance of life.

Through it, it may be possible for future science to create life when the third or neutralizing force of electricity is understood. At present we have positive and negative electricity; but no neutralizing. Electricity is in the atmosphere but in limited quantity. It divides into the three currents in our three brains:

Cerebral   positive
Spinal   negative
Visceral   neutral

The cerebral creates by its effects on the spinal brain. This makes food for the internal or middle brain. Three brains are normal to man.

At present nature has need of man's planetary body *only*. Nature has no obligation to provide man with an emotional or cerebral body. We must acquire these ourselves. There is always ample substance from which to make them.

Only three centered beings can consciously create this new body; for there is for it no natural evolution.

How are the materials meant for the new body now utilized? By Kundabuffer, used without understanding. The very stuff of which dreams are made is stuff from which other bodies could be made.

Electricity (Okidanokh) can be used mechanically or vitally. The more electric light, the less light. Electricity is being more and more prostituted to the use of the planetary body. There is a notable loss of human power to think and feel.

In Athens there was no electric light but a group of one hundred most noteworthy people.

Electricity is fixed in amount and the outgo is more than the income, squandered for the indulgence of the planetary body.

"Potential" is the neutralizing force.

Every being tends to become more and more particularized in its threefoldness. Key thrown out by what is known as evolution.

TUESDAY, 13 DECEMBER 1927

This was a reading of Beelzebub.

The fifth Decent had to do with Ashiata Shiemash. His object was how to produce a substantial and permanent change in the character of the human species.

A reform can be measured and scaled according to its effects and its difficulties. The reform as proposed attacked the whole species. Try to imagine the scale of this. Try to speculate for yourself some practical ways in which humanity may be changed.

Ashiata doubted every conclusion brought by sociology, because of its subjective conditioning and limitations. Not trusting these, he tried to induce conscious, that is, impartial intellection or he tried to prepare himself to be impartial. He could trust an impartial judgment. Then he tried to formulate his conclusions:

The human race was too far gone in subjectivity to be able to make an effective appeal to faith, hope and love. He found these on any adequate scale impossible. Consequently unlike all other religious reformers he decided not to build on these three but to find something deeper and more accessible. He found this in objective consciousness. This he believed to be the Voice of God. The presupposition with him was that this essential consciousness is not dead in man but is dormant. In certain circumstances, this latent may be brought to serve the individual as an infallible guide, showing him his duty. In this he may understand and voluntarily co-operate in the scheme of things. The slave may be turned thus into a son. He hoped by taking a certain number of people and training them in self-observation, participation and through voluntary suffering and conscious and constant effort to bring about a change.

The beginning of this discipline is first realized by the coming to life of the objective consciousness. To this must be added, ideas of cosmology to give the nature of duty, of man's place in the universe and what is to be done.

The following sentences will be intelligent only to the awakened: (most of us are bound to take them in a subjective way).

There are five points of objective morality:

1.   *The satisfaction of the planetary body*

This has no association with sense-gratification. It is strictly a fulfillment of the needs of the body and is an obligation to keep it in a state of lean health, pliable, adjustable, uncompromising, with neither excess nor deficiencies. It must answer to one's needs. To be fat and soft is to be immoral. The body should be neither indulged nor denied. Its objective criterion should be its maximum condition during the in-dwelling of the individual. Our body is occupied by a young soul and should be used for its needs. The range of the soul's life is conditioned by the planetary body, which is our sole means of life.

2.   *To improve one's being.*

What does being mean? Being cannot be defined in terms of the intellectual or physical body. It is the kernel of their nut. It is what we *are*, not what we *know*. It is what we are in *ourselves*.

Question yourself as to this being.

Are you afraid of being alone?

Can you take care of yourself?

Are you reckless?

Do you lose your head?

In an emergency will you have some suggestion, or a plan (never mind whether it is workable)?

This state of being is the only thing that grows or decreases.

The remainder of our qualities depend on our planetary bodies and on chance. It is not developed personality but is developed essence. All Saint Paul affirmed of love is equally true of essence. Try to find out what is meant by this.

This second objective morality is to improve being-effort. You are aware when you have made an effort which is an effort of being. This is the only way to improve being. Review each day the moment of maximum effort to be or to do. This must not be for calculated reason but for exercise. If done for selfish reasons it does not count. It must be gratuitous looking on life as a gymnasium.

Examine for efforts performed daily, running the great race. Gurdjieff says we should always be in a state of "puff," that is doing a little beyond our will to do. We should bully consciousness. Thus we acquire strength and become strong in spirit. To the Greeks spiritual is *spirited*.

3.   *You should always aim to know more and more of this world and the laws of its creation and maintenance.*

This is the aim of philosophy—an understanding of the universe. Bertrand Russell proposed to himself to "understand life as a problem." Now to be a philosopher is the privilege of the few; but is one of the functions of a normal human being. All others are not normal, are deficient. The dignity of man does not consist in right answers but in asking questions. We must enquire of the existing world what it all is about. What is our objective? What is that of people we meet?

We should always go about questioning our experience. It is not necessary to pick places in which to do this. Every meeting is full of material. Part of you should question what is taking place; but it is not necessary to behave provincially. You should be enquiring in all circumstances and try for understanding. Get understanding or wisdom, health, strength and wisdom. This gives one something to do for one's self, as a doctor is frequently not needed till one has exhausted his own enquiry.

Continuous effort will bring an assurance of inner strength, a stretching of intellectual faculties.

A proper effort to ponder will stretch the mind.

Memory, attention and observation may be automatic and intensified by indirect exercise of the whole mind, trying to investigate existence itself.

Wisdom is realized ignorance. Ignorance is a form of knowledge. The difference knowledge and ignorance is the difference between wisdom and knowledge. An effort to come to a conclusion will give you understanding.

The "I" can never be objectified:
First: Because of the difference between "I" and the planetary body.

Second: The difficulty of observing emotions.
Third: The difficulty of observing the mind.

The more you realize you don't know, the more you know.

In this book the cosmology is set out in a more or less regular order. But Orage defies anyone to tell him what it means.

Attempt a cosmic survey of life on this planet. Every time we inhale someone is born; and someone dies as we exhale.

The greatest artists are those who have aimed at an impossible perfection. Try to picture the planet and get the by-product.

Work on your being as hard as you can. By stretching little men become great men. True also as to emotion, getting one's second wind.

In course of formulating any question, you get into an area where the answer must lie.

Acquisition of strength comes from overcoming one's natural indisposition to make effort. We fail to realize the necessity of effort. This effort is an objective morality of mind.

4.   *To pay one's debt*

To be free to serve is our duty. Not one of us has discharged his debt to nature. To be alive is an unique experience, a miracle, whose cost to nature is the subjugation of all nature to us. We take as a birthright this physical body and all external favorable circumstance. The vast majority does nothing but childishly enjoy this gift. We are self-indulgent infants. Duty includes the recognition of services rendered and our obligation to repay. Earn your living by your quantity of effort. Each dollar represents an accumulation of human effort. How dare you squander the labor of others? You may spend weeks in pondering what unprofitable servants we are, not worth our keep. How can nature let us live? The majority of the human race must stand on her books on the debit side. Try to earn more than you spend. Man may command the lower orders of life, if he becomes more himself. If for an indulgence, he incurs a debt and does not convert this, he must pay to the uttermost farthing in Purgatory.

5.   *Service—which is helping others to self-realization*

Not gratifying others' weakness for our own praise but helping them to develop their own essences. Sociological virtues are demoralizing by gratitude which is satisfying and pleasing to us. We dare not be hard with others because we should be equally hard with ourselves. Ouspensky when asked to give pupils the technique of fasting said he could not because it was impossible for him at that time to fast. When told they wished to fast themselves, he could not himself eat and teach them fasting. The only service you can render others is to help them to discharge their objective duty.

Nothing else is really a service.

The "reason" of a being is the sum of its normal functions. A normal human being has an "I" and its functions are human reason.

Function of health

Function of strength

Inquiry for understanding

Paying for cost of keep

Service to others

A man or woman is one who discharges these five functions. These five make the Reason of a human being. Omit one of these and the being becomes abnormal. Most of us have one of these abnormal or even atrophied. These five should be as the fingers to the hand. Such a being must have an integral passion behind him. Ponder the word "passion." It is a craze lifelong and permanently. "By thy cross and passion." "Holy" equals whole as an objective morality; and everyone is whole according to the degree of his passion.

For pondering—*Recurrence*.

The aim of a tree is the production of seed. There is a difference between seed and leaves. The leaves fall and before they do so they give back to the tree. They recur, for services rendered and come back next year. But the fall of a seed is different from a leaf, which leaf gives back its life. The life of the tree passes into the seed. The seed is a dead loss to the tree; but leaves give back.

On the Tree of Life of the universe are developed seeds. Those human beings who maintain life in themselves may recur. We are recurring leaves with possibility of becoming seeds.

There is an infinite progression to being; and a progression to non-being. We are punished by our sins and not for them.

A man is responsible for all his acts except in death pangs.

The body has many wants in excess of needs; and many needs for which it has no wants.

Satisfaction of wants destroys; of needs builds.

There is a margin between needs and wants; e. g. sleep.

Objective thought is an attempt to understand the nature of things, as reasonably exhibited; i.e. to understand the reason in the mind of the creator. This starts on the assumption that the whole is intelligible, a process being played through. Yet man has a function not yet developed to comprehend in terms of our reason.

Souls are beings who have attained objective reason.

A normal cognizance of the cosmos would be the first indication of what a normal three centered being would have, a direct personal knowledge, not hearsay.

Our common birth-right is to understand the cosmos, just as a man born on one continent was able to understand the existence of others. He cannot understand a thing unless there is a correspondence with us, whether we are its product or it is our projection. If you are three centered, the cosmos must also be.

How cheaply can you buy cordiality? It is your business to discover beneath your friend's apparently foolish activities, what he really wants. The need is there, try to discover it.

The price of consciousness is effort.

"I have a body" may be turned into "I have the use of a body."

Our hope is freedom, the capacity to separate "I" from "It." The change from an unconscious to a conscious life is like changing the gear of a car. One must ask one's friends to await the process. Frequently at the beginning we may antagonize and make enemies for the doctrine.

Our business is to keep the three brains in order and working smoothly, finding out one's *needs* for food, sleep etc. and live accordingly.

There are no rules except as we find them for oneself.

"I" is composed of substance from suns and interplanetary spaces, but the body of planetary matter.

ORAGE LECTURES IN CARMEL

M.E.B.

When Orage came to Carmel, he held his first talk at the Blackman home. Of this talk, which was a very remarkable one, no one kept any notes. That which follows is all that was gathered of his remaining six talks.

The first lecture explained about self-observation, the mechanicality of our responses to our environment, and the existence of our three centers.

MONDAY, 13 AUGUST 1928

If you will review pictorially the forms of your body from childhood's earliest recollection, you will gain what is probably your first experience of the Fourth Dimension. This is done by experiencing a pictorial review of its forms; and this implies a most valuable psychological effort, guaranteed to give new experiences, which are otherwise impossible of attainment. Through this you may understand the physiological norm of your body.

The world as you know it may be defined by your possibilities of experience in thought, feeling and sensation. Thought is comparison; emotions lie between the poles of "I like" and "I don't like." All system of religion or ethics are attempts to break through these three.

The human race has completed its experiences in these three centers and all civilizations are the reshuffling of these cards.

The diatonic scale is really a physical formula, and is a description of nature in general. It consists of two tetra-chords, the last of one being the first of the next. The passage from do to mi is regular. Then comes a halftone, which indicates further progression must be different. See the "Knight's move" in chess. The peculiar character of this half tone is the necessity it creates for something new.

The human being starts at do and proceeds normally, seriatim physically do, emotionally re, mentally mi. Unless something new comes in, the scale cannot be repeated. Just here all real originality must be concentrated to discover ways of progressing other than the three means. The race is on the verge of the note Fa, which is the possible bridge between the first and second tetrachord. This bridge must be crossed by new means which are not within our experiences. When once this bridge is crossed three new possibilities may develop:

Wish will turn into will.

Thought will turn into consciousness.

Personality will turn into individuality.

These last three correspond to those parts of the brain whose use is now unknown, and whose possible use has been a great problem (see Sir Arthur Keith); from Pythagoras down it has been claimed that this three fifths is the soil from which to develop real will, consciousness and individuality.

Real will is absence of wish.

Real individuality is absence of personality.

Real consciousness is the absence of thought.

When Pythagoras spoke of the higher powers of man, he meant exactly that and not the further development of powers already possessed. We have no means at present to add this cubit to our stature; and this at once rules out all forms of concentration and meditation. It also rules out *practices* of all sorts, emotional and physical. The work of all Schools and all Religions has been to try to acquire new states of consciousness. Insanity has resulted from this attempt when made physically; a state of softened mentality when made emotionally. Higher mathematics is the entrance to an intellectual Yoga. Such men as Plotinus were emotionally infantile, behaving like spoiled children.

To be in possession of the body means to be aware of its behavior. This was the whole of the Pythagorean method.

Perceptions actively taken are to will, consciousness and individuality what passive ones are to wish, thought and emotion.

Speech always evokes corresponding associations; therefore do not observe the words of anyone but the meaning latent in the voice. Tone conveys nine tenths and one tenth is verbal association. Psychologists do not observe directly but only through manifestations.

No crowd can convey its ideas. McDougall took a politically minded man, with his ears stopped and blindfolded into a political mob. There were no "waves of crowd Psychology" through his obstructions. His bandages were removed and he at once became one of the mob. Its passion was conveyed only through contact. Telepathy undoubtedly occurs and it is not yet known why.

Any analysis of posture, gesture, movements, tone and facial expression is known as a post mortem.

The only knowledge is through personal experience.

It is a heresy that the quantity of attention which we possess is limited.

Experiment: Read one verse; write another; read aloud a third. An orchestra leader hears all the instruments simultaneously yet can pick one of them out.

Attempt at non-identification with the phenomena of the given body.

Despise any agreements based on belief. The state of belief is pleasant but the state of knowledge is difficult.

The body is conditioned; it has its own form; but our three systems are incomplete. The visceral system does not experience blood lust, the sensory is not capable. We are thus unevenly endowed.

There are three lines of heredity conditioned at moment of birth with a bias toward one center. These centers have different life periods therefore they run down at different periods. We may die in one center. Many die in mental center at an early age.

Many people can only repeat emotionally what they once felt. All connoisseurship atrophies the emotion of beauty, complete experience is impossible when one center has run down.

We are wound up for physical experiencing of life and unnecessary movements are a waste, Learn to relax; for all tension is a physical wastage.

Self-observation brings a relaxing of muscles. It is a human function to be aware of the body and in the absence of this function, the energy goes into unwise constrictions.

There is much emotional waste: regret, reproach, criticism of the past, expenditure of imaginary emotions on remote objects; worry over things of tomorrow. These are expending present emotions on Ghosts. It is a form of incest.

Emotions should be for certain and immediate use, sing for the future creates the sentimentalist. There is only one time—*this moment*.

Argument or discussion to arrive at a real discussion must proceed through octave. Where begin, what next, the what? This will take you through the octave of Logic. (Here Orage deliberately breaks off to test his audience. He then speaks of "feeding ghosts.")

A third form of emotional waste is looking for beauty, coupled with reading. He called this a present of blood to a nonentity and announce that most works of art were blood suckers.

The extreme artistic type is apt to be defective ethically. So great is the sum of the emotions which they expend upon objects that none is left for persons. Therefore, beware of a work of art. Do not spend emotion in space or time or on objects. Day dreaming is most dangerous; and that usual purposeless reading was the massaging of the cerebral system and a most extravagant form of self-abuse.

He spoke of dreams; there are three varieties from each of the three centers. It is very seldom that the three centers go to sleep at once. Really to sleep, they must all sleep, and about four hours. Otherwise we have a sense of partial sleep.

Love the day, so that all centers are exhausted at the same time. Self-observation will insure a full day and consequently induce maximum free working in the organism.

In Whitehead you can read his attempt to describe awareness before it becomes thought.

An exercise in thought:

Think of the planet

Think of its organized kingdoms, the coal of the past.

Think of the human beings on this ball, about two thousand million.

We draw thirty thousand breaths a day, and thirty thousand days are the approximate life of man.

Every time we breathe someone is born and every time we breathe out someone dies.

At any given moment every possible human experience is being gone through by some person.

Every moment is the present hour to some person.

Every possible action is being performed and simultaneously by the totality.

This is Adam Kadmon.

Try to think of the planet as the scene of every possible experience; thus you will arrive at an elevated and cosmic state of consciousness.

FRIDAY, 17 AUGUST 1928

The human body is as much a scientific specimen as anything botanical and must be considered as impersonally.

We will treat of the three categories of dreams later (answer to?).

As plants aim to produce seed, we exist for some unknown end. None of our faculties exist except from heredity or sociology. People differ not by their virtues but by inherent faculties.

There are two forms of knowledge: personal, such as toothache and common knowledge.

Awareness presupposes something of which to be aware. Read "The Mystery of Mind." (Author?)

There is no real concern for the human race as s whole; man is but one of the biological species of nature. In nature, there is a progressive series of biological forms. These can be arranged in a certain order. Here we also find the octave, i.e. matter, metal, mineral, cell, invertebrate, vertebrate and man.

Was the cell the result of chance?

Is nature the whole of the planet?

Nature converts solar energy into earth—matter.

It is now thought there are two other milky ways and that this is not an infinite universe.

Another octave: "I," nature, planet, sun, series of suns, milky way, universe.

We live in a seven fold prison of two parallel octaves.

Butterfly, caterpillar, chrysalis. What our next stage may be is as unknown to us as a caterpillar who may think he will come out of the chrysalis a bigger and better caterpillar. We merely expect more thought, emotion and sensation.

Man is at present in the half octave. Whole possible octaves of nature have been completed; the continuance of evolution depends on man, for the universe is finished.

"Man's octave, the first three notes have been uttered; it now requires the fourth, fa, bringing about sol, individuality, la, consciousness and will.

Just as the cell is the bridge between the organic and the inorganic there must also be as a bridge, a species of act, an awareness, not previously thought, felt or sensed, which is comparable in another cycle to the appearance of the cell.

It is impossible for the organism to observe itself, for the organism is the object. This entity, this imaginary "I," which in process of self-observation becomes self-conscious, comes into existence. Thus it realizes its own being. See Soddy, "Matter, Energy and Force."

The threefoldness of our knowledge comes from our own threefold nature. Metaphysics is a highly organized form of play.

All poets are the emotional centers of their own communities.

How we work: Here is a body, why change posture? Why move? There are two sets of strains, discomforts, digestion, internal chemistry images in the mind or external impressions.

We are commanded to love our enemies. This is impossible; but by changing the image in our mind it may become possible.

We can think only to foregone conclusions implicit in our environment. Thought is like the response of a piano to the touch of circumstance.

You may have curiosity, yet its ordinary exercise brings you out by the same door that in you went.

A human being is one who is psychologically aware of being attached to a biological body. "The body of this death."

"In the beginning was the word." Being preceded becoming.

"I" is—but "I" does not exist. The soul does not exist but may by doing something. "I am a worm and no man." Read "The Buddhism of the Buddha," "Friends of God of the Overland," Matthew Arnold.

The Fourth Way, not Yogi, ascetic, practical man.

Man differs from animals by virtue of his potentialities. There is waking, self and world consciousness.

Chemical affinity belongs to our biological outfit, plus the effects of what food we eat.

One "I" converses with another "I" by an especial language, a code.

WEDNESDAY, 22 AUGUST 1928

There are seven octaves in the universe such as music, mathematics and practical psychology.

There is a chemistry of transference of energy; i.e. anger makes a chemical change.

There is a psychonic theory.

A child has potentialities of vibration we have lost. We are like a piano on which only Jazz has been played, spoiled for a player of Beethoven.

A wish entertained in the visceral system makes its exit either cerebral or motor. Hence we are either intro or extrovert as our wish finds its easiest line of discharge.

Within this symmetrical biped is a threefold being; and as an experiencing organism men must be threefold.

The order of proportion of strength as manifested in given individuals between the three nerve centers cerebral, visceral and practical give the three types and by permutations you get a complete line.

There were nine muses, one for each sub-center. Plotinus wrote the Ennead.

Our whole waking life may be interpreted by our behavior just as our sleeping dreams.

I can induce in my waking state any nightmare and yet be aware of my train of thought.

Jung says that the un- or subconscious are the stored impressions of our ancestors. Freud an ancestral memory.

All of the ten thousand sense impressions of which we are not aware are stored and become our unconscious and recur to us only in abnormal states, illness, fatigue etc. There is no entrance to the psyche except by means of the five senses.

Strictly speaking, all imagination is memory. The muses were the daughters of memory.

Story of the man at the telephone and the man with the inferiority complex? (Does anyone recall this? I do not, M. E. B.)

The consciousness of possession of will gives individuality. This is not developed of itself; if tried personality results. When you have will you are conscious and hence have individuality.

Will excludes wish. Will is a gratuitous act, inclination is something done; will is a vow.

In digesting air, we use only the lower octave

Air
Gas
Magnetism
Food octave:
Solid
Liquid
Gas
Emotion
Magnetism
Sex

DATE UNCERTAIN

When one can realize a picture of oneself as clearly as that of an absent friend, it is "fa," the moment of birth. After this passage to "sol," there is growth.

Direct efforts of self-observation to unimportant times; and the important ones will follow.

Practice on your friends and then try to put yourself in this gallery. Get rid of your pet aversions by facing them and thus release energy.

The final duty of human beings is to become brain cells in the mind of God. At present, nature must act through human beings and human beings are too confused to act. Were there a few hundred clear brain cells—nature could carry on better. At present most of our ability is mortgaged to petty likes and dislikes. Animals spend all their time looking after their physical wants. Human beings should ponder for one half of their time.

Other senses than the eye have their impressions and images. All the images of all the senses combine to form a combined image. We are "under a human prejudice."

Types, spread among all peoples I must, possibly may, run the gamut.

Napoleonic	everywhere
Sage	Emerson
Philosopher	Plato
Scientist	Archimedes
Bard	Homer
Politician	Machiavelli
Statesman	Gladstone
Leader of Revolt	Cromwell
Charlatan	Cagliostro
Adventurer	Jason

PONDERING

Go to Biographical Dictionary and study men according to type. Everyone is some undeveloped type, a bud; classify your acquaintance. There is a difference between types and characters, amateurs, grave diggers, barristers.

Make a consistent survey, methodical, of the nature of human beings. Sort out their ideas. Learn as Swift said to "classify things in the bud."

All morphological changes will give you the fourth dimensional image. Do a daily exercise of your life in pictures.

Contemplate the planet, Adam Kadmon, the five races and isolated tribes. Try to assemble the experiences of Adam Kadmon as you would your own. Adam Kadmon's cells are continually changing.

Think of Mankind—Whither?

System, Organ, Tissues, Cell, Molecule, Atom, Electron. There are octaves of the atom see Eddington's "Nature of the Physical World," showing atoms grouped in octaves. Read "Astronomy and Cosmogony" by Jeans.

There is a cosmic octave: moon, earth, planets, sun, milky way, other milky ways, the whole universe.

There is an exact relation between the cosmic and the human.

The universe is a reasonable being. Its completion would be "Pralaya."

There is an order of beings: animals, man, superior beings and principalities.

Self-observation will subtly assist in the pursuit of any subject already chosen but is a parallel interest. It is a scientific self study. A study is a serious effort to arrive at the truth.

Our usual repertory has four or five facial expressions, about ten tones to our voice, three postures and a few movements The body is our only means of knowing we are alive. All experience is conditioned by the body which also prevents many desirable experiences. Whenever it becomes an objective instrument it is possible to control it. We are slaves to our habits. Take one week to observing each of the five, then one week at two, one at three, four, then at five. "Screening the ape"—observing oneself instead of the hysterics of the other person, by imitation or the reverse. "Cease to feed them with your Imitation." We have obligations to continue the body we have received and convert it from an animal into a man. It is an obligation to continue self development. Habits may be conditioned but not self-observation. An act of will is unconditioned and comes, no one knows whence. We may change from servants of God to Sons of God.

The difference between strength and weakness is a difference of wishes. A weak willed person is a democracy of wishes. The Napoleon with very few wishes gets somewhere. The Gnostics said humanity is the procession of fate.

CARMEL 1928

ORAGE TALKS ON ART

There are exact meanings to philosophy and science because of the three centers:

Philosophy—cerebral

Science—sensory-motor

Art—visceral or emotional

Religion is an attempt to remind man of his three fold nature's obligation to the world. It is a common sense effort to remind him, he should be more.

Each of us has a possible range of emotion, a keyboard which responds to external stimulation. Its general range is much restricted. Emotions may be classified:

Negative—Jealousy, Despair etc.

Positive—Love, Admiration etc.

Neutral—Absence of Positive or negative

We may pass through this on our way to positive or negative. We depend on external circumstances to arouse emotion. Take the list of emotions in the Thesaurus and cross off all you have never felt. To go through a Russian Revolution might induce new experiences. George Bernard Shaw tells of an experience visiting the front during the war, where he saw a man leaning over a wire; then saw he had lost his head; and Shaw said he thoroughly enjoyed the experience. Our lives are mostly devoid of circumstances which rouse emotion. None of us knows his possibilities nor his possible range of emotions. We are like an un-played piano.

Art, being design, functions as a complement to life. It is a being stimulation, not ordinarily applied, a trick to complete one's emotional experience and supplement it by artificial means. People who have full responses to life cannot be bothered with art. Art enters when life fails.

TUESDAY, 29 APRIL 1930

How many artists are aware that their function is to arouse emotion; and deliberately employ a technic to do this? A fully conscious artist has the capacity by artificial means to evoke an emotion which is comparable to that evoked by real life. Most artists aim only to express themselves and relieve their own emotional states. They have no awareness of the effect of thus discharging emotion. Others do not create new experiences but revive old ones, subjective entirely.

I want an artist to induce an emotion which I have heard described but have never felt. This is a piece of real life and I owe him a debt of gratitude. Thus a conscious artist supplements life.

We make our first mistake in attempting to judge; and next to attribute beauty.

In all cases, beauty is present in a work of art as a conveyer and may be taken for granted while trying to experience whatever emotion should be conveyed. Beauty is common because it is a cheap way of avoiding a careful statement of the effect produced. I have a simple rule by which to classify music. Draw two imaginary lines, below the throat and below the solar plexus. When music gives feeling above the solar plexus it is good (Classical), when the throat, it is good popular. In solar plexus, it is rubbish and all sentimental. An objective work of art produces a general effect. There is no form of art which is felt as generally as is rain in the physical world, which has the same reaction from all. Objective work of art—which has the same effect as prolonged self awareness. The Pyramids constitute an objective work of art.

People all say the same thing of the Taj Mahal, that it gives them an ecstatic delight and yet a sense of personal insignificance. It is like the presentation of the idea of a tree to a leaf.

Color has a tonal octave.

Temple music produces its intended effect. This is done as propaganda by agents of the powers.

The artist should understand human response and be master of the means to arouse them.

"I labor till Christ be formed in you."

TUESDAY, 29 APRIL 1930

QUESTION: What is partkdolg duty?

ORAGE: Duty in three languages, that is intelligent, emotional and instinctive. The intellectual effort is to understand the meaning and aim of existence. Emotional is to feel this. Instinctive is to use the planetary body to carry this out.

QUESTION: What is the debt we owe?

ORAGE: Every being is indebted for his incarnation at birth. Just as sociological works are produced at great effort on the part of somebody, so also "natural" works and laws are produced by conscious beings with great effort.

QUESTION: Isn't the imposition of Kundabuffer enough to release us from the debt?

ORAGE: But the removal of Kundabuffer left only psychological consequences. Physical handicaps are often beyond our power to deal with but psychological handicaps can be dealt with.

QUESTION: What is meant by "paying"? (The answer to this question given in notes on May 6th.)

ORAGE: Suppose that children on growing up will realize the effort their upbringing has cost. Our participation in existence, making possible our sharing in life, has cost effort.

Remark: But children do not ask to be born.

ORAGE: I invite anyone in this room to say whether he wishes to go on living. All our values are based on two desires: A long life and a happy one. Happy if possible but at any rate long. (When things are painful a part of us sometimes wishes to escape.) The normal being of every species desires to live. Thus implying that existence itself is a privilege, and for this privilege normal beings feel gratitude.

QUESTION: May we go back to the question of responsibility for psychological handicaps? How can we escape from our own conditioning, for we may be rationalizing?

ORAGE: Let us assume that certain physiological diseases cannot be cured at our present stage of knowledge; but psychological diseases can be cured.

QUESTION: What entitles us to think so?

ORAGE: Experience. For what has been conditioned can be un-conditioned.

QUESTION: I would like to feel this obligation but certain objections arise.

ORAGE: They are not intellectual objections, they are lack of emotional response. Our intellectual understanding often outstrips our feeling, e.g, we can clearly see the unequal distribution of wealth or the class system that puts incompetents in power but do we feel it? If I borrow money whether I feel my obligation or not I am still in debt.

QUESTION: But suppose I don't know that I have borrowed anything?

ORAGE: Whence did you derive the possibility of an existence? That which distinguishes a man from a dog is his occasional concern as to what a man is. A planetary machine capable of turning on itself and recognizing itself as a planetary machine. With the introduction of understanding there comes responsibility. Without any purpose, that is, on physiological considerations alone, we are merely the cruelest species of the carnivore. Consider the slavery to which we subject other species for our own egotistic purposes. Our use of other species is justified only if it is in pursuance of the objective duty of conscious development.

Partkdolg duty is the development of all three types of one's potentialities. Every living being aims implicitly or explicitly at making the most of himself. But he is usually limited to one or two of the possible fields and to the potentialities near the surface. Who will deny that that being who develops all types is truly superior?

Among these potentialities are in the intellectual center an understanding of the purpose and aim of existence. In the emotional center, a sense of obligation to make this design prevail. The possibility of practical, disinterested action. In the absence of reaching these stages we have only words, but when these things are experienced, these things can be understood. In any development, for instance, writing, if we are in advance of experience the teaching is not understood. If one continues writing, the moment comes when the pupil knows what writing is.

(Here followed a long discussion of the method.)

Self-observation, the importance of non-identification. Participation "as if" one were performing the acts. Experimentation and how little this has actually been practiced. It would bring a realization of inertia and the vacuity of invention end the value of movement against habit.

Without experience in the above all talk about intentional suffering and conscious labor are mere abracadabra. We have been trying for the past two weeks to talk in the simplest words—about will but it is impossible to convey. We cannot convey it in words for the understanding involved *must* be formal, that is, the product of experience. Pondering is the mastication of experience.

QUESTION: But won't we arrive at understanding of will through development?

ORAGE: But development except in the planetary body does not just happen. From the point of view of the planetary body, idiots satisfy nature as well as any other for they eat and excrete; they breathe air; they transform substances but they are not satisfying their emotional and intellectual potentialities. Nature does supply a model. The planetary body develops from childhood to maturity. But nature is not concerned with the development of the higher bodies. The development of the planetary body through the passive perception of sense-impressions is an analogy. Our psychic body also develops through impressions, taken not passively but consciously. These impressions are not of the external world but of its own planetary body. All development is through impressions, for we live by them.

The environment for the development of the planetary body is the external world as we register its impressions. The environment for the development of the body of the psyche is the planetary body the impressions of which must be consciously taken.

The psyche also goes through stages and it arrives at maturity when it can

301

say: I understand the meaning of life, I understand the nature of objective morality, I understand the nature of disinterested action.

"Intentional suffering" has nothing whatever to do with pain or the infliction of disagreeables. The word suffering in this system means *making an effort*. The conscious making of effort is called intentional suffering. Make effort we must but ordinarily we make it passively. To give oneself the trouble to do what one wishes to do. Weak fears, calculations etc. Overcoming these inhibitions that keep us from doing what we wish, this is called intentional suffering. Trying to discount the hypnotism of sociological conditioning. What we lack is not wish, but the will to overcome inhibitions. We must not have asceticism but a deliberate exploitation of life and joy. To be too moral is sometimes to be too weak. "Letting I will wait upon I dare not." "I would if conditions were different." Analyze these "ifs." You will find weaknesses, fears. Perhaps a conscious being would fill us with moral horror because of his ruthless disregard of many of our sociologically conditioned scruples. Our scruples may be false conditioning. In looking at achievements of an objective aim. The development of will is divine and goes on step by step.

QUESTION: Can this will ever be against Society?

ORAGE: Never. Since the value of Society itself is from the development of this kind of will in individuals. Our present response to manifestations of others both pleasant and unpleasant is mechanical.

Our first step must be to be able to defend oneself against mechanical responses to the negative emotions. These are most destructive to the organism and fatal to its purposes, such as depression, envy, hate and jealousy etc.

Yet so identified are we with our mechanical suffering that we prefer it to making a little intentional suffering to avoid it. But a remedy has been prescribed in non-identification.

QUESTION: What is the pondering relating to "Where do I come In?"

ORAGE: Who am I? I am a sum of my experience. Pondering is the reviving and comparing of concrete experiences within our recollections. Compare pondering with reflection: Reflection uses words within one's recollection. Pondering uses experiences within one's own recollection. Take a list of emotions and go over them recollecting, not in words out in reviving the experience. Can you string on a single thread all the experiences of pride that you have had? Can you review your life not as scenes but as experiences? Can you weigh and distinguish differences in intensity? This is pondering. It is impossible to ponder someone else's experiences, but "as if" someone else's. Neither identified nor not identified. An example is the surgeon.

QUESTION: Is playing a role an involuntary identification?

ORAGE: Yes, with three degrees of completeness depending on whether we use one, two or three centers. Conscious labor is defined as a live objective, a raison d'être—real reason for being. When for your life, as far as you can see it, you have a definite state to reach and all your behavior is directed toward it.

Remember Ashiata Shiemash, who was described as a "messenger"; apparently his message was not communicated to him. He had to ponder, acting on his own impulses; his aim had to be self-discovered. He is the only character in the book except Beelzebub himself who discovered conscious labor and who found his life-aim. Such a thing is remote from us for we can only formulate relatively temporary aims. Now defined in this system as the ultimate aim of every being is the attainment of self-consciousness and through this of a cosmic consciousness. But not feeling that, our idea is to adopt provisional aims which will not run counter to that and may further it. So that if I come upon you reading a book or talking or doing anything whatever and ask of you in what way the thing you are doing is related to what you intend to do, you can say I am doing this for that, which will lead to that and to that and so forth, to have purposiveness.

QUESTION: Of what use is the kind of life led at the Institute?

ORAGE: It is a metaphor picturing how energy may be expended. It is a therapy for duty.

Charles Sumner Greene

TALKS AND LECTURES WITH A. R. ORAGE

I am not inviting you to look into a mirror which shows you as you think you are, but into a mirror showing what you really are. When this portrait which is real, is reflected in our glass instead of the one we ordinarily see there, the feeling of self satisfaction will not be great, and we will wish to change the portrait.

We say our state is this
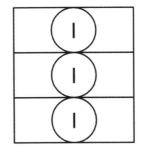
Mental ability

Emotional ability

Ability to do

I invite you to say in which respect you wish to improve.

The "I" means the lowest marks—a generous allowance.

What is your ambition to be more of in the future than you are now? This will settle your type.

Do you wish more understanding of books, art, Einstein? This is the type whose ambition it is to improve the mind.

Type two, is one who wishes to feel more, delight, more happiness etc..

The third type wishes to do more, to be more practical.

You must belong to one type, but all types are mixed for to belong to one pure type would be a misfortune, it would mean one of yoga monsters.

Types are generally a mixture of two centers pre-eminent.

If three centers were equally developed it would mean a well-round person.

The desire to improve in one center is largely hereditary.

We might everyone of us be said to be an incarnated wish or set of wishes.

There is in man an urge for growth because he is not developed,

What makes the tree go on? The fact that it is alive.

The animal is satisfied to live. Man has the wish to live, the wish to live well, the wish to live better ("The Function of Reason in Man," by a Harvard professor). The first type seeing the above phrase would run home to its mother.

The emotional and intellectual centered beings in the "Now" column wish to be less, he must wish to be more pleasing to himself. He cannot wish to be anything he has been, he can only wish for the new.

Eddington's time's arrow—everything moves in a certain direction because everything wishes to become better.

If your mind is in the state of "1," it will not change to 2 by the passing of time, etc.

Chance, shock or change of circumstances may take you out of 1 into 2 but you slip back to 1 when the former circumstances return. This is why we say we can do nothing by external means to improve the conditions in the world. Every acquirement is by our own efforts, conscious efforts; nature, time, good fortune, Providence do not help us. No-one expects to acquire an art without a technique, but here is the greatest art—transferring from "Now" to "Hence."

You may acquire great education but it is no evidence of mental power. An Oxford professor acquired 4 Oriental languages, but in point of mind he was stupid. What kind of mind do you most admire when you see it in others, or don't you care? Try to determine the kind of mind you would wish to have.

The emotional type we do not find going in search of new ideas, but in search of how they are going to have a jolly time. What the whole world is looking for is pleasurable experiences—we live largely in our emotional center. In spite of this search we do all have a goodly number of unhappy emotions.

Another sin against the Holy Ghost—it's without importance—it is the belief that it is our due to suffer and then to make others suffer more negative than positive emotions this is diabolism.

In the presence of disagreeable people, to the extent that we partake in their emotions, we lessen our ability to help them—we only add our crocodile tears to theirs.

The presence of a well person is in itself a help to a sick person (the bedside manner). The shortest out to helping anyone is to remain well yourself.

If you wish to enlarge your practical ability, I suggest you awake one morning and imagine there is nothing to eat in the house, you have no friend to whom you can appeal, and then you find you are under a vow to eat nothing until you can procure it for yourself. One day like this will be effective to enlarge your practical center. The time required to accomplish the wish for the "Hence" depends on whether you use drastic or homeopathic means. On this depends the time it takes to pass from 1 to 2. After such a situation as the above described, no situation will ruffle you.

The means (method) falls in three classes—these do not correspond with the three centers.

First self-observation: self-observation consists in the effort to be aware of your physical behavior and continuously and completely, be aware of your body and its behavior during the time you are awake, that it is your body doing or which something is taking place. Illustration—imagine the pot in which something is cooking, knowing just what was taking place in the process going on, but more important it is to know what the psyche is doing beside.

Step 2. (Pause). In this column (Means) many things are put. Every religion proposes a means by which the creature, man, may become a son of God. Education suggests a means for youth; art suggests a means for adults; proposes to transform, transcribe man—to put before man a means for betterment, and many schools and cults aim to help people to better themselves. If you have not tried many of them, you won't try this. You will try this last as the obvious is always the last thing to be discovered.

For what do you feel yourself drawn for improvement?

What is the life-belt by which you hope to be drawn into a better way? On what are you depending to bring about the change? Cards on the table, your own private table, will your best card be a trump or a low card?

Buddha said this is the only way—and he appealed to those who had the force and intelligence to try many ways, Buddha's way was self-observation of physical behavior. I call self-observation step one, because on it depends step two, and can only be understood after step one has been tried.

Step 2 is non-identification, meaning to consciously know my five manners of behavior, simultaneously being aware of all five. It does not mean be aware yourself, but be aware of yourself. I also say Orage is being aware; I don't identify myself with the organism which is mine.

We believe that while other people's behavior is not ours, we imagine our behavior is ours, but it isn't. Any behaviorist will tell you this.

All has been determined by heredity and circumstances of life. Not one cell of our body did we make, neither are we responsible for the way we part our hair. This is not an opinion but demonstrable fact. None of your behavior is any more yours than that of any other person's is yours.

Neither do we begin to have control. First admit this because it is a fact and then realize it for yourself by self-observation at the same time disclaiming it is you. It is your body but not "I."

We are trying to split personality and individuality. In order to do anything we have to imagine we have an instrument for the use of "I"; personality to be used by individuality.

Let any one person be represented by word "I"—a word we have not yet the right to use, but we say "I." Then you should have the function of discriminating between "I," and this body which we are not.

Though "I" has no function, it should be an empty circle and not a straight line. We can still say "I" will keep my eye on you, until "I" comes into existence by commencing to function. We only deny "I" because it does not yet exist. We affirm it because it can do something the body cannot do. The body cannot be aware of itself as a totality; it can think about self but cannot observe thought. If feeling it can see its emotional re-actions but it cannot see its emotions.

307

We give this mark "I" a job, that it should be aware of the body.

I am trying to talk to that part of you called "I," but you listen with that part of the organism called mind, and so something which never was will continue to speak of itself as "I." My words are not directed to your brains, but to something back of your brains, to which you begin to attach some importance, just to the extent to which "I" tries to remember that the body is not itself, are we using this second step, non-identification.

Third step: experimentation. We experiment for the reason no-one learns by experience—this is proposive experience. Every form of experience other than propose leaves "I" just where it was.

Experiment in this method is positive, active,

Illustration: If Russian refugees should theoretically make their profound deep experiences, proposive, something quite different from a pathological state would result.

No experiences are of any value—there is no telling what the effect may be on the organism, integrating or disintegrating effect.

Experiment I define as an intended experience.

Experiment without self-observation for self-understanding would be experiment for self improvement and become introspection, pathological, crazy, Illustration: the hostess who broke a piece of china, and then said she did it for consciousness sake. Suggestion for experimentation—hold cigarette in other hand. All experiments are in the direction of changing habits, so the body will cease to be an automaton, but will be amenable to my ("I") wishes. Suggestions—change the way of getting out of bed, walking down stairs, of walking down the street. We don't begin by changing good habits. They are all right, not with bad habits, as this might lead to Puritanism, so we begin with these habits that do not matter, to discover how strong habits are and what you suffer in changing them. We find ourselves rabbit-like, our way of using certain street crossings like rabbit runs. We to not do things which are observable to others, nothing is more disgusting than to be caught trying to attain consciousness in public,

Q: . . . .

A: Experiences change us we all die of experiences in the end, we can't count on experiences to better us.

Summary—Realize what we are, realize what we wish to be, and use the means.

MONDAY, 9 DECEMBER 1929

Began by reading the Sayings of Buddha, the only way. Asks for questions.
The diagram almost demands some questions.

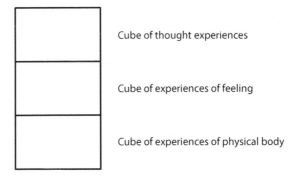

Within each of these tubes is a spherical center. This is a 3 dimensional representation of a person.

In the first cube is the center of the physical body, instinctive, motor center.

In the second cube is the center of emotions. That which we hold dear, our likes and dislikes and our wishes. "Wish" is the future tense of like (?). We like or dislike what is present, we wish for what is absent.

The question of like and dislike does not enter into thought. The degree of differences and likenesses are thought.

The third cube contains the thinking center.

We may be largely in 1 or 2 or 3. The center in which we find ourselves habitually, is our center of gravity and determines our type.

You are living in the first center when you are concerned with the matter of the body, its health, its welfare, its good times, its possessions.

Those whose interests are principally these things are the instinctive type.

We all dwell in a house with three doors. (Look for this illustration in back notes.)

When concerned largely with matters of reform, of helping others, with sympathy, discontent and wishing for the impossible etc. we are in the second center or are the emotional type.

When realizing, theorizing, studying etc. we are in the third floor. These people belong to the third type.

The point represent "I." I have put it outside but now "I" is so embedded in the body that it never gets outside. Like a chicken in a shell it may sometime emerge. Though it is true it is there we may imagine outside.

This is the first step to it emerging. We isolate it this way experimentally and also give it something to do.

"The mountain look on Marathon, Marathon looks on the sea." Though the Mountains cannot look upon the sea they can look upon something which looks upon the sea. "I" represents the mountain. It can look upon the organism and the organism can look upon the world. Only by the agency of the

309

body can "I" look upon the world. Depending on the organism "I" has only its reports.

If the organism is pathological "I" gets incorrect reports. "I" begins to observe not the reports but the reactions of the external world on the organism.

If I keenly observe the effects of the external world on the organism "I" gets a truer report. Self-observation is the ability of "I" to look upon the organism's reaction to the world,

Consciousness is the state of the organism when receiving reports of the external world.

Self-consciousness is the state of "I" observing the organism. Self-consciousness has nothing to do with your ordinary conscious state.

(Going back to the diagram) These 3 spheres are filled, imagine, with tar and move about as the body moves, one day here, one day there. I should not get the same impressions in New York as in Moscow. The tar within the center moves about according to impressions, vibrations and sensations. These depend exclusively on what circumstances my house finds itself in. We think we can move our house, take the body where we will, but it can clearly be shown not a place can we take ourselves, we have no choice, we are led about by our conditioned organisms, is are not in control of our movements.

Our personality—the structure being hereditarily and sociologically conditioned, is also subject to its experiences or to the sum of the 3 forms of impressions it has received. By the use of the word "I" we have something quit different. For the time being "I" is confined to observing. "I" can observe what effects the external world has on the organism and eventually "I" can find what parts of this external world produce effects in my emotions and intellectual centers. And possibly in time, "I" can move from passive state and the organism will move according to my own wish or will. The wish or will of "I." In terms of modern physics if returned to electrons we could be found on the point of a needle; we are simply inflated.

This organism lives on 3 forms of food without which our organism would cease to exist—they are ordinary food, air and impressions. Just as certain as we cannot live without food and air, just as impossible is it for us to live without impressions. A being in which all sense impressions were stopped for one second would die. Impressions are said to be the most important to life. We can go on without food for a time, without air for a shorter time, but only for one hundredth part of a second without impressions.

(Returning to diagram) Here we have a new conception, a second birth or immaculate conception of the body but in this conception of "I" if proper food is given, it will begin to develop a new body. We know there is nothing in our body that was not one time food or air. Similarly, in regard to our mind and emotion, we get our food from impressions.

The answer is because the nature of your emotional experiences is such that you are compelled to love or hate, we imagine our emotions ourselves.

We know for instance, we speak English because of chance, but we fancy our feelings, we choose, they are our own, pride, generosity etc., we claim as our own, but they are no more our own than the language we speak, they depend on the circumstances in which your house has been placed from time to time.

As to the mind, tell me what you think and I will tell you what your early life was, your teachers, books you read, etc. I am giving the biography of every living being. These apply to every one of us who has been conceived and sociologically brought up. Turn now to the word "I" — "I" was conceived but may never have been born. (Could you say "I" was before conception?) There are millions of conceptions which never materialize or are allowed to materialize. There are millions and millions of "I"s which have never been conceived. Think of the millions of seeds in nature which never develop. 2000 million people on this earth. How many have conceived a soul?

The first food of a child is given it before birth and generally throughout life he is receptive only to the food which the organism is given from the external world; air comes from the external, impressions from the external. Though heredity gives it its start, it depends entirely on the external world for these foods.

The "I" does not depend on the external world for food. It depends for its first food on *impressions taken of the organism*. *This is the beginning of the* WAY. SELF-OBSERVATION ★ NON-IDENTIFICATION ★ EXPERIMENTATION.

The dearest friend in the world may be suffering the other side of a stone wall and we know nothing about it.

I plead with you to take this simple step — to use the same method you use to know another, to know yourself. It is the only way to *being* (existence). If you know any other way to know yourself other than this it is not the *way*.

We begin observations on tones of voice, posture, movements, gestures and facial expressions, these same as we would on a stranger. Imagine you have been introduced to the organism bearing your name for the first time — lay siege to yourself. Be on watch for its five forms of behavior, attend to knowing it. In the course of time you will arrive at the same judgment as you would if you had met yourself as another organism.

We say 3 brains begin to collect drippings. 3 brains are passive and 3 have to do the collecting actively.

Extraordinary things happen to the organism when under the observation of "I."

Chance determines whether these 3 brains are filled and how.

When the world is positive and the organism is negative, "I" is neutralizing. For the moment "I" is neither positive nor negative. By virtue of giving "I" something to do we count its effects, the organism taking the place of the world. The organism always remains passive but takes its orders from "I" as "I" becomes positive and plays the role the world now plays.

The sole work of the "I" is comparable to that of divinity, what we call God.

God never interferes with action. "I" will guide thee with mine eye." "I" propose to play the role of God, It competes with the world. The organism is simply reacting to the world, a slave. In my awareness of it, it becomes a slave to "I" instead of the world.

Q:—

A: We flatter ourselves to say we select something else. What happens is that another image enters. But for the fact that these ideas came to me I should have preferred that action. One of the dreadful things, that it is so difficult for us to realize that we never exercise choice or refrain from some particular action.

We are not purposed to make any moral issue—to set one tradition against another, to fight like cooks. We say let the organism do what it likes on the condition that you are aware .

The organism is negative, inert, would never move but that there is in me an emotional center—there is not a quiver in me except that I receive impressions.

When I become aware the belt is shifting from the external world to "I."

Q: (Something about an abruptness in the change)

A: Every note of the scale is necessary to complete the octave. There is no abruptness, it may be a day, a-year, a life time, nature does not care.

A child cannot think, feel, act at once. We know a process of bias is necessary for collecting the drippings. The same with "I"—it accumulates observations of the organism very slowly.

The organism grows by *received* impressions. The "I" grows differently—by tak*en im*pressions.

The difficulties preclude the premature birth of "I"? If the impressions taken by "I" are confined to one type, one center the results will be a monster. The only way is the taking of total impressions—impressions of the whole organism. Then "I" develops in its 3 centers harmoniously in a balanced way.

When we say "love is blind" it means we are not in a state of thought.

When thought comes in at the door love flies out at the window.

Polyp—is a kind of creature uncertain as to whether it is animal or vegetable. Few of us know whether we are having feelings or thought—are in a state of feeling or a state of thought. When in uncertain state between the two we are polyps we may flatter ourselves and call it intuition.

(Redefines consciousness and self-consciousness) We don't mix physical pain with emotional suffering, when we hear of the death of a friend we don't say: "I have a pain in my jaw" etc.

Just as clearly as we can distinguish between light, heat and power we can distinguish between emotion, thought and instinct. As light and power may mingle, making heat, so thought and instinct may mingle producing emotion.

Consciousness looks upon the external world, self-consciousness looks upon the organism.

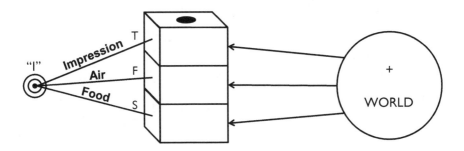

Q: about forgetting to observe?

A: Any alarm clock device is allowable. Hair shirt, Golf ticker, etc.

Say 1000 times a day "I have a body" just as you would say I have a suit of clothes or your car—you touch my car, you do not touch me—you can never again be identified.

Have a picture of 3 dimensions always moving. What better study, what better amusement, than to have a specimen of a human being always going about with you.

"I" is neither hostile nor friendly to the mistakes of the organism. The organism is related to the external world, it will exhibit the effects of a good environment or a bad. If ambition in good it will be added catalytically, if trivial it will disappear,

Does a tree care whether it is pruned or not? It will show the effects but does not care.

A dog, a rat will listen to its mother's voice when threatened.

"I" can scarcely formulate the deductions made by self-observation.

Understanding cannot be put into the same word as knowledge, but it is a form of knowledge.

Q: about memory.

A: by diagram

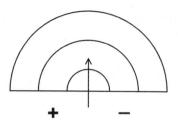

A real imagery would be able to recall tastes and smells etc. instead of just sight images.

Intuition is a half and half blending of thought and feeling.

MONDAY, 16 DECEMBER 1929

Asks for questions the answers of which would be of value to experimenting during the two intervening weeks when there will be no meetings.

Starts with familiar diagram—portrait of man.

We have common feeling, common movement, common ideas—what differentiates us from each other is the differences in experiences.

The picture on the board is not altogether flattering.

There is a brain in here and here and here—three brains.

According to our heredity and environment we fill these brains.

Our personality is built up. Our personality is always changing.

We may not tomorrow be what we were yesterday.

According to your history up-to-date, so you will be tomorrow.

According to feelings today, according to thinking today, according to doing today we will be tomorrow.

We are subject to change, but we ourselves do not change—that is we do not change in the slightest degree under our own control. Our ability to think is passive ability, our ability to move is passive ability, our ability to feel is passive ability.

All that happens in life is in fact just what happens.

We take under consideration for discussion the most important animal in the world. We each take around with us such an animal.

Q: You have spoken of good habits, what are good habits?

A: Those habits are good which adapt the organism not only to its situation but to all possible situations.

The idea being that being is most normal to who is best adapted to his environment. To find yourself ill adapted to society may mean society is not right—it may still be that you are pathological.

It is a question whether it is better to adapt to society or not.

This raises the question—what is the value of the human being, not to society, but to himself.

It is hoped that what is to my advantage is also to the advantage of society, but this is a chance. We all have to ask sooner or later:

"What have I done for myself?"

Q: (Mrs. Besse) Is it right that we live for personal advantage?

A: Yes, surely. It is first necessary to inquire what is to your own personal advantage. Let us consider what is this advantage.

The degree to which our brain can be developed is so much greater than is realized. With the brain of Plato still the range of thinkable ideas open to human beings is so vast that this is only a fragmentary part.

In the degrees of emotional experience the unrealized is so great.

In the instinctive experience there is still some to be realized.

We prescribe a thing and one thing only—that you develop your own potentialities. It is not to be thought in doing this you run into harmful apposition to anyone. We say first do for yourself before you are in a position to help others.

We define an individual as a thinking, feeling and acting possibility.

It is not likely that any of us have sinned, to say nothing of committing crimes or ever will. That is a thousand times more possible—you will omit thinking, feeling, doing what is right to think, feel and do.

Two portraits—the average, the norm.

Jesus said: "I am the way, the truth and the light." Jesus said: "Follow yourselves and you find me, follow me and you lose both yourselves and me."

"I" means a special sense. Jesus did not set himself as a special example to be followed.

He specialized to do a certain thing. We could not all be teachers.

There is something to be done by the individual—"I" is to be followed. Jesus could not save a soul. He could only supply conditions by which a soul could be saved.

There is no one so sub-human as not to wish to have more mind, more feeling, more ability (to do).

There is no religion, no mysticism, no occultism—just the state which is deplorable and the more desirable state—and to accomplish it is human work.

It is done by the acting of what we call "I." Do not associate this word with anything transcendental. (We use words so commonly).

Ask yourself what you mean when you use the word "I." You would first go back to what you have read. "I" don't like cheese" etc.

"I sometimes feel that I am." Do we think of the body as immortal?

We say—I have a handkerchief, I have a pair of shoes, I have a place to go home to tonight, meaning I have the right to use, I have the possession.

"I have a body," can you think of your body in the same way and speak in the same way as when you say "I have a pair of shoes"?

315

Then the question becomes practical. You say "I have a house."

I say—"I see down here you have a pig sty." "Here I have a hen house,"—then "here I have a soul." It is not a place a soul would like to live in. But if your home is of this kind (diagram)...

A study where you can think all possible thoughts, an artist's studio for experiencing all emotions, a gymnasium for all physical feats. When we say "I have a mansion in the skies"—it is postponement until tomorrow instead of building the mansion now.

Jesus referred to the body as a temple, not our idea of present day temple, but the temple where drama, art etc. were carried on, something for all parts of the body. Jesus said: "Did I not say unto you, your bodies are the temple of the living God." Doesn't the Bible say: "He that shall lose himself in me shall find himself"? Then Jesus said: "Give up your life" it meant that being in which you live. Treat the person (Yourself) just as objectively, impartially and friendly as you treat a friend.

When you see yourself with the same eyes with which you see others you will find yourself as a hateable person, this does not mean hateable to others.

"Until a man hates himself he cannot love God"—Bible.

Q: What makes the trinity?

A: Someone is asking for a lecture.

How, when and where and why does "I" become—and I give an answer *now*. You use the word "trinity," but this is not mysticism, I use "three brains"—an equilateral triangle. We are all triangles but not all equilateral triangles.

If the 1st logos of our trinity is developed to that degree, (drawing triangle) and the second logos to that degree we become an isosceles triangle, or this (draws another triangle) but this (draws an equilateral triangle).

Either the trinity is found in psychology or it is not found.

Asks for practical questions!

Q: What is the octave?

A: The sum of the seven notes makes the musical scale, there are seven colors in the spectrum, the eighth is the sum of the seven.

Seven centers in man if we happen to develop three.

The original octave had nothing to do with music but with phenomena occurring in all departments of physics and biology.

Q: About observing an emotional state, if bad it disappears, if good it intensifies.

A: We say an agreeable emotion is positive, a disagreeable emotion is negative.

If an emotion is positive to you it is enhancing your being.

If negative to you. you have the feeling of being less.

In a positive state it is as if you were receiving something.

In a negative state it is as if you were losing something.

Two pockets—in one you are receiving, in the other you are losing.

We never try to observe states, we observe symptoms.

Q: Is that why the emotional center of man is so little filled because the great number of emotions are negative?

A: Yes.

MRS. B: Do not people develop by negative emotions?

A: You mean developed by suffering? We are developed by stopping negative emotions—by stopping the manifestations of negative emotions the state changes.—This is not just transferring to the mind, leaving the emotion-festering in the sub-emotional center.

Q: Can positive emotions leave one without energy?

A. There is fatigue after labor and fatigue after blood-letting, negative emotions are comparable to blood-letting.

Expenditure of physical energy leave one fatigued, not weak but strengthened.

(Loosing energy against one's judgment leaves one weak)

Q: Can we have mixed emotions?

A: Can take in and give out.

The emotion of ecstasy no-one has an experience of—it is the sublimation—experience of all emotions, plus and negative most terrifying and exalted.

Consciousness—the simultaneity—awareness of all the thoughts you can think.

Intuition—a bodily state in which you are aware of all the physical states you have ever experienced—the body's remembrance of all she states it has ever experienced.

Q: About Jesus and Buddha—were they the result of H. and S.

Types of this kind always trained in a school.

Jesus went to Egypt in schools and at twenty-nine undertook public-teaching. At the end of three years—according to the narrative—He was crucified. There are also legends of His having returned to Egypt or gone to India. He was not by chance a developed human. He went to a school of training the same as Buddha and trained until He arrived at a state of complete non-identification—knew the history of the cells of the body. No-one could ever say one could arrive at this stage by chance.

The experience of this lecture attempts . . . etc.

This is why will comes in—this effort is not to be compared with any other effort for difficulty. This illustration (above) is trivial compared with what difficulty there is. Inertia is bad, bad enough but also—The union of the two is sad.

You go to sleep as a psyche and awake as a planetary body.

You note what occurs. We have no notice what occurs before judging others, we must observe what our mechanisms do, but must stop there—not judge.

It is a privilege to observe—not to do so is to be asleep.

MONDAY, 13 JANUARY 1930

Talking of being—Cell matter that reacts as itself has the character of being as being. What is the difference between one being and another.

We recognize or imagine we do, differences in beings. We consider man is a superior being than an ape; the ape higher than the fish; the fish higher than the amoeba. They differ in number, variety, co-ordination and complexity of their functions. Beings are ranked according to the totality of their functions (faculties). Our superiority is based on the above. Accepting the scientific definition of being we can now begin to establish the scale of being.

si
la
sol
fa
mi   vertebrate scale
re   invertebrate scale
do   cell scale

Strike the note *do* and the vibrations carry over to re, *re* carriers to *mi* but here the note dies unless there is a new outside shock, some thing new occurring in the individual or from the outside. Somewhere in the species all these three centers have been relatively complete.

Progress for a three centered being depends on the transition from the note *fa* to the higher triangle, otherwise the being remains beating his wings at the note *mi*.

We belong biologically to the vertebrates and the highest order having arrived at this high point man has arrived at the high vibration of the note *mi*. This is the tragedy of man—to be condemned to repeat mi, mi, mi, until the energy of mi dies down. Unless something new is initiated by man he is doomed to flap his wings until they die down.

This is the history of former civilizations. No progress on the part of man with the use of technical appliances—that we have the telephone or the motor-car does not make us superior beings, the contrary may be true. The mechanical appliances on which we lean bring about the atrophy of corresponding being powers. From our point of view no civilization is superior to another—biologically they all arrive at *mi*.

The ancient Egyptians aside from their form of knowing and doing, do not differ from our civilization. It is a fact in nature not an impulse, not a wish when any part of nature has arrived at the note *mi*—there has to be a completely new start. A new start—a new initiation.

The great initiates—why? (to initiate is to start a new work—the original impulse) They started this spark to function. This novel function can have nothing to do with knowing or feeling and doing (none of the physiological changes). It must be as different from all three as they are from each other.

Since all experiences have fallen into one of those categories—No man can by taking thought add one inch to his nature—to his being. He cannot conceive of a potentiality which has never been actualized. He will be bound to try to understand from his old familiar experiences in knowing, feeling and doing. This novel function we call self-observation—awareness, higher consciousness. This implies a plastic state but I am not plastic. I allow it is not comprehensible but better be vaguely right than sure and wrong.

If the note fa plays the role of bridge.

The "bridge" in ancient religions meant the *way*—the way of Buddha the way of Jesus. "I am the way" meaning not himself but whatever you call "I" (eye). Here give name to center in diagram.

A new form of understanding will not immediately come to you.

If your "I" can be appealed to it has the nature to understand what your three familiar activities cannot understand. To "I" the actual and potential can both be real—but you must try to observe yourself and discover by actual trial—to understand. To listen to your own tone of voice "as if" listening to another, but it is not identical. Note your posture in a state of awareness from which knowing, feeling and doing have been excluded but still active, something which appears to fly over three centers without appearing to produce any change in any of the three centers.

Being engaged in this function automatically you fall gradually into the upper triangle, but there is no giving up of the lower triangles—there is no sacrificing of any center. It is the development of the fourth center at the same time you are using the three living centers by the transition of self-observation.

As if the plant waited a long time after the stem, loaf and buds for an unfolding of the life force at its roots before it halted, waited in a state of suspended animation until sap was sent up from the roots.

This is said to be our state—a new impulse is expected for the organism to continue from this state of suspended animation as it has been in all former civilizations.

We speak of all human beings as being in state no. 1.

Now go back to scale of being—variety, complexity and co-ordination of function. There is man no.2 and man no.3

Man no.2 is superior to man no.1 and man no.3 is superior to man no.2.

Q: Is ice an illustration of this?

A: Very good.

Q: About the superior man.

The blossom, fruit, seed develop simultaneously side by side, but there is a succession—as the blossom precedes the fruit so the fruit precedes the seed. It is true there is succession, but also true there is simultaneity. All are implicit from the start.

Why I put being at the top and bottom of the diagram—all beings start at being—being, doing and knowing and go on together. We start at being and arrive at being.

When finally you in your own experiences find yourself self-observing then you will have the personal key to all that may have seemed contradictory. The test (proof) for the developing of the higher triangle is the finding of a new form of understanding.

Some question...

We do not prescribe the form that the octave takes but we take it for granted that the octave maintains.

MONDAY, 20 JANUARY 1930

Q: Does energy for self-observation take from any other energy?

A: Try to be familiar with the idea that our three brains—cerebral, visceral, spinal, each are run on its own kind of energy. True this energy is received from ordinary food, we have a power apparatus, a heating apparatus, a lighting apparatus—wiring for each apparatus.

Each current of electricity runs through a different wire and produces a different result—light, thought; heat, ability to feel; power for moving.

The energies used for self-observation is something totally different. There may be analogies but nothing like it. This force derived from self-observation is catalytic.

Your ability to think, feel and to do all increase but not directly from any use of energy you have, but from a certain friction produced by self-observation.

The coming together of the three functions we call waking up. (Following this came an explanation of dreams. The instinctive center being awake nightmare results. The thinking center being awake, intellectual problems such as algebra are solved).

Q: Why is this so, is the next question (said by O).

ORAGE: Each center receives a daily supply of energy as if the milk-man came around and left each morning a supply of milk. The quantities of energy cannot be used for any other purpose than in each center to which they belong. If you've failed during the day to use all the energy left at each door when night comes, the center which has not used its supply will continue to remain awake.

Q: How about waking tired? The center which has used its energy falls asleep first. Later, the second. Finally the third. So there is a total sleep of the whole organism for perhaps two or three hours. This is restful but not as restful as if they all feel asleep at once, it is a question of expending the energy of each center during the day. The amount of energy for each center is not equal, but in proportion to the size of the center—the distribution is not equal but equitable. This necessitates our attacking the problem of sleep. To do this review the day each night. Consider your day—realize the problem is to spend your allotment of energy each day. Ask yourself whether your three basin have been used, if you have spent in thought the whole of the basin, you will find you have used so little the wonder is that that center has slept at all. How many emotional experiences have you shirked, avoided doing something unpleasant etc. to save yourself from spending your supply of milk, you should lie awake in this center all night. Positive emotions may cause exhaustion. But this is the healthy exhaustion of a laborer working in the fields all day and going conscientiously to sleep at night, sometimes after a successful picnic when everybody had a good time during the day, the center is temporarily used up and people become irritable. Exhaustion from negative emotions, however, is different.

It can better be compared to exhaustion from being bled, and, by the way, this is an accurate comparison. You are literally being bled in your emotional center.

The potentiality of spending physical energy is so vastly greater than anyone spends. This energy then goes off in dreams about the future—material ghosts about the future—or goes off in sex. The energies must be expended. They do not evaporate. If not properly expended they poison the organism and result in sicknesses of different kinds—introspection instead of thinking, fantasy in place of feeling, and physical pleasure instead of physical enjoyment, to the detriment of the organism. If you tell me your dreams, I will tell you which of your centers are unemployed during the day.

The supply is adequate for voluntary usage but may not always be enough for all external emergencies. When being, as you thought, exceedingly exhausted, a new situation arises and you find you can go on, then the second wind is called upon, but the occasion for using second wind is rare. Energy for second wind is stored in glands, some of which are so arranged that they can feed any of the centers. (There are 273 glands, roughly speaking, of the visceral system).

Self-observation does not increase quantity of energy, but diminishes waste—there are two effects of self-observation—stops waste, this is incidental, *primarily*, it increases the energy for farther self-observation.

Learn the use of fire, of tools and of light.

By the friction of psychology, turning against itself, psychological fire is produced. In the instinctive center the proper use of tools, or *technique* is the result—in the intellectual center the proper use of language or *right ideas*—in the emotional center the conversion of negative to positive emotions i.e. a state of positive emotion, rather than dribbling away in mechanical negative responses to emotion situations.

Consciousness conserves energy by stopping up waste—it makes you feel you have more energy. Every involuntary train of thought is a leak in your thinking center—getting into a brown study—not only is your brain tired, but it is brain rot. We defy you to indulge in day-dreaming while aware of your five manners of behavior. The day-dreaming is cut off. Now this energy is yours to use in thinking.

Take the emotional center. We seldom have a genuine emotion about anything round about us. The ability to feel which we have every morning is used up and we become hard-boiled for the rest of the day.

Illustration—The man who wakes up, finds his bath water cold, breakfast late, the coffee lukewarm, the eggs bad, the wife somewhat cross, the newspaper uninteresting and stocks gone down. By the time he leaves the house he has exhausted himself in his mechanical response to all these situations, and gets to the office all tired out.

The penalty of brutality is sentimentality. This waste in the emotional center early in the day has dropped out of the emotional center but not out of the organism. A leaking gas pipe, the gas escapes in the room.

Centers are machines chemically formed for transmuting substances. What we call sentimentality is simply an escape of energy not used through the center for which it is intended. This question of leakage is most important. Not only does our physical health depend upon it but our emotional and intellectual. Consider at night what is the daily life of this organism—is there a failure in any one of the centers. What is it they are failing to do? In the vast majority of cases what is called running down is failure to use. The organism is run down by waste, by unemployment.

People say they have "to get away," the wear and tear was so great etc., but this is not what has happened. The cure against running down is always more work.

Waking consciousness differs from ordinary consciousness just as ordinary C. differs from sub-C. The energy of the centers during waking hours continues to act. When asleep, the centers continue to act just the same, the only difference is that in so-called waking states the centers interact. In sleep each center goes on independently of the others. If you fall asleep now you would continue to experience in each center what is now going on—only independently of the other centers.

The blessed state of sleep means there is nothing to recall of dreams but it does not mean that the centers have been inactive. No psychologist or group of people has ever been able at will to produce a dream. When you can do this, you are in a position to say what dreams are, what their cause, and what their effect on the organism. Scientific imagination is experimenting in psychological experiences, separately, together and in any combination. Overhaul your

322

day—on what plane you are shirking, lazy, on that plane you will find it the disturbance of your night. We say in general sleep is important, but dreams are unimportant—the necessary thing is to find the cause of your dreams, and not as psycho-analysts do the meaning. What most people call imagination, we call fancy. The ordinary form of imagination is the accidental appearance of images to your mind.

The difference between order and chaos—the difference between imagination and fancy. It is impossible for an organism to be present in more places than one at a time—a wrenched limit. When the imagination is trained, it is capable of being in more than one place at a time.

Imagination is one of the tools of psychological movement. By self-observation we could start fire...

We do not then stop at language—self-observation consists in the effort to be continually aware of the five forms of bodily behavior—tone of voice, posture, gesture etc.

Q: Probably about proper use of emotions . . .

ORAGE: Emotions escape from the visceral. The present seat of emotions is in fact the solar plexus, but the seat of real emotions is the heart.

The difference between the heart and the solar plexus is the difference between the right and wrong use of emotions. (Heart is at present nothing more than a muscle). (Perennially gay people, ordinarily considered to be in a state of positive emotion are in reality merely responding mechanically to hypnotic stimuli and therefore wasting energy negatively. Mechanical gaiety is really negative as opposed to a conscious emotion such as that of despair, which although negative, is relatively positive to the unconscious and mechanical gaiety).

Choose one intellectual faculty, e.g. that of concentration. If you could concentrate your mental energy as follows you would know the meaning of concentration. You have a watch with a minute hand. When you can watch that minute hand with no other thought in your thought for one minute, you can understand Einstein, arrange your business—-

But you can't do it for three seconds, what occurs to you is fancy not real imagination. (Here he tells the story of the man who goes to the alchemist to get the formula for turning lead into gold. The alchemist gives him the formula but just as he is leaving says, "wait a moment" and says one thing more, "while mixing the formula you must not think of the word "hippopotamus.") Of course the man fails.

The ability to concentrate excludes the possibility of fancy. In the essence of this technique to produce the fire, there will be no psychological control against fantasy.

Suppose you were to live forever, what would you do—what would be your purpose for living. You would shoot yourself because the quality and quantity of your wishes are so thin and so poor you would quickly exhaust them. If it were literally true that we were obliged to live forever, then none of us would be here another week. If our situation is that of forlorn hope on a battlefield, anything that we do would be a desperate act, and not an act of reasonable purpose.

Our waking state is so precarious; we may not reach home tonight.

But waking state and existence are not the same. *We are always.* Our waking state is an occasional accident and very precarious under conditions over which we have no control. But we shall continue to exist even though we may never have another waking state. In the absence of an organism, we continue to be. The state of being existence is not determined by the accident of an organism, but depends upon what has been done by the organism in its waking state. Personality will disappear forever.

Existence is taken to mean the continuity of being: in waking consciousness. The waking state of consciousness has a value relative to the meaning and aim of existence. Waking state has no value in itself; its only value is in exploitation for the purpose of understanding. In polite society any suggestion to the meaning and aim of existence is so objectionable, it really stinks. The vast majority of people have died in the emotional and thinking centers, and energy for these centers has gone down into their instinctive center. It is a good sign when people are violent as it means that there remains in them a possibility of awakening, although like the prodigal son they are feeding on husks. When people are indifferent they are damned. We say the atheists are one of the strictest forms of religion because they are not indifferent.

Q: How do you go about finding out the meaning and aim of existence?

That depends on the center with which you are identified. (Draw diagram.)

1	1	
2	2	
3	3	
4	4	
5	5	
6	6	
7	7	

The vast majority fall into the first column, a decreasing number in the second and practically none in the third. Instinctive answers given without thought, without instruction, without form, without emotion.

1.   One answer to meaning and aim presupposes that God is an indulgent father, of children, meaning humans only, and that he made them for one thing only—happiness.

2.   God is a stern law-giver, requires certain services and rewards good service and punishes bad. God is a taskmaster and a severe judge. In other words, to please God and avoid punishment is the thing.

3.   The provision of a school for the development of character. All that occurs disagreeable, especially to anyone else, is part of the training.

That God is a schoolmaster to produce character.

The probability is that one of these is already yours. Ask yourselves what yon conceive God to be—what do you teach your children. All answers are infantile and superstitious.

II. EMOTIONAL ANSWERS.

It is no longer a question of personal welfare. It is an emotional attitude toward God. The individual who believes he has a soul, a new form centers—the forms of religions. Christianity, Mohammedanism, Buddhism etc., Christian science, Zoroastrianism, Confucianism, all pre-supposes a relation of God to soul.

MONDAY EVENING, 3 FEBRUARY 1930

Ask for questions. Ask what it is you wish to know, or write it down.

When you're able to formulate a question clearly you are close to an answer, subjects discussed, here are the kind that should lead to questions.

"I" develops each body. Supposing "I" has no success in developing humans. It might be conceivable that three centered bodies become two centered. Nature cannot go on producing three centered beings if they do not use them. There is nothing that insures a better existence.

The condition of existence depends on "I." If "I" tries to produce a better existence there may be hope for movement up. Nature provides opportunity to run down or up the scale—involution or evolution. It remains for the individual to decide which way ho will go. Your state of being between existences is non-existence but not non-being.

You go to sleep. What is your state? For all you know it is non-existence. You were in some state. But it would not be called non-being because you re-emerge from sleep.

There are means of discovering the differences between non-existence and non-being. We do not know that without body we have no memory. We do know we have a brain. We think we think with our brain, because we have been told so. I breathe, therefore I am, I move, therefore I exist.

I think, therefore I have a brain. But modern science says it is not our brain we think with. We think with the totality of our body (Gestaltism).

We are very embryonic in the science of being. We are in the same primitive condition that the men of the Stone Age were in, say about logic.

We are just on the threshold of the science of being. We have just terms with diagram in mind, we may see the idea of being.

A being could conceivably exist or non-exist. If identified with existence, the being may go into separate existences and not remember.

He is identified with each of the beads on the string and not with the string. If, however, he is identified with the string, he remembers the beads. When out of the body, being still is. In this sense we are all immortal. But it is impossible to see the reason between one existence and another, what is the use of immortality. When you have learned to non-identify with the body and identify with being, then there is conscious continuity between existence and non-existence of the body.

I repeat, we are in the same state relative to this subject, as savages were to science. What we are not in a state of psychology to believe, no-one can convince us. I could tell you certain things that might be objective truths, they might be the truth before God, and yet we are incapable of believing them. You have no associations for them or you have the wrong associations. It is not a question merely of the amount of credulity or incredulity. Belief is not so cheap. In order to believe certain things, you have to be in the psychological state that is capable of understanding them. I defy you to believe them.

You have all been in the position of knowing a certain piece of truth, a fact about somebody, producing certain evidence, and yet having nobody believe you. On the other hand, you have also told a deliberate lie, and yet produced so plausible evidence that nobody doubted you—you have thereby lost your respect for people's ability to differentiate between the truth and a lie.

Logic alone does not convince. "A man convinced against his will is of the same opinion still." Still we have evidence.

Q: Whether this has developed in races or in families?

A: Because modern science has developed, it is not true that other sciences have not been developed in the past. The ancient Egyptian was as crazy about religion as we are about mechanics. It is conceivable that they discovered nothing. We have no reason to believe that our mechanics (last?) for 10,000 years. We can dig up from them as future races may dig up from this mechanical age. People do not know what Egyptian art means when they dig it up. What I say about this system is exactly what I teach. These people's psychology is difficult for us to believe since our psychology is conditioned by our mechanical age. There is one means which the practical way of approach—When you can non-identify from your behavior, you are on the way to discover the meaning of existence and non-existence. We do not say one is then higher. Apart from our knowledge of the rates of vibration, red, orange, yellow etc., would we say orange is a higher vibration than red? It is only science that discovers the rate of vibration. In passing from one state of being to another, we do not say one state is higher;—it is different, though it can be proved that vibration in one state is higher.

You may prefer orange to red—one existence to another. It is fortunate that you can't believe, for then you would substitute belief for knowledge.

A state of being would be self-consciousness. It is impossible to discover a state of being while identified with body. Existence is identified with the body that you happen to have.

There are 3 Indian schools, each also an experience of being. We deny that they arrive at an experience of true being. Buddha was a man like ourselves. He was born of parents, Jesus was a man like ourselves, had 3 centers—what he became is another matter. He succeeded in a single life time to become conscious. This is what *Christ* meant. Jesus was not the only Christ. Christians claim that the man Jesus had arrived at Christ; but there are others. The Jews knew this fact and that is one of their criticisms of

Christianity. Jesus attained the title Christ in schools before he started as a teacher. What happened to Jesus between the age of 15 and 39? We see his discussing with the elders. He reappeared to a fanatic, John the Baptist (Billy Sunday). Jesus asked John to baptize him; he was therefore included with John the Baptist. But they soon discovered he had something they did not.

They called him the son of God. He had become non-identified with his lowest centers. He had passed from the stage of slave to the stage of son of God.

Later when Jesus was teaching his method and was asked about John the Baptist he said: "Among all the sons of women there are non greater, but any of you are greater than he." John the Baptist was a great religious genius, but not a conscious agent of his own development. It is still possible to produce sensational notes about the Bible. Our bible was a selection of the Gospels.

There were at least 120. Some of these things are accessible to you and when the state became part of the Church at the Council of Nicaea, early in the 5th century, a formula was drawn up for the future of Christianity. All the gospels were brought together. We know Mary Magdalene was much with Jesus and that there was such scandal. Jesus had brothers and sisters. So did the disciples. (Gospel—good spell—tidings—news.)

Many statements in the gospels would not suit the Roman empire. They decided 4 were safe and certain parts of them were not safe. They cut out passages and put in sections from other gospels. These are really the canonical writings as opposed to the true and complete gospels. (Canon—rule of church, as a statutory law is rule of state). They did what propagandists would do—sent to all the existing churches or ecclesiastic groups, these compiled

327

and edited gospels. It was much as his life was worth for any ecclesiast to have in his possession any of the forbidden gospels. Heresy arose. Trials were held. The accused were indicted, refused to admit they knew the forbidden gospels, but their accusers quoted lengthy; as evidence against the offenders. These quotations were taken down in the records and it is in this way that a large number of fragments have been kept and later found. In these gospels, parables occur with different interpretations. "The Prodigal Son," in Luke and the hymn of "The robe of Glory."

One gospel is called the "Story of Mary the Mother of Jesus." There is a gospel of Mary Magdalene, of Judas, of Thomas the doubter and Peter. It appears Jesus conducted sacred dances, actually led them. In certain Welch churches, once a year, dances in the churches are performed, purporting to be taught by Jesus. In our gospels it is said—to the Jews, he was a stumbling block, to the Greeks foolishness. He was accused of losing his temper, frequently found drunk, no wonder the Jews found him a stumbling block. The church had to claim a miracle. The gospels inevitably choose themselves.

Q: Why did Jesus lead so questionable a life ?

A: That is a very interesting question. Jesus never made a model of himself. Had he been what we call a model man, he would have corrupted his followers because they would have striven to imitate him instead of living their own lives. They would forget the technique. They would worship the exponent of the method instead of practicing the method. He, that is Christ, said on one occasion: "Follow yourselves and you will find me. Follow me and you will lose both me and yourselves." In spite of this they flocked to the forest. All taught the Gospel. One of the ways of helping yourself is to try and interest others in it. It is not known what the wilderness is or what the *upper room* was. This is a question of technical language. The *upper room* meant the 3rd center. These terms are technical terms. These non canonical gospels were printed by the University Press in 1812 by professor Clearer and dug up again in 1907. Those who read them—such as Sir Bulwer, Lytton, Bakerfield—had a different outlook on religion, were more mystical.

Pistis Sophia, the complete gospel of faith by wisdom.

"Fragments of a Faith forgotten" is the name of a volume of these fragments. In this book, the line of kings was called "kingdom of heaven."

"I labor until Christ be formed in you," Paul. Judas was one of the best of Jesus disciples. Jesus said: "You must all be crucified." We have a trinity—the trinity is doomed. The coming into being was the crucifixion, the coming of the trinity into the quadrangle.

Jesus was not an initiator; he was an initiate.

The Gnostic schools may be responsible for the story of Jesus. There is no actual evidence that Jesus lived. All stories, Jewish tradition is aware of that. This is why Jews cannot stomach the parables. They have facts. They can't take Jesus as the only son of God; it would be terrible for the human race if there had been only one Christ.

All emotional states must be released by overt expression or formulation.

You can't control your emotions by reasoning, but by changing your images.

All the emotions we experience are lower emotions because they do not exist in a state of ecstasy. To bring about the state of ecstasy normally, you observe your five overt manners of behavior. You will then be following the fourth way—the human way. This is what Buddha taught when India was full of *Yogas*. *Relation of God to the soul in Buddha*. The individual who has lived in this life a soul pleasing to God goes straight to Paradise (Mohammedan).

A soul which is not goes to another place. *Christianity*—Jesus would turn in his grave to realize the conception of God by Christians. All theses religions have a value, in that they have an emotional appeal which the first does not have, but both are equally subjective , but the emotional presupposes the activity of 2 centers.

An individual knows what he knows—and also what he doesn't know.

MONDAY EVENING, 10 FEBRUARY 1930

Would you, if you had power, organize hospitals for the poor. Ask yourself such questions as: "Am I the sort of person who wishes to be of use to sufferers—to wish that others should have a good time or to educate the mind?" According to your type you are concerned in helping others in physical troubles, emotional or intellectual.

There are three permanent centers of gravity and according to inheritance you're bound to be drawn into one or another. Where you act, there is your center—your type. Question was asked about possibility of combination of centers. It is possible to combine education with pleasure—a little oil to the machine, but the wish to educate is the same. I may try to combine education and making money and distribution to charities. Who knows what is to be encouraged or discouraged? How would you prune a tree which is half developed? You would not know what branches to take off, which are to bear fruit. We would not know how to prune. Man is a creature in transformation. What is it in his nature, if conditions were favorable, he would become. A norm is that which in nature is the type man is tending towards. We have to consider what type of education would help a child to achieve his norm. To prescribe is presumption that we have God-like vision.

A man or woman does not cease to be educated. Our conception of education must extend over the whole period of life. The psyche, the soul, can be compared to a butterfly. Miracles are around us, such as the growth of the butterfly. The butterfly goes through 4 stages—1 egg, 2 caterpillar, 3 chrysalis 4 butterfly. Is there anything in an egg to suggest the miracle of a butterfly?

The human psyche goes through 4 stages. We are in the stage of the caterpillar. Our psyche is the caterpillar-stage. The next step to be looked for is the chrysalis, to be hard-shelled, self-contained, etc.

This stage is self-consciousness. From this stage we emerge into the butterfly stage. "A Caterpillar on a leaf reminds me of my mother's grave." We may be good caterpillars if we are tending toward the next stage. There are people getting on in the world, in good relationships, enjoying life, dying an old age, still in the caterpillar-stage. It is nature in us in contra-distinction to nature without, which with the help of our minds, is striving to bring about the metamorphosis. Reformers on behalf of nature try to bring about the metamorphosis. Buddha, Mohammad, Jesus, etc. were not interested in social reform or religious. They cared for none of these things, but for one thing and one only, that those they met should be on the way to becoming normal. Jesus said, "Be ye also perfect, even as your father which is in heaven is perfect." "I am the way."

First aim to develop, second aim to become ourselves.

Not for the welfare of the body, net for the welfare of the mind, but for the becoming to fulfill your norm. I protest against all the association of these phrases of Jesus. Interruption: Christ failed.

ORAGE: A message fails because of circumstances. The founder of the Roman Catholic church, Peter, was the only one who addressed as Satan—"Get thee behind me, Satan." Something so contradictory to the method Peter (stone—and on this rock shall I found my church). It is true Jesus failed, but I am discussing what his aim was. In contrast with the two kinds of reform which we call religion—education of the body, education of the mind, his aim was toward the soul, center of being or psyche. Jesus said: "I ignore your mind, I ignore your body. The body will develop; the mind will develop, if the soul does. But the development in either mind or body would be hostile to the development of the soul." (Place your center of gravity in being, and you will know and do.)

Ecstasy is a transmutation from lower emotion to higher. It is as if Orage were standing outside the body. The lower emotions are in relation to the body. Higher emotions are ecstasy. Aspiration would be a longing for the state of ecstasy.

Q: What is inspiration? Higher emotion?

Inspiration, expiration, perspiration, aspiration. Bliss means a state of ecstasy. Adoration, ecstasy. The adoration of the Magi and the adoration of the morning star when they sang together. The canticles, the Litany.

Adoration which exhibits itself in the form of praise. Revelation is the fruit of a state of inspiration, if the revelation is a truth about mankind.

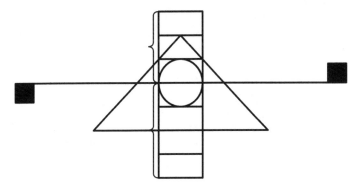

In a state of ecstasy many things may happen

ORAGE: Nirvana : Negative

Nirvana : Positive

Discussion by dressy woman on first row who afterward told Orage she would never come back, who claimed Nirvana was a state of rest and not negative.

Orage held his point that negative was not a state of rest, that negative is activity etc.

Q: Why discard the word *love* for *adoration?*

ORAGE: Adoration is a positive state of emotion but does not lead to action. Love leads to action, is a state which precedes action. Adoration and love, both positive, because both pleasant. Higher emotions have no opposites.

No opposites for ecstasy, adoration, sorrow. If you adore an object and the object is removed, you cease adoring. Nothing takes the place as an emotion. In love there is fear, desire. The state of ecstasy means standing outside and is prior to higher emotions. It is the state in which higher emotions can be experienced. Adoration is innocent of desire. We have never experienced higher emotions except vicariously through literature. We adore what is outside us, the beauty, the visions.

Q: Is fear positive?

ORAGE: This reminds me of Gilbert & Sullivan, of the man who said his wife had a whim of iron. An emotion is an impulse to actions, but of these stimuli some are agreeable and soma disagreeable. What you find to be agreeable emotion are positive for you. What you find disagreeable are negative for you. We don't say we all find the same ones positive. All have the wish for more being. If one commits suicide, it is in despair of their wish for more being. Anything that induces a plus state is positive, a minus state is negative. The most negative state may bring about the most action. Fear-accumulating weapons, more alert, expanded, but not expanded in being, but to protect your being. In a state of fear I calculate my defenses. I find them all right and my fear disappears. Anxiety is fear spread out thin. Why we like a theater with tragedy is because we set a vicarious emotion. Everything is thin, diluted. We can go out to supper. In life the same tragedy would be devastating.

MONDAY, 17 FEBRUARY 1930

Some question asked—I didn't hear.

ORAGE: Most of our lives are lived in a lie—not in the bad sense.

Someone puts a question to you, to this dark revolving mind—any psychological influence in your answer depends on the images which happen to arise to you associated with the question at the moment. On another occasion you give another answer because a different number of groups of images come up. One answer is no more true than the other. Literally we have no control over our mind. The accident of the group of images then uppermost in the mind is responsible for all our responses.

Action, feeling and thought are all mechanical, what happens to the upper most in the consciousness at the moment—so we act, feel and think.

Someone asks: What is a mood?

ORAGE: A mood is a composite of ideas, feelings and sensations uppermost at the moment. You can't forecast how you are going to act on a forthcoming occasion. You go with a certain intention. When the situation is present you find unexpected stimuli and react differently than you planned. You have a purpose for your behavior in meeting a situation. You make a resolution.

You may hold the resolution in your mind, but a scum has come over it and you may not act according to your resolution. Also feelings are rotating so they cannot forecast. If things fall out right for your purpose, to go through, it is by chance. The precariousness of our states makes it necessary for us to constantly make efforts to hold friendships and so forth. You are in love with somebody. You really feel that emotion toward them, but not constantly. There are wide blank spaces, when you have to finesse, cover the gaps.

(Draws old diagram.)

Here is another center, emotional. Make a list of these days of all emotions you have experienced and know about. You will realize how small a range of human emotions you know about. We have experienced a relatively small number. Not these you have experienced in imagination or fancy, but in actuality. I, for example, have never felt awe, adoration. I have certain descriptions of adoration, but I have not experienced it. Only occasionally I have an emotion worth talking about. Beings in whom the emotional center is paralyzed are not the most unhappy. We say their heart is as cold as a stone—worthless, hard, cold,—nevertheless they are called human. What happened is atrophy or death in the emotional center.

Points to 3rd center in diagram: Here is our beloved ability to think.

I ask what is the square of 29. You go through a process in your own mind.

You are thinking. Do you have an emotion while working this out? No. Any sensation? No. I use my arm. I have the sensation of force. I lift a chair. I feel a weight. I do not say I am thinking.

This is the power house.

This is the heating house.

This is the lighting house.

I beg you at this point to try to think of some experience which is not one of these, or a combination of forces. Some claim they have had some superior experience—beautiful or inspirational, but it turns out they all come under these 3 centers. A unique is that of the fourth center. Just as sensation is different from feeling—feeling from thinking—so this is quite new—different from any of them. It is preposterous that you can dream something which is not some combination of images that you have not received in the ordinary way. You must put imagination up here—fourth center.

It is not a mode of experience with which you are not already familiar. It is next to impossible to describe it. To be able to pass from these 3 modes of known experience to the 3 unknown modes is transition. Now let us take the emotional center. Every day of our life we have a number of emotions. Go over your emotions of the day. Have you had joy? What kind of letters did you receive in the mornings mail? Were you a little bored? Or did you hope for one of these days there will be a letter containing something—we would not like to say what. I know one lady, who used to write herself and enclose a check.

On the whole the mail is not very exciting, but on the whole no news at all is exciting, meaning, it was all what was expected. Then comes breakfast, etc. At the end of the day you find not anything very exiting has happened to you, but from the emotional point of view it has been dull—humdrum. How many days are otherwise in the course of the year. So your whole lifetime with a few exceptions has been flat. Nevertheless, such as they are, they are the sum of our emotional experiences. Just as your physical habits are set, fixed, so your emotions become habits, crystallized.

You refrain from expressing emotions which are unpleasant to you. You will then find yourself having no other kind. If you manifest unpleasant emotions these become habits. Even a pure emotion of delight when experienced by a man who is melancholy, will indicate melancholy in his manifestation and vice versa.

Aye in the very temple of delight.

Veiled melancholy has her sovereign shrine. (Keats.)

Which would you rather—it is possible to be unhappy and healthy, also happy and unhealthy. The welfare of one center is not the same as the others.

Health is the welfare of the first center. Happiness is the welfare of the second. In point of mind what do you wish to be? One may say "I wish to be intelligent, to know, to understand." I am looking for health or I am looking for

333

happiness," but how few would say "I wish to be intelligent." We are afraid of being called *highbrow*, but just as sincerely do we wish for intelligence.

We now come to how these three centers come to be filled. These 3 physical centers. The first is filled by movements—all the movements you have made since infancy have left their mark upon the muscles. We know how these contents came in. As they accumulate, they determine what the behavior of the body will be.

In the second center—all emotional experiences are there, and none which have not been experienced are there. We have only the memory of emotional experiences we have had, though we may know the names of others.

What constitutes the contents of the thinking center?

There are no words or thoughts in your thinking center that you have not already had. What does not use words or acts, we say does not think, e.g., a chair. 300 words is about the average conversational vocabulary, or vocabulary in everyday use. (It would be interesting to make a vocabulary of the words you use in one week.) A large part of our thought has to do with the words we don't use. We add new words and think we have added to our thought. They may add to your thought but not to our power. This center is determined by the words with which we have associations. The number of words you use constitute the contents of your thinking center. It is in this way you build up your thinking habits.

Never perform the same action in the same way twice.

Never feel the same way twice, etc.

Each of these 3 centers reacts with all the contents of the center.

The organism reacts always as a whole. Psychologists are now admitting this.

I say the word *home* and there is a reaction of all your verbal association.

I say "How dare you" and the whole of the contents of your emotional center reacts. A word is something more than a sound. A word is a symbol, indicating a thing or an experience. We have a word for tree, a word for feelings, such as *admiration, despair,* for conceptions such us *government* and abstract ideas such as *quietness, ponderability*. Mathematical symbols are also sounds with meaning, in that sense, words.

Our days supply of energy is spent by reaction to stimuli. The greatest fatigue comes from doing nothing.

A quantity of milk laid at the base of the brain is sufficient to equal what would supply an intellectual genius. The quantity at the door of our emotional center is enough to experience all the emotions of the greatest poets. All the energy laid at the instinctive center would supply an athlete. These 3 centers are the major reservoirs, but there are many others. These are in the glandular system. The physical center will run on mental or emotional energy, if the instinctive energy is used up and a new stimulus required action appears. This holds true for all three centers.

A new teacher will stimulate a fatigued mind.

When a center has used up its supply of milk and taken from its reserve, it sometimes robs the other centers of their supply. This has a deleterious effect on the whole of the organism. It is a catastrophe that any center should run out of milk.

When an ecstatic state is expressed it is memorable. It cannot be expressed by will, but when they do they refresh the energy. The majority of men expend their mental energy every morning by 11 o'clock. A woman has spent her emotional energy by luncheon. In fact, we generally awaken tired in the physical center. Why is this so? Because our 3 cans of milk leak.

There are many holes. They are not quite as big as the can itself. There are ways of learning to acquire new energy but why take the trouble to acquire more just to have it leak out. There are of course, 3 forms of leaks.

We have come to enjoy the leakage, though it is literally *blood* leaking out. We have come to think this leakage a desirable experience. In thinking, every mental process you have not initiated is a leak. We call it the St. Vit—a dance of the mind, e.g. drifting of thought through the mind. Then when a real problem is presented like curvature of space, you say "Oh, I can't think." How many moments during the day have you thought unintentionally.

Whenever it is unintentional, it has leaked. Every time we allow the mind to wander we are making the control of the mind more difficult. The physical brain itself wears out, but not because the thought is controlled. Day-dreaming is brain rot, destroying the physical brain. Purposive thinking constructs any condition that comes up. You imagine you are thinking, but did you intend the condition? Go to a play, hear what the dramatist makes the characters say,—but also devise words you would have them say. Otherwise you are being victimized by the dramatist. Another suggestion: Think in the most strange circumstances. In some absurd situation, think of curved space.

Mental process may be fatigued, but not exhausted. You have finished but not sapped. Difference between being sapped out and having leaked out.

A difference between expenditure of money for returns and being robbed.

We recommend mental exercises when doing physical, to find our centers can work without being dependent on the others. "Of all the experiences of the phenomena of consciousness and its experiences is the most important."

(Dewey) What we wish to do is to be aware in a single focus of all 3. When conscious you have a three fold focus.

Waste of energy—physical waste, unnecessary, waste of muscles. If you are doing nothing you will be more exhausted than by getting up and doing something. In ancient India action and inaction were both considered doing.

Always relax all muscles but those necessary to the position at the time.

In walking for example, it is a succession of falls from one leg to the other. It does not require any special effort. Gravitation should be used.

As to emotion, try to express the exact opposite to what you feel.

335

Observation is not for the purpose of finding the causes of manifestation.

This is beyond your ability. Simply observe your symptoms. You should look forward to your next negative state to find out if this method is effective as it is said to be. The same as we should try a cooking recipe. If we do not try the recipe our hunger is not ravenous. The professional psychologist is only using words. Personally, they have no psychology at all, simply telling about shades of verbal distinction. They could write an excellent essay on courage, heroism, etc. "I was so frightened I did not dare run away,"—courage.

"I had such sense of beauty." In the absence of some experiments on your part, you will never be dealing with things themselves. Self-observation is the key to practical psychology. So I appeal to you once more to make practical experiments. I swear to you, if you note your behavior, you will experience something. When Jesus was supposed to be asleep in the boat and a storm arouse and they awakened Jesus, the bible reports, he said: "Peace, be still." What he said was the key words "Observe yourselves."

Q: Does fear disappear if you observe it?

A: Certainly, because you are absorbed in your symptoms and you find fear has passed. The observer is best fitted to observe when the body is best fitted to be observed. Under drugs and drink, we say we observe, but cannot stop. But with objective observation, it does stop.

There are 2 kinds of shocks—outside and inside. Illustration: Under a change of temperature, ones style of writing changes. Indigestible food will effect one's style. You do not get angry because you think. A dog hit by a stone, bites the stone nearest it, not the offending stone. In one situation you act one way—indignant. In another—another way—you do not care.

We may be reminded, but that is not sufficient. Illustration: An alarm clock may say "Wake up," but cannot compel you to get up.

Hell is where there are no laws. Anything may happen. Our bodies are in hell. The body calls upon a savior—God.

The savior is I. In this way the I is *the light under my feet.*

What can I do for the. I : Putting bits of paper about to say "Observe yourself, you fool." The body puts up the prayer. Punish yourself if you have failed to observe. It is childish to do this to others, but wise to do to yourself. Doing penance for not observing, you will find the next day you will take self-observation more seriously. "I" cannot make "I" observe but it can call attention of "I." The age of essence determines whether "I" makes the effort, whether "I" observes. The age of essence depends upon ideas. 12 people, all equal in education, in character, in physical strength—one only will practice, by accident. They have an idea of doing something about it—magnetic center. If, as an intelligent listener to the method, a material will be created in them of which a magnetic center will be made. Whatever reaches essence must pass through magnetic center.

Both joy and sorrow will effect essence through magnetic center. Planetary body and I are most closely associated through magnetic center—called rainbow bridge.

Three schools—the three main schools in Eastern religions:

First—school to develop higher thought. Whole series of these schools. Gnani schools of yoga, abstract thought. Plato arrived at this and in a way failed.

Second school—a doctrine of the heart to develop higher emotional center, Bhakti yoga. Third school—aims at higher physical center. The maintenance of the body in a state of perfect health. Hatha yoga.

Christian science is a combination of bhakti and Hatha, a therapy.

Question about Patangis? This was a combination of Gnani and Hatha.

Never has there been a combination of the three.

This method is called the fourth yoga or the fourth way. All 3 are included in it but none of the disciples of the 3 other ways enter into the fourth way.

The fourth way is self-observation. It is more difficult than any of the techniques of any of the other ways.

Any one practiced in type of the yogi are infantile in the other 2 centers.

Super-action in any one center will draw all the energy from the other 2 and draw them dry. Each way achieve its object; but produces monstrosities.

Each school was started by a fanatic. Pupils fall into one school or another by accident. (Tells of some of the feats accomplished.) No westerners are fanatic enough to be drawn into any of the yogi—therefore for the westerner there is only the fourth way or none. Though the most difficult of all it coincides that it as simple. You are told to do one thing—observe yourself.

MONDAY, 11 MAY 1930

At least one half of the tragedy in life comes from attributing to others things which happen to us.

There is absolutely no blame.

We do not stop to think that others are as mechanical as we are. We are all liable to become unreasonable, insane or bestial.

Something will happen to submerge you, though all here are capable of fulfillment.

I would like you all to regard yourselves from now on as a story—you are the hero or the heroine—the book is half written—What do you think is likely to happen to you—do you see yourself drifting along to death or may there be reserve for your experiences in the last chapters—My last word to you—if arriving in such an occasion you have learned to look upon yourself

337

objectively. You can defy anything which may happen to you—by looking at yourself as another person, you can lift your nose above the flood.

Just at the moment when we can say "The thing that is happening to me" you will be safe.

You will have all the pangs of sympathy for him or her, but you will not be submerged. So now in fair weather, if I can hear myself speak, see myself move, etc., then the edge of the tragedy you have looked on will become amusing, ridiculous etc.

I beg of you before starting on this journey (and do not contact me) to question—you are plunging into the dark—here is a little lamp; I show you how to rub it; make sure you know how to rub it.

Simultaneously I am aware, I am thinking of our mutual problem.

So don't hesitate to ask the question which refers to your own personal situation on which you may sooner or later need light. What is waiting for me around the corner? I am not asking for philosophic questions. Is there any problems which means anything like unemployment, I am not inviting questions as to whether God created the universe but questions which concerns us.

Q: Shall I change my occupation?

Can I live with my husband any longer?

Would sexual relationship outside of marriage be possible?

How can I command the love of someone in whom I am interested?

How am I going to make more money?

A: Get on with a smaller budget.

What can I do with a mother who gets on my nerves, be tactful when I don't want to be? Should I have children etc.

Q: To what extent should I put my trust in this?

A: Sooner or later you will be skeptical. There is no subject in the world on which you can get satisfaction.

There is one question—unless I, in my own right, independent of others, become an instrument to attain knowledge.

I think there is no one living in the world for whose opinion on literature I have any respect.

There is no one living that I know whose opinion is of value to me.

I do not expect to have any further information. Still my knowledge of literature is so small that I realize I am only a worm—There is so much more to be known on literature—there is nothing more but to accrue a new mind. You pursue any subject to the end and you realize you can go no farther without a new mind. Psychological exercises stretch the mind you have by exercise—but they do not give you a new mind.

You discover your mind is not good for finding the truth. Our minds, given us biologically, are incapable of arriving at truth.

The mind of Orage under no conceivable circumstances can arrive at truth, but "I" can by looking at Orage.—When he becomes object to me then I can look upon the external world objectively.—It was not for a new mind I followed this method—it was not for any of the by-products.

I have little negative emotions, I have no problems, I have no enemies—I sleep well at night; yet none of these things have tempted me to practice self-observation. The temptation was to arrive at truth—the striving of a human being is to understand and only this would be sufficient importance to make the effort.

There is a hope that you can attain understanding—bring on an old problem a new mind.

There is a type of mind capable of attaining in which truth will strike home (book recently published "Science and Philosophy" by Haldane), interesting to read during the summer; also Eddington's "Nature of the physical world." These books would destroy the whole of agnosticism etc.

There is only one truth—our relation to God.

What does he call God?

During this writing he is confused, he arrives at everything logically.

Does anyone know that he is a brain cell in the body of God?

You know you have parents.

Do you know equally you are children to God?

Just as you have a biological relation to parents, you have psychical relations with God.

In our present mind we cannot know. To know we have to be born again.

This begins by observing ourselves—activity—self-observation is extremely subtle.

The eye of the body does not take in this.

One particle of energy at the end of the brain cell is 100.000 more energy than the atom of energy used in waking consciousness.

Energy created in the act of observing while sweeping a room is greater than the energy used in writing many master pieces.

Orage, San Francisco, August 1928, by Ansel Adams.

There was some argument about whether or not the discussion of Reason, carried on in the two preceding meetings, had been concluded. A man rather new to the group (I understand he's from Santa Fe or Taos) questioned Orage's use of "Word" in the phrase, "in the beginning was the word," stating that the latest theological interpretation was of a "Word" meaning geometrical ratio, and not the symbol of reason.

Orage said the term came from the Gnostic doctrine, older than the Greek, which implied in the word both geometrical ratio and the rational "Word." The nature of thought, according to this system, is the discrimination of degrees of likeness and difference. This ability, and the ratio of likeness and unlikeness in things discriminated, implies a corresponding ratio between the things discriminated.

ORAGE: Reason makes these discriminations. That which exists in man for active discovery of ratio is man's ratio, his reason.

A.B: What is the difference between the formal reason which is the higher part of the instinctive scale and the formal reason of the astral scale?

ORAGE: Formal reason of the instinctive scale implies one or two center activity only; in the astral scale it implies three-center activity. One center formal reason discriminates form, two center formal reason discriminates quality, and three center formal reason discriminates these two plus idea.

I. S: Then emotions and ideas have the same persistence as physical objects?

ORAGE: Yes, but the persistence is relative; chairs, metal objects and so on disintegrate 30,000 x 30,000 x 30,000 faster than ideas. It is really "as if" mental objects disintegrate. There is a corresponding difference between instinctive, emotional and mental memory. Just as overtones are produced when a violin string is played (the string vibrates in 16 parts) so every change in the human organism produces corresponding divided vibrations. Many of these fractions "pass beyond our hearing." We literally never come to the end of an event that has occurred to us. Some parts may come back, however, in memory or super-conscious states.

A.B: I felt that here are two kinds of verbal reason—one in which words associative, are adequate, and another in which we recognize words merely as inadequate symbols.

ORAGE: Verbalizing has two functions—one purely symbolic, the other in which words always point to emotional and intellectual forms. Words are one of the phenomena of the world. You can have an experience of "home" without having ever heard the word, and you can have verbal association without experience, except approximately. This experience is what we call word magic. Verbal reasoning is dangerous because words are a species—they are entities—a humanly created phenomena capable of giving experience sometimes more potent that actual experience. No one can have an original emotion or idea (any thinkable thought already exist), nor can we create living objects. But in one field we do create—with words. Insofar as this activity is not directed toward self-creation, it is limited simply to enriching the field of words.

The astral scale is so difficult to pass because of the sirens of word-magic—the first three notes of that scale.

M.J: What are the phenomena of astral formal reason?

ORAGE: Sol of that scale is the ability to distinguish all physical states; la is the same ability with emotional states, and si is the ability with mental states or ideas. These are all subjective because they are exclusively confined to the individual's experiences. Discrimination of emotions and ideas as if they were objects is the development of astral formal reason. But until your organism is as objective for you as any animate or inanimate object, you cannot have any sense of objective reason, so I avoid discussion of that.

Again, the ability to discriminate between words and their associations and between emotions and ideas is the difference between verbal and formal reason

S: Some people who don't practice self-observation do seem very conscious — pragmatically conscious, at least.

ORAGE: There may be approximations to the method, but there is no substitute. Self-conscious development by self-observation is entirely different from other consciousness.

D.K: In connection with ideas as entities, we can never subjectively see ideas any more than we actually see objects.

ORAGE: Yes, exactly. We encounter the world on three planes; the physical, emotional and ideational, and each plane is neutralized product between the experiencer and the objective world. No one plane is realer than another; our predisposition to find the physical plane more real is the result of our limited consciousness.

I'd like to go back (but I'm afraid to) to the word "ratio"—the discriminating of likenesses and differences of emotional experiences, physical events and ideas is not the same as discriminating these subjective phenomena as if they were outside personal experience.

Speculative reason is of no value aside from its verbal discrimination. Gurdjieff rates it lowest because it does not lead into formal or objective reasoning.

X: What is the meaning of the phrase "vegetable, animal and human ideas?"

ORAGE: These are ideas on different planes. We recognize planes on the biological octave—the amoeba to man. And we know there is an emotional scale—that emotions are degraded or elevated. How do we discriminate between emotional values?

B.G: The standard has been given of an emotion which contracts being as the lowest, and an emotion which expands being as the highest.

ORAGE: That is so. But this implies the ability to discriminate emotional contraction and expansion, as we know it physically. The notes of the emotional scale are related to being—to more or less being.

D.K. raised the point of the fallibility of sense perception and the necessity of an outside check for this emotional observation and discrimination.

Orage said there must be such a check and proposed a New Year's resolution to discover the means of checking. This was a long and fruitless argument with D. in which, as usual, there was a misunderstanding of the use of terms. Quite a time spent over difference in the definition of "compound "mixture" and "combination." Orage's finale point was that there could be no argument until the question has been thoroughly studied.

ORAGE: We are going on to a scale for the discrimination of ideas. This scale must be like the biological scale, ranking ideas as organisms according to their complexity and not their value to us subjectively (though the thoughts discriminated are subjective.) What criterion could we use to discriminate thoughts as we do objects?

MRS. C: Weight.

ORAGE: That is one element.

X: An octave has notes in a fixed ratio; we would have to place ideas on their scale in such ratio.

ORAGE: The rate of vibration distinguishes notes—256 passes in an octave to the vibration 512. Ideas are related to each other in ratios, but we must discover those ratios. Since we can't discover the rate of vibration of thought what criterion shall we adopt?

J.R: You once suggested clarity, range of applicability and so on.

ORAGE: And I still suggest that we must go in this direction but this sort of criterion is even more difficult than the emotional criterion, which we have admitted is difficult. I'd like to make an experiment, which isn't possible now, to put before one-hundred people, chosen at random, ten or a hundred sentences—and I'll undertake to say that nine out of every ten would place the sentences in the same order to value. We would then discover what elements were in the minds of the voters.

D.K. argued that in any scientific experiment the observers would have to be qualified to do the experiment. Orage insisted on the competency of the indiscriminate audience, since the values in the sentences are universal values, regardless of the conditioning of the person reading them. This was another long and wordy discussion, into which no one else in the group would or could thrust a tangent. Everybody is annoyed when D. carries on but nobody else has vigor or persistence such as he has in an argument, so he has the run of it when he gets Orage started.

ORAGE: This brings us back to the fact that we obviously have not the ability to discriminate formally between states of emotion or between thoughts or trains of thoughts, as we discriminate between objects. And this brings us to the method in which, seeing the organism objectively, a being is able to complete the development of the ability to see clearly and equally objectively emotional and intellectual objects.

In relation to formal reason, we are like tone deaf would-be musicians.

DISCUSSION — 14 JANUARY

LAW OF ASSOCIATION

PONDERING

H. F: We find in the law of association the raison d'être of the Gurdjieff-movements—the dances.

ORAGE: Yes. What do they imply?

H. F: That when movement of a specific gravity occurs in one center, corresponding reactions will occur in the others.

ORAGE: There are groups of associations collected in each center and corresponding groups tend to act together. In a harmoniously developed person all groups of impressions in all centers would interact harmoniously.

The easiest and most accessible means of affecting all centers is through the instinctive center, and for this purpose dances, rituals and so on are developed. Impressions so taken and self-observed are positive. Overt behavior is always the end product of three stimulated centers and this product, observed in the blend, in food for the fourth center. Dances and so on were the gospel for the motor-centered—which are 98% of all people.

I. S: What is the intellectual type? Is Hamlet an example?

ORAGE: No, Hamlet is an introvert who can "hear nothing." The centers are connected by a magnetic tie which, if lacking, permits activity in one center without reaction in the others. Sleep is this disconnection, giving the centers a chance to rest of sympathetic vibration. The magnetic tie between two, or three of Hamlet's centers had worn so thin that he approximated sleep all the time. His real complaint was, "Why, when my intellectual center is so stimulated, cannot I feel the horror of this incest and murder, and why cannot I act?"

N. T: Did the music mentioned in the chapter on art have any connection with the law of association?

ORAGE: The music of the Legomonist was "made" (not composed) in three rhythms, so that simultaneously notes a, b, and c, in different centers would be stimulated. Normally the experience with music is of having all the a's b's or c's in each center stimulated. The Legomonist music affected incongruous groups of impressions.

G. K: Doesn't our accidental conditioning produce incongruous or irrelevant reactions sometimes?

344

ORAGE: Yes, but you are mistaking what I mean by "congruous." The congruity in this relation in history, not the likeness in kind but the likeness in relation. The Legomonist would produce a non-habitual train of associations.

But we must first understand the nature of an impression—not strictly as an image, but as an image meaning the power of re-experiencing any experience received in any center. How does an impression continue in memory?

I.S: The destroyed cell structure, which is always changing must be replaced by an identical substance.

ORAGE: Yes, It must carry over activities set up in the original structure.

G. K. Suggested that an impression sets up a vibration, like music and is so related to the memory of the cell.

I. S: Does each center have its own memory, or are there three memories?

ORAGE: There are three, one for each body—for the three kinds of matter. Let us do away with the idea of memory in cells; modern physiology permits us to do this, for when cells are removed from parts of the brain the memory of that area can, in certain conditions, be regained in another area. The functions of various parts of the cortex can be taken over by the cortex as a whole.

E. K: I was wondering if real memory could come only from the true interrelation of centers.

ORAGE: I don't see the connection. We want to find something in the being, as real as the cortex, in which memory resides, or inheres.

N. T: The easiest thing is to assume activity of another body—the etheric. Physical memory—muscular reactions—seems just as strange as mental memory.

ORAGE: Yes, it is. How do new cells become successors of the cells with which they were never in contact? If memory is a function of each of the three brains, then each brain must be a separate depository of impressions.

I. S: Then if all three brains are destroyed, all memory goes?

ORAGE: Yes. There would be no receptacles. Now of what are the three brains the organs?

I. S: Of the three centers.

ORAGE: Yes. What is the physical characteristic of the three centers as differ from the physical character of the brains? What is it the body coats?

X: The psyche.

ORAGE: Yes. It is an entity, the psyche, but only incidentally planetarily coated. Physiology is merely the planetary instrument of the psyche. The center is the repository of impressions, and the brain is its instrument. So if part of the physical brain is destroyed, another method of retention (in the organism as a whole) can be devised. The organism may finesse like reproducing a tune on a piano that has a key missing. And the state of the 'tuning' of the planetary body is indicated by memory—(physical fatigue results in stumbling and fumbling, mental fatigue is absent mindedness, etc.).

Each cell in the organism is like a set of Indian boxes—one within the other, three of them—the outermost being the physiological box we see, then the astral, then the mental. Everything that passes through the first two is finally contained in the third. The process is like the development of the plant's blossom, fruit and seed, which develop simultaneously but manifest successively.

D: Are memories stored in these boxes as chemical traces?

ORAGE: That's what we want to come to.

N. T: The interior boxes aren't complete?

ORAGE: No, they are in the process of becoming complete. The most ultimate memory is in the third box—in mental matter. In each center is a field—"organized swirls"—into which every impression is received and in which they continue to act in exactly their original manner. Perhaps you have read some of the latest ideas about matter—how an atom in ether is simultaneously everywhere in its field—can never be said to be at one place in its field. The Akashic record consists of the field of cosmic ether; the psyche is like an epitomized cosmic field. The identity of individual memory is localizable but not localized (like the atom). The Akashic record is cosmic memory, the specialized field of which we call individual psyches. It is something like dropping a net into water and saying it defines a field—this definition of the individual psyche. That part of the water—the cosmic memory—defined by my neutralizing form is my psyche.

X: Is the psyche indestructible?

ORAGE: Yes, except under one circumstance. Read the chapter on Purgatory.

Within the psyche there is possible the development of three centers. I know this a difficult concept of the psyche as an ideal form, within which exists cosmic ether of which every atom is simultaneously localized and general.

L: I don't understand the difference between "I" and psyche.

ORAGE: The psyche is the instrument of "I". In the net analogy do you say the psyche is the contents of the net or do you include the boundary of the net? Is the boundary something or nothing?

D: It's nothing—not physical.

ORAGE: But nothing can produce nothing.

E. K: Is it the point at which the neutralizing force ceases to be active?

ORAGE: What a contradiction of terms! How can the neutralizing force cease to be active?

E. K: Well, the point where the active force ceases to be active.

ORAGE: That's better.

All psyches in the cosmic ether do not cease or fail to exist because of lack of coating, but coating with other forms of matter makes other bodies possible.

We can substitute as a definition of the psyches form constituted of cosmic ether—substance within the field plus the form of the field. The three emanations—the three activities of ether are differentiated into centers, but only in

346

the developed psyche. Until the mental body has been differentiated in the field it cannot be said that the soul exists.

D. K: The concept of the psyche then includes the mental body—all three bodies?

ORAGE: It includes the mental but not the physical.

L. C: Why not the physical?

ORAGE: The true physical body is the etheric body. Gurdjieff always refers to the other as the planetary body. We don't use the term etheric much because of its association with spiritualism and so on. On other planets there maybe beings with three bodies that never present any physical aspect. These four bodies explain why man is called a quaternary on this planet The physical body is modeled atom for atom on the etheric body—the planetary body is the double of the other.

N. T: This explains the use of "Tetartocosmos" in place of "Tritocosmos" in the latest versions of the book.

ORAGE: That is good. As you know, Gurdjieff prefers to illustrate the etheric body as being coated by being "dipped" into planetary matter.

A. B: Well, where does our present memory reside—in the etheric body? You said It didn't reside in the brain.

ORAGE: I will go back to that Image of the total plant - the blossom, fruit and seed; we are concerned with their development simultaneously, though in point of succession one of them is more developed than the others. The blossom in this analogy is the etheric body (the stalk and roots, I suppose are the planetary body).

A. B: But while the higher bodies are not developed, impressions intended for them are deposited in the etheric body?

ORAGE: Good.

M. R: Is "I" consciousness of the boundary of its field?

ORAGE: And also of the contents.

D. K: I'm not sure yet what you mean by an impression.

ORAGE: I know—we started in that direction. But we mustn't go off on it now. By the way, the latest word for etheric matter is "wavicle". Somewhere in that concept the persistence of memory is found.

D. K: Do you use impression in the sense of being a vibration?

ORAGE: Yes—an impression is a collection of wavicles.

DISCUSSION — 21 JANUARY

LAWS OF ASSOCIATIONS

ORAGE: Obviously we did not get to a discussion of the laws of association last week. Would anyone attempt to say with what conclusions we ended?

N. T: We were talking of memory.

ORAGE: Memory is of the psychological order; as impression is an occurrence in the matter of which we are composed. So character does not depend on memory, nor does change in being, since changes in memory are on a psychological plane and physical changes don't affect memory but the psyche of which memory is an organ. Impressions are a food, changing not necessarily the psychology but the material pattern of the mental matter or thinking center. It is relatively unimportant if memory supervenes if only the fact occurs. Memory plays a relatively small part in manifestation. Therefore self-observation is more effective as a means of determining the state of being than is introspection through memory, which can reveal only a part of the impressions received. The organism is the product of all impressions received and its behavior determined by these impressions is more integrally a part of them than that part which remains in memory. Self-observation comes in contact with the end product of all received impressions. Our body is constantly undergoing changes due to the intake of three foods, each of which must be regarded as a physical fact.

N. T: I'd like to have more elucidation of the psyche.

ORAGE: It isn't really apropos. When we are dealing with impressions we are not dealing with the psyche. Laws which govern the stratification of impression received are under discussion and it would be well to defer talk of the psyche until we have discussed these laws.

Are there any other questions? There is a great spirit of co-operation here. What question would you direct to this subject to get the material necessary to an understanding of the laws of association? I should first ask—assuming complete ignorance —what is understood by a law? By association? Is it association of similarity? Of propinquity in time and space? Of conformity? Association of what? It is" assumed that it is an association of entities, the same law that governs association of people, words, sounds, etc. Our answer obvious is an association of impressions. We take in indiscriminately a variety of foods and strangely enough the extracts assemble in the proper parts of the organism. This discrimination from indiscriminate food is by the law of association of chemicals. We must have as concrete an idea of the nature of impressions as we have of the food and air elements.

Well, at least we know that this law of association is of. The next thing is what is an impression? I made the statement in the preliminary discussion that an impression is a change brought about in the matter of which the brain is composed through the medium of a sense organ. In the absence of will, we are attached to and run by this body.

ORAGE: Stimuli are received through the five sense wires. By this medium, environment produces changes in us and regulates our behavior. Through the afferent nerves vibratory changes produce an effect which must be conceived of as a substance. Eddington makes this clear, by the way. The matter deposit by the sun on the planet is like the substance deposited by our stimulated affer-

ent nerves. So the nervous system must be regarded as a complex, differentiated wiring system attached to the dynamo of environment.

I. S: What is the unit of an impression?

ORAGE: In the case of visual stimulus it is 10,000 per second. An impression
is the duration of an external stimulus for 1/10,000th of a second.

I. S: It seemed to me that if an impression is a durable entity (an irritation)
enduring for such a time as you mention, it must take its place in the organism
as a sort of letter related to its coefficient elements.

ORAGE: I think you are confusing the physiological and the psychological
elements. The nervous system is highly differentiated and has five systems for
receiving impressions.

I. S: (interrupting) Well, if we have five systems, say, of copper, platinum,
silver, gold etc., does any impression, or irritation lasting 1/10,000th of a second leave a dross just like any other?

ORAGE: Each of the five kinds of impressions has a different source of stimulus. The deposit depends on the character of this stimulus.

N. T: Is it like different wave lengths?

ORAGE: More than that. What is the candle here aside from its value through
association?

R. A: A collection of vibrations.

ORAGE: Yes. And so it is a dynamo capable of stimulating my visual nerves
quite differently from the stimulus produced by the lamp because the lamp,
objectively speaking, has a different anthology of vibrations.

R. A: The vibrations may require the same time unit to make an impression
and yet differ in quality and character.

ORAGE: Yes, exactly. 1/10,000th second exposure to the lamp produces a different result from the same exposure to the candle, but less than 1/10,000 the
second exposure to either produces nothing. This is the quantum theory.

I. S: I'm willing to agree to all that. But how do we inject these qualities
into an impression? I don't see that we've *got* an impression yet. I'm trying to
be clear, but I want to know how we get there. (S. was very emotional and had
tried to interrupt Orage several times and partially succeeded.)

A. B: I think we're wasting a lot of time on this. We all agree about what has
just been said by Orage.

ORAGE: Well, time isn't imperative. Patience is. We introduce into the original homogeneity of the impression as stimulus for 1/10,000th of a second the
differentiation of five forms or sources for these stimuli. I further introduce
any amount of variety in the deposits these five senses leave.

I. S: But variety—how? That's where I fall off.

J. R: The unit of matter is mass, but there are different kinds of mass.

ORAGE: Yes.

B. R: There is a difference in the charges of the stimuli.

ORAGE: Yes. All that we know of matter is that it is a congeries of charges.

I. S: But why matter? This ideology then becomes the same as the substance.

ORAGE: I always assume in using "matter" that we mean that grouping of charges that produces the phenomenon of matter as we call it. You should read Eddington.

I. S: I did read Eddington!

ORAGE: The congeries of vibrations stimulating our nerves deposits at last replicas of the thing which composed this congeries. And as I say, the variations of deposit are practically innumerable in all of the five kinds.

I. S: Then I say you must change your definition and include quality as an element, and not just irritation for 1/10,000th of a second.

ORAGE: The deposit varies according to the difference in the source of the stimulus. Three things, in fact, determine the deposit: the nature of the external stimulus, (positive or negative charges in the object) the character and condition of the conducting tract (the nerve) and the nature of the deposits already contained in the receiving center—by the end product of the system.

E. K: When a similar impression comes in would it start a group by the law of association or law of similarity?

ORAGE: That would be the law of similarity, one of the laws of association. Take the center as octaves and consider the reverberations between them. These are the laws of association between centers, or within centers. We are just now concerned with the latter.

X: May I ask why every stimulation of a nerve track leaves a deposit?

ORAGE: Because it is a force.

X: But you can crumple a piece of paper without leaving a substance.

ORAGE: The creases left would, in our definition, be changes in substance and equal to an impression. Certain of the paper's particles would be changed in relation to others.

But what is it that determines in each of the centers the rules in the behavior of impressions, separating them into groups and assuming that associations are there to be related? The law of association *in* centers are in accordance with those of the octave; the laws between centers are those of Triamazikamno. Within the centers are relations of do, re, mi, sol, la, si, etc. and between centers are relations of doh, sol, and do again. What do you imagine these laws within the centers are?

B. B. G: Of association according to similarity and rate of vibration.

ORAGE: Vibration certainly has something to do with it. What vibrations? In each center we have a five-fold classification.

R. A: Won't association of impressions be according to attraction of opposites—the character of positive and negative.

ORAGE: Good, this is the first law of association. It is not of similarity, but of opposites—high-low, good-bad, etc. Try to conceive the center as a globe with opposite poles toward which impressions fall. This begins to give us a definition of mind according to this dichotomy. What other laws would you imagine to be occurring in this globe?

x: Would there be any impression in an empty center until a second impression came in?

ORAGE: Oh, I think it would be there but it wouldn't know where it was. It would measure itself against the curved space of the center.

R. A: Does the second law have to do with the breaking down of the existing contents of the center by the incoming impression?

ORAGE: Yes—the message, as it were, will be slightly changed by the contents. Swirls of impressions exist in the globe, because they must; but conceive them broken up in a sort of sociology. Their chief difference is their dichotomy. Now we come to the idea of a hemisphere on this globe.

L. M: Have we any way of distinguishing the positive or negative of an impression?

ORAGE: Yes.

L. M: Is it strictly a matter of the nature of the charge according to its source, and not a matter of whether the impression is passive received or actively taken?

ORAGE: In our sense now we are taking impressions before there is any superior force to "take" them.

J. R: This is just a case of electro-positive or electro-negative.

ORAGE: Yes.

L. M: The impression received as a unit is also positive or negative dependent on its source?

ORAGE: Yes, but in the translation from the source to the deposit it may be changed because of the conditions found in the nerve conductor, or in the contents of the center.

L. M: Well, how do we distinguish positive and negative impressions?

ORAGE: Negative is deprivation of quality; not lack of qualities but having the quality of deprivation.

J. R: Wouldn't the impressions vary in their ability to raise or lower the vibration rate of the whole center?

ORAGE: We'll come to that. We haven't yet really been able to understand the polarization of impressions. But we needn't clear up the point just now.

J. R: Propinquity in time and space would be a law.

ORAGE: It would be two laws.

R. A: According to simultaneity of external source?

ORAGE: Yes,

I. S: Asked again about the matter.

ORAGE: In the chapter on vibration it is said that when a number of vibrations cross, the point of crossing is called matter. In the enneagram the point of crossing mark the centers.

Well, we've had four laws of association mentioned: polarity, propinquity in time, propinquity in space, and according to grouping in hemispheres. These four laws are one major and three minors.

x: Is there a grouping according to weight—to specific gravity?

ORAGE: Yes, it is a very difficult conception. The whole notes of the octave, do, sol, do, have specific gravity; in them music falls. "Cadence" means "fall" you know. But does it mean heavy? Or light? Rather it means difference in vibration rate. What is the relation between gravity in this sense and gravitation? Try to think of the harmony of the spheres and of planets as notes in a scale.

Unfortunately, there is another complication and another law of association. These swirls of associations may appear to have congruity but one group will be going up scale and another will be going down scale, so there will be a law of association according to congruity in this respect also—whether the congruity is permanent or momentary, too.

Gurdjieff talks of the three centers of culture, and so on, because he is talking of the same laws of association of impressions which also control the grouping into units of every species. All entities ultimately depend on their rates of vibration.

And now we must introduce the idea of the holy Aeioua, related to this rising and falling of impressions.

L. M: In speaking of specific gravity and of planets as notes, then each planet is a point toward which centers of force converge - which is what we mean by gravity in physics. Similarly with, impressions are we to think of a series of points toward which impressions converge?

ORAGE: Yes, this is very good.

R. A: What makes impressions converge toward these points?

J. R: Each note point is a point of stability.

ORAGE: Yes—can you reformulate the question?

J. R: The question is how does an octave come to be formed?

B. H: Aren't these points restoratives?

ORAGE: Yes, but what are these restoratives? They must precede the reception of impressions. It is as if cubby holes had been prepared before the reception of impressions, but how do the first impressions know where to go to the right cubby? The character of the stimulus determines where the impression will go. If it is strong enough, the impression goes to si, the next stronger goes to la, and so on down.

If we expand our center it is a small replica of the cosmos before impressions are received, it is like the Sun Absolute. We shall find in its contents the same condition as on the Sun Absolute after God had modified the laws of 3 and 7 and put in the semitone. So we take the activity of the substance contained in a center for granted—the octavity having preceded creation, as it were. It is impossible to ask the why of this primordial octavity. We can only ask how the impressions are placed in the cubbyholes, according to the laws of association we have already mentioned.

In connection with the ascending and descending impressions I spoke of, the descending becomes food for the ascending.

x: Is there also a difference according to complexity?

ORAGE: Yes I'd like you some day to consider the difference between B flat and A sharp and whether the lower vibration absorbs the higher and vice versa.

Well, we are only on the fringes of the subject. There are still intensity of vibration, vivifyingness, and so on. The latter is a conception which makes impressions as varied in order on their own plane as vegetable matter is on this planet. Impressions are rich as vegetable foods are rich in vitamins.

I. S: Does an impression vivify the organism or other impressions?

ORAGE: It vivifies the organism.

DISCUSSION — 4 FEBRUARY

PARABLE

ORAGE: Consider the parable from the Gurdjieff point of view from which it is a truth for at least two, and usually three, centers, with interblended significance. How would you begin to write an article on the parable?

R. A: There is an organic relationship, isn't there?

ORAGE: Yes, between the things described and the images describing them.

M. J: Can you use myth and parable interchangeably?

ORAGE: No. Parables are the language, the natural speech, of mythical figures which ape the conscious representations of fully developed beings. You know how we attribute more than verbal meaning to the words of rationally developed beings—we "put more into them." For instance, there is the myth of Gurdjieff, who can't ask for a cigarette without some disciples thinking his request is parabolic—that he wants something else.

In its octave form the parable runs from the allegory through the parable with an inclusion of meanings until it reaches the oracle, capable of translation in seven forms. The idea of the parable is that the facts of one plane are made to correspond to the facts of another plane. In general Gurdjieff's book is a mythological parable, when he writes of the dispersion of races, he is writing of centers, though this seems to me one of the cruder forms of allegory.

Gurdjieff often says of his "mis-statements," "I can't say it's right, but you can't prove it is wrong."

The stories in the Biblical parables obviously did not occur. A miracle is that which is made so plausible that it is as if it occurred.

L. B: I think it has been said that parables are given in such simple terms because if an intellectual vocabulary were used the meaning would soon be altered.

ORAGE: Yes. It is always easier to remember a story than its meaning. Fairy

353

tales are the remains of difficult ideas and doctrines—Hop O' My Thumb, and little Boy Blue.

The "Tale of a Tub" is a rude likeness to a parable, but it can be read merely with intelligence and information. A genuine parable must be read for understanding—its inner significance does not show on the surface and is not on the same plane with the gross narrative. The mind that is brought to the written text is the intellect and is incapable of understanding; The mind that ponders, being blank, can understand.

Meanings change so much that even the terms of the gospel are meaningless to us—bread, fish, the upper room, and so on, are technical terms which we do not recognize now. Explicit meanings are of no value in the parable except insofar as they are in our current language, but the implicit meaning can always be arrived at.

C. Z: What is the relation of France's "Penguin Island" to the parable?

ORAGE: That is in the line of the fable, because penguins never act as he makes them. Parables are based on facts of . . .

L.C: HOW can you find the key to a parable?

ORAGE: Yes, what meaning could Gurdjieff's book have for people who had never heard of the method? What is the Bible without a key? A collection of texts from which you can select any moaning you choose. I suggest that the division of the old and new testaments has a parabolic meaning. Look up the meaning of "Testament"—its root. The Old Testament is a triad—do, re, mi; then there is the shock of the appearance of the universe incarnate, after which the narrative proceeds from the history of Jesus (Old Testament) to the history of Christ, who was born in the interval. The Old Testament should, then, be a parabolic account of the development of man through the development of the three lower centers, and the New Testament of the development through the three higher centers, with, of course, correspondences between. St. Paul translated some of the Old Testament stories into New Testament meaning—the story of Hagar. Jesus referred to the "Old Adam" and the "New Adam." "Promise" means potentiality, and very few people in the Old Testament were said to have promise. The Old Testament is historic parable; the New is psychological parable. In the absence of a key any interpretation of Gurdjieff's book, as of the Bible, can be taken as nonsense.

It is said in the Bible that "He who practices this method (self-observation) will bring out of his treasury things both old and new." You should have greater resources of memory, for instance.

Without pride, I can say that I think I could go on talking for hours about parables. You should begin to recognize this symptom in yourselves.

R. S: What is the advantage of stating a method in parable rather than in fact?

ORAGE: This is an interesting question. What do you think?

A. B: I think it's been hinted at tonight—so that the majority of people can remember the story with the meaning implicit and so that anyone who would exercise his potentialities would have material to work with.

B. G: Wouldn't people given a method intellectually, go no further?

ORAGE: Yes, Gurdjieff has said "I bury the bone." Asked why he buried it so deep he says that then the dog digs and becomes active and can understand.

Until you've had to "worry out" the meaning, you can be sure you haven't the capacity for understanding it.

J. R: Isn't this procedure auxiliary to the transmittal by initiates?

ORAGE: I hardly think. They have the pure symbols—the diagrams, etc.

R. A: The method is a sort of divining rod for finding the bone?

ORAGE: It is. As you know, Gurdjieff stresses the development of the sense of smell. He has even said he is afraid he has given too many keys, but never a key near the lock.

I. S: Is Einstein's theory a parable?

ORAGE: No, it's a code—not in language. In parable common terms are used.

L: What about Blake's Prophetic Books?

ORAGE: They are elaborate allegory and poetic imagery.

X: How about Wagner's "Ring?

ORAGE: It is allegory. Wagner started as a moralist and couldn't keep it up—he became a Christian and increasingly sentimental and beautiful and weak.

Swinburne is an infantile atheist. Like Henley's "Bloody but unbowed." He is creditable but not cosmic.

In reading poetry if you think what would be said or meant in prose, you get a double satisfaction. Music also has this double content. Most music is like most poetry—just bombast. If you reduce Wagner to prose (his own prose) you find it is just impossible platitude. Bach, Beethoven, Palestrina occasionally have something to say. Unfortunately we are in relation to most music as children are to poetry—if it sounds good we think it is good.

X: Have we a right to expect an intellectual analysis of music?

ORAGE: That is just what the poet says when he has nothing to say in his poetry.

In exactly the way that I am pleading now for the reading of content of music apart from its sonorous form, we should be able to read parables, ignoring all they ostensibly say and getting back to the real "prose" meaning.

There was some discussion of proving and disproving the statements of Gurdjieff's book.

ORAGE: The statements are of no importance.

R. B: Then how does this place the book in relation to people who have not heard of the method?

ORAGE: Well, such a person will go on for years trying to prove or disprove the statements, or he will throw the book away. In fact this is what has happened sometimes. Without "conditioning" it is not taken in. The book makes neither sense nor nonsense to such a person—but gallimaufry (a stew of which you can't tell if it is made of meat or vegetables).

A. B: I should think a third reason for using parable might be that language tends to verbalization in one center so that a three dimensional truth can't be presented just in words, though parable gets around this.

ORAGE: Yes. Parable of the equipage is a good example of this. If you really thought of your centers this way it would be a very useful working image. All the advice of moral treatises is contained in this simple story.

A. B: Because a parable is the utterance of a mythological being it need not have any bearing on the actual historicity of that being.

ORAGE: Quite right. Christianity does not depend on the historicity of Jesus.

M. M: There is a difference in tone, isn't there, between the parable, allegory and fable?

ORAGE: Yes. The parable comes from an integrated state—that's why we're not capable of writing them, or true fairy tales. A parable is "an earthly story with a heavenly meaning." It has as its content a cosmic truth.

TUESDAY, 11 FEBRUARY 1930

EVOLUTION AND INVOLUTION

Orage announced that Gurdjieff had cabled L. Gurdjieff asking her to arrange for an apartment in New York; Gurdjieff is sailing on the Paris leaving Paris February 12. During his stay in New York the Tuesday night book reading and seating are to be discontinued; the Monday night meetings and the voluntary small book readings are to continue. Orage asked for suggestions and comments, saying at the same time that it was absurd to prepare any plans or decisions until Gurdjieff's plans were known. When nothing was said, he said he hoped that the opportunity of first hand contact with the author of the book we are discussing would not be neglected; that the group's behavior at Gurdjieff's last appearance had been so passive as to be useless in increasing comprehension of the book.

There were many expressions of opinion as to Gurdjieff's stay last year:

I. S: To the effect that he has never been satisfied as to the validating authority behind doubtful statements.

E. W: That he had his money's worth many times over in the entertainment Gurdjieff provided.

B. R: That he had continually expected a new thing to happen during Gurdjieff's meetings only to be disgusted at the finish.

ORAGE: A certain psychological effort was necessary in order to get anything out of Gurdjieff; the knowledge acquired by 'eating dog' was not to be obtained lightly. You must take the attitude of a person with cancer toward his physician; you have the intensity of the dying man's wish to live. If the physician talks around the subject you bring him back. If upon the failure of Gurdjieff to keep his promise of answering questions in the first meeting, the group had failed to appear at the second, the third would have been a different story. Concerted action in leaving a meeting where questions had been treated brutally would similarly have its effect. Only one person had shown any courage last year in insisting on having his questions heard, and he had been without group support.

The discussion continued with many of what Orage called rationalizations of last year's behavior.

G. K: Questions asked in the afternoon meetings where they were not allowed were not sensible.

ORAGE: Those he had heard were sensible and important, and that all questions were important to Gurdjieff in showing where someone had stuck. Even literal questions as to names may be of first importance in understanding the parable.

I. S. was continuing along lines he had already started when M. D. asked if the topic of the evening was to be forgotten. I. S. continued. M.D. shouted "Oh, S." but he didn't stop.

When we heard him out, Orage started the discussion of Evolution and Involution.

ORAGE: On what plane do we propose to undertake the discussion—with reference to changes with the megalocosmos, or in material processes, or psychologically with respect to our own experience.

B. R: Any planes will carry over into the others. We may choose any one.

ORAGE: This assumes a relationship among the octaves which it is one of our objects to uncover. We start with man and ask, what is the class of superior order to which man belongs?

L. C: All three-centered beings.

Bipeds and mammal were suggested and rejected because of not being superior order.

N. T: The organic kingdom.

ORAGE: Yes, because man is one of its specimens. Man is note do, the organic kingdom the note re. What is the note mi? What contains the organic kingdom?

G: The planet.

Thereafter the remaining notes of the octave were given as all planets, fa; our sun, sol; all suns, la; Sun Absolute, si; Megalocosmos, do.

I. S: Is there any significance in the position of our sun at sol?

ORAGE: I had often wondered. This is the complete cosmic octave starting with man. Without question as to the planets and suns being beings, each note of the octave is under control of the next higher. The organic kingdom controls man without a doubt; the organic kingdom is controlled by the planet;

357

color in flowers, for example, being produced by chemicals in the atmosphere. One planet in particular, the moon, exercises an enormous influence on us—in the tides, the movement of sap etc.

It is impossible for the planet earth to do without the other planets. Astrology is correct in principle in recognizing the mutual influence of planets; for example, the orbits around the sun are in part determined by it. Biological life on a planet depends on the orbit, the upset of which might destroy life completely.

We started with man because we are concerned with ourselves. Theoretically we might as well have gone down the scale, monkey, vertebrate, etc. but our interest would have been merely scientific.

I. S: Why do the higher notes of the octave affect us whereas the lower notes do not?

ORAGE: It's a matter of rate of vibration.

I. S: But the lower notes do.

ORAGE: Each note sums up in itself all the lower notes and in this sense is affected by them. But it is not affected externally; it does not respond to them as it does to the higher rates of vibration. This is why we are interested in the octave building up rather than the status quo facts of the octave building flown. The old geocentric diagram of the cosmos in which men is shown centrally with the organic kingdom around him, and so on through the octave represented the same kind of interest—which is different from the interest in the facts shown in the heliocentric diagram with the sun central.

L. B: How does this octave differ from the octave ray in which the organic kingdom occupies the note fa?

ORAGE: This is the same difference as between the geocentric and heliocentric just described; there is a difference in purpose. Our octave is applied to man cosmologically considered; we accordingly have a frame of reference different from those in which man was psychologically, socio- and biologically considered. The present consideration is the most significant of all because it concerns our being; and becoming,—i.e. our successive ascent through superior orders of being. Our first step is to become one of the organic kingdom. The difficulty in conceiving the organic kingdom as a being is similar to the inability of a vegetable to see the animal kingdom as a being.

L. M: This is not an exact relationship since man is an instance of the organic kingdom, whereas the vegetable is not an instance of the animal kingdom.

This assumed that the organic kingdom of which we are aware is a whole whereas it may be but a part; that is, we may be unable to sense part of it.

I. S: What is our conception of the organic kingdom?

ORAGE: That it consists of beings; whether material or non-material, as seen from our point of view, is indifferent to the definition. Astral and mental bodies are organic.

358

I. S. started a long discussion of the validity of the existence of these non-material bodies.

ORAGE: They are verifiable though not at present verified. The verification is a matter of experience, and no authority can validate them. Astral bodies are destroyed if the planet is destroyed, and only then. Solar bodies are destroyed if and only if the sun is destroyed. For this reason a planet which supports an organic kingdom is a treasure in the universe because it provides the conditions for ascent of the octave.

I. S: What is this distinction?

It is the difference between the Trogo autoegocratic and the Egocratic systems. The Trogo applies to the status quo, that is, the maintenance of the universe, and for this process all matters in the universe are on an equal footing. The Egocratic or subjective process applies to the dynamic aspect, to aspiration and ascent of the scale. Planets on which the Egocratic process was aided were superior by this reason. The triad here is:

Egocrat—positive

Trogo autoegocrat—negative

Absolute—neutralizing.

Planets are ordinarily supposed to consist merely of minerals and metals. But to external examination we ourselves consist of just these. Saying that the planet is dead is just similar to saying that we are dead. The statement is definitely made that a planet is a being whose organs are provided by the organic kingdom. That it appears spherical to us is an illusion of our space-time frame of reference. Astral and mental bodies within the organic kingdom are the emotional and mental centers of the planet. One of these days you will be able to enter completely into one of your own centers, probably the instinctive first, and find there a complete replica of the organic kingdom—since you have acquired it in images.

The note fa in this scale—all planets—is not a true note. It is a transition note from planets to sun. The planets form a committee in its constitution—no one planet being able to act singly—so that the opportunity is open to all to pass from planet to sun. Otherwise said, the sum of all planets considered as vibration is not a single rate but a band of rates such that no single planet is discriminated against in the transition.

The Sun Absolute is the supreme being controlling all.

The octave presents two aspects: 1. ascent; 2. descent, which are mutually reciprocal. Being refers to the status of the octave as a whole; existence to movements on it.

Ascent—Evolution

Descent—Involution

Each note of the octave possesses the possibilities of ascent or descent. Asteroids are examples of destroyed planets whose dust becomes part of the organic kingdom. Within the organic kingdom species degenerate; for example the hermit crab once could make a home for itself, now it seeks shells. A position of rest in any state of being is impossible, except for a limited period, due to the action of the Heropass. Changeover from ascent to descent or vice versa is possible only at the transition notes fa and si.

Evolution is the actualization of potentialities.

Involution is the potentialization of actuality.

Any being in any state has the same potentialities as any other being; there is no loss of potentiality just as there is no loss of actuality due to reciprocal maintenance.

18 APRIL

SMALL GROUP FOR QUESTIONS

ORAGE: I suggest that you formulate questions, however crudely, and we will shake the question until we get something out of it.

E. T: I should like to have brought out more clearly the difference between ordinary meditation and being meditation.

ORAGE: I think you are confusing the word meditation with mentation. Presumably some time the phrase "being-mentation" will be commonly known and used as "subjective and objective" which date back no further than Coleridge. He got them from the German, but they are Latin in origin.

The two forma of mentation mentioned in the prologue of the book become the two dynamic streams of the epilogue. Being mentation is not a third form but an active form of the two—verbal and being mentation—which are both associative, but both of which can be either active or passive. When verbal association is active we have conscious writing (to produce a given effect purposely). When being mentation is active, associative forms are directed towards a given object.

S. R: I don't understand this.

M. M: Is this the same as pondering in which associations are brought purposively to bear on a question of action?

ORAGE: No, because we share this mentation of which I speak with animals—it is thinking in forms.

A. A: As when Hassein says: "Things are a-thinking in me."

ORAGE: Yes. The mind is always "a-thinking" and if we take a hand in it and direct the a-thinking it is active being-mentation. S. R. is asking the difference between material verbal mentation and being mentation.

S. R: Is it the result of an experience, digested?

ORAGE: Yes, and made part and parcel of your being.

A. B: I think that in any being activity, effort or mentation, the emotional center comes in.

ORAGE: I won't have the difference between these mentations made an intellectual difference, though. In being mentation we are "menting" with materials which, since they are part of experience, do have necessarily this emotional element. Instead of dealing with words and their associations (which make possible verbal logic) we have to use experiences and their associations, which make possible a being logic. The difference in the mentation is not in the intellectual process but in the materials employed.

M. M: Is the passive state of being mentation instinctive activity?

ORAGE: Yes, but then it is only a-thinking.

M. M: Is it mentation only when it is directed?

ORAGE: Yes.

S. R: That sounds like pondering.

ORAGE: Yes, but pondering I associate more with weighing of associations.

B. R: Pondering is in mentation but mentation is not in pondering?

ORAGE: Yes, very good. In being mentation not only the words but the experiences associated are brought up.

M. M: Is this the activity stimulated when we use such mantrams as "I wish to remember myself?"

ORAGE: Yes. This is active being mentation. If you call up the most vivid experience connected with each word and then you are in a state of I wish to remember myself.

B. R: Aren't we told to remember experiences non-emotionally?

ORAGE: Yes. But that is objective recollection.

B. G: Wouldn't your most vivid experience of "I" be the same as of "myself"?

ORAGE: No, for myself is my body. Ouspensky once said that his most vivid experience of "I" was once in Constantinople after leaving Tiflis—the sense of the strangeness of "I" being there—it was a state of "I-ness," and not peril of the body but rather a strangeness, simply.

B. G: Could an experience of myself be psychological as well as physical?

ORAGE: It is much better if it involves all the body. As they say experience teaches nobody; it simply provides data for learning. You can hear words a thousand times and not learn them; you must use them to know them.

Do you begin to see that being mentation is the active association of experience, just as active verbal mentation is directed verbal association? From such being mentation you can achieve new experiences. "I wish to remember myself" is a trick actually producing the wish to remember.

A. B: But, I still think it is more than an intellectual process—that as a process it is also emotional.

ORAGE: You have associations with "intellectual" which mean verbal, but I have a meaning for "intellection," which is the word Gurdjieff rejected just because of its associations with verbal reason—which allows for activity of the intellectual center in which all its sub-centers participate and use the materials of experience. I actively use this intellectual center but not words, and I arrive at a conclusion, but not in words.

L. B: What is the difference between formal understanding and being mentation?

M: Formal understanding is the conclusion you arrive at.

ORAGE: Yes.

L. B: I don't see why "being" is used and not just "mentation."

J. R: "Being" is used to differentiate it from formal logic.

ORAGE: Yes.

N. T: Isn't this being mentation the same as objective reason?

ORAGE: It is obviously one means to objective reason.

L. C: Is there a language of forms, as there is of words?

ORAGE: What would it be?

L. C: Gesture, posture, tone of voice, etc.?

ORAGE: Yes. If we take the sum of the experiences for which words stand, we have a new logic.

C. Z: To go back to dealing in experiences would be like giving up money and going back to barter?

ORAGE: Very good. Experience is the real wealth of life.

L. C: Then verbal reason leads to conclusion in words and being mentation to a conclusion expressed in behavior.

ORAGE: Yes, good, I should say, though, that being mentation can be expressed in either words or behavior.

Gurdjieff always suggested the value of being mentation in the activity of bringing up all experiences whenever you touch any object at all.

B. G: I'd like to ask .....

ORAGE: B., how do you differentiate between the intensity of one wish and another?

B. G: By the quality of suffering and the value.

ORAGE: But aside from the qualities?

S. R: By weighing the values.

ORAGE: Yes. To weigh values you have to know what it is you are weighing. Pondering is just this, but you must know what values you are pondering and propose to weigh. In the psychological exercise of weighing sentences it is purely verbal pondering. In being mentation the element pondered and the values are meanings of experiences. Belcultassi weighted his experiences this way and found them wanting.

A. B: In weighing wishes we have to look out for intensity because a real wish being harmonious would not be felt so much as some one center, emotional wishes.

ORAGE: Yes. The first sign of will appears to be the absence of wish because there is no conflict of wishes.

B. G: Is being mentation higher in the intellectual scale than pondering?

ORAGE: Yes. Being mentation is the whole octave as one, and pondering is fa. Verbal mentation is do-re-mi. Fa enters into formal or being (formal) mentation.

B. G: Is pondering always related to personal problems?

ORAGE: In the sense that it discriminates the parts of which a problem is composed. Experiences are discriminated just like numbers and pondering is this exact discrimination.

A child has formal experiences first, then learns words, We all accumulate our verbal associations much faster than we accumulate formal material. But finally over the bridge of pondering we come to have being experience to correspond with our verbal associations. Gurdjieff says this verbal association is the "grammar of the intelligentsia" he was taught as a child. But when he became a man he put away childish things—he turned to the grammar of being mentation.

B. G: Then concentration doesn't come into verbal mentation?

ORAGE: No, and words don't come into formal mentation.

Powering carries us only to the point of an establishment of values, relative to a certain object. But it leads to being mentation and association of experiences. (Wiseacring is dealing with sol-la-si of this octave in terms of do-re-mi.)

L. B: Asked a long question about whether being mentation is a "technique for observing thought and saving mental waste."

ORAGE: We cannot observe the emotions or thoughts of others, or our own. All three centers enter into every overt form of behavior (in a sense this is the basis of the difference between Behaviorism and Gestalt) Overt behavior obeys the law of Triamazikamno—there are three participants in it; the end product is observed and manifests more or less one predominant center. Learn to discriminate between these elements. The organism is threefold—"I am built up of these three elements, which arose in the organism, were concentrated in the end product, and are redistributed to "I."

L. B: My question should have been, is this observation of the end product the aspect of self-observation which covers intellectual activity?

ORAGE: Yes. If you are observing the overt forms of behavior, each center in its own way will begin to relax, tensions cease, they function normally and eliminate negative elements. A center, higher than any of the centers observed, comes into activity and exerts the Holy Aeioua.

B. R: I have the problem of being able to sustain observation quite well except when I most need it—in a crisis. Is there any ju-jitsu to aid in this?

ORAGE: As Gurdjieff said to me, you are a good fair-weather observer. And mostly in fair weather we aren't observing (noting) but just gazing at a blank.

Last Friday's discussion was an analysis of our state to show that all our physical and psychological manifestations are interrelations of our organism and its environment. From which point of view we arrive at the generality that all human beings are devoid of will—of the powers to do, to act rather than react. Then we have Gurdjieff's definition of man, to which he complains too little attention is paid, that "man is a being that *can do*." So it Follows that we do not know any men, in Gurdjieff's sense of the word; we know only men. If we take it then, that will-lessness is of the natural order, the question rises if it is possible for beings to acquire will. And also what kind of activity would be necessary to develop will as defined.

We must make an analysis of what we mean by reaction—of all the processes of which we are aware. It is hard to convince ourselves that all psychic and psycho logical phenomena are of the same order as physiological phenomena. Touch is a registration of physical contact and we don't say that the sense of touch is the cause of the contact. In exactly the same way, the process of thinking that is taking place in us now, and the effect in you perhaps subvocally, are both as devoid of will as the sense of touch is without will in physical contact.

In all this there is no more will implied than there would be in dream figures going through these movements. Who is responsible for the behavior of dream figures? We don't presume to imagine that the most phenomenal dream figure is real or initiating his own activity. But we have also to admit that we are not the initiators of the dream figure. They are not puppets, for that would imply a puppeteer. We have much the same phenomena in dream as in our waking state and if you transfer this to terms of behaviorism it must be realized that all activities if which we are aware are will-less, and will-less without any presumption of any controlling will outside.

Just as dream activities are, so are all phenomena activities of the unconscious or subconscious. This is one of the purposes of the myth to explain the influence of the moon and Kundabuffer. It is not so much the fact that man is without will that is surprising, but the fact that he believes he has it. Persuading man against scientific analysis that he has will is one of the effects of Kundabuffer. One of the first effects of self-observation would be to remove this illusion of will. One of the stages of self-observation is the conviction of will-lessness—the mechanicality of all the processes of life. It was called the Conviction of Sin in early Christianity. It is the precedent of attaining will, or salvation.

Assuming that the realization of will-lessness has been experienced, the question becomes one of whether it is possible to pass into real life—to be born again—and if so, by what means. At the very threshold of this inquiry stands the word will. And we come to the definition of will so opposite to the idea of pseudo-will which we have been believing we possessed.

It is doubtful if with only experiences of reaction we shall be able to pre-conceive the novel experience of will. So our first intellectual difficulty is to understand what is meant by will. It is obvious that if the word is intended—as it obviously is—to have a meaning, we can begin to look for this meaning in its associations, will is associated with doing—not primarily with feeling or thinking. So we must look for a new kind of doing, in one sense related to a familiar experience of doing but not just reactive doing, it must be doing with the active element rather than the reactive.

We are trying for the moment, with our reactive material, to get a purchase on the idea of that speculative "will" which is active. Have we any experi-ence within our reactive plane of a distinction between active and passive? Obviously we have all had experiences of this difference. Even in the field of reaction we make this distinction between acting and not-acting. We discover on examining our experience of this difference, that it lies in a difference of quantity of inertia overcome. When we have the sense, of obstacles and in-ertia overcome, we have the sense of acting; otherwise we have the sense of being inactive. Both are reactive but we register a sense of positive and passive. So in our definition, will is overcoming inertia, analogous to our mechanical experience of an active state. Will therefore must be of the nature of an inertia constantly being overcome.

Now let us consider the second aspect, the character of the inertia over-come. Again we have to fall back on our experience in discriminating our reactive life. Do we differentiate between the quantity and quality of effort expended? I think we do.

Don't take the words just scholastically, but refer them to your experience. Quality is the arrangement of quantity, as definite as the difference between the components of a picture and its design. The effort to assemble quanti-ties and the effort to arrange quantities are two experiences of activity in our mechanical state. And the two together are of a superior order to one alone. There is more effort in arranging design in quantities than in merely assem-bling the quantities themselves. In which activity, assembling or arrangement, is there the greater relative freedom, range of possibility? There is no doubt that from every point of view, arrangement presents greater range of pos-sibilities. So far as we know, the quantities of the universe are fixed. But the possibilities of arrangement of quantities are as great as the permutations and combinations of the quantities.

Perhaps I appear to be laboring the point, but the conclusion is that the effort associated with the assembling of quantities is less than the effort associ-ated with arrangement. The latter is a difference in kind.

The next step seems to me obvious—will in one of its aspects must be con-cerned with the arrangement of quantities, this being the only field in which the range of possibility is wider. If we therefore say now that all assemblies of quantities are according to nature and therefore mechanical, we must have an association with doing which is the arrangement of quantities. Or, will is the arrangement of matter. We define matter as inertia. Everything is material and has its quantitative aspect. Will is the arrangement of this matter. At present the permutations and combinations which we experience simply occur, and we have no knowledge of whether or not they are directed by other intelligences. The development of will, therefore, would require an activity in which matters are arranged against their disposition by nature. The unfortunate thing is that though we have experiences of "overcoming inclination" which can be shown to be simply other inclination, we must now look for an activity in which there is an absence of inclination. One unconscious wish usually overcomes a conscious wish. Can we conceive an experience in which an inclination is overcome not by a counter wish? This is why will has been said to be the absence of wish and this absence of wish which can at the same time overcome wish is called will. The difference is that we come in the course of reason to the point where no concept of will is possible according to the definition which appears to be paradoxical. The question of will is said to be the mystery of all mysteries. Yet this very force of will which creates, maintains and destroys the world is absolutely unintelligible. At the same time it is said to be absolutely necessary to develop this force.

c. z: Would the Buddhist Nirvana be a description of will?

r.a: There's no doing in that.

orage:; That's a great dispute—whether Nirvana is all doing or not-doing; all existence or non-existence. Read Santayana's "The Realm of Essence."

c. z: I was thinking of Nirvana as the absence of all wish.

orage: Yes. But all popular conceptions of Nirvana associate it with extinction.

b. r: At least it is a state of rest.

orage: But that state is one of suspended activity. Everything subsequent to will is susceptible of analysis, but will being first cause cannot be analyzed and must be approached practically and not intellectually. At the same time, all the practical schools of development claim that will can be practically realized. So we start with the assumption that will will never be analyzable or intellectually comprehensible. "I am" and "I will" are not susceptible of proof. The field of will in its respect of practicable realization must begin in small things and continue to great but the character of will in all fields is the same—the arrangement of quantities in a non-natural order.

The difference between objective art, whose works include natural objects, and pseudo-art, is that objective art is the arrangement of quantities against nature and pseudo-art follows nature. The former is designed against nature, but under its own laws, imposed by will. So the outcome of a work of will would eventually be an order of objects which nature could not produce.

B. R: Then any act of will is objective art?

ORAGE: Yes. Will operates within the law of three (art). Nature operates within law of seven.

The difference between fly and elephant efforts is the difference between quantities of effort spent for consciousness and the qualities of the efforts. Gurdjieff substitutes for the object of willing the achievement of consciousness because it is the object most nearly approximating lack of natural wishful motive.

N. T: This implies an understanding of what consciousness is though, or it might be considered something desirable.

ORAGE: Yes, and this involves another point, which is that every living creature is the embodiment of a will toward consciousness. But its will is the cause of its being and not subsequent to its creation, like its wishes are. Schopenhauer used the image of refraction of white light through a prism which breaks it up into seven colors. He said the will of man is separated through his wishes , so none of his wishes can be equal to his will. So we have to say there can never be a wish for consciousness yet every wish refracts the will to consciousness.

This is why Gurdjieff takes consciousness as the object of will since it cannot be the object of wish. Implicit in the act of self-observation is the primary manifestation of will. The creature being simply a collection of refractions cannot wish for consciousness or for self-observation.

B. R: Well, how come that?

ORAGE: You missed the point that the being itself is a concretization of the will to consciousness.

H: But he doesn't know it.

ORAGE: Yes, he does, because all his experiences are refractions of this concretization.

R. A: Is all desire to know about the universe, wish?

L. M: Don't wishes lead up to the act of self-observation?

ORAGE: Yes, they lead up to the act, but the act of self-observation is one of will. If the object of self-observation is analyzable into a gratification of it wish, then the object is not just for consciousness. The motive of any act is indifferent to the character of the act itself.

L. M: But if there is a wish in the motive, then the act is not one of will, the wish being for by-products.

ORAGE: That is true.

J. O: Isn't the act one of will, though, whatever leads up to it?

J. R: If the element of wish is present it isn't pure self-observation.

ORAGE: That is what we have always maintained.

S. R: I think there is a qualitative difference between self-awareness and self-observation with non-identification.

ORAGE: Yes, I am often taken to task for glossing over in the early days of the exposition the absolute necessity of non-identification with the organism observed.

G. B: But mightn't we wish to escape and emotional identification without impairing self-observation?

L. M: No, you can't have a wish outside your wishes.

ORAGE: Then you wish paradoxically to have no wishes.

M. R: But couldn't the refracted wishes have a sense of their unitary source?

ORAGE: Yes, we have a sense of the unitary source but we have no experience of this source until it acts. Through a transfer of the center of gravity away from the refracted wishes to the unitary source, will acts. If I can identify with "I," I don't need non-identification with Orage. There is always the possibility of identification in a single moment with "I" instead off laborious non-identification with personality. This shift in center of gravity is the two streams of which Gurdjieff speaks.

S. R: That would make awareness a do and consciousness a fa.

ORAGE: And non-identification re and simultaneity mi.

Well, let us go back to the statement that self-observation is the first step toward the development of will. But this step is not yet doing, which presupposes a period of self-observation with non-identification.

Sorry, the discussion seems to end so far exactly where it began. Every so often we have to grind out of ourselves the realization that we cannot discuss intellectually what is beyond our understanding. So we fall back on the practical steps for the development of will. How can we set out to define these steps without words? It is no longer theoretical discussion if we define the steps for the development of will in a given individual. So next week I shall try to set out to point out the practical means for the individual to develop will through his own experience. We will pass, in fact, from verbal to formal logic, to the discussion of will in terms of experience and how to bring about the experiences of the development of will.

25 APRIL

GROUP FOR QUESTIONS

H: It was said originally that the reason for starting self-observation didn't matter, and last week that was qualified somewhat. What would you call a good reason?

ORAGE: Pure curiosity. You remember Belcultassi began observing an oddity the contrast between what he wished to be and what he was. His original observation was determined by scientific curiosity. I hear people complain of depression following observation of something in themselves, but this indicates an emotional attitude and not pure observation—not the objectivity with which we would observe another's five forms of behavior. Only to the extent to which observation is objective is the aim achieved of establishing two beings—the trogoaftoegocratic planetary body and the psyche.

Verbal mentation is psyche in the planetary body; psyche itself uses images—formal mentation. When non-identification is complete, psyche is in the state of objective reason. So I would say that the motive of self-observation does in fact color self-observation in that the purest motive would be pure curiosity, or as Gurdjieff says "Impartiality." And this means "no participating in," or "non-identified."

It will be interesting to try to observe from what center of gravity these questions arise. What would you say was the center of gravity of this one? I should say that this is not indicative of a theoretical interest but of a mind driving at practice—a good question and a good sign.

C. Z: I have heard the phrase "listening to the book in all three centers" and I am not clear on how it can be done.

ORAGE: It isn't a matter of how it can be done but of understanding what it means and then wishing to hear the book that way. Remember how you listened to stories heard, when you were a child—so that you participated, your hair stood on end and your eyes shone, or you wept. That is reading with, all three centers and Gurdjieff would hope the book reading could be of that order. Of course, the difference between a child's appreciation and that necessary for this book is that it requires a developed psyche really to sympathize with the characters of this book. Which character do you find most sympathetic? It might be interesting to see one's self go through the stages of sympathy with one after another until we sympathize only with Beelzebub. Gurdjieff said Hamolinadir had no being and that Ashiata was a compassionate idiot. Reading the book with three centers is to be so absorbed and identified with the sequence of events that it is as if we were following a play.

G. K: What does the phrase "organic shame," which Gurdjieff refers to as such a virtue, really mean?

ORAGE: It is shame proper to any given organism. Shame begins when the organism begins to feel abnormality as regrettable. This abnormality is felt by the entity that constitutes the organism as improper to it.

Gurdjieff uses this in the book with special reference to women; has it any special significance in this connection?

I have heard him refer equally to its loss in men. In fact, in the last chapter he was writing while here he had passages in which he acquitted women in America of the state into which they have fallen, for it started in men, this decline, and woman only make manifest the degree to which organic shame is lost in men.

C. S: Aren't the terms men and women translatable into active and passive?

ORAGE: Yes. In this case it is only a question of where the initial impetus toward impropriety occurs.

(Orage asked if anyone knew the original Hebrew word, for "God" and its Origin. One person gave an answer correctly.)

Jehovah is made up of "Yod" and "Evoa"—Adam and Eve. The Jewish religion is regarded by objective esotericism as degraded because it dropped the responsibility for evil from Yod (God) and put it on Eve. Those "men" who shift this responsibility, slipping into their own passive part, are "men of Yod."

So organic shame is not of an organ, but of the organism which regards abnormality with fear. Only a normal organism feels it.

L. B. Asked about appealing directly to conscience, as Ashiata did, to stimulate self-observation.

ORAGE: It cannot be appealed to directly. Ashiata labored to bring conscience from the subconscious into the conscious by indirect appeal. Curiosity is the pure motive for self-observation because it doesn't color it. Like David, a prophet sets off looking for Athens, and we find a kingdom. The method provides a means of discovering one's abnormality the discovery of which inspires the observer to wish the change, which is organic shame.

H: There must be a difference between identification with the characters of the book and the characters of a play.

ORAGE: There is a difference of the Holy Aeioua—the aspiration at lower vibrations to share the experiences of higher vibrations. In the theater we identify with characters with experiences like our own, or sociologically superior to ours. In Greek drama the characters played roles of superior beings—not superior social items. To wish to be like a superior being—like the characters in the book—is the law of Holy Aeioua. Hero worship is all right if the hero is objectively superior.

C. S: Why is this Aeioua so called?

ORAGE: Have you any Idea?

C. S: It contains all the vowels.

ORAGE: Gurdjieff once described it as the sigh of objective remorse, the sound of mi aspiring to sol, with fa not clearly heard.

E. W: What can we do to revive the wish to observe?

ORAGE: This is a very serious and opportune question. Many of you must have experienced a calling toward self-observation in the last 12 months and it is difficult to recover the "first fine careless rapture." For this point in the desert there was devised the psychological trick of the mantram, "I wish to remember myself." It is assumed that if you use this device you don't wish to remember yourself but you wish to wish to remember yourself. So you associate vivid experiences with the words and it becomes a mantram.

L. C: What do you mean by doing?

ORAGE: "I did it on my own initiative"—the policy of doing purposively rather than impulsively. The conscious pursuit of whims is an act of will.

G. K: Isn't there a type of person who acts on his own initiative because of vanity?

ORAGE: Yes, but this is mechanical, as is every motive which is not an obligation to myself to act as a purposive exercise. I am preparing, though I cannot produce them at the moment, a series of phrases which give the essence of doing from the Gurdjieff point of view.

G. K: I find myself often with such a conflict of initiatives that I do nothing.

ORAGE: This has to do with your aim. The course must be determined by your objective.

G. K: When there is a conflict of initiatives I find they don't conflict in point of purpose but that the reasonableness in the procedure is hard to decide. It is really a lack of judgment.

ORAGE: Yes, in such a case I resolve myself into a committee and I debate the proposals. If you will give this committee consideration of your problem you can discover a course which any person in your position would be wise to follow.

N. T: It seems to be hard to discriminate what must be done on my own initiative and what I must do.

ORAGE: If you can say: "As a living being and before God, I did this on my own initiative," and years later you discover it wasn't on your own initiative it isn't any proof that it wasn't. Provided your Report of your state is absolutely veridical, then it *is* your state at the time.

(An example of will was the man who having dug all day went and dug three more hours "Just to see if he could." If he had never been discovered and praised for it, it would, Gurdjieff said, have been a real act of will.)

Gurdjieff calls the set of willful exertion "pressing against the cellar," it develops the muscle of will.

D. F: Is that conscious labor?

ORAGE: Yes.

L. C: If you have failed at "elephant efforts," and have to go back to making "flies" is anything lost?

ORAGE: No harm is done, only a little time is lost and discouragement incurred.

J. R: Sometimes, though, it may be necessary to try these elephant efforts to discover this inability.

ORAGE: Yes. I think it is.

G. B: Isn't there some trick or temporary incentive for doing ordinary things when the old incentive is lost?

ORAGE: Pride. When the old incentives are lost, real will is required. When the motives of the slave are lost, the motives of the master must take their place or inevitably you will fall back into slavery. Remember the young kinsman. Real being-pride is gratification in doing something purely for your own being without anyone's praise or suggestion. When we are not-slaves and not-masters we are literally nothing. If we had enough superiors to treat us as such we might develop a sense of being-pride. If we could hear what certain people say about us behind our back, we might learn something.

L. C: It seems to me that is merely sociological shame.

ORAGE: Is an incentive to real shame. Suppose you were the only person in the world, without thought of reward, or praise or hope or fear, do you think you could then do?

L.C: I don't know, but that appeals to me more than the other idea.

ORAGE: Well, if I know which idea would appeal to everyone, this question of doing would be much simpler than it is.

A. B: In the first descent, when the young kinsman failed, the failure of slave motives, wasn't there then a deliberate substitution of other kinsmen—other motives—to save the first?

ORAGE: Yes. This is a question of pride of the tribe. But this question is rather outside the pale since I thought we were to confine ourselves to questions of doing.

B. G: What can we do about making strides toward impartiality toward others? Suppose there are still people who contract our being.

ORAGE: I thought we had always considered one of the most difficult phases of self-development that of producing the opposite reaction to the one inspired by someone else.

S. G: I know, but that also seems just a practical, mechanical thing to do.

ORAGE: I have yet to see the method exhausted in regard to changing negative emotions.

B. G: How can we be impartial toward those we care for?

ORAGE: Essential relations remain in spite of non-identification and consequent impartiality. Essence relation does not presuppose a blood tie, though. Some mothers I have known have no essential relationship to their children. The condition of impartiality is unaffectability. The expression of a negative emotion is tantamount to letting blood.

N. T: The technique is simply to change the manifestation and not the emotion?

ORAGE: Yes, as Watson would tell you, the emotion *is* the manifestation.

13 MAY

LAST MEETING

ORAGE: I hope you are all gratified by the number present tonight. We are still far from that order of being that can do without meetings or a director. There is a difference between a group and a circle; the letter meets for themselves individually, to help each other and to help a common cause—"to make the world safe for consciousness." Very few of us have a sense of these three responsibilities even after six years. Some have a sense of one. The first sense of individual responsibility is that unless I spend my day advantageously from the point of consciousness and development, I am lapsing, or disloyal. This is consciousness of the first side of the triangle.

The second responsibility is towards our neighbors, the members of our tribe also striving for consciousness. When you can say that no wave of circumstance is so high that you are submerged and lose sight of the method, you have developed consciousness of the second center. This is the first crystallization of individuality. And still I hear people complain in a crisis that it is "trifling" to talk of the method at such a time!

The third form of consciousness requisite for membership in a circle has to do with the work, in which respect I think we are weakest. Jesus personality, as I have sometimes said, was not different from ours. He was not an occultist—not a Californian. He spoke of Living Jerusalem as the City of God—the circle of workers. His passion for Jerusalem was divinely paternal or parental. Theosophical literature speaks of the masters as the "elder brothers of the race"—an ideal of a being who could not act but as an elder brother. You have heard of the patriarch and matriarch; dissociate them from social associations and consider that quality which in a group distinguishes some as elders. It is something noticeable even in children, though they usually become corrupt. But when it is really present it indicates a state of being and a third center of gravity.

When a being has all three of these kinds of consciousness, he can be either a circumference or a center in a circle. Such members of a circle have a communion which is not perceptible but which is not occult either. It has risen from their common understanding, their ability to be in each other's places. It becomes unnecessary for them to meet. You will realize how far it is necessary for us to go before we reach this state.

I will be back in January for four months, but the same kind of work cannot be repeated on my return. So the terms of attendance at the group from January to April will be utterly different from those that have prevailed so far. I shall have to be independent of the group financially—no one will have to pay anything again to attend a group of mine. I shall have to see certain signs of development, of work done in those who will attend the group. I shall know these signs even if you don't, and I shall know them however you phrase them. There is an experience which comes when you know that you are losing your body and your life. Beelzebub, in the chapter on Gornahoor Harharkh's machine, thought he was going to be lost. Though the experience lasts for only a few seconds, no experience thereafter will be more than a trifle. You will have known the fact of death. This is the kind of evidence I shall require for membership in a group.

No vow of secrecy will be required because you will not conceivably be able to repeat what you hear at the group. I have a conviction that none of us can have a problem that does not impede the development of a group into a circle, and as such can be discussed objectively. But except in the absence of "other self trust" one could not give away the fact of such discussions. But can we ever trust the majority of us not to misunderstand, or not to betray confidences? A group must be selected which can be trusted to discuss problems as if we were dead and holing a post-mortem. Also it is necessary that this group should make a greater impression on the community. In six years the impression we have made is almost entirely bad, associated with cult-like beliefs. We are more like Californians than like Akhaldans. It is impossible for me to establish relations with any public institution without finding at least one enemy, and nothing I can ever do in public now will be a success. So far as I know, I have never discussed the ideas in wrong associations. This matter of associations is much more important than what you say.

The kind of works that must be undertaken by a working group here is the establishment of a school like the Pythagorean, only not under a roof; an organization without organization. Take some subject in which you are relatively expert and start a group,—if you are developing there will percolate into the group something of this magnetic influence. Not everybody can undertake such groups, but teaching must be done—teaching of the ideas—and it must be done in connection with the technique in which individuals are skilled. If such groups were formed, they could be independent, like planets, in relation to a sun which is the source of inspiration. I suggest that this work become obligatory in the New Year, with the threat that unless in eight months you are a candidate for such work you will either be compelled to attend a beginner's group or no group at all.

I aim to be absolutely independent of the group for my own needs, and the needs of the Institute, and in this position I shall be able to speak candidly and to expect candid replies in these beginning circle meetings. Seriousness and determination will of course be the first requisites for candidacy. I am too tender hearted to force the pace as Gurdjieff and Ouspensky can so ruthlessly do. But unless you are serious—you can hold me back. Sometimes I could murder you all for making it impossible for me, for instance, to get the inner meaning of Gurdjieff's book. If you had been more serious I should have *had* to extract more meaning from it to meet your seriousness.

I want to remind you once more of certain principles which you understand—to your peril, as St. Paul said to those who were hearers and not doers—for if they had not heard their not doing would have been without sin. Having heard you incur the responsibility of doing.

The end and aim of the method is to attain to the state of being in which your planetary body and all its possibilities become yours to exploit. The psyche comes into possession of a planetary body and by the law of reciprocal feeding; planetary food is eaten and transformed until it participates in higher states of being. Our feeding on nature is simply a transformation into higher substances. And when I feed upon Orage through self-observation, participation and experimentation, Orage does not suffer but comes up a step. I, as God, divinize my planetary body by feeding upon it. Self creation by reciprocal feeding between psyche and planetary body by a God is the end of the method. This attainment of the ability to exploit the planetary body is a common as well as an individual responsibility of all three center beings. There is cosmic development corresponding to that of the individual three-center microcosm.

Here enter the idea of objective morality which can, in my opinion, be set against any ethical code in existence, and from which no one can subtract anything or add anything. Those laws make necessary many acts the omission of which society or convention would never condemn. No one's example can ever be followed. Jesus, in the Uncannonical Gospels — said: "Follow yourselves and ye shall find me; follow me and ye shall lose me and yourselves."

Buddha sent a certain questioner to a butcher for his answer, saying one with objective reason can be anything he pleases.

A principle must be grasped which is contained in the five laws of objective morality and until it is grasped one cannot be said to be free from the effects of Kundabuffer; which is nothing more than the instrument of hypnotism and suggestibility.

The five points of objective morality are like the five fingers of a hand for handling situations. Number one means keeping the three brains of the body serviceable. Number two is constantly to be pondering the meaning and aim of existence—not necessarily with any hope of solution. Man exists to be the mind of God and as mind to ultimately understand the meaning and aim of existence. Preoccupation with this problem makes all other problems relatively easy. Once I defined art in life for an artist as the pursuit of ever unattainable perfection. Perhaps even for His Endlessness there is a secret even He does not understand, in the pursuit of which understanding the works of this method are tossed off like shavings.

Number three is the obligation to make being-effort—the effort of doing.

This is not necessarily a visible activity, or concrete work, but it is effort. Obligation of this kind is to keep one's self exercising—effort-making. Perhaps before January I can make for you a scale of exercises of will, from the scale of the mouse to the elephant. These would not be exercises of mind but of developing will, which is the ability to carry out whims. I have received a suggestion from Gurdjieff which makes this possible.

Number four is to cooperate with others who aim at the same objective reason.

Number five is duty to ease the burden of His Endlessness. Unless you make effort it must be made for you. Now the burden is just upon His Endlessness.

The Individual enters by self-observation into the order of being of responsibility and develops in this order of being according to these five laws of objective morality.

It is not obligatory for anyone to understand all the tenets of this work—cosmic chemistry, tables of foods, and so on—for these are specialists. But the two practical aspects are obligatory for all.

Now having perhaps unfortunately listened to this, you are capable of sin—of the refusal to convert verbal into formal understanding.

Boardman Robinson

PARABLES

The meanings for all the words in this system have their orientation.

For us all the words have a meaning relative to consciousness connected with them.

A parable is a verbal form intended to produce a certain effect.

The parable as used in this system is not to establish an analogy. It is to establish a truth in at least two centers and generally in three. It is not just the same thing as the moving center producing repercussions in the other two centers; the parable strikes the centers simultaneously.

"There is an organic relationship started between the centers by a parable." (Mike Robinson)

The figures in the Book are mythological and their language is parabolical. (Someone asked question about Odyssey. Answer: Odyssey is written in fable not parables.)

The language of these being-created figures cannot be ordinary, the parable is their language. The mythological figure is credited with the consciousness of a three centered being. (Jesus, a mythological figure spoke in parables because he had a three centered development.)

The developed conscious being puts more into his speech than a mechanical being and so more is read into what he has to say. Three meanings, one for each center, (Example: the text of John) it is said, can be read in seven forms by a conscious being. It can be read as an allegory, a parable, 3rd, 4th, 5th and 6th was not given; and the 7th can be transcendentally. It may be read in its simplest form allegorically and so on till it becomes an oracle.

QUESTION: Can parable be unconscious?

ANSWER: Yes, the parable has not only the line of the story but the state of the psyche of the writer. It is not a work of art unless done consciously.

Gurdjieff's Beelzebub is a mythological character with parabolic utterances.

In the story of the history of the races in the Book Gurdjieff does not always purport to put down facts. What he has in mind is three centers in talking of races. He says: "I don't claim it is right but you can't prove it is wrong. Why was the king's name in ancient Atlantis, Appolis? We can't prove that it wasn't.

Jesus took very familiar experiences as illustrations. In the gospels these became more complex. A miracle is not to be taken as fact, but as plausible. Five loaves and two fishes might have meant five diagrams and two statements. The truth was put into simple stories and words because a story is more likely to be handed down and its meaning may be kept intact, while less simple words would be documents which would lose more quickly their meaning and probably be tucked away in archives.

Meanings in the old fairy tales: Hop-o-my-thumb was the seventh son, the most despised, the smallest, but saved all the other six.

Little Boy Blue, full of meaning was told to propagate safely the truth it carries—the truth was the running down hill of the three centers. Much the same meaning as the story of the sleeping passenger, in the story of horse, coach, driver and sleeping passenger.

The magnetic center of young children begins to be filled by fairy tales. The new fairy tales do not do that. Perhaps "Alice in Wonderland" is the one exception. There are no good modern fairy tales as no one has the development to write one with meaning. Also the reading of a story with inner significance has no meaning without understanding in the reader. Reading a parable is an act of understanding.

The passages in the Book about Bolshevism, taken literally, are crude but they are to be taken as analogies of revolting centers. The meaning of these passages and indeed the entire Book is not to be arrived at by the mind but by a species of new understanding. A mind which ponders is capable of understanding more meaning. Kingdom of heaven, bread, upper room, etc., all had a technical meaning at the time of their use. Some current words of science used in the Book such as anode and cathode may be no more understandable in a few hundred years than the words like Elixir of Life or Philosopher's Stone, used by the alchemists of the past, are understandable by chemists today.

It is not safe to take literally the meaning of the book. The words are used only as platforms for the content that is to be understood.

Question: How does one go about getting the key to a parable?

Answer: The supposition is that something must be known of a method back of it. The key to the Bible was entirely lost or swallowed up by the church.

The Bible:
The Old Testament—(do, re, mi)
The two triads of the octave.
The New Testament—(sol, la, si)
The interval between (fa) was the history of Jesus and the history of his becoming Christ. Christ was born between the two triads, the interval.

The interval is the incarnation of the universe. See the universe in a grain of sand. The dewdrop does not slip into the sea, but the sea into the dewdrop.

Christ was a conscious creature.

In the Old Testament—the development of man, do, re, mi, parabolic history of man with three lower centers.

In the New Testament—the development of man, sol, la, si, parabolic history of man when he begins self-consciously to change in his psyche, or it might be when his psyche begins to develop.

St. Paul takes certain stories from the Old Testament and translates them into the New Testament: he calls these stories allegories.

"Promise" used in the Bible has the same meaning as "potentialities" in the Book.

"Beings with promise" meant beings on the road to the development of the higher centers. Very seldom in the Old Testament is a being spoken of as a "being of promise." It was with Abram that the process began. Abram changed to Abraham. "Ham" was the masculine for the Egyptian god Ra. Isaac, the female god of the Babylonians.

The exodus of the Jews, the crossing of the red sea, are not substantiated in history. There may never have been such occurrences but certain facts might be true and the stories were used parabolically.

Just as the Bible must be regarded as parabolical so must Gurdjieff's be taken as a kind of Bible.

The disciples astonished those about them by the things they did. He who will practice this method will himself bringing out of his treasury things both old and new.

QUESTION: Why is the method given in parable and not in fact?

One reason can be found in the parable of the sower. We may give a story that may be remembered and carried down even though the hearer did not understand. Its form would be carried ready for understanding in the future. (Allan Brown.)

If written down as fact it would lead to verbalization and intellectualizing and would not lead to formulation and understanding. (B. B. G.)

ORAGE: "I bury the bone for the dog to smell and dig it out." Until you have dug out the meaning you have not acquired the ability for understanding. By use of the method your senses become more keen.

Gurdjieff is afraid he has given too many keys to the Book. He has put a key for *every* lock but he has not placed the key by the lock.

The organic reason for using stories as parables is that there is no language for the emotional center nor the instinctive center.

The Book makes neither sense nor nonsense but something neutralizing.

Allan Brown: A third reason for using parables is found in the fact that a substantiated truth is three dimensional, it can't be expressed literally in explicate language, its presence can only be indicated by a figure.

ORAGE: Your mind must drive the horse but not be concerned with the horse; the horse must pull the cart but not be interested in the cart.

We should be able to read through the images in parables to get the content, but we are like children, if the rhyme jingles they do not look for meaning.

We are just as incapable of writing a parable as we are of writing a fairy tale.

Allegories are parables and speak to the mind. Illustration—Swift's Tale of a Tub.

Tolstoy's stories are accepted as having spiritual value, they have only psychological.

Fables are distortions of facts.

Parables are disintegrating to the ordinary paths of association as they speak to three centers.

A parable has as its content a cosmic truth.

The old definition: "An earthly story with a heavenly meaning." It would be truer to say: "A heavenly story with no earthly meaning." (This brought a laugh.)

Photo from the archives of Gj Blom, Amsterdam

Orage, by Ansel Adams.

GOOD AND EVIL

There is static and dynamic good.

Dynamically that being is good which is the process of becoming. A cross section of a being taken at any time would represent its actualized (Being?) value.

Try to understand in these discussions simultaneity of understanding—hold in mind all recollections and the whole, the complete pattern.

Two forms of effort have to be made. Not during childhood are we given a glimpse of what self-consciousness is—a glimpse of how to serve God. There is no school to which to go, no way of learning. It is because of the absence of these schools that beings on this planet differ from those on other planets. The Book says, "His grandmother did not tell him." This is at once depressing and . . .

QUESTION: Why are there no teachers?"

ANSWER: "To bring about peace on earth would be child's play compared with the undertaking of educating the human race to self-consciousness. A messenger from God would fail. Jesus failed.

There is first the difficulty of talking to a person who is constantly changing his center of gravity. In one center he is animal, in another he is childish, in another he is barbaric. The Kingdom of Heaven is unattainable until you have Objective Reason.

The emotional center is a little child. To be a little child is not to be of the Kingdom of Heaven but of the nursery. Art is like nature, it is not nature. To become like a little child is not to become a little child.

Not to use the power to be of value is the only evil.

These scrap machines are a criteria of Good and Evil. Absolute Good is associated with a plus neutralizing force. Objective reason is related to things as they are. This struggle between the plus neutralizing force and the minus neutralizing force is the drama of Good and Evil.

(The Book is called "Beelzebub's Tales to His Grandson or An Objective Critique of Man").

"Plus neutralizing is objective conscience." (Said by Benson)

I am awakened by a sense of obligation to do something for a friend—for the world, this is an urge of conscience but I have not the consciousness to accomplish the task, I am not equipped. Consciousness of obligation is an incentive toward consciousness.

Whatever the motive is when you start self-observation you will eventually, if you stick to it long enough, strike on this idea—it is like stripping a nerve—and all other motives will cease.

Faith is belief in things as yet unseen—Gurdjieff calls this "smell."

In self-observation the smell discloses the hidden treasure.

Study of the norm presupposes the study of self and study of self presupposes an interest or state in which this is possible.

Question is asked about the analogy of the car. A car is built to be driven. If we were the cars, we would not go without a driver. Answer—Car driven is implicit in the car.

HUGH FERRISS: Will self-observation without non-identification continued for a sufficiently long time bring about non-identification?

ANSWER: Yes. The rubber toy pig to be blown up illustrates the flatulent cells which God blew up in a variety of ways and sizes. (The epitome of "The Preface to Morals" is the statement about disinterestedness in critics and criticisms of virtue.)

Absolute Good as found on the Sun Absolute is not only a static form of good, these is also the dynamic form. Static good, when it ceases to be also dynamic falls into minus neutralizing.

The sin against the Holy Ghost is the destruction of potentialities.

"To be continuously aware, to observe accurately, to report accurately, constitutes the neutralizing force of impartiality." Sally Robinson.

A state of non-being has been actualized and remains as a bit of flotsam and jetsam in the stream but is no longer a part of the stream. Non-beings are in the scrap heap of the universe. Whether willfully or ignorantly, they are in the same eternal state. See Eddington on time's arrow. An atom in the center of stars goes on beating, pulsing, but registers no time. Their potentialities consists of being unable to change, to cease to be is their eternal actualization.

Denial of the power to make value is the *only* (or greatest) *evil*.

We are answerable, responsible, for the producing of those values for which the organism was created.

Sense of sin is the sense of responsibility that knowing the way you can no longer be innocent until you have attained impartiality.

Remorse of conscience is the knowledge that one is not making the effort.

Until we can understand according to essence, we cannot determine on Good and Evil—we can only know the right way and the wrong way.

TUESDAY, 12 NOVEMBER 1929

GOOD AND EVIL (MRS. GRANT)

Mr. Brown recalled the statement that there could be no criteria for Good and Evil until one lived according to essence, there could only be criteria for right and wrong.

Right and wrong are relative to fragmatic or pragmatic truth. Pragmatism professes to judge right and wrong by results, but results are provisional in time. Results are endless in point of time.

Discrimination is an intellectual exercise and is without moral value.

Objective reason is a collective term involving all three centers. Objective reason is a triangle.

Objective conscience is the Voice of God in essence—essence being a part of a cell in the universe and therefore is a part of absolute good. We define absolute as the whole taken as one. The eight planets of our system taken as one is an absolute, the total of suns is the sun absolute and the universe is the absolute.

The emotional center free from the other two centers, would give us the voice of pure essence. All essential questions arise in the emotional center.

Whichever we are gratifying our likes or our dislikes, we can be conscious of Good and Evil. (This must mean our essence likes and dislikes). All inanimate and animate beings are in a state of essence, good. Animals act according to essence and are without sin, they have no choice. The obligations of human beings are the same as animals but their obligations are not mechanical only, it is also an obligation to be conscious. The conscious obligation of a human being is to fill his place in God's plan consciously. We perform our function in two ways, mechanically and consciously. This double obligation in man brings about the spilt in man.

It should be easy to distinguish between a sociological guilt and an essence sin.

Essence has to come to understand itself. It is identical with universal life. Essence develops in respect to its understanding. Essence is untouched by sin. Essence developed is the result of identifying "I" and "It."

"I" without body persists in time but not in space. "I" still has its limits, everything which occurs to it occurs within itself. The world it then inhabits is the absolute for it. "I," consciousness, is self contained. Nothing can happen to it beyond its imaginings. A being in this state depends on its own construct of the world, and for this it is dependent on its past experiences. It would spin from its past subjectivity. Time effects it. It can shrink or grow (expand) new arrangements of images but its limitations are bounded by its recollected images.

Memory is not related only to intellect, it is more inclusive, it includes past feelings and actions.

Every absolute while still remaining an absolute may still develop within itself. Without spacial existence each absolute is unique unto itself. The relation of parts is inherent in the conception of the whole.

There may be said to be periods of imagination between periods of manifestation. A period or series of imaginations is not experience but depends on past experiences. We only have experiences when manifesting.

The chapter on Purgatory is of a creature whose imagination began to show fatigue.

"It suggests we are all cells of a ghost." (Larry Morris)

385

Certainly, we have suggested we are all dead. The force with which God imagined began to decline. We are all arrangements of God's imaginings. Being in a state of imaginings and beginning to decline God began to arrange a cosmos out of his images. This was his cosmic pattern—an arbitrary cosmos out of his images.

In this chapter Gurdjieff is trying to vivify us. The cosmic pattern superimposed presupposes that it, the pattern, has value.

"We are the hours before dawn." (Miss Johnson)

As the pattern becomes conscious to those participating in it, to that extent does the universe wake up to the object of the designer. Implicit in the design is it that the world shall become His Body in which three-brained beings shall exist in His Awakening. Body is the sum of any organization or order if experienced facts. (?) We speak of a body of knowledge. (Read Whitehead) The facts undergo no change.

This universe may be considered a work of *objective art*—created to defy time.

The second step in this—Every wish we individually experience can be regarded as a psychological entity since it continues to operate in the body. It continues to play its same role in our psychological being as a creature plays its role. The contents of our minds are also beings. So if the contents of our minds could be thrown on a screen, every group of images individualized, intellectual powers etc., we could then see in three dimensions. God has this power of concretizing His psyche (on a screen). We can be truly said to be one of the ideas occurring in God's mind. He, God, is not a participant in all this but it occurs within Him.

Absolute Good is the pattern imposed by God for His purposes. God's wrong is failure on His part to realize the developing pattern.

"I alone make Good." "I alone do Evil."

Man does wrong when he fails to maintain a catalytic state. Evil arises from the weakness projected in the forms of beings.

We have the opportunity to retrieve God's mistakes. Human responsibility occurs here, "to save Jove (God) from his nods." (Miss Johnson.)

A state of continued being was preferable to a state of non-being.

God is not guilty of evil but does evil according to His judgment—this being preferable to non-being.

Ghost cells should wake up and determine the criterion of right and wrong based on the pattern. This is what St. Paul called co-workers with God. Triple workers with God are the sons of God.

Our failure is in our not realizing his pattern. Our good is our consciousness of His pattern. God's failure is making it possible for us to manifest through experiences.

Gurdjieff arbitrarily calls being and more being good, less being and non-being evil.

God's fear of Heropass was not the cause of His choice to manifest. Emotional center had placed a higher value on being than on non-being. God's wish to manifest was not brought about by a shock.

Will exclude wish. One can act against one's wish.

We have an unspeakable amount of work to do because of God's nods.

The Atlanteans had an idea of retrieving God's mistakes. When beings can derive no more good from mistakes they past into non-beings.

The third step is—Three-centered beings contain the possibility of understanding the meaning and aim of existence.

Illustration—A private in the army is not excluded from participation with his commanding officer, nor would he mind his own rank whatever it might be. Gurdjieff's idea is that you should be independent of your status participating in any rank, in any sphere and in any function.

TUESDAY, 19 NOVEMBER 1929

GOOD AND EVIL CONTINUED

God had free desire to escape a disagreeable situation. He had two alternatives, to escape or not to escape. He did not choose the disagreeable situation. He could choose to pass into distinction or choose to will to overcome the situation.

The situation was the passing into non-being, a state of dissolution.

Gurdjieff says the universe is non-mechanical (in the sense of) being a free creation maintained by Will.

Larry Morris held that God was under compulsion. Orage held there was the alternative of doing something or doing nothing—to let time take its course. Larry held that he understood God was forced by the stimulus of fear—fear provoked Him.

ORAGE: An alarm clock going off provokes us to get up though we may continue to sleep. Choice implies that you do one thing or another and not that you do nothing. An alarm clock provoking a free agent is different from provoking a machine.

God could decide to do something about it because to do nothing was not a decision because time was already running down. God could decide among a number of plans but he could not decide to do nothing. Time would take its time. He had open to Him to decide on a positive act to oppose time, not a decision to let time take its course. This it was already doing.

God did not have a choice to be or not to be, he had a choice of how to be.

He concretized His dreams as a source for renewing His imaginings. Illustration—I am having pleasant dreams interrupted by night-mare. I review my state and discover my state (to dream pleasant dreams) is waning and the element of night-mare is increasing. I pull myself together and collect my pleasant dreams and out of them make a pattern and give them substantiality and I can then rest secure, assured that my pleasant dreams will continue.

QUESTION: (Reese Alsop) Where was the energy to renew if there was not energy to continue?

ANSWER: Time would effect the passive aspect of dreams, will, active, would overcome the passivity, the running down of time. There was no will in the passive imagining. The forming of the pattern was the concretizing of the dreams.

Contemplating is not objectivity.

Will was potentially with God. God's imaginings were subjective. When He manifested them they became objective.

QUESTION: Why were not these images able to pick themselves up again mechanically? (Nat T.)

ANSWER: Because He chose, willed, to actualize one selection of arrangements of His dreams.

We say "making his dream come true" meaning what was originally a dream, *will* made come true.

Our universe, the concretizing of one arrangement of the dreams, may be likened to a cathedral. The cathedral in question is constructed entirely of beings.

God was in a psychological state previous to His manifestation. "In His youth God took no thought of the morrow, later He took thought for the morrow." (I. Solon)

Until the emergency arose the will was not in God's consciousness. A conscious individual needs will to concretize. The whole system implies that will is not actualized but is potentially in us and should be actualized

QUESTION: (Reese Alsop) "Would you put fear at the bottom of this manifestation?"

ANSWER: "Fear of the terror, of the situation"—fear of the loss of what you hold dear, might be the occasion for an act. Fear actuating an act is not the same as causing it.

There are two elements in the universe, one to keep it stable and one to keep it developing. The second law of thermo-dynamics may be only one law of physics and not the determining law as physicists now hold. Beyond curved space there may be a curved sphere of beings. (Conscious beings?) Each being may identify with the whole sphere without prejudicing the identify of the sphere for all the other atoms. Each component atom has the possibility of occupying the whole sphere.

Gurdjieff uses this imaginary conception: Imagine a spherical ball composed of living beings from the lowest form up to ourselves—these may constitute the world of being. This sphere also has a queen bee—this is God, and He has the idea that until every being has actualized all its being the sphere shall remain.

388

When a being ceases to be, he is cast out of this sphere like the bee is cast out of the swarm, into a state of non-being. Non-being does not mean ceasing to be. One state of non-being is negative, those drifting out by inactivity, and there is another state, an active state of non-being.

I. Solon recalls his illustration of the swirl of sand storm on the desert etc.

JOHN RIORDAN: "In this sense we understand the difference between time and Heropass; God converts the passing of time when each moment of time extends over all space."

The pattern implies that all cells are good. Those that drop out are wrong and drop into a state of absolute evil.

Discussion followed on God being capable of evil as was said last week. What should have been said last week is that God did wrong in His occasional nods, but not evil, for by His nods, He did not destroy the pattern. It was a failure of consciousness not of will.

When any being by refusing to recognize his duty, will, falls out of the dynamic pattern he does wrong.

LARRY: "I would like to have right and wrong cleared up."

Illustration of a campaign for an army, all have been taken into the plan but all may not know the plan. The plan is good, its non-fulfillment is evil.

Good and Evil are already absolute in the plan. The individual does right or wrong according to his co-operation with the plan.

HUGH FERRISS: "If the individual does not know the plan of campaign how can he decide right and wrong?"

Man in the ranks receives many conflicting orders from those higher up. How does he know which to follow? These conflicting orders mean subjective ideas of right and wrong coming from society, social morality, ethics, priests etc. They come from officers higher up but not from the commander-in-chief. This state of confusion does not exempt him from the consequences of his failure to discriminate. There is the voluntary slave and the involuntary slave.

HUGH FERRISS: "There may be a technique by which the man in the ranks may come to know the campaign."

ORAGE: "We shall come to that later."

DALY KING: "Before man has the ability to choose either right or wrong he has first to be in a position to know the campaign."

Don't misunderstand the discussion, his consciousness must be in advance of his will. Knowledge of the campaign does not mean the ability to choose.

Consciousness and will are developing simultaneously. Will in not being equal to understanding is what causes purgatory. We all suffer from knowing the right way to act, but not being able to act sufficiently, (or while acting in a design we are acting wrong). A failure to develop to the extent that consciousness has developed causes the suffering of *remorse*. This discrepancy in the developing center should be adjusted.

389

B. B. G: "Beelzebub told Hassein, when he saw him weeping, that when the vibrations of the emotional center had been raised to so high a vibration he should cease pondering for a time and give the other centers to catch up." To cease activity in the center which has the high tempo, is done by the *fourth* center. It was as if Beelzebub told Hassein to self observe. This is assisting will. Self-observation is the first step, it is also *the last step*. "I keep myself in charge of myself."

"He that watcheth over Israel shall neither slumber or sleep "

(Followed by the summary of the last three evenings.)

MONDAY, 14 APRIL 1930

This is the reason why Plato "The Republic" regretfully expelled the artists. But our remedy is not so drastic. Instead of expelling or censuring the artists, we aim to keep control in our own hands. At present we are in a state of perpetual victimization. How can we control our minds? Many books purport to do this: Dimnet's "Art of Thinking" and Annie Besant's "Mind Control." Really the problem always is: How can I control my memory? Dimnet's book is just as useless as a cook book of cooking receipts on a desert island with no materials at hand. He formulates receipts without method. But in these groups we approach mind control indirectly. This indirectness is not an evasion, but a short cut. On the other hand what appears a short cut through a direct approach is really a spiral, which goes further and further from the point aimed at. The mind is an immaterial receptacle of images. It is empty at birth. Images are then continually deposited at the rate of ten thousand a second. Billions of billions of billions, mixed associated, etc. This is a witch's cauldron. In course of time groups of those adhere, crystallize, forming prejudices, opinions, "points of view". Nobody in truth has a point of view except as crystallized by chance accumulations of images. Nobody has ever "thought" there is just passing crystallization with an occasional stirring up by new impressions, as we would stir our soup with a spoon. Now assuming this is the situation, when we talk about mind control, the question arises, "with what are we going to control it?" We cannot control it with itself. We sometimes say that a man is a thinker because he pursues one line of thought excluding others. But this is merely chance crystallization. The greatest thinker is as passive as anybody else. This can be demonstrated in the biography of any great thinker.

QUESTION: What do we mean by control?

ANSWER: Determining yourself the combination of images to be made. Having ability to exploit the contents of one's own mind. What is called "making a choice" is merely becoming aware of a crystallization that has already taken place. Given the above definition of mind, that is, an immaterial receptacle of images, it is evident it cannot be controlled by itself. By what then must it be controlled? Everybody has the use of our minds except ourselves. It is lucky for us we seldom meet any who are skillful; or we could be made to do apparently of our own volition almost anything. Example—orators, publicity men etc.

HARTLEY ASHED: About Plato's theory of anamnesis; "Is there reminiscence"?

ORAGE SAYS that due to the quality or form of the mind it is not a question of the contents of the mind. Minds differ at birth in form which is capacity but Plato's is as blank at birth as an idiot's. This is different from what we call recollection. What the psychoanalysts call the sub- or pre- or unconscious is the majority of impressions which are ordinarily not subject to recall. Nothing mystical about it, nor reminiscent of other lives etc., etc. but specific images deposited during the life-time of the individual in question.

Hartley asks about the square root of eight, it is incommensurable yet has been demonstrated.

Orage answers analogy of stomach, it is a receptacle of foods but it is not merely passive. It's secretions effect the food. Can analyze the contents but we cannot at present analyze this inter-action, it is incommensurable. Similarly etc.

Going back to the question, with what can we control the mind? It seems impossible. There is something that is not mind, yet is a fact in consciousness. If we cannot find something our case is hopeless. We are condemned to passivity.

What we find, it is true, is not very much; a poor thing yet we hold it in equal value with mind. "I exist," the statement that is implicitly assumed in every aspect of life. Yet this is a statement that cannot be explicate, hence though it is the foundation stone of all psychology it is usually ignored by all psychologists.

Not body itself; one of our fake mental concepts.

Who are you apart from your biological and social history? You cannot answer. Descartes put the cart before the horse. A proof of existence cannot rest on a collateral activity. Another difficulty in answering the question is that all our experiences have been passive. Consequently we have no other experiences of inner activity than the affirmation "I am." Un roi mais un roi fainéant." All other experiences can be shown to be the product of external things. There can be no possibility of "I am" so long as "I" remains functionless. If we cannot find possibility of mind-control in "I" then there is none. For there are only two things of which we can be certain: One—"I exist"; two—"I experience."

I experience is passive. For hope we must then turn to I exist and to the first element in it: "I." But can you conceive of any function not included in the mind? Do you affirm awareness? Awareness of what? Of reactions in the body, we are never directly aware of external stimuli; we deduce external stimuli from changes in reactions. I exist, therefore I experience. We cannot experience without existence. Can we have existence without experience? Specu-

391

lations in Plotinus, Hindu-philosophy etc. All experiences can be accounted for; they are purely passive. I suffer experiences. Going back to *I exist*. Between *I experience* and *I exist* there is a relationship of passive and positive. Can we change passive into positive? Can we change experience into doings?

There is an experience potential to I, which cannot occur to *it*, which *it* cannot suffer. Being aware of the mind. The mind experiences. If I can experience the mind I am doing something the mind passively never can do. If I can of my own effort become and remain continuously aware of my own body I am doing what my mind can never do and which nothing in the universe can automatically make me do (e. g. hearing one's own voice) no conspiracy of circumstances can make me do this, yet it is possible. It is within your own power and nobody else's. Even God cannot hear your own voice; He can hear your voice, but not your own voice. This is uniquely possible to you.

This is the third affirmation of *I*. The first is the affirmation by which beings are beings:

One, I exist

Two, I experience

Three, I experience myself

We define "myself" as a concrete fact, my body. I am aware of movements of my body: posture, gesture, movements, facial expression, tones of voice. Nothing metaphysical here. It is possible but it is difficult. If one can develop ability to do this, he will find that it includes an easier ability to control his mind.

TUESDAY, 23 APRIL

The Old Group continuing a discussion begun the week before when I was not there.

Hugh Ferris

WORLD

If we take ourselves as the center, our first world is the world of human beings, our second this planet etc. The world is the skin of this planet; skin is the terminal of the nerves.

"World" always includes man, planet does not. World is planet plus man.

We come into closer use of purer electricity as we develop higher consciousness. This is the second time in the history of the world that there has been an age of electricity. If the proportion of negative and positive electricity is not kept, the numbers of three centered beings which can exist on this planet become limited and at the same time they become a nervous species of men. America at the present time is taking the lead in this.

There is a psychological use of electricity:

Individuality —positive

Consciousness—negative

Will —neutralizes them

They may be exchanged, and Will becomes positive.

Each manner of behavior, gesture, posture, etc. always has something of each center in it, though it may have more of one center than of another. Each manner of behavior is a result and contains the sum total of the three centered being—affirming, denying and reconciling, has taken place before manifesting.

Three are psychic and one is resultant. The child begins as a conception, it presupposes the reconciling. Processes take psychologically just the same whether the resultant shall appear or not. The reconciling is a precedent condition to manifestation, conception is on the piano of physiology not psychology—resultant child. Man being one third blind we can only see reconciliation as a result.

The minute there is a result, the result is subject to time, (read Edington's last chapters "Formula for Hydrogen").

Deformities from our point of view may not be deformities from nature.

Each center has three sub-centers totaling nine. A large portion of these may be negative, but all nine cannot negative to be born.

When we are dead we will have only thinks not things. That is, we become psychological. When we think psychologically we develop a hunt for the astral body but we never see the astral body.

The story of the split of the planet may be a myth or may not be but it may be of value like the story of the Garden of Eden.

I and externality itself make the world.

Do—is the first world, human beings—Tetarto cosmos.

Re—planet on which we live—Messa cosmos.

Mi—sum of planets.

Fa—solar system, planet and suns.

Sol—La—Si—Do—Man is sense organ of planet and as he is only a three centered, he is relatively stupid. A certain service should be rendered to the planet.

First purpose for nature.

Second purpose for soul.

Individuality is the consciousness of will. Self-remembering.

A thing is only a thing apprehended through the instinctive center. Self-remembering.

Every cell in the body is conditioned by the aura of the sum of sum of the cells.

Ors.—Our sun

There are three centers of our solar system:

1. Any given planet—instinctive
2. Sum of planets—emotional.
3. Sun—intellectual.

Solar energy—when it functions independently of other centers becomes objective reason.

Seven properties of Hasnamuss:

1. Depravity
2. Successful shirking of being effort
3. Disposition to appear what you are not
4. Taking delight in perverseness
5. Misleading others
6. Not appearing what you are
7. Acting non-essentially

A crystallized Hasnamuss cannot see these characteristics. Exhibitionism appearing other than what it is.

UNIVERSE

The universe may be called the neutralizing force. It can be the neutralizing force in our conscience. The body of God. The perpetual motion machine.

God defeats the effort of time to defeat him, by making an effort himself.

The government of the universe is Trogo-auto-ego-cratic, meaning—I eat myself.

There is no waste in the world. We live on something. What stops the process?

There are cells in the brain which last as long as the body-without change.

There are traveling cells in the body which are ambitious to last as long as their world (our body) lasts. If one of these traveling cells attaches itself to this point of the brain it has an access to all that is going on in its world, our body.

It can see nothing outside the body. It would have to say this body feeds on itself. It could not conceive that its world had any psychology. The cell can look in vain for any psychology in us, just so we are unable to know of the psychology of God.

The *universe* is the totality, the sum of all possible and impossible worlds.

It is possible that each brain of man is a cell in the brain of God. It always sees from an individual cellular view and can never have a view of the whole. There is always an individual view of the collective whole, but never a collective view of the collective whole.

Sex cells in the human body correspond to human beings place in nature (or universe).

According to Gurdjieff there is one change to which all matter is subject—*time*.

It is said that an operation in the abdomen does not heal readily if at all, after three operations. A cell may multiply three-hundred times and no more.

God dreaming and having a nightmare waken and begins self-observation.

Deprivation of quantity take place in a regular way. Deprivation of a quality is not only not anything but is something minus. 0 is at the absolute nothing but take away from zero and you have minus one.

Negatives are impossible until a possible comes along and then it does something—it reduces the negative. A minus 3(-3) meeting a plus 3(+3) a plus 3 is wiped out.

It is a thinkable, sensible universe.

We have to allow for properties other than those we are aware of.

I am up against the world and the world is up against me, one condition is as real as the other.

We are comparable to a cell within ourselves searching for a conception of God.

The *universe* is a neutralizing force in our experience.

WEDNESDAY, 1 MAY, 1929

If some of the talk of these meetings is over our heads it shows us the lack of our intellectual muscle.

Gurdjieff says: " Objective reason is the ability to treat ideas as if they were things."

Objective thought is discriminating between ideas with the same clarity as we discriminate between things.

Just as there is an elephant and a flea there are intellectual elephants and intellectual fleas. The same range in ideas as in things, the same scale of values.

A definition presupposes the assembling of data. Utilizing the material we have heard, what Gurdjieff calls data, we will arrive at definitions.

Taking these words and defining them, you will acquire knowledge you cannot be fooled on. Your knowledge may not be exhaustive, but it will be true as far as it goes. You will not have to subtract but add to what you already know.

Group Member:

"Nature is the objective creditor of everything."

"In nature beings are arranged according to their degree of reason."

"Reason is the sum of all the functions of man."

ORAGE: "In this sense Robinson Crusoe was superior to Wordsworth."

Reason is the objective criterion of nature. In the point of objective reason I, Orage, am inferior to a man working at a painting job—a manly function working in balance. He is shut out on one side, I Orage am shut out on another side. From the point of view of nature the painter may be more valuable. If this were not so we could all carry on our work in consciousness completely as a good carpenter carries on his work. Nature is not interested in conscious labor. In this work our danger is of becoming more and more developed in a faculty we already have. This should not be so if we work on three centers simultaneously.

Never shall we cease to be abnormal till we bring reason to an objective point.

An extraordinary man must become ordinary, meaning he must become balanced according to his inherited ratio between his centers.

Ponder these ideas as if they were ordinary things.

Wiseacreing about them begins with the failure of the memory or an incorrect paraphrasing of them. We are in danger of chewing on subjective ideas already in our minds. "Wiseacre as much as you like, as a gymnastic exercise, but do not imagine you are taking food." Orage.

Gurdjieff says: "Body and essence together make one evil." Essence is in a position to listen more to the first and second centers than to the third.

By a collection of data there will be crystallized in the mind only a concept of the normal being. With these conceptions crystallized in the mental center there will be the possibility of the other two centers trying to actualize these. The Book is a help in this.

"Nature is the agency for the transmutation of matters in the universe." (Group Member)

All the phenomena of nature takes place according to the primary and secondary laws. (See Arch Absurd and Arch Preposterous, chapters in Book.)

Nature takes man up through the scale do, re, mi: Man has to complete the scale by his own effort. Nature does no more. This does not mean that nature is anti or against man's further development. Nature fails at the note mi. Guido had an idea of the meaning of words when he named the notes of the scale.

The measuring rod of reason is the rates of vibration of man.

Nature adjusts her needs to circumstances.

The note si cannot sustain itself for long, if it does not pass into the note do, it begins to rot at the top.

Without voluntary suffering there is involuntary compulsion. We must pay in gold or in goods, but pay we must.

Orage

MAN CONSIDERED CHEMICALLY. MAN CONSIDERED PHYSIOLOGICALLY.

Man is a certain span, a certain chord, on this planet. Every species of beings has a certain span of chord. Man considered chemically is differentiated from other lower beings by quantity and arrangement of chemicals. No one can have a thought without the corresponding material. There is no psychological change without a change in chemical constituents.

Man is limited by the span of chemical materials. We therefore consider man chemically first. We consider of what substances he is composed.

"This material universe is constantly exhibiting the transmutation of substances." (Mariska)

We define a being merely as a field in which chemical changes are taking place down and up the scale. The field of battle is limited by the range of chemicals. Within the field of hydrogen 24 all the chemical changes take place which we call man. This is man's octave. If any part of the octave falls in its chemicals then the whole octave changes. It is precisely this failure of the octave man that causes the failure in all other octaves. Man is at the peak of the octave of beings and therefore his responsibility is great.

Chemicals of which man is composed are one of the manifestations of radiation, man's psychology, physiology, sociology are the other three manifestations of radiation. Viewed from each one of these four aspects man is seen to occupy a certain position.

In the scale of chemicals he is hydrogen 24.

In the physiological scale he is the note si.

In the psychological scale he is the note me.

In the sociological scale he is the note do.

Man should complete these octaves and be a complete form, as he is chemical.

Man is a certain combination of the 92 elements; these are all the elements there are.

We say man has the experience of only a fractional part of the chemicals of which he is composed. There are chemicals in man of which he does not know and which he does not use. It is not because any chemicals are absent in hydrogen 24 that man does not have all the experiences, shall we say of superman—he has the chemicals for an astral and mental body. These chemicals are unusual substances which need stimuli from without or within. The use of, or transmuting of, these chemicals is an objective duty. By our not using them we are holding up the cosmic scale of chemicals. "The whole universe waiteth and suffereth for."

Attending church is called attending "divine service," meaning serving

God. Transmutation of chemicals is serving God. There is a reward, but the objective duty remains. There may be many people who may not be said to be virtuous, but they may be tilling their field by transmuting substances. The note, middle si, has 256 vibrations per second; the number of vibrations of that octave is 512. Each octave has double the number of vibrations of the note of its source. We can analyze the musical scale into a mathematical term by the count of vibrations. Matter can likewise be mathematically computed, matter being reducible to vibrations. (See scale Hydrogen's on last page.) In this system names are given to beings higher than ourselves. Planetary gods being hydrogen 12, solar gods hydrogen 6. We sometimes speak of these as angels and archangels.

We are limited by our visual construction which gives us only a momentary and partial vision, and therefore we see only a planetary body. The rate of vibration of hydrogen 24 is lower than the rate of hydrogen 12. The rate of vibration decreases as hydrogen increases. Everything between hydrogen 48 and 24 is man, and everything between Hydrogen 24 and 12 is planetary God.

It is by grace that a dog is taken into relationship with man but by "works" that he holds that relationship. Without "works" man shoots the dog. Our deaths are never accidental though to us they sometimes appear to be.

Hydrogen has peculiar significance in the chemistry of the system. The first atom was composed of positive, negative and neutralizing. Carbon, oxygen and hydrogen equals hydrogen. Hydrogen is the name given to the compound of the threefold forces; it is the neutralizing and therefore characterizing.

In this system one proton and one electron is oxygen and carbon. The catalytic element which holds them together is hydrogen.

Carbon is related to time, oxygen is related to space, hydrogen is related to consciousness.

No birth takes place without an antecedent death; we are not talking of the transition from one octave to another. In general, man goes downwards but consciously upwards on the ladder. Harmony between transubstantiation means upwards and downwards in a state of equilibrium. By upgrading we degrade something else.

By absence of consciousness we run down in time. By conscious effort against the downward grade in time we overcome time.

We integrate the pattern of the chemical condition of our parents at the time of our conception. The catalyst is different but not the substance.

Creation is in the process of actualizing the potential.

MAN CONSIDERED PHYSIOLOGICALLY

The physiological scale is:

Metal
Mineral
Vegetable
Invertebrate, vertebrate, apes man
Sex is the highest physiological function of men—a human sex dynamo.
(Norse talk of symbolic tree (?) . . . which grew upside down roots, sap, trunk, leaves, seeds. When the seeds fell they were man.)

1.   The seed is the ultimate objective of the tree; all other elements of the tree are subservient to the seed.

2.   The seed, when ripe, is independent of the tree. in the same way man may become independent of the [*Text missing*]

3.   Each seed is the epitome of the whole tree.

Complete man is the epitome of the physiology of the planet. We, as human beings, are simply cells in the sense cells of the planet. With the lunacy of the moon and pathology of the earth as cells in the sense of cells of the earth we are in a different position. We are two transforming stations:

1.   For the transforming of chemicals.

2.   For the transforming of the forces of life.

(See next page for page omitted which belongs in middle of third page.)

Scale of hydrogens

One series of vibrations we call 1, 2, 3.

1.   Will   emotional

2.   Consciousness   intellectual

3.   Individuality   spinal

(Thinking, feeling, effort making.)

The three highest chemicals of which man is composed are three centers. (?)

Hydrogen	6	matter
Hydrogen	12	(?) higher than man
Hydrogen	24	human octave appears
Hydrogen	48	apes
Hydrogen	96	quadrupeds, vertebrate
Hydrogen	192	invertebrate
Hydrogen	384	vegetable
Hydrogen	768	mineral
Hydrogen	1536	metals

(A spider does not know of the existence of man, man does not know hydrogen 12 and 6)

Traffic moves in two ways—involution and evolution—on this highway, and man is one of the phases on the highway. We have seen that man chemically in the traffic began with the atom. In the physiological traffic man began with the cell.

We are trying to look at man as one of the links in the cosmic chain. Man discharges one of two functions, either upgrading or downgrading.

We have looked at two sides of the square which man is. Corresponding to the chemical and physical changes there are psychological and sociological changes.

Man should be simultaneously upgrading all four sides. Analogy—it is the bacteria, animal bacteria, in vegetable life that create the vitamins. Man does not really eat vegetables. Man may be considered a high form of bacteria in his function to be discharged for the cosmos. This function is only valuable to man individually if he discharges the function positively upgrading. The value to the individual is the transforming matter upwards.

Can you distinguish between man's psychological and social function and his chemical and physiological function? Chemically there are 92 elements. Chemically speaking man is a station for transforming these elements into a higher or lower order. Man would still remain a chemical entity whether he had consciousness or not.

Physiological man would still be on entity without psychology at all. There would still be a grouping of cells.

We depart from the physical to the psychological. In psychology we introduce the subject of sight. Here I invite you to try to use other kinds of eyes than those known in the physical body. Do you know such an organ of sight?

Chemically we begin with the unit—the atom.

Physically we begin with the unit—cell.

Psychologically we begin with a unit.

Sociologically we begin with a unit.

Have you an idea of what these last two units are? In these two fields we are in a pre-scientific age. The whole of psychology is a unitary impression. What defines man psychologically is the field of impressions, and a unit is one impression.

Man would be a totally different being if his field of impressions were different than it is. Man's field has its limits, its range in the cosmic octave which is dedicated to him, constituting his function.

Each kind of being has its own field of impressions. Within the field appointed to man, each man has his own status. Each man is said to have a garden in the whole field given to man. On the tilling of his own garden depends his status in the cosmic scale. Cultivate the point of view of a cosmic engineer.

We know the biological beings on this planet: invertebrate, vertebrate, man.

403

Man is the only being of the order of machines which is potentially capable of grading up substances on his own initiative. Man is the highest organism we know capable of transmuting substances. It is almost as if man were one of the psychological digestive processes of God.

There may be substances which God can get only from three-brained beings—three-centered activity.

The true psyche takes the form of the planet on which it appears. On this planet man is the threefold form; man makes the pattern of his planet.

The phase which man is in is for transforming impressions into a higher order.

(God may be indifferent to the individual if society renders what he needs but God is not society.)

God no longer desires only servants. He desires sons contributing value in three centers. As servants man contributes something. In the absence of reconciliation in a man someone has to do the reconciliation for him. There are still necessary—junior partners—conscious three-centered beings. This universe is only one of the possible frames of the time, space and purpose of God. God is an adventurer. The aspect we have of the universe has been arbitrarily chosen and maintained. This universe is not so, it is only because we have imagined so, have been trained to believe it is so.

We call Him God because we are in the frame of this God. There may be many gods of many other frames which are not the absolute. (Read the last four chapters of Eddington.) Other universes do not go through the form of actualizing it is because we are what we are that this universe exists for us. "In God we live and move and have our being."

(There is hardly a thing in Whitehead that Orage has not put in simple language. Whitehead is in the mind of God but he does not formulate simply.)

In the totality of God's psyche man may be said to be the lower mind of God. The function of man in the psyche of God is the transforming of substances.

In man's failure there will be a corresponding defect in the totality of the psyche of God.

We suffer from certain fatigue in a physical organ and cannot discharge the corresponding function. If the mind is fatigued in some part some function fails us. If memory fails, but we will improvise some kind of finesse and keep an engagement book, a notebook. Likewise if God finds a defect in His psyche he may find a substitute. (He may take a drug.)

Impressions received by man can never be received by God otherwise there would be no need for man. We are an organic necessity to God. Our function is the collection of certain types of impressions which God cannot collect. Beside collecting he has the function of transforming these impressions into form so that they become food for the totality of which man is part.

Consider—nature is a being whose function is the creation of a machine.

404

The machines have their objective duty, a capacity to do work. The being associated with the machine has the duty of doing that work defined by that machine. Nature has provided the necessary apparatus, necessary for the being to perform his work. The work being receiving and transforming food into higher forms of matter. Nature has completed its work, having provided us with transforming machines, but the work of beings is to discharge the transformation of impressions.

The totality of being-logos has the four sides.

In regard to impressions, what is the field of impressions man passively receives because he has been conditioned chemically, physiologically, psychologically? What is the boundary of our field of impressions?

We are responsive to three forms of experiences thinking, feeling and conation or effort striving etc. Our psychic life is built up of three kinds of experiences. These three kinds of experiences we passively suffer—every experience is defined as a suffering because it is passive—we irresistibly react to passive experiences. We undergo a passive transformation. (Growth, development are words that denote a direction, words from the Gurdjieff point of view we have no right to use so I use "transformation.")

Illustration: Coral islands formed by the bones of myriads of animals. (Israel Solon)

What our psychology builds up can be said to be a coral structure.

Literally these are human beings, only three-brained beings in whom it is possible for human beings to be built up. It has been said over and over and over again. "Man is of the order of the moon, he collects impressions and excretes behavior." The excreted behavior we may call growth evolution in him, but what these terms thus used denote has no relation to these ideas.

We could not live without earthworms. Read Darwin on earthworms and we will know how much we owe to the earthworms. They are totally unaware of this and never participate in the glory of their descendants.

Man has two purposes—one to serve and two to participate in the nature of divinity—"to the glory of God and man's estate." Estate—status.

Objective duty is implied in transmuting of impressions. Impressions are received by man in the octave 48. Man as hydrogen 24 is ideally defined, but he occupies the octave between 24 and 48. In this range of vibrations all three vibrations are received.

Solar beings occupy the octave from 2 to 6. Planetary beings the octave from 12 to 24. Man the octave from 24 to 48.

We receive impressions passively in the octave 24 to 48. These is no merit if your coral structure is a plateau, you have done nothing for God.

It is by chance only what range of impressions one is capable of; this is due to heredity and sociology.

Transformation is taking place by pure accident. This is according to Gurdjieff something to think about. It is a cosmic fact with a cosmic purpose. Any given three-centered structure shall of itself, on its own initiative commence transforming substance for the next higher beings planetary gods. This would be raising 48 to 24. The terrible thing is that any effort to transform 48 to 24 is lost if you do not reach 24. You drop and there is no result, the effort is lost. Many make the effort few accomplish the step, "Many are called, few are chosen." Either the thing is accomplished by this series or it is not accomplished at all. The series goes from 48 to (?), to 35 to 26 to 24. The octave is divided into three stages:

1.   do, re, mi   mechanical stage
2.   fa   self-consciousness, man
3.   sol, la, si   cosmic consciousness

We all begin without exception, do, re, mi. Everyone is born in that center of gravity, do, re, mi. In this range of impassive experiences they construct coral creatures. This does not mean that the rest of the octave is not potentially present.

For beings whose center of gravity is confined to *do, fa* it is impossible. Such are primitive beings, primitive types—there are such among ourselves:

The *re* type we call the masses.

The *mi* type—here may come a glimmering of *fa*.

Illustration: The Jews and the Promised Land, they wished to be free from something but not free for something. There are the *mi* people who can easily return to *re, do* and there are the *mi* people with magnetic center who have an attraction for sol, la, si. But for these there is the desert to be crossed. We expect the desert to be fruitless, arid, yielding only by products and unprofitable. The ability to accomplish by persistent effort awareness of the physical body—the body to which you are attached is nothing—a desert. This consciousness of the physical body is the most difficult task in transmuting in the octave from 48 to 24.

Everything you know without crossing this desert will be by report only, dreams.

After the desert is crossed comes the Promised Land for cosmic consciousness. Impressions actively received. Man may be considered a torch bearer. He receives impressions at 48 and carries them over to 24 and delivers them over to planetary gods, then man enters into the planetary order. We say man is hydrogen 24 because that is his completion of his phase in the cosmic skein the completion of the octave man.

"Take, eat, this is my body." This is not to be taken simply symbolically. Bread contains atoms of the body Kesdjan and of the soul. But if our state of consciousness is planetary (of this planet, earth) you will extract substances for your physical body only, but if your state of consciousness is cosmic you will extract the positive element from the bread for the body Kesdjan.

Impressions intellectual, impressions emotional, impressions sensed received at 48 are the order of 48. If I begin observing myself the impressions I receive are 24. We say sense impressions are passive; we don't look for them in ordinary waking state, we are like sponges.

Emotional impressions are passively received and thoughts are passively received; but we call sense positive, thoughts negative and emotions neutralizing. (In normal man thought should be positive and sense negative.)

Why do we say the duty of man is to ponder one half of his time? Pondering on passive thoughts helps to change thoughts from negative to positive. In schools pondering was not given until self-observation was accomplished. We are at a disadvantage in that the whole is put before us and not graded. We run the risk of mixing up techniques, but we have the advantage of choosing for ourselves the right technique.

When you are aware of what your body is doing you cannot be aware of what your mind is doing.

Form of behavior is like the large hand of the clock; if the large hand is out of balance how can you understand the smaller hands of thought, emotions and sensations? You cannot be sure you are observing these small hands correctly until you have mastered the self-observation of the five manners of behavior.

THURSDAY, 31 OCTOBER 1929

MAN CONSIDERED SOCIOLOGICALLY

(Mr. Brown in the chair as leader, much discussion between many people as to what was the social unit, Mr. Orage took over leadership. This was an example of a democratic form of discussion.)

("Man was born to be an individual with consciousness and will: thanks to society he is a personality with wishes and passive thoughts. Environment has wound up his three mainsprings and the unwinding of these springs covers the span of his life. Environment is the dynamo which runs the machine." B.B.G. This did not come in here.)

Chemically the atom is the unit.

Physiologically the cell is the unit.

Psychologically the impression is the unit.

Sociologically what is the unit?

"Sociologically the person is a unit of aggregation of impressions."

Not accepted.

The relation of society to us—maleficent, is the wrong idea and also our relation to society with the idea of making conditions easier, planetary conditions of human life easier, is also wrong. We do have a duty to help society to help man to function according to his cosmic purpose, to become conscious. We can only do this when our debt has been paid. (Allan Brown)

"The first step is to take the beam out of our own eye before attacking the note in our brother's eye." We have to take man as one cell in the sociological whole. One cell assists other cells but primarily it should fulfill its own function. If this function were fulfilled many of the sociological difficulties would disappear. "God has made of one blood all the nations of the Earth."

The social unit is the family—father, mother, son.

It may be hoped from this unit a threefold individual may arise. An individual is then free from society.

The unit of divine society is Father, Son and Holy Ghost.

The unit of human society is the family. To consider an individual a unit means taking an incomplete unit, for there is male and female among humans. It is necessary to have male, female and child for a complete unit.

There are three types of society discussed in the Book: the monarchical, the power handed down by heredity, the republic or democracy, elected or chosen to office and the theocratic, self-appointed government. This last is best for developing the individual.

"It is impossible to develop normally until the social coating has been seen through." (Miss Johnson.)

How do you distinguish between things which are God's and things which are Caesar's?

In the Chapter called "The First Descent," Mr. Gurdjieff said while eating meat was a disgusting thing, still we should eat meat? Meaning accommodate ourselves to society.

The individual never ceases in his responsibility no matter what society he finds himself in. ("Be ye in the world but not of it.") He lives in society but he continues to remember his function.

"Love the Lord Thy God with all thy heart, with all thy strength and with all thy soul?" it is threefold, "and thy neighbor as thyself," The value of society to an individual is the assistance it gives him to accomplish his task. There is no obligation to society; the obligation is all the other way. Society is to provide the three kinds of experiences.

In a monarchy and a republic responsibility is delegated in one by inheritance, in the other responsibility is thrust upon the office-holder.

An anarchy—meaning revolt—is society controlled by individuals, each a law unto himself, but this could only be carried out when men are individuals and society is no longer needed by man.

Never has or can a democratic form of government have a conscious leader. In a monarchy there is a chance of a ruler being conscious.

In a democracy there is the inclination to conceive equality in terms of identity. In a democracy one faction rules over another faction.

A center may be considered as a faction. One center, the instinctive, is always to be governed, therefore there remain only two kinds of government. Government by the emotional center is democratic because there is constant change, an agitation in the emotional center. Government by the third center—monarchical—there is continuity.

The theocratic organization is related to the fourth center.

(This evening has been an example of a democratic form of discussion. In the monarchical form of discussion the gaps will be filled up if you fall asleep. We have been groping blindly in our discussion this evening, with no organization. Both forms of discussion are insufficient.)

Carol Robinson

CARMEL TALKS

Mr. A. R. Orage, as many of you remember came to Carmel in August 1928 and delivered six lectures on Gurdjieff's philosophy and his method, for the harmonious Development of Man. One of the parts of this method, the physical exercises, which are a component part, Carmel has never seen. While these must be helpful the method may be practiced without them.

At the conclusion of his work here, Mr. Orage expressed a wish that the group which had made his audience might continue to meet; and to our surprise this is just what has happened. There was no picking and choosing. At first we came together once a month, then by a common wish, once a fortnight. We were fortunate in having many notes taken at the Orage talks in Carmel, and others sent to us from a New York member who had kept memoranda there. These notes have been our only text book; and each member of the group is ready tonight to tell you just what these meetings have meant to him. Realizing that we were leaderless and more or less feeling our way, we have been rather silent as to our corporate existence knowing how precarious at first was the bond which held us; but we now feel that we are really a group and that we have achieved at least a common vocabulary. But even more than any intellectual understanding, we have taken a leaf from the procedure of good Methodist brother's and every week we hold an experience meeting, telling just what progress or regress has been made in the technique of self-observation; for what we are working for is not a matter of theory but a discipline of life.

There is hope in the future that we may have more authoritative material to work with, for a short sketch of the method by Gurdjieff himself will soon be in print; and next September a book will be brought out by Ouspensky called "An Unknown Doctrine" dealing with Gurdjieff's philosophy.

Gurdjieff himself has his magnum opus, all but finished. It is now almost translated into French, German and English from its original Russian and Gurdjieff desires that it be published simultaneously in all four tongues.

Accounts of Gurdjieff origin differ. I have been variously told he was Greek, Armenian and Russian. Personally he seems to be just as incomprehensible. It is evident he must be accepted, if he is accepted at all for his message and not be regarded or revered as a messenger.

In announcing his method he does not claim it as original; but calls it a rediscovery through much labor and far travelling of what has been known to a few initiates since prehistoric times. Many other men have claimed such authority also. But Gurdjieff differs from the Joseph Smiths and of that ilk in his insistence that what he has to say be treated with skepticism.

"Whatever I say, do not accept it as I give it to you, but probe it for yourself. The method which I have found is simple and clear of comprehension, although of incredible difficulty. I believe if followed it will be of great benefit to you; but it must be worked at and its worth proved the results will not be at all immediate; they may be long delayed. No one can help you attain. Take it or leave it. "

He goes on to say that he believes in the ethics of Jesus; and that while this is true he is equally sure that man not only does not, but with his present equipment cannot put this ethic into practice. What he then proposes to do with his technique is to give a method by whose means abilities now dormant in all men may come awake. Painted on the wall of the study of his Institute at Fontainebleau is: "Our object is to strive to be able to be Christians."

Now as briefly and clearly as possible we will give you a summary of this doctrine, as it has been given by Mr. Orage, who was formerly the editor of a brilliant English weekly "The New Age" and who is known to all students of economics as an authority on Guild Socialism. But the war finished all that; and Orage, meeting with Gurdjieff, became so impressed by his doctrine that he came to bring it to America, just as that other philosopher Ouspensky, who wrote the Tertium Organum, before he meet Gurdjieff has been doing in England.

If, in trying to give you the outline of this matter, the use of some of the words does not coincide with yours, please be a little patient. There is nothing so difficult, so nearly impossible as to have one word, unless it be very concrete, meaning the same thing to a number of people. There are some words which Gurdjieff uses, not as ordinarily accepted; but in their use he is always consistent. He is a keen student of the modern sciences physics, psychology and biology, and goes so far in his premise to accept the extreme statements of the behaviorists.

He says:

1.   Man like all other animals behaves in reaction to his environment.

2.   Man differs from other animals in having a certain form of greater consciousness, in knowing that he knows; and also in having the capacity for the development of a soul.

3.   Man has a threefold nature with three brains or centers from which all his activities proceed. These are very unequally developed in different people, and are

a.   Doing: Sensory-motor or instinctive, spinal, expressed in science

b.   Being: Visceral or emotional, solar plexus, expressed in art

c.   Knowing: Intellect, brain, expressed in philosophy

The fact that one of these predominates does not at all mean that it is over developed; but merely that the others are under developed. Almost all great thinkers at present reach their preeminence at the expense of motor and emotional centers. We have grown accustomed to the artist with the mentality of a child; and to the athlete with neither mind nor heart.

The whole aim of this method is the harmonious development of our nature in an increase of being. Being is the emotional center and cannot be developed by any direct means.

That this is a fact is proven by the inability of the Christian religion, which has as its aim the cultivation of this center, to show any progress after two thousand years.

According to this method the emotional center which is the neutralizing force between mind the positive, and body the negative, can grow only through friction between the mind and the body. This means carrying on motor activities while exercising mental activities on their proper plane.

As far as can be known, evolution in bringing man into possession of his present body seems to have gone as far as it can. There seems to be difference in degree and not in kind in historic man.

If Man is to develop beyond the point to which physical evolution has naturally brought him, the work must be consciously done. Out of reason and thought, he must rise to conscious awareness. Out of his emotional diverse and unstable wishes, he must develop will; and by will Gurdjieff means always *continuous conscious effort*. Out of his instinctive personality he must develop a real individuality.

There can be little doubt to any thoughtful person that the trait most common to us all is our inertia. Under the influence of our emotions, this is frequently overcome for spaces of time, but when the incentive palls, our work ceases.

Charles Kingsley once said that as a "civilizing" agent, a ship load of whisky and trinkets on the African coast was more powerful than a ship load of missionaries. The idea of heaven which obtains in every land is one of inactivity and comfort. Ethnologists tell us that had new born children not developed the annoying habit of screaming when they needed care, the race might have ended. Why multiply words to prove what you know to be true? And here is the terrible obstacle to the practice of this method. It means an unceasing struggle, just that.

Now we may be said to have stated our problem. The end and aim of every religion has never been other than this to furnish a means to accomplish this end. Jesus said "Love your enemies, do good to them who hate you; turn the other cheek" and Gandhi, a little half naked "heathen" is the only modern exemplar. Now Gurdjieff says this may be made possible to all men if they can only be shown how to discipline themselves; and he claims that such technique has been known down through time, only it has been the property of initiates. In general religions have simply rung changes on the three centers and have sought the answer through intellectual or emotional means or through physical practices. A few in every century seem to attain; but on the whole mankind seems to have reached an impasse.

Buddha tried to make the method common property but his disciples found it so difficult that they perverted his reaching and withdrew to lonely places to practice it, thus stultifying the doctrine. In the few fragments ascribed to Pythagoras we find traces of it; also I am told in the Egyptian Book of the Dead. Plato has a great deal very plainly told; and the often quoted Greek apothegm "know thyself" has if rightly understood the whole matter in a nutshell; and leads us directly by its simple statement to a most difficult performance. Let us elaborate. How, asks Gurdjieff, do we know each other?" Only through observation of any one's behavior. Real knowledge is not obtained through what people say to us; although this contributes very much if what they say is in line with what they do. In the final determination it is conduct which settles the matter. Now, says Gurdjieff, conduct is observed from five things; the observation of:

1. Gesture
2. Posture
3. Tone of voice
4. Facial expression
5. Movements of the body

Gurdjieff says that we are so conditioned from childhood by our environment that we are a mass of illusions about ourselves. The whole psychoanalytic school confirms this opinion, though the means of release differ enormously. Gurdjieff says if we can tell what sort of folk strangers are, through observing these five things, we should be able to find out about ourselves in the same way. This cannot be done by the introspection recommended by the psychoanalyst but by a direct and simple watching our behavior, without passing either moral or aesthetic judgments upon what we see.

It is more than probable that you cannot observe these five things in yourself all at once. In that case pick one of them and do it as often as you can, following it until you have practiced the repertory. If you can accomplish a concentrated observation of any or all of these for five consecutive minutes without the slightest wandering of thought, the slightest break in your awareness, you have no need of this method or of practically anything else for you have already attained the possession of a real will, and an objective consciousness. Science tells us that we are bombarded by ten thousand impressions a second. Most of these we do not register at all in the conscious self; but enough do to make a large number of red herrings drawn across the trail of any attempt at concentration.

This means a record of our appearance and acts, made as a cine camera would make it in connection with a voice record. Now we can be quite impersonal about such a viewing of others. But can we do this thing for ourselves? We must remove such observation from any trace of emotion. We must also remove it from any moral judgments; and we begin to feel about it that Archimedes was right when he offered to move the world if he could only have a fulcrum for his lever. But Gurdjieff offers us this fulcrum when he says: "Try to do this as if you were looking at an outsider." This position is purely theoretical. Yet if you continue to persist then the effort to realize such a position will make it come to pass. This is the testimony of many who have actually made this experiment. It is as I have said held that there is an actual utilization of dormant nerve channels and brain tissue adding unspeakably to ones powers and abilities.

This matter of self-observation has one very odd property. All other exercises, which I know, do after a time develop into habits, and can with more or less success be turned over to our subconscious or automatic selves, playing an instrument, driving a car give us no conscious work; but this practice, we will all unanimously tell you is nearly as hard now as it was when we began it. And this, Gurdjieff says, is because it depends for its function on a part of the brain hitherto undeveloped. And the reason it is impossible to pursue it except by flashes is the same one.

Now he also claims, and this is the most important part of the whole matter, that an attempt at such practice, even sporadically, will, if continued over a length of time, develop in us powers at present dormant, powers which ultimately lead us to what Gurdjieff calls objective reason or objective conscience, which means the possession of a real will and not that bundle of fleeting and contradictory wishes which is our present state. And a favorite statement is that each time we practice self-observation we are administering a spoon full of food to this objective self. It may and generally will take years of work before this latent "I" can be even feebly felt to be in charge of our usual selves or "IT," before we can truth fully say "I have a body." When this is accomplished we may hope that wish may be changed into will, thought into awareness and personality to individuality.

Beyond any shadow of doubt that there is great danger if use the gains from the method as end in themselves instead of as by products, the main aim of this method is to help us to transcend the human qualities which are ours by heredity and environment. If we use the gains to arid to the abilities of our instinctive selves, we are guilty of a prostitution for which we shall pay.

The theory of Gurdjieff states unequivocally that mankind after death recurs into life here again, as the leaves of a tree drop into the soil and in a few years are again taken up into material for new leaves. But he claims that if we use this life to lift ourselves from our heredity and environment the terrifying recurring round may be lifted to a different level and the spiral carry us higher. In the same analogy the material which was once part of a leaf may become a seed and live as an independent being.

Another part of the philosophy, of especial interest to musicians, is the analogies which he finds in life and in nature to the diatonic scale and its octave. He finds this basic, a physical formula. In this scale the passage do, re, mi, is one of regular full tones but with fa there is introduced a semitone and this being passed the succeeding sol, la, si go smoothly on. He has a long and most interesting list of octaves and always there is this odd break in the fourth member. His idea is that life in plant, animal, and human being corresponds to the first, three notes, that the note of effort, the "fa" is now coming into being and that like St. Paul we may say "we know not what we shall be" any more than the caterpillar who has proceeded from the egg and gone into the chrysalis can have any idea of a butterfly. It is safe to suppose if a caterpillar could prognosticate a blessed future for himself he could only think of being a bigger and better worm.

The last and the sum of his teaching takes one to heights which are dizzying and yet which the scientists of today are putting out in all their cosmologies. There is in the universe but one spirit, one force. Of this force we are a part and just as in proportion we bring ourselves to the greatest of which we are capable, we may be more truly component, a humble assistant.

Concluding a few practical remarks may not be out of place. At once one says "have no time." May I disabuse your mind of this! It takes no reading, no stated separate work. It is something, which if it is to be of any use whatever to you, must be carried on concurrently with all your daily walk and conversation; and the little daily chores are the times when it is most difficult to practice it. You may not hope by as the old hymn put it to be "carried to the skies on flowery beds of ease." The group here gathered is ready to tell you how difficult it is but I am sure you will be told that they in almost three years of it have found it worthwhile in itself and also very worthwhile as to its by-products which I have been very careful to allude to but lightly; so easy is it for us to be acquisitive.

So far we have lost but one member who has remained living in Carmel; and for the last months no one of the group unless absolutely incapacitated has been absent. I need say no more as to the interest we have found in the study of this method.

We do not urge anyone to join the group; but if after hearing what we all have to say there are any who would be willing to give one evening a fortnight regularly to its meetings and as much effort as possible through each and every day, we would welcome you. The idea would be to form a subsidiary group until the new comers have acquired the vocabulary and some feeling of the scope of the philosophy, and when this is done that the groups should merge. We have discussed the matter very carefully and feel this is the fairest way to old students and to new.

THIS SIDE OF CARD IS FOR ADDRESS

Mrs Muriel Draper
24 E 40th St.
N.Y.c

KINDLY NOTE AND MAKE KNOWN; commencing January 8th, Mr.

Orage will hold three weekly evening classes (8:30 p. m.) in the Anderson School

(128 East 58th,) Tuesdays, for Beginners in Method; Wednesdays, English Liter-

ature; Fridays, Psychological Exercises.

Subscriptions, $2.50, $3.00 and $1.00 respectively.

A beginners' class in Physical Movements will be taken by Jessmin Howarth

in the Whitehead Studio, (180 West 59th,) on Thursday Evenings at 9, com-

mencing January 10th. ($2.00.)

Orage in California, 1928.

ORAGE METHOD

1. Man, like all other animals behaves in reaction to his environment.

2. Man differs from other animals in having the capacity for development of a soul.

3. Man has a threefold nature, with three brains or centers from which all his activities proceed.

4. Sensory-motor or instinctive, expressed in science!

5. Visceral or emotional in art

6. Intellect or reason in philosophy.

7. We know our fellow men only through observation of their behavior, that is

a. Posture

b. Gesture

c. Movement

d. Tone of voice

e. Facial expression

8. In order to know ourselves, we must observe our own behavior with equal impersonality.

9. This process of self-observation will:

a. Reveal ourselves to ourselves

b. Develop a new attitude to ourselves

c. It differs from all other attitudes in that it never becomes automatic

d. It develops new powers in us

10. Our natural impulse is to confide as much of our living as possible to habit because of innate inertia. Self-observation is to break our habit and keep us continually aware. To effect growth, this must be continuous.

11. By constant practice of self-observation and constant "Pondering," we may gradually bring about the change of:

a. Wish to will

b. Thought to consciousness

c. Personality to individuality

12. The human race has completed its experience in three centers. All religions and philosophies are reshuffling these.

13. The Diatonic scale is a physical formula of nature. The passage Do-Re-Mi being regular, Fa bringing in semitone changing to So-La-Si. The octave is basic in the universe which is an octave of octaves.

14. Man as a creature of three centers considers himself as the end and aim of creation. This system on the contrary holds that he is like all other life, merely a means of transforming energy.

15.   That he must if he do this unconsciously do it at his own expense; but if he becomes aware may transform energy and yet gain by doing so.

16.   That the "It" or natural three centers may by cooperation become a functioning part of the "I," an expression of the spirit which informs the universe.

17.   What this "I" is, its parts, its functions, we can no more comprehend than the butterfly can be comprehended by the caterpillar but, like the caterpillar we may develop.

Waldo Frank

MRS. HARES NOTES

(COURTESY OF MRS. LUHAN)

Observe movement, posture, gesture, way of walking, expression, muscle tension, be aware of where voice is placed, taste, touch, smell, respiration, etc.

Orage says at the institute they could always recognize Dr. Jung's patients from their gestures, they had unconsciously acquired his. Observation is easier when motion is rapid.

Recuperation of energy, emotional and physical, during night sufficient for full day if not misspent. Emotional energy is misspent in anticipation, regret and sympathy for ill you cannot hope to alleviate. Over expression of emotion weakens the quality.

Physical energy may be conserved by relaxation of every muscle not actually required in the work you are doing. Changing the set of muscles used in making certain efforts will conserve energy, if you are wheeling a barrel, do it first with arm muscles, then shoulder, then back, etc., relaxing others. This extends the duration of efficient effort. Observation of the physical will relieve tension, the body at all times should be so relaxed as to enable its members to be loosely flung about by another person.

Self-observation may be aided by thinking of yourself as third person, *she* is moving her shoulders, *she* walks like on ostrich, *she* is feeling the covering on the arm of her chair. Make the observation entirely impersonal, with no idea of correction or criticism. Observe yourself as some strange animal going through its daily paces, one to whom you have no personal relation. Our automatic bodies are the vehicle. We must learn to be the driver not the driven.

At the end of the day we should be able to rehearse by mental pictures the day's activities, not cerebrally. As a body might move through a fog, displacing its form, so should we be able to follow the form of our body back over the path it has taken in our vision during the day. If your day has been active, it will be easier to see yourself. You start with the first episode of the morning; then follow as closely as possible that figure which is you, as he goes through the day. You see the clothes it wears, the way it moves, don't see it as anything but the actual outside of yourself, but don't remember the mental re-actions to the physical episodes, or the reason for any action. This is difficult at first, but if you stick to just recalling the visual presentation of your day's behavior in sequence it becomes a real moving picture with you as the sole actor. At the start this takes some time but later it may become almost simultaneous. Sometimes you hear of people at the time of the death having a review of their whole life come to them all in a minute.

There are three centers acting within us, the instinctive, the emotional, and the intellectual. The instinctive or physical, is the most completely developed, the emotional less so, and the intellectual still less. They act together (some day they will act separately) and confuse each other and interfere, the emotional center being the one we employ in making these pictures. It is well to give the other two something to keep them busy so that they cannot interfere with its action. After going to bed, occupy your intellectual center with some form of counting, not so easy as to be automatic. Occupy your instinctive center by putting your arm perhaps under your back in an uncomfortable position and then the picture of your day come before you in sequence; you may have to start with a mental push so that it does move before you like the moving picture. You see yourself going through the day as a figure— observation here receives a test, your pictures will be clear according to your day's observation of your physical behavior. This is called the daily review and it is an important exercise. In some esoteric schools it is the only means employed to stimulate self-observation; it also encourages sleep.

The great difficulty is to remember to observe; may means are employed to help. The origin of hair shirts was a reminder to observe yourself, the purpose was forgotten eventually and the ascetics carried on the symbol, using it to mortify the flesh. The court jester was to remind the king that he was human. In the monastery where this technique was in practice, the Abbot had an especial acolyte to constantly remind him. In England two 'Group Members,' a man and wife had their whole household arranged with unexpected reminders, signs, etc., so they could not forget. The technique requires no extraordinary intelligence, very often mental superiority is a handicap—anyone can do it who has a wish to do it, but to remember to do it constantly is a great effort. Negative emotions, fear, anxiety, anger, etc, are dissipated by observing the physical reactions; they have their value as warnings but after they first register as such, they deplete our energy. This same energy can be used in self-observation, and by so using it, the emotion itself disappears, in a positive emotion, the emotion is intensified by observation.

By observing at the time of negative emotions the observation of your physical state employs or transmutes the energy of the fear emotion, let us say, into preparation to meet the condition which may arouse us.

IMAGINATION AND THOUGHT

Thought is the pure effort to attain the truth and takes place in the intellectual center, imagination is a combining of thought and emotion and takes place between the two centers, so is not a pure product. Fear is induced by a picture produced with the emotions and your re-action is the same to the picture as if it were real, the thought that it is real makes your re-actions such. For instance, you see a rope in the road, you think it is a snake, the picture of a snake in created in your mind and your re-action to the coil of rope is as if it wore a snake, the emotion subsides immediately however when you discover it is only a rope. It is the mental picture combined with thought that creates fear imagery.

Our makeup is of our essence which is hereditary and the social standards imposed upon us; by background, tradition and education, are our personality. We must discover if possible by self-observation what this essence is; people's way of life must be in accordance with their essence to produce a balanced and happy life. There is no success or happiness in working against essence. You must discover if you are a intellectual, emotional, or instinctive type—the instinctive type is the more predominant type, 90% of us are such.

A woman whose profession was work in psychoanalysis, who had studied with Jung and had a fair practice but was not happy in her work; discovered her essence through observing and though her life's preparation had been for her profession she discarded it and started a weaving school, the working with her hands she found satisfied her essence. This decision she arrived at through observing herself no one else could have convinced her; and had she primarily known her observation would have led to such a decision, she never would have considered it possible, nor would she have continued it.

An exercise in retrospective observation to help discover your essence may be a review of your childhood. Remember as far back as you can how you looked and how you re-acted through all the years of childhood, youth, and all intervening years. See yourself as a child of three or four, if possible, what was your appearance; remember your re-actions to as many incidents as possible, build this gradually up to the present time, carry it on from day to day and eventually you will find a recurrence in it all of the part of you which is your essence, persisting, in spite of conditions and changing circumstances. Essence is the original self without the falseness of affectations imposed upon us by education and social pressure, to discover it we must discard the personality traits. It is often very crude. "Know thyself." This is the very root of the method, and there may be found in the New Testament many such recommendations, which Christ made to those who wished to learn.

THIRD MEETING

Discussion as to different sorts of observation. They are divided into two sets. Those which you may observe objectively and those you are aware of, the ultimate aim being to someday do it all simultaneously so you are conscious of it all. The ten to observe, are: carriage, posture, gesture, movement, facial expression, rigidity of muscles, where the sound of your voice comes from, etc. The Aware group includes touch, taste, dryness or moisture of mouth, temperature of body, quickening of breath, increase of heart beats, pressure, the contracting of muscles, etc.

Everyone is born with a certain potentiality of different centers, this cannot be ceded by any effort or exercise, but we use so much less than our potentialities and waste so in meeting the supposed obligation of society. By exercises we can conserve what we have left and develop this to a higher purpose. We all at birth are supplied with a sufficient potential energy in all of our centers to last us twice as long as the ordinary lifetime, with a perfect control we could extend our life period; our intellectual center is the least developed, are less able to digest the impressions taken in by this center than the other two. Some time a center through waste may become entirely dead and can never be re-captured. The energy wasted in the emotional center may be not only conserved by its possessor, but we can make use of energy spilled over by the emotion of another. Anger is a wasteful emotion and the energy of it may be appropriated legitimately by the observer.

Direction for Observing:

Separate the "I" from Betty—this is the observer, "I" stands about ten feet behind Betty—the mechanism, as she stands, walks, moves, she may be observed but not corrected everything about her is impersonal. She is a third person, behaving as conditions impose on her, even before birth, make her behave; she has no free will. Her behavior, therefore not being her own, we need not criticize, but "I" observes it; this observation is food for "I". It grows, and in time we will be able to direct and control this mechanism which now acts so automatically and apart from the wish of the "I". This "I" cannot take a part until it is developed and this whole technique is for the development of the "I", or consciousness.

Discussion as to whether the desire for the conscious "I" is not a religious tendency, the desire to be a part of cosmic life. Orage says the procedure of this desire is first the conscious man, then super man, then God, then a part of the solar system, etc. This he calls religion but not religion in the ordinary accepted form, the precepts being so different as to make it confusing, before the theory is understood, to call a religion.

It seems that "I" within us is God, or a part of God, also that God is really made up of all the "I's" in the world, and his consciousness depends on the development of the individual consciousness. Discussion as to whether conscious direction would not destroy many chances of inspirational action. Frank cited Columbus' venture and his belief in the discovery as inspirational, that sometimes unconscious action resulted in marvelous achievement. Orage said as we are now, we are like sailing vessels blown and buffeted by winds of circumstances we sail but without direction, and where we go is determined by many things. The awakening of "I" puts a motor on the boat which allows us to go where we will.

5 JANUARY

B. asked if the exercises were not valuable to balance the intellectual effort required for the group meetings, the exercises at the Institute as well as the physical work seemed to be almost part of the whole thing. Orage says they are helpful, but not always good, and perhaps when the institute starts again they will be eliminated entirely. Personal experiences were recounted, Mrs. W. disturbed because self-observation upset her daily life, she seemed unable to efficiently do what she had efficiently done before. I, having felt the same, was glad the question was raised, ordinary obligations do not seem worthwhile. Orage says to look upon the seeming confusion as a growing pain, it is a temporary condition brought about by our inability to adjust all at once our new thought to our old life. If we have important work to do we may stop observing, put the "I" to sleep when it interferes with our efficiency, later of course, it must increase all of your efficiencies. A life whose whole course along the positive side is not enriched and aided in all directions through this method, shows that the operator is not doing it properly. Activity should be increased rather than diminished, ordinary life should go on only with the added interest of the change of motive, use every tiling as a exercise, an opportunity for self-observation, self-observation again being the opportunity to develop consciousness. Frank said he found observation diminished not only painful sensations, but also pleasurable ones; I know what he means. Orage says negative emotions should be diminished by self-observation and positive sensations intensified, but as this came under the head of emotional observation it was debarred in discussion until we reached that second step. We still are trying to get the observation of the instinctive center. Mrs. W. was also urged to eliminate emotional observation and was much surprised to have Orage tell her that she was much too emotional.

I had no personal experience worth relating, though at Saranac I did overcome an incident of fear. I thought I heard someone getting in my window which opened on the ground and by taking stock of my physical re-actions, such as heart beat increase, elevator feeling in the solar plexus, dryness of mouth and so forth. I found my fear soon relieved, it being imaginary it was easily dissipated. I find by waiting someone else often asks the question in my mind. I am not finding it so easy to get my nightly review as last summer, my improvement however is in at least remembering to try and it is my mind to observe much more to observe during the day, even if I don't do it.

Orage spoke of fact and fancy, advised allowing our thoughts to grow around facts, which as facts are indisputable, said to remember there were two thousand million people in the world, to think of this and all it signified was good, also to accustom ourselves to the thought of death. These are two thoughts which certainly diminish the importance of trivial detail and of us as individuals. If I could realize that X was to die tomorrow I certainly would not bother if Rebino throughout the ivy, I had been rooting all winter, as I did today, yet maybe I would, it may be my essence, I don't know. Orage spoke too of the physiological shock it was when we did something we believed to be wrong. I was interested to hear as eventually I think the Institute teachings will lead to acceptance of many things we think wrong now, and will lessen much of the importance of what we think right or good now. I think he would say it was well that it should be so, as we are still accepting morals with dead precepts, the symbols even sometimes of evil.

I like the group, they are all so different—the Grants, Waldo Frank, the Crowley's, Maxwell Anderson, Eunice and all. Orage says children may be helped by teaching them the exercises, so when they are ready for the cerebral part of the work their other two centers are prepared to take part. If you have a desire to indulge yourself it is as good an exercise to over-indulge as to deny. Whichever way seems to offer the best discipline to the mechanism. B: "If thy enemy asks thee to go with him one mile, go with him twain." If, for instance, you have a desire to go to the play more often than you think you should go or than seems compatible with balance of work and play, make it work by going still oftener. The world goes continually from the lower Do in the musical scale to the Mi and then has always had to return to the beginning again. One day, when consciousness has developed in enough minds, there may be hope for the world beginning a new octave. This method we are now struggling with has always been understood by some but never enough. The 'I' must be in control of the mechanism to bring this about. As it now is, the 'I' is asleep, but there are brain cells in the mechanism with a desire to grow up, a desire to attain a Christ consciousness, those are the allies which work for the 'I'. The first stop is to establish the mechanistic quality of our being as we know it to these cells.

It is known and accepted as a scientific fact that the rays of the sun deposit on the earth matter to the extent of tons a year. Now similarly moon, planets, and all within our solar system carry through their rays matter or vibration which enters the earth's surface. Orage says you can think of films spread upon the earth as the skins of an onion in layers; the layer with the highest vibration entering the farthest in; this would be in accordance with the nearness or far-ness of the body from the earth. These radiation effect us even at birth, or rather at the time of conception, and the actual deposits they make upon our embryo determines our essence. This idea is the basis of astrology. This is also the sum of our potentialities, we never increase them beyond the quality acquired at that moment. To establish the relation of the centers to the 'I', the simile of the cart the horse and the driver is useful. The cart is the instinctive center; the horse is the emotional center, the driver the intellectual and the passenger asleep is the 'I'. The cart (body) is rattled about, dragged hither and yon, often kicked to pieces by the horse (emotions); the driver does not know where he is going, he sometimes tries to drive but his destination is unknown. He drives the horse but needs direction from the passenger asleep in the cart, who only can direct him if he awakens. If he wakens he will find an ally in the driver (mind)—but how to awaken the sleeping passenger? The method of self-observation. In the brain there are cells sympathetic to the desire of 'I'

427

to awake; it is those cells which stimulate the desire to observe; it is the driver who must wake his passenger. The desire for a higher consciousness is present in all of the many circles of which the universe is made—metal, mineral, vegetable, animal worlds, man, the solar system, God,—all are struggling to develop the 'I.' Life has hitherto been always in circles, Orage spoke of a wave as it curls the crest again becomes the base. Those circles must be broken to change the routine of life consciousness; we must get out of this circle finally and prevent incarnation into the same circle again.

In time we should be able to use our centers separately and at will; we know the stimulation of one has great effect upon another; if we hear good news our emotional center is stimulated immediately the work we have been at, either mental or physical, will become easier; we will cease to feel fatigued, our body is lighter, our mind more alert, though before the news came we were tired. The physical circle is the most easily altered, so we begin by observing that. Yet even here we find some things unalterable, a characteristic walk, hand writing, etc.

There are said to be seven dimensions—the fourth dimension may be called time. The development of the 'I' tends towards the power to exercise the higher centers consciously. Christ undoubtedly was a fourth dimensional being. Many of his sayings may be interpreted as relative to the development of the 'I'—"except ye be born again," and "unless ye are as little children," refer to the birth of the 'I,' and the infancy of the 'I.' The new spirit so separate from the mechanism, the crucifixion would symbolize the death of Jesus and the birth of Christ or the 'I.' Orage quoted from unknown gospels: "Follow me and ye shall find thyself and me, follow thyself, and ye shall lose thyself and me," which means follow Christ's teachings and you will find Christ and your 'I'—follow the mechanism and both will be lost.

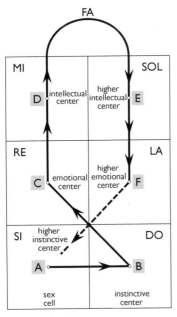

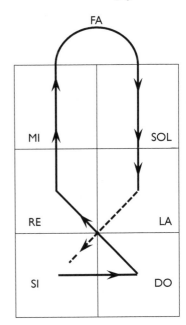

shaded spaces are
undeveloped centers

There are patterns for humans, patterns for vegetable and animal worlds. The above diagram # 1 which is representative of man in profile shows the lower centers, and the higher corresponding centers in the relation in which they exist. A is the sex cell from which we start, from there we go to B which is our instinctive center, and represents the physical body, which is a very complete automatic mechanism; this is the beginning of the scale. C is our emotional center, our next development, we begin to register like and dislike. This center has its brain in the solar plexus, the higher emotional center has its brain in the heart, and true intense feeling may register there. Most of our emotions however, register in the solar plexus. D is the intellectual center, and is situated in the front of the brain, the higher intellectual center is in the back of your brain and this is where the undeveloped brain cells lie. We use about one ninth of the brain cells we possess. After progressing through A, B, C, and D, in order to reach E you must bridge the space which corresponds to Fa, or the first semitone in the musical scale. This is the semitone so hard to surmount, and where the great effort is required. After getting past this the rest is easier, but most human effort reaches its apex at mi and then returns down the scale without ever having drawn upon the resources of the higher centers. Through accident or pathological condition a higher center is occasionally drawn upon, the result being so extraordinary that it can never be

429

confused with actions of the lower centers again and forms new criteria for future possibilities.

Our unused brain cells may be looked upon as representing the potentialities of our intellectual center and as the empty concentric (?) they are still awaiting future occupancy. The scale applied to the profile of man is again used in the cosmic universe, the fa in this scale comes between the planets and the sun. Each kingdom is faced with the problem of wakening its particular 'I.' It is the same with man as it is with the earth or organic kingdom—the planetary, sun, milky way, etc., God can only realize his 'I' through man, so our higher development is necessary for the whole cosmic attainment. Man is fa, or the bridge in God's diagram, and man's consciousness was the object of Christ's coming to the world. His life and teachings were in order to stir the effort of man to regain consciousness, so that the cosmic scale could continue upwards.

His death symbolizes the re-birth of man through the death of the body or mechanism and the birth of 'I' or consciousness. The Bible too is said to symbolize mechanism and the 'I' in the Old Testament and the New. Everything in the Old Testament has to do with the lower centers, in the new it deals with the higher. The body is often referred to in the Bible as Egypt, signifying darkness.

Figure 3 was to show how we progressed in time. We start as a child, and continue in increased stature, leaving as we come a picture much as our persons appeal in our nightly review. If we recapture this picture back through childhood we are seeing ourselves in time; it is all still there. What has happened once continues to happen always. In anything we do we act according to our personality. For instance we get out of a chair always in one way, because we are that sort of a person. If we had been born in the East we would be sitting on cushions cross-legged perhaps; at any rate, the way we get up is determined by our environment and education. But there are many other ways we could get up, not only the way we do got up, but the ways we could get up continue on and on. This is the fourth dimensional. This stream is very difficult to alter as the course is predetermined by your personality; it is set in motion for all time by your action and the potentialities of the action are set in motion too. Recurrences in time seem inevitable, but by constantly changing

430

and observing our habits we find ourselves able to use some other potentiality which could help us change or make a new stream. We can begin by changing our habits in small things, the first result that this has is to convince us of what creatures of habit we are, for the difficulty of doing anything in a way new or unaccustomed to our mechanism is proof of how mechanistic we are. It is helpful to make a list of certain things you might change in your daily habits, and make as many changes as possible even the simplest—like getting out of bed on a different side, or changing your routine of dressing, etc, would become useful. It is important to change again as soon as it becomes as familiar as to require no effort to accomplish. If you are accustomed to sleep on your right side, try sleeping on your left, even if you don't succeed the effort is of value eventually this change of habit may us move to larger field and will help us to alter our personality and change the stream of recurrence. New habits are also for fresh means of self-observation; this always is to be considered an occupation or experience—chose that which will offer the best opportunity for self-observation.

Questions asked regarding observation of other centers beside the instinctive.

ANSWERS: That all centers are observed by the observation of the physical demonstration induced by the emotional or intellectual states, the physical state itself in time of pain may be observed and the pain alleviated by observing, not the pain itself but the physical reactions in other parts of the body to this pain. The way which has done best for as is to imagine you are observing a total outsider who has been asked to report to a physician how the mechanism reacted to the pain, was the mouth dry, what muscles were tense, etc. Orage said in the institute if a member of one of the advanced groups had a headache of which he could not cure himself in three minutes observing, he was put in a lower class. The cure of ills etc., are not to be connected with the object of the Institute, this and many other benefits are by-products which accompany the pursuit of the final aim which is consciousness.

A help to sleeplessness is to put your three centers at rest. The idea is that if during the day one center had not sufficient exercise to bring a comfortable sleep, that center does not sleep soundly. If our centers are all equally exorcised, their fatigue would be equal and our rest or sleep would be very sound. A deep sleep in this way restores us in a much shorter time. At the Institute four hours of deep sleep is considered sufficient. If your centers get fidgety at night and you cannot sleep, try the following: Put the instinctive center to rest by complete relaxation, put the emotional center to rest by making a mental picture of a scene or a situation which in some past time has produced a state of complete rest in you, the center don't know the difference between the picture it re-creates, and the reality and will react to the scene as it did before. Suggest to the intellectual center by word and thought, that all is well

431

with the world, put yourself, as it were, in the hands of God, this occupation will keep this center at rest and assured.

In observation of the different centers the following sequence may be used:

1.

A.   Instinctive—Observation of movement, gestures, etc.

B.   Experimenting in movement, gesture, and changing habits in order to observe.

2.

A.   Emotional—Observation of emotions through observing the physical effects produced.

B.   Experimenting by assuming an emotion contrary to what you feel, observe facial expressions of emotions in the glass, try to assume expressions simulating different states of feeling.

3.

A.   Intellectual—Observation of mental state through observing physical.

B.   Experiment in observing, creating mental state where observation may be stimulated, day dreaming may find a legitimate use here. There is a fourth of which we will speak later—this is used in the observation of all centers simultaneously.

4.

A.   Assume a role in which you think and move and act for the sole purpose of new and different observation.

If there is no wish to develop the I, even if the mentality has full understanding, it cannot come about. The wish lies within a few brain cells which when stimulated by self-observation begin to develop; it is always through the intellectual center that the first effort made.

Things which seem so even in appearance often are not so seen in a different aspect. For instance the figure which is Orage would lose its identity if whirled in space, a rotary motion would make everything seem round. Also a point in motion becomes a circle—a point like the end of a burning stick if held in the hand while running forward and rotated at the same time, would, to the person you are running towards appear as a cylinder or cone. So our whole solar system when viewed by an outsider might have very different appearance (from) that we imagined from our knowledge. I wonder if the rings around Saturn could be satellites going around very fast.

FURTHER DISCUSSION AS TO ESSENCE AND PERSONALITY

Essence is our inheritance and birth circumstances, the planetary and solar influences wore imposed upon us even in prenatal life. Essence expressed can often accomplish more than the acquired personality. In human relations when some break has occurred, matters may often be straightened out by speaking directly from essence to essence. The use of essence is likely to bring a response from essence, it is an infantile approach, it is really us speaking to what is really somebody else without the concealment or subtlety which experience and education has taught us to use. Essence can never be changed, it has potentialities which may be developed but everything must be in line with essence. It is presumable that essence is better than acquired characteristics although there are occasionally found very bad essences.

The musical scale with three tones, then semitone is used as an example of the difficulty in carrying thought consecutively through the scale and particularly over the semitone. When we get to mi in the scale a fresh effort is required to surmount the difficulty of the next note fa, which is now from point of view of attack. This is true of all effort. In the effort of thought all questions asked at groups should be formulated in rhythm to the thought under discussion, not in rhythm to things outside the scale, and better a scale sequence with extra effort of thought when we come to a semitone, which corresponds to an obstacle to be overcome before we can begin the next sequence. This effort is necessary in order that the discussion may not disseminate and die away. This often happens and distresses us when the beginning has promised so well. There may be said to be Jujitsu of the emotional and intellectual as well as the physical. By certain attitudes and approaches the adversary may succumb in an extraordinary way.

The following is an exercise for improving and awakening the memory. Take any common object, a box of matches for instance, observe it in its totality, that is, observe everything about it that it is possible to observe, everything that went to make it in its present form, where it all came from, etc. If this could all come to you as simultaneous observation you would be working in the fourth dimension or time. Complete consciousness would enable you to register consciously all you said, heard, touched at a moment, and then nothing would go to the subconscious. Subconsciousness is formed by the unconscious registering of all things which we have not sufficiently observed while registering takes place in our vision or other senses, to keep in our memory. We can however, recapture a subconscious memory by improving our observation. The above exercise is food for this particular department, it creates new energy for memory for instance, in reconstructing a scene of your childhood after several attempts, you may discover something in that scene which had registered at the time only in your subconscious but which comes back into memory after your exercises have been practiced for a time.

Concentric circles may be drawn, imagine your mechanism placed in the very center. This is Betty. She is surrounded by an instinctive, emotional and intellectual circle area and all the other circles are now empty which are the potentialities of her higher centers.

Mrs. L. asked if there was any knowledge of this technique having reached a high development at any particular point in the world's history? Orage

433

said about a quarter of a million years ago Babylon was a center for it, and through it had become the center of the world. He spoke of the fact that the handwriting of the people in the countries surrounding even pointed toward Babylon, that is, those living North wrote down, those South up, East to the left and those West to the right. Perhaps only coincident but certainly interesting. As I understand it comparatively few people need have the technique in order to influence their time. Those who are masters are catalytic in the sense that their thought continues to influence or change life without necessarily imparting the technique to all. Those actually able to do the work will always be few, but those, if enough, can affect the lives of many. To those who through the technique reach free will through consciousness, may be given the choice of re-incarnation, that is, instead of re-incarnating back into our own circle, we could chose our circumstances the value here too that we being prepared with the knowledge acquired of the method would be more fitted to carry it to a further development in a new re-incarnation. You may not be born into the world fully conscious, but after preparation in one life you may acquire it more quickly in another. Christ willed to reincarnate in human form that He might help man to consciousness, but He also had to work through to consciousness again though it came to Him very early.

If the method is continued long enough and with enough participants it will eventually lead to the world's attaining the do of a new octave instead of the retrograde it has always made on reaching its highest accomplishment. Orage said Christ had reached, as a spirit, the state of will where He could choose his re-incarnation. He chose to be the carpenter's son on this earth in order to help us regain consciousness. Doubtless He had Himself to learn again self-observation, through His approach through His higher centers made it easier.

All the planets, sun, moon, etc., look to the earth for food. The legend is that the moon is the earth's child, the mother earth is anxious for food for her child, moon food may be said to be derived from the pro-creative desire in man, it might be considered nature's or earth's moans of deceiving man into pro-creating for her purposes. Many attempts are made in nature for production and perpetuation of species, the perfection of the species seems to have nothing to do with it. It always the creative and not the evolutive idea in which nature is interested. The moon is not dead but just coming to life; vegetation is just beginning. Some day in the cosmic scale the moon will become an earth, the earth a sun, the sun a solar system, etc. For this purpose they require the food which must be produced by man's different centers and which in his present state he is unable to supply except through his instinctive, which is most highly developed.

We, as man, have three different kinds of food given us, that which our body takes in and digests, air which we take in our lungs, and impressions which are taken in through the brain. The food taken in our circulation through the ordinary process of eating and drinking are the liquids and solids, these well digested by our bodies are food for the instinctive center. Air which we take in and on which our emotions feed, we only partially digest, which we must learn to do much better with before the planets can get what they need from it. Impressions which our intellectual center takes in (but does not digest) the sun requires for food. We must assimilate these foods consciously and actively not simply passively, or they will never become the food necessary to the higher bodies for their development. Ordinary food scale when it reaches mi is helped over fa by the coming in of air, so it continues up the scale. Air scale goes to do, re, mi and should be helped over fa by as its entrance of impressions, but we digest no impressions there comes nothing to send it up.

Behind the moon there is perhaps another planet in formation, which will in time try to be a moon, the moon is trying to be an earth, the earth a sun, the sun a solar system (it is already a part of Hercules), the whole scale wishes to move up to the new note, and it waits for man to regain his consciousness, the loss of which we might call the fall of man through Satanic influence and it is still the Satanic influence or inertia at work which keeps us unconscious, and this we must overcome. The cosmic stream runs the other way from the earth stream; it is running down and we run up—it is our affair to start it running up again. It was just as difficult for Satan to lose consciousness as it is for us to gain it. He had to cross the fa semitone in order to get from the sun active to sun passive. His desire to create by himself brought him to earth and man's mechanism is the result. Satan was a spirit of the kingdom of God as God absolute includes all.

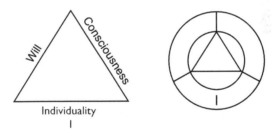

The above triangle made up of will, consciousness and individuality is the absolute in passivity, and as they become active, the meeting of will and consciousness makes individuality and the form of the triangle changes to diagram #2 and all the universes are governed by these laws. As the sun enters, that is governed by the laws of the universe, sun, planets etc., down so that the lower scale comes under many more laws, the divisions of the circle doubling with each new entry. This we find in the Athanasian creed.

Octaves begun in three ways always divide in seven, so much so that Plato introduced the word sevening. Orage suggested we make a vocabulary of words assuming a new meaning in connection with the technique.

Consciousness	Instinctive	Technique
Self-consciousness	Emotional	Bridge
Will	Intellectual	Semitone
Individuality	Impressions	Role
Essence	Realization	Man
Personality	I	Energy
Observation	She	Development
Awareness	Time	Effort
Time	Review	Positive
Simultaneity	Food	Negative
Scale	Imagination	Objective
Octave	Knowledge	Chief Features
Inertia	Cognition	Potentialities
Mechanism	Exercise	Attitude
Center	Group	
Brain	Method	

All men go to make up man's potentialities. The possibilities of every form of re-incarnations are manifested by all existing human life, we may become any one of these many any sort of man, woman, or child, whose life may be for only a month or a day. The sum total of all these experiences is the potentiality of man. There the whole of man can only be whole because of all the possibilities being included—good, bad, well, ill, maimed, poor, rich, lunatics, saints, ignorant, and intelligent. This is the Adam Cadman idea. As each man's consciousness is a part of God's consciousness, so each man's life forms part of Adam, or man, or physical life.

A similar idea is that every created object or condition is the manifestation of some wish, everything in the world is the expressed sum total of all wishes—there is nothing manifested without a wish from some quarter.

Imagine God's consciousness as a triangle filled with two hundred million triangles or a triangle for each human being in the world. Imagine God from time to time looking in a mirror, his thought reflected is made manifest, and humans or man is the thought of God. (c.f. Hermetic theory.) Mind of man in its relation to God may be considered as two thousand million triangles enclosed in the large triangle which symbolizes God—God is the highest form of conscious individuality and will. God has memory; the return of man to early stages is the manifestation of God's memory.

The active animates the masculine principle, and the passive the feminine. God is both male and female, celestial and terrestrial, the perfect image of

436

God is not man alone, but man-woman. Our body shows our relation to the universe as our bodies are similar to all systems of bodies. When thought separates from the Absolute, it becomes active; so consciousness is the first step to creation. Consciousness and will create individuality. In order to accomplish real creation in the human scale, the same system follows, the thought may create.

Digested impressions are knowledge or experience *realized*. So far our response to impressions through different centers are entirely mechanical, we respond from our experience or knowledge, but from nothing else. The only way to realize impressions is through self-observation. Impressions are also solar food, our possible contribution to the development of the sun. Negative emotions such as hate, fear, anger, etc. may be transmuted into higher motions, of which they are often the embryo. This is done by change of attitude. The amount of hate in the world is limited, there is only a certain amount. If by transmuting this into higher emotions through self-observation, we can diminish the supply, we are really diminishing the evil of the world, or stealing from the devil. Positive emotion may be increased by itself, and also by the transmuting of negative emotions into positive. In this way evil will, eventually be made good through the individual effort toward self-consciousness.

The great criticism of the League of Nations from this point of view was that it was simply a re-distribution of hate, and one individual who could consciously transmute a small part of hate into higher emotion has accomplished more for the benefit of mankind than any settlement of war conditions could possibly do. Christ brought the first brotherly love into the world, and by changing much of the hate into love, actually diminished the world's amount of existing hate.

All effort, or occupation, or daily routine, or duty, should be done, not alone for its end, but from all should be extracted a little food for consciousness, individuality and will. Every effort should be accompanied by observation, and a little super-effort, so that there is nothing that does not have its value outside its object, *over do it*. Christ said: "If your enemy asks you to go with him one mile, go with him twain." He meant always do more than is required. That which is necessary for the efficient accomplishment, and the extra for the development and food for "I".

The forth center is the Master Center. Without some development of this beyond what we already know, nothing in the way of real development can be attained. Growth is as different from development as hearing is from understanding. Exercises in self-observation are food for the fourth center. Be aware of yourself in as many different ways as possible at the same time, at all times. Be especially aware during times of emotional and intellectual activity, always observing the physical changes. In my own observation I so often am aware of a difference in temperature on part of my body, my left side in the area of about a foot feels as if a draft were blowing on it. My hands are often con-

437

tracted, my fists clenched, my shoulders hunched and rigid, this is fear. Again I feel a tingling in my extremities, or a sensation comes through the knuckles of my hands, as if there was melting wax in the joints.

Sensation, emotion, and cognition are as different from each other as cognition is from realization, which is the function of the fourth center. This center may be likened to a master gland which all the other glands contribute to.

Impressions are the combination of what we react to through the three centers which need the action of the fourth center to make them digestible. We receive about 90,000 impressions a minute, and have been doing so since the time of conception; they came through all our centers, but in the food scale they are food for our intellectual center, which is as yet too undeveloped to use them.

Essence is made of planetary influence and hereditary structure. We inherit nothing but structure, a structural peculiarity may decide the development of certain characteristics, but the ordinary inheritance idea is accounted for in this theory by personality influences.

Essence has ninety types arrived at by the combination of structure and planetary determination. The structural types are limited to twelve.

Everything is either running up or down the scale. Man is the highest animal in the organic kingdom. The scale turns metal, mineral, vegetable, invertebrate, vertebrate, monkey, man; super-man could only be in man's form. It is possible that some of the apes of today may have been men of a previous time retrograding.

The time taken for life development has been greatly underestimated; it must have taken infinitely longer than is generally supposed.

Orage in 1932, portrait by Thomas Cantrell Dugdale.

We are creatures of habit, of tradition, of education, we may wish to act differently, but our wills are not free. We behave according to the conditioning our environment has subjected us to, we are mechanisms, very perfect ones in many ways, but without the ability to perform in any but the prescribed form, we act or react always as it has been suggested we should act, either by example, tradition or education. It would be difficult to name one act of free will to locate one instance of unsuggested behavior. We have the potentiality, but at present free will, as understood by the Institute, has no part in the thing we call will, which is really only wish strengthened by tradition created or suggested by the impressions we have been receiving even before birth. We are unable to act apart from our conditioning.

Man as we know him is a mechanism, the realization of this is the first step in the direction of freedom from it.

It was asked how it was possible to determine, if one was with or without free will, and was it not possible that certain beings had reached this state of development without having acquired the method of the Institute. Orage sighted as an instance the response to anger. One with free will developed cannot be made angry, provided he wishes not to be. As we are now, with the best wish in the world to control anger it is impossible to do so if a determined attempt is made to upset our control by a skilled adversary. As we register in our physical center the reaction to our emotional, it is very difficult to feel anger and not to act it, one should try for purpose of experiment to express emotion by gesture, expression, etc. contrary to the one he is experiencing.

We cannot detach or disassociate ourselves from the mechanisms and reactions. We are at the mercy of all adverse winds. We know how a physical condition can affect our emotional and mental state, or how an emotional state may destroy our judgment, this shows the undesired influences that we are constantly subjected to against our wish or "will" as we call it. We are not reasoning beings, we are rationalizing beings, the process is we act first, then feel, then rationalize our feeling and action by our reason; it should of course go the other way. We should reason and then act. We are dependent on environment and suggestions from outside for our responses. We should be able to supply this stimulus to ourselves, to produce in our mechanism the desired result by our own suggestion and eventually to manage our reactions to all stimuli as we wish, even in direct opposition to the accepted responses.

No education along accepted lines can bring about these results. All knowledge as now understood is without significance in relation to the control of the mechanism; there is a way by which this robot may be controlled and used, by the development of a fourth center which may act as guide, philosopher and friend to the other three. Man is a three centered being with a potentiality of a fourth center; on the development of this fourth center

440

depends his possibility of free will; it is to the development of this center that the technique of the Institute is directed; there is a method of a theory, in the theory there is little that may not have been taught at previous times by various esoteric schools, but the technique according to Gurdjieff has never been taught before publicly.

Amos Pinchot

TIME. THE FOURTH DIMENSION.

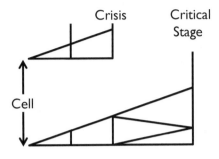

Crisis   Critical Stage

Cell

TIME TUBE

The crisis is birth. Before this is the long biological history of evolution. Afterwards the sociological phase—artificially made.

In critical stage a contraction sets in bringing one back to same point. Revert to infantilism. "Retreat back into the womb." (Freud.)

Begin with the single seed, then babe and old age. With which form do you identify yourself? Always the same "I." Fourth dimension is the ability to see simultaneously all the forms through which you have passed. It presupposes an excellent memory and an ability to recollect all the images through which you have passed. Always try to look at objects in fourth dimension. This gives inexhaustible interest.

Physically nature takes care of our body, but it doesn't take of our three brains. Education and experience take care of that.

I am the most hateful and despicable person I know. How could I lose my temper with anyone else?

Our emotions grow up as they are evoked not by recalled images but by real objects. Shelley's Skylark.

Unless the individual today can develop his potentialities the race cannot. The potentialities of the race are inherent in the individual today.

There are not only vestigial but also anticipatory organs for which no function is known.

O	Consciousness
O	Individuality
O	Will

Consciousness of self, as opposed to consciousness of outside world, requires effort.

Self-responsibility. Personality. These Qualities must be acquired.

Will is the energy to carry out that which you are conscious of. We are passive to images.

LECTURE 6

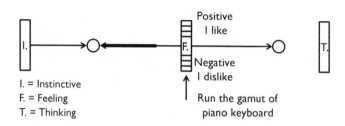

I. = Instinctive
F. = Feeling
T. = Thinking

All the sensations we receive, we either like or dislike. Negative reaction spends energy without benefit to self. It is a dead loss, devitalizing and diminishing value, whereas positive enhances value.

1 center beings—reptiles
2 center beings—mammals
3 center beings—man

The third class classifies, says is it right or wrong. Judgment enters. It implies comparisons. You can't help making them, but it is possible in third center to make conscious judgments.

We each have three centers or brains. See above diagram.

1. It is the storehouse of images since birth, 10 senses, 10,000 sense impressions per sec. Not only received but classified, even in infancy or before consciousness. We have been the victims. Idealism is the conditioning of these impressions since childhood.

Plotinus is example of super conscious intellect.

Imagination is the source of material upon which thought acts. Feeling is a classification of sensations into I like or dislike. St. Francis of Assisi is an example of emotional super-consciousness. Manifest the opposite of what you feel as an experiment. Yogi.

When I observe, the corresponding impression I receive is 3-fold. Thus as the higher centers are filled simultaneously we begin to develop them. Read "The Way of Buddha," by Woodward, Oxford Press, chapter—"The Only Way"—"Not by fasting, intellectual devotion—when you are walking, breathing, etc., be aware of whatever the body is doing. This alone is the way of salvation."

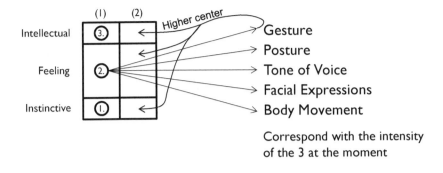

	(1)	(2)	Higher center	
Intellectual	③.	←		→ Gesture
Feeling	②.	←		→ Posture
				→ Tone of Voice
Instinctive	①.	←		→ Facial Expressions
				→ Body Movement

Correspond with the intensity
of the 3 at the moment

LECTURE 7

No offense at anything anyone can tell you about yourself; surprise is that you haven't known it. Scarred faces. Sting of offense, at self-pride. There is no sting if you know it is true. This is key to youth. Story of Socrates when someone told him he was a braggart, liar etc., and he answered—shake hands—I congratulate you. His recognition shows that they either no longer existed or else they were under control.

Diagnose yourself then find out what is to be done. You come to the state where you find yourself worthless, in utter pessimism, no good for anything. Has exactly opposite effect when discovered by yourself, at last you can be yourself as a child—natural, incapable of remorse or regret. Affectation is gone. *Cannot fall any longer. Chance to rise higher.*

Object of study: our self.

Technique: such a study as we would use on anyone else.

You cannot help another person until you have become the person to be helped. Teachers impart to students only their own prejudices unconsciously. The subjective element is so great that none is to be trusted with the lives of others until he has studied himself in the same objective manner.

Psycho-analyst treats patient for the same complex he himself has. You stand better chance if you do the opposite to what he advises. Cast out the beam (self ignorance) in your own eye first. Means of casting out is self examination. Say you do not belong to me nor I to you.

How can you call up the image of this past self? It depends largely on your mood at the time—elation or depression.

Negatives. You are worried. Go to mirror. "I see how I look when I worry." Then walk up and down room, note where you feel constriction. Hello, hello, where is the worry? Negative emotion is whatever is for you an unpleasant state. The proof of this practical psychology is the thing itself. Moment you begin to observe, the state itself disappears if negative, or is enhanced if positive.

445

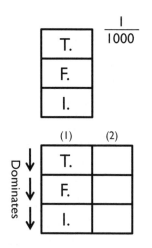

Everyone's portrait

For 99/1000 of day we are concerned with our emotional states.

For 9/10 we are doing things.

We are not concerned with 1, but with 2. Self-consciousness dominates T., F., and I., through the observing center "I."

LECTURE 8

I am the being for whom I am responsible, whatever the effort. There walks the being for who's present, past and future I am most concerned. Yet a very ordinary person, not so colossally important. Presented the picture of all dead within 100 years hence. For each breath we take someone is dying, someone is being born.

Our imagination becomes merely a hoping that all will go well. But in form, mind, emotion, being what is it we shall become?

Idealometer—instrument for measuring ideals which exactly indicates the kind of mentality, emotional experience, the kind of person you wish to become so many years hence. I wish to be—?—Resistance to facing these issues about ourselves is strong. We would rather study others, what steps are we taking to become that which we wish? What is the means?

		Now	*Means*	*Hence*
1	T.	1. We can judge fairly well. We are in the	1. Awareness.	4
2	F.	provincial slums.	2. Non-identification.	5
3	I.	2. In the city slums. Go through list of emotions. Check. 3. Adaptability to physical circumstances.	3. Experiment.	6

446

To what extent am I indebted to chance for my present position? What would a change in my present position—war, earthquake, loss of fortune,—do to me? What is your ambition in the future to be more of than it is now, principally? Modern philosophers say: in human animals it is—

The wish to live.

The wish to live well.

The wish to live better.

We cannot change without effort. Time doesn't do it, which is after nature has turned us out.

Knowledge of any kind is no indication of mental power. Test your resources; one day no money, no food, no friends. You will do either the drastic or the homeopathic. If the drastic, one experience of this sort and nothing can rumple even ripple your emotional center.

For above diagram under heading means:

Step 1: To be aware. Art, religion, science, success in business, achievement in writing, etc., all propose means for man's betterment. Likewise schools of mysticism, will power etc. All overlook the obvious—always do. What are *you* depending on to make this change? Cards down. What is your trump card? Ah, only a low one, a species of false deception.

Step 2: Non-identification. This is to regard the organism as not yours. The behavior of your body is not yours. It is determined by Biology and Sociology. Not one cell in your body have you made or controlled, not even the part of your hair. Truly you are no part of your body or of your behavior. *Goal* is use of personality by individuality.

Step 3. Experiment. Nobody learns except by experiment, purposive experiment. All experience leaves "I" where it was, except when it is positive and purposive instead of passive and incidental. Experiment is an intended experience. Constantly experiment—every form that ingenuity can devise.

Suggested experiments:

Hold cigarette in other hand. Walk down street by another route. All experiments are in the direction of a change of habits. Those that don't matter. Begin on habits that are relatively indifferent, not those that are good or bad. Observe to find how strong your habits are, how hard it is to change them, how almost impossible.

LECTURE 9

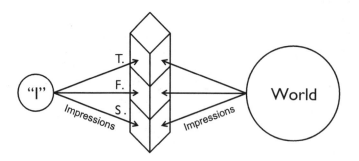

T.—Thinking cube.

F.—The wishing cube. Our wishes are to repeat or to have. Simply the future tense of liking or disliking.

S.—Our moving cube.

Thought is a comparison for likenesses and differences. Question of like does not enter into that. They differ merely in degree.

Normal being—one who has control of body, has likes and dislikes and can make comparisons. S.F.T. That which makes for difference is our like or dislike. Our type is the one we do most—T., F., or S. (S is concerned with body—its comforts, likes etc.) But we all have the same kind of structure.

"I"—our flatterer. Only a possibility, at present inside us and not an external thing as shown here, we isolate it and give it something to do that it cannot do in the body. Byron: "The Mountains look on the Marathon, and Marathon looks on the sea." Thus as Marathon so is "I" the medium, "I" can observe the body and all its actions. The body can see the external world, while "I" cannot. Only through the body can "I" see the external world. The reports it sees of external world depends on character of body, disused, abnormal, etc. May see it distorted. "I" observes the reactions of the external world on the body to which it is attached.

Self-consciousness is the ability of "I" to be aware of what is happening in the body. It is the state of "I" when aware of this body when in contact with world. It is the state in which "I" can discriminate states of consciousness.

1.	T.	F.	I.
2.	Light	Heat	Power.

We distinguish between 1. in the same way we do between 2.

Consciousness looks on external world. Self-consciousness looks on consciousness.

The impressions collected in the three accumulators are in accord with the images we collect. They depend on chance circumstances of where my movie house finds itself. Full, rich, empty, infantile, etc., collects automatically. Our personality, conditioned by heredity and environment, its content is by chance determined, according to its experiences. Through "I" there is no element of chance. Through "I" there is awareness or chance to learn how it works, and through this we move from submissive to active state and are able to direct it according to will. "I" starts at an invisible point and is not subject to analysis. "I" grows as any germ does—it must receive appropriate food.

1. Ordinary food
2. Air
3. Impressions

Exclude any one and we die. Once the conception of "I" begins, it develops only by proper food.

All our thoughts, feelings and habits have been conditioned. Our thoughts are merely a register of the contacts we have had since birth, no originality. Thus we have the normal biography of each person.

"I" and personality differ in:

1. Food it receives it must take as in pre-natal period. Positive in regard to it.
2. Food the organism receives must be from external world.

Heredity gives a start but growth depends on environment. The food of "I" does not come from our external world. It comes from impressions taken of the organism. Must not be passive. Always positively engaged in taking impressions. Thus develops consciousness, individuality, and will. This is the truly self-made individual, not the accidental. The Hindu is: Sons of their own work. Heredity and environment have nothing to do with development of "I".

External world. What it is, no one knows or can know. It has reality but no actuality. It is created or conditioned by the form of our organism. We see the illusion through colored glasses, but it is otherwise through "I." "I" grows by observing the organism in contact with the world. You will know as much of reality as you know of yourself. It is the effect of the world on the thing you know, by self-observation, non-identification, and experiment. We learn of others through observation of their behavior. By the same method you will and must learn to know your own existence and character. Take yourself as a stranger and be introduced. You are curious, and lay siege to your own symptoms. The judgment is in "I."

Only conscious impressions are deposited in "I." At present the master of the organism is in the external world. Now "I" is neutral. As we make it positive it begins to compete with external world and gradually takes the place of the external world. "I" then circles the cube. "I" is comparable to divinity. (Body is the temple of God.) "I" proposes to play the role of God. Body must

449

become the slave of "I" and not of the world. It is subjective not to the world but to "I."

Result of any action will be good if you observe yourself in the action. Let the organism do what it likes under the condition that you observe it. The organism is negative, inert, never wishes to do anything, but that there is in me an emotional center subject to impressions of external world.

Employ some device to help yourself to remember to be aware. Tomorrow is a disease of the will.

I have a body.

I am a soul.

"I" is indifferent to any wish or ambition of the organism. Under the method the wishes, etc., will probably disappear; the organism will change.

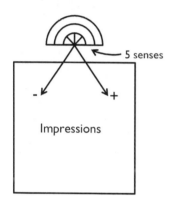

5 senses

Impressions

Deposited in the mind as an image.
Memory. Imagination is power of images received through our senses—colored by our emotions.

LECTURE 10

Our personality is constantly undergoing change with each day's experiences. Can I not regulate my books, ideas, actions, etc.? No. The sum of your I.T.E. to date will be your I.T.E. tomorrow. We defy you to change, but at the same time we do change, though not of ourselves—as the man who trims a tree. This change now is not under personal control, it does not flatter us.

Habits are good that adapt the organism, not to immediate but to any circumstance in which it may find itself. That being is most normal which is adapted to his environment—epitome of health if psycho-analysis. Criticism. Adaptation may be to a degenerate society. Ill-adaptation to bad society is no disgrace. May be disadvantageously good or bad. Merely adapt organism to immediate circumstances.

What is value of organism to himself? Do you live for society or for your own good and welfare? Two different values:

If for my good: criteria—is it for my personal advantage?

If for society's good: criteria—is it for public advantage?

We should reckon ourselves not in terms of the trifles we accomplish, but the mountains we leave untouched—the ideal—that which is possible.

The ideal portrait	At moment of conception		At 45?
●	○	◐	Newspaper chatter.
●	○	◔	Family quarrels.
●	○	◑	Aspirations after games etc. Theatre representations.

Every individual is capable of accomplishing 100% of original potentiality, but the hereditary endowment may differ—the sizes of centers not identical.

120 gospels existed after death of Jesus. We have four selected by church. Commission had instructions to destroy every other gospel. See: Fragments of a Faith Forgotten. Jesus conducted a gymnasium class for his disciples. Portrait we have now is grotesque. He was a 3—3—3, not divine.

Object of experiment is to be able to do or regulate five forms of your behavior irrespective of attack of other person. It is the five forms of others you react to—not what it said. Jesus: turn other cheek—because you are in such control of your behavior. *I* am the way, the truth and the life etc. Grotesque that Jesus set himself up to be imitated. He taught principle "I." Don't follow me. Jesus is an oddity.

I observe about your house but I have a workshop, and an artist's studio, where I can manipulate and feel, and an academy where I can think. A mansion, not in the skies. A temple was not a church but a place for crafts, art, etc., something for I.T.E.

He who shall lose himself shall find himself. Give up the attachment to the person who bears your name. Treat him no better or worse than another stranger—with these eyes you can see on the whole you are a hate-able person. Unless a man hate himself he cannot love God, cannot be identified with God.

Aesthetic emotion is the one which includes all positive and negative emotions—it is ecstatic and agonizing, the total feeling of emotional center.

Consciousness is simultaneous awareness of all the thoughts you can think.

Intuition is the body's remembrance of all the states it has experienced.

What happened to Jesus from age of fifteen to twenty-nine? He went to Egypt, etc., to school. He taught three years and then retired.

451

Buddha remembered history of all cells of body, hence stories of his many lives, frogs, etc.

LECTURE 11

New Year Resolutions—reason for being for one year. Vow to accomplish something you have wished—something pleasant—worth living to have accomplished.

Psychic wealth—the entertainment of a strong wish necessitating health.

What would you wish to accomplish this year supposing it were given as your last. It is not a task—involves no rearrangement of your life. Includes all three or part of them.

A wish emotionally to succeed.

A wish materially to succeed.

A wish that the work will have social value.

An honorable work for man to discharge, however no sacrifice of his pleasure or profit. Our sins are that of omission. Resolutions shall be superfluous—nothing happens if we do not keep them. Something that would give great delight when accomplished.

Kill suppressed wishes by taking them out and gratifying them.

Essential wishes are:

Each morning a task of the day.

Related to a task of the week;

Related to a task of the month;

Related to a task of the year.

O	S – – O Exp. N – – L I	O
O	Suffering	O
O	Tasks	O

No negative emotions—suffer purposively.

Be able to give at any moment what you are doing toward that purpose.

To follow likes and dislikes one has no reason for being—children. In grown-ups these likes and dislikes are subordinate to your reason.

Money is the blood of society. Natural that the individual should desire to possess. He doesn't—then rationalizes—beginning of psychological decadence. Money is power sociological speaking.

Vow indicates a regime under which one becomes a slave to a resolution. A like is not a wish. Likes and dislikes are states. Wishes are dynamic.

In ordinary consciousness we are conscious of environment. In self-consciousness we are conscious of self—aware of organism, which is itself registering the effect of external world. Object of this method is the attainment of self-consciousness, an active consciousness of the behavior of one organism. Beyond there is cosmic consciousness, the ability to see both external world and ones organism in relation. In Bible, this is called the Open Vision.

Read "The Conquest of Illusion." Van der Leeuw.

Realize value of values.

Realize deficiency of will.

Profitable and pleasurable New Year—in so far as it is real profit and pleasure.

LECTURE 12

KING SOLOMON'S SEAL

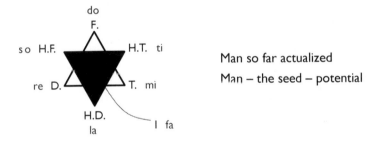

Man so far actualized

Man – the seed – potential

Potentiality is not the ideal but the means on the way to being realized. Similar to a plant not yet in blossom. Man is a being not yet fully actualized—he is as a plant—stem, leaves, and bud, but not arrived at blossom, seed and fruit. He is in the state of becoming. An animal in general is a completed being, man is incomplete. We differ now little from animal except in potentialities—several arrows in our sheath. Our completeness compares rather badly with animals—grace of movement etc. We can claim superiority on the basis of potentialities which animals do not possess.

In diagram we used the word "being" instead of "feeling." Feeling is in the sphere of being. Matter that reacts as if it felt—the characteristic of being is feeling. Beings are ranked in a certain scale according to the variety, complexity and coordination of their functions. Man to ape etc.

	do	
	re	
	mi	
Self-willed or externally induced	fa	Shock from outside or unusual exertion on part of person, or something must happen to enable transition from upper to lower triad.
	sol	
	la	
	si	Progress for man—3 center being, absolutely depends on his ability to do make transition. Otherwise being remains at point of beating his wings at mi.
	do	

Note the pathos and tragedy of man at mi, repeating mi—mi—mi. Doomed to state of a recurring decimal.

Telephones, cars, etc., do not make us superior biologically. Race in present day inferior—atrophied in organism by development through mechanical means. Our method opposite. Must have a new start—an *Initiation*. No man by taking thought can add an inch to his stature. Associations. Awareness is not associated with T., F. or I.

Bridge—The Way—Buddha—Christ.

It is only "as if" one were listening as to another person. I do not hear myself as if you hear me. No T., F., or I.

Not startling—emotional.

Not illuminating—intellectual.

Not movement—physical.

You begin to realize you are dropping into lower triad—but no cessation. It would be one form of Yogi if any center became inactive.

B.—Individuality—man no. 1

K.—Consciousness—man no. 2

D.—Will—man no. 3

Differentiation is complexity, variety, and coordination of functions.

Fa is a bridge—method is self-awareness. Man no. 4.

Blossom, seed, and fruit develop both simultaneously and successively.

Being—to knowing—to doing.

Government:

do—democracy

re—monarchy

mi—theocracy

The "I" converts from one triad to another. The Yogi jump from one center to another and remain there. No. 1. Development of "I" depends on development of 3 centers.

No matter what one is in search of—it is really more consciousness, not the object itself.

People appreciate art but not the same situations in life. Artificial art center. Pseudo-emotional life cultivated that is symbolic of real life. Should be an emotional life developed not through art but life. High form simultaneously seeks variety, complexity and coordination of experience—3 centers ¾
¾ Leonardo da Vinci.

Law of 3 prevails in essence.
Law of 7 prevails in organism.
Know the effect you intend to produce.
Mechanical monkey—conscious man.
Evolution—man no. 1 to man no. 2—pseudo to real.
Turning back—Lot's wife.

LECTURE 13

Your ideas, etc., will be carried out to a greater degree according to the extent to which your being is changed. Knowing and doing are by-products of being. Do not try to know and do more or better. Try to be more and you will as a result know and do more.

Our three brains—cerebral, spinal and visceral—are each run on a certain energy—light, heat, and power. We are a factory run on the three centers, but there is another wiring system in our organism, analogous but not identical; it is self-observation, a totally new form of energy. Its effect on the other energies is catalytic.

Energy of 3 centers must be expended each day; it does not evaporate. If it is not expended or does not function as intended, it manifests itself to the detriment of the organism as a whole, we get: imagination instead of thought, fantasy instead of feeling, physical pleasure instead of organic enjoyment.

Glands—associated with each center—are reservoirs which come to one's rescue when one has voluntarily expended all one's energy. This is second wind—273 glands in body.

All organisms are machines chemically constructed for the transfer of energy.

Sentimentality is an escape of emotional gas, but not through the center for which it was intended. Most brutal and hard-boiled are sentimental of necessity. On this phase of the subject Freud's work is authoritative.

Cure for being run-down is more work, but of the kind that has not been employed. The plane on which you are lazy is the plane on which you suffer insomnia. I., F., T. Something is wrong if you dream. You have spent the previous day badly.

Most imagination is fancy. Difference between heart and solar-plexus is the difference between the wrong and right use of emotional energy.

Meaning and Aim of Existence. Answer according to:

I — *Instinctive reason*	II — *Emotional reason*	III — *Objective reason or instinctive*
1. God is an indulgent Father of his children. He wishes them happiness.	1. Soul a. Christian b. Mohammedan c. Buddhism d. Brahmanism e. Confucianism etc.	
2. God, the stern-lawgiver, rewards and punishes. Supposition: he is a judge		
3. God's way of teaching us — school for development of character.		
Relation of God to body	Relation of God to soul	

Existence — That continuity of being exhibited in a waking state of consciousness.

III. Presupposes man is a being in the state of becoming, that be shall unfold the potentialities actual in him. This makes for health. Nothing to punish him. No one else cares about him. Otherwise he is a failure — futile waste.

Aim is the realization of our potentialities. Waking state is of use insofar as it helps that aim.

The history of all religion and folk-lore has been from 3 — 2 — 1.

LECTURE 14

Sheep give wool and mutton for their existence. Human beings give? We exist for some purpose different from that we imagine we exist. Higher mind is the ability to use the lower mind. Ability to think what you will, as long as you wish, toward a defined end. What are you thinking about? Why?

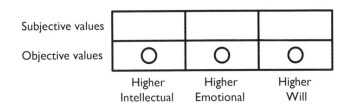

Set off in minus and plus sings the emotions you have for one day. Note the loss of capital—energy.

Regulation—always do the opposite of what you feel if it is unpleasant. Manifest the opposite. Save yourself against being chick-pecked. Express opposite opinion. Defy those events, lie to them. At that moment it becomes true. Example—cold coffee. Only lie really is the mechanical reaction of your organism. At the end of the day you will be fresh, glowing with energy. Good exercise for two weeks.

Next step: Go in search of uncomfortable situation—eagle pecks. Defy anything or anyone to bore or not to interest you. Difference between adult and child. Higher center has control, through this method, of lower center or emotion.

Third step: Higher will, the most difficult of all. Making your body do what you wish it to do. Higher will controls our physical behavior.

These three higher centers are the objective values for which man wishes to exist.

From common soldier to:

Lieutenant of Higher Intellect, and from this to

Captain of Higher Emotion, and from this to

General of Higher will.

Mind—emotion—will, is the order of development. Otherwise it is pathological. Blossom, seed and fruit. Simultaneously filled out but successively developed. See diagram Lecture 6.

In all the occult schools there is a method, a variant of Yogi—one of the three centers. Proper food in our method is not a variant; it is novel—to be aware.

Man has three centers. That is smallest epitome of law of economy.

Both the theory and practical understanding of emotional theory set forth is required. Castaway is one who has the theoretical understanding, but no practical application. All the emotions are in pairs—married unhappily - each exists at the expense of the other.

All things to all people. People impel you to act mechanically.

LECTURE 15

Subconscious interests—unfilled wishes, ungratified interests—perhaps one reason why we continue to live. This is the magnetic center, the nucleus of your psychology that has not yet unfolded itself; it has received no food. Wishes, aspirations, hopes, unformulated because unconscious, no stimulus to make them conscious. Consciousness is merely an aid to the fulfillment of wishes. We are as animals using tools in the aid of our instincts. Only as they are brought into consciousness and become explicit can we aid their development. When a question is clearly formulated you are in a short distance of an clear answer.

When "I" is in a state of body he is said to exist.

When "I" is in a state of body he is said to being.

"I" is self-conscious when you identify with:

"I" is self-conscious and non–identify with:

O	O	O	H.C.

Then there is a conscious continuity with all states of existence.

Psychological ability to understand is limited and conditioned as is one's ability to understand, e.g. higher physics. This statement was an answer to a question to show it would be useless to answer it.

Difference between being and existence is not one of 'higher' but one of being totally different.

Means to knowledge is when you can become aware of this being carrying your name, then you know state of being, self-consciousness. Must have non-identification, otherwise you are still in existence.

Read Julian the Apostle (Apostate) story of the Prodigal Son. The Hymn of the Robe of Glory.

In all religious forms they worship the model and forget the method. Jesus did not set himself up as a model.

Pistis Sophia.

The emphasis of this lecture was on the necessity for formulation.

When one is truly objective there is no fear. Thus religion that has no fear must be objective. The objective approach rules fear out of religion. (W. J. M.)

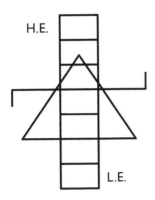

Ladder of scale of being.
Higher emotions are related to mind.
Lower emotions are related to body.
Look up list of emotions in Thesaurus.

A seed is now a tree in point of being, but it is not a tree in point of becoming. Process of actuality is important. Life is the principle of actualizing the potential.

Read Santayana's—The Realm of Essence.

Lower emotions are states of body, while higher emotions are states of mind such as ecstasy, bliss, inspiration, adoration, revelation.

Higher emotions have no opposites.

We experience higher emotions only vicariously through literature. (Here is something to live for, W. J. M.)

An emotion is an impulse to act.

The body passes back to the elements. What you have become in association with or as the proprietor of the body is important.

LECTURE 18

Waking state of consciousness—awareness of external world through sense contact plus psychological objects or processes taking place in myself, e.g. pain. When our present state of consciousness is not closely defined we imagine self-consciousness to be similar. It is as different as consciousness in sleeping and waking state. The psychological processes of which we may be aware are: varieties of sensation, of emotion, and of thought. Through this psychologists say there is no self, since all these experiences can be analyzed. To modern Psychology self is an illusion. We include the object our own body, the one we identify ourselves with, but of which biologically we are not responsible for not a single cell. Difference between an inanimate chair and an animate body is that the animation of the body is external. I reign over it but do not govern. I inhabit but do not control it. No difference between you and a tree except what you make, yet we call this body self. Self-consciousness is awareness of objects including your own body. In ordinary waking consciousness we are aware of all objects except body. In self-observation we are aware of both.

459

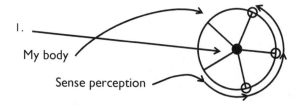

When I am aware of my body I am beginning to be self-conscious. As slowly as a child's sense develops so does awareness of self develop. In selecting our body we are trying at same time to divert attention from anything metaphysical, which is selection of thoughts and not records of facts. It is a drug. It is often hypnosis. We say there is no psychology, no divinity, no higher self. There is a concrete, the self we all see, on which we must concentrate. There is no other self. Yourself is your body.

If the energy is not used in awareness, it is used otherwise in tensions etc. A table has one wish, to retain form which only time can destroy. Animals and savages have self-consciousness, but they have not attained it. It is mechanical. Ours is an attained art that rescues us from nature.

Examples of great art. Taj-Mahal, early Gothic Cathedrals, Leonardo's Virgin of the Rocks, Chinese painting, The Tiger of the 14th Century, Pyramids, Sphinx, etc.

Aesthetic emotion is when simultaneously you feel very acutely feeling of anguish of state of your own insignificance and at the same time the grandeur of life. So glorious, you are identified with totality of life and of nothing. It is our own nothingness in relation to universe and the magnificence of universe itself.

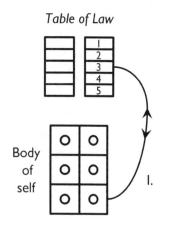

Table of Law

I alone am capable of adhering to rules of objective morality. Orage alone can adhere to laws of conventional morality. Division of consciousness is necessary to pass from convent to objective morality.

LECTURE 20

Question asked: What is God?

If you can ask question, you can speculate to some intelligible answer. Why does this planet exhibit so extraordinary a spectacle as the swarm of living beings on its surface?

Common answers

1.   Chance—Bertrand Russell.

2.   Cooperating with the forces of evolution. Breeders of pigs exercise more care than human beings.

3.   Can you conceive of a being for whom we are sheep; we exist for his well-being or advantage. He is a being, who for his own sake breeds human beings on this continent for his own profit.

If one cannot give a reason for being, I strongly suspect he is being used. Am I living merely that I shall be ripe when I did.

It is impossible to permanently maintain a state of happiness.

Society changes our likes into don't likes, and our don't likes into likes, that is it changes our likes to the extent that as a social being I am at a loss. This is good and evil. But this like and dislike through sociological pressure is changed to: yes I like it but I mustn't and yes I don't like it but I must. This induces in us a conventional morality. The child with its native likes and dislikes subject to this do and don't becomes a mere slave to its elders.

Objective morality passes from:

1. Standard of judgment "I like or dislike it."

2. Standard of my neighbor's or society's approval.

It is objective because it doesn't depend on the subject. Example as in mathematics 2 x 2 is 4.

Herbert Spencer: That is true, the opposite of which cannot be proved.

Mathematics is discovery, not an invention.

Objective morality is discovery, not an invention.

We may be at the dawn of an understanding of objective morality just as 300 years ago there was a flash—a dawn of a new mathematics—perhaps a rediscovery.

There is a type of understanding of mathematics, so there is a type who can understand objective morality. Either you have it or you have not. Conscience is to your objective morality exactly what a mathematical bent is to mathematics. There is no understanding without this. "Conscious" is as if when you pursue a certain discussion you find certain things by the way, which if you went another way, you would not have discovered because you never follow the same route again. Consciousness in objective morality is the same as mathematical understanding to mathematics. Consciousness is that which remains in your consciousness when the likes and dislikes in yourself and your neighbor have been set aside. Subordination of individual and social likes and

461

dislikes leaves practically nothing, but through the consciousness one has a criterion we can use and employ.

Conscience plays the same function toward being that good health does toward physical well being.

Your *essence* is the nucleus or entity which remains after you have been stripped of all heredity and environment. It itself wishes to be. It may be static, even eventually incapable of movement. It may die. It is still in being.

PRINCIPLES OF OBJECTIVE MORALITY

This is addressed to us now not as children of our parents, environment etc., but to the nucleus, etc., of this being entrusted with or given a body thanks to parenthood and environment.

1. Preservation and maintenance of body. You shall as a being preserve intact and always efficient for your use the body you have received. You shall keep it in working order for the development of your being. It is not enough for the being to preserve body for the efficiency of *one* of his brains, example Shaw, but in all respects, that is for all brains. Not ascetic for it would be at the expense of other brains.

2. Must be a conscious endeavor of individual to understand meaning and aim of existence. It is one of the conditions for the beings fulfilling his wish to become. Incumbent on him to discover as quickly as possible and fulfill the aim implicit in him to become. As everything in the egg points to the caterpillar, everything in the caterpillar to the chrysalis, and everything in the chrysalis to the butterfly —but there is no indication of the next stage—so the being we are has a forward looking sense of being or becoming. Conscience is a criterion of ways through which one must pass, a realization of the being that has become.

3. Being must aim at the next stage, that is, self-consciousness. You may attempt cosmic-consciousness, but beware of skipping the chrysalis stage.

4. Love of Kind. All beings have affinities, consequently each being must assist other beings, first and foremost those of its own kind.

5. Becoming must be for sake of a collectivity of all beings—God. God is the sum of living beings on this planet—knowing no other planet. Nothing metaphysical. Everyone is God, though not a part of him.

LECTURE 21

What you do outside of observation is caused by heredity, environment and provocation. To sweep the floor objectively is worth the writing of three literary masterpieces.

None of us can think, because to think implies the ability to maintain the posture of mind irrespective of external stimuli. Our behavior is determined by sense impressions over which, in our inability to think, we have no control. We are without realization of Robot state as in R.U.R.

In Behaviorism (Watson) everything we do is conditioned by heredity and sociological stimulus. All these things can be shown by scientists. The causes can be shown to have existed before. Marriage relationships are thus determined. The Agnostics said: we are examples of a procession of fate.

Eternal Recurrence—Nietzsche or The Wheel of Life—Buddha.

"Sin" in the New Testament comes from Sinai. Mean you see the vision of, and get understanding of Promised Land—the ability to act originally and not mechanically.

Moon governs life on this planet.

Read the last word of Freud, Myth of the Ego. It represents his most profound thoughts. Final conclusion is that neurotics are only exaggerated examples of everybody. All suffer one disease, inability to realize truth of their existence, thought, feeling and action are beyond their control so we try every form of compensation, flattering and praising ourselves and others.

The mental part of our behavior is easy to understand, while emotion and physical are not, because they are not directly related to mind. Specific—self-consciousness. An approximation in point of age or state of development of all 3 centers. What you do you also think, and feel whole. This is the difference between a reactive entity and an active entity.

One thing I can do you cannot do: be aware of myself doing things. One cleverness is accidental—Song of Nightingale and that of Jack Daw. They can't help it. Similarly prose style.

All one's income is spent on body. Our God is here in the flesh—Miller. Immaculate conception by parents, brought up in Egypt in bondage, and I worship him. No one more irreligious than religious and vice versa. No use for God, all his time is taken up with his God himself—of which he is fanatical. Thou shalt have no other gods before me. Philosophy, education, etc., is concerned with welfare of body in this life. Religion concerns itself with the soul and possible immortality. This method is often referred to as religious because it concerns itself with the soul, but we haven't one, only the possibility of achieving one. Souls are self-created. Nature gave us a body, the materials, a work-shop in which it may be fashioned. We are only trees, but trees half-grown; we have not yet produced seed. This seed we call the soul. Should the body be so conditioned that the body grows upon or in it, then the soil should survive and have the ability to manifest the same properties again. Fresh for a new tree. Condition of a seed is that it must be detachable or separate from the tree. L. differentiate between potential and actual soul. Egg and potential chicken. Figure of the Indian string of beads—soul and its descendants, successive incarnations. Ready to shoulder responsibility of your share of the collective life of this planet.

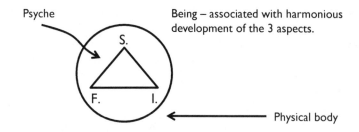

Theory is constancy of choice. Gandhi makes it one. Being is the right proportions between T. F. S. The Trinity.

Carlyle—There is no Falstaff in Christ.

LECTURE 22

Lecture opened with interpretation of word cult.

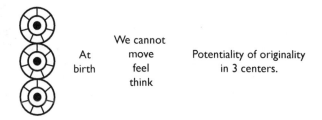

They become filled beginning with first experience. Behaviorism shows there is no freedom of choice in movements, gestures etc. Unconsciously habituated, 1 and 2 are pure automatism. In 3 we pride ourselves of having a little free-will, but no more can we think what we please then we can feel or do. It is all predetermined.

Words are the only evidence of thinking. Association between words and ideas is great. Our ideas are limited by vocabulary. Enlargement of vocabulary is enlargement of ideas, without enlargement of vocabulary there can be no new ideas. Thus "cult" depends on association in which already heard. This automatic process is what we call thinking. It is really a process of sound, not mental but verbal, having as its basis sound. You are so conditioned you believe yourself in nothing you think, feel or do, you merely react in vocabulary, feeling and muscular history. It is merely a process taking place in you. What truly constitutes each? That is, is there any escape from our present automatic state? The blind man's first answer to Jesus was I see men as trees walking. We are all vegetables as Behaviorists say, no difference from trees—only in form.

Are we biologically condemned as a special species of vegetable kingdom? Of three forms of reaction, or is it possible to really think, feel, and do? Behaviorists overlook or rather underlook hereditary element. A man convinced against his vocabulary is of the same opinion still. Read "Human Body" by Glendenning. Excellent. Also Sir Arthur Keith's "Engines of the Body."

We do nothing, everything is done in us. There is no originality. It comes only as we do something other than what we are accustomed to.

An animal is distinguished from vegetable in that it goes in search of its prey. Motor. Difference between man who T. F. and D's originally and not reactionally is also that he goes in search of something. According to Behaviorism, since I am a reactionary being, it makes no difference whether prisoner or free. Conditioned to freedom.

Recall certain things about which you are sure, certain, and use that criterion to determine certainty of new experience, belief, etc.

Thinking Originally

1. Non-mechanically—not foreseen, not predictable or implicit.

We can predict what a machine will do. Unexpected or non-conditioned. In doing it is obvious that we are mechanical.

2. In all circumstances act in a way that you have never acted before, never repeat. Exercise initiative in devising new methods, in contrast to repetition. Repetitive versus initiative. Incalculable. Distinguishes living beings from machines. This may be a new form of habit but it is non-habitual. Essence of non-mechanical is the non-repetitive. Habit is the repeated.

Originality

It shall have an aim—effort on part of individual to attain something. This is its second characteristic. First is non-mechanical.

Man by nature is an originating force in universe. He is not mechanical, but he has come there through circumstances. He is in essence a creator, an originator. Aims to avoid repetition not for sake of repetition but for something else, person trying to become conscious makes as many mistakes as anyone else only he doesn't repeat them. "If a fool is to persist in his folly he will become wise." (Blake) "10.00 to a man who calls you a liar."

LECTURE 23

Are you a mind moving toward an object, or are you a passive reagent. As a monkey, a busy person whose energy is being engaged from outside, or one whose busy-ness is controlled from self. Difference between conscious and self-conscious is that one is busied while the other is busy. One has controls outside, obligations, etc. Other has controls inside. Review your life and try to come to conclusion as you would about someone else. Is there one aspect of life that has always interested you? In frankness you will probably discover why our thinking is so small—passively half-hearted interest pursued in desultory fashion. Make a classification of the fields of knowledge. What is the most general form in which we can study the world? What is nature of physical world? Also, the phenomena life. A concretion and an abstraction.

Nature of living beings. Physical matter presenting certain forms of behavior teaching us to believe in their liveness.

Two classes of physical facts:

1. Purely physical.

2. Physics in such a state of behavior that we say it is living.

Do not compose, but occupy it. Part of, but different.

Tough-minded—concerned with universe as physics.

Tender-minded—concerned with universe from standpoint of living-beings.

Decide which you are. Chances are, if tough-minded, you will make little progress in Psychology or if tender-minded you run a serious risk of becoming fanciful, speculative and neurotic. Must know your own mind before you can make necessary counter-checks to avoid error.

Music of physics in scale. Moon (revolving) is inferior—do. A slave to the earth—re. Sun—me, etc. Real knowledge is confined to do, re, me. The rest is logically speculative. Scale in pure physics. Electron—do.

At the base of all atoms is a three-fold force:

1.   Particles—positive.

2.   Wave motion—negative or passive.

3.   Wavicle—neutralizing force.

In what do these three forces operate? A force cannot be perceived to operate in nothing. Ether—nothing (that which gives no evidence of itself or everything—since all things issue from it). Ether, that supposed original something but which is unknown until its evidences are observed, non-sensible, imperceptible, not imaginary. In the absence of effects it is without evidence, cannot be observed.

Tree is an epitome of every vegetable that preceded it. No being exists in and for itself but as a note in a scale. Do—single cell, animal or vegetable. Si—man. Every being is at a given moment in the process of moving up or down the scale, not static but dynamic. As we are in movement up or down the scale, development becomes personal.

Health—wholeness—momentum toward wholeness is momentum toward development. Is pursuit in study of universe necessary to health? Simian—inability to persist in any object.

Only as you observe this being impartially can you observe anything impartially. A personality is one whose behavior is determined by outside forces. Through self-consciousness one can transfer to individuality. When needs are living impulses we are said to exist.

466

Impulses—started by do, recognized by re and overcome by mi.

Chances that by accidental circumstances a stimulus may be given—example by a teacher. Or in yourself through your own Psychology, a stimulus or shock may aid you to carry on in your resolution. I write a book, arrive at mi, give myself a shock, reproach Miller. This second case, where individual has the relativity or objectivity to shock himself as though from the outside is rare. It is a law of physics and because of that it is a law of Psychology. Units in Psychology are qualitative. In physics quantitative. A force in physics is paralleled by an effort in Psychology. Psychology is not physics but a replica in consciousness of physical happenings. Thus self-consciousness.

All the laws of physics operate in the mind. All the laws of universe operate in the mind. A mirror in which the events of external world are reflected, we have five projecting antennae to collect images, process of thinking is our looking at them and arranging these images of the external world.

Is second triad different? If so, how? In musical structure it is identical. Only difference is in place in octave. The psychological associations with "sol" are different from those with "do." Do, re, me, are juvenile, "first fine careless rapture." Sol, la, si, are seasoned. Look at auto-biography or biography of men who have accomplished great things. Always their initial enterprise arrives at a stage when they are ready to give up, then something happens, thanks to which they go on, but they never arrive at same state of despair again. He has experienced it once. You can never exactly repeat anything you have already done. Sol, la, si, "second fine careful rapture." It becomes this through experience. Nature is once over—first triad. First is according to accident. Second triad is according to art or consciousness. First semitone is bridged from the outside. Second semitone is a self given shook. That is, birth according to nature or birth according to art or consciousness. Second triad is the beginning of consciousness.

Much unhappiness is due to one thinking one has a wish strong enough for the accomplishment of the object wished for. What is to be done? Give up your object or reduce it. Make it sizeable. Can't chew all you bite off. Don't fly so high. If not a novel write a short story. But you feel humiliation or frustration. This state of growing a trunk, of sacrificing the branches to it, we call being in a state of passion toward an object.

Two types of ambition

1.   Wishing to succeed in chosen field—best painter, or writer, wealthiest man, etc. Great sacrifice.

2.   The attainment of the ability to be perfect in a variety of fields. Da Vinci was not just a painter, etc. His object was to attain the ability to be perfect in a number of fields. He satisfied himself that he could excel. Having arrived there, you may be disposed to leave off. You want the sense of power.

Napoleon identified himself with his ambition.

Everyone has the same amount of impulse. In some of us our energies are scattered, we have no passion. The talented person. A flowery bush or a tree. Most of us are bushes, with no passion or craze so strong; that we sacrifice other things. We are mediocre. No passion by nature, what must be done? But we reject our main wish—a passion for attaining self-consciousness. It may be by taking a new trunk, or by taking even the smallest branch and developing it. Read Journal of Popuci—Japanese. Milton deliberately prepared himself for his great work by writing polemics political essays, going in politics, associating with inferior men etc., so he could write defense of God.

Essential wish is always to fulfill laws of objective morality. No one can attain perfection in this method unless he has had perfection in another line. You must know the futility of perfection before you can have perfection as an objective-human-being. You know what mediocrity is? The *futility of perfection*. It is not the attainment toward excellence in the world workshop, but excellence as a man or woman. Not as an oyster that secretes pearls, but an object in your contacts in the world of the attainment of the stature of a whole man or woman. Society is soulless. Your purpose is not to gratify society. Criterion is to what degree is it making me more whole or complete. Certainly services to society do not become less. They may become more, but do not get same approval. Illustrated by story of Socrates and Pythagoras—the bread and pastry salesman. With complete object, to the branch as a whole, perhaps some neglected branch because it be nearest to objective morality or duty. This couldn't be selected without the realization of futility of arbitrary selection of a trunk. You do not sacrifice those things which are germane.

LECTURE 25

Differences between animal and human brains.

In animals the perceptions are grouped according to form, while in human beings they are grouped according to form and name. We share memory with animals, but we have the word to recall. Animals recall when circumstances are repeated. They do not brood. We, through word or associative process, have more ready access to our memory. Man has a verbalizing mind in addition to a formal mind—ability to use words and recall at will. The semi-consciousness of man, the subconsciousness of animals.

Through images we are victimized in literature. Likewise in the theater, no one ever receives a new impression. Theater is not life; one cannot become experienced through the theater. Will the watching of spectacles on the stage provide a substitute for experience?

Our memories can be exploited by someone else's use of words, and it will be unless we exploit it ourselves. We can be as easily spent as we can spend. Can be unconscious. Some consciously evoke in our memory such images as suit their objective purpose. Life spent in the theater—a life of no experience—no one takes a play or book as a direct substitute for life—because they merely seek to recall the impressions, they are negligible. Otherwise our reactions would be as though they happened to us personally. We go to dinner afterwards because the impressions gathered are already put down as stale.

Gift of verbalization has its equal disadvantage, but it points to a possibility. If I can control images in my mind and control those coming from others, I can insulate myself against them; can resist mob suggestion, and the power of words. You can listen to words and prevent mind from making corresponding images. (You can only control your emotional responses through forms of behavior or changes of images.) As a pianist cannot produce any note at the piano that is not there, so is the artist, the word-monger, playing on our psyche, evoking undesirable word associations. By what means can the mind now controlled by others be controlled by us? Mrs. Besant's "Mind Control" and many books by other authors, Dimnet's "Art of Thinking," are useless. Not practical—recipes without method. We control mind indirectly—not an evasion but a short-cut. Mind is an immaterial receptacle of impressions. At birth it is empty. Impressions pour in in form of images at rate of 10,000 per sec. for each sense. They form groups, cohere and become crystallized into prejudices, opinions, attitudes, points of view, etc., all of which are subject to images formerly received. Thinking is exactly comparable to stirring soup with a spoon. With what am I going to control it? Cannot be controlled by self. One group with superior crystal controls the rest (even the one whom we say thinks clearly). It is impossible to control the mind through the mind. The equal and superior of the mind is not the permutations and combinations of the sense impressions recorded there (not one of the forms already there) but through the "I" that is aware of them. I exist. Indictment of Psychology is that anything which doesn't lend itself to analysis is ignored. But who are you apart from your biological and sociological history?

Error of Descartes—I think, therefore I am. But truth of existence cannot depend on such a thing as thinking. I am, therefore sometimes I think. These activities presuppose I am. We can offer no evidence as there is no experience other than images. We cannot prove it to anyone else. Mind control must be either in this factor "I" or it doesn't exist. Only two factors in our consciousness of which I am certain:

1. I exist—Active.
2. I experience—Passive.

For hope we must turn to I, and mainly "I."

Can you imagine a new color, a new taste, something of which you are capable and the mind is not capable. Can we change the passive into the positive, and suffering into doing? There is an experience potential to "I" which it cannot suffer and which cannot occur to it by chance or nature. Differs in that it cannot be evoked in it. One experience we can never have—being aware of

469

the mind. If I can, then I am doing something mind can never do, nor anything in the universe make me do. Even God nor anyone in the universe can hear your tone of voice; it is uniquely your power; no one can make you do it. It is the second active function of "I."

1st is: I exist.

3rd is: I experience "I", or myself, or my body.

I am conscious of, am aware of, take cognizance of, or note the five overt forms. It is both possible and it involves such effort of consciousness that when you can do that you can control your mind.

There are thirty conclusions that one will arrive at when one has practiced the method sufficiently. They are the same for all people.

LECTURE 26 AND 27

Read Pistis Sophia or Faith of wisdom "In Fragments of a Faith Forgotten."

Present Bible was created for political purposes. For almost no event previous to 1000 years ago we have any real evidence for. Religion of Christianity was a technique, a way or a method. Jesus on one occasion called it Yoga. "My yoke is easy and my burden light." Yoke is identical with Yoga or method or way. It was practical. There was no sanctity about use of word. It was a definite means of arriving at a certain object. The end in view was salvation. (Connotation of this word cannot be stomached today. Originally it had a sane and healthy meaning as the word health). Holiness—wholeness—is likewise of unsavory connotation, we cannot look at word unprejudiced with the verbal associations the word evokes.

One of complaints made of Jesus was that he was an ordinary person—ordinary as could be—man addressing men—but he had before his mission attained a degree of efficiency in method he proposed to teach. Difficulties:

1.   That of conveying his method to others.

2.   Jealousy of other teachers.

3.   Misunderstandings of what he had to say, namely by our inability to use words not already charged with insidious meanings or associations.

Central organization—the nucleus—had from time to time many difficulties with provincial groups, for example, doubt as to what Jesus had said. Disputes became so many that they decided to establish once for all a Canon (Statutory authority) to agree on what Jesus had said. These were considered more representative than the rest. Four Gospels were chosen. Commission was established to force the giving up of all other manuscripts. Result was four gospels and chance fragments which were declared heretical by central council. But we have inherited a prejudice against them as also against the word Gnosticism because it is Anti-Christian. Secondly, the language being different, it makes them almost a sealed book. Example "Pistis Sophia," pleroma, etc. Likewise we have really no understanding of the four gospels in the sense in which the words were originally used. Proof: no one reads the Bible any more for the purpose it was intended—practical advice on the art of living. Salvation (being saved from something). "They that are whole need not a physician" presupposes a state of need or un-wholeness. The way was a technique. Salvation implies a state that is so profoundly unsatisfactory to the individual that he wishes to be saved from it—an individual matter. Matthew Arnold: An appeal to the individual conscience. It was to the individual that the way was subscribed. The state is one that almost every individual is bound to realize. The state is automatism, scientifically Behaviorism. Not one living being by nature, ever does, says, feel, or thinks originally. Our experiences are reactions; their form, quality, intensity and kind are absolutely determined by the conditioning of the organism and the stimulus at the time employed. Accidental stimuli and conditioning. *Human beings peculiarly find* it almost impossible to entertain ideas which are intolerable for them to *entertain or from which there appears to be no remedy.*

It is impossible to realize the anguish of a sincere thinker like Freud, when he realizes all our beliefs are defenses against beliefs, that we are not active but reactive mechanisms in whom only processes of life take place.

Salvation has meaning only for those who take blinders off.

Realize truth of behaviorism and then raise question of Paul: "Who then shall raise me from this body of death." Have the manliness to admit the fact. Read "The Mysterious Stranger," by Mark Twain. "I feel disposed one of these days to blow the gaff on the whole damn human race—reveal them as they are." He kept his promise. He knew that human beings were in no way what they thought they were. Neither Twain nor Swift have been recognized as the objective critics of the human psyche which they were.

Human automatism

Two ways for you:

1. To deny it. (Orage predicts that in 10 yrs. no Psychology that is not Behaviorism will be taught in any respectable University).

2. Admitting or accepting it. Not subjectively. But not accepting in a way that you do nothing about it. There is a method of acceptance, therapeutic of the injury done by its acceptance. If automatism were incurable it would be well to deny it, but when it is curable, denial is just superstition. The sense of sin is the beginning of salvation (substitute real meaning for imaginary ones). Sin was the ancient psychological name for Behaviorism. They discovered the life processes worked in them in spite of them, a condition precedent to the realization of the means of salvation. Conversion originally meant a realization—not intellectual—that we are in truth mechanical. Processes of salvation began by act of realization, by pursuit of a method, the way. The steps were set out in simple form for anyone who realized the state from which they wished to escape.

It is universal that all human beings are mechanically determined. In this sense we are equal. If the condition is universal, the way out must be universal. The method is the same for all. Differences from Shakespeare and Goethe to Taxi drivers are superficial; they differ no more than vegetables.

"If you are not prepared to make personal experiments you merely play with other people's opinions." (Dewey) William James, practicing introspection, hit upon and rejected method of extrospection—examining self as others. Watson took up this hint, as after his diatribes against introspection, he took lit up in favor of naturalistic observation without preconception. Observed human being as any animal or vegetable. Conclusion: No thinking, only sub-vocal verbalization. No emotion, only constriction of muscles around solar-plexus. Emptied out baby with the bath (German). He also prescribes a useful extrospective exercise: attempt to observe yourself as others. See one's self as others—not mentally, but as he sees others behave. Unfortunately he was already consigned to Behaviorism.

It is this stone which the builders rejected that is to be the head of the corner, but only on Behaviorism with no Freudian escape. The experiment must be: exactly as we now observe others, observation of their five forms of overt behavior, so will we observe ourselves. Confine our attention in our own case to overt forms of behavior. No attention to thinking, feeling etc. Focus is on what we overtly do. Wait until we collect data before we come to any conclusion of the being we are.

As we wait when observing others, so we shall defer in ourselves. The judgment shall then be comparable to the judgment we arrive at in observing others. Defy anyone who has observed himself thus ever again having a bad judgment of another person. Patiently waiting for collection of sufficient data to form an opinion. When at last one sees himself as he sees others; I am the sort of person whom if I met I should not like. The five overt forms constitute the only picture another can have of us. Everything else is a deduction from them. Our response to others are passive—senses are passive—someone moves in my line of vision and I see him—can't help it. In my own case an effort is necessary, a psychological effort. Suggests a psychological effort to begin to try to observe your own behavior as if it were the behavior of someone else. There are two forms of observation: amateur and professional. The fact that a Psychoanalyst has to ask his patient a question means he is not an expert. Try to test strength of character by not degenerating into the amateur.

1. For one week hear what you say.
2. For one week observe your gestures.
3. For one week observe your facial expressions.
4. For one week observe your postures.
5. For one week observe your bodily movements.

Then combine 2,3,4,5, and at the end of nine weeks you would be objective and impartial to yourself and rid of the greatest subjectivity—non-identification.

Introspection.

1.   The phenomena (stream of consciousness in mind) are extremely difficult to define, report on etc.

2.   Bias of observer. I report what I wish to see etc. Personal Equation.

3.   Invalid, because it is not the method we arrive at understanding of others.

Even Watson in his observation of babies gave a mere deduction. In no case is Introspection a guide to self-understanding. Ruled out. Other method is "know thyself." Not training in character, cunning, concealment of feelings, but self-knowledge. What is spring of your conduct? What kind of a being are you? What is your passion, behavior, habits etc. Most people are totally unaware of the impression they make on others, their defects, potentialities, stuff they are made of. In a dream. We are not concerned with these but with those who have the curiosity to know the kind of being they are.

Vaihinger—as if—it is both like and unlike the thing in question. Simultaneously it is both my own and someone else's. Conscious objectification of that which was unconscious and subjective.

If the intelligent could cultivate the tone of voice of the dumb, the world "would be saved for the intelligent." All forms of behavior are end-products of the organism, each the complete language for that medium of the total personality. With the act of speech 5 other languages are being spoken by every person.

Asceticism was to keep observers reminded of the body they had to observe. We are so tender with ourselves we seldom inflict punishment. Behave toward yourself as you would have another pupil do. Have you exhausted toward yourself the stimuli you could apply to others.

Keep note-book and jot down what you say in the course of one day. At end of day read it as a verbatim report of another person—conclusion is—*moron*.

Self-knowledge for self-use, exploitation, development. No attempt to self-improve until you arrive at self-definition and then it is never the detail (the thing you are dissatisfied with) in question. Conscious suffering is not associated with pain—we despise that—suffering is making effort against inclination, making trouble for yourself. You suffer for things you wish to do. Deliberately giving oneself the trouble of doing what one likes. Conscious labor is one having an object.

Our life is simply a process of waiting for death, filling in time until the bell rings, without a reason d'être. Suppose you are dead and given option of returning, incarnate again, what work would you set yourself? Formulate an object for which your life is worth living—and its pursuit. That is conscious labor.

Three efforts:
1. To move
2. To think.
3. To feel.

Each has its own method of relaxation. Practice lying down for five minutes to get rid of muscle tensions. That is sufficient time, if you completely relax, to offset mental, physical and emotional fatigue. We sleep eight hours, but only four valuable; the other four are used for untying muscles. Breakages are not due to work but insufficient balance of effort—distribution. Under-employment rather than over-employment. Most fatigue is due to muscular stricture.

We wish to have the full use of our opportunity; depends on our ability to meet them. To utilize the divine gift of an animated body, to leave it more developed than when you found it—but knowledge is necessary.

LECTURE 28

What is the most intriguing, interesting, valuable, or illuminating idea that has been presented during the meetings this year? Your answer is the thread that will lead you to the light, (living consciousness—always aware of why you are alive). Life is a strenuous game—victories and defeats—has an objective—we are conscious participants in the game—we are aware of the rules of the game. A passage is made over a certain bridge; over entrance is the sign "know thyself." The bridge consists of the clue, the major interest of your life, understanding without doing is like a passive without an active force—world of women without a single man in it, or vice versa.

Obligation, necessity, or a strong wish is no good at all, only effort that counts is that consciously initiated (by your own volition, willed by yourself, under vow to yourself, no thought of approval or disapproval of others; resolution made for, by, and kept by yourself). You aim eventually to do what you like. Strong, glad, happy, laugh, smile, joy—chosen to describe the state of being of one who makes conscious effort. Orage believes Elixir of Life of Alchemists was conscious effort.

Real imagination is emotional. Provokes impressions of images which visual imagination couldn't provoke. Experiences that happen to us are of no value, unless in devoted watchfulness we watch ourselves. Watch this strange animal in its strange jungle. We would then know what it is to be alive, tingling with wonder, curiosity, and attention, at the phenomena always about us. No need to go abroad. Contrast with this other world of wonder.

"The eyes of the fool fixe on the ends of the earth, himself he sees not." (Bible)

Resolutions are of the heart and head. To be consciously accompanying this body. My delight is in another activity than that associated with body.

How do you measure an idea? Trivial or profound, comprehensive or narrow?

Consciousness follows the two laws of the universe: Involution and Evolution. Either it moves upwards, or lacking resistance it moves downwards. These laws operate in every object, animate and inanimate. The universe is time looking into space. The two laws correspond with time and space. Where they meet is an object, low or high on scale. Vegetable, worm, pig, dog, human being, planetary being or God, sun, etc. We are an embodiment between these two forces, resisting the tide of unconsciousness that is threatening to take us into complete inertia. (This was one answer to above question. Good, because it is comprehensive, covering many statements of facts.)

Second question was knowing what it is to really do. Valuable to those humans in need of knowing what doing means to those of us who realize sad pathos of behaviorism: that no one has actually done a thing. "Who shall deliver us from the body of this death?" (Paul) When awake, never rest. Be your own Satan. Do what you please; give yourself always what you wish to do; keep on improvising. *Keep yourself awake.* The absurdities and silly things.

Distinguishing Ideas.

Ideas of mind. Why?

Ideas of emotional and instinctive centers. How?

Why object to being an inert dead organism? It is average. Can be average and degenerate. Pygmies, etc. Average is not normal. In the land of the blind, the one eyed man is King. Normality is a goal. It presupposes the being in question is exercising actively all 3 centers. Intellectual genius is subnormal. Aim is to be equally capable in each center. If you haven't thought or felt or done something during the day you are abnormal. Better be mediocre in all centers than distinguished in one.

Take away body, I cannot say I exist, but I am. This is the difference between a creature and a being. Orage is a creature, I am a being.

Intellectualist—mind is limited to experiences it has had. Experience precedes think-ability (this is Dewey). In the absence of the experience of the initiated act it cannot be conceived. All thinking is conditioned. Experience had to precede the conceivability. It is a matter of technique. Fallacy of intellectualism: failure to recognize that mind is a recorder of experiences. Your experiences of "I" are already limited to those experiences you have had, if you have not already experienced "I."

Third answer was that it seemed to answer a need of the organism. On this the elaboration was: There are three types according to their wishes.

1. Those without wishes.
2. Those with conflicting wishes.
3. Those with wishes that the organism cannot gratify.

Real wish is the signature of "I," belongs exclusively to "I." In the absence of an attempt to realize "I" it is literally impossible to know what that wish is. Discovery of essential wish is proportionate to effort toward objective non-identification you make. Observation is a unique experience. You might say: "Thank you God, you may have had it but I doubt it."

Margaret Anderson

LECTURE

It is not consciousness that determines social conditions. It is social conditions that determines consciousness. The modes of production determines forms of life.

Theory rises out of material activity of man.

Problem of Theory of Knowledge. Transformation of liberty into slavery.

Problem of Theory of Things.

Needs transformation of thinking.

We think of becoming, (Chair has no direction) of human beings becoming something they are not yet.

Possibility of error.

A unity and a conflict of opposites.

Law of unity of opposites.

These opposites are simultaneously mutually exclusive and mutually connective.

Relation between conceptual and perceptual.

Percepts are at basis of concepts.

Practice at basis of theory.

All things are connected as well as disconnected.

Each object must be analyzed as it is.

Difference between animal and man is that man goes hungry, etc., amid too much food.

LAW OF CONTRADICTIONS

Same—and unlike   Individual and facades   Same at center.
Accidental and necessary (species—society goes on. Death—growth—limit)
Form   Substance   Transformed into their opposites.
Kip Rhinelander's death. Stream of consciousness
Law of Negation
Feudal monopoly negated by Free Trade
Free Trade negated by monopoly
Fundamental law of Dial
Law of Unity and Conflict of opposites
Inherent contradictory and contain opposites within themselves
Capitalism—Proletarianism
Man is a part of nature—He reflects nature.
Society is different and has different laws.
Each object has its own inner laws of motion—but each is related to each other.

478

To the proletariat it is a matter of life and death, that it reflect reality accurately.

Do any of you suffer from such spectacles as prison conditions, unemployment in England, etc? How many people cause you distress? Usually one. Resolve: I do not understand all people, out there is one person who embodies all; I will objective try to understand him. I shall purposively experiment. Reduce this person to living with me in peace and harmony. Work only as if I were enthusiastic. Read the "Psychology of I" by Daly King.

FINAL LECTURE, TUESDAY GROUP

Three senses of Obligation:
1. To yourself.
2. To your tribe.
3. To all mankind.

1.   Responsibility of circle: not an intellectual responsibility, but a fact. Unless I spend my day in a way that is to my advantage from the standpoint of objective development, I'm disloyal, or lapsing, or going down the scale. A set-back of this sort requires several days for recovery, individual responsibility. Obligation. This is consciousness, in regard to first side of the triangle.

2.   Obligation to neighbors—our tribe, to whom, if I came to a crisis, I can appeal. Not a fair weather thing. You have established a center of gravity in second side when "weather" counts not at all. Beginning of individuality is when you depend on no person or thing.

3.   Jesus was not of an occult school. He had a passion—feeling for whole of mankind, something divinely paternal. The true patriarch, or elder brother, is of conscious development. It is a stage in the point of being. When center of gravity is established in each of these three, beings become as a circle, and are at center and circumference at the same time. It is complete organization without machinery. Not occult, but a common understanding so one can put himself in the position of anyone in the circle. A member of a circle is one capable of forming a circle anywhere or nowhere, and he is independent of anyone else.

NEXT YEARS WORK

Conditions: There must be specific signs of work done. The experience is as vivid and indubitable as having been drowned. Comes at moment when you begin to realize you are losing your life in your body. Every attachment to present body seems cut, lost. This marks stage in observation. You will with non-identification-observation come to this. You will receive the shock that you are dead. Lasts but a few seconds but every experience after will be nothing in comparison. You have known in your living experience, the shock of death, or the fact of death.

Our personal problems are not ours to unravel; every situation into which a group falls is a joint responsibility. Every individual problem is one for the circle and to be discussed objectively. Impossible to give away anything told in confidence. Not sworn to secrecy. You or they have attained the state of secrecy, an inability to betray confidence of fellow members. Of those selected from the group things shall be spoken of them as if they are dead—a postmortem. It is also absolutely necessary that the group make a greater impression on the community than they do now. Absolutely necessary to have something similar to Pythagorean school, but no building or organization, because following the cosmic law it would run down the scale.

Take a subject in which you are expert and develop a group in that subject. If you are conscious, some magnetic current will develop so that pupils will discover what is in the back of your mind. Teaching must be done in the art in which individual is most skilled. This will be obligatory. Be prepared to know what you will do. Eight months to strive for this candidacy. Unless you are candid, you will be compelled to attend beginner's group or none whatever. At circle meetings, leader will speak candidly and expect candid replies. That you be serious and determined is a condition of membership. Seriousness is joint.

Sin is the responsibility of having heard and then not doing anything about it.

End and aim of method: to attain self-consciousness of being; that your planetary body is yours to exploit responsibly. By law of reciprocal being, you as a being develop by feeding on your planetary body, transforming it into higher forms. Planetary food—we eat and transform it to a form infinitely higher in substance, so when I feed on myself through observation and experimentation—conscious control, I step up the scale to that of a higher being. It is of reciprocal advantage. I, as reciprocal God, not only feed on my planetary body, but I *divine* it in the process of feeding on it. This is the aim of the ideas and method,—to become a God, that is one who can exploit responsibility of any planetary body. Psyche and planetary body. It is a common obligation on all the center beings. Simultaneously there is a cosmic development which must wait on this other development.

Here enters the five rules of objective morality. Understanding of these becomes a criterion for all conduct. You do things which under conventional morality you could not do. Makes obligatory many acts conventional morality would never commend. That is why beings in objective morality appear so strange—so lax and yet so strict.

No being in the world whose external conduct is a model to copy. Follow yourselves and you will find me. Follow me and you will lose me and yourself, etc. (Fragments of a Faith Forgotten)

Buddha: Being with objective understanding may do anything he pleases. Within the limits of your understanding you act individually.

OBJECTIVE MORALITY

Hand of five fingers. Handling of situations, the conduct of life. Art is the pursuit of an unattainable perfection.

Third rule—obligatory to make being effort—doing. Exercise for pure sake of exercise.

Will—the ability to carry out whims, or the ability to do what it takes your fancy to do.

Fourth rule—that I will not cause the feet of a little one to stumble. Better a millstone, etc.

Fifth rule—your collective effort eases burden of being who is responsible for us all.

Sin is neglect to make effort according to your understanding; refusal to convert verbal into formal understanding.

FIVE STRIVINGS

1. To have in their ordinary being--existence everything satisfying or their planetary body.

2. To have a constant and unflagging instinctive need for self-perfection in the sense of being

3. The conscious striving to know ever more and more-concerning the laws of World-creation and World-maintenance.

4. Striving to discharge the debt of their arising and their individuality of existence as early and as quickly as possible in order afterwards to be free to lighten as much as possible the sorrow of Our Common Father.

5. Striving always to assist the most rapid perfecting of other beings, both those similar to oneself and those of other forms, up to the degree of the sacred Martfotai, that is, up to the degree of self-individuality.

LECTURE 28 FINAL

Be responsible for self, irrespective of everyone else. Never blame anyone for anything that happens to us. Not like children casting blame. We are mechanical as trees with no free-will. We can blame no one. One half tragedy of life is this blaming of others for what happens to us.

Warning: sooner or later we shall encounter experiences which we are unprepared for and for which we are so unequipped that they may conquer us. Defy anything on this planet to submerge you. There is the light of a life-belt in you.

Regard yourself as engaged in writing a book, a yet unfinished story, you the hero. What do you foresee will happen to you, drifting, passing peacefully into death; or do you expect to engage in some sudden encounter. How will you meet it? If you depend on a human person you are lost. There isn't a living person that can carry you through certain crisis. *If by the arrival of such an occasion,* and you have learned to look upon yourself *objectively, you can confidently* defy any act to overwhelm you, distress you. By awareness you will lift your nose above the flood. To have that degree of detachment enabling you to say at just that moment: *this thing is happening to him.* Look at self objectively, then when crisis arise, you will have pangs of sympathy but not of identification. While weather is fair, prepare plunging into the dark—this is the light.

To be constantly present with a dummy that is behaving for you in this world is possible for you, it's experiences plus your own.

"I" independent of help from others. No one can tell me what to do. I must get a new mind. You have come to end of resources of present mind. New one can be acquired, not by any exercise of present mind; mental exercises give us use of the mind we have, but not of a new mind.

Two conclusions:

1.   No mind better than mine.

2.   My own is no good. Not an instrument for arriving at truth, only for a clever dialectical opinion.

New Mind—objective reason. As you observe him from outside, that same reason will enable you to look at external world with a new understanding. Human being strives to understand.

Literature: To write something that will change your life at once; production of real experiences and not imaginary ones. Disgust with literature, the theater, etc., is that you read or go to see a play and come out from the experience exactly as you went in. Example: You go in capable of meanness and jealousy, and come out capable of meanness and jealousy. Should be: he has gone through the fire and comes out purified.

In the beginning was the word. Adam created animals by naming their name. That brought them into existence.

Read "The Sciences and Philosophy" by Prof. Haldane. He says there is one truth—our relation to God. But he has no knowledge; it is all logically deduced. He does not speak with certainty. As certain you are children of God as that you have a father and mother.

New mind, being born again—ability to be aware—death.

Danger of apathy. Action is a subtle form that makes unnecessary the action of the organism. 1 gr. of energy of self-observation equals 30x 30.000 gr. ordinary energy.

Waking consciousness is to self-consciousness as mass energy is to atomic energy.

Energy in self-observation is far greater than reading books or discussing etc.

Energy is ability to do work.

With present minds we arrive only at the realization that we cannot arrive at truth.

Two steps:

1. Skepticism toward any mind today.
2. Development of new mind.

Psychological exercises are to mind as moving exercises are to body. They move sub-center of mind.

Emotional exercise; revive by means of images an emotional experience you had in past. Recall images. Combine images to get combination of emotions. Intentional suffering: put yourself in a situation where you know you will have distress. Most people shirk distasteful or disagreeable. Don't evade. Run the risk of being embarrassed.

Chief-feature.

Or governing motive, Napoleon's was ambition. Each of us now sacrifices everything to this main feature. Review life objectively and you will discover this. Try it in two or three others first and then in yourself. No one can be persuaded to do anything contrary to his own psychology. In the end he does it by his own consent. Provided they do not transport your body, no one in this world has power over you. You are the limits of your conditioned ability. When you say ha ha, it doesn't act so any longer; it amuses me to see it, but it loses its power, then it can't act. It is what you most despise in others, would least like to have. Think in general what your ideal is of yourself; it is the exact opposite of what you are. I am so and so—not so. I hate jealousy—you are jealous. Real knowledge is the ability to manipulate your own psychology.

To get people to do what you want them to:

1. Urge them not to.
2. Be indifferent.

The last way is to wish that they should, because your emotional state, whatever it may be, tends to produce the opposite state in other person. Cathode-Anode, poles of a magnetic bar have same relation as two people in personal relationship. Experiment with this, especially in people with whom you are on strained terms. They are doing something you dislike; appear to do the opposite of what you wish. Girl at 16 runs away to get man. Opposite at 17. Physically the man may marry; psychically he runs away.

Let go lightly in order to take hold tightly.

The way to get is the way to give.

The way to hold is the way to lose.

An idea never stands alone, but in relation to the ideas then current in the minds of those who hear them.

Orage with his son Richard, Hampstead, 1933.

LETTER FROM A. R. ORAGE TO ISRAEL SOLON

6 Radcliffe Square
London SW10
21 November 1930

My dear Israel:

I got your letter this morning and my first wish was to cable you my complete agreement with your attitude; but, on reflection, I find it better to write at some length and, in the meantime, to presume on your good judgement as you have already expressed it. I am very grateful for your expressions of personal friendliness which, as a fact, I could never doubt, if only for the reason that on my side, whatever is sincere and real in me is whole-hearted affection for you and the New York group. Whatever happens and whatever Gurdjieff may do or require you and the group to do, I feel myself so personally knit with you all that no thing can really sever our essential relations even if, externally, our paths should lie apart. What is more, I cannot conceive myself ever reproaching any one of you for anything you may find yourselves constrained to do or say. I know too well the difficulties of the situation to require any predefined line of conduct. You are like ships at sea in a storm and the first principle of navigation is to get to port. So please, my dear Israel, do what you can to assure everybody that I beg them to think of and for themselves first and last. Their best "loyalty" to me is to learn and become all they can. I feel that "loyalty" to me is confusing on still another ground. I came to New York as an agent of Gurdjieff and the institute idea—not at all in my own right or on my own responsibility. Certainly, however, Gurdjieff may say I have, only titillated—I have done my best both for the group and for Gurdjieff. But if after these years Gurdjieff himself comes along and, declaring that I have failed him as a good servant, proposes to take over the group himself, or to nominate a new agent in my place, I certainly have no complaint to make. I accepted this commission originally, I discharged it to the best of my ability, he is my superior officer and I quite naturally resign my commission at his suggestion, and all the more readily if he personally puts himself in my place. There is and can be thus, as you clearly see, no division of loyalty as between my superior officer and me. We must all, I as well as you, accept his rulings so long as we remain in his school.

But then another consideration arises. I've not been, in relation to the New York group, just an agent of Gurdjieff. Perhaps that has been my failure from his point of view. I should, perhaps have regarded the group as simply material for Gurdjieff's use in all respects, and had no such feelings about you all as would give me a qualm at whatever he might do. It may be, perhaps, that I should have treated you all like dogs (I don't mean harshly of course), or, better to say, like a flock of sheep whose wool and mutton were of value to Gurdjieff and one or two of whom might conceivably one day attain a higher state of being, through being used as wool and mutton by a presumed superman. Maybe it is so, and maybe any other attitude on my part (or that of any of Gurdjieff's agents) is titillation. My reply is simply that I couldn't either feel or pretend to feel in that relation. I, if you like to say so, fell in love with the group personally and so far from being willing to carry out my commission if it involved seeing the group shorn and encouraging it to grow wool, I found the shearing one prolonged agony and in the end, I was more disposed to side with the group than with my master. Even now I am; and as you will see, it makes my situation really desperate. On the one hand I believe that G is our common teacher and the only one we are likely to encounter. But, on the other hand, I cannot make myself his agent when it appears to me to involve hurting you; and, furthermore, I cannot refrain from crying out to you at his approach—"Look out! Be sure you get as well as give." Certainly don't consider *me*, but be sure also that you do consider yourselves. For *he* is among you who perhaps doesn't care two hoots whether you fare well or ill, provided only that collectively you serve his aim (which incidentally is not personally selfish at all) *and* at the same time are offered individually a chance, if only a bare chance of possible "salvation."

The last consideration I will state is this. It is obvious that my unwillingness to go to all lengths for Gurdjieff with the group and with myself, indicates an insufficiency of what shall I say?—Faith in him? Trust? Radical conviction that he can do no wrong? Well, to be explicit, that is the fact. I have not that absolute faith. If I were Nahom and Gurdjieff commanded me to slay my first born, I wouldn't do it. I realize that this degree of faith is perhaps essential to full participation in Gurdjieff's teachings. I realize that any degree of belief, short of this makes all services to him ultimately conditional and therefore except within limits, not to be counted upon. I know it is not the "Other-Self-Trust" which results from or leads to the sacred rite of eternal friendship. I regret that I have not got it in relation to Gurdjieff; and I envy those who have or who may find it born in them. But while I wish it for others, I have sorrowfully to avow that I haven't got it myself; nor do I see myself attaining it by any means that I can employ. "Lord," I can say, "I believe;" but I have to add, "Help thou my unbelief," because, in truth, my belief is not absolute.

I hope you will find these notes a sufficient reply to your letter, and, also, of some use to Blanche and Allan B., and Sherman and Mrs. Schwarzenbach and Muriel and, in fact, all the people who really feel the poignancy of our common situation. You are, of course, at full liberty to use this letter as you please. I have nothing to conceal from you all; and I am so far from feeling "disloyal" to Gurdjieff himself that, if it were feasible, I would send him a copy of this letter myself. I can see clearly that from *his* point of view, believing in himself so absolutely, my half or three-quarters belief in him, is titillation, and results only in the titillation of others. He *cannot* but wish either that I shall be absolutely faithful, *or* cease to be regarded or to regard myself as his chief "minister" in America. I accept this without reproach. But what I pray for is that my own friends, the best I have on earth, the New York group, may not only not suffer on my account, but that, through me, like another Moses, they may find themselves led to the Jordan and transported across by Joshua Gurdjieff!

Yours affectionately,

A. R. ORAGE

PS: I'm still planning to return to N.Y. at the end of the year.

Gurdjieff, circa 1930.

Went for the first time to Orage's beginners group, which had been meeting weekly for a month or two. Before putting down notes of this meeting, I will indicate what had evidently been said before; I gathered that the previous week Orage had asked the group to try to imagine two portraits, one on each wall:

Portrait No. 1, on your left, is of yourself as you are: your actual self.

Portrait No. 2, on your right, to be filled in later, is of yourself as you might be; that is, the full, normal development of which Portrait No. 1 shows only a stunted growth.

Portrait No. 2 is of yourself as you "should" be. The essential "should" of each being is to actualize what is now potential in him. Orage had evidently spent some time trying to disassociate in the minds of his listeners this use of the word "should" from any use based on codes, of morality, social suggestion, conventions, doctrines, etc. ,

He had warned his listeners that Portrait No. 1 was hard to arrive at No. 2 extremely so.

At the present meeting Orage said:

Important to keep two things in mind:

1.   The subject, we are discussing at these meetings and
2.   The purpose, for which we are discussing it.

Otherwise, what is said will be of no value, except as random remarks which may have an incidental interest: things heard "by the way."

The subject is ourselves. We are using this word now not in any metaphysical sense; but to mean the actual concrete body that goes by our name. Asking each person to think of himself as he things of other people; an object that can be felt, heard, seen, etc.; whose behavior can be observed; and about whom certain deductions can be drawn from his behavior (which includes his feelings and thoughts).

We habitually form deductions about others from their behavior. Unfortunately, all our conclusions are twisted both by our inadequate data, and our own bias; our personal reaction to them. We see others in relation to ourselves, not in relation to their potentialities. Yet we continue to form these conclusions and act on them, out of necessity.

An Exercise: Call up before your mind's eye some person you know well who is not present in the flesh. Ask yourself:

What type of person is he? or she?

Is he doing the things that are wise for his own happiness?

Would you feel safe in trusting him, when something of importance to yourself was at stake, with:

489

a.   Power over others?

b.   Success?

c.   Money?

In what important enterprise of your own would you invite him to take part?

How would you feel if you were condemned to spend a year alone with him?

Do you find, generally speaking, that he is:

a.   Reasonable?

b.   Dependable?

c.   Strong?

If his essential wishes were gratified, what sort of person do you *imagine* he would be? Etc. etc.

It is true that your answers to all these questions will be of limited value, because you have only a few scraps of evidence to go on and your personal bias will intervene even in considering those.

But ask yourself these questions and find out whether if it came to a matter of *very close relations* with something dear to you at stake, your opinion of him then would confirm the light opinion you fall into when nothing is at stake.

For example, Wilkins the explorer is now picking companions to go with him in a submarine under the Arctic ice to the North Pole. He has had hundreds of applications, but can take only a handful. What tests does he apply? He may reject people whom he personally finds congenial for light companionship. He must consider the seaworthiness and danger-worthiness of his personnel. Would you invite Wilkins' judgment, in such circumstances, on yourself?

It is necessary in testing persons in your mind to apply questions relative to them about a large *variety* of situations in which you may never have had a chance to see them.

Your answers of course, will not be objectively true, but the effort to make them will force you to focus your own impressions and boil them down.

Now, from this visualized image of someone else, turn to yourself. Try first to call up a picture of yourself, as you appear externally walking, sitting, talking, etc.—that is, the same sort of picture that comes into your mind when you think of someone you know. Then ask yourself all the above questions and try to answer them as candidly as you would about someone else.

This gives you the beginning of Portrait No. 1—the actual.

Portrait No. 2 cannot be started until No. 1 is *vivid*, *solid* and can be seen by you *as if it were a portrait of someone else.*

For example, Orage added, I can call up before my mind's eye a picture of my sister. It never occurs to me to identify myself with that picture.

Similarly, I can call up a mental picture of Orage without identifying myself with that.

No. 1: the actual;

No. 2: the potential, or "ought."

Orage again warned his listeners to disassociate this "ought" from the pseudo-ought's, held up by society.

A dog can be house-broken: it is a process of implanting an artificial conscience in him by the use of punishments and rewards. Similarly, we have a *house-broken civilization*. And the "progress" of civilization is ordinarily measured by the relation between punishments and rewards. Primitive societies lean more heavily on punishments; the more a civilization "progresses," the more it uses rewards, the various forms of rank, title, distinction, approval, esteem, etc. By these devices a moral code is implanted, as an artificial conscience and kept effective.

When we are members of a minority, we usually flatter ourselves that we are immune to these influences, without realizing that our indifference to the dominant code is merely the result of our having fallen under the hypnotic influence of a different code, which for us is stronger.

Imagine the present as the center of a circle. Here you stand the person you are today. Now describe a circumference which will represent a time, say five years hence. From the present moment to that circumference are many radii, by one or another of which you may travel; but five years hence you will be at *some* point on the circumference.

Now, of all those points, one represents the fullest possible development of your potentialities. Will you be going towards that, or will you be deflected, and end up at some other point? All the points represent actual potentialities of yours. What usually happens is that we go a little way along one radius, then jump to another, later to another, zigzagging continually.

The value of trying to arrive at a conception of our full development (Portrait No. 2 or the point on the circumference mentioned above) is that, to the extent that it can be formulated, it will exercise a magnetic influence on our course.

The material out of which this Portrait No. 2 will eventually be made is "the truthful formulation of essential wishes. "

It must not be imagined that this can be done at once. A thousand non-essential wishes, entertained under the suggestion of sociological influence, will first have to be stripped off; education, training, moral codes, etc. By the time we grow up we are spoiled.

How are we to be brought to recognize this deformed condition? By self-observation.

But it is practically impossible to tell another person how to perform a psychological act; for the words in which I try to tell it have different content for each hearer. The content that each word has for us is the result of all our personal associations with it up to date. If I have encountered the word "consciousness," for example, in one book, or in one discussion, and you in another, it will have different associations for each of us. Nor can we get around the difficulty by "defining our terms," for the very words we use in our definition will themselves have a different content for each of us, etc. We live in a Tower of Babel.

In the case of a concrete act, it is relatively easy to instinct. For example, I can get on a bicycle, demonstrate how to sit and pedal and then say: "Now, you sit in the saddle and do the same thing. "

But what happens, when I try to convey the idea of self-observation, is often no more grotesque than as if I said: "Get in the saddle, you should go in the house and bring me out a sandwich." I say: "No, that's not what I meant. Here, this is the saddle; now sit in it the way I was sitting." You think a moment, then exclaim, "Oh, I see" and fetch me an umbrella.

In contemporary psychology there is no definition of self-observation. The nearest to it was in one of Wundt's books. He used the term "apperception," and the meaning he gave to it was perception of the external world accompanied by a perception of the organism perceiving it. This is perhaps as near as we can come to it. But Wundt himself did not follow up the idea, and his disciples soon changed the meaning of the word beyond recognition.

Note that this use of the word apperception involves a *double* perception. When I look through a telescope, I get an image of the external world, and at the same time I remain aware I that I'm looking through an instrument called a telescope. I don't identify the telescope with myself. But in looking through the eye, we forget that the eye is also an instrument.

In self-observation we receive the ordinary image *accompanied* by this image of the instrument. It's as if the ordinary image was received with an aura around it and this *double* image, being different, will have a different subsequent history in us.

It is easy to understand why Wundt's followers did nothing with the idea he had hit upon. In the-first place, they found it practically impossible to produce the psychological state at will and consequently could not collect data to work on. In the second place, even if it could be produced, the state was obviously of very rare occurrence; and being committed to the point of view that, the normal is what is common, they were, bound to consider so rare a state, abnormal or pathological.

As an analogy of self-observation take the old-fashioned stereoscope. The picture placed in the rack was a flat picture, but by use of the double image and lenses, it was seen in perspective, as a three-dimensional view. Self-observation is a double lens

In a state of self-consciousness there is perspective, a double image:

a.   Of the external world.

b.   Of the organism perceiving it.

Since it is unavoidable in these discussions that we should use the word "consciousness" (in our Tower of Babel), let us try to have as similar a content for the word as possible. We will use it in the following sense:

Our reception of images constitutes our continuing consciousness.

Thus, if in imagination you will shut off one by one each of the channels by which images arrive (i.e. all of the senses), until there is a total absence of images, then the result will be unconsciousness.

At this point I introduced a digression by raising the point that the unconsciousness will not be complete unless we have eliminated not only the images currently arriving but those already present in memory.

Orage then discussed memory from the following point of view: You are familiar with what is called a "dying sound." This is caused either:

a.   By the receding in space of the source of sound—for example, a train whistle getting farther away or

b.   By the diminishing of the sound—for example, a note struck on a piano.

Now, the strength of any image at the moment we receive it is its maximum strength in our consciousness. But it immediately begins to run through a series of octaves, becoming less vivid, until it passes out of conscious recognition. But it remains permanently in the vibrations of the organism. A new image entering is like a radio wave entering an ether field already filled with vibrations. With some the new one has affinity, and it revives them. This is the evocation of ideas through association.

When this digression was finished, Orage asked: Do you remember the exact point from which we digressed? It is always important to keep in mind, during a digression, the main path we set out to pursue, and the point at which we left it.

This is true not only in an intellectual discussion, but in everything. The aim is to be able to digress—recreation, calls on one's time, social obligations, etc. , etc.—and to be able, when the digression is finished, to return at once to the main purpose at the point where we dropped it. A "logic of life." Otherwise no aim can ever be carried out.

The point at which we digressed was the definition of consciousness as awareness of images.

Self-consciousness = consciousness plus awareness of the organism perceiving.

The first is automatic. That is, images from the external world strike us without any effort on our part. But it requires an effort on our part to be aware of the instrument perceiving them. And the significant point is that this effort also has consequences, which are unexpected and appear to be quite unrelated to the images obtained by this effort.

To take a childish example, it's as if a youth on a South Sea Island could get food either by picking up a cocoanut that is lying on the ground at his feet, or by climbing to the top of the tree to get one there. Now let us suppose that the cocoanuts at the top of the tree are better. If he climbs up there for his, he not only gets better cocoanuts but incidentally he develops the ability to climb—a new power. So, in self-consciousness, the images are of a different kind, and consequently have different subsequent histories, the effort of climbing to get them is the beginning of the development of psychological will. These double causes induce the sense of self (individuality).

TUESDAY, 7 APRIL 1931

It is important to keep the sequences of these talks in mind. And to make an effort between meetings to digest what has been said, remembering that the brain is also a stomach. Otherwise ideas go in one ear and out the other.

Nothing is so rotting to the brain as to let a stream of images pass through it with no effort to digest them. The digestion, or assimilation, of ideas is brought about by comparing, contrasting, and measuring them with ideas already current in the mind. Even if this is done, the idea may not be *fully* grasped, but as a result of the effort made you will have extracted the ideas from it that are of personal value to you in your present condition and these ideas, or food for the mind, redound to your general health and well-being.

A man requires three foods:

What is ordinarily called, food: liquid and solid.

Air.

Impressions.

Of the first we have a pretty complete digestion; of the second we get only a few of the grosser elements, unaware that we are not getting the important vitamins; of the third we have hardly any digestion at all.

The first evidence of emotional well-being is impression-ability; the capacity to respond to a new situation or to a person, or an idea, in what is ordinarily called a naive or boyish way. One, who is always bored, incapable of delight, is emotionally senile, or paralyzed.

As our body depends on the thorough digestion of food, our emotions depend on the thorough digestion of air. Higher emotions are possible only through the assimilation of the "vitamins" of the air. This assimilation is the result of a certain kind of breathing, for which there is no name in current physiology.

Physiology has the two names, respiration and expiration. But there are two other forms, which are aspiration and inspiration. But these cannot be done mechanically. This kind of breathing comes about, and is possible only when one is in a certain attitude.

Compare psychological attitude with physical posture. Everyone knows that posture affects breathing. An attitude is a "psychological posture." In certain *attitudes* aspiration and inspiration are more possible.

494

If you are trying to aspire to something, above your ordinary plane—e.g. a higher state of being—you will find that you will be breathing differently.

The lungs are the organ for the digestion of air.

The brain is also a stomach, but the food of the brain consists of ideas. An idea is the expression of relationships between sense impressions.

It is hard to think that these are food for our growth: as real as ordinary food and air.

Ideas have the same range as foods: good, bad, spoiled, neutral, poisonous, etc. One can have a plethora; or have too few to sustain intellectual life. Or ideas may be so badly mixed by association that they become collectively poisonous to us. We are familiar with the idea that ordinary food can be taken in good order or in bad order, and we arrange our meal accordingly. The same is true of ideas.

The ideas discussed at these meetings, for example, compare with foods of which a small quantity gives a strong effect. If taken too soon after talk on light, trivial subjects, or followed immediately by such talk, bad effects result. Compare the care taken in religious services to surround the consideration of divine subjects with relative quiet. The kneeling and praying on entering the church is to provide a moment of "fast" before the intake. Similarly on leaving the church, to provide another moment of fast during which ideas may be absorbed,—or the impressions settle to their level before being mixed with impressions of a different specific gravity. Orage remembers the custom in the village church that he knew as a boy, of keeping silence until one was out of the churchyard. If this "silence" is complete—i.e. not merely on the lips but in the mind—the impressions have a chance to be absorbed while still unmixed.

In these groups we come to the discussion fresh from the affairs of everyday life, and turn back to them immediately afterward. It can be seen that it is hard to maintain a state of intellectual health. Almost no one succeeds. One must know *when* to feed.

Each of our three health's does thus depend on food selection.

Distinguish between letting ideas pass through our heads and entertaining them. In first entertaining a new idea, one abstains temporarily from other ideas. One is not making the new idea one's own, nor agreeing with it, but finding out *how it feels in the mind*. What is for you in it will be absorbed; what is not will drop out of your memory. What drops out is not for your present mental health. A while after thus *entertaining* an idea you will find yourself intellectually stronger—(like the invigoration after a meal).

Try to put yourself in the attitude of aspiring, and note the effect on your breathing. Any aspiration to excel, to become more, etc.

Aspiration is hope *plus* effort. Neither one alone constitutes aspiration. It is because of this double nature of aspiration that it was symbolized in ancient times by the two wings of the eagle on the ox. One wing was hope, the other effort.

We live three lives simultaneously. Our first stomach is in passable condition, but our emotional and intellectual stomachs are badly deranged. An invalid stomach needs an invalid diet.

Now let us apply what we have been saying to the two portraits, begun at the preceding meetings. Last week we formed the external portrait; now internal.

Instead of the external picture, imagine the three-story diagram:

3—intellectual
2—emotional
1—physical

In each of these there is a stomach. The first receives food, digests and excretes. The organ has taken what it could from the food received. Perhaps it has been accustomed to cheap food of little nourishment value; or perhaps it is in a normal condition and accustomed to the best.

We won't go into the question of the first food except to remark in passing that it is dangerous to eat if during the process you are psychologically depressed. But the care suggested here is not meant to be that of a valetudinarian, picking at food; and afraid of quantity, or strange dishes, or irregularity. A "robustness" that is not rash, but adventurous.

Now think of Portrait No. 2. It is No. 1 in a state of good health. The physical stomach is working well, selecting its food. "Good taste" is the normal selective faculty of healthy organisms.

Postponing consideration of its emotional stomach until later, look at its intellectual stomach. The brain is at its best. This does not mean that it is changed. It is still your brain, not somebody else's. That is, there is nothing supernatural, or mystical, about this matter. The brain will still be yours, not Newton's; but it will be yours at its maximum. And the result of this maximum functioning would be a sensation of satisfaction. Satisfaction is the result of normality.

It is true that you would give the impression both to yourself and to others that you had become very different, although you would not be.

Now to return to the emotional stomach, and to explain why we left it to last.

Remember the conception of three forces: positive, negative and neutralizing. What is the neutralizing force? Take as an example the play of Macbeth. The positive force is Lady Macbeth, the negative force Macbeth. The word negative does not here mean weak; the negative force is a force but only in resistance; is not self-initiating. (Compare Othello and Iago, neither one weak.) The neutralizing force is *the play*.

Another example: evolution (positive) and involution (negative). This can be taken to any profundity, but for example—growth and decay. An organism grows to a certain point, then merely changes, and then begins to decay—the organism involves.

All life consists of the opposition of these two forces. Any object at any moment is growing, changing, or decaying. Chemicals in it differ in what may be called "age," i.e. they are neither ascending nor descending their own scale.

Modern physicists, Jeans, etc., agree in stressing the negative force, as if the positive force had been applied once for all at some previous moment, and then withdrawn. They say that the universe is running down—only by decay. Impossible that this should be true.

From the widest point of view, the neutralizing force is the universe itself.

Any given note is always in process of decreasing or increasing its number of vibrations. What keeps it at the note? The balance of the two forces.

We are notes. In each of us Othello and Iago work. The will to live, to excel, to aspire—to try to become more—susceptibility to new ideas, etc., versus the will to resign—to cease to make effort—to become inert. The neutralizing force in each of us (as in every object—and the universe consists exclusively of objects) is our body. Everybody is a *field*.

Apply this to Portrait No. 1. The three forces. We can change the neutralizing—i. e. the person—not directly, but only by changing either the positive or the negative. We change the play by changing either Othello or Iago. Once, given the two characters, the play follows.

But all three are inter-related. Where does the impetus start? With the brain; that is, through the effect of a change in the brain, *in relation to* the body. Mind without body doesn't make change of emotion; and body without mind doesn't make change of emotion.

But the neutralizing force must not be thought of as merely the result of the other two. The play had to be created according to its own reason. Shakespeare is in the emotional center. And every time the brain is opposed by the body, Shakespeare writes a play, which is our emotional state.

The technical definition of man is the emotional center. He is at every moment a neutralizing force to these two practically cosmic forces.

TUESDAY, 14 APRIL 1931

It must be born in mind that these talks are preparatory to practice. Theory is discussed only that it may be put into use.

No muscle can be developed by watching someone else practice—nor by understanding what should be done.

Development pre-supposes effort.

The effort here indicated is calculated to give the maximum effect in the minimum time and with the minimum effort.

There is a danger in understanding too much if it is not accompanied by the desire, to put the understanding into practice, if only experimentally.

We are familiar with the distinction between the hearers of the word and the doers of it. The first are the intellectuals, the second the practical ones.

The danger of the second type is that they try to practice before they understand what it is that is to be done. Nine out of ten rush out with a false impression of what is involved and come to grief.

The danger of the intellectuals is that although they may acquire such a clear understanding that they can even pass it on to others, they are not moved to lift a finger to put it into practice.

Ask yourself to which type you belong. Look back over the actual events of your life, and ask yourself candidly in which way you have behaved. If you will do so, you will know which the danger you are exposed to is. This is a simple illustration of the relation that should be kept between theory and practice.

What is your own picture of yourself? Let us suppose that you have enough imagination to forget who you are, and what you have done, what you have been, etc. Then imagine that you meet yourself. What impression would you make on yourself? How would you estimate or judge this creature? What future would you think probable for him?

This is important because most of us live in the anticipation and hope of a future for ourselves that is in fact impossible. It wouldn't bear five minutes scrutiny. A false hope, which is merely the projection of our wishes, with *no relation to our potentialities*. This false hope keeps us living in a state of what is ordinarily called optimism. Yet anybody else, looking at it objectively, could pronounce it impossible.

If you will try to do this, you will be on the track of an important psychological exercise, which will develop insight.

Contrast the future to which you look forward by hope with the future, you would forecast objectively if you were somebody else.

When the false-illusory-impossible future has been eliminated, it will still leave open several futures based on possibilities.

Among our possibilities there are some which, from our own point of view, are more desirable than others. A desirable future is one that we would find, in the deeper sense of the word, agreeable to pursue, and which we would close with satisfaction. Each of us also has the possibility of several disagreeable futures.

Many people from middle age on suffer from various agonies, which might have been avoided, and also might have been forecast by any objective observer. Attachments to one's children, or money, or even health etc., of such a kind that the creature suffers. These are the result of the failure to employ, while the future was still moldable, the means to direct it.

We are not speaking now from the point-of-view of merely day-by-day happenings. The future is the rest of our lives, or perhaps longer. The factors involved are being determined now.

What kind of a future would you regard as agreeable? Ask yourself honestly. It will fall into one of three types:

    a.   Is it doing something? Is there some particular achievement the doing of which you imagine would make you happy? Do you say to yourself: If I could do that, I'd die happy?

    b.   Or is it knowing, or understanding something? Do you say: If I could once understand such-and-such, I'd die happy? People of this type are numerically, fewer than the first.

    c.   Or is it becoming something? Having become something as a result of the experiment we call life. People of this type, especially in the Occident, are very rare.

These three kinds are all. It is these or nothing. That is, nothing practicable, or even definable.

Suppose you have discovered the desire in yourself—what are the prospects of arriving at that future?

Imagine a straw floating in the middle of a lake of many currents. On which bank will it eventually land up? Call that bank its future. But the straw is making in no direction; it has no port in mind, no motive power, and no compass. Hence we can deny it, strictly speaking, any conception of a "future" whatsoever.

Now imagine a sailing boat in the hands of a skipper who is ignorant of the art of sailing. He may propose one of the three banks as his objective; but he doesn't know how to take advantage of winds, currents, etc. For all his efforts, in the absence of knowledge, he lands up on one of the other banks than the one he had proposed.

Now imagine a steamboat (an integrated person) with a skipper who knows the art of navigating. He has his own power on board, the steam. He also will encounter adverse winds, currents, storms. But he has the power plus the knowledge of direction and ports. He can guarantee that sooner or later he will arrive at his port.

The steamboat alone can be said to have a "future"—calculable in point of port and power, if not in point of time. He may suffer delays; take longer to beat up against certain currents than he expected—steamers are often delayed by storms. The time of his arrival will be determined by chance, the rest is calculable.

For the other two types there is no future.

Now let us confine ourselves to the one with a future. We began by saying that there were only three kinds of future, from which to choose.

From one point of view we may say the choice doesn't matter; it is made automatically according to type, not objectively. But what counts is that the skipper should define his port. Is it doing—knowing—being?

If it is doing, what do you propose to do? Without an answer to this question, you are a straw, condemned to drift.

499

In the effort of asking, you will find that you will eliminate several impossibilities—squeeze out some illusions. This in itself will be healthy if not pleasant. But ask yourself still more candidly. Use your imagination. Try to picture the day of your death. From having accomplished *what* would you pass contented out of this existence?

It may be something very simple that you want to do; such as having learned 15 or 30 languages; or brought up your children; or written a unique book; or accomplished some work in art; or have influenced your contemporaries—a thousand things.

At this point Orage remarked that he might paraphrase this idea in innumerable ways, but that the effect would be the same in the absence of any effort on the part of his listeners to question themselves, either at that moment or at some early time.

Note that the definition of your goal is not imposed on you from without. Ask yourself *explicitly* what you are aiming to do.

Arrival at the port presupposes that:

You have steam on board.

You know how to manipulate the vessel.

You have a compass.

The psychological correspondence of steam is will.

This implies that, having set your objective, you can compel yourself; in the face of all the hypnotic suggestions you may meet, to employ the means necessary for this end.

The accomplishment of the work you have set yourself will require that *abilities* be trained in yourself.

And for this there must be power or will. For only this enables us to choose when two propositions are presented to us.

And our whole lives are a series of choices between two alternatives. We travel along a series of continually forking roads.

When the port is defined and the will exists, the choice becomes relatively easy. For one is then immune to suggestion.

People make a great mystery of will, forgetting that it is atomic in structure, not a straight line. It is composed of particles, having in this sense an affinity with all matter.

All substance, however continuous it may appear, is made up of particles. These particles, in their final analysis, are charges of energy.

Will is a congeries of moments—the moments at each forking. At each forking there is a choice between this or that (occasionally this, that, or that); at each of these points an atom of will exists.

The development of will is brought about by the *repetition* of choices. We imagine that once we have willed, the rest will follow of itself, forgetting that will is an atom of time as well as of energy. A line is a series of points; and psychologically speaking each point equals a moment of choice between two possibilities. Alternatives.

Now let us assume that we have that power. For none of us is without a single particle of will, what we lack is enough to make a line. But ninety-nine times out of a hundred we don't know which to choose. The absence of knowledge makes it impossible to make a straight line. Consequently will is not called into play.

Have you ever been in a maze? The next time you are in London, go into the one at Hampden Court. A series of lines in which you might wander for hours, making the wrong choice at the forkings.

What would be the criterion of right choice?

Suppose, for example, there were an arrow painted at each forking—you could go through the maze without hesitating, and get out in a minimum of time.

The clear definition of a part—an *aim*—is the beginning of the making possible a choice. Choices bring into play will, and it then becomes possible to develop linear will.

Yet this will is not automatic. The other road will always have attractions. The arrow is usually found on a road that at the outset appears a little forbidding; on the other road (inclination) there are, at least at the outset, primroses. The primrose path is merely the downhill road of wishes.

Even with arrows it is necessary to choose between the in-appearance-more-desirable and the in-fact-more-desirable.

WISH VS. WILL

Wish is in relation to an object; or strictly speaking, an image of an object. This image evokes in us a wish, strong in proportion to our polarized affinity with the object. No object (or image), no wish. This is purely mechanical, and in relation to the object we are negative.

A negative electricity is produced in us by the presentation of a, to us, positively charged object. "Positively charged" means, in psychological language, possessing desirability.

In relation to the object we are like an iron filing to a magnet. If the iron filing could speak, it would probably say: "I'm crazy about that magnet. I simply must possess it." The magnet-is the cynosure of every iron filing's eye.

The filing is negatively charged; but to itself it gives the psychological impression of a great and driving passion.

Will is *choice* (according to reason and not according to wish). In wish (drawing the filing towards the magnet) there is no choice.

The essence of will is the calculation of means; that is, to what extent.

a. Is preferable to.
b. *In reference to an aim.* Will is cold.

At each forking of the road, there is will vs. wish. It's as if down one road there was a strong draught; a positive charge of desirability. Arriving at the fork, this sets up in us a negative charge, which we interpret as a wish.

We must stress the necessity of aim; because without aim no exercise of will is possible.

[*Text missing.*]

2.   If the port you have chosen is knowing, ask yourself explicitly what it is you wish to know. May be still unknown to yourself; but if you are one of those whose future is of this type, you may be sure there is something you have an ambition to know.

Your happiness depends on discovering what it is.

Happiness is the experience of being on the way towards the goal you have in view.

Ask yourself, therefore, is there something to be known, the possession of which would be bliss, progress towards which happiness, for you.

As an example of persons of this type, take Bacon, one of the few in the western world with what could truly be called a passion to know. Eventually he incurred his death in the pursuit of knowledge. In his case, what did he wish to know? He defined it himself. We will not say that his goal was possible to reach in one human life, but at least he clearly defined it. It was "to know the mind of God."

He regarded the world as an intelligible structure, created to serve some use, and he asked himself: What was the motive of the mind that created it? He used the analogy of a machine, which is defined by its use, and each part of which is intelligible only in relation to its use. In his attempt to understand the world, he studied physical laws, psychological laws, and what we would now call spiritual, or what he called "alchemical" laws, his ultimate purpose being to grasp the intent of the inventor.

Considering the altitude and intensity of his passion, we can only feel ourselves—as minds in relation to such a mind—as savages, and our little passions for knowledge trivial.

There are few men living today with even a fraction of the passion for knowledge that quite a number of men, for no apparent reason, had in the time of the Renaissance.

Yet, even though not at this altitude, we can each of us develop in our own octave.

For each of us belongs to a certain scale; which may be different for each of our centers. It is important to try to realize on which scale each of our faculties is.

For example, in the field of doing: Napoleon. Relative to the little enterprises in which most of us engage his activities were on a gigantic scale.

In the field of emotion: Francis of Assisi. And on a still higher scale—at least according to the portrait we have, which may be fictitious—Jesus, whose love for others included in a wise affection not only people unknown to him but people not yet in existence. This is a scale of emotion that is impossible to us.

Thus it is important to try to allot ourselves on our own scale. For it is possible to move up or down on any scale. And happiness consists in moving up or towards an aim. For an aim is always a little higher than our present condition.

With the end defined, happiness thus depends on the effort to rise. And complete happiness results from the maximum progress towards the aim.

In using the term "complete" happiness, think of a row of pots, from one pint to one gallon size. If they are all filled to the brim, each one experiences the sensation of fullness, although they contain different quantities. That is, we are not comparing happiness with happiness, but completeness with completeness.

At present we are half, or quarter, or less full. As we move up the scale of any one of our three pots, we experience more or less fullness.

Returning to the question: What do you wish to know?

God spare us the experience, common in fairy tales, when a fairy godmother offered to gratify three wishes. Could we answer promptly—for presumably the fairy godmother was not to be kept waiting—we may be sure that we should no sooner have enunciated our wishes—long before they had been granted—than we should bitterly regret them, and run after her, crying: "No, no, that's not what I want."

A true passion to know might perhaps assure us of a series of lives. We have no raison d'être to galvanize our lives, force left over from unfulfillment. If we had a passion that only a series of lives could satisfy, and if at the end of each there was some passion left over, then there might be something in the nature of immortality.

[*Text missing.*]

3.   Now, if you are one of those whose choice of a future lies in the field of Being.

This is the hardest category to discuss because of the obscurity of the words. Practically everybody has wrong associations; and even with the right ones the words often have no meaning.

Yet the idea can be fully explicated in four words. And each of them has an exact meaning to Orage. The words are:

Being—Becoming

Actual—Potential

To take the simpler pair first: actual and potential

a)   A thing is actual when it acts. And the proof that it is acting is always that it can *cause impressions*.

For example: why is there a dispute as to whether ether actually exists? Experiments have been made to try to detect the effect of the passage of the sun through ether, causing what is called "drift," analogous to the wave of a boat, passing through water. If this drift or friction could be perceived, it would be evidence of the actual existence of ether. Since the experiments have as yet had no result, ether remains an hypothesis.

Orage then lifted a glass ashtray from the table. "This acts. It is made up of particles containing energy, which affect the optic nerves, etc. We *assume* that the ashtray is there only because of its effects. Similarly we may take any object, including ourselves."

b)   A potential is anyone of the actuals that any present actual may become.

If brought into contact with another actual, this ashtray might become an amorphous mass of molten glass. But it could never be, say, a billy-goat. In other words, a potential is not something abstract. The ashtray has a use for me; the mass of glass would have none. Thus we can classify potentials in a series, or an order, of superior or inferior values, defined relative to use. The only reason for transforming glass into an ashtray is that this form has a use value. In economics all work is the transforming of actualities of inferior order into actualities of a superior order. Raw materials are manipulated by intelligence and machinery; the product is the same thing in a new form. Wealth consists of the selection from the potentialities of any given material for the production of actualities of a higher order.

To a non-valuing creator, such as is ordinarily assumed in current thought, any actual world is as good as any other. Eddington ends his book on the question of value. The contemporary school of science which maintains that there is no value can deal only in permutations and combinations of this pair, actual and potential.

Now let us oppose to this pair the other: being and becoming.

With these words we enter a different world, where "becoming" presumes an end. We can now measure relations between one actual and another relative to an aim regarded as desirable. For only when there is a more desirable object, can actuals be arranged from the point of view of becoming. This introduces a scale for determining progressive values in the actualizables of a being.

The ashtray was at one stage a mass of glass; that form was converted by art into its present form, because this, compared with raw glass, is an object of superior desire.

Take ourselves also as beings. As such we are susceptible of other actualizations. If it is a matter of indifference to you, or to anybody else, what you become, then there is no becoming—that is, no value, no meaning.

But if one potential can be selected as more desirable, then relative to that, coupled with an effort to actualize it, you can be said to be in a state of becoming.

In the absence of any such end you are becoming nothing; and the next actual into which you are transformed will also be nothing.

Maybe you have no passion to do or to know. Have you any to become?

Imagine yourself in the center of a circle of time. The center of the circle is this moment. The circumference represents the moment of your death, say five, or ten, or fifty years hence. When that time comes you will be occupying some point of that circumference, and it will be a concrete definite *you* that will be buried. You will then be actualizing one of the potentialities of the present you at the center of the circle. Will it be the one you essentially wish to be? In relation to this there can be striving, and in becoming one figure there is good riddance to others. Can you say: This is what I wish to be? You will find also that it is what you were designed to be and by your wish you are magnetically attached to it. This is the potentiality, the becoming of which is for you the condition of happiness and the attainment of which is bliss.

In the *effort to make* the two portraits we have talked of before, this potentiality will emerge. To reach the port steam (will) is necessary. One can then be in a "posture of advance"—but everything is contingent on the definition of the goal.

TUESDAY, 21 APRIL 1931

Let us go back to the time diagram. Let the center represent now, and the circumference ten years hence. At that time you will be actualizing some present potentiality. But which one will it be? Among all the possible ones there is one which you would regard as most desirable. We are not concerned now with what others would wish us to be. There is no satisfaction in being that. It may be useful on occasion, but it gives no gratification to our innermost self. The one that we would truly wish to be (after the water of our illusions has been squeezed out) is attached to us, by this very wish, by what we call a magnetic tie.

This constitutes conscience, which we may define as follows: conscience is a sense of right direction from where we are to where we would most wish to be.

Whether we become this depends on many things:

1)   Accident—The chances are a million to one against our drifting to the one desirable point on the circumference. It might be that we would end up in a *state of being* we should regard as ideal, but the betting is not good.

2)   The alternative is design or will. By projecting definitely the most desirable future, its attraction might then make us work towards it. It will still be hard, because we will be forced at every moment to choose, and other goals will look temporarily desirable. But the only sporting chance is on effort in that direction.

This presupposes a more or less concrete image of what you prefer to become.

3—intellectual

2—emotional

1—instinctive

Consider yourself as this diagram. You wish, because it is impossible not so to wish, to be relatively well—functioning in all three centers.

Knowing this, one would think that we would set about studying the questions of diet, etc. Of the other two cubes (centers) with which, we are not so familiar.

Let us assume that civilization, although crudely, has more or less understood the digestion of the bottom cube. But there is no tradition of diet in reference to air; and as for thinking, our understanding is so undeveloped that there is not even any discussion of right and wrong forms of the digestion of impressions. Yet both are relatively simple.

Now let us consider the time diagram again, but using it for a larger idea. The world we live in is an actual world, as concrete as ourselves; in other words, it is also a body.

At the center of the diagram put the present world, and let the circumference represent the state of that world a million, or ten million, or a hundred million years hence. Obviously it will then be different.

The radius seems long, in comparison, with the span of our lives, but the principle is the same. If we can use the word God—meaning whatever vital principle animates the world—his situation is like ours in reference to potentiality. It may be one of a million things, depending on (1) chance (the point of view adopted by science), or (2) will. We will only suggest now that, as there is a magnetic tie between ourselves as we are and that most desirable potentiality whose actualization is our secret wish, so it is with the world. This is called the will of God.

Having chosen our own point on a circumference, it becomes the object of the will of man. This parallel is given for future use, but setting it aside now, we will go back to the three cubes.

We can arrive at an approximate picture of our present status. This diagram is the creature bearing our names and occupying the center of the circle in the time diagram. Now imagine another diagram of three cubes on your right. Let this be the creature bearing your name at the point you wish to reach on the circumference of the time diagram.

It will not be hard to see that the creature at the center functions badly in some respects. But be specific: use concrete terms, not abstractions. The creature on the circumference will be the same one but functioning differently. And it will be you, not some fanciful figure ten years hence.

Try to see, understand, feel clearly what kind of being ten years hence you would most desire to be.

a.　　What will your physical state be? Will your digestion be good, or will you be chronically dyspeptic, tired—and unable to do, or enjoy doing, many things you want to do?

b. What will be your emotional condition? Will you be bored, incapable of any enthusiasms, that is, half sick? Will life present itself *afresh* to you every day, or will it be just one damn day after another? Will you be capable of real (though perhaps not shown to others) enjoyment of beauty, love, etc.?

c. What will be your intellectual state? Will you have preserved your keenness for ideas? Will you enjoy the expectation of knowing more tomorrow than today, or will you have grown dull and given up any interest in ideas?

The transition may be imperceptible, but it is obviously important.

First let us examine how our Portrait No. 1 has been arrived at. Are you capable of looking at yourself for a few moments and passing judgment? What are the materials of your judgment? What you find compared with what you would wish to be (remember again that it is not what others would wish. The measuring rod is not public opinion, or the opinion of your friends or any moral code, etc...

We come to be what we are through the interplay of two factors. We are the product of heredity and environment, meaning by environment the total series of influences to which we have been subjected through our whole lives.

Looking at the columns of cubes forming other people you know, we may see the world as a strange picture. Two thousand million of these pillars, upright by day and toppling over as the sun goes down.

Among these are a number of varieties, not infinite, but according to type, of which there are twenty-seven. These varieties are irrespective of color; races do not count in relation to cubical structure.

What does count is the distribution of contents. One race may be excellent in the bottom cube; another relatively good in the emotional; and a third yields occasionally an individual who is not completely sick in the intellectual.

In general, among all races, there are individuals who approximate the normal, in at least one cube. A few with good digestion in either the first, second or third.

Each of these types becomes distinguished for all other people by reason of being normal in *one* cube. Unfortunately this almost never happens in two cubes in the same individual; and it can safely be said that, thanks to heredity and environment, never in all three.

This suggests the beginning of a classification. If one cube alone is developed, we have one of three pronounced types:

"Weak yogis" or tame intellectuals. These are thinkers without common sense.

"Silly saints." In these the top story is usually empty and the bottom story in bad shape. Their emotions are divine, but their digestion is very bad.

"Stupid ascetics." They are masters of the physical body and can use it supremely well, but unfortunately they have the emotions of a rabbit and the mind of a babe.

These are the three main types. There are three more, much rarer, in which two cubes function relatively normally, giving us six types. Remember that each of these is what we ordinarily call extraordinary. These individuals invariably stand out as exceptional men.

But majority are those in whom no one cube is fully normal. There are, of course, degrees. . . .

We must distinguish here between normal and average. We are using the word normal in reference to those few in whom the distribution of functioning is relatively harmonious. They cannot be said to be average, nor usual; but they are normal because they are beginning to approximate efficiency.

The transition depends on our ability, after having correctly judged Portrait No. 1, to adopt such measures as will lead towards full functioning, ten years hence.

First set of cubes—subjective.

Second set of cubes—objective.

Let us try to define the terms subjective and objective. They are often used by everybody and seldom twice running in the same sense. The distinction is not that between subjective and real; nor between imaginative and concrete; - If I dared, I should use another pair of words, saying that the difference is that between a personal and a universal point of view.

What constitutes the material that has entered into the first set of cubes from birth to now? What we call experiences. We are the sum of our experiences; and these fall into three kinds: physical, emotional, intellectual. Each cube is a container. Its contents are the sum of the corresponding experiences from birth.

But where did they come from? Who regulated their number or quality? Obviously no one.

The frame work, crazy or well-built, we owe to heredity. The contents we owe to our chance contacts with the world.

Wouldn't it be strange to imagine—yet this is a current superstition of our civilization—that any one cube, under these chance conditions, should nevertheless yield a good distribution at the end? No law of probabilities would point to it.

Yet the three cubes, that is our whole body, react as a whole to any new experience. It cannot help it. The three are linked together. One touch, and there are reactions in all three. What kind of reactions? This depends on the contents of each cube.

No two sets of cubes are identical either in point of heredity or environment. The inference is that each of us is unique, and consequently that our reaction to each new experience is peculiar to ourselves. What I pronounce to be good, or beautiful, or true, may be on my part genuine. I am not lying, but I am stating something only about myself. I have said nothing about the object in question except the effect it had produced on me—not necessarily on you. This reaction we call subjective because it reports only the nature of the subject undergoing the experience.

There is no possibility of discussing what is good, beautiful, true, etc., not for lack of sincerity or truthfulness, but because it is impossible that our reports should coincide. They will differ because we differ.

Yet we use certain words in a subjective sense that have the possibility of a different meaning, which we will call objective.

Take the words good, beautiful, true.

Let us try to get down to the common sense of each of these words in relation to each cube.

The word "good" belongs to the bottom cube, and is used to describe what gives that cube its own state of well-being.

The word "beautiful" belongs to the second cube and is used to describe what produces good working order in its emotions. When it can say, I would not have the world different,—when the world appears beautiful—we call this the sensation of beauty; in its highest form it is the ecstasy of beauty (this is not aesthetic beauty, which is a ghostly, valetudinarian beauty).

The word "true" belongs to the third cube and is used to describe the experience we have when the brain stomach is working well. Remember that, even in using the word true, we are relating it to centers, and having no truck with metaphysics. This experience of truth is the result of occasional moments of good digestion.

But the individual good is often bad for others. This is the dilemma of ordinary morality, which says, "Pursue the Good, but do no bad to others."

Emotionally also, my good may involve a bad state of emotions for others. Thus Napoleon is said to have remarked that his happiness required to be nourished, on the deaths of thousands of other people.

Similarly in the case of truth: all discussions in politics, art, morality, etc, arise from the conflict of subjective truths; and in the hurly-burly that follows it is usually the loudest voice that sets up its truth.

It is not because, as individuals, we are good or bad, that this happens; but because we are compelled to see things in this way.

We use these three words as if they had a common meaning for all forgetting that they must have a meaning peculiar to each of us.

Now recall the idea of what the world aspires and wills to be. With this emerges a good, beautiful and true, which apply to all. But instead of taking a vote of the whole world and letting the majority decide, we must inquire of each idea what constitutes its principle,—what in itself, and *sooner or later for every normal* individual, is acceptable as a standard.

The difference begins in the area explored by Plato but without result. Plato assumed that the ideas of good, beautiful, true, exist absolutely on some plane of ideas without relation to any being; and that therefore they were insusceptible of having been created or changed. His inquiry was without result, because it was impossible to prove this assumption, which is contrary to all psychology, and has no parallel in our experience. Yet it was an inevitable deduction from the ideas then present in Plato's mind, although demonstrably false.

With the time-diagram for the world, having its radius of a hundred million years, in mind, draw a parallel between this and the same diagram for any person. Suppose that I have chosen my particular point on the circumference as my objective. In one sense my choice is arbitrary; in another, it is magnetically determined. My preference is "loaded," as a result of my nature, which in turn has been determined by the nature of the world from which I emerge (or of which I am a part); but having chosen my point, it then becomes the object of my will. Everything that conduces to its realization is good, beautiful, true. It is my guide in relation to any other potentiality or set of potentialities.

But the larger circle in which we are contained is the universal circle. It is all there is. Don't fall into the Hindu fancy of trying to imagine other worlds. There is only one (the very simplicity of this makes it hard to grasp), and this one cannot have unlimited possibilities: it can only actualize one of its *present* potentialities (if there are other dimensions, they too are potentialities of the present three).

In the world-diagram there is also a magnetic tie, which we can call for convenience the will of "God," determining a universal good, beautiful and true, as in the case of the individual. This represents God's most desirable potentiality; and because he, by will, has selected one potentiality, he has at the same time *defined*, among all the possible, goods, beautifuls and trues, one of each.

This may be called "absolute," not in the metaphysical sense, but because it refers to the whole.

The word absolute, in these discussions, is used always to mean "the whole taken as one."

Our "objective" is God's subjective. Conscience is awareness of his desired future, the actualizing of which corresponds to service.

Individual right or wrong, is measured by its approximation to this universal aim. If an individual's will coincides with the will of God, he is astride his proper instincts and becomes part and parcel of the process.

Let us take certain more definite illustrations. The figure on your left (Portrait No. 1) aims to have universal values. But what are his present values in:

1. Economics;
2. Art (using this word in its widest possible sense);
3. Science.

In economics our subjective good is whatever contributes to our well-being, whether it contributes to that of others or not. We must try to arrive at the conception and practice of an economics good for all; this is the secret of the attraction and value of such proposed systems as socialism, communism, etc. Their *impulse* is in the right direction, since they seek to replace a personal good by a universal good; but, unfortunately, they are lacking in ideas.

In art, the individual is satisfied with his choice, and his judgment is dogmatic. But his sense of beauty is determined by heredity, etc. An individual who arrives at will, will form judgments coinciding with the universal will.

In science the objective truth to be reached is what is true in fact, and ultimately appears true to everybody... These second and third cases are hard to conceive, but it is not so difficult in economics. There, few know how to bring about the desired aim, but many can recognize it. As a result of impartial self-observation, students of this method should eventually acquire at least some glimmering of objective beauty and science.

This is the magnetic tie. For if there were no desire, there would be no possibility of transition, but only drift. When each cube is working well, it dreams of, reaches out toward, this aim.

What is the bridge—the means of transition? Will is not enough; it must be instrumented. A means, or way for a will, must be found. Here I shall not repeat the method of self-observation, but recall to your minds the three forms of food. Each cube hungers and thirsts after rightness, its universal good, or beautiful, or true. This presupposes an absence of food, and a method of digestion when the food is supplied. The food for the emotions is described as "ideals" *peculiar to you* (not supplied by society). They are what you *wish*. When you have made concrete what you find desirable, you begin to breathe towards it; aspiration is "breathing towards." This changes the character of the breathing; the lungs function differently. This phenomenon, which is obvious to anyone who has ever experienced it, is described many, many times in the Mahabharata, where the heroes are said to be "sighing like serpents."

The food for the third cube is no longer desire but thinking (or trying to think) in universal terms. Let me remind you of the exercise that has often been recommended to students. Imagine the globe of the earth, the distribution of its total population, the status of that population from the point of view of biology, economics, race, interests, etc., etc. Assemble together as many as possible of the facts you already know but which lie scattered in your mind and focus them in a simultaneous picture. Then spin this globe. Try to get a sense of the nature of this being, mankind, which is divided into two thousand million cells. This is thinking in terms which are universal but concrete (not what are ordinarily called universal, such as time, space, etc.). The type of mind capable of this sort of perspective is sometimes called the statesman's mind, and it differs in kind from the mind of a politician or journalist, which gossip. And the effort to think in such terms produces a change in being.

Finally, this evening, I shall leave with you the memory of an ancient symbol, the Sphinx, which was calculated to lie between a temple and a pyramid.

The pyramid represented objective good, beauty and truth or an integrated individual. The temple was a place of preparation; in other words, a school for becoming pyramids. Between the school and the pyramid stood the Sphinx, a perpetual reminder to the pupil of what he needed to make the transition. He would require the wings of an eagle (aspiration), the body of a bull (ability to work), the legs of a lion (the assurance necessary, to defend himself against waves of depression, which would set him back farther than he had advanced), and the head of a virgin—sometimes represented as the head of an old woman—that is, impartial love. When you aspire, remember the Sphinx.

TUESDAY, 28 APRIL 1931

In these talks the stress is laid partly on ideas as such, and also on a practical attitude toward old and new ideas.

A mere feeding of the intellectual center may induce not only no inclination to put the ideas into the other two centers, but eventually an inability to do so. Devotion to ideas as such results in the weak yogi, who has lots of logical understanding, no emotional ability, and no practical technique. We are trying now to connect intellectual appreciation with the necessity of practice.

It is for this reason that so much emphasis is laid on diagrams, to balance a previous overstressing of the intellectual point of view. The diagram which Orage considers particularly useful in this connection, and which was given to him to be passed on at these meetings, is the time diagram of a circle in which the center represents the present and the circumference a given number of years hence.

This future point of time may be five or ten or twenty years. Let us call it ten. On the circumference we can conceive a certain number of actualities of yourself as you will be, or may be, in ten years. There is nothing metaphysical about this; it is yourself ten years older.

From the center you have at least theoretically a choice as to what part of the circumference you will reach. It is a sort of Dantean circle of hell, in which every conceivable figure may be horrifying.

Among these some are more agreeable, some less, and of them all there is one to which we are magnetically attached.

Last week we drew out illuminating and practical consequences from the analogy of our circle with the wider circle of the world. We shall now return to the personal use of the diagram.

Any move in the circle is bound to be along some radius; time passes and we cannot stand still. Assuming a sense of direction, movements toward the end in view may be chosen, and one finds questions of good and bad automatically, decided by the test of advantageous or not advantageous, relative to that aim.

In the absence of a definition of the aim, one will zigzag from radius to radius. The same time passes, but at the end of ten years one will be at the terminus of a different radius than that on which one started. Such a person has one aim today, but tomorrow or next year loses sight of it, or is incapable of finding things to think and do leading toward it. The same ten years have elapsed.

Since we are all in that state, by what means can we discover what is in fact the sympathetic figure ten years hence to which we are magnetically attached?

We can at least say at once that it differs for each of us, because each of us has different potentialities. And we can say that each of us will necessarily be contented with a choice based on his own potentialities. The definition of contentment has nothing to do with "that which" contents; it is the satisfaction of a secret desire.

What may be your ideal may not be ideal for me. "Better your own dharma though devoid of merit, in other men's eyes than another man's dharma though held by all the world to be meritorious."

Nor can one construct a figure which is merely a composite of sociological suggestion.

The figure we are seeking must be:

1. Within you.
2. One that in your secret heart you would most wish to be.
3. One that, in point of becoming, is the condition of your happiness.

There is no question here of praise or the world's approval. What would it secretly delight you to have become?

Nor can we answer as is ordinarily done in "uplift" literature. We might search all the books of ethics in the world without finding the material for the portrait of this figure.

Nor is it a question of average; the norm, the superman, etc. All of these terms have been corrupted by society. It is your secret image, and if it coincides with others, that is pure coincidence. And it is a matter of indifference if, in realizing it, you appear to be running counter to popular morality—serviceability to the world—etc.

All these are suggestions of collective morality. For the time being, let collective morality look after itself. As before God, who presumably is responsible for the effect that my sincerity produces on the world, what is it that ten years hence I would *wish to be?*

We have now dismissed one most frequent answer—the figure cannot be "constructed."

Nor can we succeed by trying to figure an ideal man or woman. All models must be ruled out, as suggested by sociology, and inadaptable to a self-initiated ideal: the will of God in the will of man.

If we abandon general methods—the holding up of ideals, etc.—to what can we turn?

Let us turn to the first portrait, on your left. This is you at the present moment in the light of your best objective judgment—such a judgment as you would give of another with whom you were intimate and about whom your most serious judgment was invited. Not a snap judgment, nor a clever one, nor one for personal interest; you are not giving it to please him, nor to amuse us, nor to get profit; but having reviewed all the knowledge at your disposal you weigh it and still hesitate....

In comparison with this standard you will discover how superficial and malicious your judgments of people are.

This judgment (we are still, speaking-of your judgment, of another person) will not be the truth; but it will at least be yours.

Now with the same sincerity, put yourself on the stand before yourself. This is, put yourself in such a *perspective*. The means for attaining this perspective is self-observation. Try to get such a picture of this person who goes by your name as you would have of another. Call upon yourself with a seriousness that will evoke the effort necessary to tell the truth.

This is the center of the circle; the figure is now actualizing one of its potentialities. It is not static. We must try to discover the direction in which it is moving in time.

About many people we can prophesy what will become of them, barring accidents, if they are still alive at a given time hence. Such a man, we can say, at forty or fifty will be living intellectually on his past, his emotions will be pre-adolescent, and physically he will be living for comfort. Or of this woman we can say that she will be practically without friends, acid in temperament, unhappy, with no interests in life, and driven to seek company that today she would be shocked to seek.

Most people at fifty or sixty become something that, had it been presented to them at twenty or thirty with the knowledge that that was what they were going to become, would have seemed not worth living for, and would have awakened thoughts of suicide.

The portrait on your left is moving along a radius of time, bound for a certain end. It should be possible to foresee that end with at least as much certainty as that with which we foresee the lives of others.

But even this does not get us much nearer to a full sense of the kind of being we would wish to be. To answer that question let us turn, while bearing Portrait No. 1 in mind, to Portrait No. 2 on our right.

This portrait is on the circumference. It is separated from the one on the left by ten years, but we are magnetically bound to it. This is what we know we "ought" to be. And it is one of our present potentialities (or else the world is a mad-house).

Can we choose a radius and stick to it? Along this line is to be found the "way" spoken of by all religious teachers; the way, or the path, or the shortest cut, or the radius, between the present actuality and a future actualizable.

Remember that we have dismissed the composite. Arjuna once asked Krishna: "What is the type of this Ideal? How does he walk? How does he speak? What does he do?"—And Krishna answered: "I cannot tell you."

We must distinguish between a model and an example. Arjuna was asking for a model; some conception to imitate—somebody whose behavior he could model for his own, with the certainty of producing the same results.

But there is no model. It is impossible that there could be actualized in flesh and blood any being that could be a model. Each circle of time, or time diagram, is unique. If yours could hold for me, God would be guilty of what he has never been, guilty of dividing where divisions are unnecessary—that is, one of us would be superfluous. In the economy of consciousness every individual is unique. A model presupposes that two or more have the same potentialities are identical.

This applies equally to founders of religions, not one of whom is a model. How ridiculous, for example, to try to make Christ's life and *external* behavior a model. His behavior was specifically that of a teacher. At that rate we should all take in each other's washing.

Or Buddha, to whom the same applies. No life, however full of vitamins, is a *model*.

But each of these may be exemplary. An example illustrates the *way* a thing should be done; not the thing done. For example, in learning arithmetic; examples are useful only for bringing out the principles involved.

We often pass from model to example without realizing that a model is to be slavishly copied (e.g. an art student copying a master); an example in order that the principle may be seized.

We should see now why we refrain from general terms in connection with Portrait No. 2. Examples might be given, but at the risk of leading to mistake.

We fall back on a principle difficult to explain unless we bear in mind the existence of a magnetic tie.

The portrait on the right is cast, and only becomes actualized by what may be called breath. To breathe into it the breath of life. Last week we called this aspiration: running along the magnetic tie and producing action, itself induced by something that at first sight may appear a paradox.

Ashiata Shiemash abandoned the idea of producing action by faith, hope, or love, because of the corruption of these functions under sociological influence. Your wish alone to develop will avail nothing. It may remain a dream. You may intellectually judge it worthy but lack the corresponding emotion; or you may approve intellectually and feel correspondingly, but have no practical ability. The same is true in the case of love, if it does not induce the threefold activity necessary. And still more so, especially in these days of faith. No one of these three can any longer evoke Sphinx like action.

On what then can we count? If archangels were to describe your potentiality to you, still you would not actualize it. Nor could all the propaganda in the world lead you to do so. Nor the inducements in the object itself, however adorable, would make you undertake the discovery and labor of becoming it. Orage realizes this about himself.

What situation is there that alone can evoke the resolution sufficient to enable us to choose and then move along the right radius, making constant choice between it and radii in other directions?

The answer is: self-hatred. This is the most powerful, and for us the only surviving, motive force. So far this is all merely a theory. The only proof can be by experiment. And as for the results of the experiment we will only say that it is impossible to make such a judgment of yourself as described, and to set down impartial statements about yourself in your present form without two things occurring:

1. A correspondingly vivid sense of the nature of the portrait on the right. This is filled in by lights corresponding to dark on the left; not by deliberate effort on your part; the complimentary colors (green-red) begin to be built up in your imagination in the figure which you feel you ought to be. As the qualities in No. 1 are denoted, those in No. 2 emerge.

(This, you will see, avoids dependence on a model. The warning should also be given that it is impossible to conceive what the portrait on the right should be without having done the one on the left. Orage tried for months to set down his Portrait No. 2 on paper, and found himself utterly unable to make the qualities fit. He was as much at loss as a novelist who, in the absence of a realization of his characters, sets down incompatible traits.)

2. The second result from such a judicial inquiry into our actual status may also be tested by experiment. It is not a picture this time, but a wish of a *three-fold character* to become it. It is neither primarily intellectual, nor emotional, nor instinctive; but the union of all three: it is in fact what we call will—that state, when three wishes are so blended that no one element is distinguishable. This is technically called conscience; the voice of God in essence; the magnetic connection between two different actualities in time; what Shelley called: "The spirit of the years to come yearning to mix itself with life."

This may now be only a ghost. As an interesting fancy we might imagine all potentialities as ghosts, wandering not in space but in time; each wishing to be actualized; but of these there is one which we wish, and when our wish and this one come together the maximum effort is produced on both sides.

By chance we have the notes this evening of someone who has set down the beginning of an attempt to survey his behavior. These notes may be considered as an example of the tentative trial; not as a model. Orage then read some of the notes:

"Reviewing my actual behavior it is evident that I have never really tried to do anything since leaving school, when I did try to get on the football team; what has come to me has come easily or not at all. There is nothing I have wanted hard enough to make effort for it. I never think about what I shall be or do in the future, but trust to luck. I read a

good deal and remember practically nothing. Last night I reviewed the thoughts that had occupied my mind during the day; any child could have thought them. At heart I love nobody. I must be a good deal of a squirt, but I'm continually maneuvering to impress others as a good fellow. I like to think that I am a dangerous man to women, but in fact I have never wanted any woman enough to run a risk. In discussions with men I am usually cagey, waiting to side with the strongest. No idea ever touches me deeply. I am never indignant except at some offense to myself. I have never lost any sleep over other peoples troubles, and usually think that those who do are showing off. I give lots of free advice which I haven't taken the trouble to think out and which I wouldn't, or couldn't, take myself . . ."

This represents only an attempt at a detached attitude which each of us should aim at being able to assume toward himself. In doing this one should avoid the assigning of motives, and try as far as possible to remain concrete, describing *actual behavior.*

From this we derive both a compensation and a task. The compensation is that we begin to realize Portrait No. 2 in brighter colors. The task is a sense of obligation, arising from conscience, and manifesting itself in a three-fold wish to become that figure.

Our way of going to work at this must be characterized by two things: ruthlessness, and a curiosity for the truth.

This is all we have in the way of assets. Our possible future lies within us. Neither gods nor powers nor angels can help. It is one's self against the world—not that the world is bad but that it offers many radii. From some absolute point of view—or say from the point of view of Einstein—this may not matter. But if there is a design in us and the world, then one radius has greater value than others, and there is predilection. (Eddington speculates that this world may have been a choice among many possible ones.)

We are less concerned here with theory than with practice, and tonight we have combined theory with experiment.

TUESDAY, 5 MAY 1931

Orage began by saying that he was going to read a chapter from a novel, "Success," by Lion Feuchtwanger. This chapter, called "Some Historical Data," represented an attempt to begin doing what had often been recommended to students of this method: i.e., to realize the environment in which they find themselves, not only on this planet but in the rest of the universe at any given time.

According to certain theories of time, it is permissible to imagine every moment of time existing simultaneously. But we can perceive each of these moments only in one dimension—as long as our cinema lasts. Everything that exists is in process of change; if nothing else, time is at work. The direction in which time is working may be determined.

In our experience there are two directions in which time works:

1.   Towards being, and more being
2.   Towards less and less being

Everything, in point of being, is continually en route toward moreness or lessness.

We have certain criteria of the direction of movement. Movements toward more being have a different taste. It's as if one of the possibilities of the will of God is towards being, and an experience associated with this we call "positive." In the opposite direction, we have an experience we call "negative."

Positive gives pleasure; negative the reverse of pleasure (not, however, necessarily pain, which is sensational, not emotional. Some emotions are more painful than pain).

This is brought up, Orage added, in response to questions he had received:

1)   What is the nature of the emotional center?
2)   How may positive emotions be brought about?
3)   How is emotional health maintained?
4)   What is the nature of the air required for feeding the emotions?

Last week we spoke of aspiration and inspiration. The attitudes in which these forms of breathing are possible are mentally induced. The other attitudes, of respiration and expiration, are induced by the body. People often say that they are "on top of the world," when they are still far from it, being merely in a state of good health on the plane of respiration. Excellent animals, but not yet human. This depends on the digestion of substances whose intake depends on the alternate rhythm of aspiration and inspiration.

To induce in the lungs the rhythm in which breathing changes from respiration to aspiration, it is not necessary to have any particular state of the body. It is induced by presenting to the emotional center certain ideas, or images, which are associated with "the promise of more being."

There are two states of pleasure: anticipation and realization. Given a reasonable prospect of success in any enterprise on which something for us hangs, and the mere prospect is pleasurable. Now let us consider ourselves for the moment simply as emotional beings—and theoretically at least we may separate ourselves into three beings. With the intellectual and emotional centers drugged, or put to sleep, we would only be instinctive; or with the physical and intellectual centers put to sleep, we would become beings run purely by emotions, etc. The point is the possibility of taking the emotional center as an entity, of whose experience we are only partially aware. We may often, for example, give a report from the mind that we are "happy," when in fact our emotions are suffering. In this sense the emotional center can experience that which promises more, or less, being to itself. This accounts for the effect of two different kinds of images; those promising more, which create pleasurable anticipation, or hope; and those, threatening less, which induce disgust, despair, hatred perhaps—all the negative states.

Negative states = fear of less being

Positive states = anticipation of more being

But the emotional center is virtually the sole controller of the movements of the body. In the old analogy, the intellectual center plays the role of driver; the instinctive center, or the body, the role of cart; the emotional center the horse. Of these, two elements are inert: the body by inertia, the brain by the fact that though it can direct, it cannot move. The emotional center is the motive power.

Now the emotional center is made to move exclusively in relation to the images presented to it. It knows nothing of the existence of the body or mind; but is aware only of the succession of images passing before it.

These images arising in the brain, are derived from two sources:

1. Through the body
2. In the mind itself

One may ask what sort of images are those that originate in the mind itself, having no sensuous origin? To use Eddington's word, they are "relata"—i.e., the sum of the *relations* in which objects stand to each other.

For example, the idea of a constellation—say the Belt of Orion. We know that there is no Belt of Orion; there are simply a number of stars whose accidental positions suggest an enclosing relationship. The constellation is an idea; all its parts—i.e. stars—are sense impressions, but the constellation is not a part of the sense impressions. It is superimposed by the mind.

Thus, the emotional center is presented with two types of images: those from ordinary sense impressions, and those from *the effort of the mind to arrange* ordinary sense impressions in certain relations. Or: images of objects, and the mind's own ideas—(patterns).

Now, recall that the body is insert save for the activity of the emotional center; that the emotional center in turn is driven by the thinking center. The effect of activity in the emotional center, whether from images or ideas, is to transfer this activity from itself to the physical body. An emotion instantly affects the behavior of the body. The medium is from brain to brain; i.e. from the emotional center directly to the organization called the lungs; in other words, emotions affect breathing.

Consequently, the rhythm of the lungs, feeding upon air, depends upon the emotional center, which in turn depends upon the images presented to it by the brain. In this way the three centers are linked up.

So long as the images, presented to the emotional center, refer only to sense impressions and not to relations, the breathing will be respiration. The person breathing will have, in relation to air, a restricted ability to digest. This person, naturally, is breathing the same air as anyone else; we all breathe all the air there is; but whether certain substances in it will or will not be digested, depends on the emotional center, which determines the quality and rhythm of breathing.

519

One of the difficulties of music is the existence of over-tones. How is it that a piano, for example, by the vibration of one string alone, can produce one tone and at least seven overtones? In theory, the mechanical explanation is this: when the note is struck, the whole string begins to vibrate—if it is, say, middle C, at a rate of 256. But while the whole string is vibrating at this rate, it also begins to vibrate in two halves, each half vibrating at double the rate of the whole string, or 512. At the same time, each half is halved into quarters of the whole string, vibrating at double the rate of the halves, or 1024; the quarters into eighths, etc,... All of this is taking place simultaneously.

The atoms composing a piece of wire, or a violin string, also beat such complex rhythms.

But man is also a mechanical instrument, and no part of any of us is vibrating at only one rhythm. There are also overtones in us: heard melodies are sweet, but those unheard are sweeter. We hear only the tones, not the overtones, although every part of the body is at every moment beating into complex rhythms, and one of the possibilities of the lungs is the simultaneous breathing in more than one rhythm:

a) The set of rhythms induced by images from sense impressions, referring to the body; and

b) The set of rhythms induced by the activity of the emotional center under the influence of images, or ideas, of relations.

Aspiration and inspiration induce different results in the body, by the digestion of different substances in the air.

The recipe for better (or, as used to be said in the old days when the word was in more repute, higher) breathing is to think in terms of relations.

This is because the promise of more being is pleasurable; a greater activity is presented with the images of a higher type of thought. Only "relata" induces the promise of more being. Even in ordinary expectations of material success or advantage, the effect on the breathing may be noticed. Compare the breathing when one is discouraged and when one is confident; one breathes more rapidly in a confident mood. On the plane of ideas proper there is not only acceleration, but a change of kind.

All the above is in preparation to repeating the advice often given *to try to see the constellation in which we exist.*

Some people are incapable of seeing a picture; they see the daubs of paint, etc., but a picture is something we make by training. So with our environment. Try to realize the constellation and our relation to it. The facts are not imaginary; the points for the centers of any constellation are concrete, not abstract; but a different mode of thought is required for contemplating relations, instead of merely the concrete points.

There is nothing fanciful about this; we need merely to name the points and form the constellation, if we can realize it. You can point out to a child, for example, each star in the Belt of Orion, but the child may still not see the constellation. Or, to take another analogy, we have all seen puzzle pictures, in which a face or some familiar object is hidden among many details. We can look at the page for a long time, turning it in various ways, and when we suddenly get a certain focus on it, the face stands out clearly. The environment in which we live may be such a puzzle picture, and by turning it, we may find it not only intelligible but familiar. For, theoretically, at least, there is no reason to suppose that the world may not be as complete an organism as any of its parts. In fact, it would be odd if man, evolving out of this world, had no relation to the world that bears him. The world is a being in process of being. Arid we may hope to take the pattern by surprise.

For we have the material, if not the mental ability to constellate. The points are all familiar objects:

To begin with, we are on a planet, which has a subordinate planet, the moon, whose possibilities are limited by its association with the earth. Superior to ourselves there is obviously the sun; superior to it the galaxy of which the sun is a constituent part; and beyond that thousands of other galaxies with myriads of suns, about some of which there may also be other planets. These are objects which may prove to be a constellation, if we can take them so. That is, take them as a whole. But it requires a genuine effort of the mind to consider all these as a constellation and simultaneously be aware of their relations:

1. Their spatial relations, and
2. Their relations of order.

Their spatial relations involve questions of distance and size. The relations of order involve the distinctions of subordinate, equal, and superior. The moon, for example, is subordinate to the earth for the simple reason that what happens on the earth is more important to the moon than what happens on the moon is to the earth. Similarly as between the earth and the sun; the slightest protuberance on the sun has great effects on the earth.

This is still continuing the question: "What is our environment?" and the first answer is the largest that can be given—our widest possible environment.

For the moment we will drop the question of spatial relations. In general, relations of space may be said to be more subtle than relations of order. Order is always defined by the test of "reciprocal influence."

If you are doing what you should, you will be instantly applying this idea to a number of other fields. This definition of order applies also to people. Beings differ in order, according to the influences they exert; for example, by inducing fear, love, or any emotion that activates the organism as a whole.

In the various orders of society what is called government is established on influence. In primitive societies this is based chiefly on fear of pain (consider the brutality of primitive societies). In periods of superstition witch doctors, of various kinds, exercise superior reciprocal influence through the fear of the unknown. In our days certain classes exercise it through the fear of starvation; this is called the economic weapon.

Now let us suppose that each of these monopolies for inspiring fear has been destroyed. There would still exist differences of order *by virtue of being*. One being is superior to another by the fact that his reciprocal influence is greater. For what, passes between them we have a word, but no corresponding image. The word is emanation.

There is a distinction between emanation and radiation. Emanation implies immediacy of contact between beings. Radiation is by an intermediary; i.e. another body.

This idea of order is important, because in our environment, both large and small, we are constantly encountering beings whose relations to us are either superior, inferior, or equal. And do what we may—since we can't change our being on the spur of the moment—the effects are in proportion to the differences of the two that meet. The superior being affects the inferior more than the inferior affects the superior.

(You should have in mind here all that is traditionally implied in various codes of morality, from noblesse oblige to the Confucian idea of the superior man: the mark of superiority is always inaccessibility to effects from inferiors).

If the earth were equally affectable by the moon, the two would be equal. Or take the relations between the moon and the galaxy: what happens on the moon is of slight importance to the galaxy as a whole; but the slightest change in the galaxy and the poor little moon is all in a flutter.

Between the earth and the sun there is no doubt a communication. All life, force, movement, on this planet depends on solar energy. As beings we are joint products of earth substances and solar energies. This we take for granted.

But we may also speculate that forces are exerted by the moon upon the earth, by other planets upon the earth, by the galaxies, etc.

The theory involved here is that the substances of our air are complex but numerable. Assuming the relations of planets, sun, galaxy, the substances will be—lunar; planetary (our planet and others); solar; and galactic. And since these substances are of different origin, they will have different influences. And since the origins differ in order, the substances differ in order.

Solar substances will have greater power than planetary, etc. Only as the particles enter our body and become part and parcel of us, are we subjects for corresponding experiences.

In respiration, generally speaking, we assimilate substances from the moon, the earth, and other planets. The substances from the sun and galaxy are digested only when the form of breathing is changed from respiration to aspiration.

Why is this so? Recall the theory of the piano string, vibrating simultaneously in several different rhythms. All substances in origin are vibratory phenomena. Matter is made up of wavicles; i.e. a focus of complex vibrations. Our body is a collection of wavicles. Every atom is beating its complex rhythms. We are aware only of those vibrations occurring in us which represent our state of being.

A being is defined by the range of the vibrations of its constituent atoms.

If we try to think in terms of relations, we induce a rhythm of breathing which sets up in our atoms no longer overtones but tones, with the result that the body acquires the possibility of experiencing effects that before were only unconscious. And since a being is defined as an entity of consciousness, that effort of thinking which affects the feeling, which in turn affects the breathing, which in turn makes possible new tones, which in turn change the state of being, leads to more rather than less.

All of this flows from the simple exercise of trying to establish constellations. We recommend beginning with our own planet. And the use of a familiar school globe often makes the exercise more interesting and easy.

Orage then picked up a copy of "Success" by Lion Feuchtwanger, from which he had announced at the beginning of the evening he was going to read a part of a chapter.

What interests us in this chapter, he went on, is the suggestion that the author had either heard of this exercise and practiced it, or that since he was an intelligent man it had occurred to him as one of the necessities of thought. We might almost say one of the decencies of thought, meaning by that only that it was disgraceful to a human mind not to try to be aware of its environment.

This chapter occurs in the midst of a long narrative, as though the author digressed for a moment to say: "You have now heard the story so far, but remember you cannot understand a thing these people did without bearing in mind their whole planetary backgrounds." Our own lives today, for example, are affected by the present world-wide economic depression. Even if we have the same incomes, and apparently lead the same lives, our relations to others are inevitably affected by what has taken place in the world at large. Whether the individual is aware of the changes in environment or not makes no difference. In fact, it is impossible to be aware of all of them; but the happenings are different, and we are affected although we may be ignorant of the causes.

Orage then read parts of the chapter in question. It is entitled "Some Historical Data" and is Chapter XIV of Book II of the novel, occurring at page 203 of the American edition (published by the Viking Press). I will copy a little of it to indicate the tone. The story is laid in Munich in the years 1921-1923.

"In those years the population of this planet numbered 1800 million people, of whom about 700 million were white. The civilization of the white races was supposed to be better than that of the others, and Europe was supposed to be the best part of the earth; but it was being gradually ousted in importance by America, in which about a fifth of the white race lived.

The white races had set up various barriers among themselves of a very arbitrary nature. They spoke various different languages; there were groups of a few million who had their own idiom that was incomprehensible to others. As far as possible they strengthened by artifice the difference between individuals and between groups, and found the most varied excuses for making war on each other. The idea, certainly, was gaining ground that it was out of place to kill human beings; but there still existed in many people a primitive lust for slaying. They used to fight each other, for example, for national reasons, that is to say, because they were born at different points of the earth's surface. Group emotions were exploited; it was considered a virtue to regard as inferior those who were born outside one's own officially determined frontiers and to shoot them down at stated times fixed by the governing body. This virtue was impressed on all from childhood, and was termed patriotism. They also fought each other for sociological reasons, using with great effect such concepts as surplus value, exploitation, class, proletarian and bourgeois. As the lines of demarcation here, too, were purely arbitrary, it was not easy for the party leaders to define the attribute which made people supporters or opponents of any particular group.

The manner of living in that epoch was not hygienic. People were crowded close in enormous buildings of stone and iron, badly ventilated, and huddled evilly together with few green spaces.

In the year of the Kruger case 379,920 people died in Germany, 14,352 of these being suicides, that is four percent of the total.

Sports and physical exercises were in high favor. The chief aim of sport was to establish a record, and extraordinary trouble was taken to specialize in physical achievements. The most popular sport was boxing, which consisted of a combat, according to certain rules, between over-trained and powerful men. But the so called six-day races were also popular... These professional followers of sport could not exercise for long their powers of foot and fist, for their over-trained muscles consumed their own strength, and these men aged and died prematurely.

The culture of that epoch was based in essentials on the ideals of the Renaissance, that is, on the literatures of ancient Greece and Rome romantically interpreted. The wisdom of the East insofar as it was embodied in books and works of art, in history and forms of life, was known by only a few hundred scholars of the white race... In the schools for children, by far the greater part of what was taught had no practical value. The events of past years were classified on an unintelligent system, based on wars and other hostilities...

Of congenital idiots and cretins, there were in Germany 36,461, of whom 11,209 were in Bavaria. The German Empire expenses for its army amounted to 338 million gold marks, for literature 3000 marks, for the campaign against venereal disease 189,000 marks.

The practice of justice in Germany at that time had little relation to ordinary life, and none at all to the best opinion of the age. It was based....

Such were the white races whom the planet whirled through space during those years, and who comprised two-fifths of its total human freight. "

Having finished reading, Orage remarked that as last week he had given an example of the kind of statements one should aim at being able to make about one's self, so this week he had happened to be able to give an example of the kind of statements one must try to make about one's environments. Only when both can be done will it be possible to arrive at a true picture of one's own norm.

Last week he had spoken of the diagram of time, in which the present was represented by the center and a given point in the future by the circumference. Along one radius and one alone, does movement produce in our emotional center that pleasurable anticipation associated with the promise of more being. Along all others pleasures are merely the passing pleasures of the body.

But why is it so difficult to discover one's own magnetic line leading towards one's own normal actualization? The answer is to be found in the world situation at the given moment. Thanks to the total environmental effects, our judgment is warped, and we are directed under the influence of mass suggestion—or, and this is equally fatal, by resistance to mass suggestion—to actualize an inferior, non-soul potentiality.

According to the nature of the total environmental influences to which we are subjected we suffer the attraction of the forked paths, which occur at every moment. At each fork, one is our magnetic path; but—thanks to the environmental influences—the other becomes at that moment overwhelmingly attractive. The chances are a million to one against our choosing the magnetic one and arriving at our normal actualization.

But if, at the moment of choice, you pause, so to speak, "to take a breath," the character of the substances digested will decide the choice. If it is merely respiration, it is equally certain that the planetary substances will remain overwhelmingly influential. If you preface the attempt by making an effort to realize your situation in regard to your environment, you will by that very fact become a little less under the influence of the environment. Not merely by the mental effort, but because the type of images presented induce a new order of breathing, which results in the digestion of new substances, etc...

From this will result:

1) Some degree of separation from the environment;

2) Hence, some possibility of realizing our norm apart from the coloration of the environment; and

3) The establishing in one's self of the experienced difference between an environmentally originated wish and a magnetically realized, essentially felt wish.

This was the end of the talk, but Orage said he might add one or two suggestions for further thought. It may be, he went on, that in our environment (the sum of which constitutes the existing civilization on this planet), there occurs a succession of seasons, which may be very long—so long as to correspond to changes in our zodiac, and determined by the relations of our solar system to other solar systems. This idea was known in ancient India, where these vast seasons were known as the Yugas (spelling) and it was announced

525

that the death of Buddha had inaugurated the Kali Yuga, or winter. In this long winter the total environmental influences are such that it is practically impossible for any individual to arrive at normal development. It is only in this state that such difficulties are encountered as we encounter; we are unlucky to have been born in winter.

Against this somewhat gloomy prospect, we can, however, perhaps set two ideas: one, that even in winter growth is possible; and secondly, that in any case, the maximum of happiness for any individual is still to strive for normality, even against the season and his contemporary environment. In earlier ages, according to an old tradition, normality was natural, and failures not more common than the failures among us to arrive at any ordinary physical development. This was the age of gold, followed by the age of silver, then the age of bronze; ours is the age of lead.

In this connection try also to think how the environment came to be what it is, and what its possibilities are for the future. Try to fit what geological, biological, and chemical facts you already know into the picture of the past of the earth. In the simian age, what was happening on this spot where we are now gathered? Then what are the potential actualizations of this planet in the future? The answers themselves are of no importance; we are abysmally uninquisitive about the earth a million years ago or a million years hence. We are interested in the present; in the past only as we try to read in the present environment what must have happened; similarly to read what will happen. Not the answers but the activity is important. These are merely *exercises* designed to bring about that exhilaration in the emotions which is the anticipation of more Being.

TUESDAY, 12 MAY 1931

The meeting began by someone asking for a recapitulation of the idea involved in the two portraits. Orage recalled the time diagram in which we let the circumference represent ten years hence. The radii are many but not infinite in number because the center is our present state of being.

Remember also the three cube diagram, bear in mind that the totality of our life is made up of three orders of experience. There is a certain life in each cube; certain tests of the degree of fullness of each and the rate at which each is developing one way or the other. None is ever stationary—each is always moving toward more being or less being: developing or involving, bringing in more varied and rich experience, or more monotonous.

Each radius is the line of one of the possible actualizations of each center. There are thus three possibilities at the end of each radius. One center may at that time be practically obsolete; no longer actively functioning.

Ten years ago a similar diagram might have been drawn for each of us. Our present center would then have been a point on the circumference. Today you are no phantom, but flesh and blood; if ten years ago you could have foreseen yourself today, the figure would have been imaginative but not imaginary. The you today was not present in time, but none the less real for that. The diagram represents the second dimension of time. Each potentiality exists in time only; whether it is to exist in space also, is to be determined by the individual.

There is one radius to which we are magnetically attached by a sort of compass within ourselves, and even when the steering apparatus is broken the compass still points north.

There is no common north for all of us; but looking at your own compass, ask yourself if you are moving towards what you would wish to become if you control your fate.

Nor is it utterly impossible to stake out a few guide posts in Portrait No. 2. Taking it by cubes:

1) Are you perfectly satisfied at present with the health of your intellectual brain or stomach? Do you derive *delight* from its activity? Will it think about the kind of problem that really interests you, or is it like a monkey picking up one little thing, dropping it and jumping at another. Can you *make it think for you?* It is impossible for you to wish to find it worse, or no better, ten years hence; to have, let's say, no longer any interest in any intellectual question; no power of concentration; no discernment, no grasp, etc. Yet most people who are intelligent at thirty-five are gradually growing intellectually atrophied at forty-five, on their way to becoming morons. There is every kind of inducement to let ourselves slide into apathy. Yet nobody can wish to be a moron; why that is so, we don't know, but none of us can.

2) Similarly in regard to the emotional center; how do you like to be described as incapable of any feeling? We have words which we apply to men and women whose emotions dry up; we call the women sour and the men crusty. They are incapable of a spontaneous reaction to a new situation; they cannot play.

3) Physically what sort of picture would please you? Would you wish to be, say, too fat to move? Or unable to sit up late at night, or get up early in the morning? Finding no delights in physical activity? Allowing for the effects of time under good conditions, it is possible to contrast the present picture with that at fifty, sixty, or seventy. Dying old is very different from dying prematurely in each center. As an example in the instinctive center (and not implying any other comparison) I can cite a man of seventy-eight whose name is familiar to you all—Lloyd George. His delight in physical activity, while he cannot do the same things he did before, is still fresh and keen. He lives, at a tempo appropriate to his age and powers, with vigor and pleasure.

Notice that we are not aiming to become fully alive in only one of these centers; i.e. to become ascetics, or saints, or intellectuals. These are the kind of ideals which, if you become them, you will find yourself transformed in a monster.

[*Text missing.*]

The contemplation of this picture of the actual serves a double purpose:

1)   It accustoms us to an objective survey of ourselves. This incidentally is of great help in dealing with others. For *no one* can objectively define others who has not objectively defined himself. We can look at the animal in question and define it, say as a camel, not a giraffe, nor a horse. At this point someone asked: Can we say that it is an awkward camel? Orage replied let us leave out any adjective except those necessary to define the type. There are for example, various breeds of dogs. Eventually we may learn to classify not only type but breed within the type.

2)   The second consequence of this effort is one that would seem quite unexpected. It is an emotional reaction to the discovery of the breed to which you belong. Imagine a dog belonging to the breed poodle which has always fancied itself a Newfoundland. It discovers that it is a poodle. Its emotional reaction is first a dislike of being a poodle, because its most cherished pleasures in the past have come from its fantasies that it was a Newfoundland (we are not implying here that one breed is better than another; our question is, to which species does this particular individual belong? For, relative to that, we may judge its evolving possibilities: to what, as a member of this breed, it may aspire.)

It is the surprise itself that is unpleasant, regardless of any question of superiority of type. If by chance the individual finds that he belongs to a type which it pleases him to belong to, then he is still due for another surprise. For he would eventually discover that there is no difference between types as such from the point of view of objective value. He may be a military conqueror, or a savior. We think one better than the other, the healer superior to the killer, because we are subject to the effects of each, and our reaction is purely personal. But from the point of view of God it is not a question of whether a given type of individual is more pleasant for his neighbors; but whether, from the point of view of developments—the actualization of potentialities—he is more active.

We are now speaking not of growth but of development. Growth is merely enlargement, or the perfection of a species. Development is the transmutation of species. There are sudden transmutations of species as well as gradual evolution. During the slow process it is according to Darwinian laws; but there are crises when behavior is according to the Mendelian laws. The latter produce new species—the former variations within species.

Perhaps each of our three brains may be the result of a Mendelian jump. We can find no history to account for their sudden appearance, even germinal.

From an objective point of view, what counts are not so much the variations. Suppose any one of us, from various lucky circumstances over which we have no control, were to acquire objective consciousness—this would be a leap. This was brought out by Jesus when the Apostles questioned him about

John, the Baptist, and he replied: "Of all the sons of women there is none greater than he, yet the least of those that has entered the kingdom of heaven is greater than he."

A Rolls-Royce, let me say, stands at the acme of the kingdom of machines; yet relative to the amoeba, at the bottom of the kingdom of life, has less value. The difference is not one of degree, but of kind; the amoeba has more value; value being defined as containing more, or less, potentiality of self-development.

The question of transmutation has a relation to the two diagrams. For one, in the absence of one of these Mendelian leaps, will find the radius, or finding it stay on it.

The preceding digression arose from the two results we noted of the attempt to make a judicial survey of Portrait No. 1: (1.) the ability to define ourselves and others; and (2.) the induced reaction of shocked surprise.

In describing animals we make no moral judgments; or if we do, it is merely a question of agreeable or not agreeable to us. In the medieval story of Reynard the Fox, which arose in the attempt to describe human types, the animals were described. We are in the habit of saying the cunning fox or the treacherous jackal; but we should be able to say simply: "The fox or the jackal is such and such an animal and treat him accordingly—beware of him if necessary." This is what in fact we do with a charged wire. We don't say it is wicked; we define *its nature and its effects*. The absence of judgment does not mean the absence of definition. Our judgments of others, if we have not made an objective judgment of ourselves, is made from the point of view of self-preservation. A is likely to be dangerous to me, B is likely to be congenial; I call A bad and B good; and I am largely unaware that I am doing this; but imagine that I am passing a real judgment on A and B.

[*Text missing.*]

The first shock is the discovery that we belong to a different type than we thought; the second that, no matter what type we belong to, *the mechanicality is the same*.

When the conception of pursuing a certain radius enters, then behavior is no longer purely mechanical, but purposive.

Having discovered the figure that should be the normal development of your present potentialities, and having experienced the wish to become this figure, it is necessary then to specify what characteristics must be actualized in order to pursue your radius with some hope of arriving.

All things start as a triangle, that is, an assembly of three forces. Nothing is initiated without all three; two produce nothing.

Space itself consists of three forces that never meet; it is not just "nothing." One of the difficulties of modern science is to distinguish between space as nothingness and space as the source of matter. The ancient Gnostics defined space by two words: A simultaneous plenum (all fullness) and vacuum (all

529

emptiness). Only at the points where three forces meet is there what we call a first atom of matter.

No enterprise can be begun without the certainty of its early demise unless the three necessary elements are present.

Hence it is important to find out what they are. In the case of this ten years course there are three alone that promise success. It is not necessary, nor even possible, that the three should be already developed. We don't require of a seed that it is a tree; merely that it contain the potentialities of normal development; given the principal, normal development then becomes a matter of environment.

Similarly, each of our potentialities exists in us as a seed of the future.

The three necessary elements are:

1) Some degree of understanding of what is meant by will; and some ability to try to exercise it. Will may be defined as "effort against inclination." But one must be careful, in applying this definition, that the effort against inclination is not merely an effort made in the direction of a greater inclination—the kind of effort indicated here is made for its own sake. As an example of effort against inclination in the direction of a greater inclination, we often overcome momentary temptations to inertia to obtain a subsequent profit, say, a hundred dollar check. The hundred dollars in this case has been a magnet overcoming the inertia, and we an iron filing between the two magnets of inertia and the check, approaching the stronger. In other words, merely overcoming difficulties proves not will but the attraction of the magnet.

At this point the question was asked: Isn't the magnetic compass we have already spoken of an inclination? Orage answered: Not an inclination, but a direction. Our organism as a whole is unaware of this compass; its inclinations are determined by its history. This point is subtle but not hair-splitting. People are too prone to assume that any subtlety must be merely hairsplitting; but it may be making a distinction of *kind*. The greatest inclination differs, in kind, from the smallest will. In the case of people of whom we say that they have a strong will, the fact is that they have merely fallen under the influence of a strong magnet, such as ambition. We speak, for example, of a Napoleonic will; we say that such people will dare fire and water, etc. A life lived under the influence of such a magnet is to a single act of will as our Rolls-Royce is to an amoeba; a whole world plane, or octave, lies between them—the difference is that between mechanical and vital. It is difficult for us, mechanically trained, even to realize the nature of this amoeba. We are various types of machines, from Fords to Rolls-Royces, of varying years, models, etc. and we think we are making a distinction of kind when in fact it is only one of degree.

Will is thus acting against inclination for no other reason. (The question was promptly asked: Isn't the desire to develop will itself an inclination? Orage answered: The wish for being may be called an urge but not an inclination).

Inclination is the sum of our past. Our psychology is only another form of our physiology. Our report of what happens is a report of what our cells are doing. What we call the inclination is a disposition of a group of cells resulting from our history, and charged to act in a certain way: psychologically this is perceived by us as an inclination.

But from the point of view of whatever it is that becomes self-determinative, we are dealing with a cell that has as yet no history. The other three centers are passably filled, and according to that filling we experience what we call our psychology. But in regard to the three centers to be developed, no passive experience can enter. For all passive experience is of a rate of vibration insufficient to penetrate. To give an analogy, we all know that there are sounds we do not hear; our sense experience is limited in range.

We need another form of action different from passive: this is what we call conscious. And the only form of conscious activity of which we can begin to have experience is self-observation.

Now what is required of an act of will? It cannot be for any motive that appeals to any one of the existing centers. It would thus *seem* an objectless activity, of the nature of whim or fancy or mere cussedness.

Objective may be defined as the pursuit of objects of will; subjective as the pursuit of objects for the development of the three lower centers.

Objectivity is difficult to understand. It does imply an object, but not an object for the three lower centers. The object is to attain will. We might say it is not an object but an aim.

There is a difference between having an object in life, and being inclined to one.

In what has been said above I have tried to *point towards* will; it is impossible to realize its nature from a definition. It is to be developed by self-observation.

Will is thus the first of the three necessary elements and it is the positive force.

2) The passive element is consciousness. The word passive is misleading, for it is assumed that it means negative; that is, nothing. The difference between positive will and passive consciousness is that consciousness aims only to be aware of what is happening. Will initiates activity against inclination; consciousness is aware of the degree of will acting and the effects produced by it in our psychology. It is important to remember that it is also an activity, but the activity of awareness of an activity.

Try always to be aware of what in fact you are doing, and when it occurs to you to act against inclination, be especially aware of how it feels and what happens.

3) The third force is the neutralizing (see notes of 7 April). This is not to be regarded as a compound of the first two; nor a resultant. It appears only when the other two are present, but at the same time is a force in itself.

This third force is equally necessary as the others; in one sense a resultant of them, in another quite different from them.

We may define it by saying that *consciousness of will constitutes individuality*.

In the absence of will there is nothing of which to be conscious; in the absence of consciousness the will is not in existence; in the absence of will and consciousness there is no possibility of individuality.

It is assumed by most people that we already have will, consciousness, and individuality; but what we have as the result of passive experience are shadows of these things:

When people speak ordinarily of will, they mean inclination according to history (desire).

When they speak of consciousness, they mean the passive awareness of happenings in the body (waking consciousness).

When they speak of individuality, they mean a series of happenings according to type (personality).

We must equip ourselves with these three forces at the outset of the radius. But it is only in regard to the first two that we can do anything *directly*. The first may be developed by self-observation and opposing inclination for no reason; the second by the effort to be on the qui vive when doing so; and let individuality look out for itself.

Occidentals are often deceived by the misleading character of most of the Indian doctrines when popularly presented. For centuries they were handed down orally, and only when India was conquered were the schools compelled to write their doctrines. Under compulsion they subtilized maliciously, so that the doctrine, as written, was both wholly right and wholly wrong. An instance: in a state of aspiration (a mental—emotional attitude) the lungs tend to breathe in a certain rhythm. Among other things, they breathe through alternate nostrils. How many Indian philosophies prescribe breathing through alternate nostrils as a means of arriving at aspiration! They invert the right order, taking an effect for the cause; and following this prescription can produce only pathological states.

The same is true in the development of individuality. It can never be directly caused, any more than emotions.

[*Text missing.*]

What can we recognize as criteria? We have three stomachs, and each of these has its own state of working well, its own joy in being alive and functioning. We are aware of this in our habit of sizing up the state in which we get up in the morning; we say we are feeling a little low, or full of zest. The lungs are perhaps at their top form and breathing would be of a certain complex rhythm. What do you regard as emotional well-being? It can be defined only in terms of the two others.

Do you recognize a state of joie de vivre in the brain? An intellectual joie de vivre? When this state in the brain corresponds to a similar state in the stomach, then the emotional state will follow.

The greatest delight for the mind of man is the employment of "cunning," with a good conscience, to a successful practical conclusion. At its peak this is "the employment of cunning, with a good conscience, to the aim of more being."

The word "cunning" is used here without any connotation of slyness, but in the sense of the canny employment of the whole of one's intelligence. The word cunning comes from the Anglo-Saxon *cunnan*, which meant both to know and to be able. In esoteric use it indicates a person who *knows and can do*. In this sense King Alfred was spoken of as a cunning man. In our use here it means going to work at a task, even such a one as the pursuit of a ten years' aim, in a common sense way.

TUESDAY, 19 MAY 1931

The present meeting will be the next to the last in this series.

We have been discussing the science of being, which has two aspects: theory and practice. I urge each of you strongly to make the effort to assemble for yourself just what you have gathered of each of these two aspects. Set your results down on paper, in parallel columns, and see to what extent you have grasped the general ideas, broadly, simply, and comprehensively; or to what extent you have merely a lot of details, without vertebrae. This is not a question of agreeing or disagreeing with the ideas, but of finding out how clearly you can focus them in your own mind, which is the prerequisite, as in the case of any ideas, for future consideration.

Orage then said that he had challenged himself that day for the main idea he had got from seven years' association with the Gurdjieff system. He had found that for his own convenience he could express it in a simple diagram.

This diagram consisted merely of an octave, in which the three lower notes were mechanical; the three upper conscious; and the bridge between them (fa) the state of transition which we call balance of normality.

The lower notes (do, re, mi) are the three mechanical-centers; each of us has his center of gravity pitched in one or another of them. All of these are sub-normal; or sub-human, defining a human being as a conscious being. Mechanical means behavioristic; which means conditioned totally by heredity and environment.

The fourth note, fa, is normality. We can pass from mechanicality to consciousness only through normality. Other ways of making this transition result in a pathological state, comparing with the normal transition as moonlight with sunlight.

The three higher notes (sol—consciousness; la—individuality; si—will) are "I" (the state of being "I").

Consciousness is the state of knowing what we know and what we don't. Of a conscious man we might say, what he knows he does know and what he doesn't know he doesn't deceive himself about. He has *experience* of the differ-

533

ence between knowledge, opinion, wish, guess, and ignorance, and he knows where his own ignorance lies. Our difficulty is that in the first place we don't know what we know; secondly, we cannot discriminate between knowledge and plausibility; and thirdly, we cannot distinguish between an objective certainty (being-certainty) and subjective-certainty (a feeling-certainty). This does not mean that the conscious man is omniscient; he is still a learner but with a criterion of knowledge.

The third note of these, si, is will. But in the absence of experience it is impossible to distinguish will from wish, particularly a strong and sustained wish. On this diagram all men fall into seven classes or degrees (falling into a further subdivision of twenty-seven types within each class). Of these seven, the three lower are mechanical: instinctive, emotional, and intellectual; the three higher are conscious: knowing, being individual, and willing. Each of these last three differs from the others just as each of the first three differs from the others.

Each of us should be able to recognize on which rung he stands. If you are intellectual, every situation, where there is no special reason for emotional disturbance, becomes a matter for thought; the center of gravity is predominantly there. And so on . . . Ask yourself in what circumstances you are most at home. What is most congenial to you?

Fa is the bridge, or path—the straight and narrow gate—through which every human being must pass if he desires to become an individual, to know, and to be able to do.

In the absence of having passed through the impartial state of balance, he cannot distinguish between individuality and personality, between will and wish.

Almost the whole of Plato's dialogues is taken up in trying to lead readers to distinguish between knowledge and opinion. Socrates professed always not to know, but in contrast with the conscious ignorance of Socrates all those who professed to know were shown to have only opinions. But Plato's dialogues were written in vain. Without experience no one can distinguish; one may theorize about it, but theoretical and actual experience are totally different; and only one who has had the experience can distinguish between the description of the two different sensations.

The same is true about individuality and personality. Nine out of ten people are convinced that they know the difference. But the possession of individuality is impossible in the absence of having acquired it by conscious effort. Otherwise there is merely an anthology of personal idiosyncrasies. There are people in history who appear to have individuality because of their oddities and they are described as unique, strange, or individual. It is important to be able to distinguish between oddities that give the impression of singularity, and the actual fact—to realize that a human being with experience of individuality as a fact is as different as an emotional from an instinctive; not in degree but in kind. His rank is determined, not because of something more, but because of something totally different in his experience.

All mechanical people have the same experience, ranging only in *degree*; consider for example any experience of terror, in war, on a sinking ship, in any entanglement of the emotions; the difference is only one of degree, according to the individual's private anthology. It is impossible to cite any experience that you and I have not had in some degree. The only uniqueness is in the selection. We all share the same world of possible experience.

We all, for example, occupy this planet. One of us may have travelled more, or less, of its surface than another; but this difference, which is only one of degree, and not of kind, is insignificant compared with the fact that we all know the same air, earth, etc.

But individuality, consciousness, and will, are experiences that differ in kind. It is no use pretending that one has had them because it is possible to give some kind of a description. The author of Uncle Tom's Cabin had never owned a slave. A critic is one who has had experience and cannot be deceived by the description.

Thus from the Gurdjieff system stands out this diagram, both terrifying and encouraging. Terrifying because we are all born and educated mechanically; yet encouraging because of the possibility in all of us of attaining a nonmechanical rank.

The first of these non-mechanical stages of being implies a specific experience indescribable in the absence of the experience itself; the same in the case of knowing and will.

The transitional state is defined as the balanced man.

Objectively speaking, men are ranked: 1, 2, 3, mechanical; 4, balanced or normal; 5, 6, 7, conscious men.

Having set out the diagram, the next important thing is the conception of the balanced or normal man. Search yourself for the answer. At bottom all men will agree. Every one discounts his own preferences if so questioned. Implicit in every individual is the conception of normality. What is necessary is a certain amount of self-questioning, *pondering*, to get at the conception; which, strangely enough, when individuality arrived at, is commonly accepted.

Men agree in everything except opinion: we are concerned here with what is not opinion in ourselves.

This balanced type is what every being aspires to become. It is as if it were only on account of some pressure, cosmic perhaps in origin, that we are not normal; but our true center of gravity is on the plane of normality. We are pressed down, but feel resistance to this oppression.

In a long illness, let us say, the real crisis is the moment when you begin to think of your illness as a normal state, to be content in the role of invalid, with no wish left for health. We can say of human beings that they are not born to be mechanical, but that under certain influences they find themselves

535

sub-normal, scarcely distinguishable from animals except in faith, hope, and a sense of normality. Animals can degenerate without sighing for their lost state, without realizing even that they are decaying. Mechanical man can still feel pressure under the artificialities of his state.

All effort for all human beings must be directed simply to becoming normal. It is not yet a question of attaining the higher ranks; any experience of individuality, consciousness, or will, by any other means being practically certain to be either pathological, or fatal to the reason, or to any further development. There are beings who because of an experience of individuality, or consciousness, or will, are unable afterwards even to aim at normality, believing normality behind them. In the Gospels those that came in not by the front door but stole in by the back door were said to be expelled with violence.

But if it is thus impossible to attain individuality, consciousness, or will, except through the straight and narrow gate of normality, it is equally impossible to attain normality without desiring the three higher ranks, or at least one of them.

The state of normality in itself is not desirable, but only because it is a gate. In itself it is technically called "The Desert." For in itself it had no color of any of the three higher ranks, and it has lost the color of each of the three lower. The aniline dyes of the three lower have faded, the lasting colors of the three higher not yet appeared. Normality in itself is not an object of desire. The passage through the desert as made possible under the stimulus of the Promised Land for which the journey through the desert appeared worthwhile.

With the Promised Land held out, the attainment of normality becomes an instrumental agency. But the difficulty is that the experience of the three higher stages is possible only from this one; and it is impossible for the three lower ones to envisage them as an object of desire, to make possible the passage across the bridge.

At this point the intellectual type may be said to have a certain advantage over the emotional and instinctive. Though it is true that an intellectual conception is not knowledge, yet it is also true that the mind is capable of analogy, symbolism, allegory, etc., so that when contemplating from below the described but as yet inexperienced, one moment of understanding of the above may be possible. This is the part played by intellectual mysticism, associated with the school of Plotinus. If you read his Enneads, you will realize that three times while contemplating the pattern of a higher man in his mind, he had the experience of being higher men; and that from these three experiences came the Enneads, and his prescription of intellectual mysticism as one method. In India this is called Raj Yoga. Raj means king; yoga means method; yoga—yoke—a means of carrying a burden. The three kings: individuality, consciousness, and will. Raj Yoga was a way of attaining one of these kingships.

The difficulty is that we seem to be indifferent to this attainment of balance. This is to be overcome by intellectual contemplation and emotional aspiration, remembering that "aspiration" includes practical effort, thus making a three-fold activity. With this diagram any competent student of the science of being has a working diagram: a *map of being*, indicating the still unattained states, the road to them, and the difficulties.

For this diagram alone the years spent in the study of this system have not been wasted.

But this example of Orage's has been cited as a inducement to the rest of you to do something similar for yourselves. Select the outstanding *vertebrae* of the system, to which for the rest of your lives you will be able to attach yourselves as a map of being. A map of being is not to be despised, even though there may be blank spaces on it. The relation between the blanks and the parts known is a part of knowledge.

Orage added that he hoped none of those in the group was without some such map, and would not mistake a description for a map. I hope you will not say, for example (he went on) that for you the major idea is self-observation. That falls into a certain octave. It is *a means* only, for those that wish to become No. 4, or cease to be No. 4 (4 fa state of balance, or normality). It is not a map of the system as a whole, but the means of transition from one part of the map to another. Nor that the main idea for you is the interchange of matters; of the three forces; or the simultaneous presence in any object of two opposing forces, one making for the intensification of the vibrations of the object and the other for the decreasing. All these are details, photographs of places, not a map.

If hereafter you are going to be left to the recollection in your own minds of what has been said in these groups, it is essential that you should form your thinking around leading ideas; the principles involved.

Who is willing to formulate what seems to him the central idea of the subject?

One woman in the group answered: "the realization of potentialities." To this Orage said: Be more specific. A potentiality is not merely a possibility, but a latent power. It may seem unnecessary to you to make clear distinctions between words, but our civilization is rotting at present from an inability to distinguish between potential and actual, in its economic life, in the field of production. Potential refers to as yet undeveloped potencies. We all have the possibility of crumbling into dust; we have the potentiality of development. But people fail to distinguish. After the age of 22 or 23 most people talk a Babu English which passes for psychology, metaphysics, etc. and which is really the illiteracy of the educated classes. There is also a quarrel with your word, "realization," which means to understand fully. It is not merely to realize but to actualize potentialities that are in question. And to actualize means to put into effect.

Another person answered: "the possibility of lifting one's self out of me-chanicality." To this Orage said: It is good so far as it goes. There is nothing static in nature: everything is either appreciating or depreciating; up is the line of potentiality, down is the line of possibility. Every being is at every moment moving in one or the other direction. But a being is an agent with a responsibility to actualize his potentialities in the positive-direction. This answer touches one of the living ideas of the system, but it is still not the bony structure.

Only beings are interested in the possibility of becoming. A being is an entity that can feel. Without feeling the question of becoming is a matter of indifference.

A man in the group (Loomis) answered: "The idea of watching what goes on in one's self. " To this Orage said: You are singling out the contempla-tive, or intellectual, aspect of a man's development, and neglecting the other two. The Cherubim were said to be complete on the plane of thought; the Seraphim on the plane of feeling; but man is capable of being a truly three-centered being. The contemplative aspect, which you stress, is the path of the intellectual yogi. It develops a being who can do and feel and think on the plane of ideas; that is, the emotional and instinctive sub-centers of his intel-lectual center are developed. But in the true centers of feeling and doing, he can neither feel nor do. It is not enough to watch. One must watch, but at the same time one must think, wish, and do. By self-observation alone it is possible to develop the soul only in one of its centers; that is, the intellectual. This is Raj Yoga. Each of the three main yogis leads to the development of one center, producing a total being on one plane. But this is not a Man, whose definition is that he is complete on all three planes.

The meeting next week will be the last of this series. Try between now and then to set down the questions that are in your mind, or a statement of what you consider you have derived from a consideration of these ideas.

TUESDAY, 26 MAY 1931

This evening is the last time that we shall meet in a group of this kind to dis-cuss these ideas.

Have any of you a serious question to ask, the answer to which would be, for the rest of your life, of some practical use?

I beg each of you to set down in your mind what significance these ideas have for you. How much better off, or worse off, are you for having consid-ered them?

The question was asked: What is will? Orage said: The effort to be non-mechanical is will. Self-observation, participation, and experiment, all three, are the bridge.

The proper framing of a question is of itself of value. Do not dart out unrelated questions, but formulate your question in the framework to which it belongs. The relating of a question to its framework helps make it possible to answer it, and already points towards the direction the answer must take.

The question was asked: How is one to develop impartiality? Orage replied: An exercise has been frequently urged in these groups, which is designed to lead towards objectivity. The exercise is of such a kind that any mind, from a baby's up, may begin it, and it may be continued as the capacity of the mind increases without the exercise becoming exhausted. Take a globe of the world and try, from an external point of view—that is, in imagination not occupying any continent on the earth to become aware of the life actually existing on its surface at this moment. You see a sphere, covered with a green paint of vegetation, through which are scattered swarming and creeping objects, some on two legs. Try to bring together and realize simultaneously all that *you already know* about them.

Thinking is only the *mobilization* of your past images. When you think you first evoke images already present in your head; assemble them, arrange them, and finally draw conclusions from them. This is true of all thinking, from the least to the greatest. The only difference in point of thought between any of us and the greatest thinker is that he has a greater command over all of his past images, can mobilize, compare, contrast them, etc., more fully and more freely than we. But each of you has as many images as he; like him you are receiving them every moment of your life. His superiority lies in the effort, not contained in the images themselves, to arrange them.

Now returning to the exercise recommended: You already know a thousand things about life on this planet, impressions that have been received at various times under various circumstances, and which lie unrelated in your mind. Make the effort to draw together all of these impressions, and try to realize simultaneously all that you know. In that moment you will become detached; you may even forget that you are a human being; and that moment will give you at least the taste of objectivity.

Similarly, if you can shut your eyes and call up a picture of yourself, as clearly as though it were a picture of someone else. This also will give a taste of objectivity. The experiment can be described, and the moment is checkable. If you cannot realize yourself as you realize some person you know who is absent, you haven't yet accomplished the first note, "do," of this method. The "re" of the method is participation but in the absence of already having accomplished "do," this will mean nothing except an intellectual conception. Participation is the possibility of being simultaneously:

a.   The acting organism, and

b.   An observer who is *as if* the actor.

A life would be well spent if it were accompanied by a steady, sustained effort to attain this experience of seeing one's self.

Incidentally, it would be a guarantee that one would be kept on one's psychological toes. If you were making this effort day in and day out, you would find that automatically many trivialities would drop out of your life; and that many reactions, which are merely leakages of energy, and devastating to the organism, would cease. The quantity of energy that each person has is approximately the same; but in one person it leaks out through a thousand holes like a sieve, another person *contains* it for his use.

He is continent (which is very different from abstinent). But unfortunately there are two kinds of continence:

1.   The first is merely mechanical; that is, the person *is obsessed* by some dominating idea. For example, Napoleon. This idea has the effect of focusing all his energy, so that none is wasted. I said "unfortunately," because such a person acts willy-nilly, like a person in a hypnotic trance.

2.   The second kind is conscious continence. That is, for a voluntarily chosen objective; for example, self-observation in the pursuit of objective reason. It has the same effect, but the person is not victimized. Eventually he becomes able to do what he has wished and striven to do.

Let us hope there are no world-shattering geniuses here in this group. Such persons are so magnetically attracted by some *external* aim—power, knowledge, fame, etc.—that, like a filing on a magnet, they are literally incapable of letting go.

Yet in the absence of some strong wish, centralizing and organizing our energy, we do nothing.

We thus seem to be between two stools: on the one hand the magnetic wish of the genius, so strong that he is dominated by it, and is incapable of any self-activating will; in other words, pathological; and on the other hand, having such diverse wishes that we can't guarantee they will be the same two years, or two days, running. The choice seems to lie between the white heat of the genius and excelling at nothing.

It is true we can't wish a wish on ourselves. We may deplore the fact that our wishes are weak, but that doesn't change them. Suppose I despise myself for being lukewarm towards something that my mind tells me I've love to love. How am I to generate the heat I need and want? That is, how am I to focus and intensify my feelings towards this objective? I cannot do it directly, but it can be done indirectly, by making use of the relation between the intellectual and the emotional centers.

Emotions are evoked in response to the images present in our consciousness. The wishes themselves live in the dark, seeing the outer world only in the images that we form of it passing through our consciousness like a cinema. We are in the habit of leaving this to the haphazard accidents of our daily experiences, reading, associations, etc.

To create a wish, or to intensify one already present, assemble out of the memory of all your images those that are associated with that wish, and keep them present in your consciousness. This was once the technical meaning of "prayer." This was what happened mechanically to Don Quixote, as a result of his reading. But we can dispense with an external stimulus. Evoke images and keep them permanent.

Perhaps you find that your wish is not intense enough to do what you wish to do. Your heredity and environment have not happened to make it so. Yet your intelligence tells you that the thing can be done. How are you to strengthen yourself?

Collect your images and mobilize them. "Who keeps one end in view makes all things serve." (Browning)—and becomes thereby a real person, only differing from a mechanical person in that he has done it consciously. The selection of aim has been his own; the means intelligent; and incidentally the *effort involved* develop the thinking center so that thereafter he can think capably about practically anything.

[*Text missing.*]

A member of the group (Wolfe) then said that to him the realization of death was the keynote of the ideas. Orage said: Call it rather a stimulus to effort. Suppose you were on the Titanic when it struck the iceberg. Such a situation may be the contingency of every moment of our lives. We forget that every time we draw a breath someone is being born, and someone is dying, somewhere on this planet.

We all know theoretically that some time we shall die. But we don't realize it as a fact. Such a realization would be two-fold:

a. A sense of unfulfilled wishes, or obligations; and

b. A sense of shame that we have lived so long, done so little, and been so ignorant.

If the realization of how little we have become could be combined with the realization that even this little might be lost, it would be the strongest incentive to seeing ourselves as we see others.

Suppose a man were hanging over a precipice on a rope which was gradually being abraded, as he climbed up it, by the edge of the precipice. He might, or might not, reach the top before it snapped. He would have a double shock: first, the realization of the imminence of death; and second, that what was dangling was only a simulacrum of a real being. It is said that this experience has been used in certain schools, with perhaps no guarantee that the danger was not real, to awaken the knowledge of death and that nothing dies.

When Orage dies, nothing dies. He is a product of nature, animated and made to look alive; but no more human than a tree or an animal. He has not become an incarnation, a vivification, of himself. Realizing this failure brings a sense of frustration, shame, etc. For we are attached to life, from an unconscious realization of our need of the body in order to attain consciousness. If we merely live out its life, we have failed. This shame was the technical meaning attached in the ancient "schools" to the word hell.

Wolfe's formulation touches a nerve of the system; touches its emotional center. We can talk for weeks about diagrams, and except for the light they throw on contemporary intellectual problems, they would not touch one's being.

We have these three steps:

Knowledge of the body: through self-observation;

Control over the body; through participation;

Proper use of the body; through experiment.

None of us can fail to realize the slow pace at which even an earnest student changes. Year after year passes, and the change is so little that one's nearest friends see no difference. The change in one's attitudes and reactions is microscopic. This fact is due to the failure to realize what Wolfe has just brought up: death and the shame of un-fulfillment.

How could a man, really knowing that he might die at any moment, keep on thinking trivial thoughts—unless they were connected with the practical details of his life, in which case he would think them as capably, practically, and quickly as possible, and dispose of them. Orage expressed himself amazed, not at the time devoted to trivial things, for our daily lives are made up of small matters that have to be dispatched, but at the importance attached to them. With the mobilization of all of a man's energies toward the central aim of his life, accompanied by the knowledge that his time was short, he would, automatically shed the trivial concerns which didn't contribute to that aim and from which he derived, in consequence, no real satisfaction even at the moment. This would be a sort of inner asceticism, brought about automatically by the rejection of what was of no value to him, and differing from ordinary asceticism in that it would be invisible to others.

[Text missing.]

Another member of the group (Morris) said that he had written down, as Orage had asked at the previous meeting, what seemed to him the framework of the system in relation to the question of being. Not in a diagram, as Orage had done, but in a series of statements. Orage remarked that that form was equally useful. Morris read his statements (given at the end of the notes on this meeting.)

Orage criticized the last statement in which Morris said that the only hope of development was hatred of our present mechanical state. Orage pointed out that this ignored the "magnetic tie," discussed in previous meetings, between ourselves as we are and as we would be if fully developed; that is, as we should be. Hatred alone is not enough; there must also be love of what we are designed to be; that is, aspiration. The statement read give only the negative side, hatred, which should be counter-balanced by love.

The danger of the formulation read was that, left alone, it leads to melancholia and despair. To the seven deadly sins the Eastern Church added an eighth, which was well known in Hindu philosophy: spiritual despair, incurred by those so unfortunate as to fall out of love with themselves as they are, without falling in love with themselves as they should be. Hatred refers to the actual, love to the potential.

Mantra are formulations used for mobilizing ideas, and keeping images present in consciousness. If repeated with a full inner effort to give them significance to one's self, the corresponding wish in the emotional center will be evoked. The prayer-wheel originated as a device to keep the mind occupied with a certain set of images. "I wish to be aware of myself. " What content can you give to the word "I"? None, as yet; but you can try to use it *as if* it already had meaning. What is the most intense association you have with the word "wish"? It is all of that ardor, and a thousand times more, that you are trying to put into that word here etc. You are speaking for the secret "I" within your heart, and some part of your mind should always be reminding you of this.

Another mantra is a simple one, which you might attempt to repeat frequently, say, a hundred times a day. With the attempt to say it *as if* it had meaning there would be a rapid development of consciousness. It is a short cut, but unfortunately no one is ever able to do it, simple as it looks. People either forget it entirely, or else the words lose all meaning to them. It is an ancient one: "More radiant that the sun, purer than the snow, subtler then the ether, this is the self, the spirit within my heart, I am that self, that self am I. "

At first this can be merely a mechanical repetition. But the process is one of making a fact by making it conscious. Spiritual facts do not occur, they are willed; and often brought about by what appear to be mechanical means. Try to repeat this *as if* it were a fact, not just verbally. You will say this is auto-suggestion, and so it is; but in the absence of acting under auto-suggestion, you are bound to act under the suggestion of others.

All of our present behavior is done under suggestion, and our hypnotist is our environment. The only counter-hypnotist is auto-suggestion. Spiritual growth takes place as normally as growth of the body, but it presupposes something to grow: that an "I" is there. Once given the germ, it grows according to its own laws.

Many of you have asked if there wasn't some short cut, instead of the drudgery of the method, and here is one if you can use it. But you will find that after three times you will begin to say it mechanically. How hard it is to try to put more and more meaning into it each time! I am trying to bring it home to yourself to have the resolution that it shall be so.

An illustration: How can you persuade a man who has always lived in poverty that he has a million in the bank he can draw on? Ouspensky told of an incident in England. A barman inherited half a million pounds from a brother in Australia, and although the lawyers explained it to him, showed him papers, gave him a checkbook and urged him to write checks, he was incapable of believing it. He listened to everything they said, and then went on as if he didn't have the money.

You have an "I" in the bank. It may be that we are all drugged on this planet, that its fumes are uncongenial to man, and breathing them in we dream. But there are times, in grief, etc., when we have moments of self-realization.

[*Text missing.*]

Many ideas have been discussed in these groups. Either dismiss them entirely, or get them down. Chew on them. Don't leave them, like a cow, in your first stomach, but like a cow bring them up again and again, and ruminate over them. Get them into the second stomach. This ability to bring ideas up and chew on them, comparing and contrasting them with others, etc., is a preventive against brain rot.

This meeting is the last day of a certain year, which so far as Orage is concerned has lasted seven years. So far as he can see it is the last meeting he will ever address in New York on this subject, and it is probable that no such meetings will be held again. He can regard this as the last night of an old year, and the eve of the new.

There is an ancient custom, still preserved among serious people, of marking such a night with something in the nature of a "vow to one's self"—and fulfillment of it is the condition of self-respect. A self-respect which is independent of any injury done to what is called self-pride, which fears nothing from the insults of others, and expects no praise, but is more severe than any taskmaster. A vow to be fulfilled on peril of having to condemn one's self henceforth to futility, and to swallowing what others may say of one with the conviction that they are justified, having failed one's self. The nature of the vow is not very important; but it should have certain characteristics:

1.   It should be possible;
2.   It should lie in the sphere of secret desirability for you;
3.   It should be instrumental; that is, on the way towards that figure of yourself that you know you should be ten years hence. This is a resolution to perform divine service, which consists in only one thing: in becoming divine. It is simultaneously a service to one's self and to that divine that is in each of us.

The attempt to fulfill such a vow is the condition of happiness. In the failure to have any such vow, or to attempt to fulfill it, one is condemned to accident, chance, etc.—drifting.

Let us seize this occasion of our last meeting and turn it to account.

Recall the ideas in your mind, and make use of the practice. You will find that there will be a progress in your realization of the meaning of much that has been said, the full meaning of which didn't strike you when it was heard. It has often been said that not for seven years will one fully realize what is contained in the buds of these ideas. But this increase in meaning will accompany a constant striving to be more conscious, more individual, and to have more will (guts).

Meaning more, being more, doing more.

Muriel Draper

CONSCIOUS OR OBJECTIVE MORALITY

A. R. ORAGE: We will talk to "I" about "It." It is left outside. Use conscious imagination to leave it outside. "It" is for the moment dead. But it is to be re-entered shortly. What should "I" do in relation to "It"?

Ordinary morality is a matter of social convention. In relation to ordinary morality, the organism is subject. But the organism becomes the object of conscious morality. In ordinary perception and observation, the organism is the subject, external objects are the objects. But with us, organism becomes the object of observation, since we observe what is observing. So the organism becomes the object of conscious morality.

The five elements of conscious morality which define the duty the "I" is obligated (under the necessity of reason) to perform with respect to the organism, are:

1.   The preservation and maintenance of its life and well-being. (Self-preservation the first law of life)

a.   No destructive acts or pursuits are to be engaged in.

b.   No suicide.

For it has been given to us by nature on trust, and it is necessary to the life of "I." Moreover, should we quit "It," we should pass on a good and even better organism to the next "I".

Figure: the duty of a responsible tenant towards the house rented from a landlord.

2.   The improvement of the organism.

a.   Acquiring new technics.

b.   Discovering possibilities and realizing them.

For we must turn over to the next "I" or to our own "I" at the next recurrence, a better equipped vehicle. (The necessity of acquiring new and many technics, not for the sake of the technics, but for the purpose of preparing the body to be used by "I," that is, pliant to demands of the technics of technics.)

These, 1 and 2, can be, and are, subscribed to by ordinary subjective morality. Everyone admits them, and displays this acceptance by evincing the corresponding wishes, namely, to preserve and improve themselves. Disregard the ordinary canons, not simply for the sake of disregarding them or being unconventional, but for the purpose of experiment. Ordinary conventions and conventional morality are equally mechanical. Not even as contrasts can they serve as guides to conscious morality.

3.   To understand the nature of man, the nature of the universe, and their mutual relations, is the duty of the "I". (To understand the nature of the organism and its relation to nature.)

Philosophy and science are not mere interests or inclinations (as they are generally considered to be), but obligations, from an objective point of view. Energies are differentiated for curiosity, that is, philosophy and science. If

546

these are not used, they turn back on some other avenue of functioning and derange it. Nervousness and sex perversion are not to be dealt with directly, but can be cured by stimulating and pursuing the curiosity to understand the nature of man and the universe.

The five types of energy. The five pointed star. Each person and situation should be made to yield an understanding of principle (psychological, social, etc.) not only mere likes and dislikes.

The capacity for reason is the saving faculty of mankind.

The spectacle of life is the great drums, which I should approach to understand. Every contact should yield something more as a subjective response. It should yield an understanding of habits, traits, motives, etc.

4. The fourth duty of the "I" is to discover and discharge its function. (To pay for its existence.) The discovery of this function can only follow from having discharge duties (1), (2), and (3).

Figure: wheel, nut, wagon. A wheel is such, not a nut. The wagon is such. Taken together, their relationship defines an inevitable function for the wheel.

5. The fifth duty of "I" is to aid their efforts to apply (1), (2), (3) and (4).

Such one of these follows from the other, and, taken relatedly, they are axiomatic, self-evident to objective reason. Although the organism may reject these five obligations, the "I" knows as true.

The effort should be to apply (1) (2) (3) (4) (5) simultaneously, that is, all in any one given action. It is the duty of the "I" to select, from among a number of possible, the one which will allow an inclusion of all five. The organism will be determined to select one by past experience. The "I" must make the effort to non-identify, select, and actualize the one in which its purpose be served.

This fivefold effort superseded the threefold one (designed for personality) or profit, pleasure, and religion.

These five elements pass quickly from the memory, since society is hostile to them, does not aid then. The difficulty is to remember. This is the main difficulty.

The difficulties in separating and developing "I" are equal for all. But organic capacities may differ by accident, one being better equipped for certain purposes than another, and hence more suitable for the conscious object of such a one as Gurdjieff. (These capacities may be: strength of personality in influencing people, many languages, diverse crafts, talents, etc.)

Can the "I" ever be completely separated from the organism? No. There are two forces at work, simultaneously, between the "I" and the organism, one, separating, and one joining the two more closely in union. (Separation and union) This antinomy always exists, so that an application of the method will yield in actual experience, at once, a sense of a greater separation and a closer union.

Remember Do, Re, Mi (organism="IT"), Fa, (transition), Sol, La, Si, ("I").

547

Interposed at every semitone are triangles: positive, negative, and neutral forces, purpose being the third or neutral force.

ENNEAGRAM

Jesus: Do, Re, Mi. Christ: Sol, La, Si. Jesus Christ, the two in one, Do, Re, Mi, becomes one in Sol, La, Si.

We are not one. We must become two, in order to become One. Duality is the precondition of One-ness.

The upper room of the early Christians. The place where psychological conditions are favorable to the "I's" learning their duty.

Governments; Due to accident. All within the organism.

Democracy: the domination of the organism by first one center and then another, due to some chance and incalculable external stimuli. So we now exist.

Socialism: the continued control of the organism by the instinctive center. Physical appetites. Leading to chase and anarchy.

Monarchy or Aristocracy: The continued control by the emotional center. The best feeling.

As Plato wished: continued domination by the intellectual center. Philosophers.

Government: Conscious. By a fourth center not contained in the organism. Theocracy.

Our "I's" become gods to the organisms.

Some beings are responsible for the whole of nature.

Some beings are responsible for man. Remember the place of man in the scale of nature, that is, Si. Man a sex call. Si of the food octave is sex.

So we are responsible as gods to our organisms.

God, for his purpose, in order to maintain perpetual motion, designed that each order of being feed on some other and be fed on.

Unfits among men are symptomatic of disease in nature. They are the pimples through which poison is drawn off. A number of "I's" becoming conscious might so utilize the energies designed for conscious usage as to being health, as, for analogy, energy used for thought cures nervousness and perversion.

Lincoln Kirstein

Love was meant by His Endlessness the creator for moral reciprocal sustain-
ing. (What are naptha minds?) (Why always by a Persian.) I always thought in
Persian and translated into Russian because one cannot think in Russian but
only in Persian.

Russian has no word for "I say it" they always use the words "I speak it."

Contemporary literature has nothing in it to develop the human mind—only
empty words. One can by proverbs and anecdotes transmit thought sometimes.

Meetings with remarkable men.

Sparrows in old times, there was a rumbling noise and a scent, then horses
and artist knew he would find that which would give satisfaction. Said the old
one, but now any rumbling noise or scent but no satisfaction.

Thought alone does not give understanding, but only with feeling also.

Asiatics find Europeans literature empty. Love par example. One does not
feel a real thought.

Newspapers satisfy by their mechanicality—they spoil man's memories and
render their minds more mechanical.

In the old days newspapers existed but only the very best men were appointed and only on oath.

Contemporary men are proud about discoveries and quite properly—but
they imagine that never before there has been this 80–143 element knowledge
existed.

Surgeons now remove organs that are put there by nature.

The philosopher stone was radium—X-ray etc.

Karapet whistle in Tiflis was to awaken people from sweet but brief dreams
and was cursed by everyone.

Rest is obtained by telling about ordinary things. Now I shall write this
book so no one shall ask all sorts of questions.

A remarkable man is one par ex: who can perform tricks but I consider a
man remain a man if he stands out by reason of his mind and his ability to
remain just and fair.

Ashokh, poet and teller of tales, his father. Illiterate but a remarkable memory. Competition opened by one chosen by lot who proposed a question as to
the meaning of a folktale or—Prizes for winners—carpets etc.

My father, an amateur Ashokh, would tell us stories always concluding
with one from Arabian Nights.—A friend of my father would spend a whole
night analyzing old stories. After the 21st song, my father stopped to fill his
pipe, and said it was a story of Lemurians which was afterward incorporated
in the Bible of the Jews and then Christians.

Marble cones found in Babylon tell the same story of the deluge. Before
seventy generations each of a hundred years there existed an island—the only

survivors were the wise men of Atlantis—this island was a center then, they were spread yet communicated with each other by pythonesses from the East, who wrote down messages.

T. S. Matthews

48 QUESTIONS

1.   The effort to realize: I have a body.

2.   The effort to realize that I descended into, and become attached to this organism (this animal) for the purpose of developing it.

3.   The attempt to realize the organism's mechanicity:

(a)   Its habitual reaction to recurrent situations

(b)   The magnetic relationship of the centers

4.   Experiment of the part of the driver (intellect), in order that he may learn his business.

5.   The formatory apparatus reporting the behavior of the organism to the "I."

6.   Formulation of observations concurrent with the act of observation.

7.   Formulation of the ideas.

8.   The attempt to understand the ideas.

9.   The attempt to relate the ideas and understand the relationships.

10.   The attempt to define terms in accordance with institute ideas.

11.   The attempt to interpret life, human beings, etc., in terms of mechanicality, types, springs, centers, etc.

12.   Describe experience; reflect on the ideas

13.   Triangulate, that is, have a three-fold purpose for each act.

14.   Assemble all you know of a given object at the moment of perceiving it.

15.   Constructive imagination:

(a)   Image the great octave.

(b)   Attempt to realize man's position in the universe.

16.   Relate each object to its position in the scale. For instance a cigarette belongs to the vegetable kingdom (mi) of the organic scale. Trees belong to the vegetable kingdom. The gold of a watch to metals (do). Man (si). The whole natural kingdom is interposed between earth (mi) and planets (fa) of the great octave.

17.   Attempt to realize the fact of two thousand million people.

18.   Attempt to realize the fact of death.

19.   Be aware of the weight of opinion.

20.   Apply the law of the octave to one's own behavior. Attempt to know when any given impulse has reached 'mi.'

21.   Peel the onion, that is, make notations of the various attitudes toward life, stripping off the superficial ones in an effort to reach the fundamental attitude.

22.   Note likes and dislikes. Find the essential wish.

23. Find the chief feature.
24. Make gratuitous efforts.
25. Cast a role for oneself.
26. Pursue an impossible task.
27. Go against inclination.
28. Push inclination beyond the limits of its natural desire.
29. If a man forces you to go one mile, go with him twain.
30. Determine what it is you really want in any given situation. Deliberately get it, or deliberately oppose the "I" to this wish. At any event, non-identify with the wish.
31. Practice mental gymnastics relative to time, space and motion.
32. Seek the concrete illustration and examples (in experience) of the ideas.
33. Try to perform, consciously, instinctive, emotional, and intellectual work at the same time.
34. Try to keep in mind that at any given moment you are actualizing one of several possibilities.
35. Try to keep in mind that when you talk these ideas to someone or to a group, human cells are at that moment instructing a group of monkey cells, within each brain.
36. Try to realize that man, oneself, is a cosmos. That this organism is the planet or globe of this "I." That the organism contains cells corresponding to the categories of nature.
37. Try to become aware of the operations of the sub-centers: the emotional and moving sub-centers of the intellectual, the intellectual and instinctive of the emotional, the intellectual and emotional sub-centers of the instinctive.
38. Try to keep in mind and realize that we are constantly receiving influences from our entire universe.
39. Try to realize that this organism is in reality a mere bubble. That, in fact, the whole material or actualized universe is related the potential universe as shadows is to substance.
40. Give all five points the necessary activity.
41. The attempt to use the formatory apparatus as a muscle, directly and independent of sub-vocalizing (inner talk).
42. The attempt to repeat a poem and a series of numbers simultaneously, using formatory apparatus for the poem, the vocalizing apparatus for the numbers.
43. Unroll the film.
44. Evoke in pictures the object to which ideas are related.
45. Supply the base, the third force, the neutralizer in all and every situation. That is, *improvise.*
46. Cast spells.

47.   Try to practice conscious morality.

48.   Try to think of the *reasonable* thing to do or say in any given situation. Each event is potentially a complete circle. But circumstances usually distort it or, at best, supply only a curve. If this much is supplied: (U) try to determine just what is reasonably necessary to complete it. Supply it, thus: (Ü)

Kathryn Hulme

BEYOND BEHAVIOR

The term 'psychology'—Greek derivation. 'Psyche' Greek name for butterfly, and 'Logos'—knowledge of. Psyche was name ancient Greeks gave to Soul. Soul imaged as a butterfly.

Review salient features of butterfly to understand what—if anything—the Greeks meant. Formation exemplifies a numerical regularity—number three its basis. Butterfly divided into three parts—head, thorax, abdomen, each in turn divided anatomically into three parts.

Life history: The egg on the surface of the leaf. Hatching, eats shell, eats leaf under it. Next, larva moults, sheds skin, grows another a bit too large. Voracious feeding. The larva repeats performance four times; on fifth moult, attains full larva size. It has increased in size, taken on more active color protection. Entire life so far just feeding and adaptation to environment; no reciprocal effect on environment.

On fifth moult, caterpillar spin silken web. Once more its skin splits, larva enters web, shrinking. Now a true chrysalis—a small cone-shaped object hanging point downward from leaf or beam.

This chrysalis is neither larva, caterpillar nor butterfly. A definite transition stage. Hard outer shell, within a formless creamy fluid without structure, containing nuclei. Curious happening—sometimes the outline tracing of the creature to be appears on shell though the liquid molecules of super-protoplasm within are still entirely formless.

At length, with no feeding visible from without, the chrysalis emerges. It is a butterfly. The overwhelming character of transformation that has taken place might be likened to a horse that had drawn up legs and tail, rolled off a jetty to live henceforward as a whale.

II

"Bigger and Better Men"—We hear of the breakup of civilization, of need for bigger and better men. General idea is that education can produce them.

Men can be divided into three main classes or types—the practical, athlete or man of affairs; the aesthetic, artist or religious; the intellectual, scientist or philosopher. A small degree of supremacy in any one of these fields militates against the other two. The greater excellence he exhibits in one, the greater his prejudices against the other two classes. Thus, no one kind of eminence is of much avail to society for its current problems—all too real. "Big men" appear, but they can be explained mechanistically—i.e. reciprocal action to environment.

Trend of modern psychology—there are broad facts impossible to deny:

William James: conception of 'stream of conscious,' as a single dynamic flow; his theory of emotion—the blend of all internal physical sensations is the emotion.

Høffding (Danish): theory of 'will.' "Consciousness as a decision takes place when an unaccustomed situation must first be met; successive repetition gradually brings about less and less involving of consciousness until response becomes habitized reflex."

Wurzburg School: investigation of so-called higher thought processes. There are elements in consciousness which are neither sensation nor feeling. These non-sensory states are called "attitudes."

Titchener: maintaining that imagery once established, eventually thins out but remains as a trace in all thought processes.

Gestalt: serious attack on whole position of analytical psychology. Maintained not only that external stimuli must be treated simultaneously in toto, but that reacting organism also presents to investigation a functioning whole which likewise, as a whole, determines the separate functionings of its constituent members.

The conflict as to possibility of "imageless thought." Can thought be carried forward in the absence of all imagery? Introspection must then be a tool. By the nature of the process there exists no means of knowing whether or not a man is capable of introspection. Who can see within him, check his statements against possible self-deception?

Watson: *Behaviorism*; asserts the whole subject of images a futile ground for research, technique of animal psychology must be transferred to human. Denied authority of introspective opinion—of any research to be called scientific which did not include those objective measurements which could be reproduced and verified anywhere.

"Unconditioned response"—at birth exist in us a small number of organic nerve pathways which are prepared to conduct stimuli through the organism and return it to the world as the physical behavior.

But these few unconditioned responses begin immediately to be modified. Baby once knocked down by dog—soon the visual element—sight of dog alone suffices to provoke the now "conditioned response," fear. This simple process of conditioning has been employed to account for all our most complicated, habitized behavior, even in so subtle a matter as language and speech, and is confirmed in these cases also by experimental evidence.

THE PICTURE OF THE HUMAN BEING

"A man then, says psychology, is a biological product of three interacting systems, the ordinary muscular, the visceral and the cerebral. These structures, having developed physiologically in the embryo in the above order, at birth begin to be filled with content in the shape of nerve modifications, muscle adaptations to particular stresses, permanent and semi-permanent tensions and so on. The body consists of just these three large muscular systems, of which physical movement and sensation are the response of the first to environment, emotions are the various changing strains in the unstriped muscles of the second, and what we call thoughts are the changes in the third which, like the other two, is also a muscle."

The three systems are inter-connected in the organism and a series of reactions in one always coincides with some series in both others. These coincident responses are almost never congruous; they are chance-joined events. Consequently the associations, instead of being aids, are interferences.

Thus, a man cannot think without suffering the intrusion of feelings, etc, etc., immense waste and friction. There is also a tendency of the three systems, a struggle to make the organism act as in such a way as to relieve the wishes (tensions) of the other two, even at their expense. Since one center is always stronger than the others, here is explained the appearance of 'types'—the athletic, the aesthetic, or the scholarly.

How then can a machine of three interacting mechanisms improve itself? Any attempt at improvement is doomed to intensify one element in our make-up at the expense of the other two—(*remember the organism reacts always as a whole*). There is no way.

THE DILEMMA

With the considerations of behaviorism, we reach a cul-de-sac. For if this inner organization of thinking, feeling and physical action must always proceed in a 'vicious circle,' what avenue of escape lies open to man, all of whose activities are comprised in those categories?

Our civilization must head toward eventual extinction.

Not so calmly can we shrug away the problem of our single destinies. We are practically defenseless against environment. Where shall we be in death who cannot so much as consciously exist through ordinary sleep?

The age-long dream of a soul—is this a loop-hole of escape? With this dream we must do the one human thing that sets us off from animals; namely, submit it to stern objective test, not of the emotions but of reason.

The hope for a soul, pervading all ages and religions, is only emotional wish-fulfillment. Nothing proves we possess a soul. It must be worked for, perhaps?

The saint, the ascetic, the yogi, they are all, equally with each other and with the rest of mankind, automatic. Even their most striking distinctions are demonstrably the play of environment upon a given mechanistic structure.

LAW OF THE OCTAVE

There is an ancient tradition in the East to the effect that the widely known diatonic scale (do-re-mi-fa-so-la-si and the next repetitive do) was originally not associated with music at all; but was a mathematical formulation, in respect of sound, of that series of phases through which all action physical, psychological, or of any other category, must pass either upwards or downwards in the phenomenal changes of nature.

In physics—the periodic table of elements. The wave theory of electronic vibration, called *Quantum*. The seven primary colors of spectrum constitute one octave. In Astronomy we know there are 8 major planets in our solar system.

In Psychology: the puzzling phenomenon with regard to process of learning. "Curves of learning" exhibit peculiar variations in their rise—ceases periodically to rise, continues for a period horizontally ("plateau").

This might mean the original psychological energy applicable for the learning expenditure carries the process over the first three stages, the notes do-re-mi, at which point the semitone stage is reached and a fresh supply of energy is needed to pass over and beyond that different psychological period.

"And it may be that in our individual growth we, as human beings, have passed through our first three stages and are stalled at the interval fa of our individual octaves. Certainly we have acquired by growth three distinctly separate, yet continuously bound-together functions, namely physical action, emotion and associative thought. Conceivably these might be, in the full octave of human functioning, the notes do-re-mi; we have run through them and are now at the last, which incidentally is the position of our planet in the octave of the solar system."

What then is to be done? . . . since all our behavior is demonstrably comprised within the categories of mechanically habitized action, emotion and thought, no more of any of these will suffice for our necessity, whether or no they take the form of religion, philosophy art or physical culture. It has already been pointed out that all known and even conceivable reforms must operate through, and in fact be, one of these first three functional activities.

A way must be discovered to elude this hopeless automatism.

IV PSYCHOLOGY OF THE FUTURE

The Only Way of Buddha. We see immediately that this impersonal observation of the three automatic functions of our organism as objective facts (entirely as objective and unrelated to anything properly called ourselves as is any other mechanism of nature, such for example as the ocean tides) is precisely *a fourth possible* activity for human beings.

This process is not a physical action, nor an emotional activity, neither must it be thought.

The valid distinction between being *conscious* of something and *thinking* about it is the significant thing here. It is also plain that for each of us the field of observation is confined (certainly at the moment) to our own bodies. We cannot be directly aware of a cool breeze, but we can be conscious of the physical effects produced by it in our bodies.

Thus we conclude, upon consideration, that we are dealing here with a real fourth activity, differing from the other three at least equally as much as they differ from each other. It is not physical action, it is not feeling, it is not thought. *It is awareness.*

We do not convince ourselves by logic that our hands are resting on a hot stove; we are aware of it. In fact long before there has been time for thought-formulation on the subject, our arm muscles have contracted reflexively and the situation been met. Now it is suggested that we be aware, not of the stove, but of the reflex, and not for the purpose of changing or guiding it, but just to be aware of it as of any other movement in nature. Between us and all external environment is interposed this automatic mechanism, our body, and it is solely through that as a medium that we are able to perceive anything of outside reality at all.

Here is the means whereby "I" can begin its existence as an entity, can conceivably achieve a meaning which is real. Assuredly "I" cannot at once, if ever, aspire to the control of this complicated organism behind which stand millions of years of biological and sociological history. But "I" can at least maintain from the outset an occasional brief, independent existence in just this way: "I" can *observe*, in the sense of being vividly aware of, the contemporary actions of the powerful machine, the body, to which it finds itself unaccountably attached.

We have an unexercised faculty by means of which direct knowledge of our own body is obtainable. This is Whitehead's "Prehension" as distinguished from our ordinary "apprehension" of external objects. Do we normally exercise this activity? We do not; it has never even occurred to us. But can we? Most certainly we can. It is a human possibility, rusted perhaps from disuse.

Supposing this activity to be initiated, what would become of the impressions resulting from our detailed awareness? Just as sensations are received into the physical-muscular system and form its content, so these impressions we may imagine, will commence to fill another physical system with content (Jane's fourth room?)—thereby eventually actualizing it, i.e. enabling it to function. Modern science finds only three systems in the human organism, but modern science is young. It has just found glands of internal secretion.

Nor is it remarkable that our hypothetical fourth system remains unknown to science for unlike the glandular system it has never functioned since it lacks all content in the form of impressions. Nothing has ever been put into it. How can anything come out?

There is a very extraordinary feature about impression-producing awareness. It is absolutely different from the processes which occur in the first three systems and which, if they are made sufficiently habitual, can proceed as we say subconsciously.

Those who attempt to collect impressions of their bodily behavior soon discover that this process *cannot become a habit.* Equally with the first impression, the ten-thousandth or the ten-millionth must be consciously taken. In fact, it is a permanent characteristic of the activity that it must of necessity always include the attribute of consciousness. Never can it exist apart from that *active* component.

And it is further to be noted that there is no necessary interference on the part of the activity, in what is otherwise happening in the organism. To be aware is simply to observe impersonally and objectively. It involves no meddling with other functions and no proposal to change what is being observed, for *this would defeat its own object which is to see, not what might or should occur, but what in fact does occur.*

Its function is comparable perhaps to that of *catalysis* in chemistry.

Self-observation, undertaken with no effect in view, produces nevertheless an effect *if* it lacks all tutorial purpose. Personal awareness tends to reduce immediately the extent and intensity of the constant interference between the other three systems. This appears to be the effect of awareness upon the organism, so much more powerful is the energy made use of by our fourth, conscious system, than the automatic energics distilled and scattered by our first three, nature-engined ones. The saving of energies ordinarily wasted through interference is one of the first noticeable results of the process.

V THE OLD NEW METHOD

Toward the construction of a technique:

At the *very* outset the gravest difficulties are to be encountered. There is in each of us a conservative party so powerful and so strongly entrenched that until we have experienced the subtlety of its devices we can form no adequate idea of its strength. For we soon find that in dealing with our own bodies the dethronement of prejudice is well-nigh beyond possibility. And yet this is just what *must* be accomplished. How can we acquire any true knowledge if all our basic observations are to be warped by a predisposition in their making?

Again we shall find that this innate prejudice regarding ourselves has its obverse and reverse sides. There will be at first a tendency to admire the complexity and apparent smoothness of operation of our machines because they are our own, and then also the temptation to criticize certain defects and awkwardnesses which tend to disparage our possession. *Above everything these at-*

titudes must be avoided, as exactly the reverse of scientific. Our awareness, our observations, must be purely objective, for the actualization of "I" is achievable from no other standpoint.

"I" cannot be responsible (since it exercises no control) for on objective mechanism of nature's. To be betrayed into a responsible identification is to fall from the position of "I" back among our introspective thoughts and mechanistic wishes.

How shall we begin? Perhaps by classifying our body according to typical muscular, visceral or cerebral dominance habitually manifested by it. Are we predominantly practical, emotional, or intellectual?

Each of the types has its two opposite manifestations. Positive muscular dominant is physically active and energetic, negative is physically lazy. Emotionally positive means optimistic, negative—pessimistic. Positive intellectual is the constructive criticizer, the one who as a rule finds himself in agreement with proposed statements; the negative is the destructive critic. Sometimes we exhibit characteristic of all three, but the question is which system guides the mechanism *usually*? To ascertain the answer, the examination of no temporary or present period will suffice; it is only how the organism tends habitually to act over long periods that counts, for *it is the time factor that points to type*. To this end we must review our life, not introspectively, but by the ordinary, exercise of *pictorial memory*, dividing it for convenience into such phases as infancy, childhood, school, married days, etc., etc. This process will take up considerable time and during it we shall inevitably have some light thrown upon the two kinds of our present characteristics: those resulting from environment (socially acquired attributes) and those resulting from heredity—our "essence"—(those which our bodies would have tended to possess in any environment).

So far this is only thought and its value is therefore supplementary to the real task, that of *awareness*, i.e. current, conscious, impersonal observation of one's own behaving organism. This latter makes no demands upon either time or upon what we are accustomed to consider as energy, since the energy used is of a different sort than that used by the first three systems; and moreover this observation must go on *simultaneously* with their functioning, so there can be no giving-up of time involved.

A beginner cannot observe the entire organism. Divide work into four stages:

1. Observation of muscular system.
2. Observation of visceral.
3. Observation of cerebral.
4. Observation of all three together.

Even the second stage is far beyond the beginner. We shall therefore stick to the simple processes, namely direct observation of the ordinary, physical occurrences manifested by our bodies.

It is possible to divide our physical events into (1) the class of behavior which everyone can observe and (2) into the class which ordinarily only ourselves can notice. Examples of the 1st are: tone of voice, customary postures, gestures, habits, and of the 2nd—sense impressions, including the kinetic, breathing, pulse-beat, temperature, etc. The point to make sure of is that the whole field is covered, and this is not impossible since the varieties of our behavior are not infinite.

Perhaps the easiest way for a serious beginning consists in the effort to be currently aware first of the general manner in which the body is acting, as for instance whether it be sitting, walking, speaking, eating, or just what its mass action is at any given moment. Even in our waking state these things go on in our sleep for we are scarcely more conscious of them, as they happen in detail, than a somnambulist. The mechanism let us say is on its way to take a train, and suddenly it breaks into a run; we now wish to be in a position to make the immediate statement, without reflection: "Now my organism is running."

Almost everyone will maintain that this is nothing new, that he has always known when such activities take place. Leaving aside the answer that often enough we "wake up" to find ourselves somewhere and have no recollection of our arrival, let it be added that this *knowing things* is precisely what we are *not* suggesting. There is a vast gulf between knowing that one is walking, and being *conscious* of the walking activity that goes currently forward in the body.

Having thus become somewhat accustomed to the feel of the thing, we can proceed farther by selecting a particular category of behavior, say tone of voice, to concentrate upon. The goal is to hear our own voice just as impersonally as we hear any other voice, whenever it speaks. Then - facial expression, etc.

The absolute understands itself only through man. That's why God never can forget man any more than man can forget God.

Prayer was never meant for supplication. "Three-fold prayer." The state of having three centers working together is prayer.

Testament means "I will to you"—the Old Testament, the New Testament—knowledge willed to us.

We cannot change our being but we can change our condition. Water into steam. Steam is a greater force than water.

Habits are the solids in the octave of our personality. We have to melt them and loosen our being.

Development cannot begin until degeneration is arrested. Habits are degenerating.

Divide the word *remember* into re-member. That's what we mean when we say: "remember ourselves"—doing self-observation. We are stopping our degeneration and doing self development. Degeneration is Involution, the running down of the octave.

Adam the unregenerate man—living in the first Do, living mechanically.

Man is at the note Do—but every completed process begins at the note Do; hence, man has the potentiality. *He is at the beginning.*

We have to *un-involve.* When the cosmos evolves, man involves. While the cosmos has been evolving we have been involving, that is our condition. In completing ourselves, we are e-volving and as we e-volve we take into ourselves the cosmos.

"And man lives in caves and looks out through small apertures" ....

The cross is the plus sign and what is on the cross?—man. The most fascinating study in the world is what the cross means. Infinite variety of *being meanings* in the cross. And the mother who weeps is nature who loses as man rises from the cross. Nature doesn't want to lose us.

It is the chief concern of man to *work on* the moon.

All waste energy of our three centers goes to the moon by gravity without intention.

Was the snake in the garden personality tempting man to serve the moon?

All our deaths go to serve the moon.

Find out about the moon. Create in yourselves a moon.

What is the moon? A split-off particle of our planet earth.

Why is the moon without reality but with influence? We never think of the moon as a reality—yet it pulls oceans.

Every outside manifestation has its psychological replica.

Why do we feel that way about the moon? Because there is something like that psychologically in us.

Some part of our psychology bears the same relation to us as the moon bears to our psychical life.

It is only when wish becomes a need that it becomes the *Magical Evocative.*

You say: What do you want? Nothing.

You say: What do you need? *Everything.*

I don't want food but I need it.

Wants are only real when they are needs, they are imaginary when not.

We die because we don't get all we need to live.

Find out the needs of our lives and become conscious of them.

"They lived happily ever after." What do I need to enable me to live happily ever after and what is happily and what is ever after?

To live happily ever after—the discovery and adoption of the means to arrive at immortality.

Find out if the means exist, where found and how to use them.

Few of us want what we need and few of us need what we want.

What we want, the moon wants, what we need—the sun needs. *Memory belongs to the moon,* awareness to the sun.

The child in the womb sings "I remember who I am"—but the first breath, the first cry, means "I have forgotten who I am."

And we keep *on* forgetting until we die.

When masculine and feminine sex fluids mix, they never could produce another individual unless that force, the third force, comes. But it takes 9 months. The "I" covers itself, coats itself, in the womb, during those nine months, with the sex fluid.

ist—to be

ex—outside.

The *ist* is now covered up in subconscious brain. The being from the Sun Absolute is now covered up and is only a potentiality.

When that "I" can develop itself, it never comes again. Mature loses the machine with which the "I" has coated itself.

We have many "I's" but they are all personality I's. Produce an "I" superior to all the personality I's—Produce an "I" with the *range of the universe.*

DEFINITION OF FATE

If you let your personality impose upon you, then it is fate.

DEFINITION OF IMAGINATION

Imagination is the building up of new creations out of *previously conceived impacts.*

Think with will. Organize your thinking. Organized—from the organ. Not from muscle extension. Think organized.

Our effort is to be free of the type imposed upon us by planetary conditions—to be free of the animal.

Planets are moods. Moods make temperament. Temperament makes outside confirmation.

We think we make effort in this method but we don't even approach the outside of it. Think of effort. Think of those men who roll 40 kilometers over stones to a shrine, doing self-observation all the while. That's effort.

Do physical work every day. Consciously, with self-observation. That takes will. We cannot think without will.

Personality—We have a saying, "He stands in his own light." He can't see his real self because of his personality.

A Persian saying: You must always hold a mirror up to yourself so you can see the Devil approaching. (Emotional center working with the body is the devil.)

Truth doesn't lie in either pan of the scales, it lies somewhere between. *Shock in the octave* comes at a certain place, but not always between two definite notes.

Life is an organization of vibrations. The circulation of blood has its vibration, the emotional viscera has its, etc., etc. Each organ has its rate of vibrations for different stages—youth, age, etc.

Man, woman, child.

Into that positive and negative sex fluid comes a third force from the Sun Absolute itself which is life. Later in your subconscious force as the I.

The agent is not the action. Positive and negative come together and the neutralizing force is lost to our sight.

The "I" is a particle of the affliction of God in the subconscious brain.

Rate of vibrations. It is the rate of vibrations, the neutralizing force, (form-giving force, a particle of the Sun Absolute) which enters the sex fluids which are *also* rates of vibrations, which produces the child.

The "I" comes and comes until it develops.

If you develop yourself you become a help in the enlarged universe. G. says you become an individual—instead of one of the thousand leaves on a tree, you become a seed.

When we die the whole of the vibrations that hold us together go into space. The vibrations of the physical organs just run down the scale and go into the earth.

NEGATIVE EMOTIONS

The commonest of the negative emotions is anger, displeasure, etc. Next after association, negative emotions are the most depleting of our 'activity'.

Negative emotions are difficult to handle because they are insusceptible to reason. When we *think* reason has come in, it is usually only another emotion that has been added.

Bodily well-being usually pulls us out of anger, the coming in of another center, physical. Child-care stresses keeping the body busy. This is calling in the physical center to equalize small rages, fears, etc. in its emotional center.

Almost all forms of negative emotion are infantile.

Some negative emotions, like despondency, despair, jealousy, need help from the outside. This usually calls in more negative emotions on the part of the helpers—they must lie, tell 'charitable' untruths and thus anger arises for being so forced.

Make a list of the dramas of negative emotions. You will find all are tragedy. If you are not secretly in love with your negative emotions, there is usually a cure. (Most people are in love with theirs. They do not want to get rid of them.)

To get rid of a negative emotion, say "I am sick." Do *not* say what made you sick. When you say I am sick, a positive attitude is at once established.

Observe manifestations of each mood in your negative emotions.

When one is angry at you, don't meet him with anger, with the same center. "Turn the other cheek"—a recommendation to turn another center.

Write a candid opinion of someone/yourself as you think they would write it to you. Something in us is never deceived. Often the result is amazingly near the truth. Often the getting of this opinion is necessary for your future life and its development.

When a bad situation arises, ask yourself:

"What did that friend expect of me?"

"What did I give him?"

Christianity has not been tried and found wanting; it has been found difficult and never tried.

In perfecting a technique of living, the great difficulty is the body. It is first necessary to organize the outside life, the life of the body.

There is no chance for a *significant relationship* with a person whose center of gravity is in the physical center. The body will always triumph . . . and your "friend" will fail you.

We always expect behavior of people without bodies. Don't trust. No illusions.

A physical center person never loves, but always hates. He hates to have his body deranged.

You project your chemistry on other people and your relations with them are a result. Your unconscious manifestations are more powerful and get more results than your so-called "conscious."

You receive what you evoke.

CHIEF FEATURE

In each one of us is a "special little quirk"—the last little thing added to the scale. This is what makes you do things as *you* do them, and not like anyone else.

In bowling balls there is a pellet of lead added, so that it must be thrown with a special quirk to make it go straight.

We must learn how to send ourselves off with a certain quirk to make up go straight. We must learn where chief feature lies, what it consists of. Chief feature is the pattern of your wishes and motives.

It is mechanical.

It is of the essence but in the emotions.

Chief feature gives you *illusion of freedom.* (Freedom is actually the absence of choice of wishes.)

Write about yourself as if of another person. In a situation, how do you behave? This gives a clue to chief feature.

Chief feature is *wish.*

Look for chief feature in 5 things:

Greed
Self-pride
Lying
Fear
Sex
"Chief feature is not nice."
Chief feature can often be a combination of one or many of these 5 things. It is always the last little thing making you act as you do. It is in every situation. Look for it.
Chief feature is imaginary. It is not real. It is emotional.
Chief feature is not ever a good thing; but once found it can be used consciously.
Chief feature is an outgrowth of your emotional attitude toward yourself.

Our body is as much an object of the outside world as a tree, a stone or a planet.
The great absurdity—science investigates a world image which we cast upon our own consciousness.
The mask—You must know you have a mask and that little exists behind it. Try to discover how this mask was started—in youth we made always for peace—adjustment to a hostile environment. Make a list of people you remember earliest in life—put down opposite the name every effect and influence they had upon you. Maybe some of these influences were what we "put on" these persons. Our three centers are like clocks—they are wound up by and with these influences. And time (material) determines the effects.
We begin by protecting our inner essential lives.
A child has more sense of reality than its parents.
We evolve a mask—sex mask, social mask, professional or national mask. Our "repertory of gestures."
We become 'mask sore'—but it is dangerous to remove our mask, even if we could. The other person has the advantage over him who momentarily lets his mask slip. A specialized cruelty then goes on.
We can build up behind our mask our essence. Then we are impervious.
Victimization is a form of exhibitionism on the part of both parties.
We cannot go back far enough in our childhood to remember or find out how we put our masks on—hence the difficulty of removing.
We have practically no manifestation we can make to show our essence. Sometimes we want to show an "essential attitude" to a friend—often we show just the opposite because we have no gesture that is not part of the mask, etc. . .

WORDS AND ASSOCIATION

We waste our minds by words.

We should non-identify with all the traditional things in words. Because of words and association, the mind is always in a state of tension, not of attention.

Poetry is a fact translated in another center. Non-identification with the traditional application of the words.

THE CINEMA

It is a recorded fact that people drowning have a complete memory of everything that has happened in life. Could we never use this power consciously? Everything that has happened to us, every experience, is there within — the impress is in some one of the three centers, never to be eradicated, generally forgotten. *Everything is there.*

Try to picture the days' events with yourself as the central figure; but impersonal. Do the day from the beginning, not backwards. Engage the mind and leave the emotional center free with its pictures. Count a series of numbers until it becomes automatic, thus engaging the mind.

1234

4321

2345

5432 and etc., up to 10. Don't try to remember. *Do it pictorially* — the unrolling of the cinema.

This method of seeing oneself pictorially in all one's daily activity, has been called a "specific against mediocrity." This is a way of keeping your life from slipping into oblivion.

Four reasons why this nightly 'cinema' is difficult:

1.   Usually no self-observation during the day. This self-observation *necessary*.

2.   Difficulty of keeping from thinking of the counting.

3.   Constant interruption due to association.

4.   Sleep.

After doing the day's cinema, try the cinema of your life.

If we could do these things, if we can teach ourselves to see, impersonally, uncritically, we should gain a mastery over the three mechanical centers. There is an "inviolate completeness" which could be property of the human being. We are approaching only the outskirts of it.

For this method, *ability to think* is the first thing needed.

Be able to think differently than as accustomed, know the world in different categories.

This method is a mathematical and material explanation of the creation, maintenance and purpose of the universe and man's responsibility to it.

A TECHNIQUE FOR SELF-OBSERVATION

Observe:
Tones of voice
Gestures
Posture
Carriage
Facial Expressions
★Weight
★Temperature

★Weight—not physiological, rather a feeling of heaviness, on awakening in morning, or of lightness. Clues to emotional state, etc.

★Temperature—not medical, rather the emotional temperature. Why a sudden hot flush? A cold clammy sensation?

Often the condition observed disappears upon observation.

But at first, with this self-observation, all we are doing is *getting data on ourselves*.

IV REPETITION

Investigate what you repeat. (In love this is fairly obvious—one always repeats.) Investigate all relationships outside the definite love relationship. You find out your weak spots if you find out where and how you repeat.

Formulate reasons for wanting to wake up and change. Make repertory complete of your weaknesses and failures. Avoid *moral*. Find out the wrong working of your centers.

Try to remember to remember to observe. Participate in your gestures observed. Try also to observe how whole trains of thought go on without our taking part in them.

MORALS

The subconscious mind sees the result of our real experiences. Conscience once uncovered needs no morals.

John the Baptist, crying in the wilderness, is a symbol of man crying in the wilderness of his own body.

Give up the idea that the universe has desirable ethical ends in view.

Give up "doing good."

Sacrifice mechanical suffering. Suffering is very real to us, therefore we identify with it. Most suffering is mechanical. But our identification with it is real.

Self-pity is the most depleting of the emotions.

Chaplin—the epitome of self-pity, which explains why all the world identifies with him.

Be careful of self-depreciation. Don't discourage the body.

You must observe yourself with non-identification otherwise your statements about yourself sound fantastic.

These ideas give no result unless worked on. *Effort is the first and last word.* The Labors of Hercules—the Augean stables are a man's personality. Clean out our own stables.

Of all the great teachers, Christ is the most cruel when he speaks of the difficulty of doing things with ourselves. One wonders how he came to be called the meek and gentle Jesus.

Make a catalogue of a friend's image of life; this will help you with your own. Make a formula which encompasses your attitude toward life. "All is lost from the beginning"—Jane's.

We only know two states now—sleeping and waking (the chart). There is an exact analogy between our personal psychology and this chart. Everything below the planet is repetition of things perfected above . . . imperfected repetition.

On the chart, God begins with "planets"!

The idea of a "personal God" is the most egotistic gesture of man—that a divine omnipotent being could be concerned with our transient little life.

Our environment is not this planet we live on. Ours is the megalocosmos—everything above the planet.

LOVE

Love is of three kinds (as far as we are in it): Instinctive, emotional and conscious.

Instinctive love has chemistry as its base. And it lasts only as long as, and is only as strong as, this chemistry.

Emotional love is pathologic. The lover is a medium through which uncontrolled power of magnetism passes. Emotional lovers are the victims of their own uncontrolled power. Emotional love *always* creates hate in the lover, then in the loved one, then back again—an eternal changing of the hate.

Instinctive love is the highest type we know, *because of its irradiations.*

Emotional love seldom produces off-spring. It is non-biological. It evokes its own slayer.

Conscious love wishes that the loved object should arrive at its own native perfections, regardless of consequences to the lover. The paradox: it always evokes the same in the lover. This love is rare among us.

"Take hold tightly, let go lightly" a proverb from Tibet. It is always hard to let go. We have fear, we are over-sensitive from past failures, or we have imagination—we cannot bear to imagine the loved one happier elsewhere with someone else.

Instinctive and emotional loves are uncontrolled and unconscious. These are dangerous states to be in. This is love without knowledge or power.

Love can be evoked in 4 associative ways:

1.   External form—reminding of someone you've been in love with, esthetic associations.

2.   Feelings influenced by other people. You love what others love, or what others hate, etc.

3.   Suggestions—influenced by praise of others, etc.

4.   Superiority—you get the idea that another person is superior. "All the rot about ideals . . ."

When associations work and run together in harmony, then we are in love.

All in lower row we take passively. We must "coat" the higher body. Self-observation makes this active—the worm must turn, and observation starts with the body.

Another picture of man.

THINK: /10.000 of a second—an impression

Every three seconds—a breath

24 hours—a day

80 years—a life

ANOTHER PICTURE OF MAN

This is how it always works—we perceive, we feel, we act. The three interconnected centers.

(At night—we jump in half sleep—one of the centers disconnecting.) This above interconnection of centers works only on the waking hours.

Study your dreams. There is a self-contained energy left over in some one of the centers. You can discover in which center you contain unused (during the day) energy. Do you have predominantly physical, mental or emotional dreams?

The three centers fall asleep separately. Sometimes one center does not sleep at all during the night. Times we awaken with a feeling of suffering, though the physical self has slept soundly—this means the emotional center was wide awake all night with some suffering.

Teach yourself to put all three centers to sleep at any time. If this could be done, we would need little sleep. Gurdjieff awakens people at the Priory, at all hours of the night, making them change beds—saying "You're not sleeping anyhow. Why not spend the night talking and learning something?"

V OUR LIFE

Consider each year of your life as a chair. See yourself sitting in it, see the chairs you will sit in. Should be able to see yourself both ways in time—back to beginnings, forward till death.

Our effort is to break this circle in time—not repeat. Recurrence.

Man, three-centered, geared to connect with, *wheel of circumstances* (running down).

These wheels are emptying their contents as they connect with the wheel of circumstances.

Numbers in centers represent relative proportional strength of center. The functioning of these three centers depends on a set of seven circumstances (accidental):

1. Heredity in general
2. Conditions at moment of conception.
3. The combination of the radiations of all planets, etc.
4. "Degree of *being*" in our parents.
5. Quality of 'being' manifested in people around us.
6. Good wishes, thoughts and actions manifested by people around us.
7. Conscious effort on our own part during childhood.

A being consists of its appetites.

Intelligence is due to innate arrangements in the nervous system. You are born intelligent. You never acquire intelligence.

Instincts are given to man to enable him to cope with his situation.

We in this method are like Lucifers, cast out from the mechanical heaven in which we live. We must realize the solemnity of the situation. We must think with terror of dying unfinished.

There are seven accidental circumstances determining the reactions' of our three centers. We die accordingly as the contents of one center are used up prematurely.

*Physica*l dying—doctors have names for it but no cure. Sport addicts often die thus. Statistics show wrestlers die at 49 years.

Emotional dying: artists die as a result of the disharmonizing in the tempo of their lives.

Mental center dies—reading, studying and associations (superfluous) provoked. "Dying by newspapers."

To *not* die in one center, get an activity that is linked up with another center. Put a regulator on the spring of each center. Do not allow one center to overwork. You give yourself up to the associations in the functioning of these centers.

Harmonious associations with the three centers is difficult to acquire. Self-observation is the first regulator. You thus begin to cut off the superfluous associations running into one center. The tragedy is that when one center dies, runs down, it affects the other two without their taking part.

I

We are in a state of arrested development.

A one-centered being is a worm.

A two-centered being is an animal, 2 dimensional.

A three centered being is a man.

We take no part in our activity. Everything is done in us from the outside.

Our whole life is wasted in yes/no argument between the three centers. The contents of these three centers were accidentally acquired. Thus, they are accidentally called forth. 1% it is ourselves, 99% of us is sociology.

The ages of our different centers differs. There can even be different ages in one center.

Physical—young face, old neck, etc. We can develop hallucinations of our centers as we "develop"—one can be retarded mentally and develop a mental hallucination, retarded emotionally and develop emotional hallucination.

The three centers like three types—physical (yogi) emotional (monk) mental (ascetic). Each is a one-centered development, developed at the expense of the other two centers.

Our brain has undergone development only for survival. It is *not* a truth-finding organ.

Everything tends to put us to sleep, suggestibility, etc.

We start with these three centers practically empty. The emotional and mental has inclinations, desires—pleasing to them. Constant repetition of the same desires makes our character. We receive 10,000 impressions per second, but we register practically not one. We always choose by our habits of yesterday—repeat, repeat, repeat.

We have no future. Our lives are an idle escape from one error into another.

Our race, etc. is indicated by a series of gestures. A human being can make 20 gestures, but makes usually only 5. Find out the repertory of your own gestures.

The agency of the will is not admitted in the scheme of psychology. What we call 'will' is only desire.

The first symptom of awakening from our sleep is to SUSPECT we are asleep.

It is more difficult to wake from our dream sleep than from our life state. Our life state (to a trained observer) gives us away.

Man collects impressions and excretes behavior and by this behavior is he known.

A need is an internal dis-equilibrium—one needs a shock to awaken—one must *want* to awaken. Do not disturb those who are "sitting pretty" unless

their need is great. One loses one's place and one must go through life standing. Standing is not comfortable, especially if a good chair has been lost.

II LAW OF THREE

In the cosmological scale, operating at three, operating at shock. The shock
can carry us beyond the status quo. The shock is self-observation. We have the
three forces in us.

The plus and the minus, sexes, electricity, etc. Science is the third force.
The third force is the neutral balancing force. The mind affirms all, the body
denies. All energy leaks away from the bottom of the triangle because it is
open at the bottom.

Some have no emotions after thirty. Some stop, mental growth at seven
or eight. Many die too soon (physical). Close up bottom of triangle, stop the
leak. A three-centered force is given us each morning. We cannot use but a
part of it; the rest is wasted. One uses only 1/10. If the bottom of the triangle
can be closed, new energy flows in, and can be stored. In psychology, the third
force is usually the motive behind the act. Problem: Find out the motives behind your acts, thoughts, etc. (Usually it is the emotional center motivating.)

Law of three operating—in fairy tales. Three princes, each with a task, the
reward being in one of the three centers.

A set-up of man, law of three.

Matter.

Emotion.

Physical

The emotions are situated in the solar plexus.

A system of nerves, across the center of the being. Like the milky way—a
galaxy of disconnected nerve centers.

Reality

Know-able

Feel-able

Do-able

Unless these three operate at once, it is not Reality. (That's why Reality is
never found.)

There is a continual argument, friction, between the three centers in man.
The body is always the tyrant.

The Cosmological Chart presents an exact analogy with our psychological
processes. The shock in our life is self-observation.

Everything we touch is degraded—air, water, food, etc. We send energy
into the planet thus. We are the digestive apparatus.

Our real function is to up-grade energy. Change the vibrations into higher instead of degrading to lower. (Some—like breathing and eating, are automatic
and must go on.) We give only quantity vibrations. We should give quality

576

vibrations to this octave. As we function, eat, drink, suffer, create, etc, vibrations are extracted from us by nature. A few quality vibrations would make up for many quantity vibrations.

We're in a situation—"the terror of the situation"—Gurdjieff. Like sheep, taken for its mutton and wool. Thus ourselves. Nature feeds us, cares for us, etc. but not from love—for profit from us. Nature takes from us with a drastic hand. Takes vibrations from us she can't get voluntarily. If we could give ONE quality vibration. . .

Wars—nature needs those vibrations. Only consciousness can change this. Deaths give vibrations to the planet—10,000 bodies going back to earth—the suffering before death is one sort of vibration—the crystallization of material substance, another. All goes back to the planet.

2

Essence is difficult to define. It must be found out by relations. Human essence is composed of 2,000 million people. 2,000 million implies history, all our evolution from the animal up. *Each one of the 2,000 million is one of your potentialities actualized.*

Mi   Essence is composed of three notes:
Re   anger, hate and fear
Do

Anything else is an 'overtone,' that which does not exist but which might. All the so-called 'good' in the world, philanthropies, etc, are possibilities not actualized. Usually you find they are motivated by one of the three notes, anger, hate or fear.

Try to find out the distribution in you of anger, hate and fear. These three can be in one center, or in all three.

We have to make an effort to get at essence. It is not your own—it is human essence. In getting at it, it is fatal to identify yourself with it. Get at motives, then more easily, you will get at essence. When you get at essence, what you learn can be applied to everything. Art, literature, etc.

There are *affirmed emotions* of humanity. In great literature, in great art, there are no emotions that have not to do with the affirmed emotions of humanity . . . something every man can understand.

Your essence is material. You can change it. Essence aspires to be soul. It has no sex differentiation. It is wishes. Wishes are planetary. You are interesting or dull according to the number of planets that were in conjunction at conception. More planets, more interesting, vice versa.

Personality is a cross-section of all streams of activity at any one moment. The pattern of your habits is personality. Personality is a mass of unfused chemicals.

Analyze yourself in respect of some person near to you. How do you recognize yourself? Your identity? How do you know yourself from another?

What is the *essential power* in you? To find out, gratify all your fancies, whims (but don't cultivate). Gratify and watch them and yourself. Whims and fancies change. An essential power does not. You must find out this power by excess.

To have essential power, you must have *essential wishes*.

Three kinds of wishes:

Potential   Actual   Ideal

Most of us spend our lives on non-actualizable wishes. Find the actualizable wishes. Most "ideal" wishes are non-actualizable. These non-actualizable wishes are mistletoe. Cut them off. Don't plod along with them. "Imagination is only excess of desire over ability," Orage.

THE "I"

Necessity to establish in yourself an unique and personal "I." We have too many "I's." Physical center "I's"are disconnected and go off in different directions. Thought must connect and fuse.

Subjugate to one single "I" the personalities in you. Say over and over again—I am. I have a body. Say it, to try to find out what it means. (I am a body is a confusion.)

3

Self-observation pumps up energy, uncovers that "I." The "I" is not defined by intelligence, gifts, talents, etc. It is simply what you are in yourself.

The body is the only vehicle, cart, vessel, instrument, etc., through and by which we can find out. Stripped of your 5 senses, what are you? What manifestation could you give that an astute psychologist could not reduce to a bodily manifestation? *99% of our 70 years is spent in sublimated animality* (caring for body, thinking of it, etc.)

Get the "I" out from the inside where it is buried, to the outside. All miraculous re-births in legend and history are just this—the uncovering of the "I."

Our first birth is passive. Our second birth is active, conscious. We are born out of our own bodies. Self-observation gets at the "I." For this 2nd birth, we must first die to our automatic selves; change values and die to the old values.

Gurdjieff says in the cerebellum there is a seed, a germ, which is a possibility of a soul. He calls it the "representative of God in the essence."

"Fragments of a Faith Forgotten," "Hermes Thrice Greater." These ancient books show these ideas are not new but have been with man always (esoteric).

TIME

In the physical center we sense time as one thing after another. In the emotional center, we experience a thing at the time. In the mental center time as a thing in immediacy.

Space
Line
Plane
Solid
Energy   + – (neutral)
Time
Succession
Recurrence
Eternity
Space is the field in which time operates.

Time is the actualization of one possibility in a situation. All others die *for you* (but remain for others).

When we start to actualize one possibility, that determines the second, because we have taken a direction. Thus the danger of making a wrong choice—all off in the wrong direction. Again, find the essential wish.

Time is the possibility of your existence.

Time can never be subjective.

Wherever a process goes on, there is time.

This method is a *technique against time.*

4 ADDENDA — 2ND CONFERENCE

This method is a psychological technique of life. Most people are technique-resisting.

In the *solar plexus* the negative emotions are situate in the left side, positive in the right side. Locate the agitation and the kind of emotion acting on you can be known.

Essence is eternal, compacted of internal relations simple or complex but individual at every level.

When we talk about our essence, we talk about our psychology.

Time is the actualization of one possibility in a situation. The minute we begin to actualize one possibility in a situation, all others are dead for us (but exist for others on earth). The moment we actualize, the next is decided. *This gives a direction in time.*

Time is *my* possibility of experience.

Time is the exhaustion of the means to renew ourselves.

Time is the unique subjective. It can never be objective. It cannot exist for you outside yourself. Your time is in you.

Eternity is the possibility of the actualization of every possibility in a situation *at the same time.*

Art is a subjective emotion backed up by craftsmanship. Art enjoys only vivid values. Mahabharata—greatest objective art.

We progress in details. The whole is often lost in details.

Essence will put you eventually in a certain current in life. You may want to change the current.

Asia is essence. Europe is personality.

Sleep is a rehearsal of death. If we could answer questions and do problems in sleep—i.e. in the sleep of our centers—this would be a sign of consciousness existent without body. This would be a small hope for immortality. This would be manifestation stripped of the 5 senses and the personality.

Cerebellum—the "seed at war"—our subconscious brain, *should* be our conscious brain. Everything that has happened to us in life is there, penned up in the cerebellum, escaping only in sleep, trances, etc.

We understand *space* in three ways:

Line
Plane
Solid
Time as:
Progression
Recurrence
Eternity
Energy as:
+ Plus
Minus
Neutralizing force

Use the pause—There is a minute pause before a certain center prompts to action. This pause is the neutral-balancing force at work. We should use this pause. Then work like chess players with ourselves. Strong personalities are a hindrance. They are too active, or too passive, in the moves. Strong personalities over-shoot the mark.

BOGACHEVSKY

Objective morality is established by life and by the commandments given to us by our Lord God Himself through his prophets and gradually becomes the basis in man of what is called conscience. By this conscience is objective morality maintained. Objective morality never changes, it can only broaden in the course of time. As for subjective morality, that is invented by man and is therefore a relative motion differing for different people and different places and is based upon the understanding of good and bad prevailing at the given time.

Subjective morality is a relative notion and if you are filled with relative notions then when you are grown up you will always and everywhere act and judge other people according to the conventional views and notions you have acquired from others. You must learn not what people around you consider good or bad—but learn to act in life as your conscience bids you. An untrammeled conscience will always know more than all the books and teachers put together. But for the present, until your own conscience is formed, you should live according to the commandment of our Teacher Jesus Christ: Always-do-unto-others-as-you-would-have-others-do-unto-you.

YELOV

It is not a question to whom a man prays but a question of his faith. Faith is conscience, the foundation of which is laid in childhood. If a man changes his religion, he loses his conscience and conscience is the most valuable thing in man. I respect conscience and since conscience is sustained by his faith and his faith by religion, therefore I respect his religion and for me it would be a great sin if I should judge his religion or disillusion him in it and thereby destroy his conscience which can only be acquired in childhood.

It's all the same. Our thoughts work day and night. Instead of letting them think of "caps-of-invisibility" or the "riches of Aladdin" let them better be occupied with something useful. In giving direction to thought, of course a certain energy is spent but no more energy would be spent for this purpose during twenty-four hours than is required for the digestion of one meal. I decided to study languages in order not only not to allow my thoughts to idle, but also not to allow them to hinder my other functions with their idiotic dreams and childish phantasies. Besides, the knowledge of language itself may sometimes be useful.

FROM KANARI

The Yogis do not teach evolution as it is conceived by modern science. Modern science teaches that mind is a by-product of the evolving material forms. The Yogi teaching says that there was mind involved in the lowest form and that mind constantly pressing forward for unfoldment compelled the gradual evolution or unfoldment of the slowly advancing degrees of organization and function. Science teaches that "function precedes organization." The Yogis say that "desire precedes function." There is ever the urge of the mind which the creature feels as dim desire and which grows stronger as time goes on. Science says all is material and mind is a by-product, the Yogis say all is mind, (even God—pure mind) with matter as a tool and instrument of expression and manifestation. Accompanying this evolution of bodies there is an evolution of souls producing the former.

Sayings of Gurdjieff's Father

1.   Without salt, no sugar.
2.   Ashes come from burning.
3.   He is deep down because you are high up.
4.   If there is "I" in one's presence, then God and the devil are of no account.
5.   All the unhappiness on earth comes from the wiseacring of women.
6.   In the dark even a louse can be worse than a tiger.
7.   Once you've shouldered it, it's the lightest thing in the world.
8.   If the priest goes to the right, the teacher inevitably must turn to the left.
9.   The cassock hides a fool.
10. A good representative of hell—a tight shoe.
11. If the teacher is the enlightened, who then is the donkey?
12. If there is no elephant and no horse, even the donkey is great.
13. He is really stupid who is to those around him "clever."
14. If a man is a coward, it proves he has will.
15. If you want to be rich—make friends with—the police.
16. If you want to be famous—make friends with—the reporters.
17. If you want to have peace—make friends with—the neighbors.
18. If you want to sleep—make friends—with your wife.
19. If you want to be full—make friends—with your mother-in-law
20. If you want to lose your faith—make friends—with the priest.
21. If you are first in the house, your wife is second; if your wife is first, then you are zero.
22. More powerful than Genghis Khan if he wishes, is the corner policeman.
23. Happy is he who sees not his unhappiness.
24. It isn't the quantity of food a man eats that denotes absence of greed.
25. Fire heats water but at the same time water puts out fire.
26. The truth is that from which one's conscience can be at peace.

BOKHARIAN DERVISH

Here it will do you no harm to say that among your favorites there have long existed in each locality special forms for outward relationship, for the reason that the *inner feeling of relationship common to all the beings of the universe* without difference of form or place of existence, has long been destroyed in them.

Good or bad relationships among them are established at the present time only by external manifestations, chiefly by politeness as it is called, that is to say, by empty words.

However much one being might inwardly wish another being food, if for some reason or other he should express himself in the wrong words . . . all would be over.

It is also interesting to note that the abnormal existence of your favorites has not only spoiled their own psyche, but it has reacted on the psyche of other forms of beings on this same planet.

Such an inner feeling is entirely atrophied in those forms of beings with which your favorites have a frequent contact, and it has been preserved only among those other forms of beings, whose form of existence is such that they have no contact at all with these biped beings of yours; as for example those called tigers, lions, bears, hyenas, snakes, falangas, scorpions, etc.

In the psyche of these forms of beings however a very strange peculiarity has been formed. These tigers, lions, etc., etc., perceive the inner feeling of fear of other beings as hostility, and hence try to destroy them in self-defense.

This strange peculiarity in their psyche was also acquired on account of your favorites. Thanks as usual to their abnormal conditions of existence, they gradually became cowards from head to foot; and at the same time, and equally completely, the peculiarity of destroying the existence of other beings entered into them.

Being thus by nature cowards of the highest degree, whenever they set out to kill other forms of beings, or accidentally meet any of them who, psychically and in other respects, are much stronger than themselves, they sweat with fear and long with all their being for a means of killing them. In this manner, in the psyche of beings who have no frequent contact with your favorite, side by side with the real function placed in them by nature—instinctively to pay respect to those forms of beings which in the gradation of the sacred reasonableness are higher than themselves, an instinct is gradually acquired and formed, owing to which the feeling of fear in others is perceived as a menace to their own life, which menace they try accordingly to destroy.

In spite of the difference of their exterior forms, all the beings of this planet lived together at first in peace and concord; and even at the present time it happens occasionally that one of your favorites so perfects himself that he realizes that all living creatures are alike to Our Endlessness; and then succeeds in completely destroying his fear of other forms of beings. In consequence not only do other forms of beings not attempt to harm him but they even pay him every respect and render him every service as a being higher in the scale of reasonableness.

If all humans had a soul
There would not be any room left on earth
And there would neither exist
Poisonous plants nor wild beasts nor even evil.

Soul is for the lazy-fantasy
Luxury for the indulger-in-suffering
The denominator of personality is in it

The way and the connection to the Maker and Creator

Leader of the will
Its presence is "I am"
It is a part of the All-being
So it was and ever will be.

Soul is the sediment of education.
It is the (prime) source of patience.
It is also the testimony
To the sense of the eternal being.

Read—Elliot—(Book on Atlantis)
The Sphinx is supposed to be a replica of a figure before a temple door in Atlantis.
The *symbol of the sphinx*—Consciousness
Body of a bull—*effort*
Claws of a lion—strength
Breasts of a virgin—*impartial love*
Wings of an eagle—*ability to soar*
Face of a conscious being.
In writings of Plato—he relates how in his travels (Egypt?) he saw the actual ground-plans of Atlantis.

 The seal of Solomon ancient and universal. 2 triangles, 2 sexes.

 The *swastika*—The one line represents our passive birth. We must turn around, be re-born in consciousness, the line is active, conscious.

There has been all knowledge in the world, but vast bodies of it have been wiped out (wars, calamities, etc.) as chalk off a slate. But all over the world we find proofs (if we can read) of a superior knowledge—Atlantis, Stonehenge, Pyramids, Mayan architecture, temples, etc.

As in the life history of the human race, so in our personal life history—there are great blocks of memory that are irretrievable to us.

Great cathedrals, monuments etc were built with a *conscious purpose*—to elevate for a moment the vibrations of people. This was a conscious attempt to leaven the masses. An attempt to force people to non-identify for even one instant.

I

This is a method of *effort*—conscious effort, not automatic, mechanical effort. As we are, there is no will. Will as we think we have it is a state of development. Will is a possibility, in a higher center. All we call development now is but an extension of one of the three centers. All our art is but an extension of the emotional center, etc. All supposed development in the world today is really a detriment.

The obligation and highest aim of man is to understand and cooperate with the laws of the universe. The universe is an intelligent creation and therefore intelligible. There are answers to everything.

Nature can do no more. Man is the highest possible development of a self-evolving form. All further development requires conscious effort. This requires labor comparable to that which nature has expended on our development thus far, millenniums of it.

In all nature's creations, a certain activity follows a certain form.

The start toward consciousness—neutral scientific observation of one's self. Begin with the body because of its speed. Body is three times faster than emotions. Emotions are three times faster than thought.

Gestures are speedy and proficient, habitized from birth. It is almost too fast for itself to observe. Here the personal equation is most pernicious; but remember the body is something *outside* the "I."

We are an animal with a formless psyche—a psyche to have form must be three-fold.

A three-fold psyche means the three centers in the brain are developed equally:

Instinctive
Emotional
Mental

Be conscious of your body, aware of emotions and mindful of your thoughts.

Feel with the mind and think what you feel—this is insurance against self-deception.

We observe at first only with the emotions—the wish to do this and that, avoid one-centered observation. This is a pathological attack.

Eradicate subjective weaknesses—greed at table, etc. Don't try to observe yourself in excess. You are then observing an over functioning organism.

Self-observation is the first step toward *freedom from associations*.

Self-observation is *not* the body observing the body (like an actress in a glass).

585

We must non-identify with the body.
There are three kinds of people:
A people are masters (Buddha, Christ, etc.)
B people are artists, interested in experience, not facts.
C people are scientists, positivists. Facts are more agreeable to them.

Magnetic-center people have a few cells in the brain *not* monkey cells. These can be developed into traits of B people.

Find out what you are—are you predominantly practical, emotional or mental. In which centers do you work and in which centers do you expect your rewards?

The law of three operates in each note.

Human development (average) goes from *do* to *mi* and back again—always within the same three.

The perfect do is known to have been struck in a room of the pyramid, and in a place in the Gobi desert.

Science proves that in a sound-proof room when the perfect note *do* is struck, it will go up in vibrations to *mi* and then drop back to *do*—as with us. . . .

Rita Romilly

FURTHER READING

RELATED TO ORAGE

Orage, A. R., Lawrence Morris, Sherman Manchester.
  Orage's Commentary on Gurdjieff's "Beelzebub's Tales to His Grandson":
  New York Talks 1926–1930.
    Book Studio, 2012.
Nott, C. S.
  Teachings of Gurdjieff: The Journal of a Pupil.
    Routledge & Kegan Paul, 1961.
  Further Teachings of Gurdjieff: Journey Through This World.
    Routledge & Kegan Paul, 1969.
Welch, Louise.
  Orage with Gurdjieff in America.
    Routledge & Kegan Paul, 1982.
Taylor, Paul Beekman.
  Gurdjieff and Orage: Brothers in Elysium.
    Red Wheel Weiser, 2001.
Martin, Wallace.
  Orage as Critic.
    Routledge & Kegan Paul, 1974.
Mairet, Philip.
  A. R. Orage: A Memoir.
    University Books, 1966.
Steele, Tom.
  Alfred Orage and the Leeds Arts Club 1893-1923.
    Orage Press 2009.

RELATED TO GURDJIEFF

Gurdjieff's Early Talks 1914–1931: In Moscow, St. Petersburg, Essentuki, Ti-
flis, Constantinople, Berlin, Paris, London, Fontainebleau, New York, and
Chicago.
  Book Studio, 2014.
Gurdjieff and the Women of the Rope: Notes of Meetings in Paris and New
York 1935–1939 and 1948–1949.
  Book Studio, 2012.
Transcripts of Gurdjieff's Wartime Meetings 1941–46.
  Book Studio, 2009.

GURDJIEFF'S WRITINGS

Beelzebub's Tales to His Grandson.
  Harcourt, Brace & Company; Routledge & Kegan Paul, 1950.
Meetings with Remarkable Men.
  E. P. Dutton, 1963.
Life Is Real Only Then, When "I Am."
  E. P. Dutton, 1978.

The Herald of Coming Good.
  Book Studio, 2014.
The Struggle of the Magicians: Scenario of the Ballet.
  Book Studio, 2014.

INDEX

abdomen, 396, 558
abnormality, 189-190, 282,
   289, 296, 369-370, 397,
   448, 475, 492, 584
Absolute, the, 8, 12, 21-23,
   45, 47, 50, 62, 65, 72, 77,
   96, 113-114, 117, 119-120,
   126, 140, 149, 152, 167,
   173-181, 184, 186, 191,
   202, 219, 254, 261, 275,
   282, 352, 357, 359, 368,
   383-386, 389, 396, 404,
   435, 437, 486, 510, 517,
   565, 567-568
absorption, 6-7, 116, 203,
   269, 277, 336, 353, 369,
   495
abstract, 140, 157, 334, 337,
   504, 520
absurd, 246, 284, 335, 356,
   397
acceptance, 21, 44, 58, 82, 90,
   158, 164, 193, 231, 245,
   318, 381, 407, 411-412,
   425, 427, 440, 471, 485,
   487, 509, 535, 547
accord, 264, 449
accumulation, 42, 288, 312,
   334, 363
accuracy, 1-3, 39, 49, 63, 72,
   106, 157, 166, 211, 245,
   321, 384, 479
accustom, xii, 210, 265, 412,
   426, 431, 465, 496, 528,
   559, 564-565, 571
acid, 514
acquaint, 233, 246, 297
acting, 12, 100, 116, 139,
   154, 178, 264, 266-267,
   274, 280, 303, 315, 365,
   389, 395, 422, 503,
   530-531, 539, 543, 565,
   580
actor, xiv, 100, 166, 422,
   539
active
   force, 346, 474
   state, 365, 389, 449

actors, xiv, 100, 166, 422,
   539, 586
acute, 43, 247, 260
adaptation, 75, 108, 314, 450,
   513, 558-559
admiration, 232, 298, 306,
   334, 563
advance, 146, 161, 185, 216,
   263, 275, 301, 389, 431,
   505, 512
adventure, 71
advice, 47, 177, 236, 246,
   356, 426, 445, 471, 517,
   520
advise, 177, 236, 426, 445
affairs, 435, 495, 558
Affectation, 445
affection, 76, 91, 225, 485,
   503
affirmation, 98, 231, 287,
   307, 391-392, 394,
   577-578
affliction, 568
Afghanistan, 2
African, 413
ages, 65, 240, 526, 560, 576
agitation, 409, 580
agony, 486
agreement, 4, 7, 165, 220,
   349, 470, 485, 497, 535,
   564
aid, 17, 83, 86, 92, 154, 281,
   359, 363, 422, 426, 458,
   467, 548
air, 3, 32, 37, 47, 50, 57, 62,
   69, 71, 73, 89-90, 93, 100,
   104-105, 114, 126, 144,
   146, 152, 175, 192, 269,
   284, 296, 301, 310-311,
   348, 434-435, 449,
   494-495, 506, 518-520,
   522, 535, 577
Akhaldans, 271, 374
Alchemists, 379, 474
alchemy, 133, 156, 196
alertness, 8, 331, 428
Alice in Wonderland, 91, 208,
   379

allegory, 206-208, 353,
   355-356, 378, 380-381,
   536
aloud, 92, 161, 193, 292
altruism, 71
amazement, 91, 164, 247, 542
ambition, 9, 252, 305, 313,
   447, 450, 467-468, 483,
   502, 530
America, x, xiv, 369, 394,
   412, 487, 523, 589
American, x, 523
Americans, 190
amusement, 3, 313
analogy, 20-22, 50, 73,
   84, 88, 199, 212, 254,
   267, 269, 275, 277, 283,
   301, 320, 346-347, 365,
   378-379, 384, 391, 403,
   415, 455, 492, 502, 504,
   512, 519, 521, 531, 536,
   549, 573, 577
analysis, 31, 69, 77, 233,
   254-255, 261, 276, 292,
   355, 364, 366, 449, 469,
   500
anamnesis, 259, 391
ancient, 65, 73, 92, 241,
   318-319, 326, 335, 378,
   471, 495, 511, 524-525,
   529, 541, 543-544, 558,
   561, 579, 585
anecdotes, 551
angels, 120, 126, 180, 183,
   194-195, 228, 257, 401,
   517
anger, 4-6, 8, 49, 69, 71, 227,
   229-230, 295, 336, 423,
   425, 437, 440, 568-569,
   578
anguish, 258, 263, 460, 471
aniline, 536
animate, 342, 385, 436, 459,
   474-475, 506, 541
annihilate, 5, 168, 269
annoy, 86, 281, 343, 413
Anulios, 257
anxiety, 332, 423

calculate, 60, 331
Calf, 234
California, iv
calmness, 150, 204, 560
camel, 211, 528
cancer, 246, 356
candidate, 374
candles, 349
capacities, 41, 83, 548
captains, 210, 457
Carbon, 401
cards, 133, 267, 291, 307, 447
care, 96, 100, 151, 212, 234,
   237, 245-246, 286, 306,
   312-313, 336, 372, 413,
   443, 461, 486, 495-496
career, xii
carelessness, 158, 370, 467
caricature, 222
caring, 142, 579
carpenter, 397, 434
carpets, 551
Carriage, 6, 220, 424, 572
cars, 219, 225, 233, 237, 282,
   290, 313, 384, 415, 469,
   503
cart, 18, 28, 94, 104-105,
   199, 204, 208, 380, 391,
   427, 519, 579
castes, 109, 127, 155, 166,
   207-208, 246, 272, 389,
   445, 515, 555, 570, 575
categories, 21, 93, 186,
   230, 293, 319, 503, 555,
   560-561, 565, 571
cathedrals, x, 183, 210, 388,
   460, 585
Catholicism, 193, 330
cats, 23, 55, 124, 195-196,
   469, 503
celestial, 8, 62, 120, 436
center of gravity, 49, 172,
   190, 193, 197, 211, 270,
   309, 330, 368-369, 373,
   383, 406, 479, 533-535,
   569
centers
   higher, 5-7, 17, 24, 30,
   32-34, 37-39, 43, 45, 48,
   51-52, 54, 67, 77, 93,
   97-98, 102, 107, 111,

117, 139, 152, 206-207,
   243, 354, 380, 428-429,
   433-434, 444, 457, 586
moving, 190, 378
sex, 59
centuries, 5, 80, 532
cerebellum, 579, 581
cerebral, 10, 74, 80, 86, 99,
   139, 223, 229-231, 285,
   293, 295, 298, 320, 427,
   455, 559, 564
chalk, 585
channels, 180, 193-194, 261
chaos, 7, 58, 84, 114, 138,
   168, 203, 278, 323
charge, 186, 203, 246, 269,
   272, 351, 390, 415, 502
charm, xii
chart, 573, 577
chasing, 36, 549
Château
   du Prieuré, 574
cheap, 290, 299, 326, 496
cheat, 114
checkbook, 543
checks, 543
cheese, 315
chemicals, 25-26, 194, 196,
   216, 230, 258, 267, 295,
   346, 400-401, 403, 526
chemistry, 196, 273, 294-295,
   376, 401, 563, 569, 573
chemists, xiv, 194
Cherubim, 120, 538
chess, 291, 581
chewing, 94, 397, 467, 544
Chicago, 589
chicken, 66, 150, 309, 463
chief feature, 12, 71-72,
   77, 85, 91, 98-100, 108,
   111, 126, 143, 161-163,
   165-166, 555, 569-570
China, 2, 225, 260, 308, 460
Chinese, 460
Christianity, 1, 44, 49, 65,
   84, 98, 190, 266, 278, 325,
   327, 329, 337, 355-356,
   364, 412-413, 470, 549,
   551, 569

churches, 193, 207, 265,
   327-328, 330, 379, 400,
   451, 495, 542
cigarettes, 40, 52, 88, 308,
   353, 447, 554
cinema, 31, 517, 540, 571
cipher, 129
circulation, 80, 196, 434, 568
civilization, xii, 3, 78-79,
   149, 236, 244, 318, 491,
   506, 508, 523, 525, 537,
   558, 560
clairvoyance, 211, 219-221,
   243
clarity, xiii, 205, 343, 396
cleaning, 48, 262, 573
climbing, 138, 141, 168,
   493-494, 541
clock, 182-183, 220, 224,
   233, 313, 335-336, 387,
   407
clothes, 313, 422
Club, iv
clues, 474, 569, 572
coal, 73, 293
coarse, 132
coat, 4, 54, 80, 101, 199-200,
   202, 269, 345-347, 408,
   567, 574
coffee, 47, 322, 457
cognizance, 289, 470
coincidences, 90, 141,
   161-162, 278, 337, 412,
   434, 509-510, 513, 560
cold, 8, 172, 225, 284, 322,
   332, 457, 501, 572
collection, 60, 347, 349, 354,
   367, 397, 404, 472, 522
color, 2, 35, 162, 194, 232,
   246, 248, 268, 299, 358,
   369-370, 469, 507, 536,
   558
colors, 35, 114, 148, 223,
   261, 316, 367, 516-517,
   536, 561
column, 190, 305, 307, 324
combinations, 15, 18, 25, 28,
   49, 60, 64-65, 168, 178,
   211, 275, 322, 329, 333,
   337, 343, 365-366, 390,

PROPER NAMES

WORD CLOUD

TOP 250 WORDS